Pediatric Medications

Pediatric Medications

An Emergency and Critical Care Reference

by

Carolyn M. Stewart, Pharm.D.
Clinical Pharmacist, Mission Bay Memorial Hospital
San Diego, California

Linda B. Stewart, R.N., M.S.N.
Patient Educator, Mercy Hospital and Medical Center
San Diego, California

This work has been developed in conjunction with Capistrano Press, Ltd.

ASPEN SYSTEMS CORPORATION®
Rockville, Maryland
Royal Tunbridge Wells
1984

Library of Congress Cataloging in Publication Data

Stewart, Carolyn M.
Pediatric medications.

"This work has been developed in conjunction with Capistrano Press, Ltd."
"An Aspen publication."
Bibliography: p. 437
Includes index.
1. Pediatric pharmacology. 2. Pediatric intensive care. 3. Pediatric emergencies.
I. Stewart, Linda B. II. Title. [DNLM: 1. Critical Care — in infancy & childhood.
2. Emergencies — in infancy & childhood. 3. Pharmacology — in infancy & childhood. QV 55 S849p]
RJ560.S7   1984   618.92'0025   84-9322
ISBN: 0-89443-869-7

Capistrano Press, Ltd.
Acquisitions Editor:
 Carmen Germaine Warner
Editorial Assistant:
 Barbara Halliburton
Illustrations:
 Glen Joyce
Book Design:
 Alice Harmon

Aspen Systems Corporation
Publisher: John R. Marozsan
Associate Publisher: Jack W. Knowles, Jr.
Editorial Director: N. Darlene Como
Executive Managing Editor:
 Margot G. Raphael
Managing Editor: M. Eileen Higgins
Printing and Manufacturing:
 Debbie Collins

Copyright © 1984 by Aspen Systems Corporation

The authors and publisher have made every effort to ensure the accuracy of the information herein, particularly with regard to drug selection and dose. However, appropriate information sources should be consulted, especially for new or unfamiliar drugs or procedures. It is the responsibility of every practitioner to evaluate the appropriateness of a particular opinion in the context of actual clinical situations and with due consideration to new developments. Authors, editors, and the publisher cannot be held responsible for any typographical or other errors found in this book.

All rights reserved. This book, or parts thereof, may not be reproduced in any form or by any means, electronic or mechanical, including photocopy, recording, or any information storage and retrieval system now known or to be invented, without written permission from the publisher, except in the case of brief quotations embodied in critical articles or reviews. For information, address Aspen Systems Corporation, 1600 Research Boulevard, Rockville, Maryland 20850

Library of Congress Catalog Card Number: 84-9322
ISBN: 0-89443-869-7

Printed in the United States of America

1 2 3 4 5

*To Kitty Stewart, with affection,
for encouragement and companionship*
C.M.S.

To Jeffrey and Gregory, who make my life worthwhile
L.B.S.

Contents

Foreword xvii
Preface xix
Acknowledgments xxi
Introduction xxiii

Section I
SPECIAL CONSIDERATIONS FOR PEDIATRIC PATIENTS 1

1. Administration of Medications 3
   DEALING WITH A CRYING CHILD 5
   GIVING ORAL MEDICATIONS 5
   MEASURING SOLUTIONS OF ORAL AND PARENTERAL
      DOSES 6
   LOCATION OF INTRAMUSCULAR INJECTIONS 6
   LOCATION OF INTRAVENOUS INJECTIONS 7

2. Pharmacology 9
   DRUG ABSORPTION 11
   PLASMA PROTEIN-BINDING CAPACITY 11
   VOLUME OF DISTRIBUTION 11
   DRUG-METABOLIZING ENZYMES 12
   RENAL FUNCTION 12
   CLINICAL STUDIES 13

Section II
AGENTS FOR CARDIOPULMONARY RESUSCITATION — 15
THE NERVOUS SYSTEM — 15

3. Adrenergics — 23
   - Dobutamine — 25
   - Dopamine — 26
   - Epinephrine — 27
   - Isoproterenol — 29
   - Norepinephrine — 30
   - Phenylephrine — 31

4. Cholinergic Blockers — 33
   - Atropine — 33

5. Adrenergic Blockers — 35
   - Phentolamine (Parenteral) — 36
   - Tolazoline — 37

6. Antiarrhythmics — 39
   - Bretylium Tosylate — 40
   - Lidocaine — 41
   - Phenytoin (parenteral) — 42
   - Procainamide — 43
   - Propranolol — 45
   - Verapamil (IV) — 46

7. Cardiotonics — 49
   - DIGOXIN PHARMACOKINETICS — 49
   - Digoxin — 50

8. Antihypertensives and Vasodilators — 55
   - Diazoxide (IV) — 56
   - Hydralazine — 57
   - Nitroglycerin (IV) — 59
   - Nitroprusside — 60
   - Reserpine (Parenteral) — 61

Section III
AGENTS FOR FLUID AND ELECTROLYTE IMBALANCES   65

9. Diuretics   67
   - Chlorothiazide   68
   - Ethacrynic Acid   69
   - Furosemide   70
   - Glycerol   72
   - Mannitol   73

10. Oral Rehydrating Solutions   75
    - Oral Rehydrating Solutions   76

11. Electrolyte Replacements   79
    - ACID-BASE BALANCE   79
    - Calcium Chloride   81
    - Calcium Gluconate   81
    - Magnesium Sulfate   83
    - Potassium Chloride   85
    - Potassium Acetate   85
    - Potassium Phosphate   85
    - Sodium Bicarbonate   87
    - Tromethamine   89

Section IV
AGENTS AFFECTING BLOOD VOLUME AND HEMOSTASIS   91

12. Colloid Plasma Volume Expanders   93
    - Albumin (Human)   94
    - Plasma Protein Fraction (PPF, Human)   95

13. Coagulants and Anticoagulants   97
    - MECHANISMS OF COAGULATION   98
    - Antihemophilic Factor (Factor VIII)   100
    - Cryoprecipitated Antihemophilic Factor   101
    - Epsilon-Aminocaproic Acid   103
    - Factor IX Complex   104
    - Fresh Frozen Plasma (FFP)   106

Phytonadione (Vitamin K$_1$) 107
Protamine Sulfate 109
Heparin 110

Section V
AGENTS AFFECTING INFLAMMATION AND ALLERGY 113

14. Corticosteroids 115
    CORTICOSTEROIDS (GENERAL STATEMENT) 118
    Desoxycorticosterone acetate 121
    Dexamethasone 122
    Hydrocortisone 123
    Methylprednisolone 124
    Prednisone 125

15. Antihistamines 127
    Chlorpheniramine 128
    Dimenhydrinate 128
    Diphenhydramine 130
    Hydroxyzine 131
    Promethazine 132

16. Bronchodilators and Antiasthmatics 135
    N-acetylcysteine 137
    Albuterol 138
    Aminophylline (Parenteral) 139
    Aminophylline (Oral) 140
    Theophylline (Oral) 140
    Isoetharine 143
    Metaproterenol 145
    Terbutaline 146

Section VI
ANTIBIOTICS 147

17. Aminoglycosides 151
    AMINOGLYCOSIDES (GENERAL STATEMENT) 152
    Amikacin 154

Gentamicin	156
Kanamycin	158
Neomycin	159
Streptomycin	160
Tobramycin	161

18. Cephalosporins — 165
CEPHALOSPORINS (GENERAL STATEMENT)	165
FIRST-GENERATION CEPHALOSPORINS (GENERAL STATEMENT)	167
Cefadroxil	168
Cefazolin	169
Cephalexin	170
Cephalothin	171
Cephapirin	172
Cephradine	173
SECOND-GENERATION CEPHALOSPORINS (GENERAL STATEMENT)	174
Cefaclor	175
Cefamandole	176
Cefoxitin	177
THIRD-GENERATION CEPHALOSPORINS (GENERAL STATEMENT)	179
Cefotaxime	181
Moxalactam	182

19. Penicillins — 185
PENICILLINS (GENERAL STATEMENT)	185
PENICILLIN G AND PENICILLIN V (GENERAL STATEMENT)	186
Penicillin G (Parenteral)	188
Penicillin G (Oral)	190
Penicillin V	190
PENICILLINASE-RESISTANT PENICILLINS (GENERAL STATEMENT)	191
Cloxacillin	192
Dicloxacillin	193
Methicillin	194
Nafcillin	195

Oxacillin	196
EXTENDED-SPECTRUM PENICILLINS (GENERAL STATEMENT)	197
Amoxicillin	198
Ampicillin	199
Carbenicillin	201
Mezlocillin	203
Piperacillin	204
Ticarcillin	205
20. Sulfonamides	**207**
SULFONAMIDES (GENERAL STATEMENT)	208
Silver Sulfadiazine	209
Sulfamethoxazole	210
Sulfamethoxazole with Trimethoprim	211
Sulfisoxazole	212
21. Tetracyclines	**215**
TETRACYCLINES (GENERAL STATEMENT)	216
Doxycycline	218
Minocycline	219
Tetracycline	220
22. Urinary Tract Anti-infectives and Antiseptics	**223**
Methenamine Mandelate	224
Nalidixic Acid	225
Nitrofurantoin	226
Phenazopyridine	228
23. Other Antimicrobials	**229**
Acyclovir	230
Amphotericin B	232
Chloramphenicol	234
Clindamycin	236
Diiodohydroxyquin	239
Erythromycin	240
Ethambutol	242
Gamma Benzene Hexachloride	243
Griseofulvin	244

Isoniazid	246
Ketoconazole	249
Mebendazole	250
Metronidazole	251
Miconazole	252
Nystatin	254
Rifampin	254
Spectinomycin	256
Vancomycin	257

Section VII
AGENTS FOR MANAGEMENT OF PAIN AND FEVER — 261

24. Narcotic Analgesics — 263
NARCOTIC ANALGESICS (GENERAL STATEMENT)	264
Codeine	266
Meperidine	267
DPT Cocktail	267
Morphine Sulfate	269

25. Mild Analgesics and Antipyretics — 271
Acetaminophen	273
Aspirin	275

26. Local Anesthetics — 279
LOCAL ANESTHETICS (GENERAL STATEMENT)	281
Bupivicaine	282
Cocaine	283
Lidocaine	284
Mepivicaine	285

Section VIII
ANTICONVULSANTS AND SKELETAL MUSCLE RELAXANTS — 287

27. Anticonvulsants — 289
Carbamazepine	292
Clonazepam	293
Diazepam (Parenteral)	295

Ethosuximide 296
Paraldehyde 298
Phenobarbital 299
Phenytoin 302
Pyridoxine HCl 304
Valproic Acid 306

28. Skeletal Muscle Relaxants 309
    Carisoprodol 310
    Dantrolene 311
    Diazepam 312
    Methocarbamol 314
    Pancuronium Bromide 315
    Succinylcholine 316

Section IX
SEDATIVES AND HYPNOTICS 319

29. Sedative-Hypnotics 321
    Chloral Hydrate 323
    BARBITURATES (GENERAL STATEMENT) 324
    Pentobarbital Sodium 328
    Secobarbital Sodium 330

Section X
AGENTS FOR HYPERGLYCEMIC AND HYPOGLYCEMIC EMERGENCIES 333

30. Glucose-lowering Agents 335
    Insulins (Regular) 338
    Insulins (Longer-acting Preparations) 340

31. Glucose-elevating Agents 347
    Dextrose 50% (IV) 348
    Diazoxide 348
    Glucagon 350

Section XI
ANTIEMETICS, ANTIDIARRHEALS, AND GASTRIC ACID INHIBITORS — 353

32. Antiemetics — 355
    - Chlorpromazine — 357
    - Diphenidol — 359
    - Hydroxyzine — 360
    - Promethazine — 361

33. Antidiarrheals — 365
    - Diphenoxylate with Atropine — 367
    - Paregoric — 368
    - Paregoric with Kaolin-Pectin — 368

34. Gastric Acid Inhibitors — 371
    - Cimetidine — 371

Section XII
TREATMENT OF POISONINGS — 373

35. Antidotes — 375
    - N-Acetylcysteine — 377
    - Activated Charcoal — 378
    - Cyanide Antidote Package — 379
    - Deferoxamine Mesylate — 381
    - Dimercaprol — 382
    - Edetate Calcium Disodium — 384
    - Syrup of Ipecac — 385
    - Methylene Blue — 386
    - Naloxone — 388
    - Penicillamine — 389
    - Physostigmine Salicylate — 391
    - Pralidoxime — 392
    - Sodium Polystyrene Sulfonate — 394

36. Antivenins 397
  Crotalidae Polyvalent Antivenin (Equine) 399
  Latrodectus mactans Antivenin (Equine) 400
  Micrurus fulvius Antivenin (Equine) 402

37. Antiserums 405
  Hepatitis B Immune Globulin 406
  Immune Human Serum Globulin (IM Use Only) 407
  Immune Human Serum Globulin (IV Use Only) 408
  Rabies Immune Globulin 409
  Tetanus Immune Human Globulin 410
  Varicella-Zoster Immune Globulin 411

Appendix 415

   VACCINES FOR ROUTINE CHILDHOOD
     IMMUNIZATIONS 415
     VACCINES FOR SPECIFIC NEEDS 415
     IMMUNIZATION SCHEDULES 421
     TREATMENT OF RABIES 421
     TETANUS PROPHYLAXIS IN WOUND MANAGEMENT 421
     PEDIATRIC DOSAGES OF COMMONLY USED
     EMERGENCY DRUGS 421
     AVERAGE PEDIATRIC WATER REQUIREMENT 421
     COMPOSITION OF COMMONLY USED IV SOLUTIONS 421
     KILOGRAM CONVERSION CHART 429
     AVERAGE BODY WEIGHTS 429
     COMPATIBILITY OF DRUGS COMBINED IN A SYRINGE 430
     CALCULATION OF DOSAGES 430
     CALCULATION OF IV DROP RATES 433
     CALCULATION OF INFUSION RATES FOR DRUGS
       GIVEN IN μg/kg/min 434

Bibliography 437

Index 441

Foreword

Health care personnel who deliver pediatric emergency care must be intimately familiar with each of the components of the human growth process so that they will be able to quickly interpret clinical findings and provide, often simultaneously, the appropriate therapeutic intervention. The emergency practitioner must make actual determinations, or in the acute situation, accurate estimates of the patient's age, size, and weight, with the understanding that these determine the different activities of direct metabolizing enzymes, the availability of drug-binding proteins, size of water compartments, and other variable factors, each of which may influence the choice of the agents, mode of action, route, dosage, and ultimately the therapeutic (or adverse) effect.

Just as the human growth process from birth to adulthood is associated with characteristic changes, emergency medicine—once considered the "poor stepchild" of the more traditional specialties—is maturing. One manifestation of its youth is the apparent dearth of practitioners, teachers, research, and texts in the emergency subspecialty areas such as pediatric emergency medications. The present volume fills a philosophical as well as a practical void. This effort represents another formal step in the growth and establishment of emergency medicine as a specialty unto its own and, at the same time, represents a major contribution in meeting a real but practical need: Pediatric emergency medications are not infrequently given incorrectly.

This text will be most helpful to the emergency medicine practitioner when used in conjunction with good clinical judgment and observed clinical responses and physical measurements that must be considered if the therapeutic modalities and resuscitative efforts are to be successful.

Thomas Clark Kravis, M.D.

Preface

The intent of this book is to provide the nurse, nurse practitioner, paramedic, and other health professionals with a concise, immediate source of clinical and pharmacological data on the use and effects of drugs that may be employed during a pediatric emergency. The information presented here deals specifically with the application and effects of these pharmacological agents in children from birth to adolescence.

Each section covers a major problem in pediatric emergency therapy, from cardiopulmonary resuscitation to poisonings. The chapters within each section are organized according to therapeutic action and indication; the individual drugs are listed alphabetically by generic name; and each individual listing includes data on administration (e.g., available forms, diluents, dosages, routes and rates of administration), indications, pharmacological actions, contraindications, precautions, adverse effects, drug interactions and incompatibilities, and antidotes specific for that particular agent.

Chapter 1, Administration of Medications, includes useful guidelines for administering medications to children and for promoting compliance and cooperation in both the child and the parent. Chapter 2 briefly discusses some of the physiological factors differentiating the newborn from the older infant and child and how these variables may alter drug action, biotransformation, elimination, toxicity, and, ultimately, dosage regimens.

The drug data have been derived from many reference sources, and the dosages included are average and therefore approximate ones. Some dosages and indications for use are still investigational; when these appear in the text, they are noted as such. The authors have been careful to state dosage guidelines that are in agreement with current standards and accepted reference sources. Every effort has been made to note circumstances under which drug response or toxicity may vary because of physiological or genetic differences and for which alterations in dosages are necessary. The authors suggest that the reader consult several appropriate sources when dealing with new and unfamiliar medications. The appropriateness of a particular opinion concerning dosages or applications of therapy should be evaluated in the context of the actual clinical situation and with due consideration to any new developments in the field of pediatric medicine. It remains the professional practitioners' responsibility to understand the benefits and possible hazards of each medication that they may be required to give. Ultimately, no therapeutic agent should be given if there is any doubt as to its safety and propriety in a given situation.

It is the authors' hope that this text will aid the health professional in providing the pediatric patient with drug therapy of the utmost benefit and safety.

Acknowledgments

Our sincere appreciation to David Rush, Pharm.D., of the Truman Medical Center, St. Louis, for his guidance and helpful suggestions in the review of the manuscript. My special thanks to Keith D. Vrhel, M.D., of San Diego for his assistance in the preparation of the chapter on anticonvulsants. My gratitude to Carmen Germaine Warner for her encouragement, inspiration, and friendship. I wish to express my thanks to American Medical International, Inc., for their encouragement of the pharmacist's active participation on the cardiopulmonary resuscitation team. Such support has allowed me and others to gain valuable practical experience in the clinical application of these medications in various emergency situations. Lastly, my thanks to Jim for his patience and understanding.

C.M.S.

Thanks are expressed to Carolyn for her invaluable assistance in the preparation of this manuscript and to Carmen Germaine Warner for convincing me that I could write. A special thank you to my parents, Joan and Burton Berry, for their support and encouragement in my career choice. And most of all, my thanks to my husband, Dick, whose love and support have guided me all along.

L.B.S.

Introduction

Whether created by an unavoidable environmental condition or by the careless placement of poisons or pills, a pediatric emergency must be treated with haste. The therapeutic agents or antidotes must be appropriate, effective, and employed quickly to avoid a life-threatening crisis.

Approximately 200 pharmacological agents are discussed in this book. These medications have been grouped into sections based on the type of pediatric emergency and further divided into chapters according to the drugs' therapeutic actions.

Most of the pharmacological agents included are "prescription" (i.e., legend) medications available on any "crash cart" or in any hospital emergency department, clinic, pharmacy, or ambulance. Some, like aspirin and syrup of ipecac, are over-the-counter (OTC) preparations. Antibiotics, while not truly "emergency" medications per se, are included because of their frequent use in the emergency department.

Each medication is listed by its generic name. In most instances the salt has been omitted in order to include the different forms that may be available. One or more trade or proprietary names are included (in parentheses) for easier identification of agents listed generically.

Information on each individual medication is listed in nine categories:

1. Administration
2. Indications
3. Actions
4. Contraindications
5. Precautions
6. Side effects/Adverse reactions
7. Drug incompatibilities

8. Drug interactions
9. Antidote

The first category, administration, begins with a list of available dosage forms and includes information on strength per tablet, capsule, injection (per milliliter), oral solutions, elixirs, and so forth. Topical preparations are included when applicable. When an injectable form is listed, designated routes of administration (e.g., intravenous [IV], intramuscular [IM], subcutaneous [SC], intracardiac [IC]) are also indicated. The size and type of prepackaged container (e.g., ampule, multidose vial, preloaded syringe) are given for information only.

When a medication must be reconstituted before use or further diluted for IV infusion, the appropriate diluents and the recommended final concentrations are given.

The information on dosage lists the amount of medication to be administered at one time or during a specific time period, usually 24 hours. Most doses are recommended on the basis of milligram per kilogram (mg/kg) of body weight, but in many cases the amount of medication per square meter (mg/m^2 or gm/m^2) of body surface area is also given. Situational recommendations are made when dosages must be determined on the basis of the patient's physiological response or disease state. The recommended dosing intervals as well as the routes of administration are included also, with the preferred route so designated when necessary.

The rate listed applies to the IV route of administration only. Medications can be given IV by "piggyback" (also called "volutrol" or "Metriset") infusion or by bolus injection (direct IV push). The choice between the two methods depends on the type of medication, the volume of the solution, and the recommended rate of administration needed to effect the desired response. When an IV bolus injection is the chosen method, the injection port closest to the insertion site of the IV line should be used. Care must be taken to ensure that the medication goes directly into the vein and not into the surrounding subcutaneous tissue.

The second category of data, indications, lists the most common applications of a medication or reasons for its use. The third, actions, describes the physiological or pharmacological changes that occur after the medication is introduced into the body.

Conditions when the use of a medication is prohibited or strongly inadvisable are cited under the fourth category, contraindications. Known hypersensitivity to the agent or to its cogeners is one of the most common. Others, such as particular disease states or physiological impairments, are listed when applicable.

The fifth category, precautions, is included to warn the health professional of problems that might develop during therapy. Physiological and genetic impairments that may alter a drug's effect or toxicity are indicated where applicable. Recommendations for dosage adjustments are noted when deemed necessary. This category also outlines areas of health teaching, idiosyncrasies of the medication, recommendations for laboratory and physical monitoring, and specific nursing care.

Side effects and adverse reactions, the sixth category, refer to expected or unexpected—and often undesirable—actions caused by the pharmacodynamics of a medication. Some side effects, while not dangerous, may simply be uncomfortable. Many may occur when the medication is properly used and therapeutic blood levels have been reached. In some cases, the side effects are dose-related, and a simple reduction of the dose will eliminate or minimize the severity of these effects. More severe adverse reactions, on the other hand, are potentially hazardous physiological sequelae of therapeutic or excessive doses of a drug or drug combination. These reactions may be an extension of the normal pharmacological action (e.g., profound hypotension with vasodilators) or may be idiosyncratic reactions (e.g., severe blood dyscrasias or anaphylactic shock) that can lead to life-threatening emergencies requiring resuscitative efforts. When a medication elicits a severe enough adverse reaction, the drug should be discontinued immediately and the appropriate antidotal treatment administered. The frequency and degree of severity of the many different side effects and adverse reactions are indicated in the text, and recommendations for discontinuing the medication are given when applicable.

Caution should be taken whenever one mixes two or more pharmacological agents in the same syringe, IV container, or tubing. Many medications are incompatible and lose chemical stability and potency when physically combined. The seventh category, drug incompatibilities, lists the most common physical and chemical incompatibilities of each therapeutic agent. Additional material can be found in the appendix.

When two or more medications are given concomitantly, the combination may have the potential to interact adversely in the patient. The resulting effect may only be mild or it may be potentially hazardous. Sometimes the actions of one or more medications may be potentiated or inhibited. Clinically significant interactions of this type are listed in the eighth category, drug interactions.

The final category of data is antidote. Some medications have specific antidotes that directly antagonize or neutralize their pharmacological effects. Most, however, have no specific antidote. Consequently, treatment of overdoses must usually be symptomatic and supportive.

With all of the aforementioned information on hand, it is hoped that the therapeutic agents listed can be given safely, appropriately, and efficaciously.

I
SPECIAL CONSIDERATIONS FOR PEDIATRIC PATIENTS

Pediatric patients are not merely small adults. Consequently, dealing with pediatric emergencies and the administration of emergency medications must take into account certain unique circumstances.

The care and handling of pediatric patients demand special psychological considerations. The pediatric emergency can be a frightening experience to both the child and the parent, and in many instances the parent is as frightened and anxious as the child is hurt. The successful administration of medical treatment requires the cooperation of both the parent and the child. Chapter 1 offers some guidelines that may facilitate the administration of medication to an often fearful, resistant child and promote cooperation and compliance while allaying the fears of both patient and parent.

The use of medications also requires special considerations with regard to selection, dosage calculations, and administration. Dosage calculations that have been empirically based on age, weight, or body surface area assume that various body compartments of infants and young children are proportional to those of adults and that certain physiological functions are fully developed. However, the disposition, efficacy, and toxicity of pharmacological agents vary greatly in infants and young children as compared to adults because of the continuous changes in body weight, composition, and tissue function that occur during infancy and early childhood. The differences between neonates and older infants and children are particularly significant with respect to the functional development of specific tissues and organ systems that govern drug absorption, metabolism, and excretion. The immaturity of these systems predisposes the newborn and full-term infant to the risk of drug accumulation and possible toxicity. Chapter 2 discusses some of the factors that influence the pharmacokinetics of therapeutic agents in the pediatric patient and that may necessitate alterations in the selection of medications and dosage regimens.

1
Administration of Medications

There are probably as many methods of administering medications as there are children who will need them. If one general rule were to be made, it would be that no one way always works. This chapter describes some of the most successful and effective methods. It includes nine rules to guide you to a more successful child-medicine confrontation. These rules are not necessarily in order of importance.

1. *NEVER give a child a choice of whether or not the child wants any medicine.* There really is no choice to be made. The medication was ordered, is necessary for recovery, and therefore must be given. Avoid such questions as "Do you want your shot now?" Of course not. A child seldom if ever wants an injection. "Will you be a good girl and take this pill?" A simple no will be the response to that! Change your questions to positive statements such as "I have some medication for you," or "It's time for some pills."
2. *Give choices that allow the child to have some control over the situation.* These might include choosing the injection site, kind of juice, or number of bandages.
3. *NEVER LIE.* Do not tell a child that a shot will not hurt or that a tube going down the nose will not be felt. Do not say that you are giving a child candy when in fact you are giving medicine that could save the child's life. This type of deceit results in distrust and fear of all people in white. Try to give an age-appropriate time frame (Table 1–1) that the child can understand: "It will hurt for the count of three. Let's count 1-2-3. See, that wasn't too long." You might want to compare the situation to one the child has already experienced. "It will feel as if I were washing a scraped elbow. Have you ever scraped your elbow?" "This (alcohol swab) will feel very cold as if I just took it out of the freezer."

TABLE 1–1 Age-Appropriate Time Frames

Age	Perception of Time
0–18 mo	Has no concept of time.
19–24 mo	Has limited ability to conceptualize time. May behave appropriately to "just a minute."
2–4 yr	Uses own time reference experiences. Relate time to events that the child has experienced. Has no understanding of yesterday, today, or tomorrow.
5–7 yr	Is learning to tell time. Is able to count and anticipate. You can show a clock and tell the child to watch for hand positions.
8 yr and over	Can usually tell time accurately. Understands concept of minutes, hours, days, yesterday, tomorrow, today.

4. *Assure each child, whatever the child's age, that it is all right to be afraid and that it is okay to cry.* (Sometimes the extent of crying that you can allow must be limited. See the following section on dealing with the crying child.) You can gain a child's confidence by being truthful and acknowledging the child's feelings.
5. *Remember that you are dealing with a child, not a small adult.* Your little patient will have child-like fears, a lack of understanding, a poor perception of cause-and-effect relationships, and a distorted or literal interpretation of word usage. Imagine the possible connotations of the following:
    - We'll need to shoot another. (x-ray film)
    - Let's hang the blood.
    - He's done. Pull the tube.
    - I'll need to sew him up.

    Keep explanations simple and brief. Use words that the child will comprehend.
6. *Do not talk in front of a child as if the child were not there.* Unless a child is in a profound coma, the child can hear. Include the child in the conversation when talking to parents and talk as if the child were actively listening. Explain what you are doing and, very simply, why you are doing it.
7. *Keep the time between explanation and execution to a minimum.* The younger the child is, the shorter the time should be. Preparations such as setting up IV solutions, injections, and instrument trays should all be done outside the child's line of sight. Syringes should remain out of sight throughout the duration as they are very anxiety provoking. Remember, keep the explanation simple. Explain what the medication will do if the child is old enough to understand.
8. *Be positive about yourself and your approach to the child.* Remember that feelings are easily conveyed to children. Expect success and you will be

more likely to succeed. Be very firm and assertive when you say, "Take your medicine *now.*"
9. *Obtain parental cooperation.* Parents may be able to calm a frightened child, persuade the child to take medication willingly, and achieve cooperation for your ensuing care. A young emergency patient may have been exposed to health professionals prior to the contact with you, and the memory of previous experiences may cause the child to be extremely frightened and resistant. You may want to explore the exact cause or event of any prior emergency with the parents. Such knowledge may provide clues for easier emergency management. If you are unable to gain cooperation even through the parents, you may have to administer oral doses of medication via a nasogastric (NG) tube. Never hesitate to use this method as a last resort.

DEALING WITH A CRYING CHILD

Crying is a child's reaction to pain and fear. The pain is easier to remedy than the fear. It would be unnatural for a child to show no reaction to a traumatic injury. (In fact, showing no reaction might be a clue to a physical or emotional defect.) When a child cannot be calmed, one of the following hints may aid in controlling the crying:

- Eliminate the pain.
- Distract the child with conversation.
- Explain the intended course of action.
- Use physical comfort measures (a pacifier, hand holding, and so forth).
- Allow the parents to hold the child (when possible).

If none of these suggestions works, expedite the treatment and release the child to the parents.

With a young child, less than 2 to 3 years of age, the presence of the parent may cause more anxiety and crying than the parent's absence would. Although a physical separation between the parent and child has occurred, the child might still be able to see the parent and not understand the need for the separation. The child might also feel deserted and wonder how the parent could allow this personal invasion and pain to occur.

GIVING ORAL MEDICATIONS

The oral route would always be the child's choice. Unfortunately, the emergency may not permit this method of administration. When it is possible to give oral medications, they should be made as palatable as possible. Many agents are available in liquid forms: syrups, solutions, elixirs, and suspensions. And many have a disagreeable taste or aftertaste. Pills and tablets can be crushed and capsules opened, then camouflaged in ice cream, juice, applesauce, or jelly. The amount used should be large enough to change the taste but not so large as to significantly increase the volume. When choosing a camouflage substance, avoid milk, formula, or other routinely eaten essential foods so the child will not learn to associate the chosen food with an unpleasant experience. Alternatively, you can have a child chew on ice chips immediately prior to taking an unpleasant medication; this procedure numbs the mouth and desensitizes the taste buds. Or you can provide a chaser to take away the aftertaste. Older children, those over 6 to 8 years, should be able to take pills but would probably appreciate a flavorful chaser. Extremely bitter pills like codeine or salty preparations like potassium need special attention. Gelatin capsules, root beer, and cranberry juice work well.

MEASURING SOLUTIONS OF ORAL AND PARENTERAL DOSES

Solutions given orally must be measured with great accuracy. Plastic medicine cups are reasonably accurate for amounts exceeding 5 ml. Syringes without needles should be used for amounts less than 5 ml. Plastic, disposable syringes without needles can be used to administer medication directly into a small child's mouth. Place the tip of the syringe between the child's gums and cheek. Nipples can be used when giving thin liquids to babies.

When calculating parenteral dosages, diluent and syringes can be used to further dilute the medication. A drug that is available in 1 mg/ml can be diluted to 0.10 mg/ml or 0.01 mg/ml by using the following procedure.

1. Using aseptic technique and a tuberculin syringe (1 ml), draw up 0.1 ml (0.1 mg).
2. In the same syringe, draw up 0.9 ml appropriate diluent. This gives a new dilution of 0.1 mg/ml.
3. Eject all but 0.1 ml of this new solution.
4. Draw up another 0.9 ml of appropriate diluent. This gives a new dilution of 0.01 mg/ml.

LOCATION OF INTRAMUSCULAR INJECTIONS

Intramuscular injections must be given in muscles large enough to accommodate the medication, yet in muscle areas free of large blood vessels and nerves. In small children, the preferred area is the midlateral thigh (the vastus lateralis muscle) or central midthigh (the rectus femoris muscle). Older children and teenagers have enough muscle mass to receive an injection safely in the ventrogluteal, posterior gluteal, and deltoid muscles. Always allow the alcohol swabbed on the skin to dry before you inject the medication. Insert the needle quickly and pull it out straight.

LOCATION OF INTRAVENOUS INJECTIONS

Intravenous injections are the most effective way to elicit a rapid response. The hand and forearm are the best locations for inserting an IV line. Because babies' hands are so tiny, feet and ankles are sometimes used. One of the most preferred locations for IV infusion is the baby's forehead or scalp. This may be very frightening for a parent to see. Explain that this is a less painful area and that it frees the baby's hands and feet. When securing an IV on a child, be sure to do it well. Many layers of tape are usually needed. Place the arm (or foot) on an arm board. Inverting a paper cup over the needle provides protection from inadvertent bumps. Using a "T" tube to connect the needle and infusion set allows for easier adjustments and tubing changes. Other extremities should be softly restrained. If possible, give infusions by means of a controlled infusion device. This procedure provides accurate infusion of fluid and prevents fluid overload.

2
Pharmacology

Determining the pediatric dosage of a medication poses some special problems. Children cannot be considered as merely small adults and, indeed, premature and newborn infants cannot even be regarded as small children. There are many qualitative differences between the neonate and the older infant and child with regard to the physiological function of organ systems responsible for the detoxification and excretion of pharmacological agents. Consequently, most rules that employ parameters of age and body weight for calculating dosages in older children and adults cannot be applied to neonates.[1]

Doses for infants and children can be determined on the basis of (1) body weight (mg/kg), in which case the calculated amount should never exceed the recommended adult dose, and (2) body surface area (mg/m^2). Appropriate dosing nomograms have been developed for this purpose (Exhibit 2–1). Dosages can then be further individualized according to clinical response; serum levels of the drug; the status of renal or hepatic function; and any disease state, allergies, or genetic abnormalities (e.g., glucose-6-phosphate dehydrogenase [G6PD] deficiency) that may alter a drug's metabolism, excretion, or toxicity.

The functional immaturity of the neonatal organ systems that govern drug absorption, biotransformation, and excretion can markedly change the pharmacokinetics of many therapeutic agents. Some of these alterations can render the newborn or premature infant particularly vulnerable to the accumulation of toxic levels of medication.[2,3] Notable differences exist between neonates and older children with regard to the processes of drug absorption, protein binding, distribution, metabolism, and excretion.

EXHIBIT 2–1 Dosage Calculation Nomogram for Children*

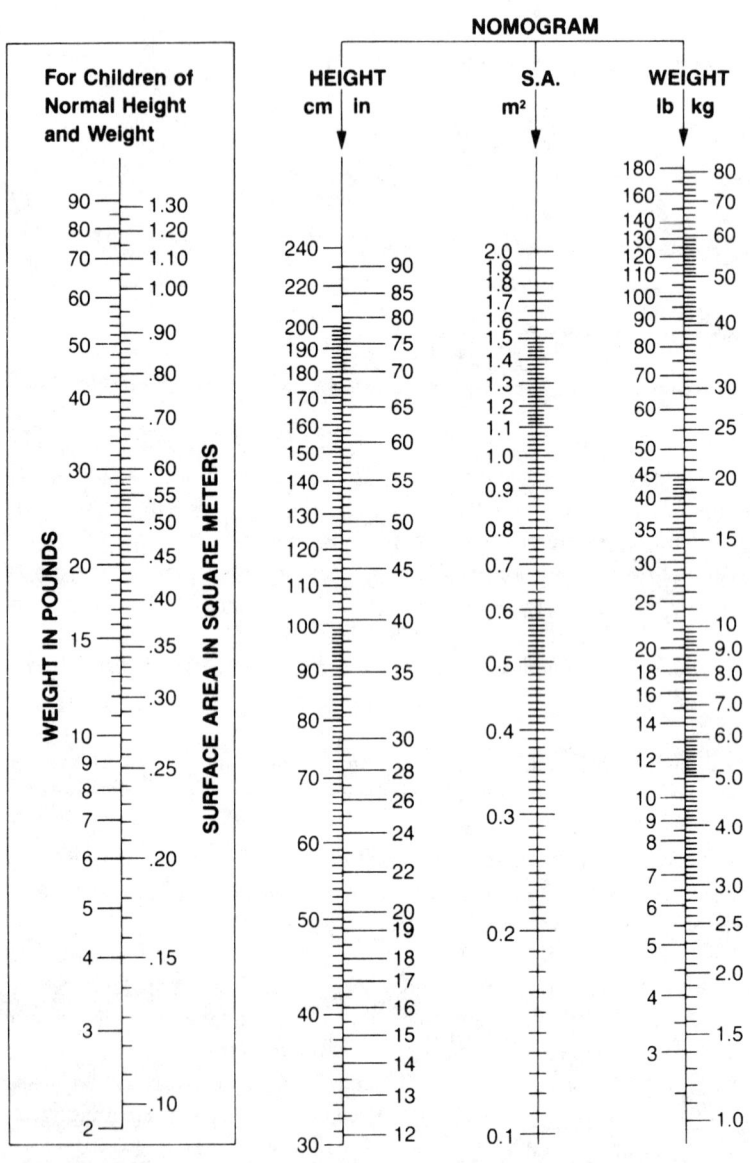

NOMOGRAM

For Children of Normal Height and Weight	HEIGHT (cm / in)	S.A. (m^2)	WEIGHT (lb / kg)

If your patient is of average size, find his weight and corresponding surface area on the first, boxed scale. Otherwise, use the nomogram to the right. Lay a straight edge on the correct height and weight points for your patient, then see the intersecting point on the surface area scale.

*Reprinted with permission from Vaughan VC III, McKay RJ Jr, Behrman RE (eds): *Nelson's Textbook of Pediatrics*, ed 11. Philadelphia, WB Saunders Co. 1979, p 2055.

DRUG ABSORPTION

For example, drug absorption is dependent on gastric pH and emptying time. After a brief initial 24-hour period of low gastric acidity, the newborn secretes little or no gastric acid for approximately the first eight days of life.[2] Normal adult values for gastric acidity are not reached until 3 years of age.[4] Gastric emptying time is also significantly delayed in the neonate, and it may take six to eight months for emptying time to approach adult values. As a result, an oral dose of a medication such as penicillin G, which would otherwise be partially destroyed by gastric acid, is more completely absorbed during the neonatal period as compared to later years. Conversely, the absorption of oral doses of therapeutic agents such as phenobarbital and phenytoin are reduced in the preterm infant, so parenteral administration of these medications is advisable.[2]

PLASMA PROTEIN-BINDING CAPACITY

Plasma protein-binding capacity is generally reduced in the neonate because of a combination of factors, including lower concentrations of plasma protein, a diminished binding capacity of fetal albumin as compared to adult albumin, and an increased serum concentration of bilirubin.[5] The latter is especially significant because this excess bilirubin can be displaced from its albumin-binding sites by certain medications and become toxic. Adult values for total plasma protein concentration and protein-binding capacity are not reached until about 10 to 12 months of age.[2] The effects of reduced protein binding vary. For instance, the activity and toxicity of highly bound drugs like phenytoin and warfarin are based upon the unbound fraction of the drug present in the plasma. If the amount of unbound phenytoin or warfarin increases as a result of reduced binding capacity, the effects and potential toxicity of the agent also increase.

Another potentially serious complication related to the newborn's reduced protein-binding capacity is hyperbilirubinemia. Some therapeutic agents, notably sulfonamides, phenytoin, aspirin, and vitamin K, are capable of displacing bilirubin from its albumin-binding sites.[6] The resulting higher serum level of unconjugated, unbound bilirubin is toxic to the central nervous system (CNS). Unbound bilirubin can freely diffuse into brain cells and cause cell death and permanent brain injury, a condition known as kernicterus. For this reason, the use of agents such as the sulfonamides is contraindicated in infants less than 2 months of age.

VOLUME OF DISTRIBUTION

The volume of distribution of certain drugs within various body compartments is also altered in the newborn. The volume of distribution represents a theoretical volume that accounts for the total amount of a dose of medication as it disperses into body water and tissues. The size of these compartments (body water and fat) determines the concentration of the drug in the blood and the amount at the site of action. Most drugs must pass through the extracellular fluid (ECF) spaces to reach their site of action. Infants have a higher percentage of total body water and ECF than older children and adults have. In premature and newborn infants, total body water accounts for about 70–80% of body weight, whereas the adult value is only about 50–55%. The amount of ECF is also significantly greater, approximately 40% in the neonate as compared to 20% in the adult.[7]

This larger compartment of body water and the infant's lower plasma protein-binding capacity result in an expanded apparent volume of distribution, especially for water-soluble medications. Consequently, to produce the same therapeutic serum concentrations, the mg/kg dose of a relatively water-soluble drug should be greater for an infant than the mg/kg dose of the same medication for an adult.[2,8] An example of the clinical application of this theoretical consideration is the larger mg/kg doses of theophylline and the sulfonamides given to infants as compared to adults. Conversely, because infants have a lower percentage of total body fat than adults and older children have, the mg/kg dose of lipid-soluble medications such as diazepam or the barbiturates is lower for neonates than for adults.[2]

DRUG-METABOLIZING ENZYMES

The activity of drug-metabolizing enzymes is reduced in neonates, particularly the enzymatic processes of hydroxylation and conjugation with glucuronic acid in the liver.[1,9] For instance, diazepam is metabolized by hydroxylation. Its half-life in full-term infants ranges from 20 to 45 hours, but in neonates it can be increased to 40 to 100 hours because of the slower biotransformation rate of the enzymes involved.[10] Hence, diazepam must be used cautiously and in reduced doses in these young infants. Caution must also be used in the administration of phenytoin and chloramphenicol since the decreased hepatic metabolism of these agents in the neonate can lead to drug accumulation and toxic levels in the serum.[1]

RENAL FUNCTION

Renal function is less efficient in newborn, premature, and full-term infants than in children and adults. Full function is not reached until 6 to 12 months of age.[2,3] Antibiotics like the penicillins and aminoglycosides, which are not extensively metabolized and which are totally dependent on good renal function for their excretion, are eliminated slowly in the newborn.[2,11] Dosages and administration intervals must be adjusted, based on the maturity of kidney function. Doses of penicillin, for example, are given only every 12 hours during the first week of life and then every 8 hours for the next three weeks as renal clearance improves. Dosage intervals for an older child would be every three to six hours. Similarly, aminoglycoside doses and frequency of administration are also reduced in neonates and young infants to avoid serious nephrotoxicity.

Water, too, poses an additional and important requirement for the renal excretion of pharmacological agents. During disease water requirements and losses may increase because of the infant's diminished intake. Aspirin, for instance, is disposed of primarily by urinary excretion. As the pH of the urine rises above 7.0, aspirin excretion accelerates. Fever, one of the indications for aspirin's use, is likewise indirectly associated with reduced renal blood flow and an acidic urine.[12] Consequently, aspirin excretion diminishes, and what would otherwise be an "average" dose may now become toxic to the infant.

CLINICAL STUDIES

Many drugs have not yet been studied in infants and children. Clinical studies for new therapeutic agents follow the path from laboratory animals to adults to, lastly, infants. This sequence offers the pediatric patient some measure of safety, but, as is often the case, this progression of clinical studies results in years of delay before neonates, young infants, and children are allowed to use new agents already approved for use in older children and adults.[12] Ideally, investigational protocols should include studies in the newborn and full-term infant so that they, as well as adults, may benefit from these newer, improved medications. Until such studies are routinely done, it is preferable to utilize those therapeutic agents that have been proved over the years to be safe and effective in the pediatric age group.

NOTES

1. Zenk KE: Drug dosing in neonates, in Pagliaro LA, Levin RH (eds): *Problems in Pediatric Drug Therapy*, ed 1. Hamilton, Ill, Drug Intelligence Publications Inc, 1979, pp 161–162.
2. Cupit GC: Pediatric therapy, in Koda-Kimble M, Katcher BS, Young LY (eds): *Applied Therapeutics for Clinical Pharmacists*, ed 2. San Francisco, Applied Therapeutics Inc, 1978, pp 874–875.
3. Morselli PL: Clinical pharmacokinetics in neonates. *Clin Pharmacokinet* 1976;1:81–98.
4. Yaffe SJ, Juchau MR: Perinatal pharmacology. *Annu Rev Pharmacol* 1974;14:219.
5. Wallace S: Factors affecting drug-protein binding in the plasma of newborn infants. *Br J Clin Pharmacol* 1976;3:510.
6. Thaler MM, Schmid R: Drugs and bilirubin. *Pediatrics* 1971;47:807.
7. Friis-Hausen B: Body water compartments in children: Changes during growth and related changes in body composition. *Pediatrics* 1961;28:169.
8. Giacoia G, Jusko WJ, Menke J, et al: Theophylline pharmacokinetics in premature infants with apnea. *J Pediatr* 1976;89:829–832.
9. Vest MF, Rossier R: Detoxification in the newborn: The ability of the newborn infant to form conjugates with glucuronic acid, glycine acetate, and glutathione. *Ann NY Acad Sci* 1963;111:183.
10. Morselli PL: Diazepam elimination in premature and full-term infants and children. *J Perinat Med* 1973;1:133.
11. McCracken GH: Pharmacological basis for antimicrobial therapy in newborn infants. *Am J Dis Child* 1974;128:407–419.
12. Shirkey HC (ed): *Pediatric Therapy*, ed 5. St Louis, The CV Mosby Co, 1975, p 21.

II
AGENTS FOR CARDIOPULMONARY RESUSCITATION

One of the most frightening medical emergencies involves the immediate threat of death because of serious cardiac arrhythmias and anoxia. Cardiopulmonary resuscitation (CPR) requires coordinated teamwork and quick action. Sudden cessation of effective cardiac output can result in permanent neurological damage or death if not treated in 4 to 6 minutes. The aim of therapy is to maintain adequate circulation of oxygenated blood while measures are being undertaken to restore normal cardiac rhythm. Since the majority of therapeutic agents used for cardiovascular support and antiarrhythmic effects act by simulating or antagonizing the effects of the autonomic nervous system, a basic review of the structure and function of this system may be helpful in understanding the pharmacological actions of these medications. For this purpose, a brief discussion of the nervous system, with particular emphasis on the autonomic division, has been included as a preface for this section.

Section II discusses adrenergics (vasopressors), cholinergic and adrenergic blockers, antiarrhythmics, cardiotonics, antihypertensives, and vasodilators.

THE NERVOUS SYSTEM

Two major systems control and integrate body functions: the endocrine system and the nervous system. The ability of these two systems to integrate activity in the brain and influence tissues and organs in the distant parts of the body depends on the transmission of information between these central and peripheral areas. The endocrine system accomplishes this transmission via blood-borne hormones. The nervous system, on the other hand, relies primarily on the rapid electrical transmission of impulses along nerve fibers. However, the transmission of an impulse across the synapses or "spaces" between individual nerve fiber endings and adjacent nerve cell bodies is accomplished by the release of small amounts of specialized chemical substances called "neurotransmitters." These substances diffuse across the synaptic spaces and attach to special receptor sites in the adjacent nerve cell body, causing it to be electrically or chemically stimulated to carry the impulse along the next length of nerve fiber. The primary neurotransmitters of the peripheral nervous system are acetylcholine and norepinephrine. (Epinephrine is the chemical transmitter for the adrenal medulla.)

The nervous system can be divided into two functional divisions:

1. The central nervous system
   - Brain
   - Spinal cord
2. The peripheral nervous system
   - Somatic system (nonautonomic)
   - Autonomic system
     - Parasympathetic ("craniosacral")
     - Sympathetic ("thoracolumbar")

A stimulus, transmitted either through the bloodstream via a hormonal substance or by a peripheral sensory (afferent) nerve fiber, is received by the integrating areas of the central nervous system, namely the medulla, hypothalamus, reticular formation, and spinal cord. It is then transmitted peripherally to the various tissues, organs, and glands via the peripheral motor (efferent) fibers. These efferent fibers are the preganglionic and postganglionic fibers of the peripheral nervous system.

The peripheral nervous system consists of the somatic and autonomic systems. The operation of the somatic system is largely "nonautomatic" in that it is associated with consciously controlled functions such as respiration and the movements of skeletal muscles. In contrast, the operation of the autonomic nervous system is "automatic" since it does not require conscious activation. It automatically controls such functions as heart rate; cardiac contractile force; regulation of blood flow and blood pressure; contraction and relaxation of the smooth muscle of the gut, bronchioles, and bladder; visual accommodation and pupil size; control of certain exocrine secretions; and the like.

The autonomic nervous system is further divided into two subdivisions: the parasympathetic nervous system (PANS) and the sympathetic nervous system (SANS). In simplistic terms, the parasympathetic and sympathetic systems act opposingly. The PANS is concerned with the energy-conserving and growth-oriented activities of the body, while the

SANS, described as the "fight-or-flight" system, expends large amounts of energy. Table II–1 illustrates some of the basic and opposing effects of these two systems.

The PANS is sometimes called the "craniosacral" system because its nerve fibers leave or enter the central nervous system via the 3rd, 7th, 9th, and 10th cranial nerves and the S-3 and S-4 sacral segments. The PANS preganglionic fibers are relatively long and often terminate directly in or very near the organ or tissue innervated (Fig. II–1). The 10th cranial or vagus nerve is especially complex with branching preganglionic fibers innervating many abdominal and thoracic organs (e.g., stomach, gut, bronchioles, liver, pancreas, heart, adrenal medulla). The postganglionic fibers are short and often located in the walls of the innervated organ. Acetylcholine is the neurotransmitter at both the preganglionic and postganglionic synapses. Medications that act primarily at these sites are called parasympathomimetic (cholinergic) if they act like acetylcholine to stimulate parasympathetic nerve activity and parasympatholytic (anticholinergic) if they block or antagonize the effects of cholinergic stimulation.

The fibers of the sympathetic or "thoracolumbar" system enter and leave only the spinal cord at the thoracic and lumbar segments. The preganglionic efferent fibers are relatively short (Fig. II–2) and enter the sympathetic nerve trunks (one on each side of the spinal cord). Each of these trunks consists of a chain of 22 ganglia connected by fibers. Some preganglionic fibers end in other specialized ganglia outside these two main trunks (e.g., cardiac, celiac, or hypogastric ganglia). The SANS postganglionic fibers are much longer and terminate in many of the same effector cells or organs as do the PANS fibers (e.g., cardiac muscle; smooth muscle of the gut, blood vessels, bronchioles). The neurotransmitter at the SANS preganglionic synapse is acetylcholine, but the mediator released at the SANS postganglionic synapse is norepinephrine (epinephrine in the adrenal medulla only). Medications that simulate or mimic norepinephrine (or epinephrine) release are called sympathomimetics (adrenergics), while those that inhibit or antagonize the activity of norepinephrine at these sites are referred to as sympatholytics (adrenergic blockers).

It should be noted that acetylcholine released at the preganglionic synapses of both the SANS and PANS acts on "nicotinic" cholinergic receptor sites, so-called because their stimulation produces the same pharmacological effects as nicotine (i.e., adrenergic effects). The actions of acetylcholine are referred to as "nicotinic" if they cause stimulation of the SANS postganglionic fibers (sympathomimetic effects) or "muscarinic" if they cause stimulation of the PANS postganglionic fibers (parasympathomimetic effects).

TABLE II–1 Effects of the Autonomic Nervous System*

Organ/Function	Receptor Type (Adrenergic)	Sympathetic (Adrenergic)	Parasympathetic (Cholinergic)
HEART			
Rate (direct)	Beta-1	Increased	Decreased (vagal)
Contractility		Increased	Decreased or no change
BLOOD PRESSURE	—	Increased	Decreased or no change
BLOOD VESSELS			
Skin, mucous membranes	Alpha	Constricted	Dilated
Skeletal muscle	Beta, alpha	Dilated	Dilated
BRONCHIOLAR SMOOTH MUSCLE	Beta-2	Relaxed (bronchodilation)	Constricted (bronchoconstriction)
GASTROINTESTINAL TRACT			
Motility/tone	Alpha, beta	Decreased (usually)	Increased
Sphincters	Alpha	Contracted	Relaxed
Secretions	—	Inhibited (?)	Stimulated
SALIVARY GLANDS	Alpha	Increased secretion (thick, mucus)	Increased secretion (watery, dilute)
URINARY BLADDER/URETER WALL	Alpha, beta	Relaxed	Contracted
METABOLIC ACTIONS	—	Fat mobilization from depots; Glycogen breakdown for energy; Increased blood sugar	No change

*Source: Goodman LS, Gilman A: *The Pharmacological Basis of Therapeutics*, ed 6. New York, Macmillan Publishing Co, Inc, 1980; Sutherland VC: *A Synopsis of Pharmacology*, ed 2. Philadelphia. WB Saunders Co, 1970.

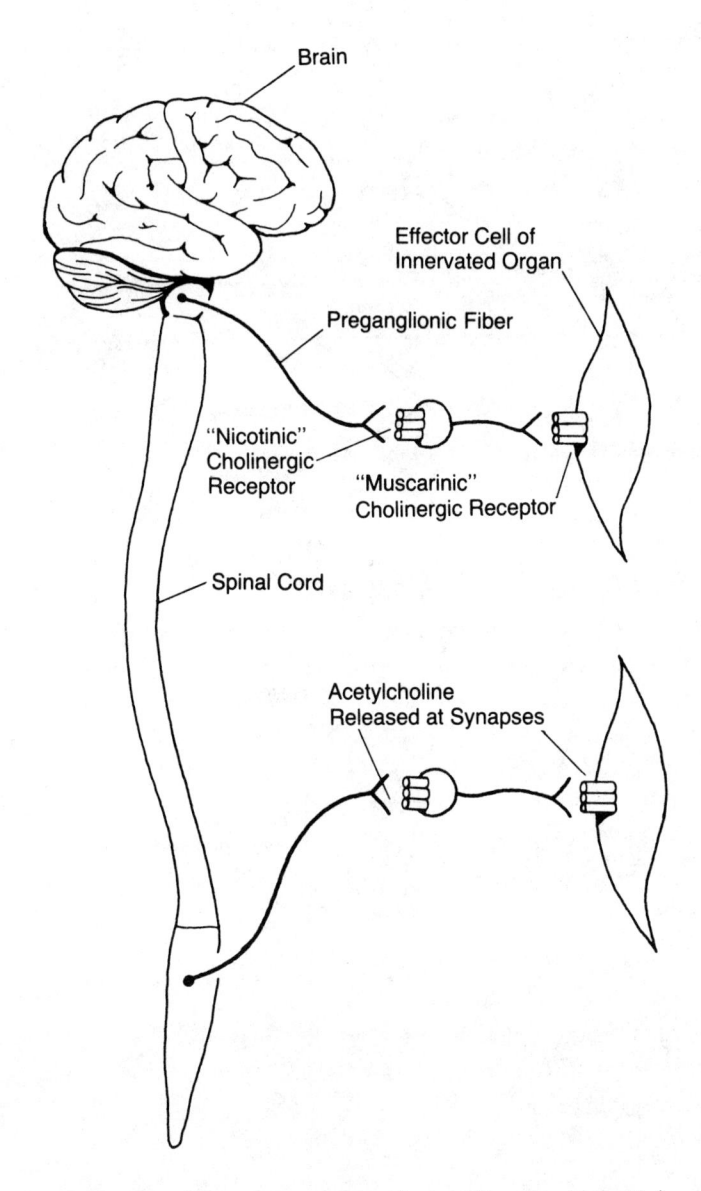

Fig. II–1 Parasympathetic Nerve Fiber (schematic)

In the somatic nervous system, neuromuscular transmission is cholinergic. Acetylcholine is released at the neuromuscular junction and stimulates the motor endplate, a specialized membrane at the site where nerve endings approach the muscle (Fig. II–3). Lower concentrations of acetylcholine cause a depolarization that spreads to the muscle cell membranes, and contraction follows. If the effect of acetylcholine is intense or

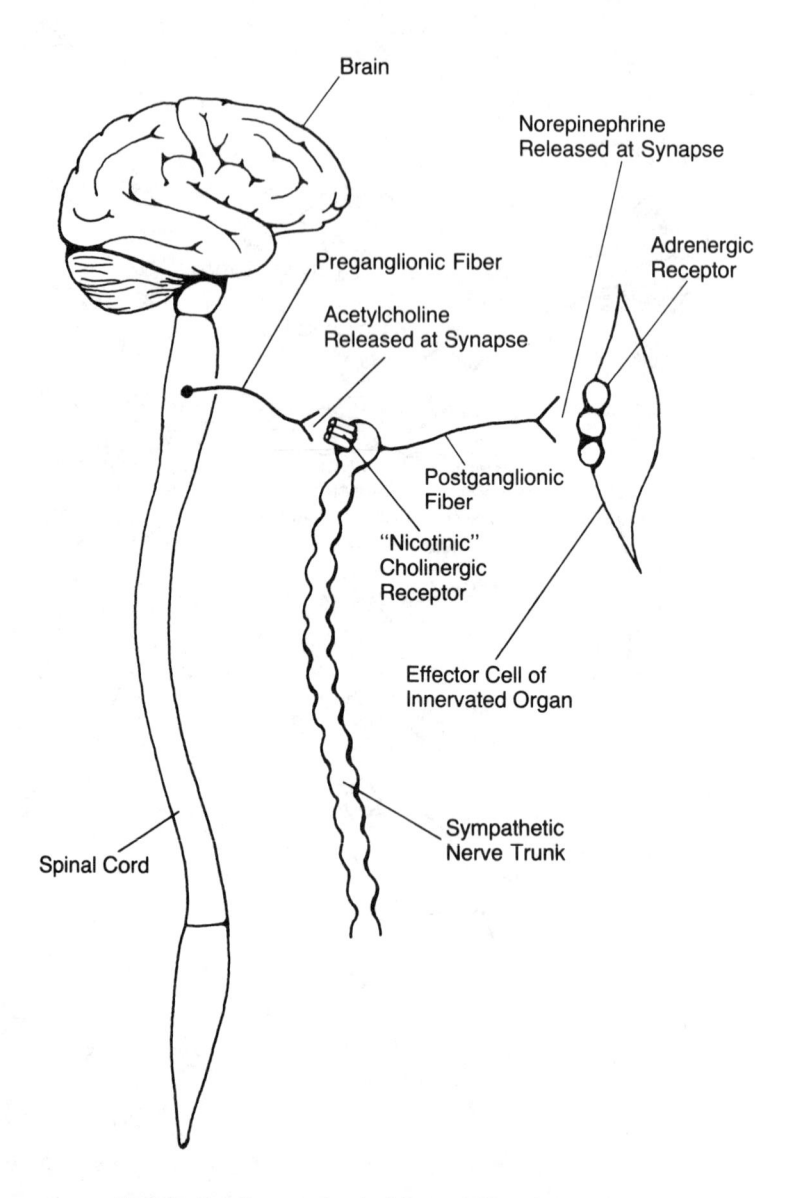

Fig. II–2 Sympathetic Nerve Fiber (schematic)

if high concentrations of this mediator are present (as may be produced by cholinesterase inhibitors or depolarizing skeletal muscle relaxants), this depolarization persists. If repolarization of the motor endplate does not occur, a flaccid paralysis results. (High doses of nicotine also cause this depolarizing effect, so the receptor site at the neuromuscular junction is also referred to as a "nicotinic" cholinergic receptor.)

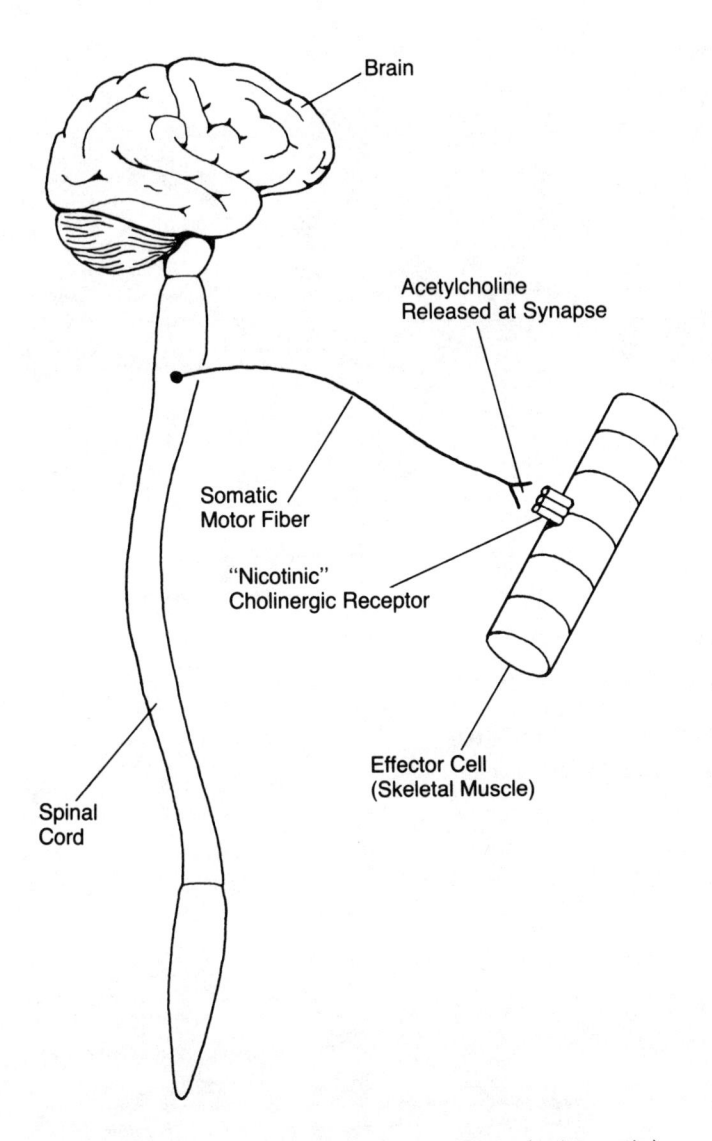

Fig. II–3 Somatic System Nerve Fiber (schematic)

3
Adrenergics

Adrenergics, classified as sympathomimetic amines, simulate or mimic the effects caused by stimulation of sympathetic nerves. The effects of these agents vary according to their action on the different types of adrenergic receptors in the cardiovascular system: alpha-adrenergic (α), beta-1-adrenergic (β_1), beta-2-adrenergic (β_2), and dopaminergic. Table 3–1 lists the different receptor types and the results of their activation.

TABLE 3–1 Adrenergic Receptors

Receptor Type	Location	Result of Stimulation
Alpha (α)	Skin, mucous membranes, intestines, kidney	Vasoconstriction of vascular beds
Beta-1 (β_1)	Myocardium	Increased heart rate, increased contractility
Beta-2 (β_2)	Bronchioles, skeletal muscle arterioles (primarily)	Bronchodilation, vasodilation
Dopaminergic	Renal/mesenteric vascular beds	Vasodilation

The adrenergics used clinically can be divided into two groups: endogenous catecholamines and synthetic sympathomimetics (Table 3–2).

TABLE 3–2 Adrenergics

Type	Primary Receptor Type Stimulated
ENDOGENOUS CATECOLAMINES	
Epinephrine (Adrenalin)	Beta-1, beta-2, alpha
Norepinephrine (Levophed)	Alpha, beta-1
Dopamine (Intropin)	Dopaminergic, beta-1
SYNTHETIC SYMPATHOMIMETICS	
Dobutamine (Dobutrex)	Beta-1
Isoproterenol (Isuprel)	Beta-1, beta-2
Metaraminol (Aramine)	Alpha
Methoxamine (Vasoxyl)	Alpha
Phenylephrine (Neo-Synephrine)	Alpha

The following medications are discussed in this chapter:

- **Dobutamine**
- **Dopamine**
- **Epinephrine**
- **Isoproterenol**
- **Norepinephrine**
- **Phenylephrine**

Dobutamine (Dobutrex)

ADMINISTRATION

Available Forms: Injectable (IV), 250 mg powder for reconstitution.

Diluent: 5% dextrose in water (D5W), normal saline (NS), sodium lactate. Suggested dilution is 250 mg in 500 ml or 1000 ml to yield concentrations of 500 µg/ml or 250 µg/ml respectively.

Dosage (Parenteral): (Not established in children) IV infusion of 2.5–10.0 µg/kg/min. Administer with controlled infusion device and adjust rates according to heart rate, blood pressure, ectopic activity, urine flow, pulmonary artery wedge pressure (PAWP), and so forth.

Rate: 2.5–10.0 µg/kg/min. Rates up to 40 µg/kg/min have been used.

INDICATIONS: Dobutamine is used for short-term inotropic support in congestive heart failure and other forms of cardiac decompensation when increased cardiac output, decreased PAWP, and decreased left ventricular end diastolic pressure (LVEDP) are desired.

ACTIONS: Dobutamine, a direct-acting catecholamine, stimulates beta-1 receptors of the heart to increase myocardial contractile force and cardiac output. It does not cause the release of endogenous norepinephrine as does dopamine, and moderate doses do not increase heart rate or decrease peripheral resistance as much as isoproterenol. High doses, however, resemble isoproterenol since they produce tachycardia and decreased peripheral resistance. Dobutamine also enhances atrioventricular and intraventricular conduction. Onset of action is rapid (1–2 minutes) but brief (minutes).

CONTRAINDICATIONS: Hypertension, idiopathic hypertrophic subaortic stenosis.

PRECAUTIONS: Continuous cardiac monitoring is necessary since dobutamine may precipitate or exaggerate ventricular ectopic activity. Use with caution when atrial fibrillation is present since ventricular rate may increase. (May need to digitalize patient to control ventricular response.) Maintain or replace plasma volume as necessary. Exaggerated pressor response may be seen in patients with preexisting hypertension. Solutions of dobutamine may discolor slightly with no loss of potency.

SIDE EFFECTS/ADVERSE REACTIONS: Ventricular ectopic beats, premature ventricular contractions (PVCs), chest pain, palpitations, increased heart rate (5–15 beats per min [bpm]), increased systolic blood pressure (10–20 mm Hg), nausea, and dyspnea may occur (most are dose-related).

DRUG INCOMPATIBILITIES: Do not mix with alkaline solutions (e.g., sodium bicarbonate, aminophylline).

DRUG INTERACTIONS: *Beta-blockers* may inhibit dobutamine's action. *Nitroprusside* and *dobutamine* together may result in higher cardiac output and lower PAWP than when either is used alone.

ANTIDOTE: Discontinue the infusion until the patient stabilizes. Additional remedial measures are usually unnecessary because of dobutamine's short duration of action.

Dopamine (Intropin, others)

ADMINISTRATION

Available Forms: Injectable (IV), 40 mg/ml in 200 mg ampules (amps), 400 mg vials; premixed solution of 400 mg/250 ml D5W (1600 µg/ml).

Diluent: D5W, NS, lactated Ringer's solution (LR). Suggested dilution is 200 mg in 500 ml diluent to yield a concentration of 400 µg/ml.

Dosage (Parenteral): Initial IV infusion is 2–5 µg/kg/min; can be increased by increments of 5–10 µg/kg/min if a satisfactory response is not observed. (Note: Safety and efficacy are not established in children, but a dosage range of 0.3–25.0 µg/kg/min has been used.)

Rate: 2–5 µg/kg/min. Maximum recommended rate is 50 µg/kg/min, but most patients usually require 20 µg/kg/min or less.

INDICATIONS: Dopamine is used for the correction of hemodynamic imbalances due to impaired cardiac function and various kinds of shock (cardiogenic, septic, and shock accompanied by oliguria). It may also be effective in chronic refractory congestive heart failure.

ACTIONS: Dopamine is a centrally acting neurotransmitter that increases cardiac output, systolic and pulse pressures, and urine flow *directly* by stimulating beta-1 receptors and *indirectly* by causing the release of norepinephrine. The effects are dose-dependent.
0.5–2.0 µg/kg/min: Acts primarily on dopaminergic receptors in the renal and mesenteric beds to cause vasodilation and increased renal flow.
2–10 µg/kg/min: Stimulates beta-1 receptors to increase myocardial contractility and cardiac output.
Over 10 µg/kg/min: Stimulates alpha receptors to cause increased systemic vascular resistance, resulting in elevated blood pressure.
Over 30 µg/kg/min: Causes prominent vasoconstriction, which decreases renal and mesenteric blood flow, resulting in a diminished output of urine.
Moderate doses (10–20 µg/kg/min): Cause increased cardiac output and contractility with little tendency to increase heart rate as isoproterenol does.

CONTRAINDICATIONS: Pheochromocytoma, uncorrected tachyarrhythmias, ventricular fibrillation.

PRECAUTIONS: Monitor blood pressure frequently (q2–5min) until it is stable or until the emergency is terminated. Maintain blood volume or replace if necessary. Hypoxia, hypercapnia, and acidosis all reduce the effectiveness of dopamine. Monitor urine output, especially when infusion rates exceed 30–50 µg/kg/min. Use with caution in patients with hyperthyroidism. Avoid extravasation of dopamine solutions as it may cause tissue necrosis. Peripheral ischemia and gangrene at the infusion site can be treated with phentolamine (Regitine); infiltrate 5–10 mg into the site. Do not use discolored solutions of dopamine.

SIDE EFFECTS/ADVERSE REACTIONS: (Primarily dose-related) Ectopic beats, tachycardia, palpitations, anginal pain, dyspnea, headache, nausea, vomiting, hypotension (low doses), and vasoconstriction (high doses) occur most frequently. Also reported are bradycardia, widened QRS complexes, aberrant conduction, azotemia, hypertension, and gangrene of the extremity that is the site of infusion.

DRUG INCOMPATIBILITIES: Do not mix with alkaline solutions (e.g., sodium bicarbonate, diphenylhydantoin, aminophylline).

DRUG INTERACTIONS: *Monoamine oxidase (MAO) inhibitors* potentiate dopamine, so reduce dopamine to one-tenth the usual dose. Use with *diphenylhydantoin* causes additive bradycardia and hypotension. *Cyclopropane* and *halogenated anesthetics* sensitize the myocardium to arrhythmias (especially ventricular) that may be induced by dopamine.

ANTIDOTE: Discontinue the infusion until the patient stabilizes. Dopamine's action is short, and no other measures are usually necessary.

Epinephrine (Adrenalin)

ADMINISTRATION

Available Forms: Injectable (SC), 5 mg/ml (1:200 suspension) in amps and vials (Sus-Phrine); injectable (IM, IV, SC), 1 mg/ml (1:1000 solution) in amps and vials; injectable (IV, IC), 1 mg/10 ml (1:10,000 solution) in preloaded syringe; solution for nebulization (1:100).

Dosage (Parenteral): Varies according to use.
As bronchodilator: 0.01 ml/kg/dose of a 1:1000 solution SC (up to a maximum dose of 0.5 ml). Can be repeated 15–20 min for 2 doses, then every 4 hours as needed (prn).
1:200 suspension of Sus-Phrine: 0.004–0.005 ml/kg. Can be repeated q8–12h (maximum is 0.15 ml/dose).
As cardiotonic in CPR: 0.1 ml/kg of a 1:10,000 solution IV or IC with defibrillation available. Can be repeated q5–10min. Can also be given via direct instillation into an endotracheal tube.

INDICATIONS: Epinephrine is used in CPR to stimulate myocardial contractility and coarsen fine ventricular fibrillation before electrical defibrillation and as a bronchodilator in the treatment of asthma, anaphylactic shock, and other hypersensitivity reactions.

ACTIONS: The catecholamine epinephrine is a potent vasopressor that acts on alpha, beta-1, and beta-2 receptors to increase both systolic and pulse pressures. However, diastolic blood pressure usually decreases. Blood vessels in skin, mucosa, and kidney are constricted (stimulation of alpha-receptors), while vessels in skeletal muscle are dilated (stimulation of beta-receptors). Epinephrine increases heart rate, stroke volume, myocardial contractility, and cardiac output. The overall effect of full stimulation of alpha and beta receptors is increased peripheral resistance and elevated blood pressure. Epinephrine also stimulates beta-2 receptors of the bronchioles to cause bronchodilation.

CONTRAINDICATIONS: (Excluding use in CPR.) Narrow-angle (congestive) glaucoma, organic brain damage, shock other than anaphylactic, coronary insufficiency and cardiac dilatation, labor, hypersensitivity to sympathomimetics.

PRECAUTIONS: Use with caution in patients who have cardiovascular disease, hypertension, diabetes, hyperthyroidism, chronic bronchial asthma, or emphysema with concurrent degenerative heart disease. Peripheral vasoconstriction and cardiac stimulation may cause fatal pulmonary edema. Avoid intracardiac use if possible. Shock in already hypotensive patients may be worsened. Monitor vital signs at least every 5 minutes throughout the emergency. Epinephrine "resistance" or tachyphylaxis may occur. Do not use discolored solutions. Check the label carefully for dosage and route of administration; do not give epinephrine suspensions or epinephrine in oil IV.

SIDE EFFECTS/ADVERSE REACTIONS: Anxiety, tremor, fear, dizziness, headache, dyspnea, palpitations, tachyarrhythmias, anginal pain, cerebral and other organ hemorrhages, pulmonary edema, hypertension, hypotension, and local tissue necrosis at the injection site may occur. Intracardiac use may produce intractable ventricular tachycardia or asystole.

DRUG INCOMPATIBILITIES: Do not use with calcium salts and alkaline solutions (e.g., sodium bicarbonate, aminophylline).

DRUG INTERACTIONS: Simultaneous administration with *isoproterenol* may induce serious arrhythmias. (The two medications can be given alternately, however.) The pressor effects of epinephrine may be potentiated by *other sympathomimetics, levothyroxine, tricyclic antidepressants, and antihistamines.* Use with *digitalis* may increase ectopic pacemaker activity. *Halogenated hydrocarbon anesthetics* and *cyclopropane* sensitize the myocardium to epinephrine-induced arrhythmias. Epinephine may antagonize the hypoglycemic effect of *oral antidiabetic agents* and *insulin*. The cardiac stimulatory effect of epinephrine is antagonized by *beta-blockers,* resulting in bradycardia.

ANTIDOTE: Counteract excessive pressor effects with rapidly acting vasodilators or alpha-adrenergic blockers.

Isoproterenol (Isuprel)

ADMINISTRATION

Available Forms: Injectable (IV, IM, SC), 0.2 mg/ml (1:5000 solution) in 1 ml and 5 ml amps.

Diluent: D5W. Suggested dilution is 1 mg in 250 ml to yield a concentration of 4 μg/ml.

Dosage (Parenteral): Initial bolus of 10–25 μg can be given IV, followed by an IV infusion of 0.1–0.5 μg/kg/min, titrated on the basis of heart rate and blood pressure (up to 1.0 μg/kg/min). Has also been given IM or SC in doses of 0.1 mg.

Rate: See dosage.

INDICATIONS: Isoproterenol is used for treatment of complete heart block (with ventricular arrhythmias), Stokes-Adams syndrome, cardiogenic shock, and low cardiac output caused by myocardial failure (excluding coronary artery disease). It is administered primarily by IV infusion to maintain heart rate in third-degree heart block and by inhalation and orally for bronchodilation.

ACTIONS: Isoproterenol is a sympathomimetic that acts exclusively on beta receptors of the heart and the vascular beds of skeletal muscle to increase heart rate, cardiac output, and systolic blood pressure. Peripheral vascular resistance, diastolic blood pressure, and central venous pressures are decreased. Isoproterenol acts on beta-2 receptors of the lung to produce bronchodilation. It also inhibits antigen-induced histamine release and stimulates insulin secretion. After IV administration, the onset of action is immediate, but duration is brief (minutes).

CONTRAINDICATIONS: Hypersensitivity to isoproterenol and other sympathomimetics, tachycardia due to digitalis toxicity, tachyarrhythmias, aortic stenosis.

PRECAUTIONS: Maintain adequate blood volume. Continuous cardiac monitoring is necessary since arrhythmias can occur. Supplemental oxygen may be necessary to provide adequate O_2 perfusion. Isoproterenol may worsen shock because of systemic vasodilation that can diminish coronary perfusion pressure and lead to myocardial ischemia. It may also worsen cardiogenic shock by increasing myocardial oxygen demands via its positive inotropic and chronotropic actions. Use cautiously in patients with tachyarrhythmias, hyperthyroidism, or limited cardiac reserve. Temporarily discontinue the infusion if the heart rate rises above 110 bpm. Do not use discolored solutions. Solutions are light-sensitive.

SIDE EFFECTS/ADVERSE REACTIONS: Headache, flushing, dizziness, nausea, tremor, hyperhidrosis, and tachycardia may occur. Doses sufficient to produce heart rates higher than 130 bpm may cause anginal pain and ventricular extrasystoles and arrhythmias.

DRUG INCOMPATIBILITIES: Do not mix with alkaline solutions (e.g., sodium bicarbonate, aminophylline, phenytoin, barbiturates, lidocaine). This medication is unstable at pH >5.5.

DRUG INTERACTIONS: Simultaneous administration with *epinephrine* may lead to serious cardiac arrhythmias. *Beta-blockers* (e.g., propranolol) may antagonize the effects of isoproterenol.

ANTIDOTE: Discontinue the medication until the patient's condition stabilizes. Adverse reactions usually dissipate quickly because of isoproterenol's short duration of action.

Norepinephrine (levarterenol) (Levophed)

ADMINISTRATION

Available Forms: Injectable (IV), 1 mg of levarterenol base per milliliter in 4 ml amps (available as the bitartrate salt; 2 mg levarterenol bitartrate = 1 mg levarterenol base).

Diluent: D5W with or without sodium chloride. (Do not use NS alone as it promotes oxidation of the drug.) Suggested dilution is 1 mg base (1 ml) in 250 ml to yield a concentration of 4 µg/ml.

Dosage (Parenteral): IV infusion of 2 µg base/min (0.5 ml/min) titrated to maintain blood pressure. (Can start at 0.1 µg/min and increase rate as needed.)

Rate: See dosage. Maximum rate is 6 µg/min (1.5 ml/min of the suggested IV dilution).

INDICATIONS: Norepinephrine is used as an adjunctive measure to produce vasoconstriction and myocardial stimulation in hypotension and cardiac standstill. It may be useful when "indirect-acting" agents fail.

ACTIONS: Levarterenol (norepinephrine) is a direct-acting catecholamine that acts predominantly by stimulation of alpha receptors. It also stimulates beta-1 cardiac receptors but to a lesser extent than epinephrine or isoproterenol do. It has a positive inotropic and chronotropic effect on the heart, but a reflex vagal bradycardia occurs (which can be blocked by atropine). Systolic, diastolic, and pulse pressures increase as total peripheral vascular resistance rises. Renal and mesenteric blood flow decreases. Myocardial oxygen consumption increases.

CONTRAINDICATIONS: Concomitant use during cyclopropane or halothane anesthesia, pregnancy (causes fetal anoxia).

PRECAUTIONS: Cardiac arrhythmias may occur in patients who have profound hypoxia or hypercarbia. Metabolic acidosis should be corrected first since it inhibits the cardiac response to norepinephrine. Monitor blood gases frequently. Monitor blood pressure frequently until the patient is stable or until the emergency is terminated. Maintain adequate blood volume. Discontinue infusions gradually to prevent rebound hypotension or vascular collapse. Avoid extravasation as tissue necrosis and sloughing may occur. Do not use discolored solutions. Solutions in ampules are light-sensitive.

SIDE EFFECTS/ADVERSE REACTIONS: The first symptom of overdose is usually headache followed by tremor, weakness, pallor, anxiety, and insomnia. Overdoses cause severe hypertension, reflex bradycardia, and decreased cardiac output.

DRUG INCOMPATIBILITIES: Normal saline promotes oxidation of norepinephrine in solution. Do not mix with whole blood or with alkaline solutions (e.g., aminophylline, sodium bicarbonate, barbiturates, phenytoin, ampicillin, metaraminol). Administer whole blood separately or via Y-tubing. Stability decreases at pH >5.5.

DRUG INTERACTIONS: Use with *MAO inhibitors* or *tricyclic antidepressants* may cause severe, prolonged hypertension. *Cyclopropane* and *halothane anesthetics* sensitize the myocardium to norepinephrine-induced arrhythmias.

ANTIDOTE: For extravasation and tissue necrosis, infiltrate the affected area with 5–10 mg phentolamine diluted with 10–15 ml NS. For systemic adverse reactions, discontinue the infusion gradually to avoid abrupt withdrawal and vascular collapse. Maintain adequate circulatory plasma volume.

Phenylephrine (Neo-Synephrine)

ADMINISTRATION

Available Forms: Injectable (IM, SC, IV), 10 mg/ml in 1 ml amps.

Dosage (Parenteral): 0.1 mg/kg as a single dose given IM or SC. IV use is not recommended but doses of 1–3 mg/m^2 diluted in D5W and given as an infusion have been used for treatment of paroxysmal atrial tachycardia.

INDICATIONS: Phenylephrine is used to control acute hypotension during anesthesia with agents that sensitize the heart to catecholamines. It is also used to maintain arterial pressure during spinal anesthesia, to treat drug-induced or hypersensitivity-induced hypotension, and to overcome paroxysmal supraventricular tachycardia in patients with hypotension.

ACTIONS: Phenylephrine is a vasopressor that causes peripheral vasoconstriction by direct stimulation of alpha-adrenergic receptors. The subsequent rise in both systolic and diastolic pressures causes a reflex bradycardia (which can be blocked by atropine). Pulmonary arterial pressure is also elevated. Since phenylephrine has almost no activity on the cardiac beta receptors, cardiac arrhythmias are rarely seen, even with large doses. The vasoconstricting effects of phenylephrine last longer than those of epinephrine or ephedrine: up to 20 minutes after IV injection, and up to 50 minutes after SC injection.

CONTRAINDICATIONS: Severe hypertension, ventricular tachycardia, hypersensitivity to phenylephrine.

PRECAUTIONS: Monitor vital signs frequently. Use cautiously in patients with hyperthyroidism, hypertension, myocardial disease, heart block, or bradycardia and during labor and delivery induced with oxytocic drugs.

SIDE EFFECTS/ADVERSE REACTIONS: Headache, reflex bradycardia, excitability, and restlessness may occur. Cardiac arrhythmias are rare, but overdoses may induce ventricular extrasystoles or tachycardia, tingling of the extremities, and a sense of fullness in the head.

DRUG INTERACTIONS: Phenylephrine may cause serious cardiac arrhythmias during anesthesia with *halothane*. Use with *tricyclic antidepressants, MAO inhibitors,* or *oxytocic drugs* may produce severe hypertensive responses.

ANTIDOTE: Treat excessive hypertension with an alpha-adrenergic blocker such as phentolamine.

4
Cholinergic Blockers

Cholinergic blockers, or anticholinergics, inhibit the action of acetylcholine on tissues that are innervated by postganglionic cholinergic receptors and on smooth muscles that respond to acetylcholine. The end result of anticholinergic inhibition often resembles overactivity of the sympathetic nervous system because the balance between sympathetic and parasympathetic tone is altered.

Because atropine typifies all members of this class of medications, the actions of cholinergic blockers are often referred to as "atropine-like." Only the prototype, atropine, is discussed in this chapter.

In contrast to atropine, parasympathomimetic agents mimic cholinergic stimulation. Physostigmine, which represents this group, is discussed in chapter 35.

Atropine

ADMINISTRATION

Available Forms: Injectable (IV, IM, SC), 0.3, 0.4, 0.5, 0.6, 1.0, 1.2, and 2.0 mg per milliliter in amps and vials; prefilled syringe with 1 mg/10 ml.

Dosage (Parenteral): Varies according to use.

For bradycardia: 0.01-0.03 mg/kg IV, SC, or via endotracheal tube; can be repeated in 5 minutes. Minimum dose is 0.1 mg; maximum dose is 1.0 mg.

For cholinergic crisis: 0.2-1.0 mg IV as needed (up to 2.0 mg).

INDICATIONS: Atropine is used in *low* doses to treat sinus bradycardia and heart block (first-degree and second-degree) and in higher doses to treat cholinergic crises caused by overdoses of anticholinesterase medication or by poisoning with organophosphate insecticides.

ACTIONS: Atropine competitively blocks the actions of acetylcholine. It lessens the degree of atrioventricular (AV) block by decreasing vagal influence, enhancing AV conduction, and increasing sinus rate (ventricular rate may also increase). Atropine reduces the motility and secretions of the gastrointestinal (GI) system, dries up mucous membranes of the respiratory tract, causes mydriasis and cycloplegia, and may elevate intraocular pressure in narrow-angle glaucoma. It readily crosses the blood-brain barrier, and high doses cause CNS stimulation while toxic doses cause CNS depression. Onset of action after IV administration is about 1–5 minutes. Cardiac effects last approximately 2 hours; systemic effects may last 4–6 hours.

CONTRAINDICATIONS: Hypersensitivity to atropine, acute glaucoma, obstructive disease of the GI or urinary tract (e.g., pyloric stenosis, obstructive uropathy), reflux esophagitis.

PRECAUTIONS: Atropine may cause paradoxical bradycardia because of central effects when given in less than therapeutic doses. Use with caution in patients with glaucoma, fever, asthma, obstructive disease of the GI tract, GI immobility, or ulcerative colitis.

SIDE EFFECTS/ADVERSE REACTIONS: (Most are dose-related and manifestations of atropine's pharmacological action.) Low doses cause initial cardiac slowing, some dryness of the mouth, and inhibition of sweating. Full therapeutic doses cause tachycardia, mydriasis, cycloplegia, constipation, and dysuria. Toxic doses produce all aforementioned symptoms as well as a burning sensation; hot, dry, scarlet-flushed skin; ataxia; dysphagia; thirst; hypertension or hypotension; excitement; hallucinations; delirium; and coma. Dermatological and hypersensitivity reactions may also occur (not dose-related).

DRUG INCOMPATIBILITIES: Do not mix with sodium bicarbonate.

DRUG INTERACTIONS: *Antihistamines, phenothiazine tranquilizers, tricyclic antidepressants, MAO inhibitors,* and *amantadine* may all potentiate the anticholinergic effects of atropine. Atropine enhances the vagal-blocking action of *procainamide* and *quinidine* and inhibits the bradycardia produced by *propranolol* (beta-blocker).

ANTIDOTE: Discontinue the medication. Treat thirst and fever symptomatically. Treat anticholinergic symptoms with physostigmine, 0.5–1.0 mg (or 0.03 mg/kg) IV or IM; dose can be repeated once in 15–30 minutes. Barbiturates or diazepam can be given to control convulsions.

5
Adrenergic Blockers

Adrenergic blockers inhibit responses both to sympathetic (adrenergic) nerve activity and to circulating sympathomimetic agents (e.g., epinephrine, norepinephrine, other sympathomimetic amines). Agents that specifically bind to either alpha or beta receptor sites to inhibit these responses are designated as either alpha-adrenergic or beta-adrenergic blockers. Medications that act by interfering with the release of norepinephrine at the adrenergic nerve terminal are referred to simply as adrenergic neuron blockers. They are nonspecific since they block sympathetic activity regardless of whether alpha or beta receptors are involved. Table 5–1 describes the three types of adrenergic blockers.

TABLE 5–1 Adrenergic Blockers

Group	Prototype Agents	Principal Action
Alpha-adrenergic blockers	Phentolamine, tolazoline	Vasodilation
Beta-adrenergic blockers	Propranolol	Decreased heart rate
Adrenergic neuron blockers	Bretylium, guanethidine	Vasodilation, bradycardia

Propranolol and bretylium are discussed in chapter 6 (Antiarrhythmics). The following two medications are discussed in this chapter:

- **Phentolamine**
- **Tolazoline**

Phentolamine (parenteral) (Regitine)

ADMINISTRATION

Available Forms: Injectable (IV), 5 mg powder in amps with 1 ml sterile water diluent.

Diluent: Sterile water for injection.

Dosage (Parenteral): Varies according to use.
Preoperative management of pheochromocytoma: 1 mg IV several minutes prior to anesthesia.
Pheochromocytoma test dose: 0.1 mg/kg (3 mg/m^2) IV as a single dose.
Treatment of tissue necrosis: 5–10 mg diluted in 10–15 ml NS and infiltrated into the area of extravasation.

Rate: IV boluses can be given rapidly.

INDICATIONS: Phentolamine is used to control hypertension caused by an excess of circulating catecholamines (e.g., pheochromocytoma). It is given IV immediately prior to surgery for pheochromocytoma and during surgical manipulation of the tumor. It has been given IV for diagnosis of pheochromocytoma, but measurement of urinary catecholamines and their metabolites is less hazardous and is now the established diagnostic method of choice. Parenteral doses have also been used for the treatment of hypertensive crisis caused by interaction between MAO inhibitors and sympathomimetics and in the clonidine withdrawal syndrome. Local infiltration is used to treat or prevent drug-induced tissue necrosis.

ACTIONS: Phentolamine antagonizes or blocks vasoconstriction by selectively blocking alpha-adrenergic receptors in the skin, mucosa, intestine, and kidney; the resulting decrease in peripheral vascular resistance lowers blood pressure. Phentolamine also stimulates gastric secretion (via histamine-like action) and causes GI stimulation.

CONTRAINDICATIONS: Coronary or myocardial insufficiency, myocardial infarction, known hypersensitivity to phentolamine or related compounds.

PRECAUTIONS: Monitor vital signs frequently. Myocardial infarction and cerebral vascular occlusion have occurred because of the profound hypotension that may occur after parenteral administration. Use cautiously in patients with peptic ulcer disease. Arrhythmias may occur.

SIDE EFFECTS/ADVERSE REACTIONS: Weakness; dizziness; flushing; orthostatic hypotension; nasal stuffiness; and gastric upset with nausea, vomiting, and diarrhea may occur. Acute and prolonged hypotensive episodes, tachycardia, and cardiac arrhythmias are more frequently reported after parenteral administration. Cerebrovascular spasm and occlusion have also been reported.

ANTIDOTE: Discontinue the medication. Treat hypotension with norepinephrine (Levophed) or dopamine.

Tolazoline (parenteral) (Priscoline)

ADMINISTRATION

Available Forms: Injectable (IV), 25 mg/ml in 10 ml vials.

Diluent: Give undiluted or further dilute in a sufficient volume of D5W or NS for continuous IV infusion. Other multiple electrolyte solutions can be used.

Dosage (Parenteral)
For neonatal hypoxemia (investigational): 1–2 mg/kg slow IV push over 10 minutes, followed by IV infusion of 1–2 mg/kg/hr.

Rate: Give IV push doses over at least 10 minutes.

INDICATIONS: Tolazoline's major clinical use is in the treatment of neonatal hypoxemia caused by pulmonary artery hypertension or pulmonary vasospasm secondary to hypoxia or acidosis (conditions collectively known as persistent fetal circulation or PFC). This use is still investigational.

ACTIONS: Tolazoline causes peripheral vasodilation and decreases peripheral vascular resistance, primarily by directly relaxing vascular smooth muscle. It has less alpha-adrenergic blocking effect than phentolamine, and the blockade is incomplete and transient with usual doses. In PFC pulmonary hypertension due to severe pulmonary vasoconstriction causes a right-to-left shunting of blood through the foramen ovale or ductus arteriosus. This leads to hypoxemia in newborn infants without apparent lung disease or in those with parenchymal lung disease, such as hyaline membrane disease (HMD). The direct, non-adrenergic action of tolazoline causes vasodilation of the pulmonary arteries, relieves the vasospasm, lowers pulmonary hypertension, and thereby improves oxygenation. Tolazoline also causes cardiac stimulation, resulting in increased heart rate and cardiac output. Blood pressure can increase or decrease depending on the net balance between the vasodilating and cardiac-stimulating effects. Tolazoline's parasympathomimetic and "histamine-like" actions can increase GI motility and gastric secretion.

CONTRAINDICATIONS: Known or suspected coronary artery disease, use after a cerebrovascular accident, hypersensitivity to tolazoline.

PRECAUTIONS: Administer bolus dose slowly. Monitor vital signs, especially heart rate and arterial blood pressure, frequently (e.g., every 15 minutes for first hour and thereafter as clinically indicated). Monitor arterial blood gases frequently. The patient must be intubated and provided with assisted mechanical ventilation. If a trial of mechanical hyperventilation fails to maintain a Pao_2 of 50 mm Hg or more, tolazoline can be administered to maintain Pao_2 over 50 mm Hg; as lung compliance and oxygenation improve, ventilator pressures can be lowered cautiously. Tolazoline infusion can be stopped when the Pao_2 can be maintained at 70 mm Hg or more with an Fio_2 of 50%. A therapeutic response to tolazoline is marked by a cutaneous flush followed by an increased Pao_2 and often a fall in the systemic arterial pressure. An adequate circulatory volume should be maintained;

plasma volume expanders should be readily available to counteract shock if necessary. Infusion of dopamine (5–10 μg/kg/min) can be given simultaneously to maintain systemic blood pressure and renal blood flow, especially if shock complicates PFC. Correction of the underlying abnormalities contributing to the patient's decreased cardiac output or to the hypoxia must be done. Acidosis should be corrected with diluted sodium bicarbonate as necessary; glucose infusions are also important. Use cautiously in infants with gastritis.

SIDE EFFECTS/ADVERSE REACTIONS: The most common side effects are a cutaneous flushing reaction and hypotension. Chilling, pilomotor erection ("gooseflesh"), and sweating may also occur. Other possible effects include abdominal distension, oliguria, hematuria, thrombocytopenia, GI and pulmonary hemorrhage, tachycardia, and arrhythmias.

DRUG INCOMPATIBILITIES: Do not mix with any other medications.

DRUG INTERACTIONS: Concurrent administration with *epinephrine* or *norepinephrine* may produce rebound hypertension after a brief hypotensive episode.

ANTIDOTE: Discontinue tolazoline. Manage hypotension with IV fluids, plasma volume expanders, or dopamine.

6
Antiarrhythmics

Cardiac arrhythmias are produced by disorders of impulse formation, by disturbances in impulse conduction, or by a combination of these factors. Antiarrhythmics regulate the electrical activity of the myocardium. They act as cardiac depressants since they reduce automaticity of ectopic foci by depressing spontaneous diastolic depolarization. They affect conduction by altering conduction velocity and the duration of the refractory period of myocardial cells.

It is helpful to ascertain the underlying cause of a cardiac arrhythmia (e.g., drug-induced or due to a particular disease state such as fever, thyrotoxicosis, congestive heart failure). This underlying cause should be corrected and the arrhythmia treated as a symptom rather than as a primary disturbance.

The following medications are discussed in this chapter:

- **Bretylium tosylate**
- **Lidocaine**
- **Phenytoin (parenteral)**
- **Procainamide**
- **Propranolol**
- **Verapamil (IV)**

Bretylium tosylate (Bretylol)

ADMINISTRATION

Available Forms: Injectable (IV, IM), 50 mg/ml in 10 ml amps.

Diluent: D5W or NS. 10 ml (500 mg) can be diluted with 40 ml of diluent to yield a concentration of 10 mg/ml for IV use.

Dosage (Parenteral): Safety and efficacy have not yet been established in children. In an extreme emergency 5–10 mg/kg/dose can be given undiluted as an IV bolus over 1 minute. The same dose can also be given as a diluted solution by rapid IV infusion over 8–10 minutes. 2–5 mg/kg/dose, undiluted, can be given IM. Maximum IM dose per site is 250 mg or 5 ml. Both IV and IM doses can be repeated in 15–30 minutes for 2 more doses if needed or q6h for prophylactic therapy. Maximum dose is 30 mg/kg/day.

Rate: Administer IV push over 1 minute (extreme emergency), rapid IV infusion of bolus over 8–10 minutes, and slow IV infusions at 1–2 mg/min.

INDICATIONS: Bretylium is used for treatment and prophylaxis of ventricular fibrillation and other life-threatening ventricular arrhythmias unresponsive to conventional treatment (e.g., lidocaine, procainamide).

ACTIONS: Bretylium is an adrenergic blocker that acts *directly* on the myocardium to increase the threshold of ventricular fibrillation by prolonging the effective refractory period and the action potential duration of the ventricles. It also acts *indirectly* by inhibiting the release of norepinephrine from the adrenergic nerve terminals and thus suppressing the excitability of sympathetic nerves. Suppression of ventricular fibrillation is usually rapid (within minutes) when the medication is administered by IV push. Suppression of ventricular tachycardia and other arrhythmias develops more slowly (20 minutes to 2 hours). Bretylium causes an initial release of norepinephrine, resulting in slightly increased blood pressure, heart rate, and frequency of ectopic beats. Subsequent adrenergic blockade produces orthostatic hypotension with little change in heart rate.

CONTRAINDICATIONS: None.

PRECAUTIONS: Monitor the patient's electrocardiogram (ECG) continuously during therapy and have electrical defibrillation available during an emergency. Keep the patient in a supine position during therapy since bretylium may cause severe hypotension. Monitor vital signs frequently. The initial release of norepinephrine caused by bretylium may aggravate digitalis toxicity, so avoid concomitant use with digitalis glycosides. Dosage reductions may be necessary in patients with renal impairment. Rapid IV infusion may cause nausea and vomiting. No more than 5 ml should be injected IM in any one site; repeated IM injections may cause tissue necrosis and atrophy. Bretylium is for short-term use only; the patient should be weaned in 3–5 days.

SIDE EFFECTS/ADVERSE REACTIONS: The most common side effect is orthostatic hypotension (seldom more than a drop of 20 mm Hg) to which tolerance may develop. Nausea, vomiting, dizziness, fainting, and bradycardia may also occur. More severe reactions include severe hypotension, bradycardia, premature ventricular contractions, angina, substernal pressure, and allergic reactions (e.g., flushing, fever, rash).

DRUG INCOMPATIBILITIES: Do not mix with any other medications.

DRUG INTERACTIONS: Use with *digitalis* may increase risk of digitalis toxicity. *Procainamide, lidocaine, quinidine,* and *propranolol* may cause additive hypotension. Use with *tricyclic antidepressants* may cause hypertension.

ANTIDOTE: Treat hypotension (supine blood pressure <75 mm Hg) with dopamine or norepinephrine infusions. Replace deficits in fluid volume as necessary.

Lidocaine (Xylocaine)

ADMINISTRATION

Available Forms: Injectable (IV), 20 mg/ml in 5 ml prefilled syringes (100 mg), pre-mixed solution of 2 gm/500 ml D5W (4 mg/ml), prefilled 1 gm and 2 gm syringes *to be diluted* for IV infusion.

Diluent: Use undiluted for IV bolus doses. Dilute in D5W or NS for IV infusion. Suggested dilution is 1 gm in 500 ml to yield a concentration of 2 mg/ml.

Dosage (Parenteral): Initial IV bolus of 1 mg/kg; can be repeated q5–10min prn up to 3 doses. Maximum dose is 5 mg/kg or 100 mg/hr. Can give subsequent IV infusion of 10–50 μg/kg/min.

Rate: Give IV boluses at 25–50 mg/min. For IV infusion do not exceed 5 mg/min.

INDICATIONS: Lidocaine is used for treatment of ventricular arrhythmias, especially premature extrasystoles and tachycardia.

ACTIONS: Lidocaine depresses diastolic depolarization and automaticity in the ventricles but has little effect on atrial tissue. Usual therapeutic doses do not slow AV conduction, depress ventricular contractile force, or change systemic arterial pressure. Large doses, however, may have a negative inotropic effect on the heart and cause CNS reactions that include convulsions and coma. Therapeutic serum levels are 2–5 μg/ml, and toxic reactions appear to be correlated with serum levels of 8–10 μg/ml. Onset of action is almost immediate after doses given as an IV bolus, but duration is brief (10–20 minutes), necessitating repeated doses or continuous IV infusions. Lidocaine is metabolized in the liver to two active metabolites: monoethylglycinexylidide (half-life, 2 hours) and glycinexylidide (half-life, 10 hours). These metabolites are excreted in the urine and may accumulate in patients who have renal impairment. The half-life of lidocaine itself may be prolonged in patients with liver disease or congestive heart failure.

CONTRAINDICATIONS: Known hypersensitivity to amide-type anesthetics; Stokes-Adams syndrome; severe degrees of sinoatrial (SA), AV, or intraventricular block.

PRECAUTIONS: Monitor the patient's ECG continually during the entire infusion period; discontinue the infusion if excessive cardiac depression occurs (e.g., prolonged PR intervals or QRS complexes). Check vital signs frequently. Use cautiously in patients with sinus bradycardia or incomplete heart block as more frequent and serious ventricular arrhythmias may occur if the heart rate is not first accelerated (e.g., by isoproterenol or cardiac pacing). Ventricular rate may be accelerated in patients with atrial fibrillation. Give with caution to neonates and to children with hepatic or renal impairment. Maintain adequate plasma volume and avoid hypovolemia. Do not confuse "lidocaine for arrhythmias" with other lidocaine preparations (with paraben preservatives) intended for use as local anesthetics or with those preparations containing epinephrine.

SIDE EFFECTS/ADVERSE REACTIONS: (Appear to be correlated with doses greater than 3 mg/kg or IV infusion rates exceeding 5 mg/min.) The major toxic effect is CNS stimulation leading to convulsions, respiratory depression, and cardiovascular collapse and arrest. Dizziness, drowsiness, diplopia, hypotension, and bradycardia may precede convulsions. Hypersensitivity reactions include urticaria, rash, and edema.

DRUG INCOMPATIBILITIES: Do not admix directly with sodium bicarbonate.

DRUG INTERACTIONS: Additive cardiac depressant effects may occur with *phenytoin* and *propranolol* and possible additive neurological toxic effects with *procainamide*. Barbiturates and chronic use of *phenytoin* may accelerate hepatic metabolism of lidocaine.

ANTIDOTE: Discontinue the infusion if signs of excessive cardiac depression occur (e.g., prolongation of PR interval and QRS complexes). Treat convulsions with small doses of ultrashort-acting barbiturates or diazepam.

Phenytoin (parenteral) (Dilantin)

ADMINISTRATION

Available Forms: Injectable (IV), 50 mg/ml in 2 ml (100 mg) and 5 ml (250 mg) amps.

Diluent: Can be given undiluted. If dilution is necessary, use NS and mix just prior to administration.

Dosage (Parenteral)
As antiarrhythmic: 1–5 mg/kg/dose given as a slow IV bolus over 5 minutes. Can be repeated as needed in 5–10 minutes. Maximum is 500 mg/4 hr.

Rate: Do not exceed 25 mg/min.

INDICATIONS: Phenytoin's major indication is for treatment of ventricular arrhythmias associated with digitalis toxicity. Its use as an anticonvulsant is discussed in chapter 27.

ACTIONS: Phenytoin depresses spontaneous depolarization in the atria and ventricles. It improves AV conduction and counteracts the depressant effect of digitalis in that tissue. Onset of action after IV administration is rapid (approximately 1–5 minutes) and lasts about 15 minutes. Therapeutic blood levels are 10–20 µg/ml.

CONTRAINDICATIONS: Hypersensitivity to hydantoins, sinus bradycardia, SA block, second-degree and third-degree AV block, Stokes-Adams syndrome.

PRECAUTIONS: Monitor the patient's ECG continuously and check vital signs frequently during IV therapy. Rapid IV rates can cause cardiovascular collapse. Follow direct IV push with saline flush to minimize venous irritation. Absorption of IM doses is erratic and this route should be avoided.

SIDE EFFECTS/ADVERSE REACTIONS: Rapid IV administration may cause tremors, dysarthria, nystagmus, drowsiness, CNS depression, myocardial depression, bradycardia, hypotension, paradoxical AV block, and cardiovascular collapse. (For other reactions and precautions, see chapter 27.)

DRUG INCOMPATIBILITIES: Phenytoin will precipitate at a pH less than 11.5. Do not admix with any other medication.

DRUG INTERACTIONS: See phenytoin in chapter 27.

ANTIDOTE: Provide symptomatic and supportive treatment. Maintain the patient's airway. Provide oxygen, assisted ventilation, and vasopressors as necessary.

Procainamide (Pronestyl)

ADMINISTRATION

Available Forms: Injectable (IV, IM), 100 mg/ml in 10 ml vials, 500 mg/ml in 2 ml vials (must be diluted before IV use); tablets, 250, 375, 500 mg; capsules, 250, 375, 500 mg; sustained-release tablets, 250, 500 mg (Procan-SR).

Diluent: D5W or NS. Suggested dilution is 500 mg in 500 ml to yield a concentration of 1 mg/ml.

Dosage (Parenteral): IV bolus dose of 2 mg/kg (diluted in D5W or NS) given slowly. Maximum is 100 mg/dose. Bolus doses can be repeated q10–15 min until the arrhythmia is controlled. Total cumulative dose should not exceed 1 gm. An IV infusion of 20–80 µg/kg/min can be given after a bolus dose.

Dosage (Oral): 40–60 mg/kg/day (1.5 gm/m^2/day) in divided doses (q4–6h).

Rate: For IV bolus doses do not exceed 25 mg/min. For IV infusions do not exceed 6 mg/min.

INDICATIONS: Procainamide is used for the treatment of ventricular extrasystoles and tachycardia associated with digitalis toxicity or not controlled by lidocaine. It may be less effective for treatment of atrial fibrillation, paroxysmal atrial tachycardia, or other supraventricular arrhythmias.

ACTIONS: Procainamide acts *directly* on the myocardium to depress pacemaker activity, conduction velocity, and automaticity in the atria, AV junctional tissue, and the ventricles. However, it has an *indirect* anticholinergic ("vagolytic") effect that increases AV conduction velocity. This indirect effect is usually the dominant one when therapeutic doses are used. Therapeutic serum levels are 4–8 μg/ml, but higher levels may be necessary to treat atrial arrhythmias. Procainamide's metabolite, N-acetyl-procainamide (NAPA) is active, and both compounds contribute to the therapeutic and toxic effects. Serum levels of both agents should be monitored simultaneously. Serum levels totalling 5–30 μg/ml (procainamide plus NAPA) are usually associated with therapeutic responses. Toxic serum levels of procainamide are about 12 μg/ml. Onset of action of IV doses is immediate and peaks in a few minutes. Procainamide is partially metabolized in the liver to NAPA and other metabolites. These and some unchanged procainamide are excreted in the urine. The drug may accumulate in patients with renal or hepatic impairment or congestive heart failure.

CONTRAINDICATIONS: Heart block greater than first-degree; myasthenia gravis; hypersensitivity to procainamide, procaine, or amide-type local anesthetics (e.g., lidocaine).

PRECAUTIONS: Monitor the patient's ECG continuously and check vital signs frequently, especially during parenteral administration. Stop the infusion if the QRS complex widens 25–50% or systolic blood pressure falls more than 15 mm Hg. Use cautiously in patients with shock since IV administration may cause serious hypotension. Dosage adjustments are necessary for patients who have renal or hepatic impairment. Use cautiously in patients with AV conduction disturbances such as digitalis intoxication or bundle branch block. Use cautiously in the treatment of atrial fibrillation or flutter (patient may have to be digitalized to control ventricular rate). Solutions should be clear or light yellow. Avoid use of amber or dark solutions.

SIDE EFFECTS/ADVERSE REACTIONS: Serious effects, especially with parenteral use, include hypotension, bradycardia, heart block, ventricular tachycardia or fibrillation, and cardiac arrest. CNS symptoms of depression, confusion, and hallucinations have occurred. Oral doses may cause gastric disturbances of nausea, vomiting, diarrhea, and anorexia. A systemic lupus-like syndrome with fever, chills, myalgia, and arthralgia may occur with prolonged oral use (incidence 50–70%). Blood dyscrasias including thrombocytopenia and agranulocytosis have been reported, as well as dermatological hypersensitivity reactions.

DRUG INTERACTIONS: Procainamide may potentiate the neuromuscular blocking action of *aminoglycosides* and *neuromuscular blockers* (surgical). Use with other *anti-*

hypertensives may cause additive hypotension. *Cholinergics* are antagonized by procainamide while *anticholinergics* (e.g., atropine) will have additive effects.

ANTIDOTE: Discontinue the infusion. Treat hypotension with vasopressors. Isoproterenol and sodium bicarbonate may reverse cardiotoxicity. Cardiac pacing may be indicated.

Propranolol (Inderal)

ADMINISTRATION

Available Forms: Injectable (IV only), 1 mg/ml in 1 ml amps; tablets, 10, 20, 40, 80 mg.

Diluent: Can be given undiluted. Dilute in D5W or NS for minidoses.

Dosage (Parenteral): Varies according to use.
For digitalis toxicity and arrhythmias: 0.05–0.15 mg/kg as a single IV dose given over 10 minutes; can be repeated in 10 minutes if needed. Maximum dose is 10 mg.
For tetralogy spells: 0.15–0.25 mg/kg/dose slow IV. Can be repeated once in 15 minutes.

Dosage (Oral)
For digitalis toxicity and arrhythmias: 0.5–1.0 mg/kg/24 hr in divided doses (q6–8h) or 0.1–0.2 mg/kg q8h.

Rate: For IV infusions do not exceed 1 mg/min.

INDICATIONS: Propranolol can be used for treatment of ventricular and supraventricular arrhythmias (including those induced by sympathomimetics and digitalis), atrial flutter and fibrillation, and paroxysmal atrial tachycardia. It is also used to control reflex tachycardia induced by vasodilating drugs, to treat anoxic spells in tetralogy of Fallot, and to manage hypertension and angina.

ACTIONS: Propranolol blocks cardiac beta-1 receptors to produce negative inotropic and chronotropic effects on the heart. This beta-blockade results in a decrease in heart rate, myocardial contractility, automaticity, and blood pressure. Atrioventricular conduction is slowed as well as the rate of SA node firing. Propranolol also blocks beta-2 receptors of the lungs to cause bronchoconstriction. Onset of action after IV administration is immediate, and duration of action depends on the dose (i.e., larger doses result in an initial half-life longer than 10 minutes). Thereafter, half-life of elimination is about 2–3 hours. Propranolol is metabolized in the liver, and its metabolites are excreted renally. It is highly protein-bound. Oral doses are higher than IV doses because much of the drug is metabolized during the first pass through the liver.

CONTRAINDICATIONS: Bronchial asthma and bronchospasm, congestive heart failure, heart block greater than first-degree, cardiogenic shock, sinus bradycardia.

PRECAUTIONS: Propranolol may induce hypoglycemia in diabetics and may impair the sympathetically mediated rebound response to acute hypoglycemia. It may mask the symptoms of sweating and tachycardia normally seen in hypoglycemia and thyrotoxicosis, so use cautiously in diabetics and in patients with hyperthyroidism. Use cautiously in patients with hepatic impairment. Propranolol may precipitate or exacerbate congestive heart failure, especially in patients with preexisting inadequate cardiac function. It may intensify AV block and lead to complete heart block and arrest. Beta-blockade may cause increased airway resistance and bronchospasm, and IV use particularly may cause laryngospasm. Monitor the patient's ECG continuously and check vital signs frequently during IV administration.

SIDE EFFECTS/ADVERSE REACTIONS: Oral doses may cause gastric upset. Light-headedness, dizziness, ataxia, paresthesias, confusion, nightmares, and mental depression may occur. More serious effects (especially after parenteral use) include bronchospasm, laryngospasm, decreased respiratory function, bradycardia, AV block, worsening of congestive heart failure, hypotension, peripheral neuropathy, and hypoglycemia. Rebound hypertension, ventricular tachycardia, and anginal pain may occur if the medication is suddenly withdrawn from patients receiving large doses.

DRUG INTERACTIONS: *Isoproterenol* antagonizes the beta-blocking effects of propranolol. The hypoglycemic effect of *insulin* and *oral antidiabetic agents* is potentiated by propranolol. Use with *phenytoin* or *digitalis* may cause additive cardiac depression and bradycardia. Use with *barbiturates, narcotics,* and *phenothiazines* produces additive hypotension. Propranolol antagonizes the bronchodilating effects of *isoproterenol, metaproterenol,* and other *bronchodilators.*

ANTIDOTE: Treat excessive bradycardia with IV doses of atropine. If there is no response, use isoproterenol cautiously. For cardiac failure administer digoxin and diuretics. For hypotension use vasopressors such as norepinephrine or epinephrine. Treat bronchospasm with isoproterenol, aminophylline, or terbutaline.

Verapamil (IV) (Calan, Isoptin)

ADMINISTRATION

Available Forms: Injectable (IV), 2.5 mg/ml in 2 ml amps. Tablets are available but are used only for treatment of angina pectoris.

Diluent: Can be given undiluted or mixed with D5W or NS.

Dosage (Parenteral): Varies according to the patient's age.
Infants and neonates up to 1 year old: Initial IV bolus of 0.1–0.2 mg/kg; can be repeated 30 minutes after the first dose if necessary. Single dose range is 0.75–2.00 mg.
Children 1–15 years old: Initial IV bolus of 0.1–0.3 mg/kg; can be repeated 30 minutes after the first dose if necessary. Single dose range is 2–5 mg. Do not exceed 10 mg/dose.

Rate: Give IV bolus doses over 2 minutes.

INDICATIONS: Verapamil is used for the treatment of supraventricular tachyarrhythmias, including paroxysmal supraventricular tachycardia and those occurring in the Wolff-Parkinson-White syndrome.

ACTIONS: Verapamil is a slow-channel calcium blocker that inhibits the flow of calcium ions into the myocardial and vascular smooth muscle cells thereby altering conduction and contraction in these tissues. Inhibiting the influx of calcium ions slows AV conduction, prolongs the effective refractory period within the AV node, and subsequently slows the ventricular rate in paroxysmal supraventricular tachycardia. By interrupting impulse reentry at the AV node and depressing depolarization and conduction in atrial fibers, verapamil restores normal sinus rhythm. It also reduces afterload and has a negative inotropic effect on the heart that may worsen congestive heart failure in patients with moderately severe cardiac dysfunction. Verapamil is metabolized in the liver and excreted in the urine as metabolized and unchanged forms.

CONTRAINDICATIONS: Severe hypotension or cardiogenic shock, heart block greater than first-degree, sick sinus syndrome (except where a functioning artificial pacemaker is present), severe congestive heart failure or left ventricular failure, patients concurrently receiving beta-adrenergic blockers (relative contraindication).

PRECAUTIONS: Monitor the patient's ECG continuously and check vital signs frequently during therapy. Use cautiously in patients with significant renal or hepatic failure since verapamil may accumulate after repeated doses. Use cautiously in patients with AV block or other types of heart failure or cardiac dysfunction. Verapamil may cause a rapid ventricular rate in patients with atrial flutter or fibrillation (cardioversion may be indicated).

SIDE EFFECTS/ADVERSE REACTIONS: Hypotension (systolic blood pressure <90 mm Hg), dizziness, and headache are the more frequent side effects. Extreme bradycardia and possible asystole may occur, especially in patients with the sick sinus syndrome. Tachycardia and occasional premature ventricular contractions may occur, as well as a worsening of congestive heart failure with pulmonary and peripheral edema. Nausea and abdominal discomfort have been reported.

DRUG INTERACTIONS: Use with *digitalis* may result in additive bradycardia. *Beta-adrenergic blockers* cause additional myocardial depression. *Antihypertensives* cause an increased hypotensive effect.

ANTIDOTE: Treat hypotension with vasopressors (e.g., norepinephrine, isoproterenol, or dopamine). Bradycardia with heart block may respond to isoproterenol, atropine, or cardiac pacing. Premature ventricular contractions and rapid ventricular rates may require cardioversion or IV doses of lidocaine.

7
Cardiotonics

One of the most important sequelae of a failing myocardium is a cardiac output inadequate for the needs of the body. The cardiotonic steroids, represented here by the digitalis glycoside digoxin, are among the most effective agents available for treatment of congestive heart failure. Digoxin produces complex alterations in the electrical and mechanical activity of cardiac tissue. Its direct action on myocardial cells increases the force of contraction without increasing oxygen consumption, increases cardiac output, and thus improves the efficiency of a failing myocardium. Digoxin's intricate *direct* and *indirect* effects on automaticity and conductivity have both therapeutic and toxic potential. Dosages must be calculated carefully and therapeutic progress monitored closely with total awareness of the toxic potential.

Although the digitalis glycosides include many other compounds, digoxin is the one commonly prescribed for pediatric use and is the only medication discussed in this chapter.

DIGOXIN PHARMACOKINETICS

Absorption: Table 7–1 describes the absorption of digoxin administered by various routes.

Elimination Half-Life: Varies according to the patient's renal function.
Normal renal function: 36 hours (1.6 days).
Anuria: 96–144 hours (4–6 days).

Metabolism: 14% in the liver (oral doses). Percentage decreases in patients with severe hepatic impairment.

TABLE 7-1 Absorption of Digoxin*

Route	Percent Absorbed	Onset of Action	Peak Action
Oral†	70–85 (elixir) 60–80 (tablets)	1–2 hr	6–8 hr
IM‡	70–85	30 min	4–6 hr
IV	100	5–10 min	1–2 hr

*Based on Lanoxin brand of digoxin (Burroughs-Wellcome).
†Absorption may be inadequate in patients who have malabsorption syndromes or rapid GI transit time (e.g., diarrhea, vomiting).
‡Peripheral circulation can be compromised in patients with congestive heart failure and may lead to unpredictable absorption of IM doses.

Excretion: Renal (primarily unchanged drug in the urine).

Serum Levels (Therapeutic)
Infants <6 months old: 0.5–3.0 ng/ml.
Older infants and children: 0.5–2.0 ng/ml.

Serum Levels (Toxic)
Infants <6 months old: 3–4 ng/ml.
Older infants and children: 3 ng/ml.

Distribution: (Biphasic) The first phase, lasting 6–8 hours, is due to distribution and equilibration in tissues and serum. Serum levels of digoxin in blood samples drawn during the first phase may be misleading and may not reflect myocardial concentrations. The second phase, 6–8 hours after administration, is due to renal elimination. Serum levels of digoxin should be determined during the second phase.

Digoxin (Lanoxin)

ADMINISTRATION

Available Forms: Injectable (IM, IV), 100 µg/ml (pediatric), 250 µg/ml (adult); tablets, 62.5, 125.0, 250.0, 500.0 µg; capsules, 50, 100, 200 µg; oral elixir, 50 µg/ml.

Diluent: D5W, NS, or sterile water for injection if dilutions are required for minivolume doses. Precipitation can result if *less* than 4-fold dilutions are used. Use the diluted product immediately.

Dosage: All doses must be individualized according to the patient's response, general condition, renal function, sensitivity, and so forth. Titrate to the smallest effective dose; reduce the dose in patients with renal or severe hepatic impairment; readjust dosage when changing from one dosage form to another. Table 7-2 gives suggested doses of digoxin tablets, elixir, and injectable forms. Doses are based on normal renal and hepatic function and ideal body weight.

TABLE 7-2 Suggested Doses of Digoxin*

Age	Digitalizing Dose (μg/kg)		Daily Maintenance Dose (% of digitalizing dose)
	ORAL	IV†	
Preterm	20–30	15–25	20–30
Full-term	25–35	20–30	25–35
1–24 mo	35–60	30–50	25–35
2–5 yr	30–40	25–35	25–35
5–10 yr	20–35	15–30	25–35
>10 yr	10–15	8–12	25–35

*Source: Adapted with permission from product literature for Lanoxin. Burroughs-Wellcome Pediatric Elixir, Research Triangle Park, NC, October, 1983.
†IV digitalizing doses are 80% of oral digitalizing doses because IV doses are absorbed completely.

Rate: For slow IV push give 0.25 mg over 5 minutes. Rapid IV push can cause systemic and coronary arteriolar vasoconstriction.

INDICATIONS: Digoxin is used for treatment of congestive heart failure (in conjunction with diuretics) and for treatment and prevention of certain cardiac arrhythmias (primarily atrial fibrillation, flutter, and paroxysmal atrial tachycardia).

ACTIONS: Therapeutic doses have complex *direct* and *indirect* effects on cardiac muscle and conductive tissue. The indirect effect is mediated through the autonomic nervous system and causes enhanced vagal action on the SA and AV nodes and conductive tissue. The net results of both direct and indirect actions are increased force of ventricular contractions (positive inotropic action), decreased heart rate via depression of sinus node pacemaker activity (negative chronotropic action), and decreased conduction velocity through the AV node. These combined effects produce improved cardiac output, decreased venous pressure, slowed heart rate, and diuresis. Manifestations of digitalis toxicity are a consequence of digoxin's direct actions. Direct excitatory effects on atrial, AV junctional, and ventricular automaticity produce atrial and nodal tachycardias as well as premature ventricular contractions, bigeminy, tachycardia, and fibrillation. Direct depression of AV conduction may result in complete AV block.

CONTRAINDICATIONS: Ventricular fibrillation, hypersensitivity to digitalis glycosides (rare).

PRECAUTIONS: Before administration of digoxin, obtain a baseline ECG, serum electrolytes (especially serum potassium), and some determination of renal function. Myocardial ischemia, hypoxia, alkalosis, and electrolyte imbalances (e.g., low potassium, high calcium, low magnesium) may predispose the patient to digoxin toxicity. Accumulation of digoxin can occur in patients on high doses or in those who have decreased renal function or hypothyroidism. Patients who have been receiving digitalis preparations within the past 2 weeks should receive only one-half the digitalizing doses. The IV route of administration is preferable since the absorption rate of oral doses can be variable. Intramuscular administration is painful; doses should be injected deeply and followed by massage of the site (used only when other routes are not feasible). Maximum dose per IM site is 0.5 mg. Incomplete AV block (especially with Stokes-Adams attacks) may develop into complete AV block when digitalis is given. Monitor the patient closely and check the ECG strip for effects prior to each dose (observe ECG for prolonged PR interval, shortened QT interval, ST depression, decreased T wave amplitude). Check the pulse rate prior to the next dose and at regular intervals during the day (hold for pulse rate <100–120 bpm for infants and <60–80 bpm for older infants). Double check (preferably with two nurses) all dosage calculations and all volumes of medication drawn up. Do not confuse *adult-strength* with *pediatric-strength* injections, *milligrams* with *micrograms,* or *digoxin* with *digitoxin.*

SIDE EFFECTS/ADVERSE REACTIONS: Early signs and symptoms of toxic effects (e.g., anorexia, poor feeding, nausea, vomiting, diarrhea, CNS symptoms) may not always be present in infants. Cardiac arrhythmias are more reliable signs of digitalis toxicity. Although almost any arrhythmia can occur, the most common ones include supraventricular tachyarrhythmias such as paroxysmal atrial tachycardia with or without heart block and junctional (nodal) tachycardia. Sinus bradycardia may also be an early sign of toxicity, even in the absence of first-degree heart block. Ventricular arrhythmias (e.g., premature ventricular contractions, bigeminy, trigeminy, ventricular tachycardia) are less common in infants and children than in adults. CNS symptoms include dizziness, headache, syncope, confusion, psychosis, and visual disturbances (e.g., blurred vision, yellow vision, halos, diplopia).

DRUG INTERACTIONS: Concomitant use with *quinidine* may increase serum levels of digoxin and predispose the patient to digoxin toxicity. Reduce the dose of digoxin by 50% when using it with quinidine. *Antacids* and *neomycin* may decrease the gastric absorption of oral doses of digoxin. *Potassium-depleting diuretics* and *calcium salts* may predispose the patient to digoxin toxicity. *Beta-blockers* (e.g., propranolol) may worsen AV block and potentiate digoxin-induced bradycardia. *Sympathomimetics* (e.g., epinephrine, isoproterenol, ephedrine) may precipitate or worsen digoxin-induced arrhythmias by enhancing ectopic pacemaker activity.

ANTIDOTE: Discontinue digoxin, continuously monitor the patient's ECG, and remove digoxin from GI tract (if applicable) by induction of emesis or gastric lavage. Administer potassium (orally or preferably IV), especially if hypokalemia occurs. Do not give potassium to patients with hyperkalemia, renal failure, or AV block. Give atropine, 0.01 mg/kg IV, for bradycardia. For AV block, tachycardia, or premature ventricular contractions, give phenytoin, 1–2 mg/kg IV slowly. This dose can be repeated q5–15min, up to 10 doses or until the arrhythmia ceases. Monitor the patient frequently for hypotension. Lidocaine, as well as propranolol (0.05–0.20 mg/kg slow IV), can be given for recurrent ventricular tachycardia or premature ventricular contractions. Avoid use of propranolol in patients with asthma, AV block, or severe congestive heart failure.

8
Antihypertensives and Vasodilators

Constricted blood vessels can cause pain, tissue necrosis, and, most notably, hypertension. The latter is an important risk factor for the development of major cardiovascular complications, including stroke, congestive heart failure, and progressive renal failure. Effective reduction of blood pressure reduces the frequency of most hypertensive complications.

Proper use of vasodilators and antihypertensives allows for improved blood flow to the heart, brain, and peripheral areas of the body. These agents are used for the management of hypertensive crises or where controlled hypotension is required.

The following medications are discussed in this chapter:

- **Diazoxide (IV)**
- **Hydralazine**
- **Nitroglycerin (IV)**
- **Nitroprusside**
- **Reserpine (parenteral)**

Diazoxide (IV) (Hyperstat, IV)

ADMINISTRATION

Available Forms: Injectable (IV), 15 mg/ml in 20 ml amps (300 mg).

Dosage (Parenteral): Safe use in children has not been established.
For hypertensive crises: 5 mg/kg (0.3 ml/kg) or 150–175 mg/m² by rapid IV bolus. Can be repeated in 30 minutes if necessary. Additive doses can be given q4–24h, depending on the response.
Minibolus technique: Small boluses of 1–3 mg/kg by IV push q5–15min up to a maximum of 150 mg. This technique may cause a more gradual reduction in blood pressure and thus fewer circulatory and neurological risks associated with acute hypotension.

Rate: Give IV boluses rapidly, within 30 seconds.

INDICATIONS: Diazoxide is used parenterally for emergency treatment of hypertensive crises such as malignant hypertension and hypertensive encephalopathy (it is ineffective against hypertension due to pheochromocytoma). It has been used orally for management of idiopathic hypoglycemia of infancy and hypoglycemia due to hyperinsulinemia (see chapter 31).

ACTIONS: Diazoxide, a nondiuretic thiazide derivative, produces a prompt fall in both diastolic and systolic blood pressures by directly relaxing arteriolar smooth muscle. Heart rate and cardiac output are increased. There is significant retention of sodium and water (an action opposite that of thiazide diuretics), and expanded plasma volume and frank edema may result. Diazoxide also inhibits insulin release to cause hyperglycemia. The onset of action is generally rapid, within 5 minutes. Blood pressure may increase rapidly after 10–30 minutes and then more slowly over the next 2–12 hours. Parenteral doses of diazoxide are highly protein-bound (90%). Since only the unbound form is active, rapid IV administration is usually necessary to obtain high levels in the plasma and at arteriolar receptor sites before most of the diazoxide becomes protein-bound.

CONTRAINDICATIONS: Compensatory hypertension associated with aortic coarctation or arteriovenous shunt, hypersensitivity to diazoxide or thiazides (unless benefits outweigh risks).

PRECAUTIONS: Since the fall in blood pressure is not directly correlated to the amount of drug given, monitor the patient's blood pressure every 1–2 minutes until stable, then every 15 minutes for 1 hour, and then every hour for 24 hours. The patient should remain recumbent for at least 30 minutes after IV injection (ambulatory patients should have their blood pressure measured while they are sitting and then while standing before surveillance is ended). Sodium and water retention may necessitate pretreatment with IV doses of furosemide. Use cautiously in patients with congestive heart failure or diabetes mellitus (insulin dosages may need adjustment). Use with caution in patients who have impaired cerebral or cardiac circulation or who are currently receiving medications such as vasodilators or potent diuretics where additive hypotensive effects may be detrimental. Avoid extravasation as it is extremely painful (pH is about 11.6).

SIDE EFFECTS/ADVERSE REACTIONS: Frequent and serious reactions include sodium and water retention, edema, and hyperglycemia. Infants and neonates may be at increased risk for altered carbohydrate metabolism, hyperbilirubinemia, and kernicterus. Profound hypotension may cause myocardial and cerebral ischemia, confusion, dizziness, unconsciousness, and convulsions. Gastric upset, parotid swelling, anorexia, "tightening in the chest," sweating, flushing, and sensations of warmth have also been reported. Cardiac effects may include both supraventricular tachycardias and bradycardias. Hyperuricemia, hypertrichosis, and hypersensitivity reactions (e.g., rash, urticaria, blood dyscrasias) may also occur.

DRUG INTERACTIONS: Diazoxide may displace *coumarin* and its derivatives from protein-binding sites, resulting in increased anticoagulant activity. Concomitant use with *potent diuretics* and other *antihypertensives* may lead to profound hypotension. Use with *thiazide diuretics* may cause additive hyperuricemia and hyperglycemia.

ANTIDOTE: Treat hypotension with sympathomimetics such as norepinephrine. Treat hyperglycemia with conventional therapy (insulin, potassium, and so forth).

Hydralazine (Apresoline)

ADMINISTRATION

Available Forms: Injectable (IM, IV), 20 mg/ml in 1 ml amps; tablets, 10, 25, 50, 100 mg.

Diluent: NS or D5W if dilutions are required. Admixtures in D5W may discolor after 12 hours.

Dosage: (Parenteral)
For hypertensive crisis: 0.15 mg/kg IV or IM q6h until desired effect is attained. Maximum dose is variable; the range is 1–4 mg/kg/day.

Dosage (Oral): 0.75 mg/kg/day in divided doses (q6h); can be increased gradually over 3–4 weeks up to 10 times the initial dose if indicated.

Rate: If given as IV bolus, do not exceed 10 mg/min.

INDICATIONS: This potent hypotensive agent is used orally for treatment of chronic forms of hypertension and parenterally for hypertensive emergencies such as those associated with acute glomerulonephritis and hypertensive encephalopathy. It may be given in combination with other antihypertensives or diuretics.

ACTIONS: Hydralazine lowers blood pressure by directly relaxing arteriolar smooth muscle. It has little effect on capacitance vessels (veins). Diastolic blood pressure is lowered, often more than systolic pressure, which causes a reflex stimulation of the heart; cardiac output and heart rate are consequently increased. The antihypertensive effect usually begins 15 minutes after IV administration and lasts approximately 2–6 hours. Onset of action of oral doses begins in about 30 minutes and lasts 2–4 hours. Hydralazine is metabolized in the intestinal wall and the liver. Some of the medication is inactivated during the first pass through the liver (rate is determined by acetylator type*). The metabolites are excreted in the urine. Plasma levels of hydralazine are increased and possibly prolonged in patients with impaired renal function.

CONTRAINDICATIONS: Hypersensitivity to hydralazine, coronary artery disease, rheumatic mitral valve disease.

PRECAUTIONS: Use cautiously in patients with coronary artery disease (may precipitate angina or myocardial infarction), congestive heart failure, or cerebral vascular accidents. Dosage adjustments may be necessary for patients with renal impairment; use cautiously in cases of advanced renal failure. A metabolite of hydralazine causes an "antipyridoxine" effect of peripheral neuritis that can be treated with pyridoxine (vitamin B_6). Periodic blood counts are advised during prolonged therapy. Use cautiously in slow acetylators (genetically determined) as they are more susceptible to hypersensitivity reactions. Prolonged therapy with doses higher than 400 mg/day may produce an arthritis-like syndrome clinically similar to systemic lupus erythematosus (SLE); keep the dose lower than 200 mg/day. Slow acetylators are particularly prone to the development of this condition.

SIDE EFFECTS/ADVERSE REACTIONS: Common side effects are headache, tachycardia, palpitations, nausea, vomiting, anorexia, diarrhea, and angina pectoris. (These can be minimized by reducing the dosage or by adding beta-blockers such as propranolol.) Other possible side effects include nasal congestion, flushing, dyspnea, lacrimation, edema, dizziness, tremors, peripheral neuritis (symptoms include paresthesias, numbness, tingling), muscle cramping, mental depression or psychotic reactions, hypersensitivity reactions (drug fever, rash, urticaria, arthritis-like symptoms), GI hemorrhage, and blood dyscrasias (anemia, leukopenia, agranulocytosis, purpura). Prolonged therapy with high doses may cause a "lupus-like" syndrome characterized by arthralgia, fever, splenomegaly, and LE cells in the peripheral blood.

DRUG INTERACTIONS: Concomitant use with *beta-blockers, diuretics, reserpine, guanethidine,* and other *antihypertensives* necessitates *lowered* doses of hydralazine.

ANTIDOTE: Discontinue hydralazine. Support of the cardiovascular system is of primary importance. Treat shock with volume expanders without resorting to the use of vasopressors, if possible. If a vasopressor is necessary, use one that is least likely to precipitate or aggravate cardiac arrhythmias (e.g., dopamine or levarterenol). Digitalization may be necessary. Renal function should be monitored and supported as required.

---

* Slow acetylators have a relative deficiency of the hepatic enzyme, N-acetyltransferase. Rapid acetylators include most American Indians, Eskimos, and Orientals and about 50% of American Negroes and Caucasians. The remainder of the population are slow acetylators.

Nitroglycerin (IV) (Tridil, Nitroglycerin for Injection)

ADMINISTRATION

Available Forms: Injectable (IV), 5 mg/ml in 5 and 10 ml amps and vials. *Must be diluted before use.*

Diluent: D5W or NS. Suggested dilution is 25 mg in 500 ml or 250 ml to yield concentrations of 50 µg/ml and 100 µg/ml, respectively. Note: Avoid concentrations greater than 400 µg/ml as the propylene glycol in the diluent may precipitate. Do not admix with any other medications.

Dosage (Parenteral): Safety and effectiveness in children have not been established. Initial IV infusion of 5 µg/min. Titrate with 5 µg/min increments q3–5min until the desired response is observed. If there is no response at 20 µg/min, use larger increments of 10–20 µg/min.

Rate: See dosage. Must be administered with an infusion control device.

INDICATIONS: Nitroglycerin infusions are used for control of hypertension during cardiovascular surgical procedures, for treatment of congestive heart failure associated with acute myocardial infarction, and for treatment of angina pectoris that does not respond to recommended doses of organic nitrates and beta-blockers.

ACTIONS: Nitroglycerin causes direct relaxation of vascular smooth muscle. Although the effects of venous dilation predominate, higher doses cause arteriolar dilation as well. The resulting venodilation reduces left ventricular end diastolic pressure (preload), and arteriolar relaxation reduces systemic vascular resistance and arterial pressure (afterload). Heart rate may be slightly increased by reflex response to the reduced systolic and diastolic blood pressures. Elevated central venous and pulmonary capillary wedge pressures are reduced as pulmonary vascular resistance decreases. Effective coronary perfusion pressure is usually maintained but could be compromised if blood pressure falls or if heart rate increases excessively.

CONTRAINDICATIONS: Hypersensitivity to organic nitrates, uncorrected hypovolemia, increased intracranial pressure, constrictive pericarditis, pericardial tamponade.

PRECAUTIONS: Since doses must be titrated to individual response, continuous monitoring of blood pressure, heart rate, and pulmonary capillary wedge pressure is necessary. Use cautiously in patients with renal or hepatic impairment. Excessive hypotension may compromise effective organ perfusion and increase the risk of ischemia and thrombosis. Nitroglycerin adsorbs to many plastics, so glass infusion bottles and special nitroglycerin infusion sets (not polyvinyl chloride) must be used.

SIDE EFFECTS/ADVERSE REACTIONS: The primary side effect is headache. Tachycardia, hypotension, nausea, vomiting, restlessness, apprehension, muscle twitching, retrosternal discomfort, palpitations, dizziness, vertigo, and abdominal pain may also occur.

DRUG INCOMPATIBILITIES: Do not admix with any other medication.

ANTIDOTE: Severe hypotension and reflex tachycardia can be treated by elevating the patient's legs and decreasing or temporarily discontinuing the infusion until the patient's condition stabilizes (hemodynamic effects of nitroglycerin are short). If further therapy is needed, alpha-adrenergic agonists (e.g., phenylephrine, methoxamine) can be used.

Nitroprusside (Nipride)

ADMINISTRATION

Available Forms: Injectable (IV), 50 mg sterile powder for reconstitution. *For IV infusion only.*

Diluent: Preservative-free sterile water can be used for initial reconstitution. Final dilution for IV infusion should be in D5W only. Suggested dilution is 50 mg in 500 ml D5W to yield a concentration of 100 μg/ml.

Dosage (Parenteral): 3 μg/kg/min (average) by IV infusion via an infusion control device. Range is 0.5–10.0 μg/kg/min.

Rate: Adjust to achieve desired effect. It is recommended that the rate *not* exceed 10 μg/kg/min or 800 μg/min. Administration must be via a controlled infusion pump.

INDICATIONS: Nitroprusside is used for treatment of hypertensive crises, especially those associated with acute left ventricular failure. It has also been used in combination with vasopressors for management of cardiogenic shock and for preload and afterload reduction.

ACTIONS: Nitroprusside is a potent, rapidly acting vasodilator that directly relaxes both arteriolar and venous smooth muscle, producing peripheral vasodilation. It lowers both arterial and venous pressure, and a slight increase in heart rate occurs as a reflex response. Cardiac output decreases because of a reduction in venous tone and return (preload reduction). Diastolic pressure may be lowered to 40% of pretreatment levels. Onset of action is rapid (within 1–2 minutes), but duration is short (less than 10 minutes), so continuous infusion is necessary to maintain a hypotensive response.

CONTRAINDICATIONS: Arteriovenous shunt, coarctation of aorta, known hypersensitivity to nitroprusside.

PRECAUTIONS: Monitor blood pressure continuously until stable and at frequent intervals throughout crisis therapy. Solutions are light-sensitive but are stable for 24 hours if protected from light; cover the infusion bottle and change the solution q24h. Reconstituted nitroprusside has a slight brownish tint; do not use highly discolored solutions. Do not mix with any other drugs or preservatives. Avoid extravasation. The patient should remain in a recumbent position during therapy. Nitroprusside is metabolized to cyanide in tissues and to thiocyanate in the liver. Use cautiously in patients with renal or hepatic impairment as cyanide or thiocyanate toxicity may occur. Use with caution in patients who have vitamin B_{12} deficiency or hypothyroidism (thiocyanate inhibits iodine uptake). Monitor blood levels of thiocyanate daily during prolonged use (levels should not exceed 10 mg/100 ml). Monitor blood pH, lactate-pyruvate ratio, and mixed venous blood O_2 content daily.

SIDE EFFECTS/ADVERSE REACTIONS: Most side effects are usually due to a rapid reduction of blood pressure; these include nausea, vomiting, nasal stuffiness, sweating, headache, agitation, muscle twitching, dizziness, palpitations, and substernal distress. Signs and symptoms of thiocyanate toxicity (usually appear when blood levels of thiocyanate are 5–10 mg/100 ml) include tinnitus, blurred vision, fatigue, delirium, anorexia, rash, pink skin, dilated pupils, dyspnea, and coma. Massive overdoses produce signs of cyanide poisoning (e.g., profound hypotension, metabolic acidosis, methemoglobinemia, dyspnea, coma).

DRUG INCOMPATIBILITIES: Do not mix with any other medications.

DRUG INTERACTIONS: *Dopamine* and nitroprusside together may result in higher cardiac output and lower pulmonary vascular resistance (synergistic action).

ANTIDOTE: Discontinue nitroprusside. Administer amyl nitrate perles by inhalation for 15–30 seconds until 3% sodium nitrite solution can be administered IV push, followed by sodium thiosulfate IV (solutions and instructions contained in Cyanide Antidote Package). Hydroxocobalamin (vitamin B_{12}) given as an IV infusion (0.1 mg/kg) has been used to manage cyanide toxicity.

Reserpine (parenteral) (Serpasil, others)

ADMINISTRATION

Available Forms: Injectable (IM), 2.5 and 5.0 mg per milliliter.

Dosage (Parenteral)
For hypertensive crisis: 0.07 mg/kg/dose (2 mg/m²/dose) as a single IM dose. Can be repeated in 12–24 hours (has been given q4–6h). Note: Patients over 25 kg should receive an initial dose of at least 1–2 mg.

INDICATIONS: Parenteral reserpine has been used in the management of hypertensive crises such as acute hypertensive encephalopathy and renal hypertension. However, reserpine has a slow onset of action, and its sedative effects may make neurological evaluation of the patient difficult. Therefore, other antihypertensives such as sodium nitroprusside, hydralazine, and diazoxide are usually preferred. Reserpine has also been given parenterally to lessen the tachycardia, palpitation, and agitation experienced by patients with thyrotoxicosis ("thyroid storm"), although propranolol is used more frequently for this purpose.

ACTIONS: Reserpine reduces blood pressure by depleting catecholamine (norepinephrine, epinephrine) and serotonin stores in many organs, including the heart, blood vessels, adrenal medulla, and brain. It also prevents the sympathetic nerve fiber endings from taking up these catecholamines again. The effects of this peripheral and central amine depletion are (1) a reduction in SANS activity, causing a decrease in heart rate, cardiac output, and blood pressure; (2) a reflex increase in the tone of the PANS (because of SANS inhibition), causing increased GI motility, increased gastric secretion, and miosis; and (3) CNS and behavioral sedation. The vasodilation produced by reserpine causes flushing, a feeling of warmth, and nasal congestion. Catecholamine depletion begins within an hour of reserpine administration. Following a single IM dose, antihypertensive effects occur within 2 hours, peak within 2–6 hours, and persist several hours. The drug is widely distributed in body fluids, particularly in fat; its half-life may be prolonged in obese patients. Reserpine is extensively metabolized, and both metabolites and unchanged drug are slowly excreted in the urine and feces. Reserpine crosses the placenta and is excreted in breast milk.

CONTRAINDICATIONS: Hypersensitivity to reserpine and other rauwolfia alkaloids; past history of bronchial asthma or allergy (may increase the possibility of drug sensitivity); for long-term use: active peptic ulcer, ulcerative colitis, or extreme mental depression.

PRECAUTIONS: The hypotensive response after IM administration is slow and may be unpredictable; severe hypotension has occurred. Nasal stuffiness is common and usually well tolerated; however, avoid use in neonates who are obligate nose breathers. Use cautiously with digitalis, quinidine, or procainamide as cardiac arrhythmias may occur. Use with caution in epileptic patients (large doses). Exercise caution in hypertensive patients with renal insufficiency since the lowered blood pressure may further compromise renal blood flow and function.

SIDE EFFECTS/ADVERSE REACTIONS: Reserpine frequently causes nasal congestion, dry mouth, lethargy, drowsiness, gastric upset, acid hypersecretion, nausea, vomiting, and anorexia. Other CNS effects include dizziness, dyspnea, nervousness, anxiety, and nightmares. Cardiovascular side effects include angina-like symptoms, bradycardia, and arrhythmias (particularly when used concurrently with digitalis or quinidine-like drugs). Water retention, edema, conjunctival congestion, rash, and pruritus may also occur. Large doses have produced a parkinsonian syndrome, other extrapyramidal reactions, and convulsions. It may also precipitate biliary colic.

DRUG INTERACTIONS: Concomitant use with *digoxin, quinidine,* or *procainamide* may produce cardiac arrhythmias. Pressor response to parenteral *epinephrine* and other *direct-acting sympathomimetics* may be enhanced. Use with *MAO inhibitors* may cause hypertension and excitation. Additive CNS depression occurs if given with *barbiturates, narcotics, sedatives,* etc.

ANTIDOTE: Discontinue reserpine. Signs of overdose include hypotension, bradycardia (although hypertension and tachycardia have occurred in young children), CNS depression, respiratory depression, hypothermia, diarrhea, vomiting, flushed skin, conjunctival congestion, drooping eyelids, miosis, and extrapyramidal symptoms (stiffness, leg pain, tremors). Atropine can be given IV to counteract the bradycardia and parasympathetic effects. Severe hypotension should be treated with direct-acting pressor agents (e.g., levarterenol). Avoid fluid overload when attempting to raise arterial pressure. Because the effects of reserpine are prolonged, observe the patient closely for at least 72 hours.

III
AGENTS FOR FLUID AND ELECTROLYTE IMBALANCES

The proper management of fluid and electrolyte problems in children demands precision in selecting the amounts of volume replacement and the type of solution. The relationship between electrolytes, body water, osmolality, and pH is one of dynamic equilibrium that is continually shifting to maintain homeostasis. Any condition that upsets this homeostasis by causing increased loss or retention of necessary electrolytes or by altering the total fluid volume must be corrected promptly because children are more vulnerable to these imbalances and their sequelae than adults are.

The aims of fluid and electrolyte therapy are as follows:

- To treat shock
- To replace abnormal losses already sustained
- To provide water, electrolytes, and nutriments for maintaining daily needs
- To avoid creating new disturbances as a result of the therapy

Monitoring should include the following:

- Daily weight (if possible)
- Daily intake of water and electrolytes
- Daily output and specific gravity of urine
- Serum levels of sodium, potassium, bicarbonate, and chloride and serum osmolality on admission and frequently until stable

This section discusses oral rehydrating solutions, individual electrolyte solutions for treatment of specific ion imbalances, and diuretic agents for the treatment of fluid overload.

9
Diuretics

The salt and water balance of the body is under the immediate control of the kidneys. Diuretics inhibit salt and water retention and thus reduce the volume of extracellular fluid by increasing urine output. They are used primarily to prevent or alleviate edema when the fluid overload compromises the function of the cardiovascular and respiratory systems. Diuretics are also used to promote diuresis in oliguric conditions.

The following medications are included in this chapter:

- **Chlorothiazide**
- **Ethacrynic acid**
- **Furosemide**
- **Glycerol**
- **Mannitol**

Chlorothiazide (Diuril)

ADMINISTRATION

Available Forms: Injectable, 500 mg, powder for reconstitution; tablets, 250, 500 mg; oral suspension, 50 mg/ml.

Diluent: Sterile water for injection or NS.

Dosage (Parenteral): Not recommended.

Dosage (Oral): 20 mg/kg/24 hr (60 mg/m^2/24 hr) given in 2 divided doses.

Rate: If IV infusion is used, do not exceed 100 mg/min.

INDICATIONS: Chlorothiazide is used to alleviate edema associated with congestive heart failure and many other disorders. It may also be used in the management of hypertension (either alone or with other antihypertensives). It is used primarily for long-term therapy.

ACTIONS: Chlorothiazide is a moderately potent diuretic representative of a large class of thiazide diuretics that all have identical mechanisms of action. They act on the proximal and early distal tubules of the renal nephron to block the reabsorption of sodium, chloride, potassium, bicarbonate, and water. These ions are therefore excreted with an accompanying volume of water. Thiazides are usually ineffective for treatment of severe renal impairment in which creatinine clearance (CrC) rates are 25 ml/min or less. Onset of action after oral administration is within 30 minutes, and duration is about 6–12 hours. Chlorothiazide is excreted primarily unchanged in the urine.

CONTRAINDICATIONS: Anuria, hypersensitivity to thiazides or sulfonamide derivatives.

PRECAUTIONS: Monitor and evaluate vital signs (especially blood pressure), fluid intake and output, serum electrolytes, BUN, and CO_2 at frequent intervals during therapy. Correct electrolyte imbalances as necessary. Use cautiously in patients who have severe renal disease (azotemia may develop) or hepatic impairment (minor alterations in fluid and electrolyte balance may precipitate hepatic encephalopathy or coma). Hypersensitivity reactions may occur in patients who have a history of allergy or bronchial asthma. Measure blood levels of glucose frequently as thiazides may cause hyperglycemia; diabetics may need dosage adjustments of their hypoglycemics. Chlorothiazide may increase serum levels of uric acid, so use with caution in patients who have gout. The thiazide diuretics cross the placenta and may induce severe fetal jaundice and thrombocytopenia. These agents displace bilirubin from albumin-binding sites, so avoid their use in already jaundiced neonates and infants. IV administration can irritate veins and cause phlebitis. Avoid extravasation. Do not give IV injections simultaneously with blood (administer blood separately or via Y-tubing).

SIDE EFFECTS/ADVERSE REACTIONS: Common side effects include electrolyte imbalances, gastric disturbances, dizziness, headache, dehydration, and orthostatic hypotension. Severe dehydration and excessive loss of potassium and chloride may cause hypokalemic-hypochloremic metabolic alkalosis, embolism, or thrombosis. Paresthesias, muscle weakness, hyperglycemia, glucosuria, and hyperuricemia may occur. Hypersensitivity reactions include skin eruptions, photosensitivity reactions, purpuras, fever, respiratory distress, blood dyscrasias, cholestatic jaundice, and anaphylaxis.

DRUG INTERACTIONS: Chlorothiazide may antagonize the hypoglycemic effects of *insulin* and *oral antidiabetic agents*. Concomitant use with *CNS depressants, narcotics,* or *antihypertensives* causes additive hypotension. Chlorothiazide may predispose patients to *digitalis* toxicity by lowering serum levels of potassium. Excessive potassium loss may occur with *corticosteroids*.

ANTIDOTE: Discontinue the medication. Replace losses in fluid volume and electrolyte deficits as indicated. Treat hypersensitivity reactions appropriately.

Ethacrynic acid (Edecrin)

ADMINISTRATION

Available Forms: Injectable (IV), 50 mg (lyophilized powder for reconstitution); tablets, 25, 50 mg.

Diluent: Reconstitute the contents of the vial with 50 ml of D5W or NS; the resulting concentration is 1 mg/ml. Use a diluent with pH over 5. If the solution is hazy or opalescent, do not use it. Doses can be further diluted in NS for intermittent (IVPB) infusion.

Dosage (Parenteral): 0.5–1.0 mg/kg/dose given slowly IV. If the response is unsatisfactory, the same dosage can be repeated in 1 hour. Up to 3 mg/kg/dose has been used in severe pulmonary edema.

Dosage (Oral): Initially, 25 mg as single daily dose. Increase by 25 mg increments to desired effect; maintain on alternate day schedule if possible. Alternatively, 1–2 mg/kg/day given in single or divided doses (2 or 3 times a day [bid or tid]).

Rate: Give IV bolus dose slowly over several minutes into the tubing of a running IV infusion. IV piggyback doses can be given over 20 minutes.

INDICATIONS: Like furosemide, ethacrynic acid is an extremely potent diuretic of greatest benefit in treating acute congestive heart failure or pulmonary edema. It may also be given in conjunction with IV albumin for severe compromising edema caused by the nephrotic syndrome. Ethacrynic acid may also be effective in patients refractory to other diuretics or in patients with severe renal impairment (e.g., glomerular filtration rates less than 5 ml/min).

ACTIONS: Ethacrynic acid induces rapid diuresis in the same manner as furosemide. It inhibits sodium, chloride, and water reabsorption in the ascending limb of Henle's loop and in the distal and proximal portions of the renal tubule. Urinary excretion of water, sodium, chloride, potassium, calcium, and magnesium are all increased. Like furosemide, ethacrynic acid's action is not affected by the acid-base balance of the patient. Diuresis usually occurs within 5 minutes after IV administration, peaks within 15–30 minutes, and lasts for about 2 hours. After oral doses, diuresis usually begins in 30 minutes, peaks in about 2 hours, and may persist 6–8 hours. Like furosemide, some of the drug is metabolized in the liver, and the metabolite and unchanged ethacrynic acid are excreted primarily in the urine. There is some excretion in the bile.

CONTRAINDICATIONS: Anuria; hepatic coma; increasing oliguria, azotemia, or electrolyte imbalance; development of severe, watery diarrhea; hypersensitivity to ethacrynic acid; pregnancy; lactation.

PRECAUTIONS: See furosemide; the same precautions for excessive fluid and electrolyte loss apply. See also chlorothiazide. Administer IV doses slowly to avoid tinnitus and possible deafness.

SIDE EFFECTS/ADVERSE REACTIONS: See furosemide. In addition, temporary or permanent deafness has been reported, especially if rapid IV administration is used, if the patient has severe renal impairment, or if the drug is used concurrently with other ototoxic medication.

DRUG INCOMPATIBILITIES: Diluents with pH 5 or less (e.g., D5W) may produce a hazy or opalescent solution, which should not be used. Ethacrynic acid is incompatible with blood, blood derivatives, hydralazine, procainamide, reserpine, and tolazoline solutions.

DRUG INTERACTIONS: See furosemide.

ANTIDOTE: See furosemide.

Furosemide (Lasix)

ADMINISTRATION

Available Forms: Injectable (IV, IM), 10 mg/ml in 2, 4, 10 ml amps; tablets, 20, 40, 80 mg; oral solution, 10 mg/ml.

Diluent: Can be given undiluted.

Dosage (Parenteral): 1–2 mg/kg/dose slow IV push or IM. If the response is unsatisfactory, the dose can be increased (no sooner than 2 hours) by 1 mg/kg/dose until the desired effect is achieved. Maximum is 6 mg/kg/dose.

Dosage (Oral): 1–2 mg/kg/dose. Can replace parenteral therapy. Daily maintenance doses can be divided into 2 doses.

Rate: For slow IV push do not exceed 20 mg/min.

INDICATIONS: Furosemide is a potent "high-ceiling" diuretic that is effective for rapid reduction of edema secondary to cardiac, hepatic, or renal dysfunction. It is particularly useful in the management of acute congestive heart failure and pulmonary edema. It may also be used for long-term management of hypertension, for acute treatment of hypercalcemia when effective diuresis will decrease serum levels of calcium, and as adjunctive therapy for increased intracranial pressure.

ACTIONS: Furosemide causes rapid diuresis by inhibiting the reabsorption of sodium, chloride, and water in the loop and ascending limb of the loop of Henle and in the distal and proximal renal tubule. Response to furosemide is independent of acid-base balance. Urinary excretion of water, sodium, chloride, magnesium, and calcium is increased. Potassium loss is increased proportionally to the amount of fluid flowing through the distal tubule of the nephron. After IV administration diuresis occurs within 5 minutes, peaks in 20–60 minutes, and lasts for about 2 hours. With oral doses onset occurs within 30 minutes, peaks in 1–2 hours, and lasts for 6–8 hours. Diuretic response may be prolonged in patients with severe renal impairment.

CONTRAINDICATIONS: Anuria; hepatic coma; hypersensitivity to furosemide; hypersensitivity to sulfonamides; pregnancy; increasing oliguria, azotemia, or electrolyte imbalance.

PRECAUTIONS: See chlorothiazide. In addition, excessive depletion of electrolytes and dehydration resulting in circulatory collapse or vascular thrombosis may occur if diuresis is too rapid. A transient hearing loss may occur if the IV infusion rate exceeds the recommended rate. Furosemide may precipitate digitalis toxicity if the serum level of potassium is lowered excessively. It can potentially cause fetal or neonatal jaundice by displacing bilirubin from albumin-binding sites; use cautiously in infants who have preexisting high serum bilirubin, low serum albumin, or acidosis.

SIDE EFFECTS/ADVERSE REACTIONS: Many of the toxic effects are due to the profound effect on electrolyte and water balance. Excessive electrolyte imbalances may cause cramps, neuromuscular weakness, hypokalemic-hypochloremic metabolic alkalosis, tetany, and impaired glucose tolerance. Dehydration with thromboembolism, orthostatic hypotension, elevations of BUN, and circulatory collapse may occur. Other possible side effects include transient deafness, tinnitus, vertigo, and dizziness. Allergic interstitial nephritis, hyperuricemia, jaundice, and acute pancreatitis have been reported. Hypersensitivity reactions, gastric disturbances, and blood dyscrasias are similar to those of the thiazide diuretics.

DRUG INTERACTIONS: (See also chlorothiazide.) Additive ototoxicity may occur with *aminoglycosides* and additive nephrotoxicity with *aminoglycosides* and *cephaloridine*.

ANTIDOTE: Discontinue the medication. Replace losses in fluid volume and electrolyte deficits as indicated. Treat hypersensitivity reactions appropriately.

Glycerol (USP) (Glycerin)

ADMINISTRATION

Available Forms: Oral solution, 50% v/v (Osmoglyn) and 75% v/v (Glyrol) in 180 ml bottles, 96% (USP) in various sizes of containers.

Dosage (Oral)
For cerebral edema: 0.5–1.0 gm/kg given orally or via nasogastric tube q6h.

INDICATIONS: Glycerol (glycerin) is given orally to lower intracranial pressure (ICP) in patients with cerebral edema. After initial treatment with IV mannitol, glycerol may be added to produce chronic osmotic diuresis and reduce ICP. Because only a small percentage of a glycerin dose is excreted by the kidneys, it may be preferred over mannitol for patients with severe renal impairment. Glycerin solutions are more concentrated than mannitol, and smaller volumes can be given, an advantage for patients in whom there is a danger of overloading the cardiovascular system.

ACTIONS: Glycerol, like mannitol, produces tissue dehydration and reduces cerebrospinal fluid pressure by osmotic diuresis. It elevates the osmotic pressure of the plasma to such an extent that water is drawn from extravascular tissue spaces into the blood stream and excreted. Glycerin also reduces intraocular pressure. Peak effects occur 30–60 minutes after oral administration. Within 2–3 hours most of the dose is metabolized by the liver to carbon dioxide and water or utilized in glucose or glycogen synthesis.

CONTRAINDICATIONS: Severe dehydration, intracranial hemorrhage.

PRECAUTIONS: Monitor urine output, serum electrolytes, and osmolality as clinically indicated. Administration of less concentrated solutions (50 or 75%) may minimize nausea and vomiting. If sedation is required, light sedation is preferred because heavy sedation may cause more nausea and vomiting. Use cautiously in patients with cardiac disease as the shift in body water may aggravate pulmonary edema and congestive heart failure. Use cautiously in diabetics because slight hyperglycemia may occur. Use with caution in already dehydrated patients.

SIDE EFFECTS/ADVERSE REACTIONS: Nausea, vomiting, diarrhea, mild headache, dizziness, and thirst are common reactions. Dehydration, hyperglycemia, glycosuria, and pulmonary edema may occur.

DRUG INTERACTIONS: There is an additive osmotic diuretic effect when used with *mannitol* or *urea*. Glycerol may increase *insulin* requirements in diabetics.

ANTIDOTE: Discontinue glycerol. Treat dehydration with hypotonic fluids. Treat adverse reactions symptomatically.

Mannitol (Osmitrol, Mannitol)

ADMINISTRATION

Available Forms: Injectable (IV), see Table 9-1.

Diluent: Can be given undiluted.

Dosage (Parenteral): Varies according to use.
Test dose for oliguria in acute renal failure: 0.2 gm/kg given over 5–10 minutes. A positive response is a urine flow of 30–50 ml/hr for 1–3 hours.
For cerebral edema: 0.25–0.50 gm/kg/dose given IV over 30 minutes; can be repeated q4–6h as needed. Maximum dose in infants and children is 1 gm/kg.

Rate: Adjust rate to maintain a urine output of at least 30–50 ml/hr (5–10 ml/kg/hr).

TABLE 9-1 Solutions of Mannitol for Injection

Concentration %	(mg/ml)	Size (ml)
5	50	1000
10	100	500, 1000
15	150	150, 500
20	200	250, 500
25	250	50

INDICATIONS: Mannitol is used most frequently for the emergency reduction of increased intracranial pressure associated with cerebral edema. It is often combined with glycerol, corticosteroids, or potent IV diuretics (e.g., furosemide) for this purpose. During acute renal failure precipitated by such conditions as shock, massive hemorrhage, burns, sepsis, or transfusion reactions, single doses of mannitol may promote an adequate urine flow when oliguria or anuria persist even though CVP, blood pressure, and circulatory volume have been restored with IV fluids and other measures. Mannitol may prevent or reverse acute functional renal failure before there is evidence of renal tubular damage or irreversible failure. It is also used to reduce intraocular pressure and to promote urinary excretion of toxins or drugs after overdoses.

ACTIONS: Mannitol is a rapidly acting osmotic diuretic. It is filtered by the renal glomerulus but not reabsorbed by the tubules. Its presence in the renal tubule draws water and accumulated toxins with it. Reabsorption of sodium and water is impaired since the increased rate of flow of tubular fluid overwhelms the capacity of the transport system. Excretion of other ions such as potassium, chloride, calcium, and magnesium is also increased. After a single IV dose diuresis begins in about 20–30 minutes, peaks in 30–60 minutes, and lasts about 3–8 hours. It should produce an output of 5–10 ml/kg/hr of relatively dilute urine. Repeated or large doses can cause fluid and electrolyte imbalances and also induce a "rebound" increase in ICP. This greatly limits the benefits of long-term use; consequently, oral glycerol and IV corticosteroids are usually given concomitantly for their prolonged effects in the management of cerebral edema.

CONTRAINDICATIONS: Anuria or impaired renal function not responding to a test dose of mannitol, dehydration or hyperosmolar serum, severe pulmonary congestion or edema, active intracranial bleeding, edema associated with abnormal capillary fragility or membrane permeability.

PRECAUTIONS: Administer with an in-line filter in place. Use only clear, crystal-free solutions. Solutions more concentrated than 15% may crystallize (warm solution to redissolve crystals). Measure urine output hourly or more frequently. Monitor fluid and electrolytes (especially sodium and potassium) and central venous pressure frequently. Avoid extravasation. Do not mix with infusions of blood. Discontinue use if the patient develops signs of progressive renal dysfunction, congestive heart failure, or pulmonary congestion. Maintain adequate fluids to prevent dehydration because of osmotic diuresis. Avoid doses greater than 1 gm/kg in infants and children.

SIDE EFFECTS/ADVERSE REACTIONS: Headache, nausea, chills, vomiting, dizziness, thirst, lethargy, confusion, a sense of constriction or chest pain, and allergic reactions may occur during infusion. Serious effects include fluid and electrolyte imbalances, circulatory overload with pulmonary edema, rebound increases in intracranial pressure, water intoxication, hypertension, tachycardia, congestive heart failure, aggravation of intracranial bleeding, and intraocular hemorrhage. Convulsions may occur (due to hyponatremia), and too rapid diuresis may lead to dehydration and hypovolemia. Extravasation can cause thrombophlebitis and tissue necrosis.

DRUG INCOMPATIBILITIES: Do not mix with blood or concentrated solutions of sodium chloride or potassium chloride.

ANTIDOTE: Discontinue the infusion. Treat fluid overload with diuretics (furosemide).

10
Oral Rehydrating Solutions

A deficit in the volume of extracellular fluid can be caused by an abrupt reduction in fluid intake or by an acute loss of secretions and excretions through vomiting, infantile diarrhea, high fever, or fistulous drainage. Parenteral and oral hydrating solutions are used to expand the intravascular and, subsequently, the extracellular volume; to maintain isotonicity and circulatory efficiency; and to permit renal perfusion.

Fluid volume in children represents a higher percentage of body weight than in adults. Children adjust to imbalances less promptly than adults, and there is a smaller margin between overhydration and volume depletion. For example, while a 10% loss of body fluid in a 70 kg adult may not require immediate correction, a 10% loss in a 7 kg child may be a critical emergency. Calculation of volume and administration rates must be accurate, and the patient's state of hydration must be monitored frequently (Table 10–1).

TABLE 10–1 Relationship between Loss in Body Weight and Dehydration

Loss in Body Weight (%)	Severity of Dehydration
5	Mild
5–10	Moderate
10	Severe
15	Shock

During acute loss of fluids, it is useful to assume that the total loss in body weight has been lost as water (i.e., 1 gm = 1 ml). Thus, a 1 kg decrease in body weight equals an acute loss of approximately 1000 ml of fluid. Knowledge of exact weight loss in infants is the most accurate method of clinically assessing fluid replacement. A guide for calculating the normal daily range of fluid requirements for children and a table listing the composition of commonly used parenteral hydrating solutions and noncolloid plasma volume expanders can be found in the appendix.

Parenteral replacement of fluid losses is indicated for infants and children who are experiencing severe dehydration (10 to 15% weight loss), severe vomiting or gastric distension, or who are unable to take fluids orally. Commercial electrolyte solutions for oral use have been used widely and successfully for patients who have milder degrees of dehydration (5 to 10% weight loss) and even for those who are vomiting.

Oral rehydrating solutions

ADMINISTRATION

Available Forms: Various preparations are available (see Table 10–2).

Dosage (Oral): Varies with the severity of the condition. About 150 ml/kg is administered during the first 24 hours, with one-half the calculated amount given in the first 8 hours if possible.

INDICATIONS: Oral rehydration solutions are used for maintenance of water and electrolytes during mild to moderate diarrhea, for prevention of dehydration, and for reestablishment of oral intake following corrective parenteral therapy for severe diarrhea.

TABLE 10–2 Oral Rehydrating Solutions*

Solution (Source)	Na^+	K^+	OTHER CATIONS	Cl^-	BASE	OTHER ANIONS	Carbohydrates (%)
HYDRA-LYTE (Jayco) Powder (packet dilutes to 1 qt)	84	10	none	59	HCO_3 15 Citrate 20	none	Glucose plus sucrose: 2.0
INFALYTE (Pennwalt) Powder (packet dilutes to 1 qt)	50	20	none	40	HCO_3 30	none	Glucose 2.0
LYTREN (Mead Johnson) Liquid (ready to use)	30	25	Ca 4 Mg 4	25	Citrate 29	SO_4 4 PO_4 5	Glucose plus corn syrup: 7.7
ORAL ELECTROLYTE-SOLUTION (Wyeth) Liquid (ready to use)	30	20	Ca 4 Mg 4	30	Citrate 23	PO_4 5	Glucose 7.5
PEDIALYTE (Ross) Liquid (ready to use)	30	20	Ca 4 Mg 4	30	Citrate 28	none	Glucose 5.0
PEDIALYTE R.S. (Ross) Liquid (ready to use)†	60	20	none	50	Citrate 30	none	Glucose 2.5
WHO Oral Rehydration Salts‡ Powder (packet dilutes to 1 liter)	90	20	none	80	HCO_3 30	none	Glucose 2.0

*Adapted with permission from *Med Lett* 1983;25(629):20.
†To be marketed in May 1983.
‡Available from Jianas Brothers Packaging, 2533 SW Blvd, Kansas City, Mo; KBI, Berlin; ALLPACK, Waiblingen, West Germany; Geymont Sud, Anagni, Italy; others. Also available as Oralite—Beecham; Elotrans—Fresenius, Bad Homburg; Oral Rehydration Salts—Servipharm, Basel; Salvadora—LUSA, Lima.

ACTIONS: These solutions replace fluid and electrolyte losses (particularly sodium, potassium, and chloride) caused by diarrhea. Since stool is relatively hypotonic, and since losses of water are usually greater than losses of electrolytes under normal circumstances and with milder degrees of diarrhea, the best oral replacement solutions are those with low osmolality. Ideally, preparations containing 50–60 mEq sodium/liter are preferred for infants, who have a higher insensible water loss. The solutions with higher concentrations of sodium (90 mEq/liter) can be used in children and in those infants with cholera-induced diarrhea in which sodium losses are especially great. Diarrhea invariably causes substantial losses of potassium. If not replaced, these losses may lead to hypokalemia, metabolic alkalosis, gastric distension, and paralytic ileus. These oral rehydrating solutions therefore contain approximately 20 mEq potassium/liter. The higher concentrations of glucose (5.0–7.5%) in some of the earlier formulations tend to produce an osmotic effect that can worsen diarrhea. Using the preparations with only 2.0–2.5% glucose avoids this osmotic effect of unabsorbed carbohydrate and promotes the absorption of sodium from the intestine.

CONTRAINDICATIONS: Severe dehydration (10–15% weight loss), severe vomiting or gastric distension, inability to drink.

PRECAUTIONS: Infants should be offered frequent small amounts of the solutions initially, if tolerated; however, frequent feedings can increase the gastrocolic reflex and may aggravate diarrhea. Avoid large volume feedings in the initial vomiting stages. Do not administer cold solutions as they can increase colonic activity and worsen the diarrhea. Infants who finish the prescribed amount of solution in less than 24 hours should be offered plain tap water to avoid the development of hypernatremia. Monitor fluid intake and output frequently and body weight daily.

SIDE EFFECTS/ADVERSE REACTIONS: Osmotic diarrhea may occur if higher glucose concentrations are used. Hypernatremia and hyperosmolality may occur if diarrhea or vomiting persists and insufficient amounts of water or dilute solutions or too concentrated electrolyte solutions are given.

ANTIDOTE: Discontinue oral rehydrating solutions. Parenteral therapy may be necessary to correct fluid and electrolyte imbalances.

11
Electrolyte Replacements

A variety of integrated physiological processes keep the fluid, electrolyte, and pH balance of the body remarkably constant despite the many stresses placed upon it. However, profound imbalances in the amount and composition of cellular fluids can result from trauma, surgical procedures, and a variety of disease states. Under such circumstances, the body may not be able to make the rapid and appropriate readjustments necessary to reestablish homeostasis. The clinician must be able to anticipate and correct these deficits or imbalances with suitable electrolyte replacements.

ACID-BASE BALANCE

The body's acid-base balance determines and maintains the pH of extracellular fluid within the normal range of 7.35–7.45. The pH must be kept within the narrow limits of 7.0–7.8 to sustain life. To review briefly, the acidity or alkalinity of a fluid depends on the concentration of hydrogen ions [H^+] in the solution: An increase in hydrogen ions makes it more acid, a decrease makes it more alkaline. For convenience this concentration is expressed as the negative logarithm of the hydrogen ion concentration, or pH. An acid solution has a pH below 7.0; an alkaline solution has a pH above 7.0; a neutral solution is pH 7.0.

The body minimizes deviations in the pH of ECF by means of the following:

- Chemical buffering capacity of ECF
- Alterations in respiratory activity
- Renal mechanisms
- Ion-exchange mechanisms (shifts of H^+, Na^+, and K^+ in and out of cells)

A buffer system can bind up surplus hydrogen ions or release them to prevent fluctuations in pH. The major buffering system of the body is the carbonic acid (H_2CO_3)–bicarbonate (HCO_3^-) system. Excess hydrogen ions combine with HCO_3^- to form carbonic acid, which dissociates to water and CO_2. The latter is excreted through the lungs. Excess bicarbonate is excreted by the kidney along with sodium and potassium ions. Thus, through these various mechanisms, the body can partially "compensate" for an acid-base disorder.

The pH of a carbonic-acid-bicarbonate buffer can be expressed mathematically by the Henderson-Hasselbalch equation:

$$pH = pKa + \log([HCO_3^-]/[H_2CO_3]), \text{ where } pKa = 6.1 \text{ (constant)}.$$

In other words, if the ratio of the concentrations of bicarbonate and carbonic acid changes, the plasma pH will change accordingly. At the normal pH of 7.4, most of the carbonic acid is neutralized, so $[H_2CO_3] = 1$ and $[HCO_3^-] = 20$. Therefore, the normal ratio of bicarbonate to carbonic acid is 20:1. In acidosis the plasma pH drops below 7.35; in alkalosis it rises above 7.45.

Table 11–1 lists the four primary acid-base disturbances and the changes that occur during these imbalances.

TABLE 11–1 Primary Acid-Base Disturbances

Condition	pH*	HCO_3^-*	PO_2*	PCO_2*	Compensatory Changes
Metabolic acidosis	Decreases	Decreases	Increases	Compensatory decrease	Decrease in PCO_2, acid urine
Metabolic alkalosis	Increases	Increases	Decreases	Compensatory increase	Increase in PCO_2, alkaline urine
Respiratory acidosis	Decreases	Compensatory increase	Decreases	Increases	Conservation of HCO_3^-, acid urine
Respiratory alkalosis	Increases	Compensatory decrease	Increases	Decreases	Excretion of excess HCO_3^-, alkaline urine

*Normal values are pH, 7.35–7.45; HCO_3^-, 20–28 mEq/liter; PO_2, 80–100 mm Hg; PCO_2, 35–45 mm Hg.

The following electrolyte replacements are included in this chapter:

- **Calcium chloride**
- **Calcium gluconate**
- **Magnesium sulfate**
- **Potassium chloride**
- **Potassium acetate**
- **Potassium phosphate**
- **Sodium bicarbonate**
- **Tromethamine**

Calcium chloride
Calcium gluconate

ADMINISTRATION (CALCIUM CHLORIDE)

Available Forms: Injectable (IV, IC), 100 mg/ml (10%) in preloaded 10 ml syringes (contains 1.36 mEq Ca^{++}/ml or 27.3 mg Ca^{++}/ml). (1 mEq Ca^{++} = 20 mg Ca^{++}.)

Diluent: For slow IV infusion dilute in D5W or NS.

Dosage (Parenteral)
For cardiac resuscitation: 0.2–0.5 ml/kg (5–10 mg Ca^{++}/kg) slow IV (preferred) or IC; can repeat dose in 10–20 min prn. Average dose is 0.3 ml/kg.

Rate: Maximum recommended for IV infusion of undiluted calcium chloride is 0.7–1.5 mEq/min (0.5–1.0 ml/min).

ADMINISTRATION (CALCIUM GLUCONATE)

Available Forms: Injectable (IV, IC), 100 mg/ml (10%) in 10 ml vials (contains 0.47 mEq Ca^{++}/ml or 9.4 mg Ca^{++}/ml). (1 mEq Ca^{++} = 20 mg Ca^{++}.)

Diluent: For slow IV infusion dilute in D5W or NS.

Dosage (Parenteral): Varies according to use.
For cardiac resuscitation: 1–2 ml/kg/dose (9–18 mg/kg) slow IV (up to 5 ml in premature infants; up to 10 ml in full-term infants).
For severe hypocalcemia with seizures or tetany: 1–2 ml/kg/dose, diluted and given slowly IV over 5–10 minutes. Begin with lower dose (up to 5 ml in premature infants; up to 10 ml in full-term infants). Monitor ECG during the infusion.
For asymptomatic hypocalcemia: 45–90 mg/kg/day of elemental Ca^{++} (5–10 ml/kg/day) given as a diluted IV solution over 24 hours.

Rate: As for calcium chloride.

INDICATIONS: Calcium salts are administered IV during cardiac resuscitation to improve weak or ineffective myocardial contractions. They are often useful in electromechanical dissociation when the heart rate is inadequate to maintain circulation as evidenced by low blood pressure and weak pulses. Calcium salts may also restore electrical rhythm in some instances of ventricular standstill when epinephrine has failed. The calcium chloride salt is usually preferred for emergency use because it produces higher, more predictable levels of ionized calcium than does the gluconate salt; however, calcium gluconate is recommended for use in infants and neonates because it causes less acidosis. Calcium salts are also given IV to treat tetany caused by acute hypocalcemia, hypermagnesemia, and certain poisonings (e.g., fluoride, oxalic acid, carbon tetrachloride). In addition, they are used as adjunctive therapy to relieve muscle spasms or cramps associated with lead colic and certain insect bites. Neonates with hypocalcemia induced by exchange transfusions with citrated blood and other patients with asymptomatic hypocalcemia may be given calcium salts by IV infusion or orally.

ACTIONS: Calcium is essential in a number of physiological processes. These include transmission of nerve impulses; contraction of cardiac, skeletal, and smooth muscle; renal function; respiration; blood coagulation; mineralization of bones and teeth; and regulation of certain hormonal control mechanisms and secretory processes. Nearly 99% of the body's calcium is stored in the bones and teeth. When serum levels of calcium fall, additional amounts are mobilized from this reservoir by parathyroid hormone or vitamin D. The remaining 1% of calcium is present in serum and body fluids. Three forms of calcium are distributed in the plasma. The first form, approximately 45–50% (of the total plasma calcium), is ionized; the second form, 5–10%, is complexed to citrate, phosphate, or other anions; and the remainder, 40–45%, is non-ionized and bound to serum proteins (albumin, primarily, and globulin). Both the ionized and complexed forms are readily diffusible through cell membranes and hence are physiologically active. The protein-bound fraction is inactive. There is a reciprocal imbalance between the ionized and protein-bound forms: If the concentration of one form increases, the concentration of the other decreases. If serum pH increases (alkalosis) or the plasma protein level rises, the concentration of ionized (active) calcium decreases and tetany can result. Conversely, in acidosis or hypoalbuminemia, serum levels of ionized calcium increase.

Normal serum levels of calcium are 4.5–5.5 mEq/liter (9–11 mg/100 ml); levels may be lower in neonates. Hypocalcemia occurs commonly in the newborn after exchange transfusions with citrated blood and after high-phosphate diets that use whole cow's milk. Other causes include respiratory distress syndrome (RDS), asphyxia, hypoxia, prematurity, overcorrection of acidosis, sepsis, hypoparathyroidism, intestinal malabsorption of calcium and magnesium, steatorrhea, low intake of vitamin D, hypoproteinemia induced by liver disease or nephrosis, renal disease, hyperkalemia, hyperphosphatemia, acute pancreatitis, fluoride poisoning, and drugs such as potent diuretics, glucagon, corticosteroids, and bicarbonate. Signs and symptoms of hypocalcemia include muscle spasms and cramps, tetany, circumoral tingling, paresthesias, numbness, carpopedal spasm, positive Chvostek's and Trousseau's signs, and ECG changes (prolonged QT intervals and lengthened ST segments). Neonates commonly become jittery and irritable and have high-pitched cries, hypotonia, and seizures.

CONTRAINDICATIONS: Hypercalcemia, ventricular fibrillation, digitalis toxicity.

PRECAUTIONS: The chloride salt is more irritating and more likely to cause acidosis than the gluconate salt; use this form cautiously in patients with respiratory acidosis or failure, and avoid its use in neonates. Use both forms cautiously in patients with renal impairment and in those patients receiving digitalis preparations. Do not give any calcium salt SC, IM, or by accidental intramyocardial injection, as severe tissue necrosis may result. Avoid extravasation and rapid IV rates. Monitor ECG and blood pressures continuously during acute IV calcium therapy, especially with large doses. Monitor serum levels of calcium periodically during therapy. In newborns, rapid administration of IV calcium through the umbilical artery may be a precipitating factor in necrotizing enterocolitis. If an umbilical vein catheter is used, make sure that it bypasses the liver and is pushed up into the inferior vena cava. Otherwise, necrosis of the liver could result from extravasation into hepatic tissue.

SIDE EFFECTS/ADVERSE REACTIONS: Rapid administration of IV doses with resultant hypercalcemia may cause vasodilation, hypotension, bradycardia, a shortened QT interval, cardiac arrhythmias, syncope, and cardiac arrest. IV injection also causes irritation of veins; tingling sensations; a feeling of heat waves; and a chalky, calcium taste in the mouth. Hypercalcemia may occur after large doses are given to patients in chronic renal failure. Oral doses cause gastric upset and constipation.

DRUG INCOMPATIBILITIES: Calcium forms precipitates with sodium bicarbonate and phosphate salts and chelates tetracyclines.

DRUG INTERACTIONS: Oral doses cause decreased absorption of *tetracyclines*. Calcium salts may precipitate serious arrhythmias in patients receiving *digitalis*.

ANTIDOTE: Discontinue the infusion. Keep the patient well hydrated and administer furosemide to facilitate calcium excretion. Disodium edetate can be used cautiously.

Magnesium sulfate

ADMINISTRATION

Available Forms: Injectable (IV, IM), 100 mg/ml (10%) in 10, 20 ml amps; 250 mg/ml (25%) in 10 ml amps; 500 mg/ml (50%) in 2, 10, 20 ml amps, 30 ml vials; (1 gm $MgSO_4$ = 8.12 mEq Mg^{++}).

Diluent: Can be given undiluted IM or added to D5W or NS for infusion. Avoid solutions containing calcium or phosphate.

Dosage (Parenteral): Varies according to use.
For seizures or tetany due to hypomagnesemia: 0.2 ml/kg (of a 50% solution) IM q12h (q4–8h may be necessary in severe cases).
For acute hypomagnesemia: 0.1–0.2 ml/kg (of a 50% solution) IM or well diluted IV q12h.
For hypertension or seizures in acute nephritis: 0.2 ml/kg (of a 50% solution) IM q4–6h as needed.

Rate: For IV use do not exceed 150 mg/min (15 ml of a 1% solution per minute).

INDICATIONS: Magnesium sulfate is used to treat acute magnesium deficiency arising from a variety of clinical conditions. Its primary use, however, is as a CNS depressant for prevention and control of seizures. It is also used to control hypertension, convulsions, and encephalopathy associated with acute nephritis.

ACTIONS: The body contains large stores of magnesium. Almost all of it (99%) is intracellular, stored in bones and muscle. Only about 1% is present in the serum. About 30% of this extracellular magnesium is protein-bound; the rest is ionized. Presumably, as with calcium, only the ionized form is active. As with calcium, the amount of ionized (active) magnesium present in plasma depends on serum pH: The level of ionized magnesium is increased in acidosis and decreased in alkalosis. The parathyroid hormone regulates serum levels of magnesium (and calcium), and the adrenal hormones control its renal excretion.

Magnesium is essential for a number of physiological processes, including the synthesis and metabolism of carbohydrates and proteins, enzyme activation, and neuromuscular function. Normal serum levels are 1.5–2.5 mEq/liter. Excess magnesium causes pronounced CNS depression and peripheral vasodilation. It blocks neuromuscular transmission, and the resulting decrease in the amount of acetylcholine released by an impulse causes peripheral muscular paralysis (curare-like effect). It suppresses spontaneous rhythms of the heart by prolonging conduction time and slowing SA impulse formation. Magnesium losses can occur with vomiting, diarrhea, intestinal drainage, malnutrition, malabsorption syndromes, prolonged diuresis, prolonged IV therapy without added magnesium, renal disorders, hypoparathyroidism, and other endocrine disorders. Hypomagnesemia may be a problem in neonates who are being fed high-phosphate cow's milk formulas instead of colostrum; also malabsorption of both magnesium and calcium is common in neonates and infants. About one-half of the infants with hypocalcemia also have low serum levels of magnesium. This hypocalcemia is usually unresponsive to therapy unless the magnesium deficits are treated concurrently with magnesium salts. The clinical picture of hypomagnesemia resembles hypocalcemia and is characterized by tetany (with positive Chvostek's sign), coarse tremors, choreiform or athetoid movements, disorientation, delirium, and convulsions. These symptoms can be aggravated by high intake of calcium, phosphate, or potassium.

CONTRAINDICATIONS: Heart block, myocardial damage.

PRECAUTIONS: Magnesium is excreted solely by the kidneys, so use cautiously in patients with renal impairment. Urine output should be maintained at approximately 25 ml/hr. Maintain adequate hydration. Monitor serum levels of magnesium before each dose and levels of calcium and other electrolytes at intervals throughout the therapy. Check vital signs, especially blood pressure and respirations, and monitor the patient's ECG frequently during infusions. Knee jerk is present when normal serum levels are reached and maintained; disappearance of this patellar reflex is a useful clinical sign of toxicity. Avoid rapid rates of infusion. Hypomagnesemia should be suspected when presumed hypocalcemia does not respond to the usual therapy.

SIDE EFFECTS/ADVERSE REACTIONS: Rapid IV push may produce a feeling of intense heat in the throat that radiates down the body. Toxic effects are correlated with blood levels:

- >4 mEq/liter: Decreased deep tendon reflexes, hypotension, nausea, vomiting
- >7 mEq/liter: Drowsiness, hyporeflexia, muscular weakness, flushing, sweating, CNS depression
- >10 mEq/liter: Disappearance of deep tendon reflexes, respiratory and muscle paralysis, heart block
- >12 mEq/liter: Coma, death

Cardiac effects include prolonged PR and QRS intervals, tall T waves, premature ventricular contractions, and various degrees of heart block.

DRUG INCOMPATIBILITIES: Magnesium sulfate forms precipitates with calcium, phosphates, carbonates, tartrates, and alkali hydroxides.

DRUG INTERACTIONS: Concomitant use with other *CNS depressant drugs* (e.g., narcotics, sedative-hypnotics) causes additive CNS depression. Magnesium may enhance or prolong neuromuscular blockade if given with *neuromuscular blockers* (surgical). *Thiazide diuretics* and *furosemide* increase magnesium excretion.

ANTIDOTE: Discontinue the infusion. Calcium gluconate 10% can be given IV to reverse respiratory depression or heart block caused by magnesium intoxication.

Potassium chloride
Potassium acetate
Potassium phosphate

ADMINISTRATION

Available Forms (Potassium Chloride): Injectable (IV), 2 mEq/ml in 10, 15, 20 ml vials; oral solution, 20 mEq/15 ml (10%), 40 mEq/15 ml (20%); extended-release tablets, 300 mg (4 mEq), 600 mg (8 mEq); 750 mg (10 mEq); powder for oral liquid, 15, 20, 25 mEq packets for reconstitution.

Available Forms (Potassium Acetate): Injectable (IV), 2 mEq each of potassium and acetate per milliliter in 20 ml vials.

Available Forms (Potassium Phosphate): Injectable (IV), 4.4 mEq potassium and 9 mEq phosphate per milliliter in 15 ml vials.

Diluent: Any dextrose, saline, or multiple electrolyte solution can be used. All IV doses of KCl *must* be diluted before administration; the concentration should not exceed 40 mEq/500 ml.

Dosage (Parenteral): Varies according to use.
For hypokalemia: Up to 3 mEq/kg/24 hr diluted for IV infusion.
For digitalis toxicity: 0.3 mEq/kg/dose well diluted and given slowly IV over *not less than* 1 hour.

Dosage (Oral): Same as for IV doses. Give in divided doses with meals. Normal daily requirement is 1–3 mEq/kg.

Rate: For IV infusion do not exceed 20 mEq/hr.

INDICATIONS: Potassium supplements are used for treatment or prevention of potassium depletion due to various causes (e.g., diuretics, vomiting, diarrhea, excessive sweating, GI drainage, malnutrition, dialysis, metabolic alkalosis, diabetic acidosis, renal disease, burns and crushing injuries, certain metabolic diseases, steroid therapy, prolonged IV therapy without potassium additives). Potassium salts can also be used cautiously to treat digitalis-induced arrhythmias precipitated by hypokalemia. Potassium chloride is usually the salt of choice since hypochloremia frequently accompanies potassium depletion. In rare instances in which metabolic acidosis accompanies hypokalemia (e.g., renal tubular acidosis) and an excess of chloride could aggravate the problem, an alkalinizing salt such as potassium acetate may be used. Potassium phosphate may be given for conditions in which phosphate depletion is common (e.g., diabetic ketoacidosis).

ACTIONS: Potassium is the major cation of the intracellular fluid. It is essential for maintaining acid-base balance and intracellular osmolality; for contraction of cardiac, skeletal, and smooth muscle; and for nerve conduction, tissue synthesis, renal function, and carbohydrate metabolism. The normal daily potassium requirement is 1–3 mEq/kg (40 mEq/m^2). Normal serum (or extracellular) concentrations of potassium are usually 3.5–5.0 mEq/liter, but levels up to 7.7 mEq/liter may be normal in neonates. In contrast, the intracellular concentration of potassium is about 150 mEq/liter. Since this intracellular level cannot be measured clinically, the serum level of potassium is monitored instead. However, serum levels do not necessarily reflect actual cellular stores or indicate deficits. Potassium, as well as calcium and magnesium, exists in a state of equilibrium. Although the total amount of potassium in body fluids is constant, this ion is continually moving in and out of cells in response to a variety of factors, so serum levels of potassium are constantly changing. Some factors influencing the movement of potassium include serum levels of glucose, oxygen, insulin, and sodium and serum pH. For instance, in acidosis, the serum concentration of potassium *increases* about 0.6 mEq/liter for each 0.1 unit drop in pH. Consequently, plasma levels may appear elevated even though intracellular levels are low and vice versa.

The kidney is the major route of potassium excretion, and the extracellular fluid (serum) is the avenue by which potassium enters or leaves the cells and the kidneys. The ultimate determinant of potassium deficits or excesses is renal output and excretion. The kidneys cannot conserve potassium as they do sodium, and frequently potassium is lost in an effort to retain sodium. Laboratory findings that reflect a developing potassium deficit include an increased plasma pH (alkalosis), decreased serum levels of potassium and chloride, increased plasma levels of bicarbonate, decreased urine pH, and an increased concentration of potassium in the urine. Symptoms of hypokalemia include lassitude; widespread weakness of intestinal, skeletal, and respiratory muscles; cramps; and paralytic ileus. The cardiac effects of hypokalemia vary from arrhythmias to heart block potentiated by digitalis. ECG patterns show a broadened (low voltage) T wave, presence of a U wave (most prominent in the anterior precordial leads), depressed ST segments, and a prolonged QT interval.

CONTRAINDICATIONS: Acute or chronic renal disease, azotemia, oliguria or anuria, hyperkalemia, untreated adrenal insufficiency, acute dehydration, potassium-sparing diuretics, heat cramps.

PRECAUTIONS: Intravenous doses must be well diluted (no more than 40 mEq/liter) and administered slowly (no more than 20 mEq/hr). Make sure these solutions are well mixed before administration. If potassium is added to an IV solution in a hanging container, make sure the container is *inverted* and *mix* the contents to avoid pooling of KCl at the bottom of the container. Monitor serum levels of electrolytes and serum pH frequently. The patient's renal function must be adequate; measure urine output continually. Monitor the patient's ECG if rates of IV administration are about 20 mEq/hr. To avoid serious hyperkalemia, replace potassium deficits slowly, usually over 3–7 days, depending on the severity of the deficit. Potassium supplements given orally should be administered as a liquid, diluted in juice or water, and given with meals to minimize gastric upset and saline cathartic effects. Tablets must be swallowed and *not* allowed to dissolve in the mouth.

SIDE EFFECTS/ADVERSE REACTIONS: Oral doses cause nausea, vomiting, diarrhea, and abdominal discomfort. Enteric-coated and wax-matrix preparations may cause small bowel ulcerations. Intravenous administration is extremely painful and irritating to veins. Hyperkalemia is the most common and serious hazard. Changes in the patient's ECG are the most important indicator of potassium poisoning:

- 6–8 mEq/liter: Tall, peaked T waves; prolonged PR interval; flattened P waves
- 8–9 mEq/liter: Disappearance of P wave, atrial arrest, widened QRS complex
- Over 9 mEq/liter: Widened, aberrant QRS complexes; fusion of QRS and RS-T segments; idioventricular rhythms; ventricular tachycardia; fibrillation; or asystole

Other clinical signs and symptoms are muscle weakness, paresthesias, listlessness, mental confusion, cold skin, gray pallor, flaccid paralysis, peripheral vascular collapse, and hypotension.

DRUG INTERACTIONS: Concomitant use with *potassium-sparing diuretics* (e.g., triamterene, spironolactone) may cause serious hyperkalemia. Use with *sodium bicarbonate* and *glucose-insulin* infusions causes hypokalemia.

ANTIDOTE: Discontinue potassium. Give glucose-insulin infusion (10–25% dextrose with 10 units insulin/20 gm dextrose) to drive K^+ into cells. Administer sodium bicarbonate IV to correct acidosis and shift K^+ into cells. Calcium gluconate 10% can be given slowly IV to block potassium's cardiac toxicity. Sodium polystyrene sulfonate (Kayexalate) can be given rectally or orally to lower serum potassium via ion resin exchange (binds 1 mEq K^+/gm resin). Action is slow, so do not use this method in emergency situations or use only in conjunction with more intensive treatment. Dialysis (hemodialysis) may be necessary if the aforementioned measures fail.

Sodium bicarbonate

ADMINISTRATION:

Available Forms: Injectable (IV), 1 mEq/ml (8.4%) in 10 ml (pediatric) and 50 ml preloaded syringes, 0.892 mEq/ml (7.5%) in 50 ml preloaded syringes, 0.5 mEq/ml (4.2%) in 10 ml preloaded syringes.

Dosage (Parenteral)
For correction of acidosis: 1–2 mEq/kg/dose (1–2 ml of an 8.4% solution/kg/dose) over several minutes. For neonates, dilute 1:1 or use 0.5 mEq/ml (4.2% solution).

Rate: Give IV bolus doses over several minutes. *Do not exceed* 10 ml (10 mEq)/min.

INDICATIONS: Sodium bicarbonate is used as an alkalinizing agent in the emergency treatment of metabolic acidosis associated with cardiac arrest, diabetic ketoacidosis, renal insufficiency, lactic acidosis, severe diarrhea, asthma attacks, or dehydration and for salicylate or ammonium chloride overdoses. The action of sodium bicarbonate is brief, and prolonged use may cause complicating metabolic alkalosis. The most important goal of treatment, however, is to stop the metabolic disturbance that has produced the acidosis and to restore the electrolytes and fluids that have been lost. When this is accomplished, the acid-base balance is automatically restored. (Normal body pH is 7.35–7.45.)

ACTIONS: Sodium bicarbonate provides base ions (HCO_3^-) to buffer the excess hydrogen ion concentration [H^+] and raise blood pH (8.4% $NaHCO_3$ provides 1 mEq each of Na^+ and HCO_3^- per milliliter). The body's buffer systems, ion-exchange mechanisms, and respiratory and renal responses assist in compensatory corrections of the acid-base imbalance. Either of the following formulas may aid in calculating the initial doses:

1. mEq of $NaHCO_3$ needed =
   0.3 × body weight (kg) × base deficit (mEq/liter)
2. mEq of $NaHCO_3$ needed =
   0.5 × body weight (kg) × desired increase in serum HCO_3^- content (mEq/liter)

CONTRAINDICATIONS: (Excludes use in CPR.) Respiratory or metabolic alkalosis, hypertension, edema.

PRECAUTIONS: Rapid injection (10 ml/min) in neonates and children less than 2 years of age may produce hypernatremia, a decrease in cerebrospinal fluid (CSF) pressure, and possible intracranial hemorrhage. To prevent development of metabolic alkalosis, only raise the CO_2 content of serum to 18–20 mEq/liter and allow readjustment of ventilation to normal. Subsequent doses should be based on arterial blood gases and serum pH. Replace fluid volume and electrolyte losses (especially potassium) as indicated. Severe alkalosis may lead to hyperirritability or tetany by decreasing the serum levels of ionized calcium. Use cautiously in patients with congestive heart failure, hypertension, edema, severe cardiomyopathy, or renal impairment or shutdown.

SIDE EFFECTS/ADVERSE REACTIONS: Rapid IV administration, especially, can cause hypernatremia, decreased CSF pressure, intracranial hemorrhage, edema, circulatory overload, electrolyte imbalances, alkalosis, and tetany.

DRUG INCOMPATIBILITIES: Do not mix with calcium salts, sympathomimetics, atropine.

ANTIDOTE: Discontinue sodium bicarbonate. Give sodium chloride infusion. If hypokalemic, administer potassium chloride. Treat tetany with calcium gluconate 10% given IV.

Tromethamine (THAM, THAM-E, Tris Buffer)

ADMINISTRATION

Available Forms: Injectable (IV), 0.3M isotonic solution (when reconstituted). Sodium content is 0.03 mEq/ml.

Diluent: Sterile water for injection. Commercial preparation kit contains 1000 ml sterile water for injection, diluent transfer device, and an administration set with needle. D5W can also be used for reconstitution. Final concentration is isotonic (0.3M).

Dosage (Parenteral): Depends on severity and progression of the metabolic acidosis. Known base deficit: Milliliters of 0.3M tromethamine needed = body wt (kg) × base deficit (mEq/liter).
In absence of exact measurements of pH and $Paco_2$: Give 3–5 ml of 0.3M solution per kilogram slow IV push initially. Subsequent dosages should be determined by base deficit.

Rate: Administer initial IV bolus (25% of calculated amount) over 5–10 minutes. Give IV infusions over 4–6 hours.

INDICATIONS: Tromethamine is an organic buffer used to counteract metabolic acidosis, especially when the latter is accompanied by respiratory acidosis as occurs in cardiac and respiratory arrest. The buffer alkalinizes without adding carbon dioxide or excess sodium. It is preferable to sodium bicarbonate in conditions in which elimination of sodium or CO_2 is restricted, such as in infants with severe cyanotic congenital heart disease. In such cases, excess sodium or CO_2 from the administration of sodium bicarbonate would aggravate heart failure and the already present respiratory acidosis. Tromethamine has also been given to correct metabolic acidosis associated with the respiratory distress syndrome of newborns and with attacks of paroxysmal dyspnea in those with cyanotic congenital heart disease. It is not indicated for the treatment of usual cases of salicylate intoxication but may be of value as an adjunct in severe cases in which marked respiratory acidosis and respiratory collapse occur.

ACTIONS: Tromethamine attracts and combines with the hydrogen ions of an acid, resulting in an acidified form of the buffer that is excreted in the urine. The acid anions are either excreted or metabolized. The reaction is represented as follows:

$$\text{tromethamine} + \text{HA} \longrightarrow [\text{tromethamine-H}^+] + \text{A}^-$$
$$\text{(acid)} \qquad \text{(acidified form)} \quad \text{(acid anion)}$$

If the acid is carbonic acid (H_2CO_3) or lactic acid, the products of the reaction are the acidified buffer and bicarbonate (HCO_3^-) or lactate anion, which are also excreted or metabolized. Thus, tromethamine reduces the hydrogen ion concentration without producing CO_2. It also acts as a weak osmotic diuretic; it increases the flow of alkaline urine containing increased amounts of electrolytes. It is not appreciably metabolized. The ionized (or acidified) form of the buffer is rapidly excreted in the urine at a rate dependent upon the infusion rate.

CONTRAINDICATIONS: Anuria or uremia (because of the possible development of hyperkalemia), chronic respiratory acidosis, status asthmaticus, pregnancy.

PRECAUTIONS: Administer only one-half of the calculated amount initially, then check arterial blood gases and pH. Do not attempt to raise blood pH higher than 7.25–7.30 because a too rapid rise produced by tromethamine can cause respiratory depression or arrest by nullifying the respiratory drive of the acidotic patient. Equipment for assisted ventilation should be readily available (if the patient is not already being mechanically ventilated). Tromethamine is highly alkaline (pH = 10.6); administer solutions through a large needle or indwelling venous catheter placed in a *large* vein. If possible, elevate the limb receiving the infusion. Discontinue the infusion if extravasation occurs. Arterial blood gases, serum pH, bicarbonate, glucose, and electrolyte determinations should be made before, during, and after administration of the buffer. Use cautiously in patients with renal impairment as hyperkalemia and drug accumulation can occur; monitor serum potassium and ECG in these patients. Avoid large doses or too rapid administration. Hypoglycemia can be minimized by mixing the buffer in D5W instead of sterile water. If more concentrated solutions (greater than 0.3M) are to be given via the umbilical vein, take care that the catheter is placed beyond the liver area and within the inferior vena cava. Hyperosmolar solutions infused into the liver can cause liver cell destruction. If the position of the catheter cannot be determined, infuse a dilute solution slowly.

SIDE EFFECTS/ADVERSE REACTIONS: Local reactions commonly include tissue inflammation, necrosis, sloughing, thrombophlebitis, and venospasm. Large doses or rapid infusion rates may result in hypoglycemia, serum hyperosmolarity, and respiratory depression. Hyperkalemia may occur in patients with renal impairment. Liver cell damage and hemorrhagic necrosis have been reported in newborns who received infusions of hypertonic (1.2M) solutions through the umbilical vein.

DRUG INCOMPATIBILITIES: Do not mix with any other medications.

DRUG INTERACTIONS: Use with other *CNS depressants* (barbiturates, narcotics, etc.) may cause additive respiratory depression.

ANTIDOTE: Discontinue tromethamine. Maintain an adequate airway and assist ventilation as necessary. If extravasation occurs, discontinue the medication; infiltrate the affected area with 1% procaine and hyaluronidase to reduce venospasm and dilute the buffer remaining in the tissues. Local infiltration with phentolamine (Regitine) and local nerve block may be useful.

IV
AGENTS AFFECTING BLOOD VOLUME AND HEMOSTASIS

Significant loss of circulating blood volume, whether caused by acute bleeding or other types of trauma, requires immediate replacement of the deficit to prevent shock and severely compromised cardiovascular function. Dextrose and many other electrolyte solutions (see the appendix) can be used for immediate volume replacement. These solutions are referred to as "crystalline" or noncolloid volume expanders. The "noncrystalline" or colloid plasma volume expanders often used in emergency situations include normal human albumin (formerly called "salt-poor") and plasma protein fraction (PPF). These two preparations are discussed in chapter 12.

The normal viscosity of the blood is regulated and maintained by an intricate and complex system of coagulation factors. Alterations and derangements of blood coagulation induced by certain diseases or medications can be treated with or modified by appropriate coagulants and anticoagulants. These agents are discussed in chapter 13.

12
Colloid Plasma Volume Expanders

One of the most urgent therapeutic emergencies is the treatment of shock associated with acute blood loss, severe burns, acute dehydration, or septicemia. The immediate need is to expand the circulating blood volume until whole blood (if indicated) or concentrated blood components are available.

When temporary maintenance of blood volume is desired, the colloid plasma volume expanders can be used instead of whole blood or plasma. These volume expanders are valuable in cases of shock because they are retained within the vascular system where they increase the osmotic pressure of the blood above that of the extracellular or interstitial fluid spaces. As a result, water is drawn from the ECF space into the blood, and the circulating plasma volume is increased. A major advantage of these solutions over whole blood or pooled plasma is that they have been heat-treated to eliminate the danger of transmitting viral hepatitis. In addition, because they require no typing or cross matching, they are immediately available for emergency use.

The following medications are included in this chapter:

- **Albumin (human)**
- **Plasma protein fraction (PPF, human)**

Albumin (human) (Albumisol, Albutein, Buminate, others)

ADMINISTRATION

Available Forms: Injectable (IV), 50 mg/ml (5%) in 50, 250, 500 ml bottles; 250 mg/ml (25%) in 20, 50, 100 ml vials. (Commercial preparations contain 130–160 mEq of sodium per liter or 7–8 mEq sodium per 50 ml.)

Diluent: The 5% preparation can be given undiluted. The 25% solution should be diluted to 5% with NS: 4 ml albumin solution + 16 ml saline = 20 ml of a 5% solution.

Dosage (Parenteral): Dosage and duration of therapy depend on the patient's condition and response. All doses given are for a 5% solution (1 gm = 20 ml).
For hypovolemic shock: 10–20 ml/kg/dose slow IV; can be repeated in 15–30 minutes.
For burns: 10 ml/kg/dose slow IV, plus electrolyte solutions.
For hyperbilirubinemia: 20 ml/kg slow IV given 1–2 hours before the exchange transfusion.

Rate: Initial rate in hypovolemia can be as rapid as possible. As blood volume returns to normal, administer 5% solutions no faster than 2–4 ml/min and 25% solutions no faster than 1 ml/min.

INDICATIONS: Albumin can temporarily increase circulating blood volume and maintain cardiac output in the treatment of shock associated with acute blood loss, hypovolemia, severe burns, septicemias, and so forth (see also plasma protein fraction). In hypoproteinemic states it helps restore and maintain the normal colloid osmotic pressure of the plasma by raising the plasma protein level. Albumin may also be useful as an adjunct to exchange transfusions in the treatment of hyperbilirubinemia and erythroblastosis fetalis in newborns. It reduces the number of exchange transfusions required by increasing the amount of bilirubin removed with each transfusion. Albumin has also been used as adjunctive treatment of cerebral edema when limited fluid intake is necessary.

ACTIONS: The oncotic pressure of albumin causes a shift of fluid from interstitial spaces to the circulation. Albumin normally constitutes 50–60% of the circulating plasma proteins and exerts 80–85% of the oncotic pressure of the blood. When given IV to a well-hydrated patient, each volume of 25% albumin can draw 3.5 volumes of additional fluid into the circulation within 15 minutes. In dehydrated patients, albumin produces little or no clinical improvement. The hemodiluting effects persist for many hours in hypovolemic patients but are dissipated in a few hours in patients with normal blood volume.

CONTRAINDICATIONS: Severe anemia, cardiac failure, use of the 25% solution in a dehydrated patient.

PRECAUTIONS: The 5% solution is preferred for infants and children. As blood pressure increases, observe injured patients carefully to detect new bleeding points that were inapparent at lower pressures. To prevent hypervolemia and possible circulatory overload, avoid large doses in patients with low cardiac reserve, anemia, or normal serum albumin levels. Rapid IV administration may cause vascular overload. Dehydrated patients need additional fluids to replace those withdrawn from tissues by the osmotic pressure of albumin. Monitor blood pressure, pulse rate, fluid and electrolyte balance, central venous pressure (if applicable), hemoglobin, hematocrit, and urine output as necessary during therapy. Use only clear and sediment-free solutions. Because these solutions are preservative-free, use them within 4 hours after breaking the seal on the container.

SIDE EFFECTS/ADVERSE REACTIONS: Untoward reactions are infrequent but may be due to allergy or protein overload. Reactions include chills, fever, nausea, and urticaria. Since albumin is more highly purified than PPF, hypotensive episodes rarely occur. Vascular overload may result in pulmonary edema and circulatory failure.

DRUG INCOMPATIBILITIES: Do not mix with any other medications, especially protein hydrolysates, solutions containing alcohol, or levarterenol.

ANTIDOTE: Slow the rate of administration or discontinue the infusion. Treat allergic reactions with antihistamines.

Plasma protein fraction (PPF, human) (Plasmanate, Plasmatein)

ADMINISTRATION

Available Forms: Injectable (IV), 50 mg/ml (5%) in 50, 250, 500 ml bottles. A 5% solution in NS contains stabilized human plasma proteins: alpha and beta globulins, gamma globulin (<1%) and albumin (90%); sodium (130–160 mEq/liter); and potassium (not more than 2 mEq/liter).

Diluent: Give undiluted.

Dosage (Parenteral)
For hypovolemic shock: 10–20 ml/kg IV. Subsequent dosage is determined by the patient's condition.

Rate: Do not exceed 10 ml/min. As plasma volume approaches normal, decrease the rate of administration to 5–8 ml/min.

INDICATIONS: Plasma protein fraction (PPF) is given to counteract hypovolemia and hemoconcentration associated with various types of shock (e.g., caused by burns, hemorrhage, surgery) and any other conditions where a blood volume deficit exists. Plasma protein fraction is preferred over pooled plasma for treatment of hypovolemia and as a protein source in hypoproteinemia. Because PPF does not contain coagulation factors, it cannot be used to correct coagulation defects.

ACTIONS: The oncotic pressure of PPF causes a shift of fluid from the interstitial spaces into the circulation.

CONTRAINDICATIONS: Severe anemia, cardiac failure, patients on cardiopulmonary bypass, circulatory overload.

PRECAUTIONS: Monitor vital signs and blood pressure frequently. A rapid rise in blood pressure may reveal bleeding points that were not apparent at lower pressures. PPF may contain Hageman factor fragments that can cause hypotension if the infusion is administered rapidly. Because of the added protein, fluid, and sodium load, use cautiously in patients with hepatic, renal, or cardiac failure. Dehydrated patients may require additional fluids to replace those withdrawn from tissues by the oncotic action of PPF. Monitor fluid and electrolyte balance, urine output, hemoglobin, and hematocrit during therapy. Do not use solutions that are turbid or contain sediment. Because these solutions are preservative-free, use them within 4 hours of breaking the seal on the container.

SIDE EFFECTS/ADVERSE REACTIONS: Flushing, erythema, urticaria, nausea, vomiting, chills, fever, headache, back pain, and hypersalivation may occur, but the incidence is low. Rapid rates of administration (>10 ml/min) may result in hypotension. Pulmonary edema and circulatory overload may occur after rapid infusion, in patients with no albumin deficiency, or in those with normal or increased circulatory volumes.

DRUG INCOMPATIBILITIES: Do not mix with any other medications, especially protein hydrolysates, solutions containing alcohol, or levarterenol.

ANTIDOTE: Discontinue the infusion. Treat hypersensitivity reactions symptomatically.

13
Coagulants and Anticoagulants

Coagulants and anticoagulants have opposing effects: The former promote blood clotting and the latter prevent it. When bleeding is encountered, an accurate diagnosis should be established quickly. Bleeding, other than that caused by surgery or physical trauma, may be associated with abnormalities in the body's coagulation mechanism. Such bleeding may arise from deficiencies or defects in either clotting factors or platelets.

Hemorrhage during the first few days of an infant's life is often caused by a relative deficiency in the vitamin-K-dependent factors (II, VII, IX, X). This hemorrhagic disease of the newborn is the result of neonates not receiving or being able to utilize this vitamin and is more common in premature rather than full-term infants. Consequently, vitamin K should be administered prophylactically to all newborns at birth. Bleeding in the first 24 hours after birth may also be the result of the mother's having used certain medications during her pregnancy (e.g., aspirin, phenytoin, phenobarbital, coumarin anticoagulants).

Hemorrhage in sick infants and children may be associated with platelet consumption and disseminated intravascular coagulation (DIC), which can be precipitated by overwhelming bacterial, viral, or rickettsial infections; shock (cardiogenic, anaphylactic, or hypovolemic); acidosis; anoxia; localized tissue damage (burns, premature placental separation); transfusion reactions from incompatible blood; vascular injury; necrotizing enterocolitis; thrombosis; and neoplastic disease, to name a few. Any significant liver disease can interfere with the hepatic production of clotting factors and lead to coagulation defects.

In otherwise healthy infants and children, bleeding may be due to hereditary clotting factor deficiencies (hemophilia), platelet deficiencies or abnormalities, vitamin K deficiency, occult infections, immune disorders, or certain medications.

Emergency therapy involves correcting the underlying pathology and administering the appropriate blood components as indicated by the diagnosis.

Some coagulants are given systemically to overcome specific coagulation defects, whereas others (e.g., topical thrombin) are applied locally to control surface bleeding and capillary oozing. Only the following systemic coagulants are covered in this chapter:

- **Antihemophilic factor (Factor VIII)**
- **Cryoprecipitated antihemophilic factor**
- **Epsilon-aminocaproic acid**
- **Factor IX**
- **Fresh frozen plasma**
- **Phytonadione (vitamin K)**
- **Protamine sulfate**

The anticoagulants disrupt the normal clotting mechanisms and thereby inhibit clot formation by interfering with or inhibiting the activity of different coagulation factors. Anticoagulant therapy centers primarily around the use of heparin and the coumarin derivatives. Since the onset of action of heparin is immediate when administered IV, it is the only emergency anticoagulant discussed.

MECHANISMS OF COAGULATION

A basic knowledge of the complexities of blood coagulation is useful in understanding both the therapeutic effects of coagulants and anticoagulants and the role of adequate laboratory monitoring during treatment. Fig. 13–1 shows the basic mechanisms.

Most of the coagulation factors exist as inactive or precursor forms. Consequently, the blood remains fluid until clotting is started by surface contact with injured tissue, lysed platelets, or a wettable surface such as glass. The clotting cascade can be initiated through either the *intrinsic* or the *extrinsic* system (Fig. 13–1). In the intrinsic system, all the necessary clotting factors are present in circulating blood, but it still takes several minutes for whole blood to coagulate. The extrinsic system bypasses the time-consuming early reactions, and clotting occurs in seconds, as is observed when blood is placed in a test tube. This extrinsic system is the basis for clinical blood coagulation tests such as the Quick one-stage prothrombin time.

13: Coagulants and Anticoagulants 99

Intrinsic System

Surface Contact
(Collagen, Skin)
↓
XII ——→ XII*
(Hageman)   Activated

↓
XI* Plasma Thromboplastin Antecedent (PTA)
↓

(IX)⁺ ——→ IX* Activated

Plasma Thromboplastin Component (PTC)

Ca⁺⁺ | VIII Antihemophilic Factor (AHF)
↓

(X) ——→ X* ←—— (X)
(Stuart-Prower)   Activated

Extrinsic System

III Tissue Thromboplastin

Ca⁺⁺

(VII) Proconvertin

↓

V + Phospholipids
↓

(II) ——→ II Activated
(Prothrombin)   (Thrombin)

Ca⁺⁺

(Fibrinogen) I ——→ Ia (Fibrin, Loose Polymer)

(Fibrin Stabilizing Factor) XIII*

↓

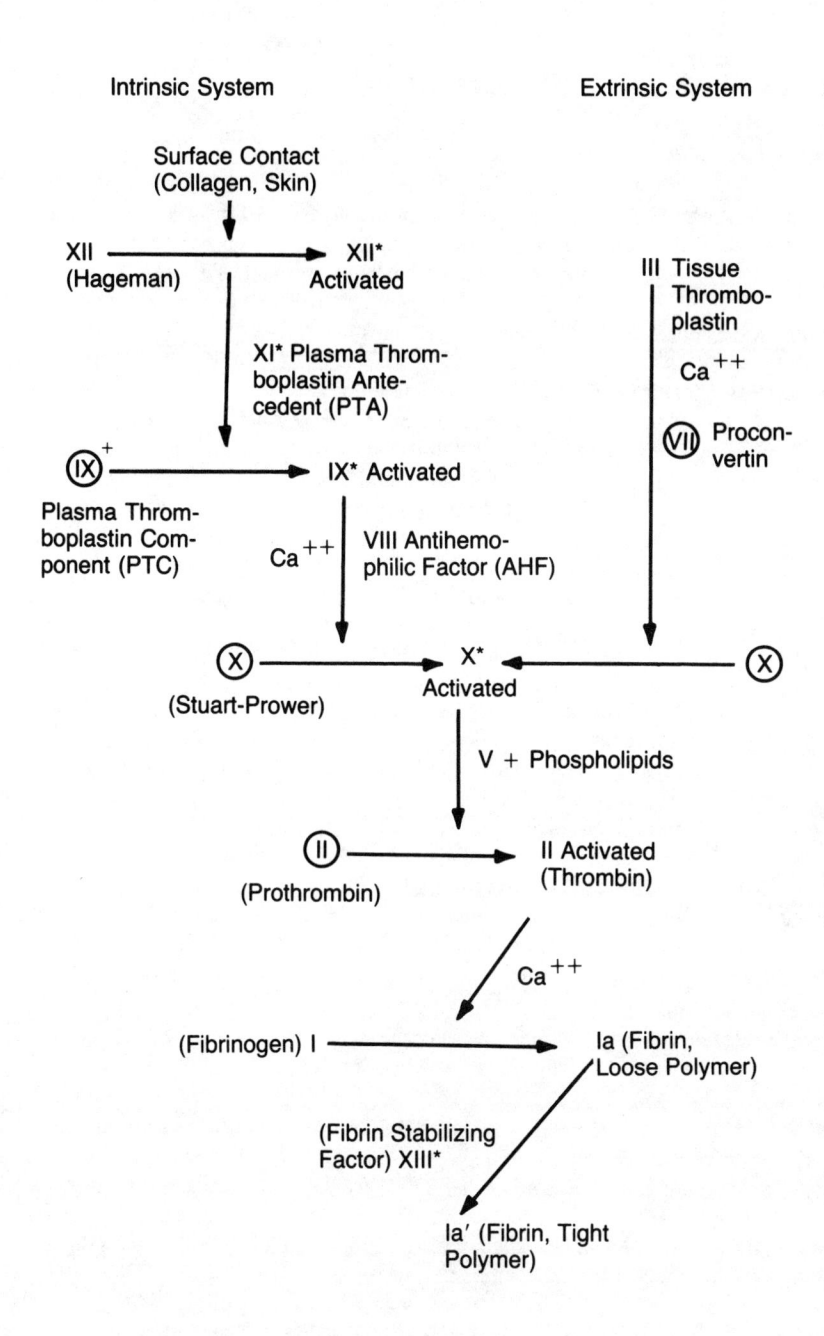

Ia' (Fibrin, Tight Polymer)

*Heparin-sensitive Factors
⁺Factors Circled Are Vitamin K-Dependent and Coumarin-Sensitive.

Fig. 13–1 Clotting Cascade

Antihemophilic factor (Factor VIII)

ADMINISTRATION

Available Forms: Injectable (IV), 250 units/25 ml, 500 units/10 ml, 1000 units/30 ml; both powder and diluent (NS) provided. Units per vial may vary, but final reconstituted volume can be no less than 5 Factor VIII units/ml.

Diluent: NS. Dilute according to package directions.

Dosage (Parenteral): Individualized according to the severity and location of hemorrhage. Dosages can be calculated by using the following formula:
units of AHF required =
(estimated plasma volume [ml]) ×
(desired increase in AHF level [% of normal] /100)
where estimated plasma volume (ml) = 0.05 × body weight in *grams*.
Hemostatic levels of AHF can be maintained for prolonged periods either by repeated "booster" injections at regular intervals (e.g., q6h for the first 2 doses, then q12h thereafter) or by a continuous infusion of the clotting factor.

For hemorrhage: Generally requires plasma levels of AHF of 30% of normal. Average dose is 25–50 units/kg IV.

For joint hemorrhage: Generally requires plasma AHF levels of 5–10% of normal. Average dose is 10–25 units/kg IV.

For soft tissue bleeding: Average dose is 10–30 units/kg IV.

For abdominal bleeding: Generally requires plasma AHF levels of 20–30% of normal. Average dose is 25–50 units/kg IV.

For CNS hemorrhage: Generally requires plasma AHF levels of 20–30% or more of normal. Average dose is 25–50 units/kg IV.

For surgery (postoperatively): May require plasma AHF levels of 40–60% of normal.

Rate: 10–20 ml of reconstituted solution can be injected over a 3 minute period. Decrease the rate if a significant increase in pulse rate is noted.

INDICATIONS: All AHF preparations can be used for the treatment and prevention of hemorrhage in patients with classic hemophilia (hemophilia A). They can also be used in patients who are not true hemophiliacs but who have acquired circulating Factor VIII inhibitors. Replacement therapy is required in patients with AHF deficiency when spontaneous, traumatic, or surgical bleeding is present. Patients with von Willebrand's disease must use the cryoprecipitated preparation.

ACTIONS: Antihemophilic factor is essential for conversion of prothrombin to thrombin in the normal clotting mechanism and for the maintenance of effective hemostasis. The average normal AHF activity in plasma is 100%, but in patients with classic hemophilia AHF activity is less than 5%. One AHF unit is equal to the activity present in 1 ml of normal freshly pooled plasma less than 1 hour old. An IV injection of 1 AHF unit/kg will raise the plasma antihemophilic activity by about 2%. AHF is utilized more rapidly when tissue necrosis or hemorrhage is present. Commercially prepared AHF products are freeze-dried extracts of pooled fresh plasma. Cryoprecipitated AHF, obtained by a selective rapid-freezing technique, can be prepared by the blood bank laboratory. While the commercial freeze-dried products are more stable and easier to store and administer, they are more expensive than the cryoprecipitates, and there is a greater risk of transmitting viral hepatitis and possibly acquired immune deficiency syndrome (AIDS) because they are prepared from pooled plasma. (The newly licensed Hemofil T [Hyland] is a heat-treated clotting factor concentrate that may have a much lower risk of transmitting hepatitis or AIDS.)

CONTRAINDICATIONS: None.

PRECAUTIONS: Because of the risk of transmitting viral hepatitis or AIDS, use cautiously in neonates and infants and in patients with liver disease. Because AHF contains trace amounts of A and B isohemagglutinins, intravascular hemolysis can occur if large amounts are given to patients with blood groups A, B, or AB. Commercially prepared AHF preparations cannot be used to treat von Willebrand's disease (they do not contain a necessary plasma factor missing in these patients); the cryoprecipitated product must be used instead. Mix commercial preparations according to package directions; use the packaged needles, diluent, and filter. Use the reconstituted preparation within 3 hours of mixing. Monitor therapeutic effects with assays for activated partial thromboplastin time (APTT) and Factor VIII prior to and at regular intervals during treatment.

SIDE EFFECTS/ADVERSE REACTIONS: Most side effects are related to rapid rates of infusion. These include headache, flushing, tachycardia, paresthesia, nausea, vomiting, back pains, hypotension, loss of consciousness, tightness in the chest, and visual disturbances. Acute viral hepatitis; hemolytic anemia in patients with blood types A, B, and AB; and elevated fibrinogen levels may occur. (Hyperfibrinogenemia has been implicated in hemolytic anemia, fibrinolysis, and increased bleeding tendency due to platelet malfunction.)

Cryoprecipitated antihemophilic factor

ADMINISTRATION

Available Forms: Injectable (IV), volume and concentration vary. Each unit contains an average potency of 80 units of AHF (Factor VIII) and at least 150 mg of fibrinogen per 15 ml.

Diluent: Thaw the contents of the vial at room temperature (25–30°C). Then add 10–15 ml NS and mix well to ensure complete removal of all the material from the container.

Dosage (Parenteral): The following formula can be used:
number of bags of cryoprecipitated AHF required = (desired Factor VIII level [%]) × (patient's plasma volume [ml]) / (100 × 80*)
*Average units of Factor VIII per unit of cryoprecipitated preparation

Rate: Give diluted cryoprecipitate at 10 ml/min.

INDICATIONS: Cryoprecipitated AHF provides concentrated Factors VIII, XIII, and I (fibrinogen) necessary for the treatment of hemophilia A and for the control of bleeding associated with Factor VIII deficiency and von Willebrand's disease (vascular hemophilia). It is also the preferred blood component for supplying fibrinogen to correct those deficiencies that may arise in severe liver disease and in disseminated intravascular coagulation with fibrinolysis. For most bleeding caused by a known deficiency of Factors I and VIII, fresh frozen plasma is usually sufficient to raise the serum concentration to 20% of normal to stop soft tissue bleeding. However, for serious hemorrhaging, replacement therapy of hemophilia A, or preoperative preparation and postoperative control of bleeding in these patients cryoprecipitate is preferred because it is more concentrated than fresh frozen plasma (FFP). It can raise these factors to the higher levels needed to control bleeding in these conditions without causing fluid overload. With respect to the transmission of viral hepatitis, AIDS, and other diseases, cryoprecipitate is considered safer than the commercial lyophilized factor concentrates because it is obtained from a single volunteer donor rather than from pooled plasma.

ACTIONS: Cryoprecipitated AHF is prepared from the fresh frozen plasma of a single donor; the concentration of Factor VIII is approximately 8–10 times that of normal plasma. The Factor VIII content (expressed as units) in different containers may vary, depending on the donor and manufacturer. Each unit, however, usually contains an average of 80 units of Factor VIII and at least 150 units of fibrinogen in less than 15 ml of plasma. For each unit per kilogram of Factor VIII administered, plasma levels will rise by 2%. Cryoprecipitate must be used within 6 hours of thawing because Factor VIII degrades quickly (about 50% in 5–8 hours). Rapid infusion, loading doses, and repeated injections may therefore be necessary.

CONTRAINDICATIONS: Laboratory evidence of coagulation defects for which this product is not indicated.

PRECAUTIONS: Compatibility testing is unnecessary, but ABO-compatible material is preferred. Use the product within 6 hours after thawing if the container has not been entered; if it has, use the solution within 4 hours. Do not refreeze after thawing. Do not use if there is evidence of container breakage or thawing during storage. Monitor therapy with periodic determination of APTT; these become prolonged when Factor VIII levels fall below 40% of normal. Monitor plasma levels of Factor VIII and fibrinogen periodically in patients with hemophilia A or hypofibrinogenemia, respectively. Antibodies or inhibitors to Factor VIII develop in about 8–16% of patients receiving cryoprecipitate. If these are present, larger doses and local measures (e.g., topical hemostatic preparations) may be necessary to stop mild bleeding. For serious bleeding, the use of commercial factor concentrates (e.g., Konỹne or Proplex) is indicated because these preparations have activated factors that bypass Factor VIII and allow coagulation to proceed. Cryoprecipitate has a very minimal risk of transmitting hepatitis or AIDS.

SIDE EFFECTS/ADVERSE REACTIONS: Side effects may include febrile and allergic reactions. Hyperfibrinogenemia is possible if large amounts are used. In rare cases, if a large volume of ABO-incompatible material is used, the recipient may develop a positive direct antiglobulin test and hemolysis. Transmission of viral hepatitis, AIDS, and other diseases is possible.

DRUG INCOMPATIBILITIES: Do not mix with any other medication.

ANTIDOTE: Discontinue cryoprecipitate infusion. Treat adverse reactions symptomatically.

Epsilon-aminocaproic acid (EACA) (Amicar)

ADMINISTRATION

Available Forms: Injectable (IV), 250 mg/ml in 20 ml vials; tablets, 500 mg; oral syrup, 1.25 gm/5 ml.

Diluent: Must be diluted before IV use. Loading doses can be diluted in D5W, NS, or Ringer's solution. Use 250 ml or a volume sufficient to permit administration over 1 hour. Dilute subsequent doses in a sufficient volume of D5W, NS, or Ringer's solution to allow a constant 24-hour infusion. The usual concentration of infusion solution is 0.2 mg/ml.

Dosage (Parenteral): 100 mg/kg/dose (3 gm/m^2/dose) slowly IV initially, followed by 30 mg/kg/hr as a continuous IV infusion until bleeding is controlled. Maximum dose is 18 gm/m^2/day.

Dosage (Oral): 100 mg/kg/dose (3 gm/m^2/dose) initially, followed by 30 mg/kg (1 gm/m^2) qh until bleeding is controlled. The oral syrup is preferable for young children. Maximum dose is 18 gm/m^2/day. Note: Usually, therapy is continued for at least 8 hours.

Rate: Infuse loading doses over at least 1 hour; for continuous infusion give 30/mg/kg/hr.

INDICATIONS: Epsilon-aminocaproic acid (EACA) is used as an adjunct to antihemophilic Factors VIII or IX to control excessive bleeding in the oral cavity and nose in patients with hemophilia. Injury to the tongue, buccal mucosa, and frenulum is a common cause of bleeding in young hemophiliacs; saliva contains fibrinolytic activators that promote fibrinolysis, which encourages further bleeding. Persistent dental bleeding may also be caused by loss of deciduous teeth or by extraction of permanent teeth. In addition to topical application of thrombin-soaked gauze to the tooth socket, EACA can be given orally to prevent clot breakdown and further bleeding. Persistent nosebleeds not controlled by simple external pressure may also respond to EACA therapy. Although it is effective in stopping the hematuria commonly seen in hemophiliacs, EACA is not recommended for treatment of this condition because the drug can cause intrarenal fibrin deposition, which can lead to decreased renal function and azotemia.

ACTIONS: EACA promotes hemostasis by inhibiting the clot-digesting process (fibrinolysis). The drug inhibits the activation of profibrinolysin (plasminogen) and possibly also the action of fibrinolysin (plasmin). The tendency of blood to clot is balanced by a number of reactions that usually prevent clotting inside the blood vessels and break down any clots that do form. One of these anticlotting mechanisms is the body's fibrinolytic system; it is this process that is inhibited by EACA. The active component of the fibrinolytic system is fibrinolysin (plasmin). This enzyme not only breaks down clots by lysing fibrin but also attacks Factors V and VIII and fibrinogen. When fibrinogen is broken down, it liberates substances that inhibit thrombin (thus preventing further coagulation). Fibrinolysin (plasmin) is formed from its inactive precursor, profibrinolysin (plasminogen). Profibrinolysin is converted to fibrinolysin by certain activator substances such as plasma streptokinase, thrombin, tissue activators, and activated Factor XII. By inhibiting this conversion, EACA prevents fibrinolysis, prevents the breakdown of clots that have already formed, and promotes hemostasis. Oral doses of EACA are rapidly absorbed by the GI tract and distributed into red blood cells and other tissue cells. The therapeutic blood level for antifibrinolytic activity is 130 μg/ml. Most of the drug is rapidly excreted, unchanged, in the urine. The kidney concentrates EACA by filtration and reabsorption; renal disease may cause accumulation of EACA.

CONTRAINDICATIONS: Active intravascular clotting with possible active fibrinolysis and bleeding, DIC without concomitant use of heparin, uremia or severe renal disease.

PRECAUTIONS: Avoid rapid IV administration. Monitor vital signs, especially heart rate and blood pressure, at regular intervals during IV administration. Adjunctive therapy with whole blood, clotting factors, and topical hemostatic agents may also be required in severe cases of bleeding. Use cautiously in patients with cardiac, hepatic, or renal disease. EACA must *not* be used in patients with DIC without also administering heparin; it is therefore important to differentiate bleeding caused by hyperfibrinolysis from that caused by DIC.

SIDE EFFECTS/ADVERSE REACTIONS: Side effects include nasal stuffiness, conjunctival suffusion, headache, rash, tinnitus, myopathy, muscle weakness, nausea, cramping, and diarrhea. Rapid IV administration can cause significant hypotension, bradycardia, and other arrhythmias. Thrombophlebitis may occur with IV use. Intrarenal obstruction from fibrin deposition, glomerular capillary thrombosis, clots in the renal pelvis and ureters—all leading to decreased renal function—have been associated with use of EACA. A fatal case, involving cardiac and hepatic lesions with cerebrovascular hemorrhage, has been reported.

DRUG INCOMPATIBILITIES: Do not mix with fructose IV solutions.

DRUG INTERACTIONS: None significant.

ANTIDOTE: Discontinue EACA. Treat adverse reactions symptomatically.

Factor IX complex (Konȳne, Proplex)

ADMINISTRATION

Available Forms: Injectable (IV), approximately 500 Factor IX units/vial with diluent.

Diluent: Sterile water for injection is supplied. Recommended dilution is 20 ml per 500 unit vial (25 units/ml). Concentration should not exceed 50 units/ml.

Dosage (Parenteral): The amount needed to achieve normal hemostasis depends on the degree of Factor IX deficiency, the levels desired, the patient's weight, and the severity of bleeding. Coagulation assays performed prior to therapy and at reasonable intervals during treatment are the best guide to dosage. Maintenance doses are given to maintain hemostatic levels of at least 20–30%. Hemostatic levels can be maintained for prolonged periods either by repeated booster injections at regular intervals (e.g., q6h for the first 2 doses, then q12h hereafter) or by a continuous infusion of the clotting factor. Duration of treatment varies; it may be up to 1–3 weeks after surgery or until wounds heal.

In general: 1 unit/kg infused IV can be expected to raise the plasma activity by 1%. (Note: Commercial preparations are labeled only with Factor IX activity.)

For soft tissue bleeding: Loading doses of 10–30 units/kg may be necessary.

For CNS or intra-abdominal bleeding: A loading dose of 25–50 units/kg may be required.

INDICATIONS: Human Factor IX complex is used primarily for treatment of hemophilia B (Christmas disease) or when one or more of the factors contained in this preparation is required to prevent hemorrhage. In newborns with hemorrhagic disease caused by a proven deficiency of Factors II, VII, IX, or X, Factor IX complex should be used only in life-threatening circumstances. (Usually administration of phytonadione and FFP is sufficient therapy in these neonates.)

ACTIONS: Factor IX complex is a freeze-dried concentrate of the human coagulation Factors II, VII, IX, and X. One unit of each factor is defined as the average factor activity present in 1 ml of normal fresh plasma less than 3 hours old. Factors VII, IX, and X are necessary for conversion of Factor II (prothrombin) to thrombin. Normal plasma activity for each factor is 100%. Patients whose plasma levels of Factor VII are less than 10% of normal and patients with hemophilia B whose plasma levels of Factor IX are less than 5% of normal may hemorrhage. Both commercial preparations are allegedly free of thrombin, thromboplastin-like activity, and anticomplement activity. Anti-A and anti-B agglutinins are present at clinically insignificant levels; hence, typing or cross matching is not required before use.

CONTRAINDICATIONS: Known liver disease, evidence of or suspected intravascular coagulation or fibrinolysis.

PRECAUTIONS: Factor IX complex can transmit viral hepatitis, so use cautiously in newborns and infants and in patients with liver disease and only when potential benefits outweigh potential risks. It may also transmit AIDS. Large doses may supply enough anti-A and anti-B agglutinins to cause intravascular hemolysis in patients with blood groups A, B, or AB. Monitor Factor II, IX, and X levels when high or repeated doses of the complex are given. Coagulation assays (activated partial thromboplastin time) should be performed prior to therapy and at reasonable intervals during treatment. Factors II and X have a long postinfusion half-life, so avoid overdoses. Because serious hypersensitivity reactions have occurred, a test dose is recommended before the full dose is given. Reconstitute the contents of the vial aseptically according to the manufacturer's instructions. Use within 3 hours of mixing as vials contain no preservative. *Do not refrigerate* reconstituted complex as precipitation of active ingredients may occur.

SIDE EFFECTS/ADVERSE REACTIONS: Transient fever, chills, headache, flushing, and tingling may occur, particularly if the complex is given rapidly. Serious hypersensitivity reactions (e.g., anaphylactic shock) have been reported after injections of Konȳne.

DRUG INCOMPATIBILITIES: Do not mix with any other medications, especially protein-containing solutions.

DRUG INTERACTIONS: *Coumarin* and *indandione* anticoagulants cause a reduction in the levels of Factors II, VII, IX and X.

ANTIDOTE: Discontinue the medication. Treat hypersensitivity reactions symptomatically as necessary.

Fresh frozen plasma (FFP)

ADMINISTRATION

Available Forms: Injectable (IV), the volume varies because it is collected from single donors and frozen. One unit contains about 400 mg fibrinogen, about 200 units each of Factors VIII and IX, and other labile clotting factors.

Diluent: Give undiluted. Thaw at room temperature (25–30°C) with gentle agitation. Use within 6 hours after thawing.

Dosage (Parenteral): Varies according to use.
For acute bleeding: 10 ml/kg IV. Repeat dose q12h as needed.
For hemophilia (Factor VIII or IX deficiency): 15 ml/kg IV initially, followed by 10 ml/kg q12h.

Rate: Administer at 10 ml/min. Use a clot filter.

INDICATIONS: Fresh frozen plasma (FFP) usually contains amounts of all the coagulation factors needed to control bleeding of nonsurgical origin, such as hemorrhagic disease of the newborn, liver disease, hemophilia (A, B, and von Willebrand's), and disseminated intravascular coagulation. It is usually the first-choice blood component for active bleeding in an emergency setting because it replaces all of the clotting factors immediately. FFP will usually supply enough Factors VIII and IX to raise the plasma concentration to about 20% of normal. This is often enough to stop soft tissue bleeding but not adequate to stop surface bleeding. If higher plasma levels are needed, Factor VIII or IX concentrates should be given to avoid volume overload.

ACTIONS: FFP is the anticoagulated clear liquid portion of whole blood, separated and frozen within a few hours of collection. The risk of transmitting viral hepatitis or AIDS is probably very minimal because the product is obtained from a single donor rather than prepared from pooled plasma. FFP provides all the coagulation factors, including fibrinogen and labile Factors V, VIII, and IX. It is also a source of plasma proteins for expansion of circulatory volume in situations where coagulation is a problem.

CONTRAINDICATIONS: Coagulation abnormalities that can be corrected with specific therapy (e.g., vitamin K, cryoprecipitated AHF, or AHF concentrates).

PRECAUTIONS: Thaw at room temperature (25–30°C) with gentle agitation; use within 4–6 hours. Administer the plasma through a clot filter. Do not use this component if there is evidence of container breakage or prior thawing. Recipients must be ABO-compatible. FFP may, theoretically, transmit viral hepatitis, AIDS, and other diseases, but the risk is very minimal. In dehydrated patients, maintain circulatory volume with additional IV fluids as needed. (See also albumin, PPF.)

SIDE EFFECTS/ADVERSE REACTIONS: Adverse reactions are usually infrequent but include fever, chills, hepatitis, allergic reactions and a positive direct antiglobulin test, and, possibly, hemolysis (from antibodies in plasma). Circulatory overload may occur if FFP is given too rapidly or if large volumes are used.

DRUG INCOMPATIBILITIES: Do not mix with any other medications.

ANTIDOTE: Discontinue FFP infusion. Treat allergic reactions symptomatically.

Phytonadione (vitamin K$_1$) (AquaMEPHYTON, Mephyton)

ADMINISTRATION

Available Forms: Injectable (IV, IM, SC), 1 mg in 0.5 ml amp (neonatal), 10 mg/ml in 1.0, 2.5, 5.0 ml containers (AquaMEPHYTON); tablets, 5 mg (Mephyton).

Diluent: D5W, 5% dextrose in NS (D5/NS), or NS only. Use the diluted preparation immediately and discard unused portions.

Dosage (Parenteral): Varies according to use.
For hemorrhagic disease of the newborn:
- Prophylaxis: 0.5–1.0 mg IM or SC as a single dose at birth
- Treatment: 1–2 mg IM, SC, or IV as a single dose

For prothrombin deficiencies:
- Infants <1 year old: 2 mg IM, SC, or IV as a single dose
- Older infants and children: 5–10 mg IM, SC, or IV as a single dose

Dosage (Oral)
For prothrombin deficiencies:
- Infants <1 year old: 2 mg as a single dose
- Older infants and children: 5–10 mg as a single dose

Rate: For IV administration do not exceed 5 mg/min (3 mg/m^2/min).

INDICATIONS: Phytonadione is used to prevent or treat hemorrhagic disease of the newborn and to treat bleeding episodes due to excessive hypoprothrombinemia produced by overdoses of oral anticoagulants. It can also be used to counteract the hypoprothrombinemia caused by poor nutrition, vitamin K deficiency, hepatic disease, or certain drugs (e.g., salicylates, broad-spectrum antibiotics, quinidine). For infants and pregnant women at term, phytonadione is preferred to the other vitamin K preparations because the incidence of hyperbilirubinemia and hemolytic anemia is lower, especially in premature infants and patients with G6PD deficiency.

ACTIONS: Phytonadione has the same activity as naturally occurring vitamin K, which is required for the hepatic biosynthesis of the blood coagulation factors II (prothrombin), VII (proconvertin), IX (plasma thromboplastin component), and X (Stuart-Prower factor). In adequate doses phytonadione reverses the inhibitory effect of the coumarin anticoagulants on these factors. Although dietary sources of vitamin K are usually adequate (except for the first 5–8 days of the neonatal period), vitamin K deficiency can occur in breast-fed infants, those on milk-substitute formulas, those receiving prolonged hyperalimentation, or patients with malabsorption syndromes. Phytonadione is ineffective in hypoprothrombinemia due to hereditary causes or severe liver disease. Parenteral administration causes an increase in coagulation factors in 1–4 hours; oral administration increases these factors in 6–12 hours. After parenteral administration bleeding is usually controlled in 3–8 hours, and the prothrombin time may return to normal in 12–14 hours.

CONTRAINDICATIONS: Bleeding disorders that are not vitamin-K-dependent, hypersensitivity to phytonadione, severe hepatic dysfunction (when repeat doses do not produce a satisfactory response).

PRECAUTIONS: Dose, route, frequency of administration, and duration of therapy depend on the severity of the prothrombin deficiency. Therapy should be regulated by repeated measurements of prothrombin times. Use IM or SC routes cautiously in hypoprothrombinemia because hemorrhage or hematoma may occur at the injection site. Avoid rapid IV administration. Oral use in patients with decreased bile secretion may necessitate concurrent administration of bile salts to ensure phytonadione absorption. Infusion bottles must be protected from light. In emergency situations transfusions of plasma or FFP along with IV doses of phytonadione may be indicated. Avoid high doses as they may reexpose the patient to the hazard of intravascular clotting (heparin should be readily available).

SIDE EFFECTS/ADVERSE REACTIONS: Phytonadione is relatively nontoxic, but severe reactions may occur after IV injections. These include flushing, dizziness, hyperhidrosis, tightness in the chest, cyanosis, dyspnea, bronchospasm, rapid and weak pulse, peripheral vascular failure, hypotension, shock, hypersensitivity or anaphylactic reactions, cardiac or respiratory arrest, and death. Doses given IM or SC may cause swelling, pain, and nodules at the injection site. High doses (10–25 mg) may cause hyperbilirubinemia, hemolytic anemia, and hemoglobinuria in neonates but to a lesser extent than other vitamin K analogues.

DRUG INCOMPATIBILITIES: Do not mix with any other medications.

DRUG INTERACTIONS: Phytonadione directly antagonizes the activity of *coumarin* and *indandione oral anticoagulants*.

ANTIDOTE: Discontinue the medication. Treat intravascular clotting with heparin. Treat allergic reactions with antihistamines, epinephrine, and corticosteroids as necessary. Give symptomatic support as necessary.

Protamine sulfate

ADMINISTRATION

Available Forms: Injectable (IV), 10 mg/ml in 5 ml amps and 25 ml vials; also 50 mg powder for reconstitution.

Diluent: Can be given undiluted. If further dilution is required, use D5W or NS.

Dosage (Parenteral): In general, 1 mg of protamine sulfate is given slowly IV for every 1 mg of heparin administered within the last 4 hours. The maximum dose should not exceed 50 mg at any one time. One milligram of protamine must neutralize at least 80 units of heparin sodium derived from bovine lung tissue (1 mg = 120 units) or at least 100 units of heparin sodium derived from porcine intestinal mucosa (1 mg = 140 units).

Rate: Inject a 1% solution (10 mg/ml) IV over 1–3 minutes.

INDICATIONS: Protamine sulfate is the pharmacological antidote for heparin overdoses. It should not be used if only minor bleeding occurs since withdrawal of heparin will usually correct minor overdoses. Serious bleeding will require administration of protamine and possibly blood transfusions.

ACTIONS: Protamine sulfate acts as a heparin antagonist. It is a strongly basic compound that reacts with strongly acidic heparin to form a stable, inactive salt. Different amounts of protamine are required to neutralize heparin derived from different sources: 1 mg will neutralize about 90 units of heparin (sodium salt) derived from bovine lung tissue and about 115 units of heparin (sodium salt) derived from porcine intestinal mucosa. Since blood levels of heparin decrease rapidly after it is administered, the dose of protamine required to treat heparin overdoses also decreases rapidly as time elapses. Protamine neutralizes heparin within 30–60 seconds after IV administration, and its effects last up to 2 hours. Paradoxically, protamine has an anticoagulant action of its own. It is a true antithromboplastin and may prolong clotting time, but very high doses are required to achieve this effect (not clinically significant).

CONTRAINDICATIONS: Hypersensitivity to fish (protamine is derived from fish).

PRECAUTIONS: Coagulation assays (either activated partial thromboplastin time or activated coagulation time) should be used to monitor protamine's effect; the tests are usually performed 5–15 minutes after administration. Heparin rebound and bleeding may occur several hours after protamine administration, so repeat the coagulation tests in 2–8 hours.

SIDE EFFECTS/ADVERSE REACTIONS: Rapid IV injection may cause acute hypotension, bradycardia, dyspnea, transient flushing, and a feeling of warmth. Fatal reactions resembling anaphylaxis have occurred. Other hypersensitivity reactions include urticaria and angioneurotic edema.

DRUG INCOMPATIBILITIES: Protamine is physically incompatible with *cephalosporins* and *penicillins*. Avoid mixing with any other medications.

ANTIDOTE: Discontinue the infusion. Facilities to treat shock should be available. Treat hypersensitivity reactions symptomatically.

Heparin

ADMINISTRATION

Available Forms: Injectable (IV, SC), derived from bovine lung tissue, 1000, 5000, and 10,000 units per milliliter (1 mg = 120 units); derived from porcine intestinal mucosa, 1000, 2000, 2500, 5000, 7500, 10,000, 15,000, 20,000, 30,000, and 40,000 units per milliliter (1 mg = 140 units); solution for heparin-lock flush, 10 and 100 units per milliliter (derived from porcine intestinal mucosa).

Diluent: D5W or NS for IV infusion. Bolus doses can be given undiluted.

Dosage (Parenteral)
For disseminated intravascular coagulation: IV bolus of 50–100 units/kg followed by 100 units/kg q4h by intermittent IV infusion. Or 50 units/kg IV bolus, then 400–600 units/kg/24 hr (or 20,000 units/m^2/24 hr) as a continuous IV infusion. Dosage range is 50–200 units/kg/4 hr. Monitor serum levels of fibrinogen and fibrin split products and platelet counts.

Rate: Give IV boluses at 1000 units/min.

INDICATIONS: Heparin is indicated in the treatment of children with disseminated intravascular coagulation (DIC) when gangrenous thrombosis, skin necrosis, or purpura fulminans is present. In patients with meningococcemia (or other types of fulminant sepsis) who have laboratory evidence of DIC, heparin may prevent tissue damage caused by fibrin deposition. Severe DIC resulting from massive hemolysis after a mismatched transfusion or from certain types of snake venom may also respond to heparin therapy. Heparin flush solutions are used to maintain the patency of "heparin locks," and diluted heparin can be added to IV infusions to keep the tubings and infusion sites clot-free. It is also employed as an anticoagulant in blood transfusions, dialysis procedures, extracorporeal circulation, and blood samples for laboratory purposes.

ACTIONS: Heparin acts rapidly at multiple sites in the normal coagulation pathway. Small doses act as a catalyst to accelerate the rate at which antithrombin III (heparin cofactor) neutralizes thrombin and activated Factor X. This neutralization prevents the conversion of prothrombin to thrombin. Larger doses inactivate thrombin and earlier clotting intermediates and thus prevent the conversion of fibrinogen to fibrin. Heparin also prevents the formation of a stable fibrin clot by inhibiting fibrin stabilizing factor (Factor XIII). Heparin may prevent the formation of new clots, but once a thrombus has formed, heparin has little effect; it cannot lyse established thrombi because it has no fibrinolytic activity. The plasma half-life of heparin is 1–2 hours in healthy individuals but is prolonged with increasing doses or in patients with renal impairment.

CONTRAINDICATIONS: Known hypersensitivity to heparin, any bleeding tendency or active bleeding. The latter two may be the result of hemophilia; hemorrhagic blood dyscrasias; subacute bacterial endocarditis (SBE); severe liver or kidney disease; active tuberculosis (TB); perforated ulcer; intracranial or hidden hemorrhage; ulcerative lesions; visceral carcinoma; postoperative oozing of blood; eye, brain, or spinal cord surgery; or the use of heparin prior to surgery without antagonization or adequate time for dissipation of heparin effects. Do not institute heparin therapy if suitable blood coagulation tests cannot be performed.

PRECAUTIONS: Therapy involving large doses of heparin should be monitored by measuring the APTT. The accepted therapeutic range is 1.5–2.5 times the control value in seconds. For continuous IV treatment, determine APTT immediately prior to therapy, every 4 hours during the early stages (unless loading doses were given), and daily thereafter. For intermittent IV or SC therapy, measure APTT prior to initiation of treatment, prior to each dose during the early stages, and daily thereafter. Dosages may need to be increased in patients with febrile conditions and decreased in those with renal impairment. *Do not* give heparin injections IM since severe hematomas may result. Doses should be given IV or by *deep* SC injection only. Do not massage the injection site before or after injection. Avoid IM administration of any medication in patients receiving heparin therapy. Continuous IV infusion is usually recommended over intermittent IV injection because of a more constant degree of anticoagulation, greater ease in adjusting doses, and a lower incidence of bleeding complications. Administer with a constant-rate infusion pump if possible. Use cautiously in patients with a history of allergies or during pregnancy, especially during the last trimester and the immediate postpartum period (increased risk of maternal hemorrhage). Periodic platelet counts are recommended for patients receiving heparin therapy for periods longer than 5 days, and the medication should be discontinued if significant thrombocytopenia appears.

SIDE EFFECTS/ADVERSE REACTIONS: Hemorrhage, ranging from local ecchymoses to major bleeding complications, is an inherent adverse effect, but its frequency and severity can be minimized by careful clinical monitoring. Rare hypersensitivity reactions of chills, fever, pruritus, urticaria, asthma, rhinitis, and anaphylaxis have occurred. Unique allergic vasospastic reactions that develop 6–10 days after initiation of heparin therapy and last 4–6 hours have been reported. Symptoms include pain, ischemia, and cyanosis in the limb with the infusion site and generalized vasospasm with tachypnea, cyanosis, headache, feelings of oppression, and itching and burning of the plantar areas of the feet. Chest pain, arthralgia, headache, and hypertension may occur in the absence of vasospastic reactions. (Protamine sulfate has no antagonizing effect on allergic vasospasms.) Acute but reversible thrombocytopenia has been reported (not dose-related). Adrenal hemorrhage with acute adrenal insufficiency has occurred. Deep SC injections can cause local irritation, pain, hematoma, necrosis, and histamine-like reactions at the injection site. Also reported but rare are alopecia, suppression of renal function, hypoaldosteronism, and priapism. Long-term use (months) may cause osteoporosis and spontaneous fractures.

DRUG INCOMPATIBILITIES: Heparin is strongly acidic and is inactivated by certain basic compounds (e.g., gentamicin, amikacin, tobramycin, kanamycin, streptomycin, ampicillin, methicillin). Acidic compounds (e.g., narcotic analgesics, erythromycin, tetracyclines, vancomycin, hydroxyzine, promethazine, dimenhydrinate, hydrocortisone) may cause solutions of heparin to precipitate.

DRUG INTERACTIONS: There is a theoretical increased risk of hemorrhage with concomitant use of drugs that inhibit platelet aggregation (e.g., *aspirin, dextran, dipyridamole, glyceryl guaiacolate, ibuprofen, indomethacin, phenylbutazone*). Use during therapy with *streptokinase* or *urokinase* may increase the risk of hemorrhage.

ANTIDOTE: Withdrawal of heparin will usually correct minor bleeding or overdoses within a few hours. Protamine sulfate can be given if severe hemorrhage or overdose occurs (see protamine sulfate listing for dosage). *Caution:* Use of protamine in patients with DIC may result in complete coagulation of circulating blood. Severe bleeding may necessitate administration of whole blood or platelets. Treat acute adrenal hemorrhage or insufficiency with corticosteroids IV.

V
AGENTS AFFECTING INFLAMMATION AND ALLERGY

Section V introduces those agents used in the treatment and prevention of inflammatory and allergic responses associated with a wide variety of diseases and infectious processes. Chapter 14 reviews the anti-inflammatory corticosteroids, which have widespread effects on almost every cell type of the body. When properly used, they offer symptomatic relief from many acute and chronic inflammatory processes; when improperly used or when therapy is poorly monitored, they cause a multitude of adverse reactions.

Chapters 15 and 16 discuss the antihistamines and the bronchodilators and antiasthmatics. The antihistamines, by antagonizing the systemic effects of histamine, produce a generalized response that relieves the many symptoms of hypersensitivity reactions. Bronchodilators and antiasthmatics, on the other hand, produce a more localized response, the reversal of bronchoconstriction associated with various forms of obstructive lung disease.

14
Corticosteroids

The corticosteroids are natural hormones secreted by the adrenal cortex or synthetically produced analogues of these hormones. Traditionally they are separated into two categories, glucocorticoids and mineralocorticoids, on the basis of their predominant biological activities. The glucocorticoids (represented by cortisol) suppress inflammation, stimulate protein catabolism and carbohydrate storage, and suppress the release of adrenocorticotropic hormone (ACTH). The mineralocorticoids (represented by aldosterone) regulate the retention of sodium and the depletion of potassium. The adrenal glands also secrete small amounts of the sex hormones (androgens and estrogens); significant amounts may be produced in certain adrenal disorders.

The secretion of glucocorticoids is cyclical: high in the morning and low in the evening. The rate is regulated by the amount of corticotropin (ACTH) released by the anterior pituitary in response to decreasing serum levels of cortisol. Secretion of the sodium-retaining hormone, aldosterone, is under the influence of the renin-angiotensin system of the kidney.

Numerous synthetic corticosteroids have been prepared by modifying the chemical structures of the natural hormones to produce agents with greater potency and different degrees of mineralocorticoid or glucocorticoid (anti-inflammatory) activity. Table 14–1 contrasts the relative potency of some of the synthetic corticosteroids as compared to cortisol.

Dosages vary according to the type and severity of the condition being treated, the prognosis, the estimated duration of the disease state or symptoms, and the patient's response and tolerance. Doses can be classified as follows:

- Physiological replacement: Equivalent to 20 mg hydrocortisone per day
- Maintenance or low: Equivalent to 5–15 mg prednisone per day

TABLE 14–1 Relative Potency of Corticosteroids*

Compound	Anti-inflammatory Potency	Mineralocorticoid Potency	Equivalent Dose (mg)	Duration of HPA† Suppression (hr)
Desoxycorticosterone	0	4.0	5.00	No data
Hydrocortisone (cortisol)	1.0	1.0	20.00	24–36
Cortisone	0.8	0.8	25.00	24–36
Prednisone	4.0	0.8	5.00	24–36
Prednisolone	4.0	0.8	5.00	24–36
Methylprednisolone	5.0	0	4.00	24–36
Triamcinolone	5.0	0	4.00	48
Dexamethasone	30.0	0	0.75	>48
Betamethasone	30.0	0	0.60	>48

*As compared to hydrocortisone (cortisol), which is arbitrarily assigned a value of 1.0.
†HPA = Hypothalamic-pituitary-adrenal axis.

- Moderate: Equivalent to 0.5 mg prednisone per kilogram per day
- High: Equivalent to 1–3 mg prednisone per kilogram per day
- Massive: Equivalent to 15–30 mg prednisone per kilogram per day

Special mention is made concerning the use of desoxycorticosterone (DOCA) and hydrocortisone sodium succinate in adrenal crisis (acute adrenocortical insufficiency). Both agents have a high degree of mineralocorticoid activity (DOCA more than hydrocortisone). The retention of sodium and water induced by them is necessary in the management of this syndrome. Adrenal crisis in infants and children is a true medical emergency with a rapidly fatal outcome if not appropriately treated within a few hours. In the neonate, adrenal insufficiency with severe adrenal hemorrhage may resemble intracranial hemorrhage, respiratory distress, or severe acute infection. In older children, it must be distinguished from diabetic coma, CNS disturbances, and acute poisonings.

Acute adrenal crisis can appear abruptly or insidiously. It can be precipitated by acute illness, fulminating infections (such an meningococcemia), trauma, surgery, exposure to excessive heat or temperature fluctuations, and other stressful situations. Signs and symptoms include nausea, vomiting, diarrhea, dehydration, hypotension, hyponatremia, hypoglycemia, hyperkalemia, fever (which may be followed by hypothermia), confusion, circulatory collapse, and coma.

Only the corticosteroids with major applications in emergency medicine are discussed in this chapter:

- **Desoxycorticosterone acetate (DOCA)**
- **Dexamethasone**
- **Hydrocortisone**
- **Methylprednisolone**
- **Prednisone**

CORTICOSTEROIDS (GENERAL STATEMENT)

INDICATIONS: The natural and synthetic corticosteroids are used in the diagnosis and treatment of a variety of adrenal function disorders and as anti-inflammatory agents. Some disorders that respond to palliative therapy with corticosteroids are various autoimmune diseases (e.g., rheumatic and collagen diseases), endocrine disorders (e.g., primary and secondary adrenocortical insufficiency), dermatological diseases, acute seasonal or allergic rhinitis, contact or atopic dermatitis, certain inflammatory ocular disorders, bronchial asthma and other respiratory diseases (e.g., TB, respiratory distress syndrome [RDS]), various hematological disorders, nephrotic syndrome, certain neoplastic diseases (e.g., acute leukemia of children), various gastrointestinal diseases (e.g., ulcerative colitis), and hypercalcemia. Many of these chronic disorders require prolonged corticosteroid therapy and respond well to alternate-day therapy with intermediate-acting agents. (The patient's 48 hour requirement for steroids is administered as a single oral dose every other morning. Prednisone, prednisolone, methylprednisolone, and triamcinolone are the intermediate-acting agents commonly used.)

The major benefit of corticosteroids in emergency medicine is their anti-inflammatory action. Systemically, they provide prompt palliation of symptoms of various allergic states such as rhinitis; bronchial asthma; hay fever; dermatoses; and hypersensitivity reactions to drugs, serum, and transfusions. In emergency situations (anaphylaxis, shock, status asthmaticus), parenteral corticosteroids are useful adjuncts to epinephrine, cardiopulmonary support, and bronchodilators. The prolonged action of the corticosteroids is valuable for the long-term management of cerebral edema. They are often used with mannitol for immediate and long-term reduction of elevated intracranial pressure (ICP) because they do not aggravate intracranial bleeding or cause the rebound increases in ICP often seen with mannitol. They are also used to reduce tracheal swelling. Topically, they may give relief in allergic, inflammatory, and pruritic dermatoses. Local injections of corticosteroids into inflamed joints, tendons, soft tissues, and bursas provide long-term relief and may be desirable since systemic side effects are minimized. (Note: Corticosteroid therapy is not curative and is rarely indicated as the primary method of treatment, but rather as adjunctive, supportive therapy.)

ACTIONS: The corticosteroids have widespread effects because they influence the function of most cells in the body. Their effects on metabolism include an enhancement of gluconeogenesis, the breakdown of proteins and their conversion to glucose for energy utilization or storage by the liver; a decrease in glucose utilization, which accentuates hyperglycemia ("anti-insulin" effect); and a breakdown and redistribution of fat from peripheral to central areas of the body. Other biological effects include suppression of the immune response and inflammation by a variety of mechanisms such as reducing the activity and volume of the lymphatic system, antagonizing histamine activity, inhibiting macrophage activity in inflamed areas, and depressing antigen-antibody reactions. These drugs also stimulate erythroid cells of the bone marrow and prolong RBC and platelet survival time. Physiological amounts help maintain muscle strength, while excessive amounts induce muscle atrophy. Corticosteroids also modify the brain's excitation threshold, inhibit calcification and the formation of bone growth matrix, reduce calcium absorption from the gut, promote renal excretion of calcium, and inhibit the deposition of collagen and the formation of scar tissue. In addition, they suppress the production of steroids by the adrenal cortex by inhibiting the release of corticotropin (ACTH) by the anterior pituitary (negative feedback mechanism).

CONTRAINDICATIONS: Hypersensitivity to corticosteroids or any of the individual agents, systemic fungal infections (manufacturer's warning).

PRECAUTIONS: Vary according to the type of therapy.
Short-term high-dose therapy: High-dose therapy should not be continued longer than 48–72 hours. Prophylactic antacid therapy (q2h) may be indicated to prevent the formation of peptic or stress ulcers. Monitor blood pressure and fluid and electrolyte balance.
Prolonged therapy with higher than physiological replacement doses: (More than 20 mg of hydrocortisone or its equivalent daily) Use the smallest dosage, for the shortest period of time, that will control specific symptoms. Regulate doses in children according to the severity of the disease rather than on the basis of body weight. Alternate-day therapy may minimize adrenal-pituitary suppression and maintain normal growth patterns in children. Monitor growth and development parameters in children and infants. Gastric irritation can be reduced by giving oral doses with meals or antacids. Diagnosis of inflammatory conditions should be made before corticosteroid therapy is started. These agents can mask symptoms of and increase the severity or susceptibility to bacterial, viral, or fungal infections. Do not use in patients with active viral infections or with bacterial infections not controlled by antibiotics. Do not give vaccines or immunizations during high-dose corticosteroid therapy; corticosteroids can inhibit the antibody response and cause neurological complications. In patients with TB, restrict the use of corticosteroids to those who have fulminating or disseminated disease being currently treated with antitubercular therapy.

Abrupt withdrawal may precipitate acute adrenal insufficiency. Taper doses gradually, usually over 7–10 days (some patients require several weeks or months). Adrenal suppression may persist up to 12 months in some patients who have received large doses for prolonged periods. If severe stress occurs during this withdrawal time, replacement doses of steroids may be necessary to treat adrenal insufficiency. Psychic derangements may appear during therapy, and emotional instability or psychotic tendencies or both may be aggravated by these agents.

Use cautiously in patients with congestive heart failure, hypertension, convulsive disorders, renal impairment, osteoporosis, or herpes simplex ocular infections (possible corneal perforation). Hypothyroidism and cirrhosis enhance corticosteroid effects, so dosage adjustments may be necessary in these cases. Because these agents impair glucose tolerance, they may aggravate or precipitate diabetes mellitus. Doses of insulin and oral antidiabetic medication may require adjustments. Use cautiously in patients with nonspecific ulcerative colitis (if probability of perforation or abscess formation exists), diverticulitis, latent peptic ulcer, or recent intestinal anastomoses.

Corticosteroids may damage the fetus or cause fetal hypoadrenalism when administered to pregnant women. Weigh risk against benefits. These medications are excreted in breast milk; avoid giving them to women who are nursing infants.

High doses in children may cause acute pancreatitis with pancreatic destruction. They may also cause increased intracranial pressure with papilledema (pseudotumor cerebri), particularly following a reduction in dosage or a change in the type of steroid being administered. Increased dosages may be necessary during periods of stress, trauma, surgery, etc. Anaphylactic reactions have occurred after parenteral therapy in sensitive individuals, especially those allergic to the paraben preservatives present in some injectable forms. During long-term therapy, periodically evaluate weight, height, chest and spinal x-ray films, hematopoiesis, electrolyte balances, glucose tolerance, ocular pressure, and blood pressure.

SIDE EFFECTS/ADVERSE REACTIONS: The incidence of harmful effects after short-term administration of even massive doses of corticosteroids is low. Administration by the IV route may cause burning or tingling of the perineal area and hypersensitivity reactions. Intramuscular administration has caused delayed pain, sterile abscesses, and atrophy at the injection site. Parenteral therapy may also cause hyperpigmentation or hypopigmentation.

Prolonged therapy produces adverse effects that are directly related to the drugs' pharmacological effects. Fluid and electrolyte disturbances include sodium and fluid retention, hypokalemia and alkalosis, hypocalcemia, hypertension, and congestive heart failure. Musculoskeletal effects include osteoporosis, muscle weakness or myopathy, compression and long bone fractures. Gastric upset, peptic ulcer, hemorrhage, and acute pancreatitis may occur. Signs and symptoms of CNS effects include psychic derangements, vertigo, headache, convulsions, and increased intracranial pressure with papilledema (pseudotumor cerebri). There may be an increase in the incidence and severity of bacterial, viral, and fungal infections. Oral inhalation therapy may cause fungal superinfections of the mouth and pharynx. Skin reactions include impaired wound healing, acne, hirsutism, petechiae, ecchymoses, facial erythema, and a suppressed reaction to skin tests. Posterior subcapsular cataracts, increased intraocular pressure, and glaucoma may occur. Endocrine effects include growth suppression, cushingoid state, adrenal-pituitary suppression and unresponsiveness to stress, hyperglycemia, and menstrual irregularities. Increased protein breakdown may lead to a negative nitrogen balance. Abrupt changes in the serum levels of corticosteroids may cause a steroid withdrawal syndrome characterized by anorexia, nausea, vomiting, lethargy, headache, fever, joint pain, myalgia, desquamation, weight loss, and hypotension. Acute adrenal insufficiency with hyponatremia and hyperkalemia may occur after abrupt withdrawal of prolonged high-dose therapy.

DRUG INCOMPATIBILITIES: Corticosteroids are incompatible with various injectable medications, but the compatibility varies according to the concentration of the medications and the resulting pH and temperature of the final solutions. Specialized references should be consulted for more specific information.

DRUG INTERACTIONS: Concomitant use with *potassium-depleting diuretics* may worsen hypokalemia. Use with *salicylates* and other ulcerogenic medications increases the risk of GI ulceration. *Barbiturates, phenytoin,* and *rifampin* (all hepatic-enzyme inducers) stimulate metabolism of corticosteroids, so larger doses of steroids may be necessary. Steroid-induced hypokalemia increases the risk of arrhythmias or *digitalis* toxicity.

ANTIDOTE: Taper the dosage gradually as indicated by the patient's condition. Treat adverse reactions symptomatically.

Desoxycorticosterone acetate (DOCA)

ADMINISTRATION

Available Forms: Injectable (IM), 5 mg/ml in oil (DOCA acetate).

Dosage (Parenteral)
For adrenal crisis (acute adrenocortical insufficiency): 1–2 mg/day (1.5–2.0 mg/m^2/day) as a single IM dose qd for 3–4 days as needed. Adjust dosage on the basis of fluid, electrolyte, and cardiac status. Up to 5 mg/day has been given.

INDICATIONS: Desoxycorticosterone acetate (DOCA) is a potent parenteral mineralocorticoid used in conjunction with other therapeutic measures (e.g., IV hydrocortisone, vasopressors, glucose-saline solutions, antibiotics) for the management of adrenal crisis (acute adrenocortical insufficiency or Addison's disease). It is also given in conjunction with parenteral hydrocortisone or cortisone acetate to restore mineral balance in infants and children who have acute salt-losing forms of congenital adrenal hyperplasia (adrenogenital syndrome). Intramuscular doses of DOCA are for short-term therapy only (approximately 3–4 days). Long-term control of water and electrolyte balance is accomplished by oral doses of hydrocortisone and liberal salt intake alone. Difficult-to-control cases may require implantation of DOCA pellets under the skin or oral administration of a mineralocorticoid such as fludrocortisone acetate (Florinef).

ACTIONS: DOCA has an intense sodium-retaining activity that rapidly restores serum sodium and potassium to normal levels. It acts on the distal renal tubule to cause sodium reabsorption while promoting excretion of potassium and hydrogen. Its effects are directly antagonized by spironolactone, an aldosterone antagonist. The sodium retention results in edema, hypertension, and lowered serum levels of potassium.

CONTRAINDICATIONS: Hypersensitivity to DOCA, hypertension, congestive heart failure.

PRECAUTIONS: Use IM route only. Give doses into upper, outer quadrant of buttocks (if not feasible, give doses SC); do not inject IM doses into upper extremities. Adequate glucocorticoid therapy must be given also. Monitor vital signs frequently as well as serum levels of sodium, potassium, and glucose. When rehydrating patients, avoid fluid overload; total parenteral fluid should not exceed the maintenance fluid requirements for normal children and infants. Amounts can generally be decreased by one-half after 24 hours of steroid and fluid therapy. If edema occurs, restrict dietary sodium; spironolactone (Aldactone) can be given to directly counteract DOCA's pharmacological actions. Potassium supplements may be necessary. Avoid use of morphine in patients in adrenal crisis. Watch for evidence of concurrent infection and treat with appropriate antimicrobials if necessary. After initial stabilization, oral maintenance therapy (or implantation of DOCA pellets) should be initiated. Stress reactions (e.g., acute illness, trauma, surgery) may precipitate adrenal crisis requiring additional doses of DOCA and glucocorticoids.

SIDE EFFECTS/ADVERSE REACTIONS: Irritation may occur at site of injection. More serious side effects include generalized edema, hypernatremia, hypertension, and cardiac enlargement. Resulting hypokalemia can produce cardiac arrhythmias and extreme muscle weakness and paralysis of the extremities. Arthralgia, tendon contractures, and hypersensitivity reactions have been reported.

DRUG INTERACTIONS: Use with *dietary sodium supplements* causes additive sodium retention and edema. Use with *spironolactone* inhibits mineralocorticoid activity.

ANTIDOTE: Discontinue DOCA. Treat edema by restricting sodium and fluid. Spironolactone can be given in doses up to 300 mg 3 or 4 times a day (tid–qid) for several days until manifestations of overdosage are controlled.

Dexamethasone (Decadron, others)

ADMINISTRATION

Available Forms: Injectable (IV, IM), 4, 10, and 24 mg per milliliter; injectable (IM, intralesional, intra-articular) long-acting suspension, 8 mg/ml; tablets, 0.25, 0.50, 0.75, 1.50, 4.00 mg; oral elixir, 0.5 mg/5 ml; topical, various preparations for topical and ophthalmic use; for oral inhalation, metered inhaler that delivers 100 μg per metered spray.

Diluent: Can be diluted with D5W or NS for IV infusion.

Dosage (Parenteral): Varies according to use.
For increased intracranial pressure: 4 mg IV push *stat*, then

- Neonates: 0.5–1.0 mg IV or IM q6–8h
- Children <5 years old: 1 mg IV or IM q6h
- Children 5–10 years old: 1.5 mg IV or IM q6h
- Children >10 years old: 2–4 mg IV or IM q6h

The dosage can be reduced after 2–4 days and gradually discontinued over 5–7 days. Can change to oral doses when feasible.

For shock: 2 mg/kg IV initially, then 1 mg/kg/24 hr in divided doses. Treatment is usually not extended beyond 48–72 hours.
For prevention of RDS: 4 mg IM 3 times a day to the mother, 2 days before delivery.

Dosage (Oral)
For inflammation or allergy: 24–340 μg/kg/24 hr depending on the severity of symptoms. Taper doses gradually.

Dosage (Oral Inhalation)
For refractory bronchial asthma: 2 inhalations tid–qid. Maximum is 8 inhalations/day.

Rate: Can be given by rapid IV push.

INDICATIONS: Dexamethasone is used parenterally for reduction of intracranial pressure and as adjunctive therapy of shock (especially septic and anaphylactic). Oral doses are used primarily to reduce inflammation in various allergic conditions. Oral inhalation can be used for treatment of bronchial asthma and related bronchospastic states in patients who are not responding well to conventional therapy. Dexamethasone has been used investigationally for the prevention of RDS or hyaline membrane disease in premature infants.

ACTIONS: See corticosteroids (general statement). Onset of action occurs in 6–12 hours with peak effects within 12–24 hours.

CONTRAINDICATIONS: See corticosteroids (general statement).

PRECAUTIONS: See corticosteroids (general statement).

SIDE EFFECTS/ADVERSE REACTIONS: See corticosteroids (general statement).

DRUG INCOMPATIBILITIES: See corticosteroids (general statement).

DRUG INTERACTIONS: See corticosteroids (general statement).

ANTIDOTE: See corticosteroids (general statement).

Hydrocortisone (Solu-Cortef, Cortef)

ADMINISTRATION

Available Forms: Injectable (IV, IM), 100, 250, 500 mg and 1 gm vials as sodium succinate salt (Solu-Cortef), (also available as acetate ester for intra-articular, intrabursal use); tablets, 5, 10, 20 mg (Cortef); oral suspension, 2 mg/ml; topical, various preparations for dermatological, rectal, and ophthalmic use.

Diluent: Provided by manufacturer. Can be further diluted with D5W or NS for IV infusion.

Dosage (Parenteral): Varies according to use.
For adrenal crisis: 1 mg/kg IM or IV initially; 50–250 mg can be added to IV glucose-saline solutions for the first 24 hours. (At the same time hydrocortisone or cortisone acetate can be given IM in the same doses so that slow release of corticosteroid is accomplished. These doses are repeated q24h until the crisis is controlled.)

For shock: 25 mg/kg IV initially, followed by 12 mg/kg/24 hr in divided doses.
For status asthmaticus: 5–10 mg/kg IV push or infusion q4–6h as indicated. Usual dose is 100 mg q4–6h.

Dosage (Oral): Varies according to use.
For physiological replacement: 560 µg/kg/24 hr (16 mg/m^2/24 hr) divided into 3 doses.
Pharmacological dose: (Varies with allergic or inflammatory disease.) 2–8 mg/kg/24 hr (60–240 mg/m^2/24 hr) divided into 3–4 doses.

Rate: Give IV bolus doses over at least 30–60 seconds. High doses of 500 mg should be given over at least 2 minutes.

INDICATIONS: Parenteral and oral doses of hydrocortisone are given as replacement therapy in acute and chronic adrenocortical insufficiency because this drug has both glucocorticoid and mineralocorticoid effects. The water-soluble form (e.g., Solu-Cortef) is given parenterally in inflammatory conditions when an immediate response is needed (e.g., acute adrenocortical insufficiency, status asthmaticus, shock, anaphylaxis). It is limited to very short-term administration (less than 48–72 hours) because its strong mineralocorticoid effects promote salt and water retention. These effects, however, make Solu-Cortef particularly beneficial for the management of certain forms of adrenal crisis in which large amounts of sodium and water are lost. The other hydrocortisone analogues (e.g., dexamethasone, prednisone) are preferred for maintaining anti-inflammatory effects. Topically, hydrocortisone is used to treat various dermatoses and eye inflammations.

ACTIONS: See corticosteroids (general statement).

CONTRAINDICATIONS: See corticosteroids (general statement).

PRECAUTIONS: See corticosteroids (general statement).

SIDE EFFECTS/ADVERSE REACTIONS: See corticosteroids (general statement).

DRUG INCOMPATIBILITIES: See corticosteroids (general statement).

DRUG INTERACTIONS: See corticosteroids (general statement).

ANTIDOTE: See corticosteroids (general statement).

Methylprednisolone (Solu-Medrol, Medrol)

ADMINISTRATION

Available Forms: Injectable (IV, IM), 40, 125, 500 mg and 1 gm vials (Solu-Medrol), repository injection also available as Depo-Medrol; tablets, 2, 4, 16 mg; capsules, 2, 4 mg; topical, ointment, and retention enemas available.

Diluent: Provided by the manufacturer. Can be further diluted with D5W or NS for IV infusion.

Dosage (Parenteral): Varies according to use.
For shock: 25 mg/kg IV initially, followed by 12 mg/kg/24 hr in divided doses.
For other inflammatory conditions: Give the oral dose IM or IV.

Dosage (Oral)
Pharmacological dose: (Varies with allergic or inflammatory disease.) 40–170 μg/kg/24 hr (13–50 mg/m^2/24 hr) divided into 3–4 doses.

Rate: Administer IV boluses no faster than 100 mg/min.

INDICATIONS: Methylprednisolone is used to treat inflammatory and allergic conditions and other diseases that respond to glucocorticoids. It lacks significant mineralocorticoid properties, and so it is not recommended for replacement therapy unless a mineralocorticoid is given concurrently.

ACTIONS: See corticosteroids (general statement).

CONTRAINDICATIONS: See corticosteroids (general statement).

PRECAUTIONS: See corticosteroids (general statement).

SIDE EFFECTS/ADVERSE REACTIONS: See corticosteroids (general statement).

DRUG INCOMPATIBILITIES: See corticosteroids (general statement).

DRUG INTERACTIONS: See corticosteroids (general statement).

ANTIDOTE: See corticosteroids (general statement).

Prednisone (Deltasone, Meticorten)

ADMINISTRATION

Available Forms: Tablets, 1.0, 2.5, 5.0, 10.0, 20.0 mg.

Dosage (Parenteral): Varies according to use.
Pharmacological dose: (Varies with allergic or inflammatory disease.) 0.5–2.0 mg/kg/24 hr (15–60 mg/m^2/24 hr), taken with meals if possible.
For nephrosis: (Initial dose per 24 hr):

- Children 1.5–4 years old: 30–40 mg in divided doses (q6h)
- Children 4–10 years old: 60 mg in divided doses (q6h)
- Children >10 years old: 80 mg in divided doses (q6h)

For rheumatic carditis: 2 mg/kg/24 hr (60 mg/m^2/24 hr) divided into 4 doses for 2–3 weeks, then 1.5 mg/kg/24 hr (45 mg/m^2/24 hr) divided into 4 doses for 4–6 weeks.

For tuberculosis: 2 mg/kg/24 hr (60 mg/m^2/24 hr) divided into 4 doses for 2 months, then gradually withdraw the drug.

For asthma: Initially 20–40 mg/24 hr in divided doses. Taper by 5 mg/day until low maintenance dose of 5 mg/24 hr is achieved. For chronic asthma, use alternate-day therapy if possible.

INDICATIONS: Prednisone is indicated for the treatment of inflammatory or allergic conditions and other diseases that respond to corticosteroid therapy. Because it has very low mineralocorticoid activity, it is inadequate as the sole agent for treatment of adrenocortical insufficiency. A supplemental mineralocorticoid such as fludrocortisone must also be given.

ACTIONS: See corticosteroids (general statement).

CONTRAINDICATIONS: See corticosteroids (general statement).

PRECAUTIONS: See corticosteroids (general statement).

SIDE EFFECTS/ADVERSE REACTIONS: See corticosteroids (general statement).

DRUG INCOMPATIBILITIES: See corticosteroids (general statement).

DRUG INTERACTIONS: See corticosteroids (general statement).

ANTIDOTE: See corticosteroids (general statement).

15
Antihistamines

Medications capable of antagonizing the effects of histamine are classified as antihistamines. They are available as single agents or in combination with other ingredients such as decongestants, expectorants, analgesics, and antitussives. The antihistamines discussed in this chapter include only those that act on H_1-receptor sites.

These agents competitively antagonize the stimulatory effects of histamine on H_1-receptors in the smooth muscle of the GI tract, uterus, large blood vessels, and bronchial tree. They also effectively antagonize the edema, wheal and flare formation, and itching that accompany endogenous histamine release. Although these medications block the action of histamine on these receptor sites, they do not inactivate or prevent the release of histamine. In addition, because of their structural similarity to atropine and related alkaloids, antihistamines produce atropine-like effects both centrally and peripherally.

These agents are not curative and only offer symptomatic relief of hypersensitivity and allergic reactions, colds, motion sickness, vertigo, and nausea.

The following medications are discussed in this chapter:

- **Chlorpheniramine**
- **Dimenhydrinate**
- **Diphenhydramine**
- **Hydroxyzine**
- **Promethazine**

Chlorpheniramine (Chlor-Trimeton, others)

ADMINISTRATION

Available Forms: Injectable (SC), 10, 20, 50, and 100 mg per milliliter; tablets, 4 mg (scored); tablets (prolonged-action), 8, 12 mg; oral syrup, 2 mg/5 ml.

Dosage (Parenteral): 0.35 mg/kg/24 hr (10 mg/m^2/24 hr) SC in divided doses (q6h). Do not give IM or IV to children.

Dosage (Oral): 0.35 mg/kg/24 hr (10 mg/m^2/24 hr) in divided doses (q6h). Single dose (prolonged-action form) is 0.2 mg/kg (6 mg/m^2).

INDICATIONS: Similar to diphenhydramine. However, chlorpheniramine is ineffective for motion sickness or treatment of drug-induced extrapyramidal symptoms.

ACTIONS: See diphenhydramine.

CONTRAINDICATIONS: See diphenhydramine.

PRECAUTIONS: See diphenhydramine.

SIDE EFFECTS/ADVERSE REACTIONS: Similar to diphenhydramine. However, chlorpheniramine is less sedative.

DRUG INTERACTIONS: See diphenhydramine.

ANTIDOTE: See diphenhydramine.

Dimenhydrinate (Dramamine)

ADMINISTRATION

Available Forms: Injectable (IV, IM), 50 mg/ml in 1 ml amps, 5 and 10 ml vials; tablets, 50 mg; oral liquid, 3.1 mg/ml; suppositories, 100 mg.

Diluent: Can be diluted with NS for IV use.

Dosage (Parenteral): 5 mg/kg/24 hr (37.5 mg/m^2/24 hr) IM divided into 4 doses. Maximum is 300 mg/day.
For prevention of motion sickness: Give a dose 30 minutes before exposure to motion.
Note: IV doses are not established for children.

Dosage (Rectal or Oral): Same as parenteral dose, or
Children 2–6 years old: Up to 25 mg orally q6–8h.
Children 6–12 years old: 25–50 mg orally q6–8h.

Rate: If IV route is used, give dose slowly over at least 2 minutes.

INDICATIONS: Dimenhydrinate is used primarily for treatment and prevention of the nausea, vomiting, and vertigo of motion sickness. It is used also as a postoperative antiemetic, but it may be less effective than the phenothiazines in controlling nausea and vomiting that are not related to vestibular stimulation.

ACTIONS: As with other antihistamines, dimenhydrinate has antihistaminic, antiemetic, anticholinergic, and CNS-depressant effects. The exact mechanism of its antiemetic action is not known but is believed to be due to inhibition of vestibular and reticular stimulation in the central nervous system. Tolerance to the CNS-depressant effects usually occurs in a few days. Onset of action usually occurs within 20–30 minutes after oral or IM administration and within 30–45 minutes after rectal administration.

CONTRAINDICATIONS: Known hypersensitivity to dimenhydrinate or diphenhydramine (see diphenhydramine).

PRECAUTIONS: Drowsiness is common, but paradoxical CNS stimulation may occur in children. Use cautiously in patients with conditions that may be aggravated by anticholinergic effects (e.g., narrow-angle glaucoma, myasthenia gravis, cardiovascular disease). Use cautiously in patients with convulsive disorders and asthma. Since dimenhydrinate may mask symptoms of ototoxicity (especially vestibular), it should be administered cautiously to patients receiving other ototoxic medications. It has proved teratogenic in animals, so avoid using it in pregnant patients. IM injections are painful.

SIDE EFFECTS/ADVERSE REACTIONS: Drowsiness is the most common side effect, but tolerance to this may develop. Anticholinergic effects include tinnitus; mydriasis; dry mouth, mucous membranes, and respiratory passages; urinary retention; tachycardia; and hypotension. Gastric upset may occur. Accidental overdose occurs frequently in infants and children. Symptoms resemble those associated with atropine overdose (flushing, dilated pupils, ataxia, excitation, hallucinations, confusion, convulsions, coma, respiratory failure, and cardiovascular collapse).

DRUG INTERACTIONS: Concomitant use with *alcohol, tranquilizers, sedative-hypnotics*, and other *CNS depressants* may cause additive CNS depression. Dimenhydrinate may mask early symptoms of ototoxicity in patients receiving *aminoglycosides* or other ototoxic drugs. Additive anticholinergic effects may occur if given with *MAO inhibitors, atropine*, or other *anticholinergic* compounds.

ANTIDOTE: Discontinue dimenhydrinate. Give supportive treatment (e.g., assisted ventilation, limited external stimulation to minimize CNS excitation). Short-acting barbiturates or diazepam can be given for management of convulsions (use cautiously).

Diphenhydramine (Benadryl)

ADMINISTRATION

Available Forms: Injectable (IV, IM), 10 mg/ml in 10 and 30 ml vials, 50 mg/ml in 1 ml syringes and amps; capsules, 25, 50 mg; elixir, 12.5 mg/5 ml (2.5 mg/ml).

Diluent: Compatible with many IV solutions. Can be diluted in D5W or NS for IV use (up to 50 mg/50 ml).

Dosage (Parenteral): 5 mg/kg/24 hr (150 mg/m^2/24 hr) given IV or *deep* IM in divided doses (q6h). Maximum is 300 mg/24 hr.
For anaphylaxis or phenothiazine idiosyncrasy: Single dose of 1.5 mg/kg as an IV bolus.

Dosage (Oral): Same as parenteral dosage.

Rate: For IV bolus doses do not exceed 25 mg/min. For IV infusions, dose in 50 ml can be given over 30 minutes.

INDICATIONS: Diphenhydramine is widely used for symptomatic treatment of mild to severe allergic reactions. It is often used for hypersensitivity reactions to blood or plasma and as an adjunct to epinephrine and other standard measures employed during anaphylactic reactions. It can be used as an antidote for dystonic, extrapyramidal reactions to phenothiazines and butyrophenones (e.g., haloperidol) and can be given alone or with other centrally acting anticholinergics for treatment of mild cases of parkinsonism.

ACTIONS: Diphenhydramine shares the histamine-antagonizing, anticholinergic, antiemetic, local anesthetic, and sedative actions of other antihistamines.

CONTRAINDICATIONS: Known sensitivity to diphenhydramine and other structurally related compounds; lower respiratory tract impairment, including asthma, and acute asthma attacks. Use in neonates and premature infants is not recommended.

PRECAUTIONS: See dimenhydrinate. Dosage adjustments may be necessary for patients with severe renal failure.

SIDE EFFECTS/ADVERSE REACTIONS: The incidence of drowsiness and sedation is high. Atropine-like effects, epigastric distress, thickening of bronchial secretions, tightness in the chest, stuffiness, wheezing, and paradoxical excitation also occur. Cardiovascular side effects include hypotension, headache, tachycardia, palpitations, and extrasystoles. Rare blood dyscrasias (hemolytic anemia, leukopenia, agranulocytosis) and hypersensitivity reactions have been reported also.

DRUG INTERACTIONS: See dimenhydrinate.

ANTIDOTE: See dimenhydrinate.

Hydroxyzine (Atarax, Vistaril)

ADMINISTRATION

Available Forms: Injectable (IM), 25 and 50 mg per milliliter in 1, 2, and 10 ml vials; tablets, 10, 25, 50, 100 mg (Atarax); capsules, 25, 50, 100 mg (Vistaril); oral syrup, 10 mg/5 ml (Atarax); oral suspension, 25 mg/5 ml (Vistaril).

Dosage (Parenteral)
For antiemesis: 1.1 mg/kg (30 mg/m^2) IM as a single dose.

Dosage (Oral)
For antiemesis, antianxiety, or sedation: 2 mg/kg/day (60 mg/m^2/day), divided into 4 doses.

- Children <6 years old: Maximum is 50 mg/day.
- Children >6 years old: Maximum is 100 mg/day.

INDICATIONS: Hydroxyzine is used to control emesis and to reduce preoperative and postoperative narcotic requirements. It is also used as a mild calming agent to reduce anxiety, tension, and agitation associated with emotional or psychoneurotic states. It may be useful in the relief of histamine-induced pruritus and urticaria.

ACTIONS: Hydroxyzine is an antihistaminic compound that exhibits CNS depressant, anticholinergic, antiemetic, antispasmodic, mild gastric antisecretory, and local anesthetic effects. It has some minor skeletal-muscle-relaxant activity and produces only minimal circulatory or respiratory depression. Onset of action of oral doses is within 15–30 minutes, and IM doses probably act more rapidly. The metabolic fate of hydroxyzine is unknown. Hydroxyzine may be teratogenic and it is not recommended for nursing mothers.

CONTRAINDICATIONS: Hypersensitivity to hydroxyzine, early pregnancy.

PRECAUTIONS: Do not administer IV, SC, or by inadvertent intra-arterial injection. In children inject into the midlateral muscles of the thigh. Hydroxyzine may produce transient drowsiness; caution ambulatory patients accordingly. Reduce dosages of other CNS depressants (e.g., narcotics, sedatives) if used with hydroxyzine. Replace fluid and electrolytes lost through emesis as indicated.

SIDE EFFECTS/ADVERSE REACTIONS: Hydroxyzine has a low incidence of toxicity. Transient drowsiness and dry mouth commonly occur. Doses given IM may produce pain and discomfort at the injection site. Inadvertent intra-arterial injection causes endarteritis, thrombosis, and digital gangrene. Doses given SC cause tissue induration. Rarely (particularly with high doses), involuntary motor activity, tremor, convulsions, dizziness, urticaria, and various rashes have occurred.

DRUG INCOMPATIBILITIES: Do not mix with barbiturates, diazepam, or other benzodiazepines in the same syringe. Hydroxyzine *can* be mixed with atropine, morphine, meperidine, pentazocine, promethazine, or scopolamine in the same syringe, however.

DRUG INTERACTIONS: Hydroxyzine causes additive CNS depression when used with *alcohol, narcotics, sedative-hypnotics, tricyclic antidepressants,* or other *CNS depressants.* (Reduce dosage of these agents accordingly.)

ANTIDOTE: Discontinue the medication. If ingestion was recent, empty the stomach with gastric lavage. Induced emesis may not be effective. Monitor vital signs. Treat adverse reactions symptomatically and supportively. Hypotension can be treated with IV fluids or levarterenol (do not use epinephrine because hydroxyzine antagonizes the vasopressor effect). Support respiration.

Promethazine (Phenergan)

ADMINISTRATION

Available Forms: Injectable (IM, IV), 25 and 50 mg per milliliter in 1 ml amps and syringes; tablets, 12.5, 25.0, 50.0 mg; oral syrup, 6.25, 12.50, and 25.00 mg per milliliter; suppositories, 25, 50 mg.

Diluent: Can be diluted in D5W or NS for IV use. Do not exceed a concentration of 25 mg/ml.

Dosage (Parenteral): 0.5 mg/kg/dose (15 mg/m²/dose) given q4–6h deep IM.
As antihistamine: Full dose at bedtime and one-fourth dose in the morning or prn.
As antiemetic: 0.25–0.50 mg/kg/dose IM q4–6h prn.
Preoperative dose: 0.5–1.0 mg/kg/dose IM.

Dosage (Oral or Rectal): Same as parenteral dose.
For motion sickness: Full dose repeated q12h prn.

Rate: If given IV administer no faster than 25 mg/min.

INDICATIONS: Promethazine is a phenothiazine derivative with potent antihistaminic properties. It is used primarily as an antiemetic in motion sickness and for nausea and vomiting associated with surgery. Because of its prominent sedative action, it is useful as a preoperative medication and as an adjunct to analgesia with narcotic and non-narcotic analgesics. However, this pronounced sedative effect limits its usefulness as an antihistamine in ambulatory patients.

ACTIONS: Promethazine has antiemetic, antihistaminic, and anticholinergic effects similar to those of other antihistamines. Although it can produce CNS excitation, CNS depression with sedation is more common with therapeutic doses. It has no significant effects on the cardiovascular system in normal doses, but rapid IV administration may cause hypotension. Onset of action is rapid (within 3–5 minutes) after IV administration and within 20 minutes for all other routes. Promethazine is metabolized by the liver and excreted in the urine and feces.

CONTRAINDICATIONS: Known hypersensitivity to promethazine or other phenothiazines, patients who are comatose or receiving large doses of other CNS depressants.

PRECAUTIONS: Use cautiously in patients with cardiovascular disease, impaired liver function, asthmatic attacks, or conditions aggravated by anticholinergic action. Promethazine may suppress the cough reflex; use it carefully in children with acute or chronic respiratory impairment. Neonates, infants, and children, especially those acutely ill and dehydrated, may be more susceptible than adults to the dystonias and extrapyramidal symptoms. Paradoxical excitability and abnormal movements may follow a single dose. Epileptic patients may experience increased severity of convulsions. Giving excessive amounts for pain without providing adequate analgesic coverage may cause restlessness and motor hyperactivity. Use cautiously in patients with bone marrow suppression since the medication may cause additional leukopenia and agranulocytosis. Chemical irritation and tissue necrosis can occur if doses are given SC or if extravasation occurs during IV administration. Inadvertent intra-arterial injection may cause serious arteriospasm and gangrene. Administer IV doses slowly to avoid hypotension. Solutions are light-sensitive and should not be used if severely yellowed.

SIDE EFFECTS/ADVERSE REACTIONS: The most common adverse reactions are sedation, confusion, and disorientation. Nightmares and CNS excitation may occur in children receiving single high doses of 75–125 mg. Other reported CNS stimulatory effects include tremors, hysteria, convulsive seizures, oculogyric crises, and catatonia-like states. Anticholinergic effects; extrapyramidal symptoms; gastric upset; and cardiovascular effects including tachycardia, bradycardia, hypotension, and hypertension may occur. Hypersensitivity, photosensitivity, and blood dyscrasias occur rarely.

DRUG INTERACTIONS: Use with *barbiturates* and *narcotic analgesics* causes additive sedation and CNS depression. (Reduce doses of each of these by 25–50% when given together with promethazine.) Additive anticholinergic effects occur when promethazine is given with *atropine* and *atropine-like compounds*. Promethazine reverses the vasopressor effect of *epinephrine*. Additive antihistaminic effects occur when it is used with other *antihistamines*.

ANTIDOTE: Discontinue promethazine. Treat adverse reactions symptomatically and supportively. *Do not use CNS stimulants*. Treat severe hypotension with norepinephrine or phenylephrine (alpha agonists). *Do not use epinephrine* as it may further lower blood pressure. Convulsions can be treated with diazepam or short-acting barbiturates. Anticholinergic antiparkinson medications (e.g., benztropine) or diphenhydramine may control extrapyramidal symptoms. Mechanically assisted ventilation may be necessary.

16
Bronchodilators and Antiasthmatics

A large percentage of pediatric patients seen in the emergency department have diseases of an allergic nature that range from hypersensitivity reactions and bronchial asthma to life-threatening conditions such as status asthmaticus and anaphylaxis. Emergency management of these acute conditions includes the administration of bronchodilators, steroids, and fluids and supportive treatment with oxygen and mucolytic agents. Long-term management also includes the elimination and avoidance of the offending allergen and hyposensitization when indicated.

Mucolytic agents (e.g., N-acetylcysteine) are often used as adjunctive therapy for patients with various inflammatory lung diseases or cystic fibrosis. These agents reduce the viscosity of abnormal pulmonary secretions.

Bronchodilators act by inhibiting the contractions of the smooth muscles of the bronchioles to overcome bronchospasm and decrease airway resistance. The two major groups of bronchodilators are the adrenergics (e.g., epinephrine, isoproterenol, metaproterenol, terbutaline, albuterol) and the xanthine derivatives (e.g., aminophylline, theophylline). Corticosteroids (see chapter 14) may be useful early in status asthmaticus and in severe acute or chronic bronchial asthma refractory to conventional therapy. The corticosteroids can be given by mouth or by oral inhalation, which may minimize some of the systemic adverse reactions seen with long-term oral systemic use.

The adrenergics epinephrine and isoproterenol are covered in chapter 3. The following medications are discussed in this chapter:

- **N-Acetylcysteine**
- **Albuterol**
- **Aminophylline (parenteral)**
- **Aminophylline (oral)**

- **Theophylline (oral)**
- **Isoetharine**
- **Metaproterenol**
- **Terbutaline**

N-Acetylcysteine (Mucomyst)

ADMINISTRATION

Available Forms: Solution for nebulizer inhalation, 10 and 20% in 4, 10, and 30 ml vials.

Diluent: NS or water can be added when used for nebulization.

Dosage (Nebulization): With face mask, mouthpiece, or tracheostomy, 6–10 ml of a 10% solution or 3–5 ml of a 20% solution 2–4 times a day (bid–qid).

Dosage (Direct Instillation): Into tracheostomy or through percutaneous intratracheal catheter, 2–4 ml of a 10% solution or 1–2 ml of a 20% solution q1–4h as necessary.

INDICATIONS: N-Acetylcysteine is given by nebulization or by direct instillation into the trachea as adjunctive therapy to reduce the viscosity of abnormal pulmonary secretions in patients with various inflammatory lung diseases or cystic fibrosis. It has also been used investigationally as an antidote for acetaminophen overdose (see chapter 35).

ACTION: N-Acetylcysteine is a derivative of the naturally occurring amino acid L-cysteine. Its mucolytic action apparently "opens" disulfide linkages in the mucoproteins thereby decreasing viscosity.

CONTRAINDICATIONS: Known hypersensitivity to acetylcysteine.

PRECAUTIONS: Because of the large amounts of secretions that may be produced during treatment, a suction apparatus must always be available. N-Acetylcysteine may cause bronchospasm, especially in asthmatic patients, which can be relieved by nebulized, bronchodilating agents. Solutions have a slight, disagreeable odor. A color change (light purple) may occur without causing any significant change in efficacy. To minimize contamination, store opened vials in the refrigerator and use within 96 hours. Certain materials in nebulizers (e.g., iron, copper, and rubber) may react with N-acetylcysteine. Continued nebulization of the medication with a dry gas will result in increasing concentrations, so dilute with water or normal saline before nebulizing.

SIDE EFFECTS/ADVERSE REACTIONS: Bronchospasm may occur in susceptible asthmatic patients, especially with 20% solutions. Other side effects include stomatitis, rhinorrhea, hemoptysis, and nausea (due to the disagreeable odor).

DRUG INCOMPATIBILITIES: Do not mix with hydrogen peroxide, trypsin, chymotrypsin, tetracyclines, or erythromycin. (Nebulize these separately.)

ANTIDOTE: Discontinue N-acetylcysteine. Administer a bronchodilator by nebulization to counteract bronchospasm if necessary.

Albuterol (Proventil, Ventolin)

ADMINISTRATION

Available Forms: Tablets, 2, 4 mg (Ventolin); metered inhaler, delivers 90 µg per metered dose (Proventil, Ventolin).

Dosage (Oral)
Children >12 years old: 2–4 mg tid or qid. Can be gradually increased by 2 mg increments up to a maximum of 8 mg qid.

Dosage (Inhalation)
Children >12 years old: 1–2 inhalations q4–6h prn.

INDICATIONS: Albuterol is used for symptomatic relief of bronchospasm in patients with bronchial asthma or other forms of reversible obstructive airway disease.

ACTIONS: Albuterol causes bronchodilation by preferentially stimulating beta-2 receptors of the bronchial tree. In normal doses, it usually has minimal stimulant effects on the beta-1 receptors of the heart, but in high doses, it may cause cardiac and CNS stimulation. Recommended oral doses generally decrease airway resistance and improve pulmonary function within 30 minutes after administration. Peak effects occur in 2–3 hours and last up to 6 hours. Oral inhalation produces therapeutic effects within 15 minutes; these last up to 4 hours.

CONTRAINDICATIONS: Known hypersensitivity to albuterol or any components of the inhaler.

PRECAUTIONS: The occasional cardiovascular stimulation that occurs necessitates cautious use in patients who have hypertension, cardiovascular disorders, or hyperthyroidism or who are unusually responsive to sympathomimetics. Large doses may aggravate diabetes mellitus. Paradoxical bronchospasm may occur with use of the aerosol preparation. Excessive use of inhaled sympathomimetics has caused fatalities due to severe acute asthmatic crisis and hypoxia. Safety and effectiveness in children less than 12 years old have not been established.

SIDE EFFECTS/ADVERSE REACTIONS: The most frequent side effects include nervousness, headache, and tremor. Also reported are tachycardia, palpitations, weakness, dizziness, vertigo, insomnia, flushing, nausea, irritability, chest discomfort, angina, CNS stimulation, an unusual taste in the mouth, and muscle cramps. The inhaler may cause irritation and drying of the oropharynx.

DRUG INTERACTIONS: *Propranolol* and other *beta-blockers* inhibit the bronchodilating effects of albuterol. Concomitant use with other *sympathomimetics* may potentiate cardiovascular stimulant effects. *MAO inhibitors* and *tricyclic antidepressants* may increase the cardiovascular toxicity caused by albuterol.

ANTIDOTE: Discontinue albuterol. Provide symptomatic treatment as needed. Cardioselective beta-blockers (e.g. metoprolol) can be used judiciously for treatment of excessive cardiac stimulation.

Aminophylline (parenteral) (theophylline ethylenediamine, Aminophyllin, others)

ADMINISTRATION

Available Forms: Injectable (IV), 25 mg/ml in 10 and 20 ml vials and amps.

Diluent: Can be diluted in D5W, NS, LR, or Ringer's solution for IV infusion. Dilute doses for intermittent infusions (up to 250 mg in 50 ml, 250–500 mg in 100 ml). For continuous IV infusions doses up to 2500 mg can be diluted in 500–1000 ml of solution.

Dosage (Parenteral): Varies according to use.
For acute asthma in patients *not* currently receiving theophylline products: See Table 16-1.

TABLE 16–1 Intravenous Doses of Aminophylline for Acute Asthma*†

Age or Clinical Condition	Loading Dose‡ (mg/kg/hr)	Maintenance Dose§ (mg/kg/hr)
Neonates‖	6.0	0.18
Infants <1 yr	6.0	0.24–0.90
Children 1–9 yr	6.0	1.00
Children >9 yr and young adult smokers	6.0	0.80

*Adapted from Hendeles L, Weinberger M, by permission of the *American Journal of Hospital Pharmacy*, 1982;39:249.
†For those patients not currently receiving theophylline preparations.
‡Based on 1.2 mg aminophylline per kilogram (1 mg theophylline per kilogram) for each 2 µg/ml desired increase in theophylline serum concentration.
§Based on initial infusion rates necessary to produce a steady-state serum concentration of theophylline of 10 µg/ml. Because clearance of theophylline varies even within these categories, these maintenance infusion doses should not be maintained beyond 12–24 hours without measurement of serum theophylline. Final dosage requirements, which may be higher or lower, should then be guided by this measurement.
‖Neonates with apnea may require maintenance infusion rates of up to 1.1 mg/kg/hr initially. Serum concentrations of theophylline should be maintained at 7–14 µg/ml to prevent recurrence of apnea.

For acute asthma in patients currently receiving theophylline products: Loading doses of 0.6 mg of aminophylline per kilogram (0.5 mg of theophylline per kilogram) are expected to cause a 1 µg/ml increase in the serum level of theophylline. When possible, determine the time, amount, route, and form of the patient's last theophylline dose. If a serum theophylline level can be rapidly obtained, defer the loading dose. *If a serum theophylline level cannot be obtained,* and if, in the clinician's judgment, there is sufficient respiratory distress to warrant a small risk, a loading dose of 3.0 mg of aminophylline per kilogram (2.5 mg of theophylline per kilogram) can be given. This loading dose is expected to raise the serum concentration by approximately 5 µg/ml.

For intermittent dosing: Loading dose of 6 mg/kg given slowly IV, followed by up to 20 mg/kg/day slowly IV in divided doses (q6–8h). Monitor serum theophylline levels.

Rate: For IV administration do not exceed 25 mg/min. Dilute loading doses in 50–100 ml diluent.

Aminophylline (oral)
Theophylline (oral)

ADMINISTRATION

Available Forms (Aminophylline): Tablets, 100, 200 mg; oral solution, 105 mg/5 ml (Somophyllin); rectal suppositories, 250, 500 mg; rectal solution, 100 mg/ml in 3.0 and 4.5 ml squeeze bottles (Rectalad), 60 mg/ml in 90 and 150 ml bottles (Somophyllin Rectal).

Available Forms (Theophylline): See Table 16–2.

TABLE 16–2 Some Available Theophylline Preparations

Dosage Form	Strength (mg or mg/5 ml)
Tablets	100, 125, 200, 250
Tablets (prolonged-release)	100, 200, 300 (Theo-Dur) 250, 500 (Theolair-SR) 300 (Quibron-T/SR Dividose)
Capsules	100, 200, 250
Capsules (prolonged-release)	60, 125, 250 (Slo-Phyllin Gyrocaps) 65, 130, 260 (Aerolate) 100, 200, 300 (Slo-BID) 50, 75, 125, 200 (Theo-Dur Sprinkles)
Oral solution	27.0, 37.5, 53.0
Oral suspension	100 mg (Elixicon Pediatric)
Rectal solution	250, 500 mg (Fleet Theophylline)

Dosage (Oral): Varies according to use.
For acute asthma in patients *not* currently receiving theophylline products: See Table 16–3.

TABLE 16–3 Oral Doses of Aminophylline and Theophylline for Acute Asthma*†

Age or Clinical Condition	Loading Dose (mg/kg)	Maintenance Dose	
		NEXT 12 HR (mg/kg q4h)	BEYOND 12 HR (mg/kg q6h)
6 mo–9 yr	7 (6)	4.7 (4.0)	4.7 (4.0)
9–16 yr (and young adult smokers)	7 (6)	3.5 (3.0)	3.8 (3.0)

*For patients not currently receiving theophylline products.
†Numbers in parentheses refer to theophylline (anhydrous) doses. Other numbers refer to aminophylline (dihydrate). Doses and dosing intervals are for the short-acting, *non*-sustained-release preparations.

For acute asthma in patients currently receiving theophylline products: Follow the guidelines outlined for parenteral doses of aminophylline. A rapidly absorbed oral dosage form should be used (e.g., elixir or *non*-sustained-release tablets).

For chronic asthma: Initial dose of 16 mg/kg/day or 400 mg/day (whichever is less) given in divided doses (q6–8h). This can be increased by 25% at 2–3 day intervals as long as no intolerance is observed or until maximum maintenance doses are reached. Maximum daily doses of aminophylline without measurement of serum concentration are as follows. The numbers in parentheses refer to doses of anhydrous theophylline.

- Age 6 months to 9 years: 28.2 mg/kg/day (24 mg/kg/day) in divided doses (q6–8h)
- Age 9–12 years: 23.5 mg/kg/day (20 mg/kg/day) in divided doses (q6–8h)
- Age 12–16 years: 21.2 mg/kg/day (18 mg/kg/day) in divided doses (q6–8h) or 1100 mg/day, whichever is less
- Age >16 years: 15.2 mg/kg/day (13 mg/kg/day) in divided doses (q6–8h) or 900 mg/day, whichever is less

Note: When using the prolonged-release preparations, the daily doses should be divided (q8–12h).

INDICATIONS: Theophylline and aminophylline are used for symptomatic treatment of bronchial asthma and reversible bronchospasm that may accompany chronic bronchitis, chronic obstructive pulmonary disease (COPD), and emphysema. Oral preparations are used for mild to moderate cases of acute asthma and as adjunctive therapy of COPD. Parenterally, aminophylline relieves periodic apnea in Cheyne-Stokes respiration and acute bronchospasm or status asthmaticus resistant to adrenergics. Investigationally, oral and IV forms have been used to stimulate respiration and myocardial contractility in infants with neonatal apnea and to reduce bronchospasm associated with cystic fibrosis and acute descending respiratory infections.

ACTIONS: Theophylline and aminophylline (the ethylenediamine salt of the latter is approximately 80% theophylline) are xanthine derivatives that directly dilate bronchial smooth muscle to relieve bronchospasm, decrease airway resistance, and improve oxygen flow rates and vital capacity. In addition, they dilate vascular smooth muscle, thus decreasing peripheral vascular resistance and venous pressure. Heart rate may be increased not only by a reflex response to lowered blood pressure but also by theophylline's direct positive inotropic and chronotropic effects (usually in doses larger than those required for bronchodilation). Theophylline stimulates all levels of the CNS. Stimulation of vasomotor and vagal centers produces vasoconstriction and bradycardia, but the overall effect on the cardiovascular system depends on whether CNS or peripheral effects dominate. Stimulation of the medullary respiratory center can increase the rate and depth of respiration. Therapeutic levels of theophylline stimulate the vomiting center while toxic levels activate the cortex and spinal cord to produce seizures. Theophylline also produces diuresis by renal vasodilation, increased cardiac output, and improved renal blood flow. Therapeutic blood levels of 10–20 µg/ml are usually necessary for optimum bronchodilation. In premature infants, levels of 7–14 µg/ml may be sufficient to reduce apnea. Theophylline is metabolized in the liver at rates that may vary among individuals. Neonates and premature infants have extremely slow elimination rates and lowered protein-binding of theophylline; the plasma half-life may be 15–58 hours (as compared with 4–8 hours in older infants and children). Not until age 3–6 months do the elimination rate and half-life approach those seen in older children. Unchanged theophylline and its metabolites are excreted in the urine and feces.

CONTRAINDICATIONS: Hypersensitivity to theophylline or other xanthine derivatives, concurrent use of other xanthine medications (e.g., theobromine, caffeine), active peptic ulcer disease.

PRECAUTIONS: Children are especially sensitive to the adverse effects of theophylline, particularly the CNS effects. Use cautiously in newborns and young children and in patients with peptic ulcer disease; hyperthyroidism; glaucoma; diabetes mellitus; impaired hepatic, renal, or cardiac function; or hypertension. Absorption of rectal doses (especially suppository forms) is erratic and unpredictable; avoid use of these forms. Rectal administration may cause the medication to be expelled by stimulation of the defecation reflex and rectal irritation. Give IV injections slowly and cautiously. Avoid IM administration as it is extremely painful. Gastric irritation can be minimized by giving oral doses with meals. Theophylline is secreted in breast milk and may cause adverse reactions in breast-fed infants.

During therapy, monitor vital signs (especially blood pressure and heart rate) frequently. Because theophylline has a low therapeutic index, careful determination of dosages is essential. Individuals may metabolize the medication at different rates, so appropriate doses must be calculated and carefully monitored by response and tolerance, pulmonary function tests, and theophylline serum levels. If previous administration of any theophylline preparation has been excessive (more than 8 mg/kg/12 hr) or if the patient is experiencing excitation, tremor, frequent vomiting, hematemesis, or convulsions, further use of this bronchodilator should be carefully considered or postponed for at least 6 hours after the last administered dose.

Note: Because of the lowered plasma protein binding and expanded volume of distribution of theophylline in premature infants and neonates, a given serum level of the drug in these patients may reflect a higher plasma-tissue ratio than the same serum level in adults. Thus, a given serum concentration would mean a larger amount of theophylline in the body tissues of an infant than in the body tissues of older children or adults. Such higher tissue levels can predispose neonates and premature infants to theophylline poisoning.

SIDE EFFECTS/ADVERSE REACTIONS: (Most are dose-related and occur with serum levels >20 μg/ml.) Both oral and parenteral forms cause gastric irritation and CNS stimulation. Common GI side effects include nausea, vomiting, epigastric pain, anorexia, abdominal cramps, and hematemesis. CNS effects, which are often more severe in children, include headache, irritability, restlessness, nervousness, insomnia, dizziness, and convulsions. Severe toxic reactions are manifested by persistent vomiting, maniacal behavior, thirst, fever, tinnitus, delirium, convulsions, and vasomotor collapse. Cardiovascular effects include tachycardia, palpitation, and increased pulse rate. Rapid IV injection causes syncope, cardiac arrhythmias, sudden and profound hypotension, and cardiac arrest. Other side effects include tachypnea, hypersensitivity reactions (especially to the ethylenediamine component of aminophylline), dehydration, diuresis, and hyperglycemia.

DRUG INCOMPATIBILITIES: Incompatible drugs include epinephrine, norepinephrine, isoproterenol, penicillins, antihistamines, phenothiazines, narcotic analgesics, tetracyclines, erythromycins, methylprednisolone, hydrocortisone, insulin, and phenytoin.

DRUG INTERACTIONS: Concomitant use with *ephedrine*, other *sympathomimetic agents*, or other *xanthine derivatives* may cause additive cardiac and CNS toxicity. *Erythromycin, clindamycin*, and *lincomycin* may increase serum levels of theophylline by reducing its hepatic metabolism. *Propranolol* may antagonize the bronchodilator effect of theophylline. Theophylline increases the renal excretion of *lithium carbonate* thereby reducing lithium's effectiveness. *Cimetidine* may reduce the elimination rate of theophylline and thus increase the toxic effects of theophylline.

ANTIDOTE: Discontinue theophylline. Gastric lavage and emetic medication can be used to treat acute overdoses. Avoid use of sympathomimetics. Administer fluids, oxygen, and other supportive measures to overcome hypotension and dehydration and to correct acid-base imbalance. Control seizures with short-acting barbiturates or IV doses of diazepam. Treat hyperthermia with cooling blankets, etc. If respiratory depression occurs, maintain a patent airway and assist ventilation. Monitor serum levels of theophylline until they fall below 20 μg/ml.

Isoetharine (Bronkosol)

ADMINISTRATION

Available Forms: Solution (for oral inhalation), 5 mg/ml (0.5%) and 10 mg/ml (1.0%) in 2, 10, and 30 ml vials.

Dosage (Oral Inhalation)
For IPPB use: 0.5 ml of 0.5% solution, diluted in 2 ml NS and given q4h. Administer each dose over 15–30 minutes.

INDICATIONS: Isoetharine is a bronchodilator that provides symptomatic relief of acute bronchial asthma and the reversible bronchospasm associated with chronic bronchitis, emphysema, and general anesthesia. Administration of the solution via IPPB or oxygen aerosolization is the preferred method of treatment for emergency cases. Routine use of the metered oral inhaler (Bronkometer) is not recommended in children as it may cause overdependency and excessive use.

ACTIONS: Isoetharine primarily stimulates beta-2 adrenergic receptors in the bronchioles and blood vessels; it has little or no effect on alpha receptors. Therapeutic doses produce relaxation of bronchiolar smooth muscle and bronchodilation, thereby decreasing airway resistance. Peripheral blood vessels are also dilated. High doses, on the other hand, cause cardiac and CNS stimulation, resulting in the annoying side effects of tachycardia and nervousness. Tachycardia may also be a reflex response to the blood pressure changes produced by vasodilation. Bronchodilation occurs promptly after oral inhalation, peaks in 5–15 minutes, and usually lasts 1–4 hours.

CONTRAINDICATIONS: Hypersensitivity to isoetharine or any component of the solution.

PRECAUTIONS: Solutions for oral doses should be diluted at least 1:3 with NS or sterile water. Acidosis may reduce the effectiveness of isoetharine and should be identified and corrected before the drug is administered. Severe paradoxical bronchoconstriction may occur 1.5–3.0 hours after use; this is unresponsive to treatment until isoetharine is discontinued. Repeated or excessive use can cause tolerance (tachyphylaxis). Because of the possibility of cardiac arrhythmias or arrest, avoid giving isoetharine within 1 hour of injections of aqueous epinephrine or within 4 hours of SC injections of epinephrine suspension (Sus-phrine). Use cautiously in patients with hyperthyroidism, hypertension, cardiac asthma, or cardiac disease.

SIDE EFFECTS/ADVERSE REACTIONS: (Primarily dose-related) Side effects include increased heart rate, palpitations, arrhythmias, hypotension or hypertension, nausea, weakness, cough, and bronchial irritation or edema. CNS effects include tremor, nervousness, anxiety, excitement, dizziness, vertigo, and headache. Paradoxical bronchoconstriction ("lung-lock") may occur as a delayed reaction; acute bronchospasm may occur immediately and could be a hypersensitivity reaction to the active drug or to components of the metered inhaler.

DRUG INTERACTIONS: Concurrent use with *epinephrine* or other *sympathomimetics* causes additive CNS and cardiac stimulation (arrhythmias). *Beta-blockers* (propranolol) can antagonize the bronchodilating effects of isoetharine.

ANTIDOTE: Discontinue isoetharine. Treat adverse reactions symptomatically.

Metaproterenol (Alupent, Metaprel)

ADMINISTRATION

Available Forms: Tablets, 10, 20 mg; metered inhaler, approximately 0.65 mg/metered dose; inhalant solution, 5% for handbulb nebulizer or intermittent positive pressure breathing (IPPB); oral syrup, 2 mg/ml.

Diluent: Dilute doses for IPPB treatment with 2.5 ml NS.

Dosage (Oral): Varies according to the patient's age.
Children 6–9 years old (or <27 kg): 10 mg (or 5 ml syrup) tid–qid.
Children >9 years old (or >27 kg): 20 mg (or 10 ml syrup) tid–qid.

Dosage (Metered Inhaler): 1–2 inhalations taken at least 2 minutes apart and repeated not more than q3–4h.

Dosage (Solution for Inhalation): For IPPB, 0.2–0.3 ml diluted with 2.5 ml NS q6–8h.

INDICATIONS: Metaproterenol produces bronchodilation for symptomatic treatment of bronchial asthma and reversible bronchospasm as may occur in bronchitis and emphysema.

ACTIONS: Metaproterenol primarily stimulates beta-2 receptors and thereby produces relaxation of bronchial and vascular smooth muscle. It has a lesser effect on beta-1 cardiac receptors, except in high doses, which may produce cardiac and CNS stimulation. Metaproterenol significantly decreases airway resistance and improves pulmonary flow. It has a longer duration of action and less cardiac toxicity and is more effective orally than isoproterenol. Peak effects occur about 1 hour after oral administration or inhalation and last about 4 hours.

CONTRAINDICATIONS: Preexisting cardiac arrhythmias associated with tachycardia.

PRECAUTIONS: Excessive use of metaproterenol via an oral inhaler may lead to tolerance and paradoxical bronchoconstriction. If these occur, discontinue the medication to avoid cardiac toxicity. Use cautiously in patients with hypertension, hyperthyroidism, diabetes mellitus, cardiac disease, or hypersensitivity to sympathomimetics. Monitor vital signs as necessary. The use of metaproterenol in children under 6 years of age has not been established.

SIDE EFFECTS/ADVERSE REACTIONS: Primary side effects include tachycardia, palpitations, tremor, nervousness, headache, dizziness, nausea, vomiting, and a bad taste in the mouth.

DRUG INTERACTIONS: Use with other *sympathomimetic agents* may cause additive toxicities. *Propranolol* antagonizes the bronchodilating effects of metaproterenol.

ANTIDOTE: Discontinue metaproterenol. Treat symptoms of excessive beta-adrenergic stimulation appropriately (use cardioselective beta-blockers).

Terbutaline (Bricanyl, Brethine)

ADMINISTRATION

Available Forms: Injectable (SC), 1 mg/ml in 1 ml amps; tablets, 2.5, 5.0 mg.

Diluent: Give SC doses undiluted.

Dosage (Parenteral)
Children >12 years old: 3.5–5.0 µg/kg as a single dose SC. Usual dose is 2.5 mg.

Dosage (Oral)
Children >12 years old: 2.5 mg tid. Maximum daily dose is 7.5 mg.

INDICATIONS: Terbutaline is used as a bronchodilator in the symptomatic treatment of bronchial asthma and reversible bronchospasm as may occur in bronchitis and emphysema.

ACTIONS: This sympathomimetic agent stimulates primarily beta-2 receptors of the bronchi and peripheral vasculature. It has little effect on the beta-1 cardiac receptors except when used in high doses; then it may cause some cardiac and CNS stimulation. Terbutaline significantly decreases airway resistance, increases pulmonary flow rates, and produces some peripheral vasodilation. It has a longer duration of action than either ephedrine or metaproterenol. Following SC injection, onset of action is within 15 minutes, peak action occurs within 30–60 minutes, and duration lasts 2–4 hours. After oral use, improvement in pulmonary function occurs within 30 minutes to 2 hours and peak effects in 2–3 hours. Duration of action is 4–8 hours.

CONTRAINDICATIONS: Known hypersensitivity to sympathomimetic amines.

PRECAUTIONS: Use cautiously in patients with diabetes mellitus, hypertension, hyperthyroidism, or cardiac disease associated with arrhythmias. Pending further data on pediatric use, terbutaline is not recommended in children under 12 years of age. Monitor vital signs as necessary.

SIDE EFFECTS/ADVERSE REACTIONS: Common side effects include tachycardia, nervousness, tremor, palpitations, and dizziness. Also reported are nausea, vomiting, anxiety, and muscle cramps.

DRUG INTERACTIONS: Avoid use with other *sympathomimetics* because of possible additive cardiovascular side effects. *Propranolol* may antagonize the bronchodilator effects of terbutaline.

ANTIDOTE: Discontinue terbutaline. Treat excessive beta-adrenergic stimulation with beta-blockers.

VI
ANTIBIOTICS

The concept of antibiosis (i.e., the destruction of one organism by another) has, over the centuries, led to the development of modern day antibiotics. These extracts of living organisms (molds, etc.) or their synthetic equivalents are employed against infection caused by other organisms. The ideal antibiotic should exhibit selective toxicity against the infectious agent without harming the host. At concentrations tolerated by the host, it will interfere with some metabolic or synthetic process that exists only in the infecting organism and not in the cells of the host. The penicillins most closely illustrate this concept of selective toxicity: They are pathogen-specific and relatively nontoxic. However, other antibiotics, such as chloramphenicol, interfere with metabolic processes of the host cell and consequently can cause complications and some severe toxicities.

Over the years resistance has developed to many antimicrobial agents, especially among gram-negative bacteria, rendering some existing antibiotics ineffective. In addition, new disease entities (e.g., Legionnaire's disease and toxic shock syndrome) have been identified that have required the development of definitive therapy. Research continues in an effort to develop antimicrobials that are more pathogen-specific, harmless or less toxic to human cells, and to which pathogens are not resistant.

Antibiotics are usually classified according to their mechanism of action, spectrum of activity, and structural similarities. The general term for agents that kill microorganisms is microbicidal. This can be further refined to indicate the specific organism affected (e.g., fungicidal, amebicidal, rickettsicidal). Antibiotics effective against bacteria can be bactericidal (causing cellular death of the organism) or bacteriostatic (causing an arrest of bacterial growth and further multiplication). The following list is a common categorization; examples are given in parentheses.

1. Agents that inhibit cell wall synthesis or activate enzymes that disrupt cell walls (penicillins, cephalosporins, vancomycin)
2. Agents that act on cell membranes to alter permeability and function and thus allow leakage of cell contents (polymyxin B, colistin sulfate, amphotericin B, miconazole)
3. Agents that inhibit protein synthesis by altering the function of microbial ribosomes (tetracyclines, chloramphenicol, clindamycin, erythromycin)
4. Agents that bind to 30 S ribosomal subunits to cause a misreading of the messenger RNA code, resulting in abnormal polypeptides (aminoglycosides)
5. Agents that alter nucleic acid metabolism (rifampin)
6. Agents that block certain metabolic processes essential for microbial growth (sulfonamides, trimethoprim)

The selection of an appropriate antibiotic should be made on the basis of a positive, or at least a tentative, identification of the causative organism as determined by clinical evidence; a gram stain of blood, urine, or wound exudates; and culture and sensitivity (C&S) tests. However, because there is often a 24 to 48 hour delay in receiving C&S test results, the physician must often initiate therapy for serious infections immediately by selecting a broad-spectrum antibiotic that covers the most likely suspected pathogens. (To assist in the selection of the appropriate antimicrobial agent, an additional category, antimicrobial spectrum, has been included in the discussion of each antibiotic or class of antibiotics.)

Culture samples should be obtained prior to administration of the antibiotic, and laboratory studies should be completed as soon as possible to assure correct diagnosis and optimal therapy. The need for *in vitro* sensitivity tests depends on the clinical situation and the organism identified. For example, *Streptococcus pyogenes* (one of the group A beta-hemolytic streptococci) and pneumococci are generally always sensitive to penicillin G. However, *Staphylococcus, Proteus,* and *Pseudomonas* species, which often develop resistance, should be tested for susceptibility to certain antibiotics. For serious infections, therapy is usually initiated parenterally until control is achieved; then it may be practical to switch to oral therapy. Milder infections can usually be treated on an outpatient basis with oral doses of appropriate antibiotics.

Other factors to be considered in choosing an antibiotic or combination of antibiotics include the type (site) of infection (e.g., systemic, local, or meningeal), the patient's age, genetic factors, allergies, status of the host's immune or defense mechanisms, and other concurrent disease states. Renal or hepatic impairment can often produce alterations in the metabolism and excretion of certain antibiotics. Without appropriate dosage adjustments, these agents or their metabolites may accumulate to toxic levels in the serum. Where applicable, suggested adjustments in dosages for patients with reduced renal function are given under the heading of renal impairment as part of the information on administration. Every attempt should be made to select the most appropriate and least toxic agent possible.

17
Aminoglycosides

The aminoglycosides are potent and widely used antibiotics reserved primarily for treatment of serious infections caused by susceptible gram-negative bacteria. They share many pharmacological properties, have a similar antibacterial spectrum, and exhibit certain common toxic effects.

The following aminoglycosides are discussed in this chapter:

- **Amikacin**
- **Gentamicin**
- **Kanamycin**
- **Neomycin**
- **Streptomycin**
- **Tobramycin**

AMINOGLYCOSIDES (GENERAL STATEMENT)

RENAL IMPAIRMENT: Because the aminoglycosides are eliminated almost entirely unchanged by the kidney, administration to premature infants and neonates and other patients with renal insufficiency can cause drug accumulation resulting in nephrotoxicity and ototoxicity. Consequently, dosage adjustments are necessary under these conditions (particularly when the creatinine clearance is 70 ml/min or less). Appropriate changes in the amount and frequency of the dose to be administered should be determined by periodically measuring serum levels of the aminoglycoside. The narrow therapeutic range of these antibiotics has prompted the development and wide use of numerous dosing methods that include various formulas, computer-assisted kinetic programs, and nomograms. Most of these are based on serum creatinine values and use calculated rather than actual creatinine clearances as the indicator of the degree of renal function or impairment. (A simple formula for estimating glomerular filtration rate in children, derived from body length and serum creatinine, has been developed by Schwartz et al.[1]) Aminoglycoside dosing nomograms (such as those developed by Sarubbi and Hull[2] and Chan et al.[3]) have been used to predict loading and maintenance doses in adults; these are based on calculated creatinine clearances without lengthy pharmacokinetic calculations.

While these nomograms may be useful for initial dosage adjustments in renal impairment, they have not been extensively evaluated for accuracy and efficacy in the pediatric population. In fact, a study demonstrated that because of the wide variability in serum concentrations that occur after the administration of equal aminoglycoside doses to adults with similar renal function, use of these nomograms has resulted in prolonged subtherapeutic as well as toxic blood levels of antibiotic. The study concluded that the individualized method of calculating doses tailored to the patient's individual pharmacokinetics and clinical condition and supported by periodic measurements of serum concentrations allows for more accurate and appropriate dosage adjustments that ensure therapeutic concentrations throughout the prescribed dosing intervals and help prevent potentially toxic levels. In addition, using adult kinetic values for calculating doses in the newborn may not be valid because renal function, creatinine clearance, volumes of distribution, and serum half-lifes are so variable during the first month of life. Any kinetic calculations or nomograms used should only be considered as guidelines and should not replace measurements of aminoglycoside concentrations in the serum.

In neonates the glomerular filtration rate (GFR), a major indicator of renal function, is particularly low (about 30–50% of adult values) during the first week of life. Consequently, the half-lifes of the aminoglycosides, as well as other medications excreted primarily unchanged by the kidney, can be prolonged 2–4 times in premature and neonatal infants as compared with older infants and children. However, this difference is limited mainly to the first week of life. During this period of significant renal insufficiency, dosage adjustments are necessary. As the GFR reaches adult capacity (on the basis of body surface area) by about 3 weeks of age, aminoglycoside excretion subsequently increases and serum half-life decreases. The volume of distribution of the aminoglycosides in infants and young children is much larger, almost 2–3 times the adult volume. Aminoglycoside kinetics also appear to differ in older infants and children as compared with adults. Studies with tobramycin, for instance, suggest that because of the larger volume of distribution in children 2–8 years old and the more rapid renal clearance and shorter serum half-life in children more than 8 years old, both the peak and the trough serum levels of tobramycin are lower than those achieved by the same mg/kg dose in adults. The studies further recommend that to maintain therapeutic serum levels, slightly larger doses should be administered every 4 hours instead of the usual every 8 hours. Other pharmacokinetic research with amikacin has demonstrated that after the first 2 weeks of life, the renal clearance of this aminoglycoside is accelerated as the GFR progressively increases with advancing chronological age (regardless of birth weight). Again somewhat larger than conventional doses are suggested for infants older than 14 days in order to maintain serum levels within the therapeutic range.

ANTIMICROBIAL SPECTRUM: The aminoglycosides are effective against a variety of gram-negative organisms, most notably gram-negative rods such as *Pseudomonas* and the *Enterobacter-Klebsiella-Serratia* group. The usefulness of these antibiotics against gram-positive bacteria is limited mainly to penicillin-resistant staphylococci. Bacterial resistance and cross-resistance can be a problem with the individual antibiotics of this class. Resistance to streptomycin is common and develops rapidly. Complete cross-resistance can occur between neomycin and kanamycin, and there is partial cross-resistance between all the aminoglycosides. Once bacterial cross-resistance develops between any members of this class, it is usually complete. Culture and sensitivity tests should always be done to determine the susceptibility of a particular organism to the aminoglycoside being considered for treatment.

INDICATIONS: Indications vary among the different aminoglycosides. Gentamicin, kanamycin, tobramycin, and amikacin are used parenterally to treat septicemias (including neonatal) and pulmonary, soft tissue, and bone infections caused by sensitive gram-negative rods. Streptomycin is used synergistically with other antibiotics to treat TB and bacterial endocarditis. Neomycin and kanamycin are given orally to control diarrhea due to enteropathic *Escherichia coli* and to sterilize the bowel preoperatively. Neomycin and gentamicin are also used topically in creams and solutions to treat serious wound or burn infections and to irrigate peritoneal and pleural cavities.

ACTIONS: The aminoglycosides are rapidly bactericidal to susceptible organisms. They appear to inhibit the synthesis of bacterial cell protein by irreversibly binding to 30 S ribosomal subunits. These antibiotics are poorly absorbed when given by mouth but well absorbed when given parenterally. Topical application to denuded areas or irrigation of closed cavities or infected wounds may result in significant systemic absorption. The aminoglycosides are poorly protein-bound (<30%) and are widely distributed throughout the body tissues except for the central nervous system and the humors of the eye. They are excreted unchanged by the kidney and are concentrated in the urine.

CONTRAINDICATIONS: Cross-allergenicity between all the aminoglycosides has been demonstrated. In general, they are contraindicated in those patients who have shown previous hypersensitivity to any member of this antibiotic group (see individual drug listings for further contraindications).

PRECAUTIONS: The aminoglycosides are potentially nephrotoxic, ototoxic, and neurotoxic. The degree of nephrotoxicity and ototoxicity depends on the dosage and duration of therapy, the patient's renal function and degree of hydration, and the concurrent administration of any other potentially nephrotoxic or ototoxic medications (see drug interactions). Cautious use of these antibiotics in neonatal and premature infants is particularly important because their immature renal function can lead to reduced elimination rates and potentially toxic serum levels. Monitor blood levels of aminoglycosides closely; avoid prolonged excessively high peak and trough levels as they are both associated with an increased risk of toxicity. (For determination of these levels, blood is drawn 30–60 minutes *after* the dose to obtain the peak concentration and *just before* the next dose to obtain the trough value.) Monitor the patient's renal function and check the results of urinalysis frequently and maintain adequate hydration of the patient throughout therapy. Prolonged therapy (i.e., longer than 7–10 days) should be avoided.

SIDE EFFECTS/ADVERSE REACTIONS: Aminoglycoside nephrotoxicity (usually reversible) is most frequently manifested by transient proteinuria; renal casts; decreased specific gravity of the urine; and increasing BUN, serum creatinine, and nonprotein nitrogen (NPN). Occasionally, severe azotemia may develop. All of these antibiotics are potentially toxic to the eighth cranial nerve, causing ototoxicity or vestibular and cochlear damage. Some aminoglycosides (e.g., kanamycin and neomycin) impair auditory acuity more frequently than others (e.g., streptomycin and gentamicin), which affect primarily vestibular function. Patients developing cochlear damage may not experience the symptoms of vertigo that usually forewarn of toxic effects on the eighth nerve; in such patients partial or total deafness can result, especially after high doses. Aminoglycosides can also cause various degrees of neuromuscular blockage resulting in apnea, particularly when IV doses are given too rapidly or when general anesthetics or neuromuscular blockers (e.g., succinylcholine) are administered concomitantly. (Apnea can be counteracted by prompt IV administration of calcium or an anticholinesterase agent such as neostigmine.)

DRUG INCOMPATIBILITIES: See individual drug listings.

DRUG INTERACTIONS: Additive nephrotoxicity can occur when aminoglycosides are given concurrently with *cephalosporins,* potent *diuretics,* or the *polymyxins.* Use with potent diuretics such as *furosemide* and *ethacrynic acid* should be avoided as ototoxicity may be potentiated. Additive neurotoxicity may occur if these antibiotics are given with *general anesthetics* or *neuromuscular blockers.*

ANTIDOTE: See individual drug listings.

Amikacin (Amikin)

ADMINISTRATION

Available Forms: Injectable (IM, IV), 100, 500 mg in 2 ml vials, 500 mg in 2 ml syringes, 1 gm in 4 ml vials.

Diluent: Dilute doses for IV infusion in D5W or NS (up to 500 mg/100 ml).

Dosage (Parenteral): Varies according to the patient's age.
Neonates up to 1 month old: 10 mg/kg IM or IV to start, then 15 mg/kg/day IM or IV in divided doses (q12h). Note: Studies[4] have recommended higher doses for infants

older than 2 weeks because increasing GFR and renal clearance of amikacin after this age progressively lower serum levels produced by the currently recommended neonatal doses. Suggested dosages are as follows:

- Infants 1–15 days old: Loading dose of 7–12 mg/kg IM or IV, then 4–7 mg/kg IM or IV q8h
- Infants > 15–30 days old: Loading dose of 13–18 mg/kg IM or IV, then 7–10 mg/kg IM or IV q8h

Infants (>1 month old) and children: 15 mg/kg/day IM or IV in divided doses (q8–12h). Maximum is 1.5 gm/day.

Rate: Administer IV doses over 30–60 minutes, depending on the concentration and volume of diluent. Infusions for infants require 1–2 hours.

RENAL IMPAIRMENT: Dosage adjustments are necessary and should be guided by periodic determination of serum concentrations.

ANTIMICROBIAL SPECTRUM: Similar to that of gentamicin (the prototype aminoglycoside). Amikacin is active against some strains that are resistant to other aminoglycosides; these include *Proteus, Pseudomonas, Serratia*, and *Providencia*. However, there are strains of bacteria resistant to amikacin that may be susceptible to gentamicin or tobramycin.

INDICATIONS: Same as for gentamicin. In addition, amikacin is used to treat infections caused by gram-negative bacteria resistant to gentamicin, tobramycin, or kanamycin.

ACTIONS: See aminoglycosides (general statement). Therapeutic serum levels are 15–30 µg/ml.

CONTRAINDICATIONS: Hypersensitivity to amikacin or other aminoglycosides.

PRECAUTIONS: See gentamicin. Avoid trough levels of 5–10 µg/ml and prolonged peak serum levels of 30–35 µg/ml as both are associated with an increased risk of toxicity.

SIDE EFFECTS/ADVERSE REACTIONS: See gentamicin. Also, ototoxicity and nephrotoxicity have been reported clinically, but few vestibular disturbances have been noted.

DRUG INCOMPATIBILITIES: See gentamicin.

DRUG INTERACTIONS: See gentamicin.

ANTIDOTE: See gentamicin.

Gentamicin (Garamycin, others)

ADMINISTRATION

Available Forms: Injectable (IV, IM), 40 mg/ml in 1.5 ml (60 mg) and 2.0 ml (80 mg) vials and syringes; pediatric strength, 10 mg/ml in 2 ml vials; intrathecal, 2 mg/ml in 2 ml amps; topical ointment or cream, 0.1% (15 gm).

Diluent: Can be diluted in D5W or NS for IV use. Do not exceed a concentration of 1 mg/ml. Use sufficient volume so that the entire dose can be given over 30–60 minutes.

Dosage (Parenteral): Varies according to the patient's age.
Premature infants and neonates (up to 1 week old): 5 mg/kg/day given IM or IV in divided doses (q12h).
Infants and neonates (1–4 weeks old): 7.5 mg/kg/day given IM or IV in divided doses (q8h).
Children: 6.0–7.5 mg/kg/day given IM or IV in divided doses (q8h).

Rate: Administer IV doses over 30–60 minutes, depending on the concentration and volume of infusion. Infusions for infants require 1–2 hours.

RENAL IMPAIRMENT: Dosage adjustments are necessary and should be guided by periodic determination of serum concentrations.

ANTIMICROBIAL SPECTRUM: Gentamicin is effective against *E. coli, Proteus* (both indole-positive and indole-negative), *Pseudomonas aeruginosa,* organisms of the *Klebsiella-Enterobacter-Serratia* group, *Providencia, Citrobacter, Salmonella,* and *Shigella.* It has limited activity against gram-positive organisms but can be used to treat penicillin-resistant and methicillin-resistant staphylococci although other antibiotics are preferred. It can also be used in patients who are allergic to penicillin and cephalosporin. Penicillin and gentamicin have a synergistic effect against *Streptococcus faecalis* (enterococci).
Resistant organisms: Most streptococci (including *Streptococcus pneumoniae* and enterococci), anaerobes such as bacteroides and clostridia, rickettsiae, mycobacteria, fungi, yeasts, and viruses.

INDICATIONS: Systemic use of gentamicin should be restricted to serious infections caused by susceptible gram-negative organisms. It is effective in bacterial neonatal sepsis; septicemia; CNS infections (meningitis); urinary, respiratory, and GI tract infections (including peritonitis); skin, bone, and soft tissue infections; and burns. It has been used in conjunction with penicillin for treatment of group D streptococcal endocarditis. Gentamicin may be effective against serious staphylococcal infections when potentially less toxic drugs are contraindicated.

ACTIONS: See aminoglycosides (general statement). Therapeutic serum levels for most susceptible organisms are 4–10 μg/ml.

CONTRAINDICATIONS: Known hypersensitivity to gentamicin, previous toxic or hypersensitivity reactions to other aminoglycosides.

PRECAUTIONS: Gentamicin is potentially ototoxic, nephrotoxic, and neurotoxic, especially with higher doses or prolonged therapy (longer than 10 days) and in patients with renal impairment. To minimize toxicity, avoid trough concentrations greater than 2 µg/ml and peak serum levels greater than 12 µg/ml. Monitor renal, vestibular, and auditory functions (if the patient is old enough for serial audiograms). Keep the patient well hydrated during treatment; perform a urinalysis periodically for presence of casts, reduction in specific gravity, or proteinuria. Dosage adjustments are necessary for patients with renal impairment. Use cautiously in patients with neuromuscular disorders (e.g., myasthenia gravis, parkinsonism) as muscle weakness may worsen. Superinfections with nonsusceptible organisms may occur as well as cross-resistance with other aminoglycosides. Culture and sensitivity tests should be done to ensure bacterial susceptibility to gentamicin.

SIDE EFFECTS/ADVERSE REACTIONS: Nephrotoxicity in susceptible patients (see precautions) is manifested by proteinuria; urinary casts; rising BUN, NPN, and serum creatinine; or oliguria. Ototoxicity may occur; signs and symptoms are tinnitus, a roaring in the ears, and auditory impairment in the high-tone range. Vestibular damage (with dizziness, vertigo, ataxia, and a Meniere-like syndrome) usually occurs more often than auditory damage. CNS symptoms and neurotoxic effects include lethargy, confusion, depression, visual disturbances, muscle twitching, numbness, skin tingling, convulsions, pseudotumor cerebri, and acute organic brain syndrome. Intrathecal use can cause arachnoiditis or burning at the injection site. Other reported reactions include transient hepatomegaly; splenomegaly; elevated hepatic enzymes; and dermatological and hypersensitivity reactions including rash, urticaria, burning, laryngeal edema, fever, and anaphylactoid reactions. Various blood dyscrasias and purpura may occur as well as GI upset with nausea, vomiting, increased salivation, anorexia, and stomatitis. Respiratory depression, apnea, pulmonary fibrosis, hypotension, or hypertension may occur.

DRUG INCOMPATIBILITIES: Gentamicin is incompatible with many medications, including penicillins (notably carbenicillin and ticarcillin) and cephalosporins if directly admixed. Do not admix with any other medications.

DRUG INTERACTIONS: Gentamicin causes increased nephrotoxicity when used with *cephalosporins,* other *aminoglycosides, polymyxins, ethacrynic acid,* or *furosemide;* increased ototoxicity when used with *potent diuretics* and other *aminoglycosides;* and increased neuromuscular blockade when used with other *aminoglycosides, anesthetics,* or other *neuromuscular blockers.* Gentamicin is synergistic with *carbenicillin* and *ticarcillin* against *P. aeruginosa,* but the combination *in vitro* in the same IV solution can decrease the serum half-life of gentamicin (use separate IV lines). Synergism with *penicillin G* against enterococci also exists.

ANTIDOTE: Discontinue gentamicin. Supply assisted ventilation and give neostigmine for apnea. Peritoneal dialysis or hemodialysis may be helpful in eliminating the antibiotic from the bloodstream. Forced fluid diuresis to maintain the urine output at 15–20 ml/kg/hr has been successful in accelerating gentamicin excretion and subsequently lowering plasma levels.

Kanamycin (Kantrex, Klebcil)

ADMINISTRATION

Available Forms: Injectable (IM, IV), 500 mg/2 ml and 1 gm/3 ml in vials, 500 mg/2 ml in syringes; pediatric strength, 75 mg/2 ml in vials; capsules, 500 mg.

Diluent: For IV use dilute doses in D5W or NS to a sufficient volume so that the entire dose is administered over 30–60 minutes. The concentration should not exceed 2.5 mg/ml.

Dosage (Parenteral): Varies according to the patient's age.
Infants (1 week old) and children: 15–20 mg/kg/day given IM (preferred) or slow IV in divided doses (q8–12h). Maximum is 1.5 gm/day.
Neonates up to 1 week old, <2 kg: 15 mg/kg/day IM or IV in divided doses (q12h).
Neonates up to 1 week old, >2 kg: Up to 20 mg/kg/day IM or IV in divided doses (q12h).

Dosage (Oral)
For suppression of intestinal bacteria: 50 mg/kg/day (1.5 gm/m^2/day) in divided doses (q4–6h) for 5–7 days.

Rate: Give IV doses slowly over 30–60 minutes, depending on the concentration and volume of infusion.

RENAL IMPAIRMENT: Dosage adjustments are necessary when used parenterally. Adjustments should be guided by periodic determination of serum concentrations.

ANTIMICROBIAL SPECTRUM: Similar to other aminoglycosides. Susceptible organisms include *E. coli*, most strains of *Enterobacter, Klebsiella, Serratia, Proteus, Neisseria, Salmonella, Mycobacterium, Vibrio*, and *Staphylococcus*.
Resistant organisms: *Pseudomonas*, anaerobes (e.g., bacteroides, clostridia), streptococci (including enterococci and *S. pneumoniae*), rickettsiae, fungi, viruses, and yeasts. Some strains of *E. coli, Mycobacterium*, and *Staphylococcus* develop resistance to kanamycin rapidly and cross-resistance to other aminoglycosides. Cross-resistance with neomycin is complete.

INDICATIONS: Kanamycin is used parenterally to treat neonatal coliform infections (notably those due to *E. coli*) and orally for treatment of diarrhea due to enteropathogenic *E. coli*. It can also be used orally for the suppression of intestinal flora prior to abdominal surgery. If used as an intraperitoneal irrigation for peritonitis or during bowel surgery, instillation should be postponed until the effects of anesthesia and muscle-relaxing medications have dissipated.

ACTIONS: See aminoglycosides (general statement). Therapeutic serum levels for most susceptible pathogens are 15–30 µg/ml.

CONTRAINDICATIONS: Hypersensitivity to kanamycin or to other aminoglycosides, intestinal obstruction (with oral form), long-term parenteral use of kanamycin.

PRECAUTIONS: Parenteral use carries the same precautions as for gentamicin. Avoid trough levels of 5–10 μg/ml and peak serum levels of 35 μg/ml as they are associated with potential toxicity. Prolonged use of oral doses may induce a malabsorption syndrome characterized by increased fecal fat and decreased absorption of lipids, protein, iron, electrolytes, vitamin K, vitamin B_{12}, and other substances; it may also interfere with the absorption of certain medications. Although absorption of oral doses of kanamycin is negligible, the presence of ulcerated or denuded areas may increase intestinal absorption and potential toxicity. Many strains of coliform bacteria have developed resistance to kanamycin, and C&S tests should be done. Alternative antibiotics such as gentamicin or tobramycin may be indicated for infections caused by these strains.

SIDE EFFECTS/ADVERSE REACTIONS: See gentamicin. Oral use may cause nausea, vomiting, diarrhea, and malabsorption syndrome.

DRUG INCOMPATIBILITIES: See gentamicin.

DRUG INTERACTIONS: See gentamicin. Also, kanamycin may impair GI absorption of *digitalis* and *vitamin K*.

ANTIDOTE: See gentamicin.

Neomycin (Mycifradin, Neomycin)

ADMINISTRATION

Available Forms: Tablets, 500 mg; oral solution, 125 mg/5 ml; irrigation solution, 40 mg/ml with 200,000 units polymyxin B per milliliter in 1 ml amps (Neosporin GU Irrigant); topical, various ophthalmic, otic, and dermatological preparations.

Dosage (Oral): Varies according to the condition.
For diarrhea due to enteropathic *E. coli*: 50 mg/kg/day given in divided doses (q6h) for 3 days.
For preoperative bowel sterilization: 90 mg/kg/day given in divided doses (q4h) for 3 days.
For hepatic coma: 2.5–7.0 gm/m²/day in divided doses for 5–6 days. Can also be given as 1% retention enema if the patient is unable to take oral medication.

RENAL IMPAIRMENT: Dosage adjustments are necessary. See kanamycin.

ANTIMICROBIAL SPECTRUM: Same as for kanamycin.

INDICATIONS: Neomycin is the most toxic of the aminoglycosides and therefore has only limited clinical usefulness. Because it is poorly absorbed from the GI tract, neomycin has been used effectively in the treatment of epidemic diarrhea of the newborn caused by susceptible strains of enteropathogenic *E. coli*. Neomycin is also given orally to eliminate most pathogenic bacteria from the bowel prior to intestinal surgery and to decrease enteric ammonia-producing organisms during the treatment of hepatic coma. It is also combined with polymyxin B for use as a bladder irrigant.

ACTIONS: See aminoglycosides (general statement).

CONTRAINDICATIONS: Hypersensitivity to neomycin, serious toxic reactions to any of the other aminoglycosides, intestinal obstruction.

PRECAUTIONS: See kanamycin. Neomycin is highly nephrotoxic and ototoxic, causing irreversible cochlear damage and deafness. Loss of hearing may first appear several weeks after neomycin has been discontinued and may progress to complete deafness. In newborn and premature infants, avoid administering excessively large oral doses for prolonged periods. Approximately 10% of an administered dose may be absorbed, and in patients with decreased renal function enough neomycin may accumulate to produce toxic effects. Monitor renal function (and auditory, if feasible) prior to and during therapy.

SIDE EFFECTS/ADVERSE REACTIONS: See kanamycin. Nausea, vomiting, diarrhea, and a malabsorption syndrome are the most common adverse reactions. Neomycin is extremely ototoxic, nephrotoxic, and neurotoxic. Contact dermatitis may occur after topical use.

DRUG INTERACTIONS: See gentamicin and kanamycin.

ANTIDOTE: See gentamicin.

Streptomycin

ADMINISTRATION

Available Forms: Injectable (IM), 500 mg and 1 gm per milliliter in syringes; 1, 5 gm vials (powder).

Diluent: Reconstitute with sterile water or NS for injection.

Dosage (Parenteral): Varies according to use.
For general use:

- Older children: 40 mg/kg/day IM in divided doses (q12h) for up to 10 days. Maximum is 2 gm/day.
- Premature and full-term newborns: 20–30 mg/kg/day IM in divided doses (q12h) for up to 10 days.

For tuberculosis: 20 mg/kg/day as a single dose IM with other antitubercular agents.
For tubercular meningitis: 1 mg/kg/day (diluted to 5 mg/ml) given intrathecally.

RENAL IMPAIRMENT: Dosage adjustments are necessary.

- Mild impairment (CCr 50–80 ml/min): Give dose q24h.
- Moderate impairment (CCr 10–50 ml/min): Give dose q24–72h.
- Severe impairment (CCr <10 ml/min): Give dose q72–96h.

ANTIMICROBIAL SPECTRUM: Streptomycin is bactericidal for a variety of gram-positive, gram-negative, and acid-fast organisms. The most susceptible are *Brucella, Mycobacterium, Francisella, Shigella,* and *Pasteurella (Yersinia).*
Resistant organisms: Bacteroides, clostridia, rickettsiae, yeasts, viruses, and fungi. Many organisms develop resistance to streptomycin rapidly, and cross-resistance may develop to other aminoglycosides.

INDICATIONS: Streptomycin is used primarily for the treatment of tuberculosis in conjunction with other antitubercular agents. It is often combined with penicillin to treat endocarditis due to enterococci and *Streptococcus viridans.* It is also the drug of choice in tularemia. Streptomycin is no longer preferred for treatment of plague because it virtually always precipitates a Herxheimer-like reaction that can be fatal.

ACTIONS: See aminoglycosides (general statement). Peak serum concentrations should not exceed 25–30 μg/ml.

CONTRAINDICATIONS: Hypersensitivity to streptomycin, previous hypersensitivity reactions to other aminoglycosides.

PRECAUTIONS: As for gentamicin. Injections given IM may cause pain and sterile abscesses at the injection site. To delay development of resistance during prolonged therapy (e.g., for TB or endocarditis), streptomycin should be combined with other antibiotics.

SIDE EFFECTS/ADVERSE REACTIONS: In general, adverse reactions resemble those associated with other aminoglycosides. Streptomycin has greater toxic effects on the vestibular rather than the auditory function of the eighth cranial nerve, although deafness may occur. Dizziness is usually the first warning sign of vestibular toxicity, and tinnitus may be a sign of auditory damage. Optic and peripheral neuritis may occur as well as nephrotoxicity and blood dyscrasias. Hypersensitivity with skin eruptions is the more common adverse reaction. Greatly excessive doses in infants can cause cardiovascular collapse.

DRUG INTERACTIONS: See gentamicin.

ANTIDOTE: See gentamicin.

Tobramycin (Nebcin)

ADMINISTRATION

Available Forms: Injectable (IM, IV), 40 mg/ml in 2 ml vials and syringes; pediatric strength, 10 mg/ml in 2 ml vials; ophthalmic solution, 0.3% (Tobrex).

Diluent: For IV use dilute in D5W or NS in a sufficient volume so that the entire dose is administered over 30–60 minutes. Do not exceed a concentration of 1 mg/ml if possible.

Dosage (Parenteral): Varies according to the patient's age.
Premature infants and neonates (up to 1 week old): 4 mg/kg/day IM or IV in divided doses (q12h).
Infants (>1 month old) and children: 3–5 mg/kg/day IM or IV in divided doses (q6–8h). Up to 7.5 mg/kg/day can be given for life-threatening infections.
(Note: Kinetic studies by Hoecker et al have suggested that because of the rapid renal clearance and larger volume of distribution of tobramycin in children 2–18 years old, a dose of 8–10 mg/kg/day (240–300 mg/m^2/day) in divided doses (q4h) should be given to achieve and maintain therapeutic serum concentrations in this age group.[5])

Rate: Administer IV doses over 30–60 minutes, depending on the concentration and volume of the infusion. Infusions for infants require 1–2 hours.

RENAL IMPAIRMENT: Dosage adjustments are necessary and should be guided by periodic determination of serum concentrations.

ANTIMICROBIAL SPECTRUM: Similar to that of gentamicin, but tobramycin may have greater activity against *P. aeruginosa* and some strains of *Proteus* (e.g., *Proteus vulgaris*).

INDICATIONS: Same as for gentamicin. Tobramycin is particularly useful for infections due to gentamicin-resistant strains of *Pseudomonas* or *Proteus*. Culture and sensitivity tests should be done to ensure susceptibility of the organism in question.

ACTIONS: See aminoglycosides (general statement). Therapeutic serum levels for most susceptible organisms are 4–10 μg/ml.

CONTRAINDICATIONS: Known hypersensitivity to tobramycin, previous hypersensitivity or toxic reactions to any other aminoglycoside.

PRECAUTIONS: See gentamicin. Avoid trough levels greater than 2 μg/ml and prolonged peak serum levels greater than 12 μg/ml as they are associated with potential nephrotoxicity and ototoxicity.

SIDE EFFECTS/ADVERSE REACTIONS: See gentamicin. Both auditory and vestibular toxicity can occur, but the vestibular portion is more susceptible to damage. Potential nephrotoxicity and neurotoxicity are the same as for gentamicin.

DRUG INCOMPATIBILITIES: See gentamicin.

DRUG INTERACTIONS: See gentamicin.

ANTIDOTE: See gentamicin.

NOTES

1. Schwartz GJ, Haycock MB, Edelman CM, et al: A simple estimate of glomerular filtration rate in children derived from body length and plasma creatinine. *Pediatrics* 1976;58(2):259–263.
2. Sarubbi FA, Hull JH: Amikacin serum concentrations: Predictions of levels and dosage guidelines. *Ann Intern Med* 1978;89:612–618.
3. Chan RA, Benner EJ, Hoeprich RD: Gentamicin therapy in renal failure: A nomogram for dosage. *Ann Intern Med* 1978;76:775–778.
4. Prober CG, Yeager AS, Arvin AM: Effect of chronologic age on the serum concentrations of amikacin in the sick term and premature infants. *J Pediatr* 1981;98(4):636–640.
5. Hoecker JL, Pickering LK, Swaney J, et al: Clinical pharmacology of tobramycin in children. *J Infect Dis* 1978;137(5):592–596.

18
Cephalosporins

The cephalosporins are semisynthetic antibacterial agents that are closely related structurally and pharmacologically to the penicillins. Over the years, a number of cephalosporin derivatives have been synthesized, and many more are under investigation for release. They differ primarily in their extended gram-negative spectrum and in their higher cost. Traditionally, this class of antibiotics has been divided into three categories: first-generation, second-generation, and third-generation cephalosporins.

CEPHALOSPORINS (GENERAL STATEMENT)

RENAL IMPAIRMENT: Because most cephalosporins are excreted in their unchanged forms by the kidney, renal insufficiency can cause drug accumulation. Dosage adjustments are usually recommended when creatinine clearances fall below 50 ml/min (moderate renal impairment). The dosages and dosing intervals for patients with renal insufficiency vary among the different cephalosporins; see the individual derivatives for appropriate adjustments.

ANTIMICROBIAL SPECTRUM: The cephalosporins are effective against a variety of gram-positive and gram-negative organisms, but the degree of activity varies among the different derivatives. For instance, the first-generation cephalosporins exhibit greater activity against gram-positive cocci than the other generations, but the second-generation and third-generation agents are considerably more effective against gram-negative enteric bacteria. The differences in the chemical structures of the cephalosporins account for this group's resistance to the enzyme penicillinase, which is produced by certain strains of staphylococci and which is responsible for the degradation of the penicillin compounds. However, some gram-negative bacteria (e.g., certain strains of *Enterobacter* and *Klebsiella*) produce an enzyme (cephalosporinase) that can inactivate cephalosporins. Some bacterial cross-resistance exists between these antibiotics and methicillin with regard to staphylococci. Methicillin-resistant staphylococci are usually resistant to the cephalosporins also. It must be remembered that bacterial sensitivity patterns vary between hospitals and geographical locations. Minimum inhibitory concentrations (MICs) listed by the manufacturer are based on achievable serum concentrations in certain tissues and may not be applicable to other sites of infection where the cephalosporins penetrate poorly (as in the CSF). Also, *in vitro* sensitivity does not necessarily imply that the same organism will be sensitive to that particular antibiotic *in vivo*. Culture and sensitivity tests are still the mainstay of successful antibiotic therapy.

INDICATIONS: Cephalosporins are effective treatment for a variety of conditions caused by susceptible gram-positive and gram-negative organisms: respiratory, urinary, biliary tract, skin, soft tissue, genital, and bone and joint infections; septicemias; and endocarditis. They are also used for preoperative prophylaxis. They are particularly useful for treatment of gram-negative bacillary infections in patients with reduced renal function, especially if the causative organisms are resistant to the aminoglycosides. Culture and sensitivity tests should be done, however, to determine cephalosporin effectiveness against gram-negative bacteria.

Although these antibiotics are useful alternatives to the penicillins, penicillin G is still the antibiotic of choice for nonallergic individuals who have infections caused by susceptible pneumococci, group A beta-hemolytic streptococci, enterococci, and nonpenicillinase-producing staphylococci. It is highly effective in most instances and far less expensive. Ampicillin remains the antibiotic of choice for infections caused by sensitive strains of *E. coli, Hemophilus influenzae, Salmonella,* and *Shigella* in those patients not allergic to it.

ACTIONS: The cephalosporins, like the penicillins, are bactericidal by virtue of their inhibition of cell wall synthesis. Certain cephalosporins are not significantly absorbed from the GI tract, and so only parenteral forms of these derivatives are available. The cephalosporin preparations specifically for oral use are well absorbed, are stable in the presence of gastric acid, and produce high blood levels of the drug. Therapeutic MICs for most susceptible bacteria are usually 1–32 µg/ml, levels achievable with recommended doses. These antibiotics are widely distributed in most body tissues and fluids. Because they do not reach significant concentrations in the cerebrospinal fluid, they are not (with the possible exception of moxalactam) recommended for treatment of meningitis. Cephalosporins cross the placenta and may be excreted in breast milk. Some derivatives (cephalothin, cefoperazone, and cephapirin) are partially metabolized in the liver, but the majority are excreted unchanged by the kidney.

CONTRAINDICATIONS: Hypersensitivity to any cephalosporin, cross-hypersensitivity to penicillins and cephalosporins (incidence is <10%).

PRECAUTIONS: Cephalosporins show a cross-allergenicity with penicillin, so use cautiously in patients who are hypersensitive to the penicillins or who have multiple allergies. These broad-spectrum antibiotics can cause superinfections with nonsusceptible organisms such as yeasts and enterococci. Prolonged use or highly concentrated solutions of parenteral doses have been associated with thrombophlebitis. (For other specific precautions, see the individual agents.)

SIDE EFFECTS/ADVERSE REACTIONS: The cephalosporins are relatively nontoxic. Orally administered forms can produce gastric upset. All forms can cause superinfections, alterations in liver enzymes, and hypersensitivity reactions. Some cephalosporins have been associated with pseudomembranous colitis caused by a toxin-producing *Clostridium*. Mild cases may respond to discontinuance of the cephalosporin, but moderate or severe cases may require treatment with oral doses of vancomycin and replacement of fluids and electrolytes. Bleeding disorders characterized by prolonged prothrombin times have been associated with some of the third-generation derivatives. (For more specific adverse reactions, see the individual drug listings.)

FIRST-GENERATION CEPHALOSPORINS (GENERAL STATEMENT)

INJECTABLE

- **Cefazolin (Ancef, Kefzol)**
- **Cephalothin (Keflin)**
- **Cephapirin (Cefadyl)**
- **Cephradine (Velosef)**

ORAL

- **Cefadroxil (Duricef, Ultracef)**
- **Cephalexin (Keflex)**
- **Cephradine (Velosef, Anspor)**

RENAL IMPAIRMENT: See the individual drug listings.

ANTIMICROBIAL SPECTRUM: First-generation cephalosporins are very active against gram-positive cocci such as staphylococci (including penicillinase producers) and nonenterococcal streptococci (e.g., group A, group B, *S. viridans*, and *S. pneumoniae*). Susceptible gram-negative organisms include *E. coli*, *Proteus mirabilis*, *H. influenzae*, and *Klebsiella*. Cefazolin is also active against some strains of *Enterobacter* and enterococci in urinary tract infections only. (First-generation derivatives are not as active as the aminoglycosides against these gram-negative enteric bacteria and susceptibility is often unpredictable, so C&S tests are recommended.)
Resistant organisms: Indole-positive *Proteus*, *Pseudomonas*, *Serratia*, *Mima-Herellea*, enterococci (*S. faecalis*), and methicillin-resistant staphylococci. First-generation cephalosporins are clinically ineffective against *Neisseria gonorrhoeae* and *Neisseria meningitidis*, fungi, yeasts, viruses, amoebas, and acid-fast bacilli.

INDICATIONS: The major use in pediatric therapy is for penicillin-allergic patients with gram-positive coccal infections (e.g., streptococcal pharyngitis, staphylococcal and streptococcal skin infections, sinusitis, otitis). Because these agents reach high concentrations in the urine, they are effective for treatment of urinary tract infections. Studies have shown that the orally administered cephalosporins produce predictably high blood levels comparable to those achieved after parenteral administration. Consequently, these oral derivatives have been used effectively for treatment of serious and chronic staphylococcal infections such as osteomyelitis and pyarthrosis. First-generation cephalosporins are not clinically useful for gonorrhea, syphilis, or meningitis. (See also cephalosporins, general statement.)

ACTIONS: See cephalosporins (general statement).

CONTRAINDICATIONS: Known hypersensitivity to cephalosporins.

PRECAUTIONS: Cross-hypersensitivity with penicillins is possible, so use cautiously in patients who are sensitive to penicillin. Therapy of beta-hemolytic streptococcal infections should continue for at least 10 days. Impaired renal function (severe oliguria, creatinine clearance rates less than 50 ml/min, or serum creatinine greater than 5 mg/100 ml) requires dosage adjustments. Prolonged use may result in overgrowth of nonsusceptible organisms such as yeasts and enterococci. IV doses of more than 6 gm/day for longer than 3 days have been associated with thrombophlebitis; change or alternate infusion sites as necessary; 10–25 mg hydrocortisone can be added to IV infusions to reduce inflammation. A false-positive reaction for urinary glucose may result with Clinitest tablets (copper-reduction method) but *not* with Tes-Tape, Clinistix, or Keto-diastix (glucose-oxidase method). Direct Coombs' tests may give false-positive results. Pseudomembranous colitis has been associated with cephalosporin use, so consider this diagnosis when diarrhea develops. Cephalosporins may accumulate or have a prolonged half-life in premature infants and neonates. Doses given IM may be extremely painful (especially cephalothin).

SIDE EFFECTS/ADVERSE REACTIONS: Oral doses commonly cause gastric upset, nausea, vomiting, diarrhea, glossitis, abdominal pain, and heartburn. Skin and hypersensitivity reactions include pruritus and a serum-sickness-like illness consisting of mild urticaria, drug fever, and joint pain. Anaphylactoid reactions have occurred. Superinfections with yeasts and pseudomembranous colitis may occur with prolonged use. Elevations in renal and liver enzymes, blood dyscrasias (eosinophilia, neutropenia, leukopenia, thrombocytopenia) have been reported. Local reactions include pain at the injection site and thrombophlebitis.

DRUG INCOMPATIBILITIES: Do not mix with aminophylline, aminoglycosides, tetracyclines, penicillins, erythromycin, levarterenol, or methylprednisolone (precipitates occur within 1 hour).

DRUG INTERACTIONS: *Probenecid* decreases renal excretion of cephalosporins thereby producing higher and more prolonged blood levels of these antibiotics. Concomitant use of *aminoglycosides* and *parenteral cephalosporins* may cause additive nephrotoxicity.

ANTIDOTE: Discontinue the medication. Treat hypersensitivity reactions with supportive and appropriate therapy.

Cefadroxil (Duricef, Ultracef)

ADMINISTRATION

Available Forms: Capsules, 500 mg; tablets, 1 gm (Duricef only); oral suspension, 125, 250, and 500 mg per 5 ml (powder for reconstitution).

Dosage (Oral)
Infants and children: 30 mg/kg/day in divided doses (q12h).

RENAL IMPAIRMENT: Dosage adjustments are necessary.

- Mild to moderate impairment (CCr 25–50 ml/min): Normal daily dose given in 2 divided doses (q12h)
- Moderate impairment (CCr 10–25 ml/min): Normal daily dose given q24h
- Severe impairment (CCr <10 ml/min): Normal daily dose given q36h

ANTIMICROBIAL SPECTRUM: See first-generation cephalosporins (general statement).

INDICATIONS: See first-generation cephalosporins (general statement).

ACTIONS: See cephalosporins (general statement).

CONTRAINDICATIONS: See first-generation cephalosporins (general statement).

PRECAUTIONS: See first-generation cephalosporins (general statement).

SIDE EFFECTS/ADVERSE REACTIONS: See first-generation cephalosporins (general statement).

DRUG INCOMPATIBILITIES: None.

DRUG INTERACTIONS: See first-generation cephalosporins (general statement).

ANTIDOTE: See first-generation cephalosporins (general statement).

Cefazolin (Ancef, Kefzol)

ADMINISTRATION

Available Forms: Injectable (IV, IM), 250, 500 mg, 1 gm vials (powder); sodium content is 2 mEq/gm.

Diluent: For IM use reconstitute with sterile water or NS. For IV use doses can be further diluted in D5W or NS (500 mg to 1 gm in 50–100 ml for intermittent IV infusions). Also stable in many multiple electrolyte solutions.

Dosage (Parenteral): Varies according to the patient's age and condition.
Newborns up to 4 weeks old: 30–40 mg/kg/day IV (preferred) or IM in divided doses (q12h).
Infants (1 month or older) and children:

- Mild to moderate infections: 25–50 mg/kg/day IM or IV in divided doses (q6–8h)
- For severe infections: Up to 100 mg/kg/day IM or IV in divided doses (q6–8h)

Rate: Administer intermittent IV infusions over 15–30 minutes (preferred). Give direct IV push doses (500 mg to 1 gm) over 3–5 minutes.

RENAL IMPAIRMENT: Dosage adjustments are necessary.

- Mild to moderate impairment (CCr 40–70 ml/min): 60% of normal daily dose given in divided doses (q12h)
- Moderate impairment (CCr 20–40 ml/min): 25% of normal daily dose given in divided doses (q12h)
- Severe impairment (CCr 5–20 ml/min): 10% of normal daily dose q24h

ANTIMICROBIAL SPECTRUM: See first-generation cephalosporins (general statement).

INDICATIONS: See first-generation cephalosporins (general statement).

ACTIONS: See cephalosporins (general statement).

CONTRAINDICATIONS: See first-generation cephalosporins (general statement).

PRECAUTIONS: See first-generation cephalosporins (general statement).

SIDE EFFECTS/ADVERSE REACTIONS: See first-generation cephalosporins (general statement).

DRUG INCOMPATIBILITIES: See first-generation cephalosporins (general statement).

DRUG INTERACTIONS: See first-generation cephalosporins (general statement).

ANTIDOTE: See first-generation cephalosporins (general statement).

Cephalexin (Keflex)

ADMINISTRATION

Available Forms: Capsules, 250, 500 mg; tablets 1 gm; oral suspension, 125 and 250 mg per 5 ml (powder for reconstitution); pediatric drops, 100 mg/ml (powder for reconstitution).

Dosage (Oral): Varies according to use.
Infants (1 month or older) and children:

- Mild to moderate infections: 25–50 mg/kg/day in divided doses (q6h)
- Otitis media and more severe infections: 75–100 mg/kg/day in divided doses (q6h)

RENAL IMPAIRMENT: Dosage adjustments are necessary.

- Mild impairment (CCr 50–80 ml/min): Normal daily dose given in divided doses (q6h)
- Moderate impairment (CCr 10–50 ml/min): Normal daily dose given in divided doses (q8–12h)
- Severe impairment (CCr <10 ml/min): Normal daily dose q24–48h

ANTIMICROBIAL SPECTRUM: See first-generation cephalosporins (general statement).

INDICATIONS: See first-generation cephalosporins (general statement).

ACTIONS: See cephalosporins (general statement).

CONTRAINDICATIONS: See first-generation cephalosporins (general statement).

PRECAUTIONS: See first-generation cephalosporins (general statement).

SIDE EFFECTS/ADVERSE REACTIONS: See first-generation cephalosporins (general statement).

DRUG INCOMPATIBILITIES: None.

DRUG INTERACTIONS: See first-generation cephalosporins (general statement).

ANTIDOTE: See first-generation cephalosporins (general statement).

Cephalothin (Keflin)

ADMINISTRATION

Available Forms: Injectable (IM, IV), 1, 2, 4 gm vials (powder); sodium content is 2.74 mEq/gm (Neutral).

Diluent: For IM use reconstitute with sterile water or NS. For IV use doses can be further diluted in D5W or NS (25–50 ml). Also stable in multiple electrolyte solutions.

Dosage (Parenteral): Varies according to the patient's age.
Newborns (1–4 weeks old): 40–60 mg/kg/day IV (preferred) or IM in divided doses (q8–12h).
Infants (1 month or older) and children: 80–160 mg/kg/day IV (preferred) or IM in divided doses (q8–12h).

Rate: Administer intermittent IV infusions over 15–30 minutes (preferred). Give direct IV push doses at 1 gm/10 ml over 3–5 minutes.

RENAL IMPAIRMENT: Dosage adjustments are necessary.

- Mild to moderate impairment (CCr 25–50 ml/min): 75% of normal daily dose given in divided doses (q6h)
- Moderate impairment (CCr 10–25 ml/min): 50% of normal daily dose given in divided doses (q6h)
- Severe impairment (CCr <10 ml/min): 25% of normal daily dose given in divided doses (q8h)

ANTIMICROBIAL SPECTRUM: See first-generation cephalosporins (general statement).

INDICATIONS: See first-generation cephalosporins (general statement).

ACTIONS: See cephalosporins (general statement).

CONTRAINDICATIONS: See first-generation cephalosporins (general statement).

PRECAUTIONS: See first-generation cephalosporins (general statement).

SIDE EFFECTS/ADVERSE REACTIONS: See first-generation cephalosporins (general statement).

DRUG INCOMPATIBILITIES: See first-generation cephalosporins (general statement).

DRUG INTERACTIONS: See first-generation cephalosporins (general statement).

ANTIDOTE: See first-generation cephalosporins (general statement).

Cephapirin (Cefadyl)

ADMINISTRATION

Available Forms: Injectable (IM, IV), 500 mg, 1, 2 gm vials (powder); sodium content is 2.36 mEq/gm.

Diluent: As for cephalothin.

Dosage (Parenteral)
Infants (3 months or older) and children: 40–80 mg/kg/day IM or IV in divided doses (q6h).

Rate: Administer intermittent IV infusions over 15–30 minutes (preferred). Give direct IV push doses at 1 gm/10 ml over 3–5 minutes.

RENAL IMPAIRMENT: Manufacturer's recommendation for patients (adults) with severe renal impairment (CCr <10 ml/min) is 15–30 mg/kg/day in divided doses (q12h).

ANTIMICROBIAL SPECTRUM: See first-generation cephalosporins (general statement).

INDICATIONS: See first-generation cephalosporins (general statement).

ACTIONS: See cephalosporins (general statement).

CONTRAINDICATIONS: See first-generation cephalosporins (general statement).

PRECAUTIONS: See first-generation cephalosporins (general statement).

SIDE EFFECTS/ADVERSE REACTIONS: See first-generation cephalosporins (general statement).

DRUG INCOMPATIBILITIES: See first-generation cephalosporins (general statement).

DRUG INTERACTIONS: See first-generation cephalosporins (general statement).

ANTIDOTE: See first-generation cephalosporins (general statement).

Cephradine (Velosef, Anspor)

ADMINISTRATION

Available Forms: Injectable (IM, IV) 250, 500 mg, 1 gm in vials, 2, 4 gm in infusion bottles (powder, Velosef), sodium content is 6 mEq/gm (vials only); tablets, 1 gm (Velosef); capsules, 250, 500 mg; oral suspension, 125 and 250 mg per 5 ml (powder for reconstitution).

Diluent: See cephalothin. Do not use LR.

Dosage (Parenteral)
Infants (1 month or older) and children: 50–100 mg/kg/day IM or IV in divided doses (q6h).

Dosage (Oral): Varies according to use.
Infants (9 months or older) and children:

- Mild infections: 25–50 mg/kg/day in divided doses (q6–12h)
- Otitis media or more severe or chronic infections: Up to 1 gm qid

Rate: See cephalothin.

RENAL IMPAIRMENT: See Table 18–1. Further modification may be necessary for children.

TABLE 18–1 Dosage Adjustments of Cephradine for Patients with Renal Impairment*

Creatinine Clearance (ml/min)	Dosage Interval (hr)
<20	6–12
15–19	12–24
10–14	24–40
5–9	40–50
5	50–70

*Adult recommendations based on a maintenance dose of 500 mg.

ANTIMICROBIAL SPECTRUM: See first-generation cephalosporins (general statement).

INDICATIONS: See first-generation cephalosporins (general statement).

ACTIONS: See cephalosporins (general statement).

CONTRAINDICATIONS: See first-generation cephalosporins (general statement).

PRECAUTIONS: See first-generation cephalosporins (general statement).

SIDE EFFECTS/ADVERSE REACTIONS: See first-generation cephalosporins (general statement).

DRUG INCOMPATIBILITIES: See first-generation cephalosporins (general statement).

DRUG INTERACTIONS: See first-generation cephalosporins (general statement).

ANTIDOTE: See first-generation cephalosporins (general statement).

SECOND-GENERATION CEPHALOSPORINS (GENERAL STATEMENT)

INJECTABLE

- **Cefamandole (Mandol)**
- **Cefoxitin (Mefoxin)**

ORAL

- **Cefaclor (Ceclor)**

RENAL IMPAIRMENT: See the individual drug listings for specific information.

ANTIMICROBIAL SPECTRUM: Same as that of the first-generation cephalosporins but with an expanded activity against gram-negative *E. coli, H. influenzae* (including ampicillin-resistant strains), *Klebsiella,* and *Proteus* (including indole-positive strains, except for cefaclor). Although the specific spectrum of activity differs, cefamandole and cefoxitin (but not cefaclor) are generally more active against gram-negative bacteria and less active against gram-positive bacteria than are the first-generation derivatives. Cefamandole is more effective against *E. coli* and *Enterobacter* while cefoxitin has greater activity against anaerobes (notably bacteroides and clostridia) and *N. gonorrhoeae.* Cefaclor has greater effectiveness against gram-positive cocci and *H. influenzae* (including ampicillin-resistant strains).
Resistant organisms: *Pseudomonas,* enterococci (*S. faecalis*), methicillin-resistant staphylococci, *Serratia,* etc.

INDICATIONS: As for the first-generation cephalosporins. However, the extended antimicrobial spectrum of the second-generation derivatives permits the use of single agents against gram-positive cocci, *Klebsiella,* and *H. influenzae,* which are often responsible for such conditions in young children as pneumonia, pyarthrosis, cellulitis, and epiglottitis. These antibiotics provide more effective treatment of urinary tract infections and peritonitis caused by *Enterobacter, Proteus,* or *E. coli.*

ACTIONS: See cephalosporins (general statement).

CONTRAINDICATIONS: Known hypersensitivity to cephalosporins.

PRECAUTIONS: As for first-generation cephalosporins. In addition, increased activity against gram-negative organisms may suppress vitamin-K-producing gut bacteria, causing vitamin K deficiency and hypoprothrombinemia, with or without bleeding (primarily in debilitated patients with already deficient stores of this vitamin). IM doses are painful.

SIDE EFFECTS/ADVERSE REACTIONS: As for first-generation cephalosporins.

DRUG INCOMPATIBILITIES: As for first-generation cephalosporins.

DRUG INTERACTIONS: As for first-generation cephalosporins.

ANTIDOTE: As for first-generation cephalosporins.

Cefaclor (Ceclor)

ADMINISTRATION

Available Forms: Capsules, 250, 500 mg; oral suspension, 125 and 250 mg per 5 ml (powder for reconstitution).

Dosage (Oral): Varies according to use.
Infants (1 month or older) and children:

- Mild infections: 20 mg/kg/day in divided doses (q8h)
- Otitis media, sinusitis, or more severe infections: 40 mg/kg/day in divided doses (q8h). Maximum is 1 gm/day.

RENAL IMPAIRMENT: In severe impairment, careful clinical observations and laboratory studies should be made because the safe dosage may be lower than that usually recommended.

ANTIMICROBIAL SPECTRUM: See second-generation cephalosporins (general statement).

INDICATIONS: See second-generation cephalosporins (general statement). In addition, cefaclor has proven to be especially effective for acute otitis media and sinusitis caused by a variety of gram-positive and gram-negative bacteria, including ampicillin-resistant *H. influenzae*.

ACTIONS: See cephalosporins (general statement).

CONTRAINDICATIONS: See second-generation cephalosporins (general statement).

PRECAUTIONS: See second-generation cephalosporins (general statement).

SIDE EFFECTS/ADVERSE REACTIONS: See first-generation cephalosporins (general statement).

DRUG INCOMPATIBILITIES: None.

DRUG INTERACTIONS: See first-generation cephalosporins (general statement).

ANTIDOTE: See first-generation cephalosporins (general statement).

Cefamandole (Mandol)

ADMINISTRATION

Available Forms: Injectable (IM, IV), 500 mg, 1, 2 gm vials (powder); sodium content is 3.3 mEq/gm.

Diluent: For IM use reconstitute with sterile water or NS. Doses can be further diluted in D5W or NS (1–2 gm in 50–100 ml) for intermittent IV infusion. Also stable in multiple electrolyte solutions.

Dosage (Parenteral): Varies according to use.
Infants (1 month or older) and children:

- Mild to moderate infections: 50–100 mg/kg/day IM or IV in divided doses (q4–8h)

- Severe infections: Up to 150 mg/kg/day IM or IV in divided doses (q4–8h). Maximum is 12 gm/day.

Rate: Administer doses for intermittent IV infusions over 15–30 minutes (preferred). Give direct IV push doses at 1 gm/10 ml over 3–5 minutes.

RENAL IMPAIRMENT: Dosage adjustments are necessary.

- Mild impairment (CCr 50–80 ml/min): 75% normal daily dose given in divided doses (q6h)
- Moderate impairment (CCr 25–50 ml/min): 75% normal daily dose given in divided doses (q8h)
- Severe impairment (CCr 2–25 ml/min): 25–50% normal daily dose given in divided doses (q8–12h)

ANTIMICROBIAL SPECTRUM: See second-generation cephalosporins (general statement).

INDICATIONS: See second-generation cephalosporins (general statement).

ACTIONS: See cephalosporins (general statement).

CONTRAINDICATIONS: See second-generation cephalosporins (general statement).

PRECAUTIONS: See second-generation cephalosporins (general statement). In addition, a "disulfiram" reaction (nausea, vomiting, flushing, hypotension) has occurred following alcohol ingestion in a few patients receiving cefamandole. C&S testing should be done with a cefamandole disc instead of the standard cephalosporin test discs.

SIDE EFFECTS/ADVERSE REACTIONS: See first-generation cephalosporins (general statement).

DRUG INCOMPATIBILITIES: See first-generation cephalosporins (general statement).

DRUG INTERACTIONS: See first-generation cephalosporins (general statement).

ANTIDOTE: See first-generation cephalosporins (general statement).

Cefoxitin (Mefoxin)

ADMINISTRATION

Available Forms: Injectable (IM, IV), 1, 2 gm vials (powder); sodium content is 2.3 mEq/gm.

Diluent: See cefamandole. Also, 0.5% lidocaine can be used for IM dosages.

Dosage (Parenteral)
Infants (3 months or older) and children: 80–160 mg/kg/day IM or IV in divided doses (q4–6h). Maximum dose is 12 gm/day.

Rate: See cefamandole.

RENAL IMPAIRMENT: Dosage adjustments are necessary.

- Mild impairment (CCr 30–50 ml/min): Normal daily doses given in divided doses (q8–12h)
- Moderate impairment (CCr 10–29 ml/min): Normal daily doses given in divided doses (q12–24h)
- Severe impairment (CCr 5–9 ml/min): 50% of normal daily dose given in divided doses (q12–24h)
- No renal function (CCr <5 ml/min): 50% of normal daily dose given (q24–48h)

ANTIMICROBIAL SPECTRUM: See second-generation cephalosporins (general statement).

INDICATIONS: See second-generation cephalosporins (general statement). In addition, cefoxitin is particularly useful for intra-abdominal and gynecological infections in which aerobic and anaerobic bacteria (notably *Bacteroides fragilis*) are often found together. Cefoxitin has also been useful for treatment of penicillin-resistant gonorrhea and gonorrhea in patients allergic to the penicillins.

ACTIONS: See cephalosporins (general statement).

CONTRAINDICATIONS: See second-generation cephalosporins (general statement).

PRECAUTIONS: See second-generation cephalosporins (general statement). In addition, cefoxitin has been reported to cause pseudomembranous colitis (can be treated with oral doses of vancomycin). Cefoxitin has shown *in vitro* activity against certain *Enterobacter* species. Susceptibility testing should be done with a cefoxitin disc instead of the standard cephalosporin test discs.

SIDE EFFECTS/ADVERSE REACTIONS: See first-generation cephalosporins (general statement).

DRUG INCOMPATIBILITIES: See first-generation cephalosporins (general statement).

DRUG INTERACTIONS: See first-generation cephalosporins (general statement).

ANTIDOTE: See first-generation cephalosporins (general statement).

THIRD-GENERATION CEPHALOSPORINS (GENERAL STATEMENT)

INJECTABLE

- Cefotaxime (Claforan)
- Moxalactam (Moxam)

Note: Moxalactam is not a true cephalosporin but rather an oxa-beta-lactam with all the characteristics of a cephalosporin. Cefoperazone, another third-generation cephalosporin agent, has not yet been approved for use in pediatric patients.

RENAL IMPAIRMENT: See the individual drug listings for adjustments.

ANTIMICROBIAL SPECTRUM: The third-generation cephalosporins are usually less active against gram-positive cocci than the first-generation and second-generation agents. However, the third-generation derivatives are effective against a considerably expanded spectrum of gram-negative organisms, including most enterobacteria. Relative to the second-generation cephalosporins, these newer derivatives are more effective against *Enterobacter, Klebsiella, E. coli, Proteus,* other coliforms resistant to the aminoglycosides and other cephalosporins, *Salmonella, Shigella, Neisseria,* and *H. influenzae* (including ampicillin-resistant strains). In addition, *Serratia, Providencia, Citrobacter,* and some clostridia (except *Clostridium difficile*) are sensitive to the third-generation cephalosporins. Their activity against *Bacteroides* and *Pseudomonas* is variable.
    Cefotaxime and moxalactam appear to be less effective against *P. aeruginosa* than cefoperazone or the newer penicillins, mezlocillin and piperacillin. Moxalactam is more effective against *Bacteroides* (notably *B. fragilis*) and other anaerobes than either cefotaxime or cefoperazone. Culture and sensitivity tests should be done to determine the susceptibility of *Pseudomonas* and *Bacteroides.* Both cefotaxime and cefoperazone have greater activity against gram-positive cocci than does moxalactam; only cefoperazone has *in vitro* activity against enterococci, but C&S tests should be done.
Resistant organisms: Enterococci, *Listeria,* fungi, and viruses. Some strains of *Enterobacter, P. aeruginosa,* indole-positive *Proteus,* and *Serratia* develop resistance during therapy. Methicillin-resistant staphylococci should also be considered resistant to the third-generation cephalosporins.

INDICATIONS: The third-generation cephalosporins are particularly useful for the treatment of gram-negative bacillary infections in patients with reduced renal function or when the causative organisms are resistant to the aminoglycosides. These derivatives can be used for children with infections caused by strains of *H. influenzae* that are resistant to both ampicillin and chloramphenicol. Intravenous administration of moxalactam and cefoperazone results in proportionately higher levels of these cephalosporins in cerebrospinal fluid than are obtained with cefotaxime. Since moxalactam, however, produces the highest concentrations in the CSF, it is the only cephalosporin currently approved for the treatment of meningitis caused by susceptible coliform bacilli, *H. influenzae,* or *Neisseria.*

(However, since CNS infections in neonates and children can frequently be complicated by streptococci or *Listeria monocytogenes*, ampicillin may have to be used in conjunction with moxalactam until the results of C&S tests are known.) A few studies have indicated that the third-generation cephalosporins alone are as effective as the combination of clindamycin and an aminoglycoside in the treatment of intra-abdominal and soft tissue infections caused by mixed populations of aerobic and anaerobic bacteria. Because moxalactam shows higher *in vitro* activity against *Bacteroides*, it may be the preferred third-generation derivative for those mixed infections in which *B. fragilis* is a causative agent. Single IM doses of cefotaxime combined with an oral dose of probenecid are an effective alternative therapy for gonorrhea in patients allergic to penicillin or for penicillin-resistant gonococci. The reduced activity against gram-positive cocci makes third-generation cephalosporins less effective than the first-generation or second-generation agents for streptococcal, pneumococcal, or staphylococcal infections.

ACTIONS: See cephalosporins (general statement). Also, the third-generation cephalosporins are highly resistant to degradation by beta-lactamase, an enzyme produced by certain strains of gram-negative bacteria and *Staphylococcus aureus*, that normally inactivates first-generation and second-generation derivatives. Both cefotaxime and moxalactam are excreted mainly through the kidney; thus, dosage adjustments are necessary for patients with renal impairment. Cefoperazone, on the other hand, is excreted mainly in the bile, so renal insufficiency does not affect serum levels or elimination of this antibiotic. However, hepatic dysfunction or combined renal and hepatic insufficiency can cause accumulation of cefoperazone. Dosage adjustments are necessary for patients with severe hepatic impairment.

CONTRAINDICATIONS: Hypersensitivity to cephalosporins.

PRECAUTIONS: As for first-generation cephalosporins. Also, both prolonged prothrombin times and hypoprothrombinemia (with or without bleeding) have been associated with treatment with moxalactam and cefoperazone. (This bleeding diathesis has not as yet been reported with cefotaxime.) Hypoprothrombinemia is probably caused by antibiotic-induced suppression of the gut flora responsible for synthesis of vitamin K, and the condition can be reversed by the administration of this vitamin. Check prothrombin times periodically throughout therapy with these cephalosporins. A "disulfiram-like" reaction (nausea, vomiting, hypotension) has been reported following alcohol ingestion (up to 48 hours after drug administration) in patients receiving moxalactam and cefoperazone. Superinfections with yeasts, enterococci, and certain strains of clostridia and *Pseudomonas* may occur. Since resistant strains of some gram-negative bacteria (notably *Enterobacter*, *P. aeruginosa*, and *Serratia*) can develop during therapy, C&S tests should be done periodically until the infection is eradicated. Pseudomembranous colitis has been reported (thought to be due to a toxin secreted by *C. difficile*). Observe the patient for development of severe diarrhea. If diarrhea develops, a differential diagnosis of colitis should be made and the antibiotic discontinued if necessary.

SIDE EFFECTS/ADVERSE REACTIONS: As for first-generation cephalosporins.

DRUG INCOMPATIBILITIES: As for first-generation cephalosporins.

DRUG INTERACTIONS: As for first-generation cephalosporins. Also, third-generation cephalosporins show synergistic activity against *Enterobacter* and *P. aeruginosa* when given with aminoglycosides.

ANTIDOTE: As for first-generation cephalosporins.

Cefotaxime (Claforan)

ADMINISTRATION

Available Forms: Injectable (IM, IV), 500 mg, 1, 2 gm vials (powder); sodium content is 2.2 mEq/gm.

Diluent: For IM use reconstitute with sterile water or NS. Doses can be further diluted in D5W or NS (1–2 gm in 50–100 ml) for intermittent IV infusions. Also stable in multiple electrolyte solutions.

Dosage (Parenteral): Varies according to the patient's age.
Premature or full-term neonates (up to 1 week old): 25–50 mg/kg IM or IV q12h.
Neonates 1–4 weeks old: 25–50 mg/kg IM or IV q8h.
Children 1 month–12 years old, <50 kg: 50–180 mg/kg/day IM or IV in divided doses (q4–6h).
Children >50 kg: Same as adult dose.

- Uncomplicated infections: 1 gm IM or IV q12h
- Moderate to severe infections: 1–2 gm IM or IV q6–8h
- Life-threatening infections: 2 gm IV q4h

Rate: Administer intermittent IV infusions over 15–30 minutes (preferred). Give direct IV push doses at 1 gm/10 ml over 3–5 minutes.

RENAL IMPAIRMENT: For patients with a creatinine clearance less than 20 ml/min, give 50% of the normal daily dose at the same intervals.

ANTIMICROBIAL SPECTRUM: See third-generation cephalosporins (general statement).

INDICATIONS: See third-generation cephalosporins (general statement).

ACTIONS: See third-generation cephalosporins (general statement).

CONTRAINDICATIONS: See third-generation cephalosporins (general statement).

PRECAUTIONS: See third-generation cephalosporins (general statement).

SIDE EFFECTS/ADVERSE REACTIONS: See first-generation cephalosporins (general statement).

DRUG INCOMPATIBILITIES: See first-generation cephalosporins (general statement).

DRUG INTERACTIONS: See third-generation cephalosporins (general statement).

ANTIDOTE: See first-generation cephalosporins (general statement).

Moxalactam (Moxam)

ADMINISTRATION

Available Forms: Injectable (IM, IV), 1, 2 gm vials (powder); sodium content is 3.8 mEq/gm.

Diluent: See cefotaxime. Doses for IM use can be diluted in 0.5% lidocaine.

Dosage (Parenteral): Varies according to the patient's age and condition.
For neonates up to 1 week old: 50 mg/kg IV or IM q12h.
For neonates 1–4 weeks old: 50 mg/kg IV or IM q8h.
For infants (>1 month old) and children: 50 mg/kg IV or IM q6–8h.
For gram-negative meningitis: Give an initial loading dose of 100 mg/kg, then follow the previously given schedules for each age group.
For serious infections: Up to 200 mg/kg/dose can be given.

Rate: See cefotaxime.

RENAL IMPAIRMENT: Dosage adjustments are necessary.

- Mild impairment (CCr 50–80 ml/min): 75–100% normal daily dose given in divided doses (q8h)
- Moderate impairment (CCr 25–50 ml/min): 50% normal daily dose given in divided doses (q8h)
- Severe impairment (CCr 2–25 ml/min): 25% normal daily dose given in divided doses (q12h)
- No renal function (CCr <2 ml/min): 25% normal daily dose q24h

ANTIMICROBIAL SPECTRUM: See third-generation cephalosporins (general statement).

INDICATIONS: See third-generation cephalosporins (general statement).

ACTIONS: See third-generation cephalosporins (general statement).

CONTRAINDICATIONS: See third-generation cephalosporins (general statement).

PRECAUTIONS: See third-generation cephalosporins (general statement).

SIDE EFFECTS/ADVERSE REACTIONS: See first-generation cephalosporins (general statement).

DRUG INCOMPATIBILITIES: See first-generation cephalosporins (general statement).

DRUG INTERACTIONS: See third-generation cephalosporins (general statement).

ANTIDOTE: See first-generation cephalosporins (general statement).

19
Penicillins

In the years since the first crude product was obtained in the 1940s, the penicillin molecule has been chemically refined, and a number of natural and semisynthetic cogeners have been produced. The development of these semisynthetic derivatives has resulted in compounds that are resistant to destruction by gastric acid and penicillinase and active against both gram-positive and gram-negative organisms. Although numerous other antibiotics have been developed, penicillin is still one of the most widely prescribed antibacterial medications.

For the purposes of discussion, the penicillins are divided into three categories:
1. Penicillin G and penicillin V
2. Penicillinase-resistant penicillins
3. Extended-spectrum penicillins

PENICILLINS (GENERAL STATEMENT)

RENAL IMPAIRMENT: Dosage adjustments are recommended for patients with insufficient renal function and for premature and neonatal infants.

ANTIMICROBIAL SPECTRUM: Both penicillin G and V are active against many gram-positive and gram-negative cocci and gram-positive bacilli. The extended antibacterial spectrum of the new semisynthetic derivatives includes penicillinase-producing staphylococci and more gram-negative organisms such as *Enterobacter, Klebsiella, H. influenzae, Proteus,* and some strains of *Bacteroides* and *Pseudomonas.* (See the different classes of penicillins for a more complete spectrum.)

INDICATIONS: For patients who are not allergic to it, penicillin G is the antibiotic of choice for most systemic and local infections due to susceptible gram-positive and gram-negative cocci. In addition, the extended-spectrum penicillins are useful for a variety of infections caused by susceptible strains of both gram-positive and gram-negative aerobic and anaerobic bacteria. Culture and sensitivity tests should be done to assure the effectiveness of any penicillin against staphylococcal and enterococcal organisms and of the newer derivatives against gram-negative bacteria.

ACTIONS: Because they inhibit cell wall synthesis, the penicillins are bactericidal, but only for actively growing cells. Dormant bacteria or organisms that lack cell walls (e.g., viruses) are not affected by these antibiotics. The penicillins are also inactive against yeasts and fungi because their cell walls differ chemically from those of bacteria. After oral or parenteral administration, penicillins are widely distributed in most body tissues and fluids; the exceptions are nerve, eye, cardiac, and skeletal tissues and abscess fluid. Only small amounts diffuse into the CSF. When the meninges are inflamed during meningitis, however, the levels of these antibiotics in CSF are higher in general (up to 10–30% of serum levels) and even more so with ampicillin. The penicillins cross the placenta and are excreted in breast milk. Most of these agents are excreted unchanged in the urine, but some are partially activated in the liver. In patients with impaired renal function and in premature and neonatal infants, penicillin excretion rates are slower. During renal impairment, a larger percentage of penicillin undergoes hepatic metabolism. Consequently, liver disease may further delay the excretion of these antibiotics in patients who have concomitant renal impairment.

CONTRAINDICATIONS: Hypersensitivity to any penicillin.

PRECAUTIONS: Because some cross-allergenicity exists between the penicillins and cephalosporins, use penicillins cautiously in patients who are hypersensitive to the cephalosporins. Prolonged therapy can result in superinfections with yeasts and other nonsusceptible organisms. High IV doses of those penicillins available as sodium or potassium salts can produce hypernatremia or hyperkalemia, especially in premature infants and neonates and in other patients who have insufficient renal function. (For more specific precautions, see the individual groups of penicillin derivatives.)

SIDE EFFECTS/ADVERSE REACTIONS: Generalized reactions include gastric upset (oral doses) and hypersensitivity reactions that range from mild rashes to anaphylactic shock (both oral and parenteral doses). The parenterally administered preparations can also cause electrolyte imbalances and thrombophlebitis. Some of the extended-spectrum derivatives have been associated with bleeding episodes and abnormal values in coagulation tests such as bleeding time, platelet aggregation, and prothrombin time. (Refer to the individual groups of penicillin derivatives for more specific side effects and adverse reactions.)

PENICILLIN G AND PENICILLIN V (GENERAL STATEMENT)

INJECTABLE
- Penicillin G sodium
- Penicillin G potassium
- Benzathine penicillin G (Bicillin)
- Procaine penicillin G (Wycillin)

ORAL
- Penicillin G (Pentids)
- Phenoxymethyl penicillin V (Pen-Vee, Pen-Vee K, V-cillin, V-cillin K, others)

RENAL IMPAIRMENT: See the individual drug listings.

ANTIMICROBIAL SPECTRUM: These penicillins are very effective against gram-positive cocci, including nonpenicillinase-producing staphylococci, alpha-hemolytic and group A beta-hemolytic streptococci, gonococci, meningococci, and pneumococci. The spirochetes (e.g., *Treponema pallidum* and *Treponema pertenue*) and gram-positive bacilli (e.g., clostridia, *Bacillus anthracis*, *Corynebacterium diphtheriae*, and *L. monocytogenes*) are also sensitive. Some strains of *Bacteroides* (oropharyngeal strains), and *Actinomyces*, *Streptobacillus*, and *Pasteurella multocida* are also inhibited by penicillin G. Sensitivity testing should be done on all staphylococcal and enterococcal *(S. faecalis)* cultures.
Resistant organisms: Nearly all enteric and other gram-negative bacilli, penicillinase-producing staphylococci, fungi, viruses, amoebas, plasmodia, and mycobacteria.

INDICATIONS: In patients who are not allergic to it, penicillin G is the antibiotic of choice for treatment of infections caused by susceptible streptococci, pneumococci, non-penicillinase-producing staphylococci, and gram-negative cocci. Conditions amenable to penicillin G therapy are upper respiratory, skin, and soft tissue infections; fusospirochetal gingivitis; pharyngitis; otitis media; and mild erysipelas. It is also indicated for long-term prophylaxis of rheumatic fever, acute glomerulonephritis, or SBE caused by group A beta-hemolytic streptococci. Parenterally, penicillin G salts are used for treatment of syphilis, gonococcal and clostridial infections (other than botulism), meningitis, and septicemias due to sensitive organisms.

ACTIONS: See penicillins (general statement).

CONTRAINDICATIONS: Hypersensitivity to any penicillin.

PRECAUTIONS: Because penicillin G may be partially destroyed by gastric acid, the more acid-stable penicillin V is used when oral doses are indicated. Serious and sometimes fatal anaphylactic reactions have occurred, particularly after parenteral administration. These reactions are most likely to occur in patients with multiple allergies. Use cautiously in patients with severe allergies, asthma, or hypersensitivity to cephalosporins (possible cross-hypersensitivity). Patients should always be asked about previous reactions to penicillin before being given the antibiotic. For streptococcal infections, therapy should be continued for a minimum of 10 days to ensure eradication of the bacteria and prevent sequelae (e.g., acute rheumatic fever or glomerulonephritis). Culture and sensitivity tests should be done in suspected staphylococcal infections. Prolonged use may cause superinfections with yeasts or fungi.

During prolonged therapy with high doses, periodic tests for renal function and blood counts are recommended. Dosage adjustments are recommended for patients with severe renal impairment. Use cautiously in these patients as kidney damage (e.g., interstitial nephritis, proteinuria, hematuria, fever, acute renal failure) has been reported. (Such damage is probably a hypersensitivity reaction and is seen more often with methicillin.) High IV doses (>20 million units/day) or high intrathecal doses (10,000 units), especially in patients with renal impairment, may cause neurological toxicity, muscle irritability, and convulsions. Use high IV doses cautiously in patients with cardiac impairment. Large IV doses of the potassium salt cause hyperkalemia with cardiac arrhythmias; large IV doses of the sodium salt cause fluid retention. Avoid use of the potassium salt in neonates with underdeveloped renal function. Avoid rapid IV rates. Monitor fluid and electrolyte balance during high-dose therapy. Deep IM injection may cause painful sciatic nerve irritation and paralysis. Inadvertent IV injection of procaine penicillin has caused "pseudoanaphylactic" reactions and cardiac arrest.

SIDE EFFECTS/ADVERSE REACTIONS: Oral administration frequently causes gastric upset with nausea, vomiting, diarrhea, and black hairy tongue. Phlebitis may occur after repeated IV use; sterile abscesses may occur at IM injection sites. Hypersensitivity reactions (reported incidence, 1–10%) range from mild rashes of maculopapular eruptions to severe exfoliative dermatitis. Serum-sickness-like reactions include fever, chills, edema, arthralgia, and prostration. Severe and occasionally fatal anaphylaxis has occurred, particularly after parenteral use. High doses of the potassium salts may cause hyperkalemia, cardiac arrhythmias, hyperreflexia, and convulsions. High IV doses of the sodium salt may induce or worsen congestive heart failure. Other hypersensitivity reactions include development of a positive direct Coombs' test associated with hemolytic anemia. Other blood dyscrasias such as thrombocytopenia (with purpura), leukopenia, eosinophilia, and agranulocytosis may occur. A Jarisch-Herxheimer reaction frequently follows a penicillin dose in syphilis patients and is characterized by fever, headache, chills, muscular aches, exacerbations of lesions, and leukocytosis.

DRUG INCOMPATIBILITIES: Do not admix with acidic drugs such as ascorbic acid, tetracyclines, cephalosporins, prochlorperazine, hydroxyzine, promethazine, and vitamin B with C complex or with alkaline drugs such as aminoglycosides, aminophylline, and sodium bicarbonate.

DRUG INTERACTIONS: Concomitantly administered *probenecid* increases and prolongs serum levels of penicillin by decreasing the renal excretion of penicillin. (*Phenylbutazone, indomethacin, aspirin,* and *sulfinpyrazone* also decrease renal excretion of penicillin.) Synergistic or potentiated activity against enterococci (*S. faecalis*) has been demonstrated when penicillin G is combined with an *aminoglycoside* antibiotic. *In vitro* combinations of *bactericidal* antibiotics (such as penicillins) and *bacteriostatic* antibiotics (such as *chloramphenicol, tetracyclines, erythromycins,* and *clindamycin*) tend to be less active than the bactericidal antibiotic alone because the bactericidal agents are more effective against actively growing bacteria than against the resting cells that are induced by bacteriostatic agents.

ANTIDOTE: Discontinue penicillins. Treat hypersensitivity reactions with appropriate agents such as antihistamines, corticosteroids, epinephrine, aminophylline, oxygen, and other supportive measures.

Penicillin G (parenteral)

ADMINISTRATION

Available Forms: Injectable (IM, IV), aqueous (powder for reconstitution): sodium salt, 1 and 5 million unit vials (1.7 mEq sodium/million units), potassium salt, 1, 5, 10, 20 million unit vials (1.7 mEq potassium/million units); injectable (IM only): procaine salt, 300,000 and 600,000 units per ml in 1, 2, and 4 ml syringes (Wycillin, Crysticillin), benzathine salt, 600,000 units/ml in 1.0, 1.5, 2.0, and 4.0 ml syringes (Bicillin L-A), procaine-benzathine combinations, 300,000 units of each in 1, 2, and 4 ml syringes (Bicillin C-R).

Diluent: For IV use reconstitute and further dilute in D5W or NS (up to 5 million units in 50 ml, 5–10 million units in 100–250 ml, 10 million units in 500–1000 ml).

Dosage (Aqueous Penicillin G): Varies according to the type and severity of infection. For most susceptible infections:

- Neonates up to 1 week old: 50,000–100,000 units/kg/day IV in divided doses (q12h)
- Neonates 1–4 weeks old: 50,000–250,000 units/kg/day IV in divided doses (q8h)
- Children: 25,000–300,000 units/kg/day IV in divided doses (q6h). Up to 400,000 units/kg/day for meningitis.

For neonatal gonococcal ophthalmia or conjunctivitis: 50,000 units/kg/day IV in divided doses (q12h) for 7 days (in conjunction with saline eye irrigations and chloramphenicol or tetracycline eye drops).
For neonatal gonococcal septicemia or meningitis: 75,000–100,000 units/kg/day IV in divided doses (q6–8h) for 7-10 days.

Dosage (Procaine Penicillin G): 0.5–1.0 million units/m^2/day IM in divided doses (q12–24h).

Dosage (Benzathine Penicillin G): Varies according to the patient's weight.
For infants and children <30 kg: 300,000–600,000 units as a single IM dose.
For children >30 kg: 900,000–1.2 million units as a single IM dose.

Rate: Administer IV infusions over 20–40 minutes with due regard for the potassium content.

RENAL IMPAIRMENT: Patients with severe renal impairment should be given no more than one-third to one-half the maximum daily dose at the normal intervals.

ANTIMICROBIAL SPECTRUM: See penicillin G and penicillin V (general statement).

INDICATIONS: See penicillin G and penicillin V (general statement).

ACTIONS: See penicillins (general statement).

CONTRAINDICATIONS: See penicillin G and penicillin V (general statement).

PRECAUTIONS: See penicillin G and penicillin V (general statement).

SIDE EFFECTS/ADVERSE REACTIONS: See penicillin G and penicillin V (general statement).

DRUG INCOMPATIBILITIES: See penicillin G and penicillin V (general statement).

DRUG INTERACTIONS: See penicillin G and penicillin V (general statement).

ANTIDOTE: See penicillin G and penicillin V (general statement).

Penicillin G (oral) (Pentids, others)
Penicillin V (Pen-Vee, Pen-Vee K, V-cillin, V-cillin K, others)

ADMINISTRATION

Available Forms (Penicillin G): Tablets, 200,000 units (125 mg), 400,000 units (250 mg), 800,000 units (500 mg); oral solution, 200,000 and 400,000 units per 5 ml (125 and 250 mg per 5 ml) after reconstitution.

Available Forms (Penicillin V): Tablets, 125, 250, 500 mg; oral solution, 125 and 250 mg per 5 ml after reconstitution.

Dosage (Oral): Varies according to use and the patient's age.
For pneumococcal infections:

- Infants and children <12 years old: 15–56 mg/kg/day (25,000–90,000 units/kg/day) in 3–6 divided doses
- Children 12 years and older: 250–500 mg q6h until afebrile

For staphylococcal infections and Vincent's gingivitis:

- Infants and children <12 years old: 15–56 mg/kg/day (25,000–90,000 units/kg/day) in 3–6 divided doses
- Children 12 years and older: 250–500 mg q6–8h

For streptococcal infections:

- Infants and children <12 years old: 15–56 mg/kg/day (25,000–90,000 units/kg/day) in 3–6 divided doses for 10 days
- For children 12 years and older: 125–250 mg q6–8h for 10 days or 500 mg q12h for 10 days

For rheumatic fever prophylaxis: 125–250 mg bid
For prevention of bacterial endocarditis before surgery:

- Children <30 kg: 1 gm given 30–60 minutes preop, then 250 mg q6h for 8 doses

- Children >30 kg: 2 gm given 30–60 minutes preop, then 500 mg q6h for 8 doses

RENAL IMPAIRMENT: See penicillins (general statement).

ANTIMICROBIAL SPECTRUM: See penicillin G and penicillin V (general statement).

INDICATIONS: See penicillin G and penicillin V (general statement).

ACTIONS: See penicillins (general statement).

CONTRAINDICATIONS: See penicillin G and penicillin V (general statement).

PRECAUTIONS: See penicillin G and penicillin V (general statement).

SIDE EFFECTS/ADVERSE REACTIONS: See penicillin G and penicillin V (general statement).

DRUG INCOMPATIBILITIES: See penicillin G and penicillin V (general statement).

DRUG INTERACTIONS: See penicillin G and penicillin V (general statement).

ANTIDOTE: See penicillin G and penicillin V (general statement).

PENICILLINASE-RESISTANT PENICILLINS (GENERAL STATEMENT)

INJECTABLE
- Methicillin (Staphcillin)
- Oxacillin (Prostaphlin)
- Nafcillin (Unipen)

ORAL
- Cloxacillin (Tegopen)
- Dicloxacillin (Dynapen, Veracillin)
- Nafcillin (Unipen)
- Oxacillin (Prostaphlin)

RENAL IMPAIRMENT: See the individual drug listings.

ANTIMICROBIAL SPECTRUM: Same spectrum as penicillin G and V but also effective against penicillinase-producing staphylococci. (Some strains of *S. aureus* and *Staphylococcus epidermidis* may develop resistance to methicillin. These strains are usually resistant to the other penicillinase-resistant penicillins and to most cephalosporins.)

INDICATIONS: These agents are indicated primarily for treatment of infections due to penicillin-resistant staphylococci. Most frequently treated conditions are skin, soft tissue, and respiratory tract infections; bacterial endocarditis; suppurative osteomyelitis; and pseudomembranous enterocolitis caused by penicillinase-producing staphylococci. High IV doses of these agents can be used for successful management of staphylococcal meningitis.

ACTIONS: See penicillins (general statement). All penicillinase-resistant antibiotics undergo some hepatic inactivation (methicillin the least), and nafcillin is excreted primarily by the liver. Because of this, there is little prolongation of the half-lifes of these drugs even in patients with severe renal disease. Of the four oral preparations, dicloxacillin has the best gastric absorption with the highest peak serum levels, but this is offset by its high degree of protein binding (98%). In comparison, cloxacillin produces the greatest antibacterial concentration of free antibiotic in the plasma. Gastric absorption of the oral preparations is best when they are taken on an empty stomach.

CONTRAINDICATIONS: Hypersensitivity to any penicillins.

PRECAUTIONS: (See also penicillin G and penicillin V [general statement].) Oral doses of these agents are indicated only for mild to moderate infections. Severe infections require parenteral administration. Culture and sensitivity tests should be done in suspected staphylococcal infections to determine susceptibility of the causative organism to these agents. Penicillin G is the antibiotic of choice for staphylococcal infections caused by strains that are sensitive to it. Resistance to methicillin can develop among staphylococci via a nonpenicillinase mechanism. Also, methicillin is a powerful inducer of penicillinase in certain bacteria. Methicillin-resistant strains of staphylococci should be considered resistant to other penicillinase-resistant penicillins as well as to cephalosporins. The rate of renal elimination of these penicillins is slow in very young infants because of their reduced renal function. (Single doses may persist for 12 hours or more, so adjust doses accordingly.) Routine blood cell counts and evaluation of renal function are necessary during prolonged therapy. Kidney damage (notably interstitial nephritis) may occur with the use of these antibiotics, particularly with methicillin; it is important to distinguish this condition from urinary tract infections.

SIDE EFFECTS/ADVERSE REACTIONS: As for penicillin G. In addition, a reversible bone marrow depression with anemia, neutropenia, and granulocytopenia has occurred, particularly with methicillin. Interstitial nephritis manifested by hematuria, albuminuria, pyuria, oliguria, rash, and fever may occur, particularly with methicillin, but also with oxacillin, nafcillin, and ampicillin. (Both of these adverse reactions are probably hypersensitivity reactions.) Pain may occur with IM doses and thrombophlebitis during IV infusion.

DRUG INCOMPATIBILITIES: As for penicillin G.

DRUG INTERACTIONS: As for penicillin G.

ANTIDOTE: As for penicillin G.

Cloxacillin (Tegopen)

ADMINISTRATION

Available Forms: Capsules, 250, 500 mg; oral solution, 125 mg/5 ml after reconstitution.

Dosage (Oral): Use in neonates has not been established.
For mild to moderate infections:

- Children <20 kg: 50 mg/kg/day in divided doses (q6h); up to 100 mg/kg/day for severe infections. Give 1-2 hours before meals.
- Children 20 kg or more: 250-500 mg q6h; up to 1 gm q6h for severe infections. Give 1-2 hours before meals.

RENAL IMPAIRMENT: No dosage adjustments are necessary.

ANTIMICROBIAL SPECTRUM: See penicillinase-resistant penicillins (general statement).

INDICATIONS: See penicillinase-resistant penicillins (general statement).

ACTIONS: See penicillins (general statement).

CONTRAINDICATIONS: See penicillinase-resistant penicillins (general statement).

PRECAUTIONS: See penicillinase-resistant penicillins (general statement).

SIDE EFFECTS/ADVERSE REACTIONS: See penicillinase-resistant penicillins (general statement).

DRUG INCOMPATIBILITIES: None.

DRUG INTERACTIONS: See penicillinase-resistant penicillins (general statement).

ANTIDOTE: See penicillinase-resistant penicillins (general statement).

Dicloxacillin (Dynapen, Veracillin)

ADMINISTRATION

Available Forms: Capsules, 125, 250, 500 mg; oral suspension, 62.5 mg/5 ml after reconstitution.

Dosage (Oral): Use in neonates is not recommended.
For mild to moderate infections:

- Children <40 kg: 12.5-50.0 mg/kg/day in divided doses (q6h); up to 100 mg/kg/day for more severe infections. Give 1-2 hours before meals.
- Children 40 kg or more: 125-500 mg q6h; up to 1 gm q6h for more severe infections. Give 1-2 hours before meals.

RENAL IMPAIRMENT: No dosage adjustments are necessary.

ANTIMICROBIAL SPECTRUM: See penicillinase-resistant penicillins (general statement).

INDICATIONS: See penicillinase-resistant penicillins (general statement).

ACTIONS: See penicillins (general statement).

CONTRAINDICATIONS: See penicillinase-resistant penicillins (general statement).

PRECAUTIONS: See penicillinase-resistant penicillins (general statement).

SIDE EFFECTS/ADVERSE REACTIONS: See penicillinase-resistant penicillins (general statement).

DRUG INCOMPATIBILITIES: None.

DRUG INTERACTIONS: See penicillinase-resistant penicillins (general statement).

ANTIDOTE: See penicillinase-resistant penicillins (general statement).

Methicillin (Staphcillin)

ADMINISTRATION

Available Forms: Injectable (IM, IV), 1, 4, 6 gm vials (powder); sodium content is 2.9 mEq/gm.

Diluent: For IM use reconstitute with sterile water or NS. For IV use further dilute with D5W or NS (1 gm/50 ml). Also stable in multiple electrolyte solutions. Use within 8 hours. Do not mix with any other medications in the same container.

Dosage (Parenteral): IV doses are not established by the manufacturer, but some studies have suggested 100–400 mg/kg/day in divided doses (q4–6h).
Newborns up to 1 week old: 50–100 mg/kg/day IM in divided doses (q12h).
Infants (>1 week old) and children: 100 mg/kg/day IM in divided doses (q6h).

Rate: For direct IV push do not exceed 500 mg over 2–3 minutes. IV infusions can be given at a rate appropriate for the volume of dilution.

RENAL IMPAIRMENT: Dosage adjustments are necessary.

- Mild to moderate impairment (CCr 50–80 ml/min): Normal dose q6h
- Moderate impairment (CCr 10–50 ml/min): Normal dose q8h
- Severe impairment (CCr <10 ml/min): Normal dose q12h

ANTIMICROBIAL SPECTRUM: See penicillinase-resistant penicillins (general statement).

INDICATIONS: See penicillinase-resistant penicillins (general statement).

ACTIONS: See penicillins (general statement).

CONTRAINDICATIONS: See penicillinase-resistant penicillins (general statement).

PRECAUTIONS: See penicillinase-resistant penicillins (general statement).

SIDE EFFECTS/ADVERSE REACTIONS: See penicillinase-resistant penicillins (general statement).

DRUG INCOMPATIBILITIES: See penicillinase-resistant penicillins (general statement).

DRUG INTERACTIONS: See penicillinase-resistant penicillins (general statement).

ANTIDOTE: See penicillinase-resistant penicillins (general statement).

Nafcillin (Unipen)

ADMINISTRATION

Available Forms: Injectable (IM, IV), 500 mg, 1, 2 gm vials (powder), sodium content is 2.9 mEq/gm; tablets, 500 mg; capsules, 250 mg; oral solution, 250 mg/5 ml after reconstitution.

Diluent: For IM use reconstitute with sterile water or NS. Can be further diluted in D5W or NS (25–50 ml) for intermittent IV infusion. Concentrations of 2–4 mg/ml should be used within 24 hours.

Dosage (Parenteral): IV doses have not been established for neonates, but some clinicians have used the doses listed.
Neonates: 20 mg/kg/day IM in divided doses (q12h) or 40–60 mg/kg/day IV in divided doses (q8–12h).
Infants and older children: 50 mg/kg/day IM in divided doses (q12h) or 50–60 mg/kg/day IV in divided doses (q6h).

Dosage (Oral): Varies according to the patient's age.
Neonates: 30–40 mg/kg/day in divided doses (q6–8h) taken on an empty stomach.
Infants and older children: 50 mg/kg/day in divided doses (q6h) taken on an empty stomach.

Rate: Dilute IV doses in at least 15–30 ml of fluid and infuse over 5–10 minutes.

RENAL IMPAIRMENT: No dosage adjustments are necessary.

ANTIMICROBIAL SPECTRUM: See penicillinase-resistant penicillins (general statement).

INDICATIONS: See penicillinase-resistant penicillins (general statement).

ACTIONS: See penicillins (general statement).

CONTRAINDICATIONS: See penicillinase-resistant penicillins (general statement).

PRECAUTIONS: See penicillinase-resistant penicillins (general statement). Avoid extravasation of IV doses as severe tissue sloughing may occur.

SIDE EFFECTS/ADVERSE REACTIONS: See penicillinase-resistant penicillins (general statement).

DRUG INCOMPATIBILITIES: See penicillinase-resistant penicillins (general statement).

DRUG INTERACTIONS: See penicillinase-resistant penicillins (general statement).

ANTIDOTE: See penicillinase-resistant penicillins (general statement).

Oxacillin (Prostaphlin)

ADMINISTRATION

Available Forms: Injectable (IM, IV), 500 mg, 1, 2, 4 gm vials (powder), sodium content is 3.2 mEq/gm; capsules, 250, 500 mg; oral suspension, 250 mg/5 ml after reconstitution.

Diluent: For IM use reconstitute with sterile water or NS. For IV use further dilute with D5W or NS to 10–100 mg/ml (up to 2 gm in 50 ml, over 2 gm to 4 gm in 100 ml). Can be added to larger infusion volumes, including multiple electrolyte solutions, but use within 6 hours.

Dosage (Parenteral): Doses higher than 150 mg/kg/day have been associated with azotemia, albuminemia, and hematuria in newborns and infants.
For mild to moderately severe infections:

- Neonates: 25 mg/kg/day IM or IV in divided doses (q6h). Alternatively, 50–100 mg/kg/day IV in divided doses (q12h) for the first week of life, then 100–200 mg/kg/day IV in divided doses (q6h)
- Children <40 kg: 50–100 mg/kg/day IV or IM in divided doses (q6h)
- Children 40 kg or more: 250–500 mg IM or IV q4–6h

For severe infections:

- Children <40 kg: Dosage can be increased to more than 100 mg/kg/day IV or IM in divided doses (q4–6h)
- Children 40 kg or more: 1 gm q4–6h, up to 8 gm/day

Dosage (Oral): Varies according to the patient's weight. For mild to moderate infections only:

- Children <40 kg: 50 mg/kg/day (1.5 gm/m^2/day) in divided doses (q6h) taken 1–2 hours before meals
- Children 40 kg or more: 500 mg q4–6h taken 1–2 hours before meals

Rate: Administer IV bolus doses (1 gm/20 ml) over 10 minutes. Doses diluted to 50 ml can be given over 15–30 minutes.

RENAL IMPAIRMENT: Dosage adjustments are usually not required, but periodic urinalysis is recommended.

ANTIMICROBIAL SPECTRUM: See penicillinase-resistant penicillins (general statement).

INDICATIONS: See penicillinase-resistant penicillins (general statement).

ACTIONS: See penicillins (general statement).

CONTRAINDICATIONS: See penicillinase-resistant penicillins (general statement).

PRECAUTIONS: See penicillinase-resistant penicillins (general statement). In addition, oxacillin may cause hypersensitive hepatotoxic effects resulting in elevated levels of liver enzymes, cholestatic jaundice, and hepatic dysfunction.

SIDE EFFECTS/ADVERSE REACTIONS: See penicillinase-resistant penicillins (general statement).

DRUG INCOMPATIBILITIES: See penicillinase-resistant penicillins (general statement).

DRUG INTERACTIONS: See penicillinase-resistant penicillins (general statement).

ANTIDOTE: See penicillinase-resistant penicillins (general statement).

EXTENDED-SPECTRUM PENICILLINS (GENERAL STATEMENT)

INJECTABLE

- Carbenicillin (Geopen)
- Mezlocillin (Mezlin)
- Piperacillin (Pipracil)
- Ticarcillin (Ticar)

ORAL

- Amoxicillin (Amoxil, Larotid, Polymox)
- Ampicillin (Omnipen, Polycillin, others)
- Carbenicillin (Geocillin)

RENAL IMPAIRMENT: See the individual drug listings.

ANTIMICROBIAL SPECTRUM: See the individual drug listings.

INDICATIONS: See the individual drug listings.

ACTIONS: See penicillins (general statement).

CONTRAINDICATIONS: Hypersensitivity to any penicillin.

PRECAUTIONS: Overgrowth with yeasts or fungi may occur. (For more specific information, see the individual drug listings.)

SIDE EFFECTS/ADVERSE REACTIONS: As for penicillin G. Hypokalemia and metabolic acidosis may occur with some extended-spectrum penicillins (not ampicillin or amoxicillin). IM doses may cause pain and erythema at the injection site. Thrombophlebitis may occur with IV use.

DRUG INCOMPATIBILITIES: See penicillin G. Do not mix with any aminoglycosides in the same infusion fluid.

DRUG INTERACTIONS: Concomitantly administered *probenecid* increases and prolongs serum levels of these penicillins. There is synergistic activity with *gentamicin* and *tobramycin* against *Pseudomonas* (can use lower penicillin dosages).

ANTIDOTE: See penicillin G.

Amoxicillin (Amoxil, Larotid, Polymox)

ADMINISTRATION

Available Forms: Capsules, 250, 500 mg; oral suspension, 125 and 250 mg per 5 ml when reconstituted; pediatric drops, 50 mg/ml when reconstituted.

Dosage (Oral): Varies according to use and the patient's age.
Infants <6 kg: 25–50 mg q8h (drops).
Infants 6–8 kg: 50–100 mg q8h (drops).
Children <20 kg:

- For mild to moderate infections: 20 mg/kg/day in divided doses (q8h)
- For lower respiratory tract and severe infections: 40 mg/kg/day in divided doses (q8h)

Children 20 kg or more:

- For mild to moderate infections: 250 mg q8h
- For lower respiratory tract and severe infections: 500 mg q8h

RENAL IMPAIRMENT: See ampicillin.

ANTIMICROBIAL SPECTRUM: See ampicillin.

INDICATIONS: Amoxicillin is used in children primarily for urinary, respiratory, and GI tract infections; and bacterial otitis.

ACTIONS: See penicillins (general statement).

CONTRAINDICATIONS: See extended-spectrum penicillins (general statement).

PRECAUTIONS: See ampicillin.

SIDE EFFECTS/ADVERSE REACTIONS: See ampicillin.

DRUG INCOMPATIBILITIES: None.

DRUG INTERACTIONS: See extended-spectrum penicillins (general statement).

ANTIDOTE: See extended-spectrum penicillins (general statement).

Ampicillin (Omnipen, Polycillin, others)

ADMINISTRATION

Available Forms: Injectable (IM, IV), 125, 250, 500 mg, 1, 2 gm vials (powder), sodium content is 2.8–3.4 mEq/gm; tablets, 125 mg (chewable); capsules, 250, 500 mg; oral suspension, 125, 250, 500 mg per 5 ml when reconstituted; pediatric drops, 100 mg/ml when reconstituted.

Diluent: For IM use reconstitute with sterile water for injection; use the solution within 1 hour. For IV use can be further diluted (up to 30 mg/ml) in NS (stable for 8 hours at 25°C). Ampicillin degrades rapidly in D5W. Use concentrations of 10–30 mg/ml within 2 hours.

Dosage (Parenteral): Varies according to use and the patient's age.
Neonates up to 1 week old:

- For septicemia or meningitis: 50–100 mg/kg/day IV (preferred) or IM in divided doses (q12h) with an aminoglycoside

Neonates 1–4 weeks old:

- For septicemia or meningitis: 100–200 mg/kg/day IV (preferred) or IM in divided doses (q8–12h) with an aminoglycoside

Children <40 kg:

- For mild infections: 25–50 mg/kg/day IM or IV in divided doses (q6h)
- For moderately severe infections: 50–100 mg/kg/day IM or IV in divided doses (q6–8h)
- For severe infections: 150–200 mg/kg/day IV (preferred) or IM in divided doses (q3–4h)
- For meningitis: 200–400 mg/kg/day IV in divided doses (q3–4h) given with chloramphenicol IV

Children >40 kg:

- For moderate infections: 1–2 gm/day IV or IM in divided doses (q6h)
- For severe infections and meningitis: 8–14 gm/day IV (preferred) or IM in divided doses (q3–4h)

Dosage (Oral): Same as parenteral doses for mild and moderately severe infections. Should be taken on an empty stomach for maximum absorption.

Rate: Administer direct IV push doses no faster than 1 gm/10 min (more rapid rates may cause convulsive seizures). Avoid infusions of large volumes of dilute concentrations (e.g., 2–10 mg/ml) because these lose activity within 4 hours.

RENAL IMPAIRMENT: Dosage adjustments are necessary.

- Moderate impairment (CCr 10–50 ml/min): Normal daily doses q8h
- Severe impairment (CCr <10 ml/min): Normal daily doses q12h

ANTIMICROBIAL SPECTRUM: Same general gram-positive spectrum as penicillin G but has an extended gram-negative spectrum that includes *H. influenzae, N. gonorrhoeae, N. meningitidis,* certain *Salmonella* and *Shigella* strains, nonpenicillinase-producing strains of *P. mirabilis,* and many *E. coli* strains. Enterococcal infections *(S. faecalis)* also respond, but additional coverage with aminoglycosides is recommended in certain cases.
Resistant organisms: Penicillinase-producing staphylococci, most *Klebsiella* strains, *Pseudomonas,* and *Serratia.* Many enteric bacilli (e.g., *E. coli, Proteus*) and strains of *H. influenzae* are developing resistance, however.

INDICATIONS: Use of ampicillin in children is indicated primarily for urinary, respiratory, and GI tract infections; bacterial otitis; and meningitis. Urinary tract infections and SBE caused by penicillin-G-resistant enterococci may respond to ampicillin. Because it reaches high concentrations in the bile, it is useful for GI and biliary infections due to susceptible organisms. *Shigella* enteritis and *N. gonorrhoeae* infections respond well to ampicillin. It is the antibiotic of choice for chloramphenicol-resistant typhoid fever and also can be used to treat typhoid carriers. Ampicillin is given parenterally to children with bacterial meningitis caused by susceptible *H. influenzae, N. meningitidis,* or pneumococci.

ACTIONS: See penicillins (general statement).

CONTRAINDICATIONS: See extended-spectrum penicillins (general statement).

PRECAUTIONS: As for penicillin G. Also, a high incidence of erythematous maculopapular rash (so-called "ampicillin rash") is associated with ampicillin (and amoxicillin), particularly when used in patients with infectious mononucleosis or other viral infections.

Carbenicillin (Geocillin, Geopen)

ADMINISTRATION

Available Forms: Injectable (IM, IV), 1, 2, 5 gm vials (powder), sodium content is 4.7 mEq/gm; tablets, 382 mg of base (Geocillin).

Diluent: For IM use reconstitute with sterile water for injection or 0.5% lidocaine. Can be further diluted with D5W or NS for IV infusions (up to 4 gm in 50 ml, over 4 gm in 100 ml). Can be further diluted in D5W, NS, or multiple electrolyte solutions for continuous IV infusions.

Dosage (Parenteral): Varies according to use and the patient's age.
Neonates <2 kg:

- For sepsis: (Slow IV preferred) 100 mg/kg IV or IM initially, then 75 mg/kg q8h during the first week of life and 100 mg/kg q6h thereafter

Neonates 2 kg or more:

- For sepsis: (Slow IV preferred) 100 mg/kg IV or IM initially, then 75 mg/kg q6h for the first 3 days of life and 100 mg/kg q6h thereafter

Children:

- For urinary tract infections caused by *Proteus* or *E. coli:* 50–100 mg/kg/day IM or IV in divided doses (q4–6h)
- For urinary tract infections caused by *Pseudomonas, Enterobacter,* or enterococci: 50–200 mg/kg/day IM or IV in divided doses (q4–6h)
- For severe systemic infections caused by *Proteus* or *E. coli*: 300–400 mg/kg/day IV or IM in divided doses (q4–6h)
- For severe systemic infections caused by *Pseudomonas* or anaerobes: 400–500 mg/kg/day IV or IM in divided doses (q4–6h)

Dosage (Oral): Do not crush tablets as they are extremely bitter and unpalatable.
Children:

- For urinary tract infections only: 50–100 mg/kg/day in divided doses (q6h)

Rate: Administer IV doses as slowly as possible to avoid vein irritation. For neonates give IV doses over at least 15–20 minutes. Give IV bolus doses (e.g., 1 gm/5 ml) over

10–15 minutes. Doses diluted to 50 ml should be given over 30 minutes. Administer large doses (>5 gm) over 30–60 minutes.

RENAL IMPAIRMENT: Dosage adjustments are necessary.

- Moderate impairment (CCr 10–30 ml/min): Give doses q6–12h.
- Severe impairment (CCr <10 ml/min): Give doses q12–16h.
- Severe renal plus hepatic impairment: Give doses q24h.

ANTIMICROBIAL SPECTRUM: Gram-positive and gram-negative spectrums are similar to those of ampicillin. Additional susceptible organisms include more strains of *Proteus* (indole-positive), *Enterobacter*, some ampicillin-resistant strains of *H. influenzae* and *E. coli*, enterococci (*S. faecalis*), and anaerobes such as bacteroides and clostridia. High concentrations are needed to inhibit certain strains of *P. aeruginosa* and *B. fragilis*. Some newer strains of *Serratia* and *Citrobacter* may also be sensitive.

Resistant organisms: Penicillinase-producing *Proteus* species and staphylococci, *Klebsiella*, and many *Serratia* species. *P. aeruginosa* may develop resistance rapidly, and such resistance can be transferred to strains of *E. coli*.

INDICATIONS: Oral carbenicillin is indicated only for urinary tract infections due to susceptible gram-negative pathogens, including enterococci. Parenteral doses of carbenicillin (and ticarcillin) are used for systemic infections caused by susceptible anaerobic bacteria, *Pseudomonas*, indole-positive *Proteus*, and *E. coli* strains. (There are insufficient clinical data to recommend their use in meningitis due to ampicillin-resistant *H. influenzae*.) These antibiotics should be given concomitantly with gentamicin (or tobramycin) for deep tissue or systemic *Pseudomonas* infections (synergistic effect).

ACTIONS: See penicillins (general statement).

CONTRAINDICATIONS: See extended-spectrum penicillins (general statement).

PRECAUTIONS: As for penicillin G. Also, bleeding tendencies associated with abnormal coagulation tests and platelet dysfunction have been reported, particularly in patients with renal impairment (warrants drug discontinuation). High doses in patients with renal impairment may cause CNS toxicity and convulsions. High doses may also cause hypokalemia; monitor serum levels of potassium periodically. High doses with these sodium salts may cause fluid retention; use cautiously in patients with congestive heart failure, etc. During prolonged therapy, periodic renal and hepatic function tests and coagulation studies are advised. Superinfections with *Klebsiella* and *Serratia* may occur.

SIDE EFFECTS/ADVERSE REACTIONS: See extended-spectrum penicillins (general statement). In addition, oral doses of carbenicillin can cause GI upset, nausea, vomiting, diarrhea, dry mouth, flatulence, and a furry tongue. Nausea and an unpleasant, bitter aftertaste can occur with both oral and IV (rapid rate of administration) carbenicillin.

DRUG INCOMPATIBILITIES: See extended-spectrum penicillins (general statement).

DRUG INTERACTIONS: See extended-spectrum penicillins (general statement).

ANTIDOTE: See extended-spectrum penicillins (general statement).

Mezlocillin (Mezlin)

ADMINISTRATION

Available Forms: Injectable (IM, IV), 1, 2, 3, 4 gm vials (powder); sodium content is 1.85 mEq/gm.

Diluent: For IM use reconstitute with sterile water or 0.5–1.0% lidocaine; maximum dose per injection is 2 gm. Can be further diluted with D5W or NS (1 gm/50 ml) for intermittent infusion. For continuous IV infusion, can be diluted to 10 mg or more per milliliter with D5W, NS, or multiple electrolyte solutions.

Dosage (Parenteral): Varies according to the patient's age.
Neonates <2 kg: 75 mg/kg IV q12h for the first week of life, then 75 mg/kg q8h thereafter.
Neonates 2 kg or more: 75 mg/kg IV q12h for the first week of life, then 75 mg/kg q6h thereafter.
Infants >1 month old and children <12 years old: 300 mg/kg/day IV (preferred) or IM in divided doses (q4h).

Rate: Infuse IV doses slowly over 30 minutes. Bolus doses are not recommended; if used, however, the manufacturer suggests 1 gm/10 ml given over 5 minutes. Give IM injections slowly (e.g., 2 gm over 12–15 seconds).

RENAL IMPAIRMENT: Dosage adjustments are necessary.

- Mild to moderate impairment (CCr >30 ml/min): Give normal doses q6h.
- Moderate impairment (CCr 10–30 ml/min): Give 75% normal dose q6–8h.
- Severe impairment (CCr <10 ml/min): Give 50% normal dose q6–8h.

ANTIMICROBIAL SPECTRUM: Mezlocillin shares the gram-positive spectrum of ampicillin, carbenicillin, and ticarcillin. The gram-negative spectrum is also similar with the notable addition of *Klebsiella* species, including *Klebsiella pneumoniae*. Mezlocillin is more effective than the other extended-spectrum penicillins against *Pseudomonas, Citrobacter, Serratia, Proteus, E. coli*, and certain anaerobes (including *B. fragilis*).
Resistant organisms: Penicillinase-producing staphylococci. *Pseudomonas* species may develop resistance fairly rapidly.

INDICATIONS: Mezlocillin is effective in the treatment of peritonitis; abscesses; and urinary tract, deep tissue, and systemic infections due to susceptible pathogens. It is not approved for use in meningitis.

ACTIONS: See penicillins (general statement).

CONTRAINDICATIONS: See extended-spectrum penicillins (general statement).

PRECAUTIONS: As for carbenicillin, except that superinfections with *Klebsiella* and *Serratia* are unlikely.

SIDE EFFECTS/ADVERSE REACTIONS: See extended-spectrum penicillins (general statement).

DRUG INCOMPATIBILITIES: See extended-spectrum penicillins (general statement).

DRUG INTERACTIONS: See extended-spectrum penicillins (general statement).

ANTIDOTE: See extended-spectrum penicillins (general statement).

Piperacillin (Pipracil)

ADMINISTRATION

Available Forms: Injectable (IM, IV), 2, 3, 4 gm vials (powder); sodium content is 1.98 mEq/gm.

Diluent: For IM use reconstitute with sterile water or 0.5–1.0% lidocaine for injection (1 gm/2 ml). For IV use can be further diluted with D5W, NS, or LR. Dilute doses in at least 50 ml diluent.

Dosage (Parenteral): Not established for children less than 12 years of age or neonates.
For uncomplicated urinary tract infections: 6–8 gm/day IV or IM in divided doses (q6–12h).
For complicated urinary tract infections: 8–16 gm/day IV in divided doses (q6–8h); up to 24 gm/day.
For pneumonia (community-acquired): 6–8 gm/day IM or IV in divided doses (q6–12h).
For other pneumonias and severe systemic infections: 12–18 gm/day IV in divided doses (q4–6h); up to 24 gm/day.

Rate: Give IV doses slowly over 30 minutes. Bolus doses are not recommended; if used, the manufacturer suggests 1 gm/5–10 ml given over 3–5 minutes. IM injections should not exceed 2 gm/dose.

RENAL IMPAIRMENT: Dosage adjustments are necessary.

- Mild to moderate impairment (CCr >40 ml/min): No adjustment necessary
- Moderate impairment (CCr 20–40 ml/min): 3–4 gm q8h
- Severe impairment (CCr <20 ml/min): 3–4 gm q12h

ANTIMICROBIAL SPECTRUM: As for mezlocillin. Piperacillin may be slightly more effective than mezlocillin against *Pseudomonas, Citrobacter, Serratia, Proteus, E. coli,* and certain anaerobes (including *B. fragilis*).

INDICATIONS: As for mezlocillin.

ACTIONS: See penicillins (general statement).

CONTRAINDICATIONS: See extended-spectrum penicillins (general statement).

PRECAUTIONS: As for mezlocillin.

SIDE EFFECTS/ADVERSE REACTIONS: See extended-spectrum penicillins (general statement).

DRUG INCOMPATIBILITIES: See extended-spectrum penicillins (general statement).

DRUG INTERACTIONS: See extended-spectrum penicillins (general statement).

ANTIDOTE: See extended-spectrum penicillins (general statement).

Ticarcillin (Ticar)

ADMINISTRATION

Available Forms: Injectable (IM, IV), 1, 3, 6 gm vials (powder); sodium content is 5.2–6.5 mEq/gm.

Diluent: For IM use reconstitute with sterile water for injection or 0.5–1.0% lidocaine. For IV use can be further diluted with D5W or NS to 10–50 mg/ml. For bolus doses dilute 1 gm in 20 ml or more. For intermittent infusion, dilute up to 3 gm in 50 ml, over 3 gm in 100 ml.

Dosage (Parenteral): Varies according to the patient's age.
Neonates <2 kg: For sepsis: 100 mg/kg IV initially, then 75 mg/kg q8h during the first week of life, and 100 mg/kg q4h thereafter.
Neonates >2 kg: For sepsis: 100 mg/kg IV initially, then 75 mg/kg q4–6h for the first 2 weeks of life, and 100 mg/kg q4h thereafter.
Children:

- For uncomplicated urinary tract infections: 50–100 mg/kg/day IM or IV in divided doses (q6–8h)
- For complicated urinary tract infections: 150–200 mg/kg/day IV in divided doses (q4–6h)
- For severe systemic infections: 200–300 mg/kg/day IV in divided doses (q4–6h)

Rate: Administer IV doses slowly to avoid vein irritation. For neonates give IV doses over at least 15–20 minutes; IV bolus doses (e.g., 1 gm/20 ml), over 10–15 minutes. Doses diluted to 50 ml should be given over 30 minutes.

RENAL IMPAIRMENT: Dosage adjustments are necessary.

- For mild impairment (CCr 50–80 ml/min): Normal dosage q4–6h
- For moderate impairment (CCr 10–50 ml/min): Normal or slightly reduced dose q8h
- For severe impairment (CCr <10 ml/min): Slightly reduced dose q12h
- For severe renal plus hepatic impairment: Slightly reduced dose q24h

ANTIMICROBIAL SPECTRUM: As for carbenicillin.

INDICATIONS: As for parenteral carbenicillin.

ACTIONS: See penicillins (general statement).

CONTRAINDICATIONS: See extended-spectrum penicillins (general statement).

PRECAUTIONS: As for carbenicillin. Superinfections with *Klebsiella* and *Serratia* may occur.

SIDE EFFECTS/ADVERSE REACTIONS: See extended-spectrum penicillins (general statement).

DRUG INCOMPATIBILITIES: See extended-spectrum penicillins (general statement).

DRUG INTERACTIONS: See extended-spectrum penicillins (general statement).

ANTIDOTE: See extended-spectrum penicillins (general statement).

20
Sulfonamides

The sulfonamides in use are all derivatives of the prototype drug, sulfanilamide, the first sulfa developed in the 1930s. The importance of these antibiotics in the treatment of many infectious diseases (notably meningitis) has diminished as bacterial resistance to them has increased and more effective antibiotics have been developed. They have, however, maintained a prominent place in the treatment of urinary tract infections. These agents are usually ineffective topically for wound, skin, and mucous membrane infections because they are inactivated by purulent exudates.

There are four major categories of sulfonamides:

1. Those that are rapidly absorbed and rapidly excreted (e.g., sulfisoxazole)
2. Those that are rapidly absorbed and slowly excreted (e.g., sulfamethoxazole)
3. Those that are poorly absorbed when given orally and therefore are used primarily for local antibacterial effect in the gut and in ulcerative colitis (e.g., sulfasalazine)
4. Those that are applied topically (e.g., silver sulfadiazine)

The sulfonamides covered in this chapter include the following only:

- **Silver sulfadiazine**
- **Sulfamethoxazole**
- **Sulfamethoxazole with trimethoprim**
- **Sulfisoxazole**

SULFONAMIDES (GENERAL STATEMENT)

RENAL IMPAIRMENT: See the individual drug listings.

ANTIMICROBIAL SPECTRUM: The sulfonamides are effective against common urinary tract pathogens, including susceptible *E. coli, Klebsiella-Enterobacter, P. mirabilis* and other indole-positive *Proteus,* and staphylococci. *H. influenzae* (including ampicillin-resistant strains), *S. pneumoniae,* certain *Shigella* species, *Nocardia,* and *Pneumocystis carinii* are also susceptible.
Resistant organisms: Notably *Pseudomonas* species, but many bacteria develop a high degree of resistance during therapy. These include strains of *Klebsiella-Enterobacter, Proteus, H. influenzae,* pneumococci, meningococci, enterococci, staphylococci, anaerobic streptococci, spirochetes, clostridia, gonococci, and *Shigella.*

INDICATIONS: The development of resistance has greatly limited the clinical usefulness of the sulfonamides. Their primary use is in the treatment of acute, recurrent, or chronic nonobstructive urinary tract infections due to susceptible bacteria. They are also used in children for the treatment of acute otitis media caused by susceptible strains of *H. influenzae* and *S. pneumoniae.* Bacillary dysentery due to susceptible *Shigella* strains is usually treated with a sulfa-trimethoprim combination. This combination is also used orally and parenterally for treatment of *P. carinii* pneumonia. The sulfonamides are also used to treat chancroid, trachoma, inclusion conjunctivitis, nocardiosis, and toxoplasmosis (adjunctive therapy with pyrimethamine). Topical preparations are used in the prevention and treatment of burn infections (e.g., silver sulfadiazine) and in certain ophthalmic conditions such as blepharitis, conjunctivitis, and corneal ulcers (sulfacetamide ophthalmic solution).

ACTIONS: Sulfonamides interfere with the utilization of para-aminobenzoic acid (PABA), which inhibits the biosynthesis of folic acid essential for the growth of certain microorganisms. Only those microorganisms that synthesize their own folic acid are inhibited by the sulfonamides. These antibiotics are usually bacteriostatic, but in extremely high concentrations (as is achieved in urinary tract infections) they may be bactericidal. Oral doses of most sulfonamides are well absorbed; these are widely distributed in most body fluids, and the levels of some in the CSF may be 35–80% of plasma levels. These antibiotics are metabolized in the liver, and the metabolites and some unchanged drug are excreted via the kidneys. Therapeutic blood levels are 5–15 mg/100 ml.

CONTRAINDICATIONS: Hypersensitivity to sulfonamides, infants less than 2 months of age (except as adjunctive therapy with pyrimethamine in the treatment of congenital toxoplasmosis), porphyria, and severe renal or hepatic impairment.

PRECAUTIONS: Maintain adequate fluid intake and urine output (at least 1200 ml/day) to prevent crystalluria and renal damage. Alkalinization of urine may be necessary if the urine is highly acidic and urine output is low. Evaluate renal function periodically. Weekly blood counts should be done if prolonged sulfonamide therapy is required. Possible cross-hypersensitivity exists for all sulfonamides and for sulfonamide derivatives (e.g., thiazide diuretics, oral hypoglycemics). Use cautiously in patients with severe allergy, bronchial asthma, impaired renal or hepatic function, urinary obstruction, G6PD deficiency, or porphyria. Dosage adjustments are necessary in notable renal impairment (CCr 15–30 ml/min). Use of sulfonamides may worsen megaloblastic anemia due to folate deficiency; oral folic acid supplements may be indicated. Avoid use in newborn infants as kernicterus may result from sulfonamide displacement of protein-bound bilirubin. Discontinue if fever, rash, jaundice, or purpura develops. Avoid prolonged exposure to sunlight as photosensitivity reactions may occur. *In vitro* sulfonamide sensitivity tests may not be reliable, so coordinate test results with bacteriological and clinical response. Administer IV doses slowly and avoid extravasation. Sulfonamides should *never* be used for treatment of group A beta-hemolytic streptococcal infections (e.g., pharyngitis, tonsillitis).

SIDE EFFECTS/ADVERSE REACTIONS: Hypersensitivity reactions range from common mild rashes and pruritus to less frequent but severe forms of exfoliative dermatitis, erythema multiforme (Stevens-Johnson syndrome), and anaphylactoid reactions. Children are especially susceptible to the Stevens-Johnson syndrome, which has a high mortality rate (about 25%). Signs and symptoms of the syndrome include fever, severe headache, stomatitis, conjunctivitis, rhinitis, and cutaneous lesions. Photosensitivity, drug fever, serum-sickness and lupus-like reactions also may occur. Oral use may cause gastric upset with nausea, vomiting, diarrhea, and anorexia. CNS effects include headache, lethargy, dizziness, ataxia, and mental depression. Peripheral neuritis, psychoses, and convulsions have been reported (rare). Toxic nephrosis with oliguria, anuria, and crystalluria may occur. Blood dyscrasias include granulocytopenia, leukopenia, thrombocytopenia, and aplastic and hemolytic anemias. Sulfonamides may precipitate acute hemolytic anemia in G6PD-deficient patients. Mild, chronic hemolytic anemia may develop during prolonged therapy. Rarely, goiter, hypothyroidism, hypoglycemia, hepatitis, and pancreatitis may occur.

DRUG INTERACTIONS: Sulfonamides may potentiate the activity and toxicity of *oral anticoagulants, oral hypoglycemics, phenytoin,* and *methotrexate* by displacing these medications from their protein-binding sites. *PABA* and *local anesthetics* derived from PABA (e.g., procaine, benzocaine, tetracaine) antagonize the antibacterial activity of the sulfa drugs.

ANTIDOTE: Discontinue sulfonamides. Treat hypersensitivity reactions symptomatically.

Silver sulfadiazine (Silvadene)

ADMINISTRATION

Available Forms: Topical, cream (1%) in 50 and 400 gm jars.

Dosage (Topical): Following cleansing and debriding, with a sterile, gloved hand, apply cream to a 1 mm ($\frac{1}{16}$ inch) thickness to burned surface once or twice a day. Continue therapy until the area is ready for grafting.

ANTIMICROBIAL SPECTRUM: Most strains of *Pseudomonas, Enterobacter, Klebsiella, E. coli, Proteus,* staphylococci, streptococci (including enterococci), clostridia, corynebacteria, *Providencia, Serratia,* and some *Candida* species.

INDICATIONS: This sulfonamide is used to prevent and treat infections and thereby reduce morbidity and mortality in patients with second-degree and third-degree (partial and full-thickness) burns.

ACTIONS: Unlike other sulfonamides, silver sulfadiazine acts on the cell wall (bacteria) and cell membrane (bacteria and other microorganisms) to produce a microbicidal effect. Its action is not dependent on inhibition of microbial folic acid synthesis, and it is not inhibited by PABA as other sulfonamides are.

CONTRAINDICATIONS: Hypersensitivity to sulfonamides and methylparabens. If the burn area is extensive and there is increased risk of systemic absorption, it is probably contraindicated in pregnant women at term, neonates (<1 month old), premature infants, and patients with G6PD deficiency.

PRECAUTIONS: Use cautiously in patients with hepatic or renal impairment and in other high-risk patients (see contraindications). Fungal superinfection may occur. Apply cream under sterile conditions. Cover with dressings only if necessary and reapply the antibiotic as needed. Concomitant daily hydrotherapy and mechanical debridement are advisable, especially in patients with third-degree burns.

SIDE EFFECTS/ADVERSE REACTIONS: Occasional pain, burning, itching, and rashes have been reported. Silver sulfadiazine does not cause electrolyte disturbances even after prolonged contact as does mafenide cream. If the burn area is extensive (e.g., 20%), systemic absorption may occur, and other adverse reactions related to systemic sulfonamides may occur.

ANTIDOTE: The cream is easily washed off. Treat hypersensitivity reactions as necessary.

Sulfamethoxazole (Gantanol)

ADMINISTRATION

Available Forms: Tablets, 500 mg; oral suspension, 500 mg/5 ml (also available with phenazopyridine, Azo-Gantanol tablets).

Dosage (Oral): Varies according to the patient's age and condition.
Neonates with congenital toxoplasmosis: 75 mg/kg/day in divided doses (q12h) for 30 days. Give with pyrimethamine (2 mg/kg/day for 3 days, then 1 mg/kg/day for remainder). Folinic acid, 1 mg/kg/day IM as single dose, can be given to lessen antifolate toxicity.
Infants (>2 months old) and children: 50–60 mg/kg (1.2 gm/m^2) initially, then 50–60 mg/kg/day (1.2 gm/m^2/day) in divided doses (q12h). Maximum is 75 mg/kg/day.

RENAL IMPAIRMENT: With creatinine clearances of 15–30 ml/min, give normal doses (q24h). Avoid use if CCr <15 ml/min.

ANTIMICROBIAL SPECTRUM: See sulfonamides (general statement).

INDICATIONS: See sulfonamides (general statement).

ACTIONS: See sulfonamides (general statement).

CONTRAINDICATIONS: See sulfonamides (general statement).

PRECAUTIONS: See sulfonamides (general statement).

SIDE EFFECTS/ADVERSE REACTIONS: See sulfonamides (general statement).

DRUG INCOMPATIBILITIES: None.

DRUG INTERACTIONS: See sulfonamides (general statement).

ANTIDOTE: See sulfonamides (general statement).

Sulfamethoxazole with trimethoprim (Bactrim, Septra, Bactrim IV, Septra IV)

ADMINISTRATION

Available Forms: Injectable (IV), 16 mg trimethoprim (TMP) and 80 mg sulfamethoxazole (SMX) per milliliter in 5 ml amps; tablets (single-strength), 80 mg TMP and 400 mg SMX; tablets (double-strength), 160 mg TMP and 800 mg SMX (DS); oral suspension, 8 mg TMP and 40 mg SMX per milliliter.

Diluent: For IV use dilute each 5 ml ampule in 75–125 ml D5W *only*. Mix prior to use and administer within 2 hours. Do not add to any other IV solutions or medications.

Dosage (Parenteral): Doses are based on trimethoprim (TMP) concentration.
For infants (>2 months old) and children:

- For *Pneumocystis carinii* pneumonia: 15–20 mg/kg/day slow IV in divided doses (q6–8h) for up to 14 days
- For severe urinary tract infections: 8–10 mg/kg/day slow IV in divided doses (q6–12h) for 14 days
- For shigellosis: 8–10 mg/kg/day slow IV in divided doses (q6–12h) for 5 days

Dosage (Oral): Same as parenteral dosage.

Rate: Administer IV infusions over 60–90 minutes.

RENAL IMPAIRMENT: Dosage adjustments are necessary.

- Mild to moderate impairment (CCr >30 ml/min): Follow standard regimen.
- Moderate impairment (CCr 15–30 ml/min): Give one-half usual dosage.
- Severe impairment (CCr <15 ml/min): Use *not* recommended.

ANTIMICROBIAL SPECTRUM: See sulfonamides (general statement).

INDICATIONS: See sulfonamides (general statement).

ACTIONS: See sulfonamides (general statement).

CONTRAINDICATIONS: See sulfonamides (general statement).

PRECAUTIONS: See sulfonamides (general statement). Also, addition of trimethoprim to sulfa drugs has been associated with an increased incidence of folate and vitamin B_{12} deficiencies that result in megaloblastic and pernicious anemia as well as other blood dyscrasias, including neutropenia, thrombocytopenia, and leukopenia. These deficiencies occur especially with prolonged use (more than 14 days). Leucovorin, 3–6 mg/kg IM for 3 days, as well as vitamin B_{12} IM may reverse the hematopoietic toxicity.

SIDE EFFECTS/ADVERSE REACTIONS: See sulfonamides (general statement).

DRUG INCOMPATIBILITIES: Do not mix with any other medications.

DRUG INTERACTIONS: See sulfonamides (general statement).

ANTIDOTE: See sulfonamides (general statement).

Sulfisoxazole (Gantrisin)

ADMINISTRATION

Available Forms: Injectable (IV, SC), 400 mg/5 ml amps; tablets, 500 mg; oral suspension, 500 mg/5 ml; topical, ophthalmic drops and ointment; also available with phenazopyridine (Azo-Gantrisin tablets).

Diluent: For IV use (not recommended) dilute ampule with sterile water for injection (e.g., 5 ml amp in 35 ml water). Do not exceed 50 mg/ml.

Dosage (Parenteral)
For infants (>2 months old) and children: 50 mg/kg (1.25 gm/m²) initially slow IV, then 100 mg/kg/day in divided doses (q6h).

Dosage (Oral)
For neonates:

- For congenital toxoplasmosis: 100–150 mg/kg/day in divided doses (q6h) given with pyrimethamine. Caution: Can cause kernicterus. See also sulfamethoxazole.

For infants (>2 months old) and children: 75 mg/kg (2 gm/m^2) initially, then 150 mg/kg/day (4 gm/m^2/day) in divided doses (q4–6h). Maximum is 6 gm/day.

Rate: Give IV doses slowly over 10–30 minutes.

RENAL IMPAIRMENT: Dosage adjustments are necessary.

- Moderate impairment (CCr 15–30 ml/min): Give normal doses q8–12h.
- Severe impairment (CCr <15 ml/min): Give normal doses q12–24h.

(If high urinary levels are desired, continue with normal doses q6h.)

ANTIMICROBIAL SPECTRUM: See sulfonamides (general statement).

INDICATIONS: See sulfonamides (general statement).

ACTIONS: See sulfonamides (general statement).

CONTRAINDICATIONS: See sulfonamides (general statement).

PRECAUTIONS: See sulfonamides (general statement).

SIDE EFFECTS/ADVERSE REACTIONS: See sulfonamides (general statement).

DRUG INCOMPATIBILITIES: Do not mix with any other medications.

DRUG INTERACTIONS: See sulfonamides (general statement).

ANTIDOTE: See sulfonamides (general statement).

21
Tetracyclines

The tetracyclines are broad-spectrum antimicrobial agents. Although many tetracycline cogeners have been developed since the introduction of chlortetracycline in 1948, only three of the analogues are discussed in this chapter:

- **Doxycyline**
- **Minocycline**
- **Tetracycline**

TETRACYCLINES (GENERAL STATEMENT)

RENAL IMPAIRMENT: See the individual drug listings.

ANTIMICROBIAL SPECTRUM: The tetracyclines are primarily active against mycobacteria, mycoplasmas (and L forms), rickettsiae, chlamydiae (e.g., the psittacosis-lymphogranuloma-venereum-trachoma group), *Brucella, Vibrio cholera* and other *Vibrio* species, *Bordatella pertussis, Pasteurella (Yersinia pestis)*, spirochetes (*Borrelia, Leptospira,* and *Treponema*), *Shigella,* and some protozoa (amoebas). Other organisms usually susceptible include staphylococci, aerobic and anaerobic streptococci, gram-positive bacilli (*B. anthracis,* clostridia, *L. monocytogenes*), *Actinomyces, H. influenzae* and *Hemophilus ducreyi* (chancroid), and *N. gonorrhoeae*. Although tetracyclines are active *in vitro* against some strains of *Mima-Herellea, Bacteroides, Enterobacter-Klebsiella,* and *E. coli,* many of these organisms are resistant or become resistant.

Resistant organisms: Most strains of *Proteus* and *Pseudomonas* and all yeasts, fungi, and viruses. Tetracycline therapy, particularly when prolonged, can result in overgrowth of resistant strains of staphylococci, *Klebsiella, Enterobacter, Proteus,* and *Candida*. Many resistant gram-positive and gram-negative enteric organisms have emerged. Cross-resistance with chloramphenicol can occur with some gram-negative bacteria.

INDICATIONS: The tetracyclines are among the first-choice antibiotics for treatment of infections caused by rickettsiae, *Borrelia* (relapsing fever), *Mycoplasma pneumoniae, V. cholera, Pasteurella tularensis* (tularemia), *Brucella,* and *Chlamydia* (e.g., psittacosis, ornithosis, lymphogranuloma venereum, trachoma, inclusion conjunctivitis, and keratoconjunctivitis). Treatment of brucellosis and plague (*Y. pestis*) usually requires the addition of streptomycin. Tetracyclines are acceptable alternative agents for treatment of bacillary dysentery due to sensitive strains of *Shigella,* for susceptible gonococcal infections in patients allergic to penicillins, and as adjunctive therapy in acne and intestinal amebiasis. They are used as alternative antibiotics for prophylaxis and treatment of acute and chronic bronchitis caused by *H. influenzae, S. pneumoniae,* or *Klebsiella*. Tetracyclines have been used also as alternative antibiotics for local and systemic infections caused by certain gram-negative organisms (see antimicrobial spectrum), but C&S tests should be done to determine the effectiveness of a tetracycline for these conditions.

ACTIONS: These bacteriostatic antibiotics inhibit microbial growth by blocking the attachment of the transfer-RNA-amino-acid complex to the ribosome. Consequently, no amino acid is available to the messenger RNA for further production of polypeptides and protein synthesis is inhibited. The tetracyclines are active against organisms that lack cell walls such as mycoplasma and certain bacterial variants (e.g., protoplasts and L forms) that may develop and persist during treatment with other antibiotics that act by inhibiting the synthesis of bacterial cell walls (e.g., penicillins and cephalosporins).

Tetracyclines are usually given orally and are readily but incompletely absorbed from the GI tract (doxycycline and minocycline have the best absorption). It is often necessary to give an oral loading dose to achieve therapeutic serum levels quickly. These antibiotics form poorly absorbed, insoluble complexes with calcium, magnesium, iron, aluminum, and other metal ions. Consequently, the absorption of tetracyclines is impaired when taken with milk or milk products, food, vitamin and mineral preparations, cathartics, or antacids. Parenteral doses should be used only if patients are unable to take these agents orally. The tetracyclines can be given IV for serious infections in patients who have malabsorption syndromes or who are comatose. Administration of IM doses is extremely painful, even with some of the preparations containing 2% lidocaine. Topical use is of little or no value except in some ocular infections.

These agents diffuse readily into most fluids and tissues including cerebrospinal fluid. They have an affinity for fast-growing tissues, liver, tumors, and areas of new bone and tooth formation, particularly before birth and during the first 3 years of life. Tetracyclines are concentrated in the liver and excreted in bile. Most are excreted chiefly by the kidneys as unchanged antibiotic. Tetracycline has a half-life of approximately 9–10 hours, but the newer analogues, doxycycline and minocycline, have extended half-lifes of nearly 20 hours, which allows for smaller doses at longer intervals.

CONTRAINDICATIONS: Hypersensitivity to any tetracycline, infants and children less than 8 years of age.

PRECAUTIONS: Avoid use of all tetracyclines during the period of bone and tooth development (last half of gestation, infancy, and childhood up to 8 years of age). These antibiotics can cause temporary depression of bone growth in these age groups because they bind calcium and phosphates. They can cause permanent tooth discoloration (yellow-gray-brown) and enamel hypoplasia even after short-term use. Renal impairment may lead to accumulation of tetracyclines, with possible nephrotoxicity and hepatotoxicity, so dosage reductions are necessary. All tetracyclines (with the exception of doxycycline) have an "antianabolic" effect that can cause a negative nitrogen balance leading to azotemia, hyperphosphatemia, and acidosis, especially in patients with renal impairment. Outdated or degraded tetracyclines have caused a form of acute renal tubular acidosis and nephrotoxicity known as the Fanconi syndrome. Make sure all tetracyclines dispensed are within their stated expiration dates and are stored properly. The diminished renal excretion of doxycycline and minocycline may make them better choices for use in patients with compromised renal function as accumulation of these two may not be significant. Preexisting hepatic as well as renal insufficiency may lead to hepatotoxicity. Use cautiously or avoid altogether during pregnancy and the postpartum period (especially in patients with pyelonephritis) since they can cause fatty infiltration of liver and hepatic failure. Tetracyclines can also cause rare pseudotumor cerebri and tense bulging of the fontanelles in infants and increased intracranial pressure in older children. Superinfections, primarily with yeasts, may occur, and an overgrowth of *S. aureus* may induce diarrhea or enterocolitis. Avoid prolonged exposure to sunlight as photosensitivity reactions of exaggerated sunburn may occur (not reported to occur with minocycline). During long-term therapy, periodic blood, renal, and hepatic studies should be performed. Do not give oral doses of tetracyclines with food, milk, milk products, or antacids. Give at least 1 hour before ingestion of these substances. Patients hypersensitive to one tetracycline are hypersensitive to all of them.

SIDE EFFECTS/ADVERSE REACTIONS: Gastrointestinal effects of nausea, vomiting, anorexia, diarrhea, glossitis, stomatitis, proctitis and vaginitis (with *Candida* overgrowth), and black hairy tongue may occur. Dermatological and hypersensitivity reactions include various rashes, exacerbation of SLE, and anaphylactoid reactions. Photosensitivity reactions may occur and persist for a considerable time after the medication has been discontinued. Hyperpigmentation of skin, nails, and mucous membranes has been reported. Blood dyscrasias include hemolytic anemia, thrombocytopenia, neutropenia, and eosinophilia. Dizziness, light-headedness, and vertigo are reported CNS effects. A high incidence of thrombophlebitis is associated with IV use. Rapid IV infusion can cause nausea, vomiting, fever, chills, and hypotension. Hepatic failure, nephrotoxicity, and pancreatic damage are associated with high IV doses, blood levels of tetracycline greater than 15 µg/ml, or dosages higher than the recommended maximum of 2 gm/day (especially in pregnant women with preexisting pyelonephritis).

DRUG INCOMPATIBILITIES: Avoid diluting in solutions containing calcium (Ringer's solution or lactated Ringer's solution can be used, however). Avoid direct admixture with aminoglycosides, penicillins, narcotics, sedative-hypnotics, antiemetics, sodium bicarbonate, or hydrocortisone.

DRUG INTERACTIONS: Decreased gastric absorption of tetracyclines occurs with *antacids, iron, mineral supplements,* and *sodium bicarbonate*. Concomitant use may decrease the bactericidal effect of *penicillins*. Increased prothrombin time (due to interference with bacterial synthesis of vitamin K) may occur alone with tetracycline and particularly with concomitant use of *oral anticoagulants*. Increased nephrotoxicity has been reported when tetracyclines are used with the general anesthetic *methoxyflurane*.

ANTIDOTE: Discontinue tetracycline. Treat adverse reactions symptomatically, and institute supportive measures where necessary.

Doxycycline (Vibramycin)

ADMINISTRATION

Available Forms: Injectable (IV), 100, 200 mg vials (powder); capsules, 50, 100 mg; oral suspension, 25 mg/5 ml (powder for reconstitution).

Diluent: Dilute with D5W or NS for IV infusion. Diluted IV solutions of 0.1–1.0 mg/ml must be used within 12 hours to ensure stability. If D5LR or LR is used, infusion must be completed within 6 hours after mixing to ensure stability. Protect solutions from direct sunlight.

Dosage (Parenteral): Varies according to the patient's weight.
Children >8 years old and 45 kg or less: 4.4 mg/kg IV in divided doses (q12h) for the first day, then 2.2–4.4 mg/kg/day in divided doses (q12–24h), depending on the severity of infection.
Children >8 years old and >45 kg: 200 mg IV in divided doses (q12h) for the first day, then 100–200 mg/day IV, depending on the severity of infection.

Dosage (Oral): Varies according to the patient's weight.

Children >8 years old and 45 kg or less: 4.4 mg/kg in divided doses (q12h) for the first day, then 2.2–4.4 mg/kg/day in divided doses (q12–24h), depending on the severity of infection.

Children >8 years and >45 kg: 200 mg in divided doses (q12h) for the first day, then 100–200 mg/day, depending on the severity of infection.

Rate: Administer IV doses in 50–100 ml of diluent over 30–60 minutes.

RENAL IMPAIRMENT: Dosage adjustments usually are not necessary.

ANTIMICROBIAL SPECTRUM: See tetracyclines (general statement). There is evidence that some strains of staphylococci resistant to other tetracyclines may be susceptible to doxycycline *in vitro*.

INDICATIONS: See tetracyclines (general statement). Doxycycline may be the antibiotic of choice for treating extrarenal infections in patients with renal insufficiency. However, for urinary tract infections, use plain tetracycline, which has a higher rate of renal clearance.

CONTRAINDICATIONS: Hypersensitivity to any of the tetracyclines.

PRECAUTIONS: See tetracyclines (general statement). Doxycycline is not "antianabolic" and does not cause further renal damage or azotemia as do other tetracyclines.

SIDE EFFECTS/ADVERSE REACTIONS: The toxic potential of doxycycline appears to be low and limited mainly to GI, allergic, and photosensitivity reactions. Same warnings, however, for use in pregnant women and young children.

DRUG INCOMPATIBILITIES: See tetracyclines (general statement).

DRUG INTERACTIONS: See tetracyclines (general statement). In addition, *phenytoin* may increase metabolism of doxycycline thereby resulting in lower serum levels of the antibiotic.

ANTIDOTE: See tetracyclines (general statement).

Minocycline (Minocin)

ADMINISTRATION

Available Forms: Injectable (IV), 100 mg vials (powder); capsules, 50, 100 mg; tablets, 100 mg; oral syrup, 50 mg/5 ml.

Diluent: Reconstitute with sterile water for injection. Further dilute to 100 mg/500 ml with D5W or NS.

Dosage (Parenteral)
Children >8 years old: 4 mg/kg IV to start, then 4 mg/kg/day IV in divided doses (q12h).

Dosage (Oral)
Children >8 years old: 4 mg/kg to start, then 4 mg/kg/day in divided doses (q12h).

Rate: Administer IV infusions slowly (e.g., give doses diluted to 500 ml over 3–6 hours).

RENAL IMPAIRMENT: Use lower dosages and extend dosage intervals. Keep serum levels of minocycline below 15 µg/ml. Monitor renal and, especially, hepatic function tests.

ANTIMICROBIAL SPECTRUM: See tetracyclines (general statement). Minocycline tends to show greater *in vitro* activity against staphylococci (including tetracycline-resistant strains), most strains of gram-positive cocci (except enterococci), and many strains of gram-negative bacilli. Clinical importance of these differences may not be significant as tetracyclines are generally not antibiotics of choice for infections caused by these bacteria.

INDICATIONS: See tetracyclines (general statement). Also, as with doxycycline, minocycline can be used for extrarenal infections caused by susceptible organisms in patients with renal impairment. Minocycline has also been used to eliminate meningococci from the nasopharynx of asymptomatic *N. meningitidis* carriers when the risk of meningococcal meningitis is high. It is *not* indicated for treatment of meningitis, however.

CONTRAINDICATIONS: Hypersensitivity to any of the tetracyclines.

PRECAUTIONS: See tetracyclines (general statement). Although minocycline is more completely metabolized than other tetracyclines, the percentage of unchanged antibiotic excreted renally is less. However, in patients with renal failure significant accumulation of minocycline and possible hepatotoxicity may still occur.

SIDE EFFECTS/ADVERSE REACTIONS: Similar to other tetracyclines. Minocycline does not appear to cause as many phototoxic reactions as the other agents do. It causes more vestibular side effects than other tetracyclines. Transient and reversible effects include dizziness, vertigo, and ataxia.

DRUG INCOMPATIBILITIES: See tetracyclines (general statement).

DRUG INTERACTIONS: See tetracyclines (general statement).

ANTIDOTE: See tetracyclines (general statement).

Tetracycline (Achromycin, Sumycin, Tetracycline)

ADMINISTRATION

Available Forms: Injectable (IV), 250, 500 mg vials (powder containing ascorbic acid); injectable (IM), 100, 250 mg vials (with ascorbic acid and 2% lidocaine); capsules, 100, 250, 500 mg; oral suspension, 125 and 250 mg per 5 ml; also available with amphotericin B or nystatin added.

Diluent: For IM use reconstitute with sterile water; use IM preparations only. For IV doses use only those preparations specifically indicated for IV use. Reconstitute and further dilute in D5W or NS (up to 250 mg/100 ml; less volume has been used, but administration must be slow).

Dosage (Parenteral): Varies according to the patient's age.
Neonates: Not generally recommended, but IV doses of 10–15 mg/kg/day in divided doses (q12h) have been given.
Children >8 years old: 15–25 mg/kg/day as a single IM injection or in 2 divided doses (q12h). Maximum is 250 mg/day. Or, 10–20 mg/kg/day IV in divided doses (q12h), depending on the severity of infection.

Dosage (Oral)
Children >8 years old: 25–50 mg/kg/day (0.6–1.2 gm/m^2/day) in divided doses (q6h).

Rate: Avoid rapid IV administration as thrombophlebitis may result. Give doses over 30–60 minutes.

RENAL IMPAIRMENT: It has been suggested that patients with creatinine clearances of 10–30 ml/min should receive loading doses and then normal calculated dosages every 1–2 days.

22
Urinary Tract Anti-infectives and Antiseptics

In the high concentrations achieved in the urine, these agents are generally bactericidal for susceptible urinary tract pathogens. Their antibacterial effects are totally localized in the kidney and bladder. They are not effective for bacterial infections in blood or tissues outside the urinary tract since serum levels of these agents after oral administration are low.

The following medications are included in this chapter:

- **Methenamine mandelate**
- **Nalidixic acid**
- **Nitrofurantoin**
- **Phenazopyridine**

Methenamine mandelate (Mandelamine)

ADMINISTRATION

Available Forms: Tablets, 250, 500 mg, 1 gm (enteric-coated), also available with phenazopyridine as Azo-Mandelamine; granules, 500 mg, 1 gm packets; oral suspension, 250 and 500 mg per 5 ml (Forte).

Dosage (Oral): Initially, 100 mg/kg/day, then 50 mg/kg/day in divided doses (q8h). Maximum dose is 3 gm/day.

ANTIMICROBIAL SPECTRUM: Methenamine mandelate is effective against gram-positive and gram-negative urinary pathogens, including *Enterobacter, E. coli, Klebsiella, Proteus, P. aeruginosa, S. aureus,* and streptococci (including *S. faecalis*).
Resistant organisms: Urea-splitting strains of *Pseudomonas, Proteus,* and *Enterobacter* because these bacteria raise urinary pH. However, they may become susceptible if an acidic urine (pH 5.5) is maintained.

INDICATIONS: Methenamine mandelate is indicated for prophylaxis and treatment of acute and chronic urinary tract infections and for antisepsis of infected residual urine that sometimes accompanies neurological diseases. It can be used for long-term therapy because of its relative safety and its nonspecific bactericidal action (usually bacterial resistance does not develop).

ACTIONS: In the presence of acidic urine (pH <5.5), methenamine mandelate is hydrolyzed to ammonia and formaldehyde; the latter has a nonspecific bactericidal action against gram-positive and gram-negative organisms. The antibiotic has no effect on systemic infections outside the urinary tract. Mandelamine is readily absorbed, and almost all of the dose is excreted in the urine. The antibiotic crosses the placenta and is excreted in breast milk.

CONTRAINDICATIONS: Renal insufficiency or when urine acidification is contraindicated or unattainable.

PRECAUTIONS: Urinary pH should be monitored and maintained at 5.5 or less for maximum antibacterial activity. Supplementary acidification can be accomplished by administration of ascorbic acid or by a diet rich in acid-forming foods (e.g., cranberry juice, meat, eggs, high-acid juices). Mandelamine is ineffective in alkaline urine, so avoid alkalizing foods. Do not administer concomitantly with sulfonamides as they may precipitate in the renal tubules in the presence of formaldehyde and an acidic urine. Higher than recommended doses may produce dysuria with bladder irritation and painful urination (presumably due to high urinary concentrations of formaldehyde), so reduce the dose and the degree of urine acidification.

SIDE EFFECTS/ADVERSE REACTIONS: The most frequent side effects are gastric disturbances of nausea, vomiting, diarrhea, anorexia, and abdominal cramps. Occasionally, a generalized rash may occur. Dysuria with bladder irritation; painful, frequent urination; albuminuria; and hematuria may occur with higher than recommended doses.

DRUG INTERACTIONS: *Urinary alkalinizing agents, antacids, carbonic anhydrase inhibitors* (e.g., acetazolamide), and *thiazide diuretics* may alkalinize urine and decrease methenamine's antibacterial effectiveness. Concomitant use with *sulfonamides* may cause crystalluria.

ANTIDOTE: Discontinue mandelamine. Treat adverse reactions symptomatically.

Nalidixic acid (NegGram)

ADMINISTRATION

Available Forms: Tablets, 250, 500 mg; oral suspension, 250 mg/5 ml.

Dosage (Oral)
Children >3 months old: 55 mg/kg/day (2.25 gm/m²/day) in divided doses (q6h) for 1–2 weeks. For prolonged therapy, reduce dose to 33 mg/kg/day (1 gm/m²/day).

ANTIMICROBIAL SPECTRUM: Nalidixic acid is bactericidal for most gram-negative urinary pathogens, including most strains of *Proteus, Klebsiella, Enterobacter,* and *E. coli*. Resistant organisms: *Pseudomonas,* enterococci, other gram-positive bacteria, yeasts, fungi, etc.

INDICATIONS: Nalidixic acid is used primarily for treatment of acute urinary tract infections caused by susceptible gram-negative organisms, particularly *Proteus* species resistant to other antibiotics. The usefulness of nalidixic acid is limited, however, by the rapid development of resistance and by its toxicity.

ACTIONS: Nalidixic acid appears to halt bacterial replication by inhibiting DNA synthesis. It is bactericidal in the high concentrations achieved in the urine. Oral doses are rapidly absorbed. The antibiotic is partially metabolized in the liver, and some unchanged nalidixic acid along with several metabolites are excreted by the kidney. Therapeutic concentrations are achieved in the urine even in patients with severe renal impairment, but metabolites may accumulate.

CONTRAINDICATIONS: Hypersensitivity to nalidixic acid, infants less than 3 months old, history of convulsive disorders or cerebrovascular insufficiency.

PRECAUTIONS: Bacterial resistance, especially with underdosage, may develop rapidly (within 48 hours after initiation of therapy). Prior C&S tests should be done, and if the clinical response is unsatisfactory, the tests should be repeated during therapy. Use cautiously in infants and children, particularly those with seizure disorders, because nalidixic acid may cause increased intracranial pressure and convulsions. (Risk increases with high doses, but toxicity is usually reversible upon discontinuance of drug.) Use cautiously in patients with severe renal or hepatic impairment as metabolites may accumulate. Keep the patient well hydrated. Perform periodic blood counts and renal and liver function tests if treatment continues for longer than 2 weeks. Avoid prolonged, direct exposure to sunlight as photosensitivity reactions may occur for up to 3 months after discontinuation of the antibiotic. Nalidixic acid may cause false-positive reactions in tests for urinary glucose that use the copper reduction method (e.g., Clinitest) but not in ones that use the enzyme method (e.g., Keto-diastix, Clinistix). It may give incorrect values for urinary 17-keto-steroids and ketogenic steroids with certain test methods.

SIDE EFFECTS/ADVERSE REACTIONS: Gastric upset with nausea, vomiting, diarrhea, and cholestasis may occur. CNS effects include drowsiness, weakness, vertigo, dizziness, and occasional headaches. Reversible visual disturbances, including overbrightness of lights, changes in color perception, and difficulty in focusing and in depth perception, may occur (reduce dosage or discontinue the antibiotic). Increased intracranial pressure with bulging anterior fontanelle, papilledema, brief convulsions, and rare toxic psychoses may occur in susceptible patients (see precautions). Allergic responses of rashes, urticaria, pruritus, photosensitivity, arthralgia, and anaphylactoid reactions may occur. Rare blood dyscrasias include thrombocytopenia, leukopenia, and hemolytic anemia, especially in G6PD-deficient patients. Metabolic acidosis is a rare side effect also.

DRUG INTERACTIONS: *Nitrofurantoin* may decrease the antibacterial effect of nalidixic acid. Increased anticoagulant effects may occur with *oral anticoagulants*.

ANTIDOTE: Discontinue nalidixic acid (the antibiotic is rapidly excreted). Supportive therapy, IV fluids, and anticonvulsant therapy may be indicated.

Nitrofurantoin (Furadantin, Ivadantin, Macrodantin)

ADMINISTRATION

Available Forms: Injectable (IV), 180 mg vials (powder); capsules, 25, 50, 100 mg; oral suspension, 5 mg/ml.

Diluent: For IV use (Ivadantin) reconstitute with D5W or sterile water for injection. Further dilute in 25–50 ml D5W or NS for IV infusions.

Dosage (Parenteral)
Children <55 kg or 12 years or older: 6.6 mg/kg/day IV in 2 divided doses.

Dosage (Oral): Varies according to use.
Infants (>1 month old) and children: 5–7 mg/kg/day divided into 4 doses. Give with food or milk. Reduce to one-half of this dose if therapy is continued beyond 10–14 days and to one-quarter dose if continued beyond another 10–14 days.
For prophylaxis: One-half of a single dose at bedtime (qhs) after last voiding.

Rate: Administer IV infusions at 2–3 ml/min.

ANTIMICROBIAL SPECTRUM: Nitrofurantoin is usually effective against *E. coli*, enterococci (e.g., *S. faecalis*), staphylococci (including *S. aureus*), most strains of *Klebsiella-Enterobacter, Salmonella, Shigella,* and some indole-positive *Proteus* species.
Resistant organisms: *Pseudomonas,* most strains of *Proteus* (including indole-negative ones), and *Serratia.* Some strains of *Klebsiella* and *Enterobacter* have become resistant.

INDICATIONS: Nitrofurantoin is used for treatment of initial and recurrent urinary tract infections caused by susceptible bacteria. It should not be used for infections outside the urinary tract, for upper urinary tract infections, or for renal abscesses.

ACTIONS: Nitrofurantoin is bacteriostatic in low concentrations but bactericidal in the high concentrations achieved in the urine. It presumably acts by interfering with several enzyme systems necessary for bacterial growth. It has an advantage over many other antimicrobials because development of bacterial resistance is slow and limited and cross-resistance occurs infrequently. Nitrofurantoin is partially metabolized by the liver and excreted in the urine. Acidification of the urine increases tubular reabsorption of the antibiotic. It crosses the placenta and is excreted in breast milk.

CONTRAINDICATIONS: Anuria, oliguria, or significant renal impairment (e.g., CCr <40 ml/min); pregnant women at term and infants less than 1 month of age; hypersensitivity to nitrofurantoin.

PRECAUTIONS: As with all urinary tract infections, C&S tests should be done prior to and during therapy, and follow-up cultures should be performed to determine if the infection has been eradicated. Continue treatment for at least 1 week and for 3 days after the urine is sterile. Renal function must be adequate (e.g., CCr >40 ml/min) or therapeutic concentrations in the urine may not be achieved. Keep the patient well hydrated and monitor urine output and fluid and electrolyte balance. Urine may be discolored (brown). Severe, irreversible peripheral neuropathy has been reported, particularly in patients with renal impairment, anemia, vitamin B deficiency, electrolyte imbalances, diabetes mellitus, or debilitation. (Discontinue nitrofurantoin at the first sign of numbness, tingling of extremities, and muscle weakness.) Hemolytic anemia (reversible) may be induced in patients with G6PD deficiency or in infants (<1 month old) with immature enzyme systems. (Discontinue drug at first sign of hemolysis.) Acute, subacute, and chronic pulmonary reactions (diffuse interstitial pneumonitis or pulmonary fibrosis with rashes, fever, chills, angioedema, myalgia) have been reported. Acute reactions may develop within 8 hours to 3 weeks after initiation of therapy, and subacute or chronic reactions may occur 1–6 months into therapy. Avoid prolonged therapy (e.g., >14 days) with nitrofurantoin. Superinfections, particularly with *Pseudomonas*, may occur. Nitrofurantoin should be taken with food or milk to minimize gastric irritation and maximize absorption.

SIDE EFFECTS/ADVERSE REACTIONS: Dose-related GI reactions of anorexia, nausea, and vomiting are the most frequent side effects. Diarrhea and abdominal pain are less frequent. Various hypersensitivity reactions occur; most hazardous are acute or chronic pulmonary reactions (see precautions). Signs and symptoms include fever, chills, cough, chest pain, pleural effusions, and dyspnea progressing to diffuse interstitial pneumonitis or fibrosis. Pulmonary function may be permanently impaired even after cessation of therapy. Other hypersensitivity reactions include asthmatic attacks, cholestatic jaundice, hepatitis (rare), drug fever, arthralgia, lupus-like syndrome, and anaphylactoid reactions. Long-term therapy may cause chronic active hepatitis and severe hepatic necrosis. Rashes, pruritus, and urticaria may occur as well as blood dyscrasias (reversible) such as hemolytic anemia, megaloblastic anemia, and granulocytopenia. Peripheral neuropathy, headache, dizziness, nystagmus, and drowsiness may also occur.

DRUG INTERACTIONS: Nitrofurantoin may decrease the antimicrobial effect of *nalidixic acid*. *Probenecid* increases the serum levels or toxicity or both of nitrofurantoin by blocking tubular secretion.

ANTIDOTE: Discontinue nitrofurantoin. Treat adverse reactions symptomatically.

Phenazopyridine (Pyridium)

ADMINISTRATION

Available Forms: Tablets, 100, 200 mg; also available in combination with sulfonamides (e.g., Azo-Gantrisin, Azo-Gantanol) and with methenamine (e.g., Azo-Mandelamine).

Dosage (Oral): 12 mg/kg/day (350 mg/m^2/day) in 3 divided doses given after meals.

INDICATIONS: Phenazopyridine relieves the symptoms of pain, burning, urgency, and frequency that are associated with urinary tract infections.

ACTIONS: Phenazopyridine is an azo dye that, when taken orally, is excreted in the urine and exerts a topical analgesic effect on the urinary tract mucosa. It is probably metabolized in the liver and is rapidly excreted by the kidneys.

CONTRAINDICATIONS: Moderate to severe renal impairment, severe hepatitis.

PRECAUTIONS: Yellowish skin or sclerae due to impaired renal excretion indicate accumulation of phenazopyridine and necessitates discontinuance. Hemolysis may occur in patients with G6PD deficiency. Caution patients that their urine may appear reddish-orange and may stain fabric. Phenazopyridine should be discontinued once pain and discomfort are relieved, usually in 3–15 days.

SIDE EFFECTS/ADVERSE REACTIONS: Occasionally gastric disturbances and headache or vertigo may occur. High doses, prolonged therapy, or renal impairment may lead to methemoglobinemia, hemolytic anemia, skin pigmentation, and transient acute renal failure. Hypersensitivity reactions of jaundice and hepatitis have occurred.

DRUG INTERACTIONS: Phenazopyridine may interfere with tests for urinary glucose. False-negatives and delayed reactions may occur with glucose-oxidase reagents (Clinistix, Tes-Tape); the copper sulfate method (e.g., Clinitest) is not affected. The results of other urinary laboratory tests may be affected by this dye.

ANTIDOTE: Discontinue phenazopyridine. Treat methemoglobinemia with IV doses of methylene blue (1–2 mg/kg) or oral doses of ascorbic acid (100–200 mg). Monitor renal and hepatic function and institute supportive measures as indicated.

23
Other Antimicrobials

Other antimicrobials include miscellaneous antibacterial agents, antiviral agents, antifungal agents, amoebicides, agents for treatment of lice and scabies, and anthelmintics. The following medications are discussed in this chapter:

- Acyclovir
- Amphotericin B
- Chloramphenicol
- Clindamycin
- Diiodohydroxyquin
- Erythromycin
- Ethambutol
- Gamma benzene hexachloride
- Griseofulvin
- Isoniazid
- Ketoconazole
- Mebendazole
- Metronidazole
- Miconazole
- Nystatin
- Rifampin
- Spectinomycin
- Vancomycin

Acyclovir (Zovirax)

ADMINISTRATION

Available Forms: Injectable (IV), 500 mg (lyophilized powder); sodium content is 2 mEq/vial; ointment, 5% in polyethylene glycol base.

Diluent: For IV use dissolve the contents of the vial in 10 ml sterile water for injection. Shake well to assure complete dissolution. Final concentration is 50 mg/ml. Further dilute calculated dose in D5W, NS, or multiple electrolyte solutions to a final concentration that does not exceed 10 mg/ml. Refrigerated solutions may precipitate but will redissolve at room temperature.

Dosage (Parenteral): Varies according to use.
For mucosal or cutaneous herpes simplex infections in immunocompromised infants and children: 5 mg/kg (250 mg/m^2) IV q8h for 7 days.
For severe disseminated herpes simplex infections in nonimmunocompromised infants and children: 5 mg/kg (250 mg/m^2) IV q8h for 5 days.
For disseminated varicella-zoster infections in nonimmunocompromised infants and children: 5–10 mg/kg (250–500 mg/m^2) IV q8h for 5 days. Note: The therapy for varicella-zoster (VZV) is investigational. The dosage range is 15–45 mg/kg/day given for 5–10 days.

Dosage (Topical)
For initial episodes of herpes genitalis and mild mucocutaneous herpes simplex infections: Apply a sufficient quantity to cover all lesions q3h six times daily for 7 days. Use a finger cot or rubber glove during application.

Rate: Infuse IV doses over 1 hour.

RENAL IMPAIRMENT: Dosage adjustments are necessary.

- Mild impairment (CCr 50 ml/min): Give 5.0 mg/kg q8h.
- Moderate impairment (CCr 25–50 ml/min): Give 5.0 mg/kg q12h.
- Moderate to severe impairment (CCr 10–25 ml/min): Give 5.0 mg/kg q24h.
- Severe impairment (CCr 0–10 ml/min): Give 2.5 mg/kg q24h.

ANTIMICROBIAL SPECTRUM: Acyclovir is active *in vitro* and *in vivo* against herpes simplex virus, types 1 and 2 (HSV–1, HSV–2). It is also active against varicella-zoster virus, cytomegalovirus (CMV), and Epstein-Barr virus (EBV), but higher serum concentrations of acyclovir are needed to inhibit these and often the addition of other antiviral agents is required. Resistance to acyclovir has developed, primarily with the widespread use of the topical preparation. Overgrowth with nonsusceptible viruses may occur.

INDICATIONS: Acyclovir (IV) is a new antiviral agent useful for the treatment of disseminated herpes simplex (HSV–1, HSV–2) infections (including encephalitis) in neonates, infants, and children. Good results have also been obtained with the drug in herpes zoster (VZV) infections although its use for this condition is still investigational. High doses have been given for cytomegalovirus pneumonias, but acyclovir's efficacy here is questionable. Although acyclovir possesses greater *in vitro* activity than vidarabine and idoxuridine against other viruses (CMV, EBV), combination therapy with other antiviral agents appears necessary to treat these infections. Intravenous acyclovir is currently approved by the Food and Drug Administration (FDA) for treatment of (1) initial and recurrent forms of mucosal and cutaneous herpes simplex infections in immunocompromised children and (2) severe initial episodes of genital herpes in nonimmunocompromised patients. Acyclovir ointment is indicated only for the initial (primary) episode of genital and mucocutaneous herpes simplex infections. It is of questionable value in the prevention and treatment of recurrent herpes genitalis or herpes labialis. Acyclovir is not indicated for ocular herpes infections. Vidarabine, idoxuridine, or trifluridine are applied topically for the treatment of keratoconjunctivitis and recurrent epithelial keratitis caused by HSV-1 and HSV-2.

ACTIONS: Acyclovir is selectively toxic to body cells infected with herpes virus. It is taken up to a greater extent by infected cells than by normal host cells and then converted by a number of viral enzymes (e.g., viral thymidine kinase) to its active form, acyclovir-triphosphate. This "false nucleotide" competitively inhibits viral-induced DNA polymerase and ultimately stops further replication of the herpes virus. Since the normal body cell enzymes cannot effectively convert acyclovir to its active form, noninfected cells and their processes of DNA replication are not affected by the drug. This accounts for acyclovir's low toxicity. The mechanism of action in EBV and CMV infections appears to be a premature termination of DNA chains. Acyclovir shortens the duration of viral shedding, shortens the duration of lesion pain, and hastens the resolution of skin lesions. It does not cure latent viral infections, and reactivation of the infection is common, shortly after completion of therapy. Peak plasma levels, inhibitory to HSV-1, HSV-2, and VZV, are achieved after recommended IV doses. Acyclovir penetrates the meninges well; concentrations in the CSF of up to 50% of plasma levels are reached after IV infusion. Topical administration of the ointment can produce some systemic absorption, resulting in low serum levels. Acyclovir is excreted unchanged by the kidney, so renal impairment can cause higher and more prolonged serum levels of the drug and thus increase the risk of toxic reactions.

CONTRAINDICATIONS: Hypersensitivity to acyclovir.

PRECAUTIONS: Varies according to the route of administration.
For IV use: To prevent phlebitis or inflammation at the injection site, IV doses should be well diluted. Avoid concentrations greater than 7–10 mg/ml. Infuse doses slowly over at least 1 hour to minimize renal tubular damage. Keep the patient well hydrated and maintain a good urine output, especially within the first 2 hours following the acyclovir infusion. Monitor renal function with appropriate laboratory tests (e.g., serum creatinine, urinalysis, BUN) periodically. Dehydration, concomitant use of other nephrotoxic medications, and renal disease may predispose the patient to renal damage by acyclovir. Use cautiously in patients with underlying neurological abnormalities or conditions that might cause encephalopathic changes (e.g., renal, hepatic, or electrolyte abnormalities; severe hypoxia). Initiate therapy as soon as possible for best clinical results.

For topical use: Apply the ointment with a gloved hand or finger cot. Do not use the ointment in the eye. Widespread and repeated use has produced viral resistance to acyclovir. Do not use prophylactically for prevention of recurrent infections.

SIDE EFFECTS/ADVERSE REACTIONS: Too rapid IV infusion rates (less than 10 minutes) or bolus injections can cause crystalluria, a rise in serum creatinine and BUN, and renal tubular damage leading to acute renal failure. Inflammation at the injection site and phlebitis occur frequently, especially if the doses are not well diluted. Other reactions reported (1%) include nausea, sweating, headache, hypotension, hematuria, lethargy, tremors, confusion, hallucinations, agitation, seizures, and coma. With topical use pruritus, rash, and stinging or burning at the application site may occur.

DRUG INCOMPATIBILITIES: Acyclovir is incompatible with blood products and protein solutions.

DRUG INTERACTIONS: *Probenecid* can decrease renal excretion of acyclovir and prolong its half-life and serum levels.

ANTIDOTE: Discontinue acyclovir. Treat adverse reactions symptomatically. Acyclovir is dialyzable in the event of anuria or acute renal failure.

Amphotericin B (Fungizone)

ADMINISTRATION

Available Forms: Injectable (IV), 50 mg (powder).

Diluent: Reconstitute with preservative-free water. Further dilute with D5W to a concentration of 0.1 mg/ml (e.g., 50 mg/500 ml D5W); D5W must have a pH above 4.2). Do *not* use NS as it will cause the antibiotic to precipitate. Protect the final solution from light and cover the infusion container with foil.

Dosage (Parenteral): Duration of therapy varies according to the type and severity of infection (e.g., 1–4 weeks, up to several months). The maximum dose of 1.5 mg/kg/24 hr must never be exceeded.
Test dose: 0.1 mg/kg/24 hr given IV over 20–30 minutes. If tolerated in 6 hours, can increase to initial dose.
Initial dose: 0.25 mg/kg/24 hr by slow IV infusion. If tolerated, can be increased daily by 0.25 mg/kg increments until maintenance dose is achieved.
Maintenance dose: 1 mg/kg/24 hr (30 mg/m^2/24 hr) slow IV *daily*; or 1.5 mg/kg/24 hr (45 mg/m^2/24 hr) given on *alternate days*.

Rate: After initial test dose, give further IV doses slowly over 6 hours.

RENAL IMPAIRMENT: In severe renal dysfunction, administer doses q36h. If BUN exceeds 40 mg/100 ml or serum creatinine exceeds 3 mg/100 ml, discontinue the antibiotic or reduce the dose.

ANTIMICROBIAL SPECTRUM: Amphotericin B is active against *Coccidioides immitis, Cryptococcus neoformans, Histoplasma capsulatum, Paracoccidioides brasiliensis, Aspergillus* species (including *Aspergillus fumigatus*), *Sporothrix schenckii*, and several *Candida* and *Rhodotorula* species.
Resistant organisms: All bacteria, rickettsiae, and viruses. Resistance has developed among some species of *Candida* and *Coccidioides*.

INDICATIONS: Amphotericin B is indicated for serious life-threatening systemic fungal infections and fungal meningitis (e.g., cryptococcosis, North American blastomycosis, coccidioidomycosis, aspergillosis, disseminated sporotrichosis, histoplasmosis, candidiasis, and invasive phycomycosis) caused by susceptible organisms.

ACTIONS: Amphotericin B is fungistatic in the concentrations used clinically. It binds to the sterols in fungal cell membranes to produce a dysfunctioning nonselective barrier that causes potassium and other cellular components to be lost. Its distinctive toxicity occurs because it also binds to some mammalian cells (such as certain kidney and erythropoietic cells). Because oral doses are poorly absorbed, amphotericin B must be given parenterally. It is highly protein-bound and must be given intrathecally to achieve fungistatic levels in CSF. Its elimination half-life is longer than 24 hours, and a single IV dose may take over a week to be eliminated. Renal impairment causes accumulation of the medication and an increased risk of toxicity.

CONTRAINDICATIONS: Hypersensitivity to amphotericin B (unless the condition is life threatening and can be treated only by this agent).

PRECAUTIONS: Use should be restricted to patients with severe, potentially fatal forms of infections caused by susceptible organisms; diagnosis should be firmly established by cultures or histological tests or both. It should be used only in hospitalized patients who can be under close clinical observation. Dosage adjustments are necessary in patients with renal impairment. Alternate-day therapy may reduce the incidence of anorexia and phlebitis. Adverse reactions to IV infusions can be minimized by prior administration of aspirin, antihistamines, antiemetics, and corticosteroids; adding small amounts of heparin (e.g., 1200–1600 units) to the infusion solution and the use of a scalp-vein needle may reduce thrombophlebitis. If treatment is interrupted longer than 7 days, re-institute therapy at the lowest dosage level and increase the dose gradually. Monitor vital signs, renal and hepatic function, and electrolyte balance (especially potassium) frequently. Use freshly made solutions; cover the infusion bottle with foil to protect the solution from light. Do not give electrolyte solutions through the same tubing used for amphotericin B; do *not* administer through any in-line filters.

SIDE EFFECTS/ADVERSE REACTIONS: (Incidence is high and many are dose-related.) The most common side effects are headache, fever, chills, nausea, vomiting, anorexia, diarrhea, cramping, epigastric pain, muscle and joint pain, and irritation and phlebitis at the injection site. Nephrotoxicity includes hypokalemia, azotemia, renal tubular acidosis, nephrocalcinosis, excretion of urine with a low specific gravity, increased BUN and serum creatinine, and decreased creatinine clearance rates and renal plasma flow. (Alkalinization of urine and gradual increases in dosage may minimize renal toxicity.) Less frequent or rare reactions include anuria, oliguria, cardiovascular toxicity (arrhythmias, ventricular fibrillation, arrest, hypotension or hypertension—all generally due to rapid IV infusion rates), coagulation defects, blood dyscrasias, hemorrhagic gastroenteritis, rashes, anaphylactoid reactions, acute liver failure, and neurotoxicity (e.g., vertigo, tinnitus, blurred vision, diplopia, hearing loss, convulsions, peripheral neuropathy).

DRUG INCOMPATIBILITIES: Incompatible with electrolyte solutions and preservatives. Do not mix with any other medications.

DRUG INTERACTIONS: Use with *corticosteroids* may increase hypokalemia. Amphotericin B-induced hypokalemia may increase the risk of *digitalis* toxicity. Concomitant use of *nephrotoxic antibiotics* (e.g., aminoglycosides) may increase the renal toxicity of amphotericin B.

ANTIDOTE: Discontinue amphotericin B. Treat adverse reactions symptomatically (see precautions and side effects/adverse reactions).

Chloramphenicol (Chloromycetin)

ADMINISTRATION

Available Forms: Injectable (IV), 1 gm vials (succinate salt, powder), sodium content is 2.25 mEq/gm; capsules, 250 mg; oral suspension, 30 mg/ml (palmitate salt, powder); topical preparations for otic, ophthalmic, and dermatological use.

Diluent: Reconstitute with sterile water or D5W for injection. For IV push doses do not exceed a concentration of 100 mg/ml (1 gm/10 ml). For IV infusion can be further diluted with D5W, NS, or multiple electrolyte solutions.

Dosage (Parenteral): Varies according to the patient's age.
Infants (up to 2 months old) and children with immature metabolic processes: 25 mg/kg/day IV in divided doses (q6h).
Infants (>2 months old) and children: 50 mg/kg/day IV in divided doses (q6h); up to 100 mg/kg/day initially for short periods during severe infections.

Dosage (Oral): Same as parenteral dosage. Change to oral doses as soon as feasible.

Rate: Administer direct IV push doses in concentrations no greater than 100 mg/ml over 1 minute. Give intermittent IV infusions over an appropriate time period, depending on the volume of infusion.

RENAL OR HEPATIC IMPAIRMENT: Use the lower doses and monitor serum levels of the antibiotic; avoid peaks greater than 25 µg/ml or troughs greater than 10 µg/ml.

ANTIMICROBIAL SPECTRUM: Chloramphenicol is active against many strains of gram-positive and gram-negative cocci and bacilli, rickettsiae, chlamydiae, and mycoplasmas. Most notably sensitive are *Bacteroides, H. influenzae* (including ampicillin-resistant strains), and *Salmonella* (especially *Salmonella typhi*).

Resistant organisms: Many *Pseudomonas* species (especially *P. aeruginosa*), spirochetes, fungi, etc. Many strains of staphylococci, *E. coli*, *H. influenzae*, and *Salmonella* have developed resistance.

INDICATIONS: Chloramphenicol is used primarily for treatment of acute typhoid fever and other serious *Salmonella* infections, especially those unresponsive to ampicillin. Because chloramphenicol reaches appreciable levels in CSF, it is very effective for meningitis caused by susceptible *H. influenzae, Bacteroides,* or *N. meningitidis*. It is effective for treatment of rickettsial infections and psittacosis and as an alternative to tetracycline for treatment of Rocky Mountain spotted fever or Q fever. Chloramphenicol's broad antibacterial spectrum and good ocular penetration make it very useful topically for eye infections. It is *not* recommended for routine treatment of typhoid carriers.

ACTIONS: Chloramphenicol inhibits protein synthesis and further microbial growth by binding to 50 S ribosomal units to prevent formation of polypeptide bonds. Oral doses are rapidly absorbed and recommended dosage regimens usually achieve the necessary therapeutic blood levels of 5–20 µg/ml. The antibiotic is metabolized in the liver and excreted by the kidneys. Accumulation of the active form (unchanged chloramphenicol) occurs in newborns and premature infants and in children with marked hepatic impairment. Renal impairment can cause accumulation of inactive metabolites (dosage adjustments may not be necessary here). The antibiotic is well distributed in most body fluids and tissues, including CSF. It crosses the placenta and is excreted in breast milk.

CONTRAINDICATIONS: Hypersensitivity or previous toxic reactions to chloramphenicol. Chloramphenicol *must not* be used for treatment of trivial infections or where it is not indicated (e.g., colds, influenza, antibacterial prophylaxis).

PRECAUTIONS: Reserve for use in serious infections unresponsive to less toxic or contraindicated antibiotics. Baseline blood cell counts should be followed by periodic studies (e.g., q2–3days) during therapy; discontinue the antibiotic upon the appearance of any blood cell abnormality thought attributable to chloramphenicol; avoid concurrent therapy with other bone-marrow-depressing drugs. Avoid repeated courses of treatment. Use with extreme caution in premature and newborn infants as their immature hepatic and renal functions may cause drug accumulation (see "gray syndrome" under adverse reactions); monitor serum levels in susceptible patients. Dosage adjustments and careful monitoring of serum levels are necessary in patients with hepatic impairment but less so in patients with renal impairment. Use cautiously in pregnant women at term and in nursing mothers because chloramphenicol may induce "gray syndrome" in fetuses or nursing infants. Superinfections, notably with fungi, may occur.

SIDE EFFECTS/ADVERSE REACTIONS: Severe bone marrow depression may produce serious and fatal blood dyscrasias (e.g., hypoplastic anemia, thrombocytopenia, granulocytopenia, aplastic anemia [incidence approximately 1 in 40,000]). The marrow depression may be reversible or irreversible. The reversible form (dose-related and a true toxic reaction that subsides if chloramphenicol is discontinued) is associated with anemia, reticulocytopenia, leukopenia, and vacuolization of erythroid cells. The irreversible form, probably an idiosyncratic reaction, is not dose-related and may occur after a single dose or after prolonged therapy. It is characterized by aplastic anemia (with or without pancytopenia) and may occur weeks or months after therapy. Gastrointestinal effects include nausea, vomiting, diarrhea, glossitis, stomatitis, or enterocolitis. Neurotoxic reactions include headache, mild depression, confusion, and delirium. Prolonged therapy can cause optic and peripheral neuritis. Hypersensitivity reactions include fever, rashes, urticaria, angioedema, and anaphylaxis. In neonates a fatal toxicity known as the "gray syndrome" may result from abnormally high serum levels due to inadequate hepatic inactivation of chloramphenicol in the immature liver. The syndrome occurs primarily in infants less than 2 weeks of age but may occur in full-term infants with excessive serum levels of 90 µg/ml or more. Signs usually appear after 3–4 days of therapy but may occur sooner. They include flaccidity, abdominal distension, lack of sucking, vomiting, ashen gray color, irregular and rapid breathing and, finally, vasomotor collapse. Death usually occurs within a few hours after the onset of the syndrome.

DRUG INCOMPATIBILITIES: Physically incompatible with methicillin, gentamicin, phenothiazines, barbiturates, narcotics, tetracyclines, sulfonamides, and vancomycin.

DRUG INTERACTIONS: Chloramphenicol may suppress the antibody response, so avoid concomitant administration with *tetanus toxoid* or other active *immunizing agents*. Therapeutic doses may inhibit hepatic metabolism of many medications normally inactivated by the liver and may enhance their toxicity (e.g., *tolbutamide, phenytoin, phenobarbital, dicumarol*).

ANTIDOTE: Discontinue chloramphenicol. Termination of therapy upon early evidence of "gray syndrome" frequently reverses the process and leads to complete recovery. Otherwise treat the syndrome symptomatically and supportively.

Clindamycin (Cleocin)

ADMINISTRATION

Available Forms: Injectable (IM, IV), 150 mg/ml in 2 and 4 ml amps; capsules, 75, 150 mg (HCl salt); oral suspension, 75 mg/5 ml (granules for reconstitution, pediatric).

Diluent: IV doses can be diluted with D5W or NS; do not exceed concentrations greater than 6 mg/ml (e.g., 300 mg/50 ml).

Dosage (Parenteral)
Infants (>1 month old) and children:

- Moderately severe infections: 15–25 mg/kg/day (350 mg/m^2/day) IV or IM in divided doses (q6–8h)
- Severe infections: 25–40 mg/kg/day (450 mg/m^2/day) IV or IM in divided doses (q6–8h), but no less than 300 mg/day, regardless of body weight

Dosage (Oral)
Infants (>1 month old) and children: Dosages given are for pediatric suspension. Amounts in parentheses refer to capsule form.

- Mild infections: 8–12 mg/kg/day (HCl salt) in divided doses (q6–8h)
- Moderately severe infections: 13–16 mg/kg/day (8–12 mg/kg/day HCl salt) in divided doses (q6–8h)
- Severe infections: 17–25 mg/kg/day (16–20 mg/kg/day HCl salt) in divided doses (q6–8h)

Children <10 kg: Give at least 37.5 mg q8h, regardless of body weight.

Rate: For IV infusions do not exceed 30 mg/min (e.g., 300 mg/10 min).

RENAL IMPAIRMENT: Dosage adjustments usually are not necessary.

ANTIMICROBIAL SPECTRUM: Clindamycin is active against most aerobic gram-positive organisms such as staphylococci (including penicillinase-producing strains), streptococci (except *S. faecalis*), pneumococci, and *C. diphtheriae*. It is also active against certain anaerobes, notably *B. fragilis*, *Actinomyces* species, peptococci, and peptostreptococci. Clostridia are more resistant than most anaerobes to clindamycin. Most *Clostridium perfringens* are susceptible, but sensitivity testing should be done for other clostridia.
Resistant organisms: All other gram-negative organisms, fungi, viruses, etc. Staphylococci, especially *S. aureus*, slowly develop resistance. Erythromycin-resistant *S. aureus* may also be resistant to clindamycin. Other gram-positive cocci and bacteroides have developed resistance. Cross-resistance between clindamycin and lincomycin is complete.

INDICATIONS: Clindamycin is indicated for treatment of serious infections caused by susceptible anaerobic bacteria, notably *B. fragilis*. In infections caused by mixed populations of aerobes and anaerobes, it can be combined with an aminoglycoside. It can be used alone for serious respiratory tract, skin, and soft tissue infections caused by susceptible gram-positive organisms resistant to penicillins and erythromycins or in patients who are allergic to these antibiotics. Clindamycin is also used for treatment of acute osteomyelitis and joint infections caused by sensitive staphylococci. Oral or topical clindamycin is used for treatment of acne vulgaris unresponsive to tetracycline and erythromycin. It should not be used for minor bacterial infections or for infections treatable with less toxic agents. Because of its poor CNS penetration, clindamycin should not be used in the treatment of meningitis. Clindamycin is not suitable for treatment of gonococcal infections.

ACTIONS: Clindamycin may be bacteriostatic or bactericidal, depending on the concentration of the antibiotic achieved at the infection site and the susceptibility of the infecting organism. As with erythromycin and chloramphenicol, it inhibits bacterial protein synthesis by binding to the 50 S ribosomal subunits in sensitive organisms. Clindamycin should *not* be given with erythromycin or chloramphenicol because they all compete for the same binding sites and antagonize each other. Gastric absorption of clindamycin is good and is not retarded by the presence of food in the stomach. The antibiotic is distributed in many body fluids and tissues, including synovial fluid and bone, but reaches no significant levels in CSF. It crosses the placenta and is excreted in breast milk. Clindamycin metabolites (both active and inactive) are excreted in urine, bile, and feces. Severe renal or hepatic impairment does not appear to cause any significant accumulation of the antibiotic. The usual recommended parenteral or oral doses of clindamycin produce serum levels well in excess of MICs necessary for treatment of susceptible organisms.

CONTRAINDICATIONS: Hypersensitivity to clindamycin or lincomycin.

PRECAUTIONS: Nonspecific colitis and diarrhea as well as potentially fatal pseudomembranous colitis have occurred during clindamycin therapy. Symptoms may develop within a week following initiation of therapy or may not occur until several weeks after the antibiotic has been discontinued. If significant or persistent diarrhea occurs, clindamycin should be discontinued or, if necessary, continued only with close observation of the patient. An endoscopic examination should be done. Such colitis can be treated with cholestyramine resin to bind up the toxin or with oral doses of vancomycin to inhibit the organism. Do not give antiperistaltic agents such as Lomotil as they will worsen the condition. Fluid and electrolyte replacements and corticosteroids may be necessary in severe cases. Use cautiously in patients with a history of GI disease (particularly colitis), in those with very severe renal or hepatic impairment (monitor serum levels of clindamycin), and in those atopic individuals with multiple allergies. Capsules contain a tartrazine dye that may cause allergic reactions (including bronchial asthma) in susceptible patients, particularly those with aspirin hypersensitivity. During prolonged therapy, periodic liver and kidney function tests and blood counts should be done. Superinfections, particularly with yeasts, may occur. Give IV doses slowly to avoid apnea and hypotension. Give oral doses with full glasses of water to avoid esophageal irritation. Monitor liver function tests and blood cell counts when treating newborns or infants.

SIDE EFFECTS/ADVERSE REACTIONS: Frequent reactions include GI upset with nausea, vomiting, abdominal cramps, and diarrhea. Hypersensitivity reactions range from mild rashes (primarily morbilliform-like) and urticaria to rare, severe Stevens-Johnson-like syndromes and anaphylactoid reactions. Jaundice, abnormalities in liver function, and blood dyscrasias (neutropenia, thrombocytopenia, eosinophilia, agranulocytosis) have occurred. Rare polyarthritis has been reported. Rapid IV infusion may cause syncope, hypotension, and cardiac arrest (rare). IV use may cause thrombophlebitis, redness, swelling, and pain at the infusion site. Sterile abscesses may occur with IM use. Neuromuscular blockade with apnea has also been reported.

DRUG INCOMPATIBILITIES: Physically incompatible with aminophylline, ampicillin, barbiturates, calcium gluconate, magnesium sulfate, phenytoin.

DRUG INTERACTIONS: Concomitant use may cause increased neuromuscular blockade with *general anesthetics* and other *surgical neuromuscular blockers*. *Antiperistaltic antidiarrheal agents* may worsen the risk and severity of diarrhea associated with the use of clindamycin. *Chloramphenicol* and *erythromycin* may antagonize the antibacterial effect of clindamycin. *Kaolin-pectin* markedly reduces the gastric absorption of oral doses.

ANTIDOTE: Discontinue clindamycin. Provide symptomatic and supportive treatment (see precautions).

Diiodohydroxyquin (Iodoquinol, Yodoxin)

ADMINISTRATION

Available Forms: Tablets, 210 mg (Yodoxin), 650 mg (Iodoquinol).

Dosage (Oral)
Children: 30–40 mg/kg/day, in divided doses (q8–12h) given after meals for 20 days. Do not repeat the course of treatment sooner than 2–3 weeks.

ANTIMICROBIAL SPECTRUM: See indications.

INDICATIONS: Diiodohydroxyquin is considered the antibiotic of choice for intestinal amebiasis (dysentery) due to *Entamoeba histolytica*. It can be used alone for mild cases or asymptomatic carriers or combined with emetine or chloroquin for acute, severe cases. It has been used as alternative therapy for giardiasis and ballantidiasis.

ACTIONS: This virtually unabsorbed amoebicide works in the intestinal lumen by an unknown mechanism. Some systemic absorption may occur, however.

CONTRAINDICATIONS: Hypersensitivity to iodine or any 8-hydroxyquinoline agents, hepatic damage, preexisting optic neuropathy, renal impairment.

PRECAUTIONS: Use cautiously in patients with thyroid disease (some systemic absorption of iodine may occur). Diiodohydroxyquin may increase serum levels of protein-bound iodine. Discontinue the antibiotic if hypersensitivity reactions (e.g., rashes) occur. Give doses after meals. Tablets can be crushed and added to applesauce or chocolate syrup.

SIDE EFFECTS/ADVERSE REACTIONS: The most frequent side effects are gastric upset, nausea, vomiting, diarrhea, abdominal cramps, and perianal itching. Fever, chills, vertigo, and headache may occur also. Prolonged high-dose therapy is associated with neurotoxicity (e.g., optic neuritis, optic atrophy, peripheral neuropathy, and permanent loss of vision), especially in children.

DRUG INTERACTIONS: Diiodohydroxyquin may interfere with thyroid function tests by increasing serum levels of protein-bound iodine, an effect that may persist up to 6 months after discontinuance of therapy.

ANTIDOTE: Discontinue diiodohydroxyquin. Treat adverse reactions symptomatically.

Erythromycin (Erythrocin, E.E.S., Ilosone, Ilotycin, others)

ADMINISTRATION

Available Forms: Injectable (IV), 500 mg and 1 gm vials (lactobionate salt), 250, 500 mg, 1 gm vials (gluceptate salt); tablets, 125, 250, 400, 500 mg; chewable tablets, 125, 200, 250 mg; capsules, 125, 250 mg; oral suspension, 125, 200, 250, and 400 mg per 5 ml; suppositories, 125 mg (Erythrocin); topical preparations for dermatological and ophthalmic use.

Diluent: Reconstitute with sterile water for injection *only*; do not use NS. Doses for IV infusion can be diluted in D5W or NS (500 mg or less in 100 ml, 500 mg to 1 gm in 250 ml). If D5W is used, the pH should be adjusted to more than 6 with 0.5 ml sodium bicarbonate (1 mEq/ml) in each 100 ml diluent. Use solutions for IV infusion within 8 hours.

Dosage (Parenteral): Use in neonates is not recommended.
Infants (>1 month old) and children:

- Severe infections: 10–20 mg/kg/day (300–600 mg/m^2/day) IV in divided doses (q6h)
- Very severe infections: Up to 50 mg/kg/day IV in divided doses (q6h); maximum is 4 gm/day

Dosage (Oral)
Infants (>1 month old) and children: 30–50 mg/kg/day in divided doses (q6h).

- Severe infections: Dose can be doubled
- Rheumatic fever prophylaxis: 250 mg bid

Rate: Administer IV infusions slowly enough to minimize pain along the vein (e.g., give dilutions of 100 ml over 20–60 minutes). *Do not give IV push.*

RENAL IMPAIRMENT: Dosage adjustments are usually not required.

ANTIMICROBIAL SPECTRUM: The most sensitive organisms are gram-positive bacteria including penicillin-resistant staphylococci, streptococci, pneumococci, corynebacteria, clostridia, *L. monocytogenes,* and *B. anthracis.* Others are *M. pneumoniae, Legionella pneumophila,* atypical mycobacteria, gonococci, *T. pallidum, B. pertussis,* and some *Actinomyces,* chlamydiae, and rickettsiae. Many strains of *H. influenzae* are sensitive to erythromycin, but sulfonamides are usually added for more effective therapy. **Resistant organisms:** All other gram-negative bacilli, yeasts, fungi, and viruses. Resistant strains of *H. influenzae* and staphylococci (especially *S. aureus*) have developed, and cross-resistance with clindamycin and lincomycin may occur.

INDICATIONS: Erythromycin can be used as alternative therapy in penicillin-allergic patients for treatment of mild to moderate respiratory tract, skin, and soft tissue infections caused by group A beta-hemolytic streptococci, pneumococci, or staphylococci (including penicillin-resistant strains). It is also indicated for upper and lower respiratory tract infections caused by *M. pneumoniae* and *L. pneumophila*. It is frequently combined with sulfonamides for treatment of *H. influenzae* infections. Erythromycin may be the antibiotic of choice for whooping cough (due to *B. pertussis*). It has been used as an adjunct to antitoxin in the treatment of diphtheria and in the prevention or eradication of *C. diphtheriae* in diphtheria carriers. It can be used as an alternative in penicillin-allergic individuals for treatment of early syphilis and gonorrhea.

ACTIONS: As with clindamycin and chloramphenicol, erythromycin inhibits growth of susceptible organisms, but it may be microbicidal in high concentrations or against highly susceptible organisms. It inhibits protein synthesis by irreversibly binding to 50 S ribosomal subunits. Oral doses of erythromycin are not stable in gastric acid; many oral forms are enteric-coated, buffered, or in special ester derivatives to protect them from inactivation by stomach acid and to facilitate their absorption in the duodenum. Erythromycin is well distributed in most body tissues and fluids except for CSF. It crosses the placenta and is excreted in breast milk. The antibiotic is partially metabolized in the liver and primarily excreted unchanged in the bile; very little is excreted in urine. Severe hepatic impairment may increase the half-life of erythromycin somewhat, but renal impairment has an insignificant effect.

CONTRAINDICATIONS: Hypersensitivity to erythromycin.

PRECAUTIONS: Use cautiously in patients with hepatic impairment as erythromycin may worsen jaundice and accumulation of the antibiotic could occur. Monitor liver function tests in these patients. Estolate salts can cause reversible hepatotoxicity and cholestatic jaundice. (Although this occurs primarily in adults, use of this form in pediatrics should probably be avoided.) As with all group A beta-hemolytic streptococcal infections, a minimum of 10 days therapy is required. Prolonged therapy may cause fungal overgrowth. IV administration is extremely painful; infusions must be well diluted and given slowly or intermittently. Oral doses can be given with meals.

SIDE EFFECTS/ADVERSE REACTIONS: The incidence of serious side effects is very low. Most common are gastric upset with nausea, vomiting, diarrhea, cramping, and abdominal pain (erythromycin stimulates GI motility). Hypersensitivity reactions are usually mild and include urticaria and rashes, but anaphylaxis has been reported. Elevations of liver enzymes may occur, and the estolate salt may cause reversible hepatotoxicity and cholestatic jaundice. Venous irritation, thrombophlebitis, and pain are associated with IV administration. Rare reversible hearing loss has been reported after large IV doses (4 gm or more daily).

DRUG INCOMPATIBILITIES: Do not mix with cephalosporins, aminophylline, barbiturates, tetracyclines, phenytoin. Unstable in acidic media (e.g., pH <5).

DRUG INTERACTIONS: Erythromycin may increase serum levels and potential toxicity of *theophylline* and *theophylline derivatives* (e.g., aminophylline, oxytriphylline). It antagonizes the antimicrobial action of *lincomycin, clindamycin,* and *chloramphenicol* (competitive binding sites); and it may antagonize the microbicidal action of *penicillins* and possibly *cephalosporins*.

ANTIDOTE: Discontinue erythromycin. Treat adverse reactions symptomatically.

Ethambutol (Myambutol)

ADMINISTRATION

Available Forms: Tablets, 100, 400 mg.

Dosage (Oral): Use in conjunction with other antitubercular medications.
For children 6–13 years old: 10–15 mg/kg/day as a single dose.
For children >13 years old: 15–20 mg/kg/day as a single dose. Maximum is 25 mg/kg/day.

RENAL IMPAIRMENT: Dosage adjustments are necessary. Do not exceed 15 mg/kg/day if creatinine clearance is 70–100 ml/min. Further reductions are necessary if clearance is less than 70 ml/min.

ANTIMICROBIAL SPECTRUM: Ethambutol is active against mycobacteria, including *Mycobacterium tuberculosis*.
Resistant organisms: Other bacteria, fungi, and viruses.

INDICATIONS: Ethambutol is used in combination with other antitubercular medications for treatment of pulmonary tuberculosis. The preferred combination of rifampin and isoniazid makes it possible to give two bactericidal drugs, thereby reducing the total duration of therapy. Although ethambutol is only bacteriostatic, it can be valuable in combination therapy by inhibiting the growth of mutant bacilli, which are resistant to rifampin and isoniazid. Ethambutol has largely replaced para-aminosalicylic acid (PAS) as the usual combination drug for isoniazid. Treatment with ethambutol does not require taking large numbers of tablets, and the drug has fewer GI side effects than PAS.

ACTIONS: Ethambutol is bacteriostatic. It diffuses into actively growing, susceptible tubercle bacilli and inhibits cell metabolism and stops replication, apparently by inhibiting RNA synthesis. Dormant bacilli are not affected. *In vitro* resistance to ethambutol develops slowly, and bacilli resistant to isoniazid, PAS, and rifampin are usually susceptible to ethambutol. However, ethambutol-resistant strains can develop rapidly (sometimes within 4 months) if this medication is used alone for antitubercular therapy. Ethambutol does not appear to produce cross-resistance to any other antitubercular medications. Oral doses are readily absorbed, and peak concentrations appear in the plasma within 2–4 hours. Ethambutol rapidly enters red blood cells, but there is little accumulation in any other body tissues or fluids. Ethambutol is detoxified by the liver to some extent; 50% is excreted as unchanged drug in the urine and about 20% in the feces. Renal impairment may cause drug accumulation and toxic serum levels.

CONTRAINDICATIONS: Optic neuritis, children less than 6 years old or those too young to cooperate in vision testing, hypersensitivity to ethambutol.

PRECAUTIONS: Eye examinations for visual acuity, color vision, and visual fields should be done prior to and at monthly intervals during therapy. Instruct patients to report any decreased visual acuity; however, make certain that any variations in vision are not due to underlying pathological conditions. To minimize the risk of ocular toxicity, avoid doses of 25 mg/kg/day or higher. Reduce the dosage in patients with renal impairment and monitor the serum concentration of ethambutol periodically. Patients on prolonged therapy should have periodic laboratory assessment of renal, hepatic, and blood functions. The manufacturer cautions against the use of ethambutol in children less than 13 years of age.

SIDE EFFECTS/ADVERSE REACTIONS: The most serious adverse effect is optic neuritis; its incidence is related to the dosage and duration of therapy. Optic neuritis is often reversible if the drug is discontinued promptly when symptoms appear, but it may take up to a year to regain normal vision. Severe damage may be irreversible. Signs of optic neuritis are changes in visual acuity (lateral and bilateral), narrowing of visual fields, central and peripheral scotomas, and loss of red-green color discrimination. Gastrointestinal effects include nausea, vomiting, anorexia, gastric upset, and pain. Peripheral neuritis with numbness and tingling in the extremities has been reported and is not amenable to treatment with thiamine or pyridoxine. Other adverse reactions include dermatitis, pruritus, dizziness, headache, malaise, mental confusion, disorientation, hallucinations, joint pain, and anaphylaxis (rare). Ethambutol may increase serum levels of uric acid and thus cause abnormal liver function tests.

DRUG INTERACTIONS: None significant.

ANTIDOTE: Discontinue ethambutol. Treat adverse reactions symptomatically.

Gamma benzene hexachloride (Kwell)

ADMINISTRATION

Available Forms: Topical, cream (1%), lotion (1%), shampoo (1%).

Dosage (Topical): Use with extreme caution in infants and young children.
For scabies: Apply thin layer of cream or lotion to dry skin (neck to toes) and leave on for 8–12 hours. Remove by washing.
For head lice: Shampoo hair and skin of surrounding areas for 4 minutes. Rinse the drug off and then remove mites with tweezers or a fine-tooth comb. Alternatively, apply lotion or cream to hair and scalp, leave on for 12 hours, and then remove by showering. Can be repeated in 7 days if necessary.
For crab lice: Shampoo affected hairy areas (pubic region, axilla, thigh, trunk) for 4 minutes and then rinse the drug off. Alternatively, apply a thin film of lotion or cream to affected areas, leave on for 12 hours, and then wash off. Can be repeated in 7 days if necessary.

INDICATIONS: Gamma benzene hexachloride is used for topical treatment of scabies (*Sarcoptes scabiei*), head lice (*Pediculus capitis*), crab or body lice (*Pediculus pubis* or *Pediculus corporis*), and mites.

ACTIONS: Gamma benzene hexachloride is a scabicide and pediculicide. Usually only one application is necessary. Because this medication may be too neurotoxic in infants and young children, some clinicians recommend 10% crotamiton cream, 10% sulfur, or 28% benzyl benzoate lotion for scabies and pyrethrins with pipronyl butoxide (RID) for lice. Cutaneous absorption is greater when the antibiotic is applied to the head and neck, axilla, pubic region, or damaged or occluded skin. The drug is stored in body fat, metabolized in the liver, and excreted in the urine.

CONTRAINDICATIONS: Hypersensitivity to gamma benzene hexachloride or any components of the topical preparations.

PRECAUTIONS: Use with extreme caution in young children and infants (greater risk of CNS toxicity); care should be taken to prevent oral ingestion by thumb sucking. *Do not administer orally.* Treat family members if necessary; clothing, bedding, combs, and hairbrushes should be washed in hot water to prevent reinfestation. Do not use additional creams, ointments, or oils on the treated areas of skin as percutaneous absorption of gamma benzene hexachloride may be enhanced. Avoid getting the drug in the eyes; flush thoroughly with water if this occurs. Do not apply to acutely inflamed, weeping, or raw skin surfaces. Discontinue use if contact dermatitis or primary irritation develops.

SIDE EFFECTS/ADVERSE REACTIONS: Contact dermatitis and eczematous eruptions may occur because of skin irritation. Acute poisoning (via ingestion or increased cutaneous absorption) causes serious CNS, hepatic, and renal effects. Symptoms include vomiting, muscle spasms, tremors, convulsions, respiratory depression, apnea, cardiac arrhythmias, ventricular fibrillation, pulmonary edema, hematuria, bladder irritation, and hepatitis.

ANTIDOTE: Discontinue the medication by washing it off thoroughly. For accidental ingestion empty the stomach via lavage and administer saline cathartics to dilute bowel contents and hasten evacuation (avoid *oil* enemas and laxatives as they increase absorption of gamma benzene hexachloride). Support respiration. Treat CNS manifestations with IV doses of diazepam and phenobarbital and muscle spasms with IV doses of calcium if necessary. Do not give epinephrine as it may precipitate ventricular fibrillation.

Griseofulvin ("Microsize"—Grisactin, Fulvicin U/F, Grifulvin V; "Ultramicrosize"—Gris PEG, Fulvicin P/G)

ADMINISTRATION

Available Forms: Tablets, 125, 250, 500 mg ("microsize"); 125, 165, 250, 330 mg ("ultramicrosize"); capsules, 125, 250 mg ("microsize"); oral suspension, 125 mg/5 ml ("microsize").

Dosage (Oral): Duration of therapy depends on the clinical response and the type of infection being treated. See Actions.
For "microsize" preparations:

- Children (>2 years old): 10 mg/kg/day (or 300 mg/m^2/day) as a single daily dose given with food or milk

For "ultramicrosize" preparations:

- Children (>2 years old): 5 mg/kg/day as a single daily dose given with food or milk

ANTIMICROBIAL SPECTRUM: Griseofulvin is effective against various species of *Microsporum, Trichophyton,* and *Epidermophyton.*
Resistant organisms: All bacteria, *Candida,* and other fungi.

INDICATIONS: Griseofulvin is an antifungal agent for treatment of ringworm infections of the skin, hair, and nails (e.g., tinea corporis, tinea cruris, tinea pedis [athlete's foot], tinea barbae, and tinea unguium [onychomycosis]). It should not be used for tinea versicolor, bacterial infections, or other fungal infections such as candidiasis or other deep mycoses.

ACTIONS: Griseofulvin is fungistatic. It primarily disrupts fungal cell division and may also cause production of defective DNA, which further stops cell replication. After oral administration, the drug is deposited in keratin precursor cells and becomes tightly bound to the newly formed keratin, which then becomes highly resistant to further fungal infection. Thus, infected hair, skin, and nails are gradually replaced with new tissue not infected with the dermatophyte. Griseofulvin also produces some vasodilation. Gastric absorption is influenced by the particle size of the drug: The ultramicrocrystalline ("ultramicrosize") preparation is more completely absorbed than the microcrystalline ("microsize") form. Consequently, the dose for the ultramicrosize tablet is one-half that of the microsize one. Absorption is further enhanced by taking the drug with food or milk. Griseofulvin is concentrated in skin, hair, nails, liver, fat, and skeletal muscle, but the highest concentrations are found in the outermost horny layers of the skin. Fungistatic levels appear in the skin within 4–8 hours after an oral dose. In warmer climates, skin levels may be higher because griseofulvin, dissolved in perspiration, is deposited in outer skin layers as the perspiration evaporates. Griseofulvin is metabolized in the liver; its major metabolite is inactive. It is excreted primarily in the urine with some elimination through the feces and perspiration.

CONTRAINDICATIONS: Porphyria, hepatocellular failure, hypersensitivity to griseofulvin.

PRECAUTIONS: Give doses with food or milk. Prior to therapy, identify the fungi responsible for the infection. Griseofulvin should not be used for fungal or bacterial infections for which it is not indicated or for trivial infections that will respond to topical medications alone. Therapy must be continued until the infecting organism is completely eradicated; palms, soles, and nails respond more slowly than less keratinized skin. Infections in fingernails and toenails may require at least 4–6 months of therapy; tinea corporis, 2–4 weeks; tinea capitis, 4–6 weeks; and tinea pedis, 4–8 weeks. Concomitant use of topical preparations (e.g., compresses soaked in 1:40 dilutions of Burow's solution, tolnaftate [Tinactin], haloprogin [Halotex], or 2% miconazole [Micatin]) is usually necessary. To control sources of infection and reinfection, good hygienic measures to keep skin and feet clean and dry should be followed. Photosensitivity reactions (sunburn) may occur, so caution patients against exposure to intense artificial or natural sunlight. Periodic laboratory tests for renal and hepatic function and blood counts are indicated for patients on prolonged therapy. Since griseofulvin is derived from a species of *Penicillium*, there is a theoretical possibility of cross-allergenicity with penicillins. However, patients allergic to penicillin have used griseofulvin without adverse effects.

SIDE EFFECTS/ADVERSE REACTIONS: A frequent side effect is severe headache, especially in the early stages of therapy. Common hypersensitivity reactions are rashes and urticaria. Angioneurotic edema occurs rarely. Griseofulvin may cause gastric upset with nausea, vomiting, and diarrhea. Also reported are fatigue, insomnia, mental confusion, tingling of hands and feet (rare), and transient diminution of hearing. Oral thrush, photosensitivity reactions, and a systemic lupus-like syndrome have occurred. An estrogen-like effect has also been reported in children. Griseofulvin can cause leukopenia and should be discontinued if granulocytopenia develops.

DRUG INTERACTIONS: *Barbiturates* decrease griseofulvin blood levels, so higher antifungal doses may be required. Griseofulvin can decrease prothrombin times and the activity of *warfarin-type anticoagulants*. Concomitant use with *alcohol* may cause tachycardia and flushing.

ANTIDOTE: Discontinue griseofulvin and treat adverse reactions symptomatically.

Isoniazid (INH, Nydrazid, others)

ADMINISTRATION

Available Forms: Injectable (IM), 100 mg/ml; tablets, 50, 100, 300 mg; oral syrup, 50 mg/5 ml. Note: Isoniazid is also available in combination with pyridoxine, rifampin, or para-aminosalicylic acid.

Dosage (Oral): Varies according to use.
For active TB: 10–30 mg/kg/day, depending on disease severity. Give in single or divided doses (q8–12h). Maximum is 300–500 mg/day.
For TB prophylaxis: 10 mg/kg/day in single or divided doses (q12h). Maximum is 300 mg/day.
For conversion of positive tuberculin skin test in a patient with no manifest disease: 15 mg/kg/day in single or divided doses (q12h). Continue therapy for 1 year.

Dosage (Parenteral): Same as oral doses. Use only when oral administration is not feasible.

RENAL IMPAIRMENT: Reduce dosages as necessary for patients with moderate to severe renal impairment (e.g., creatinine clearance of 10–30 ml/min).

ANTIMICROBIAL SPECTRUM: Isoniazid is active against mycobacteria, including *M. tuberculosis*. It is a highly specific antibiotic and is ineffective against all other organisms. Resistance to isoniazid is fairly common in areas outside the US (Southeast Asia, Mexico, Philippines), but resistant organisms have been isolated in the US from patients who have not received isoniazid therapy. Resistance can develop rapidly if the drug is used *alone* to treat active TB but does not seem to be a problem when it is used alone for preventive therapy.

INDICATIONS: Isoniazid is used in combination with other antitubercular medications for treatment of all forms of active tuberculosis caused by susceptible mycobacteria. To avoid the emergence of isoniazid-resistant organisms, a two-drug regimen (e.g., isoniazid plus rifampin or ethambutol) is frequently given to all patients with clinically active disease that involves hilar adenopathy, pleural effusion, and lobar lesions. Triple therapy (e.g., isoniazid, rifampin, and either ethambutol or streptomycin) is indicated for serious cases that require hospitalization, for patients with extensive pulmonary and other organ involvement, and for miliary TB and TB meningitis. When isoniazid resistance is known or suspected, therapy should be changed to a regimen that includes at least two new antitubercular medications as part of a new triple-drug regimen. Other medications used include PAS, cycloserine, pyrazinamide, and ethionamide. Isoniazid is used alone only as prophylactic therapy for a tuberculin-negative patient who is exposed to active TB or to prevent clinical reactivation of the disease in those individuals with dormant infections or "healed" lesions. (For more detailed information on preferred therapy of tuberculosis, see Stead WW, Bates JH: Tuberculosis, in Isselbacher KJ, Adams RD, Braunwald E, et al (eds): *Harrison's Principles of Internal Medicine*, ed 10. New York, McGraw-Hill Inc, 1983, pp 1019–1030.)

ACTIONS: Isoniazid is bactericidal for actively reproducing mycobacteria. It appears to interfere with DNA synthesis and certain metabolic processes; it is effective only on actively growing, sensitive organisms and does not affect dormant mycobacteria. The antibiotic is readily absorbed from the GI tract and injection sites and is widely distributed in body tissues and fluids, including the CSF. It crosses the placenta and is excreted in breast milk. Isoniazid is acetylated in the liver to several metabolites that are excreted by the kidney. Hepatic insufficiency can prolong the plasma half-life of the drug. (The rate of liver acetylation is genetically determined. About 50% of the US population are "slow acetylators"; approximately one-half of American Negroes and Caucasians and the majority of American Indians, Eskimos, and Orientals are "rapid inactivators" of isoniazid.) Although some individuals metabolize the drug more rapidly than others, this is clinically insignificant as long as the doses are given daily. If intermittent therapy is used (e.g., if there are 5 or more days between doses), the "rapid acetylators" may inactivate isoniazid too quickly and a poor therapeutic response occurs. Isoniazid can induce pyridoxine (vitamin B_6) deficiency. Supplemental pyridoxine (10–30 mg/day) can be given, especially to malnourished patients who may not be receiving adequate amounts of this vitamin in their diets.

CONTRAINDICATIONS: Acute hepatic disease, development of severe hepatic hypersensitivity reactions to isoniazid (including drug-induced hepatitis), hypersensitivity to isoniazid.

PRECAUTIONS: If possible, give daily doses (along with the patient's other antitubercular medications) as a single dose before breakfast to achieve a single combined peak concentration for maximum effect on the tubercle bacilli. Although isoniazid-associated liver disease rarely occurs in children, it is advisable to check patients monthly for signs and symptoms of hepatic toxic reactions (e.g., anorexia, malaise, nausea, vomiting, fever, jaundice, dark urine); notify a physician immediately if these occur. No more than a 1 month supply of the antibiotic should be dispensed at once, and inquiry about any adverse reactions should be made each time the patient is seen. If signs and symptoms of hepatic toxic reactions occur, discontinue the drug temporarily and draw a blood sample for liver function tests (e.g., SGOT, SGPT, LDH, serum bilirubin, alkaline phosphatase). A threefold elevation in any of these enzymes necessitates the discontinuation of isoniazid. If only mild elevations occur, the drug can be restarted in small, gradually increasing doses to determine if the toxic effect is drug-induced. Carefully monitor use of isoniazid in those patients with preexisting hepatic disease, severe renal impairment, or convulsive disorders. Periodic ophthalmic examinations are indicated if visual disturbances develop. Periodic blood counts should also be done.

SIDE EFFECTS/ADVERSE REACTIONS: These are generally dose-related and usually appear within the first 3 months of therapy. The incidence is higher in "slow acetylators" and malnourished patients. The most common reaction is peripheral neuritis, often preceded by tingling sensations in the hands and feet (treat with pyridoxine supplements). Other neurological toxic effects include optic neuritis and atrophy, tinnitus, vertigo, ataxia, muscle twitching, hyperactive reflexes, mental derangement, convulsions, toxic encephalopathy, and psychosis. Gastrointestinal and hepatic effects include nausea, vomiting, dry mouth, epigastric distress, elevated liver enzymes, jaundice, and hepatitis. Various blood dyscrasias such as hemolytic or aplastic anemia, leukopenia, and agranulocytosis have been reported. Other hypersensitivity reactions are rashes, fever, chills, swollen lymph nodes, keratitis, and vasculitis. Pyridoxine deficiency, pellagra, hyperglycemia, dyspnea, metabolic acidosis, and gynecomastia may develop. A rheumatoid and systemic lupus-like syndrome has also been reported. Local irritation can occur at IM injection sites.

DRUG INTERACTIONS: *Aluminum hydroxide gel* can decrease gastric absorption of isoniazid, so separate doses of the two by at least 1 hour. Isoniazid can inhibit the metabolism of *phenytoin* (mainly in "slow acetylators"), which can result in phenytoin toxicity. Large doses given with *disulfiram* can produce coordination difficulties and behavioral changes. Isoniazid may have MAO-inhibiting properties, so avoid its use with *meperidine*.

ANTIDOTE: Discontinue isoniazid. If ingestion of overdose is recent, perform gastric aspiration and lavage. Maintain an adequate airway and assist respiration. Perform blood gas, serum electrolyte, and blood glucose determinations immediately. Treat metabolic acidosis with IV sodium bicarbonate prior to using IV diazepam or barbiturates for controlling seizures. Doses of pyridoxine given IV (in amounts equal to that of the ingested isoniazid) may be useful in terminating seizures. Forced diuresis with furosemide or mannitol should be initiated immediately to hasten the renal excretion of the drug and should be maintained for up to 6–12 hours after apparent clinical recovery to prevent relapse. In cases of life-threatening overdoses, peritoneal dialysis or hemodialysis may be beneficial.

Ketoconazole (Nizoral)

ADMINISTRATION

Available Forms: Tablets, 200 mg.

Dosage (Oral): Do not use in children less than 2 years old. Duration of therapy varies with the type of infection: mucocutaneous candidiasis, maintenance therapy; candidiasis, minimum of 1–2 weeks; other mycoses, minimum of 6 months.
Children <20 kg: 50 mg daily.
Children 20–40 kg: 100 mg daily.
Children >40 kg: 200 mg daily.

RENAL IMPAIRMENT: Renal failure would not be expected to significantly alter the half-life of ketoconazole; however, severe hepatic impairment may do so.

ANTIMICROBIAL SPECTRUM: Ketoconazole is active *in vivo* against *Candida, Blastomyces dermatitidis, C. immitis, H. capsulatum, Paracoccidioides brasiliensis,* and *Philaphora* species. It is active *in vitro* against dermatophytes (*Trichophyton, Microsporum, Epidermophyton* species), other yeasts (*C. neoformans*), and various other fungi, including actinomycetes, eumycetes, and phycomycetes.

INDICATIONS: Ketoconazole is used for treatment of systemic fungal infections such as blastomycosis, coccidioidomycosis, paracoccidioidomycosis, histoplasmosis, chronic mucocutaneous candidiasis, and those caused by resistant dermatophytes. It has been useful against griseofulvin-resistant ringworm. It is *not* recommended for fungal meningitis. Because of incomplete data, use of ketoconazole in systemic candidiasis cannot be recommended. Pending more complete and well-controlled trials, amphotericin B is the agent of choice for serious systemic mycoses.

ACTIONS: Ketoconazole impairs the synthesis of ergosterol, which is a vital component of fungal cell membranes. The resulting changes in membrane composition produce enhanced permeability and, possibly, cellular death. Absorption of oral doses is rapid, and peak antifungal MICs are reached in 1–2 hours. Ketoconazole absorption is dependent on an acidic gastric pH; if the gastric pH is raised by antacids or by a physiological condition such as achlorhydria, absorption of ketoconazole is decreased. The compound is highly protein-bound (98–99%). Concentrations in the CSF are negligible after oral doses, and data on the distribution of ketoconazole in other tissues are unavailable. Ketoconazole is known to be excreted in breast milk, however. It is metabolized in the liver, and nearly all of the inactive metabolites and some unchanged ketoconazole are excreted in the bile and feces. Only a small amount (2–4%) is eliminated unchanged in the urine.

CONTRAINDICATIONS: Hypersensitivity to ketoconazole.

PRECAUTIONS: Patients with achlorhydria or insufficient gastric acidity may need to dissolve the tablet in 4 ml of 0.2N HCl; the mixture should then be ingested through a glass or plastic straw to protect the teeth and followed with a cup of tap water. If concomitant antacids, anticholinergics, or H_2-blockers (cimetidine, ranitidine) are needed, they should be given at least 2 hours after the dose of ketoconazole. Monitor liver function tests (e.g., SGOT, SGPT, SGGT, alkaline phosphatase, bilirubin) before therapy and at periodic intervals (monthly) throughout prolonged therapy, particularly in patients who have concurrent liver disease or impaired hepatic function. Discontinue ketoconazole if values for liver function tests are significantly elevated or signs and symptoms of hepatocellular dysfunction appear (see side effects/adverse reactions).

SIDE EFFECTS/ADVERSE REACTIONS: Ketoconazole is usually well tolerated compared with amphotericin B and miconazole. Signs and symptoms of GI upset are primarily nausea and vomiting. Other reported reactions include abdominal pain, pruritus, headache, dizziness, sedation, fever, chills, rash, photophobia, gynecomastia, and cholestatic hepatitis. Transient increases in liver enzymes have been observed. Several cases of potentially serious idiosyncratic hepatocellular dysfunction have been reported. (Signs and symptoms of such hepatotoxicity include unusual fatigue, anorexia, nausea, vomiting, jaundice, dark urine, and pale stools.)

DRUG INTERACTIONS: Concomitant use of *antacids, anticholinergics, cimetidine,* or *ranitidine* can decrease absorption of ketoconazole.

ANTIDOTE: Discontinue ketoconazole. Treat accidental overdoses with gastric lavage with sodium bicarbonate solutions.

Mebendazole (Vermox)

ADMINISTRATION

Available Forms: Tablets (chewable), 100 mg.

Dosage (Oral): Safe use in children less than 2 years old has not been established. Tablets can be chewed, swallowed whole, or mixed with food. No fasting or purging is necessary during treatment.
For pinworms: Single dose of 100 mg. Can be repeated in 3 weeks.
For other helminthic infections: 100 mg bid (in AM and PM) for 3 consecutive days. Course can be repeated in 3 weeks.

INDICATIONS: Mebendazole is indicated for treatment of enterobiasis (pinworm infection), ascariasis (roundworm infection), trichuriasis (whipworm infection), hookworm infections caused by *Ancylostoma duodenale* or *Necator americanus,* and mixed helminthic infections.

ACTIONS: Mebendazole appears to inhibit the uptake of glucose and other nutrients in susceptible helminths and to cause degenerative changes in helminthic intestinal cells. Secretory substances accumulate, which results in cellular autolysis of the organism. There is insignificant systemic absorption of oral doses, and most of the drug is excreted in the urine within 3 days.

CONTRAINDICATIONS: Hypersensitivity to mebendazole, pregnancy, children less than 2 years old.

PRECAUTIONS: Cure rates may be lower in patients with massive infections or increased GI motility. Hygenic precautions must be stressed and practiced to prevent reinfection.

SIDE EFFECTS/ADVERSE REACTIONS: Because of its poor absorption, mebendazole is virtually nontoxic. A few cases of transient diarrhea and abdominal pain have been associated with massive infestations and expulsion of the helminths.

ANTIDOTE: Discontinue the medication.

Metronidazole (Flagyl, Flagyl IV, Flagyl IV RTU)

ADMINISTRATION

Available Forms: Injectable (IV), 500 mg (powder) or 5 mg/ml in 100 ml solution (Flagyl IV RTU); tablets, 250, 500 mg.

Dosage (Parenteral): Safety and efficacy of IV use in children has not been established.

Dosage (Oral): Varies according to use.
For amoebic dysentery or liver abscess: 35–50 mg/kg/day in divided doses (q8h) for 10 days.
For giardiasis: 15 mg/kg/day in divided doses (q8h) for 10 days.

ANTIMICROBIAL SPECTRUM: Metronidazole is effective against several protozoa including *Trichomonas vaginalis*, *E. histolytica*, and *Giardia lamblia*. Susceptible anaerobic bacteria include bacteroides (including *B. fragilis*), *Fusobacterium*, clostridia, *Eubacterium*, peptococci, and peptostreptococci.
Resistant organisms: Other gram-negative microorganisms, all aerobic bacteria, fungi, viruses, etc.

INDICATIONS: Pediatric use of metronidazole is limited primarily to oral treatment of acute intestinal amebiasis (dysentery), amoebic hepatitis, and liver abscess due to *E. histolytica*. Metronidazole has been used effectively in giardiasis. It has also been used as an alternative to penicillin for treatment of acute ulcerative gingivitis (Vincent's stomatitis).

ACTIONS: The precise mechanism of action is unknown. Oral doses are well absorbed, primarily in the small intestine. Metronidazole is well distributed in body fluids, including CSF and breast milk. A small amount of the antibiotic is metabolized in the liver, but most of it is excreted unchanged in the urine. Anuria usually does not necessitate dosage changes because metronidazole is readily dialyzable.

CONTRAINDICATIONS: Hypersensitivity to metronidazole or other nitroimidazole derivatives, first trimester of pregnancy, active CNS disease, evidence or history of blood dyscrasias (especially bone marrow suppression).

PRECAUTIONS: Use cautiously in patients with CNS diseases since the medication may induce convulsive seizures and peripheral neuropathy; appearance of abnormal neurological signs necessitates prompt discontinuance of metronidazole. Use cautiously in patients who have or are prone to blood dyscrasias as leukopenia may result; differential white cell counts should be done periodically if therapy extends beyond 1 week. Metronidazole is carcinogenic in rodents, so avoid its use in pregnant patients. Aspiration of pus from amoebic liver abscesses must still be done during therapy with metronidazole. Known or previously unrecognized candidiasis may worsen during therapy. Metronidazole causes a "disulfiram-like" reaction if alcohol is consumed during therapy (signs and symptoms include flushing, vomiting, abdominal cramps, and headaches). Severe hepatic disease may cause accumulation of metronidazole metabolites and increased risk of toxicity. The urine may turn a darkened reddish-brown.

SIDE EFFECTS/ADVERSE REACTIONS: (Incidence is usually low.) Nausea is the most frequent complaint, sometimes accompanied by headache, vomiting, diarrhea, anorexia, abdominal cramping, or epigastric distress. Also reported are a metallic taste in the mouth, furry tongue, glossitis, stomatitis, and overgrowth of *Candida*. The most serious toxicity involves CNS effects of seizures, peripheral neuropathy, ataxia, vertigo, confusion, irritability, depression, and insomnia. Hypersensitivity reactions include rash, urticaria, nasal congestion, and dry mucous membranes. Reversible leukopenia, cystitis, dysuria, polyuria, incontinence, and joint pains resembling serum sickness may occur. ECG tracings may show flattened T waves.

DRUG INTERACTIONS: Ingestion of *alcohol* during therapy with metronidazole causes a "disulfiram-like" reaction.

ANTIDOTE: Discontinue the medication. Treat adverse reactions symptomatically.

Miconazole (Monistat IV)

ADMINISTRATION

Available Forms: Injectable (IV), 10 mg/ml in 20 ml amps (diluent is polyethylene glycol 40 [PEG-40] and castor oil); topical, cream, lotion.

Diluent: For IV infusion or bladder irrigation dilute dose in at least 200 ml D5W or NS.

Dosage (Parenteral): Do not use in children less than 1 year old. 20–40 mg/kg/day IV in divided doses (q8h). Maximum is 45 mg/kg/day or 15 mg/kg/infusion. Therapy may continue for several weeks, depending on the clinical response.

Dosage (Bladder Irrigation): 200 mg diluted and instilled into the bladder 2–4 times/day or by continuous drip.

Rate: Administer IV infusions over 30–60 minutes.

ANTIMICROBIAL SPECTRUM: Miconazole is active *in vitro* against a variety of pathogenic fungi and yeasts, including *C. immitis, H. capsulatum, P. brasiliensis, B. dermatitidis, C. neoformans,* and *S. schenckii.* It is less active against *Aspergillus* and *Candida* organisms unless higher serum concentrations of miconazole are used. Some gram-positive cocci and bacilli are susceptible also.
Resistant organisms: Gram-negative bacteria, protozoa, and viruses.

INDICATIONS: Miconazole is given IV for treatment of severe systemic and meningeal fungal infections, particularly in those patients who fail to respond to or who cannot tolerate amphotericin B. It is used for pulmonary and disseminated forms of coccidioidomycosis, and paracoccidioidomycosis and for chronic mucocutaneous candidiasis. Its clinical role in the treatment of systemic candidiasis and cryptococcosis is unclear. When treating fungal meningitis or urinary bladder infections, supplement IV infusions with intrathecal administration or bladder irrigation.

ACTIONS: Miconazole alters the permeability of fungal cell membranes and interferes with intracellular enzymes, resulting in intracellular necrosis. It is rapidly metabolized in the liver, but only a small amount is excreted in the urine, so dosage adjustments are not necessary in patients with renal impairment. It is not known if it crosses the placenta or is excreted in breast milk.

CONTRAINDICATIONS: Hypersensitivity to miconazole. (Note: Contains paraben preservatives.)

PRECAUTIONS: Intravenous doses of miconazole should not be used for common or trivial fungal infections; use should be restricted to hospitalized patients only or to ambulatory patients under conditions that permit close clinical monitoring. Monitor electrolytes, hematocrit, hemoglobin, and lipids during therapy. Nausea, vomiting, and pruritus can be minimized by treating beforehand with an antihistamine and antiemetic, reducing the dosage, slowing the infusion rate, or avoiding administration at mealtime. Use cautiously in patients with hepatic impairment. Administer through a central line or change the infusion site q48–72h to minimize thrombophlebitis.

SIDE EFFECTS/ADVERSE REACTIONS: Miconazole is generally less toxic than amphotericin B. The most common adverse reactions are phlebitis and pruritus (with or without rashes). Nausea, vomiting, diarrhea, drowsiness, febrile reactions, anorexia, and flushing may also occur. Occasionally, transient decreases in hematocrit, anemia, thrombocytopenia, leukopenia, platelet changes (without associated bleeding problems), hyponatremia, and hyperlipemia (probably due to PEG-40-castor-oil vehicle) have been reported but are not serious. Rapid IV injection of an undiluted solution may cause transient tachycardia and cardiac arrhythmias.

DRUG INCOMPATIBILITIES: Do not mix with any other medications.

DRUG INTERACTIONS: Miconazole reportedly potentiates the anticoagulant effects of *coumarins.*

ANTIDOTE: Discontinue the infusion. Treat emesis and severe pruritus with antiemetics and IV doses of diphenhydramine. Treat adverse reactions symptomatically.

Nystatin (Mycostatin, Nilstat)

ADMINISTRATION

Available Forms: Tablets, 500,000 units; oral suspension, 100,000 units/ml; topical, powder, cream, ointment; vaginal tablets, 100,000 units.

Dosage (Oral): Varies according to the patient's age.
Premature and full-term newborn infants: 100,000 units (1 ml suspension) q6h instilled slowly, allowing it to spread over lesions before being swallowed.
Infants and older children: 1–2 million units/day divided into 3–4 doses. Have the patient retain the suspension in the mouth as long as possible before swallowing.

ANTIMICROBIAL SPECTRUM: Nystatin is effective against a variety of pathogenic and nonpathogenic yeasts and yeast-like fungi, most notably all *Candida* species and *Geotrichum lactis*.
Resistant organisms: Bacteria, protozoa, and viruses.

INDICATIONS: Nystatin is used orally for treatment of thrush and intestinal candidiasis and topically for cutaneous fungal infections.

ACTIONS: Nystatin probably acts by binding to sterols in fungal cell membranes; the result is a change in permeability that allows leakage of intracellular components. It is ineffective against bacteria and trichomonads. There is no appreciable absorption of oral doses.

CONTRAINDICATIONS: Hypersensitivity to nystatin or any components in the ointment or cream.

PRECAUTIONS: When treating thrush, wipe off the plaques with gauze before applying the antibiotic; affected areas can be painted with a nystatin-soaked cotton swab. To prevent relapse, continue treatment of the infection for at least 48 hours after clinical cure. Oral tablets contain a tartrazine dye that may cause hypersensitivity reactions in susceptible patients, particularly those who are allergic to aspirin.

SIDE EFFECTS/ADVERSE REACTIONS: Nystatin is virtually nontoxic and nonsensitizing. Large oral doses may cause gastric distress, nausea, vomiting, or diarrhea. Occasionally, hypersensitivity or irritation to topical preparations may occur.

ANTIDOTE: Discontinue nystatin.

Rifampin (Rifadin, Rimactane)

ADMINISTRATION

Available Forms: Capsules, 300 mg.

Dosage (Oral): Varies according to use. Note: For those unable to swallow capsules, the contents can be mixed with small amount of jelly or applesauce.

For clinical tuberculosis and other mycobacterial infections:

- Children and infants (>1 week old): 10–20 mg/kg/day given as a single dose on an empty stomach. Use in conjunction with at least one other antitubercular medication. Maximum dose is 600 mg/day.
- Infants <1 week old: 10 mg/kg/day given as a single dose

For meningococcal carriers:

- Infants 3 months to 1 year old: 10 mg/kg/day given in divided doses (q12h) for 2 days
- Children 1–12 years old: 20 mg/kg/day given in divided doses (q12h) for 2 days

For acute and chronic diphtheria carriers: 20 mg/kg/day given for 7 days.
For *Legionella* pneumonia: 20 mg/kg/day given for 2 weeks.
For *H. influenzae* carriers: 20 mg/kg/day given for 4 days.

RENAL IMPAIRMENT: No dosage adjustments are necessary.

INDICATIONS: Rifampin's principal use is in combination with other antitubercular medications (notably isoniazid) for the initial treatment and the retreatment of pulmonary tuberculosis. It should not be used alone for TB therapy because bacterial resistance develops rapidly. Ethambutol can be added to the isoniazid-rifampin regimen to inhibit the growth of mutant bacilli resistant to the latter two medications. Rifampin is superior to isoniazid for sterilizing pulmonary lesions that contain dormant tubercle bacilli. It is also effective in eliminating meningococci from the nasopharynx of asymptomatic carriers in situations where the risk of meningococcal meningitis is high; it should not be used for treatment of active meningococcal disease, however. Rifampin may be used to treat acute and chronic carriers of diphtheria, *Legionella* pneumonia, and carriers of *H. influenzae*. Combined with parenteral vancomycin, rifampin has been effective in severe methicillin-resistant staphylococcal infections that are unresponsive to penicillins or cephalosporins.

ANTIMICROBIAL SPECTRUM: Rifampin is effective against mycobacteria. It is also active against many gram-positive and gram-negative cocci, such as staphylococci, streptococci, pneumococci, and meningococci, and species of *Legionella* and *C. diphtheriae*. Higher serum concentrations are necessary to inhibit some of the susceptible gram-negative bacilli (e.g., *H. influenzae, Proteus, Pseudomonas, Enterobacter-Klebsiella*). *In vitro* resistance develops rapidly when rifampin is used alone for treatment of tuberculosis and other bacterial infections.

ACTIONS: Rifampin stops bacterial replication by inhibiting RNA polymerase and, consequently, RNA synthesis within the bacterial cell. The drug is bactericidal for actively dividing organisms and bacteriostatic for dormant organisms. Rifampin is well absorbed from the GI tract, especially if taken on an empty stomach. It is widely distributed in body tissues and fluids such as CSF and pleural fluids. Highest concentrations are found in the liver, bile, urine, lung, and kidney. Peak plasma levels are usually achieved in 2–4 hours after administration. Rifampin crosses the placenta and is excreted in breast milk. It is metabolized in the liver to an *active* metabolite. Both unchanged rifampin and the metabolite are excreted through the bile and reabsorbed into the circulation. Fifty percent of an oral dose is eliminated in the feces; only 20% is excreted in the urine. Impaired hepatic function, especially with obstructive jaundice, can cause higher and more prolonged serum levels. There is no such cumulative effect in renal impairment.

PRECAUTIONS: Rifampin can impart a brick-red color to urine, feces, tears, sputum, and sweat. Rifampin has caused severe liver dysfunction with jaundice; fatalities have occurred in patients with preexisting liver disease and in those concurrently receiving other hepatotoxic medications. Use with extreme caution in patients with hepatic impairment. Monitor liver function closely with periodic tests for liver enzymes and serum bilirubin. Treatment with rifampin for tuberculosis should be continued until maximal clinical improvement and sputum conversion are attained (usually within 6–9 months, but this is variable). The manufacturer has not established dosages for children less than 5 years of age, but clinicians have successfully treated infants with rifampin.

SIDE EFFECTS/ADVERSE REACTIONS: The most frequent side effects are heartburn, epigastric distress, anorexia, flatulence, nausea, vomiting, and diarrhea. Also reported are headache, drowsiness, fatigue, ataxia, dizziness, impaired concentration, mental confusion, and visual disturbances. High doses can produce a "flu-like" syndrome with fever, muscle weakness, pain in the extremities, and sore mouth and tongue. Other hypersensitivity reactions include rashes, edema, pruritus, and urticaria. Superinfections with *Candida* may occur. Blood dyscrasias include eosinophilia, leukopenia, thrombocytopenia, purpura, and a positive Coombs' test; rifampin may decrease hemoglobin levels and cause hematuria and hemoptysis. Jaundice, transient abnormalities in liver enzyme tests, and serious and fatal hepatic dysfunction may occur.

DRUG INTERACTIONS: Rifampin may decrease prothrombin time, so increased doses of *oral anticoagulants* may be indicated. Rifampin accelerates hepatic metabolism of *quinidine, warfarin,* and *corticosteroids*. *PAS* may decrease the gastric absorption of rifampin, so administer these two drugs at least 8–12 hours apart.

ANTIDOTE: Discontinue rifampin. Treat adverse reactions symptomatically.

Spectinomycin (Trobicin)

ADMINISTRATION

Available Forms: Injectable (IM), 2, 4 gm vials.

Diluent: Dilute with sterile water for injection. Use 3.2 ml per 2 gm vial or 6.2 ml per 4 gm vial; final concentration is 400 mg/ml.

Dosage (Parenteral): Varies according to the patient's age.
Children <8 years old: 40 mg/kg as a single IM injection.
Children >8 years old: The Centers for Disease Control (CDC) recommend use of oral tetracycline or cefotaxime IM.

RENAL IMPAIRMENT: Dosage adjustments are not necessary.

ANTIMICROBIAL SPECTRUM: Spectinomycin is effective against the majority of strains of *N. gonorrhoeae,* including the penicillinase producers. No cross-resistance has been demonstrated between spectinomycin and penicillin.

INDICATIONS: Spectinomycin is reserved for the treatment of uncomplicated gonorrhea (vulvovaginitis, urethritis) in children allergic to penicillins and in those less than 8 years of age in whom tetracyclines are contraindicated. It is also recommended for uncomplicated gonococcal infections caused by penicillin-resistant strains of *N. gonorrhoeae* and for those infections not responding to other antibiotics such as ampicillin, amoxicillin, or tetracycline. Spectinomycin is not indicated for the treatment of pharyngeal gonococcal infections or for syphilis.

ACTIONS: Spectinomycin is usually bacteriostatic. It appears to inhibit protein synthesis in susceptible bacteria by binding to 30 S ribosomal subunits. Spectinomycin resistance may develop through mutation or a plasmid-mediated resistance factor in certain bacteria. Oral doses of the antibiotic are not absorbed, but rapid absorption occurs after IM administration. Peak serum concentrations are reached in 1 hour and antibacterial serum levels persist for at least 8 hours. Within 48 hours 70–100% of the drug is excreted in the urine as unchanged spectinomycin and as an active metabolite. Despite its total elimination through the kidneys, no renal toxicity has been reported, so dosage adjustments in renal impairment are probably not necessary.

CONTRAINDICATIONS: Hypersensitivity to spectinomycin.

PRECAUTIONS: After adding the diluent, shake the vial vigorously to ensure a uniform suspension before withdrawing the dose. Administer IM injections deep into the upper outer quadrant of the gluteal muscle; use a 20-gauge needle. Safe and effective use in neonates has not been established (penicillin-resistant gonococcal infections in neonates are best treated with gentamicin or cefotaxime).

SIDE EFFECTS/ADVERSE REACTIONS: Spectinomycin is usually well tolerated. Occasional side effects include pain at the injection site, urticaria, rash, pruritus, dizziness, headache, nausea, vomiting, fever, chills, nervousness, and insomnia.

DRUG INTERACTIONS: None significant.

ANTIDOTE: Treat adverse reactions symptomatically.

Vancomycin

ADMINISTRATION

Available Forms: Injectable (IV), 500 mg vial (powder for reconstitution); oral solution, 10 gm powder for reconstitution (500 mg/6 ml after reconstitution).

Diluent: For IV use reconstitute the contents of the vial with sterile water. Further dilute the calculated dose in 100–200 ml D5W or NS for intermittent infusion. For continuous IV infusion dilute the dose in a sufficient volume to permit administration over 24 hours.

Dosage (Parenteral)
For systemic staphylococcal infections:

- Infants and newborns: 10 mg/kg/day IV in divided doses (q12h)
- Older children: 44 mg/kg/day IV in divided doses (q6–12h)

Dosage (Oral)
For enterocolitis caused by *C. difficile* or *Staphylococcus:* 44 mg/kg/day in divided doses (q6–12h).

Rate: Administer IV piggyback doses over 30–60 minutes. For continuous infusion give over 24 hours.

RENAL IMPAIRMENT: Dosage adjustments are necessary.

ANTIMICROBIAL SPECTRUM: Vancomycin is active against staphylococci (including penicillinase producers), streptococci, enterococci, pneumococci, gonococci, corynebacteria, and clostridia.
Resistant organisms: Other gram-negative organisms, yeasts, and fungi.

INDICATIONS: Vancomycin is a potent antistaphylococcal antibiotic. Its principal indication for parenteral use is the treatment of serious methicillin-resistant *S. aureus* infections in which penicillin and cephalosporins are ineffective. It has been particularly beneficial for infants with meningitis caused by methicillin-resistant staphylococci. Oral vancomycin is the preferred treatment for staphylococcal enterocolitis and for the antibiotic-associated colitis ("pseudomembranous" colitis) produced by *C. difficile*. Vancomycin is also given parenterally to treat serious gram-positive coccal infections in patients who are allergic to penicillins or cephalosporins. Combined with gentamicin, it is effective against endocarditis caused by enterococci or by *S. epidermidis, S. aureus,* or *Streptococcus bovis*. It can be used alone for endocarditis caused by *S. viridans*. Intravenous vancomycin plus oral rifampin can be especially synergistic against staphylococci. This combination has been used to successfully treat CNS and hemodialysis shunt infections produced by staphylococci when surgical removal of the appliance has not been beneficial.

ACTIONS: Vancomycin is bactericidal; it inhibits bacterial cell wall synthesis at a site different from that affected by penicillin. There is no cross-resistance with any other antibiotics, and the development of vancomycin resistance is rare. Oral doses are not absorbed from the GI tract, so it must be given IV to achieve bactericidal levels in the blood. Its half-life in patients with normal renal function is about 6 hours. After IV administration vancomycin is widely distributed in many body tissues and fluids. Although it does not diffuse readily into the CSF through normal meninges, low concentrations do penetrate into the CSF during meningitis. CSF concentrations of vancomycin approach 15% of the serum concentrations during meningitis. If necessary, high levels can be achieved by also administering the antibiotic intrathecally or instilling it into the CSF via an Ommaya reservoir. Intravenous doses are excreted mostly in the urine; oral doses are eliminated primarily in the feces. Impaired renal function delays excretion of vancomycin, and the resulting high serum levels can cause toxic reactions. Normal serum half-life is 6 hours; in anuric patients, it is nearly 8 days.

CONTRAINDICATIONS: Hypersensitivity to vancomycin. *Do not give IM.*

PRECAUTIONS: Dilute IV doses in 100–200 ml of fluid and infuse them slowly over 30–60 minutes (or as a 24 hour infusion) to minimize thrombophlebitis, hypotension, and histamine-like reactions. Also rotate the injection sites. The drug may cause damage to the eighth cranial nerve, primarily in the hearing function, and permanent damage has resulted. Risk is greater if large doses are given, if treatment is prolonged, if renal impairment is present, or if other ototoxic medications (e.g., potent diuretics) are being given concurrently. High-risk patients old enough to be tested, particularly those who complain of tinnitus, should be given serial auditory function tests. Use vancomycin cautiously in neonates as their renal function is underdeveloped. Since vancomycin is also nephrotoxic, periodic urinalysis and renal function tests (e.g., BUN, serum creatinine) should be done.

ADVERSE REACTIONS: The most common side effect, which occurs shortly after IV administration, is a histamine-like reaction known as "red-neck" syndrome. It is characterized by fever, chills, paresthesia, erythema at the base of the neck and on the upper back, and pruritus. Rapid IV administration can cause a shock-like state, vascular collapse, and anaphylaxis. Vancomycin is very irritating to tissues; IM use can cause necrosis and IV administration often produces pain and thrombophlebitis. Ototoxicity, characterized by high-tone hearing loss and tinnitus, is associated with serum concentrations of 60–80 µg/ml; deafness (reversible and irreversible) may occur, especially in those patients with renal impairment. Other rare side effects include superinfection, drug fever, eosinophilia, leukopenia, and nephrotoxicity.

DRUG INCOMPATIBILITIES: Do not mix with D10W, protein hydrolysates, or alkaline medications.

DRUG INTERACTIONS: Additive ototoxicity and nephrotoxicity can occur if vancomycin is used concurrently or sequentially with *cephalosporins, gentamicin, tobramycin, amikacin, kanamycin, neomycin, furosemide,* or *ethacrynic acid.*

ANTIDOTE: Discontinue vancomycin. Treat hypersensitivity reactions symptomatically.

VII
AGENTS FOR MANAGEMENT OF PAIN AND FEVER

Pain and fever are not pathological in themselves but are symptoms of some other physiological disease process. The relief of pain and discomfort should be attempted in order to provide comfort, promote cooperation, and make further investigation and diagnosis more tolerable.

This section discusses the narcotic analgesics, mild analgesics and antipyretics, and local anesthetics.

24
Narcotic Analgesics

One of the most commonly encountered symptoms in clinical emergency medicine is pain. It can range from mild to intolerable and can be described as dull, burning, aching, sharp, piercing, throbbing, continuous, intermittent, radiating, localized, or referred. The mechanisms and perception of pain are complex. An oversimplified definition describes pain as the distress experienced when certain sensory nerves are stimulated. The important factor in treatment, however, is that reaction to pain is highly individualized: The same degree of sensory nerve stimulation may not cause the same amount of discomfort in each person. The choice of medication or combinations of medications used for analgesia depends on the cause, severity, and chronicity of the pain and on the personality of the patient. Non-narcotic preparations should be used whenever possible, but often the narcotic analgesics provide the most effective relief.

The following narcotic analgesics are included in this chapter:

- **Codeine**
- **DPT cocktail**
- **Meperidine**
- **Morphine sulfate**

The milder analgesics, aspirin and acetaminophen, are discussed in chapter 25.

NARCOTIC ANALGESICS (GENERAL STATEMENT)

INDICATIONS: Narcotic analgesics are effective in the management of moderate to severe pain and generally should not be used for mild pain that is due to benign conditions or for pain that can be satisfactorily relieved by non-narcotic analgesics.

ACTIONS: The precise mechanism of action of the narcotic analgesics is not completely defined. Acting within the CNS, they appear to alter the patient's psychological response to painful stimuli and reduce the associated anxiety and apprehension. Pain is relieved without loss of consciousness, although therapeutic doses often produce some alterations in consciousness or behavior (e.g., euphoria, dysphoria, sedation). The mechanism of the transmission of pain stimuli and the perception of these sensations by the CNS are still obscure. Pain is a sensation that has its own sensory apparatus: a system of receptors and sensory nerve fibers that form an intricate network throughout the body. The sensory fibers specific for pain transmission form pathways (nerve tracts) that enter the spinal cord and brain stem and end in certain areas of the brain. Pain stimuli are relayed along these pathways to the CNS where the sensations are perceived and an emotional response is elicited from the patient. Narcotics may exert their analgesic effect by modifying the transmission of pain stimuli along some of these pathways or by preventing the access of pain information to the areas of the brain responsible for mediating the emotional components of the pain experience. Research has also demonstrated the existence of specialized opiate receptors that are present in high concentrations in certain areas of the CNS such as the midbrain and the gray matter of the cortex. These receptors appear to be of different types and to mediate different clinical effects. For example, when activated, some receptors elicit analgesia and euphoria; others produce sedation, respiratory depression, miosis, dysphoria, or physical tolerance. The narcotic analgesics (and some of the non-narcotic ones) may bind to a variety of these opiate receptors and thereby produce the desirable effects of analgesia and euphoria as well as the adverse effects of respiratory depression, sedation, and the like. Small to moderate doses of these analgesics are used to relieve constant pain; larger doses are used to alleviate intermittent, sharp, traumatic, or visceral pain. Narcotics depress respiration by a direct effect on respiratory centers in the brain stem (dose-related effect). The response to hypercapnia is depressed, and hypoxia becomes the stimulus for respiration, so oxygen should be given cautiously in narcotic-induced respiratory depression. Narcotic analgesics suppress the cough reflex via a direct action on the medullary cough center. Initial nausea and vomiting are probably due to a direct stimulation of the chemoreceptor trigger zone (CTZ), but subsequent doses may suppress the CTZ and diminish these emetic effects. Cerebrospinal fluid and intracranial pressures may be increased because of narcotic-induced hypoventilation, hypercapnia, and cerebrovascular dilation. High doses may precipitate seizures.

Narcotic analgesics have an "antiperistaltic" effect on intestinal smooth muscle that results in constipation. However, these agents increase smooth muscle tone and enhance the nonpropulsive type of contractions that cause GI spasm, particularly in the biliary and urinary tract, sphincters, and colon (this effect is partially blocked by atropine). They also have an antidiuretic effect, which decreases urine flow, and they can inhibit release of thyroid stimulating hormone (TSH) and ACTH.

These agents usually cause miosis, and "pinpoint" pupils indicate overdosage. (In contrast, meperidine usually causes little change in pupil size; overdoses tend to produce mydriasis.) Narcotics cause histamine release resulting in peripheral vasodilation, orthostatic hypotension, flushing, pruritus, red eyes, and sweating. They also impair reflex activity from baroreceptors in the carotid and aortic arches, which further aggravates hypotension. Large doses and rapid IV administration can cause hypotension, syncope, fainting, tachycardia, bradycardia, and respiratory depression.

Some narcotic preparations are well absorbed when administered orally or rectally, but others must be given parenterally to be most effective. Narcotic analgesics are readily absorbed from the GI tract and after parenteral administration. However, the effect of a dose given orally is usually less than that of the same dose given parenterally. The potency of oral doses depends on the extent to which the drug is metabolized on its first pass through the GI mucosa and the liver. Oral doses usually have a slower onset, a lower peak effect, and a more prolonged duration of action than parenteral doses. Consequently, parenteral administration is superior in situations where severe pain must be relieved quickly. Oral use provides the more sustained analgesia desirable in the treatment of chronic pain. Narcotic analgesics are distributed in many tissues, readily cross the placenta, and are excreted in breast milk to some extent. They are metabolized primarily in the liver, and both unchanged and metabolized forms are excreted in the urine. Renal or hepatic impairment may cause systemic accumulation of these analgesics.

CONTRAINDICATIONS: Hypersensitivity to individual agents is an absolute contraindication. However, allergy to one narcotic does not necessarily imply allergy to all narcotics; often a derivative from another class can be used. Relative contraindications are head injuries or intracranial lesions associated with increased intracranial pressures, shock, and severely decreased plasma volume.

PRECAUTIONS: Use cautiously in patients with diminished respiratory reserve (e.g., obstructive pulmonary disease, acute asthma, cor pulmonale, severe obesity), preexisting respiratory depression, hypoxia, hypercapnia, or comatose states and in those concomitantly taking phenothiazines or other CNS depressants. Because they suppress the cough reflex and decrease ciliary activity, narcotics should be used cautiously in patients with excessive respiratory secretions (e.g., bronchitis, bronchial asthma). Use with caution in patients with biliary colic, ulcerative colitis, urethral strictures, head injuries, intracranial lesions, elevated CSF pressures, seizure disorders, shock, hypotension, hypothyroidism, Addison's disease, or severe renal or hepatic impairment and in patients with atrial flutter or other supraventricular tachycardias (ventricular rate may increase). Use cautiously in newborns with immature hepatic function; observe newborns closely for signs of respiratory depression if their mothers received narcotics during labor.

Narcotics may interfere with neurological evaluations and may mask symptoms of acute abdominal conditions. Both psychological and physical dependence and tolerance may develop with prolonged use (e.g., 2 weeks), but children may be particularly susceptible to the physical dependence, which may develop after even a few days. Tolerance develops to the CNS depressant effects of narcotics, so increasing the dosage does not necessarily increase the likelihood of respiratory toxicity. However, if doses are withheld or temporarily discontinued and then must be restarted, re-institute therapy with smaller doses to allow for the diminished tolerance and to avoid the possibility of toxicity. Always try to use the smallest effective dose and use it as infrequently as possible. Caution patients that performance of potentially hazardous activities may be impaired because of narcotic-induced drowsiness, reflex slowing, and mental impairment. Avoid IV use as it is associated with an increased incidence of respiratory and circulatory depression. Routinely monitor vital signs at frequent intervals during narcotic administration.

SIDE EFFECTS/ADVERSE REACTIONS: Respiratory depression is the most potentially dangerous acute effect, but it rarely occurs with the usual doses. Other effects include nausea, vomiting, constipation, atelectasis, histamine release (flushing, urticaria, wheals, red eyes), and cardiovascular reactions (bradycardia, tachycardia, hypotension). CNS reactions include sedation, drowsiness, lethargy, mental clouding, impairment of mental and physical performance, euphoria, dysphoria, fear, anxiety, mood changes, dizziness, vertigo, and psychic dependence. (Meperidine can cause CNS stimulation, tremors, and convulsions, however.) Increased CSF and intracranial pressure may occur. Other adverse reactions include miosis, spasm of biliary and urinary tracts (resulting in biliary colic and urinary retention), and an antidiuretic effect. Rapid IV administration may cause respiratory and circulatory collapse, coma, and cardiac arrest. Initial signs and symptoms of narcotic withdrawal include restlessness, yawning, sweating, lacrimation, rhinorrhea, tremor, nausea, vomiting, diarrhea, "gooseflesh," and mydriasis. Then more severe symptoms follow: muscle spasm, severe aching pains, abdominal cramps, hot and cold flashes, sneezing, hyperthermia, tachycardia, hypertension, and increased respirations.

DRUG INCOMPATIBILITIES: Incompatible upon direct admixture with barbiturates, chlordiazepoxide, diazepam, aminophylline, phenytoin, sodium bicarbonate, heparin, methicillin, and iodides.

DRUG INTERACTIONS: Increased CNS depression may occur with concomitant use of the following agents: other *narcotic* or *non-narcotic analgesics, sedative-hypnotics, antianxiety agents, phenothiazines*, other *CNS depressants, general anesthetics* (including alcohol), *tricyclic antidepressants,* and *MAO inhibitors.* Reduce the dose of one or both agents if used together or in close succession. Use with *anticholinergics* can increase the risk of paralytic ileus.

ANTIDOTE: Discontinue the narcotic. Signs and symptoms of overdose include respiratory depression, miosis, extreme somnolence, stupor or coma, skeletal muscle flaccidity, cold clammy skin, bradycardia, hypotension, apnea, circulatory collapse, and cardiac arrest. Support respiration by providing an adequate airway and assisting ventilation. IV doses of naloxone (0.01 mg/kg) can be given q2–3min until respiratory depression is reversed. *Do not use analeptic agents.* Other supportive measures should be employed as necessary (e.g., oxygen, IV fluids, vasopressors).

Codeine

ADMINISTRATION

Available Forms: Injectable (IM, SC), 30 and 60 mg per milliliter; tablets, 15, 30, 60 mg; soluble (hypodermic) tablets, 15, 30, 60 mg. Also available combined with other analgesics, e.g., aspirin (ASA) with codeine, 15–60 mg/tablet; acetaminophen (Tylenol) with codeine, 15–60 mg/tablet; cough syrups with codeine, 10 mg/5 ml.

Dosage (Parenteral): 3 mg/kg/day (100 mg/m^2/day) IM or SC, in divided doses (q4h) prn.

Dosage (Oral): Varies according to use.
For analgesia: Same as parenteral dose.
For antitussive effect: Use one-third to one-half the analgesic dose.

INDICATIONS: Codeine is useful for relieving mild to moderate pain due to a variety of causes and is usually given orally. It is also effective as an antitussive.

ACTIONS: See narcotic analgesics (general statement). Codeine is a morphine derivative with about only one-twelfth to one-sixteenth the analgesic potency of morphine. The analgesic effect of 30 mg of codeine is approximately equivalent to that of 650 mg of aspirin. Oral doses are two-thirds as effective as parenteral doses. After oral or subcutaneous administration, onset of action occurs in 15–30 minutes, and analgesia lasts 4–6 hours. Codeine is excreted in breast milk.

CONTRAINDICATIONS: Hypersensitivity to codeine.

PRECAUTIONS: See narcotic analgesics (general statement). Oral doses of codeine are extremely bitter; the taste can be camouflaged by encasing the tablets in gelatin capsules or by mixing them with applesauce or jelly. Avoid IV use.

SIDE EFFECTS/ADVERSE REACTIONS: Minimal side effects occurring with oral dosages include nausea, vomiting, constipation, dizziness, light-headedness, sedation, euphoria, and pruritus. Codeine is usually less addicting than morphine. Larger parenteral doses produce most of the adverse effects of morphine. IV use has caused anaphylaxis.

DRUG INCOMPATIBILITIES: See narcotic analgesics (general statement).

DRUG INTERACTIONS: See narcotic analgesics (general statement).

ANTIDOTE: See narcotic analgesics (general statement).

Meperidine (Demerol)
DPT cocktail

ADMINISTRATION

Available Forms: Injectable (IM, IV, SC), 25, 50, 75, and 100 mg per milliliter in prefilled syringes and multidose 20 ml vials; tablets, 50, 100 mg; oral elixir, 50 mg/5 ml; DPT ("lytic") cocktail, meperidine combined with promethazine (Phenergan) and chlorpromazine (Thorazine) in the same syringe.

Dosage (Parenteral): 6 mg/kg/day IM or SC in divided doses (q4h). Maximum is 100 mg/dose. Avoid IV use; significant respiratory depression occurs when this route is used.

Dosage (Oral): Same as parenteral dosage.

Dosage (DPT ["Lytic"] cocktail): Meperidine 2 mg/kg, promethazine 1 mg/kg, chlorpromazine 1 mg/kg, given as a single IM injection. Maximum meperidine dose is 50 mg.

INDICATIONS: Meperidine is used for relief of moderate to severe pain. The DPT cocktail is used to produce rapid, heavy sedation prior to painful procedures that do not require general anesthesia.

ACTIONS: See narcotic analgesics (general statement). Meperidine has a more rapid onset but a shorter duration of action than morphine. Oral doses are about one-half as effective as parenteral doses. The analgesic potency of 75–100 mg of meperidine given parenterally is approximately equivalent to that of 10 mg of morphine. In equianalgesic doses meperidine appears to produce less smooth muscle spasm, biliary colic, constipation, and cough suppression than morphine. Peak of analgesia is about 60 minutes after oral use, 40–60 minutes after SC administration, and 30–50 minutes after IM injection. Duration of analgesia is 2–4 hours for all routes.

CONTRAINDICATIONS: Hypersensitivity to meperidine, use of MAO inhibitors currently or within the last 14 days. Other relative contraindications are as for narcotic analgesics (general statement).

PRECAUTIONS: See narcotic analgesics (general statement). Also, meperidine's "vagolytic" effects may particularly aggravate atrial flutter and other supraventricular tachycardias and increase ventricular response rate. Meperidine and its metabolite (normeperidine) have excitatory effects that may precipitate seizures in patients with convulsive disorders. In patients taking MAO inhibitors, meperidine may cause either hyperexcitability, convulsions, hyperpyrexia, hypertension, and tachycardia or a syndrome that resembles acute narcotic overdose (e.g., coma, respiratory depression, cardiovascular collapse).

SIDE EFFECTS/ADVERSE REACTIONS: Respiratory and cardiovascular toxicity is similar to that of other narcotic analgesics. Nausea, vomiting, dizziness, sedation, and sweating are most common. In contrast to morphine, meperidine may cause more anticholinergic effects of dry mouth, palpitations, and tachycardia. Large doses may cause syncope, tremor, muscle twitching, delirium, hallucinations, and seizures. Subcutaneous injections may cause pain, local tissue irritation, induration, and sterile abscesses at the injection site. In susceptible patients, withdrawal symptoms can begin within 3–4 hours after the last dose and become maximal in 8–12 hours. See narcotic analgesics (general statement).

DRUG INCOMPATIBILITIES: See narcotic analgesics (general statement).

DRUG INTERACTIONS: See narcotic analgesics (general statement). For reactions with *MAO inhibitors* see precautions.

ANTIDOTE: See narcotic analgesics (general statement).

Morphine sulfate

ADMINISTRATION

Available Forms: Injectable (IM, IV, SC), 2, 4, 8, 10, 15 mg in 1 or 2 ml prefilled syringes or amps; oral solution, 2 and 4 mg per milliliter.

Dosage (Parenteral): 0.1–0.2 mg/kg/dose IM or SC; can be repeated q4h prn. Maximum is 15 mg/dose. IV dose is one-half of the IM or SC dose, diluted and given slowly.

Dosage (Oral): This route is not advisable for rapid relief of severe pain.

Rate: For IV boluses dilute with water or NS and administer slowly over 2–5 minutes.

INDICATIONS: Morphine is indicated for relief of severe pain only.

ACTIONS: See narcotic analgesics (general statement). Morphine is the prototype for narcotic analgesics. The analgesic potency of all other narcotic and non-narcotic derivatives is based on that of 10 mg of morphine. It should be given parenterally when rapid relief of pain is desired. Onset of action is slower and peak effects are lower, but duration of action is more sustained after oral doses. Maximum analgesia usually occurs about 20 minutes after IV injection, 30–60 minutes after IM injection, and 50–90 minutes after SC administration. Duration of action is approximately 4 hours but may be 2–7 hours, depending on the patient. Morphine causes more biliary tract spasm and colic than equivalent doses of meperidine.

CONTRAINDICATIONS: Hypersensitivity to morphine, increased intracranial pressure, bronchial asthma, respiratory depression.

PRECAUTIONS: See narcotic analgesics (general statement). Because it is extremely addicting, morphine should be used cautiously in children. Addiction may occur within 2 weeks or, in some adolescents, after a few doses. Newborn infants of morphine-addicted mothers must often be treated for withdrawal symptoms. In susceptible patients withdrawal symptoms can begin within 24 hours of the last dose and become maximal in 32–76 hours.

SIDE EFFECTS/ADVERSE REACTIONS: See narcotic analgesics (general statement).

DRUG INCOMPATIBILITIES: See narcotic analgesics (general statement).

DRUG INTERACTIONS: See narcotic analgesics (general statement).

ANTIDOTE: See narcotic analgesics (general statement).

25
Mild Analgesics and Antipyretics

Mild analgesics and antipyretics are commonly referred to as the "nonnarcotic" analgesics. They are most effective in relieving headaches, muscle and joint pain, and discomfort associated with fever and infections. The agents covered in this chapter can also reduce fever, one of the most common symptoms of illness in pediatric patients.

Fever or pyrexia in a child can be caused by a variety of factors, including a hot environment, exercise, dehydration, endocrine disorders, and certain medications that can impair the peripheral and central regulation of body temperature or increase the body's metabolic rate (e.g., anesthetics, sympathomimetics, thyroid hormones). However, in the majority of instances, fever is usually due to some bacterial or viral infectious process. It is of primary importance to determine the origin of the fever if possible and then to treat both the symptoms and the cause.

Fever is usually defined as an elevation of body temperature above the "normal" value of 37.0°C (98.6°F), but the temperature may vary with the route of measurement; for example, normal oral temperature is 35.8–37.3°C (96.5–99.2°F), while rectal values are 36.2–38.0°C (97.2–100.4°F). The body temperature appears to be regulated by the anterior hypothalamus, which establishes a "set-point" temperature. A fine balance between heat production and heat loss is maintained around this "set-point" temperature by the autonomic nervous system, which varies the blood supply to the body surface and aids in heat loss or conservation. Fever is usually the result of an elevation in the "set-point" temperature in response to various stimuli, including pyrogens produced by certain bacterial infections. The body then attempts to balance heat production and loss around this higher level. The treatment of fever should ideally include sponge baths to facilitate heat loss and antipyretics to act on the hypothalamus to lower the "set-point" temperature.

Evaluation of fever should take into account the child's age. Newborns with sepsis or serious illness often have no fever and, in many cases, may even be hypothermic. The only signs may be decreased appetite, lethargy, and irritability. For infants less than 6 months of age, the presence of fever always requires a systematic and thorough examination to determine if an infectious process is taking place. Unlike adults, children may often run temperatures as high as 40.0–40.5°C (104–105°F) with benign illnesses; it may be helpful to reduce body temperature to less than 39.4°C (103°F) with sponging and antipyretics to make the child more comfortable and cooperative and to make physical assessment easier.

The following mild analgesics and antipyretics are included in this chapter:

- **Acetaminophen**
- **Aspirin**

The non-narcotic analgesics such as propoxyphene (Darvon), pentazocine (Talwin), and butorphanol (Stadol) are not discussed here because they are not recommended for use in children less than 14 years old or, in some cases, less than 18 years old.

Acetaminophen (Datril, Liquiprin, Tempra, Tylenol)

ADMINISTRATION

Available Forms: Tablets, 325, 500 mg; chewable tablets, 80, 120 mg; capsules, 325, 500 mg; oral elixir, 32 mg/ml; pediatric drops, 100 mg/ml (calibrated dropper); oral suspension, 48 mg/ml (Liquiprin), 65 mg/ml; rectal suppositories, 120, 300, 500, 600 mg; in combination with 16–60 mg codeine/tablet.

Dosage (Oral): Table 25–1 lists single doses to be given 4–5 times/day. Maximum is 5 doses/day.

TABLE 25–1 Oral Doses of Acetaminophen*

Age	Weight (lb)	Dose (mg)	Pediatric Drops[†] (ml)	Elixir[‡] (tsp)	Chewable Tablets[§]
Up to 3 mo	6–11	40	0.4	—	—
4–11 mo	12–17	80	0.8	0.50	—
12–23 mo	18–23	120	1.2	0.75	1.5
2–3 yr	24–35	160	1.6	1.00	2.0
4–5 yr	36–47	240	2.4	1.50	3.0
6–8 yr	48–59	320	3.2	2.00	4.0
9–10 yr	60–71	400	4.0	2.50	5.0
11–12 yr	72–95	480	—	3.00	6.0
>12 yr	325–650 mg q4–6h prn				

*Single doses to be given 4–5 times/day.
[†]100 mg/ml
[‡]32 mg/ml
[§]80 mg

INDICATIONS: Acetaminophen is used to alleviate mild to moderate pain of low intensity and nonvisceral origin. It also reduces fever and discomfort associated with bacterial and viral infections. Acetaminophen is the alternative choice for patients who are allergic to aspirin, who cannot tolerate aspirin, or who have bleeding disorders.

ACTIONS: Acetaminophen acts on the hypothalamic temperature-regulation center to produce antipyresis. Heat dissipation is increased as a result of vasodilation and increased peripheral blood flow. Unlike aspirin or other salicylates, acetaminophen does not have anti-inflammatory, antiplatelet, or uricosuric activity, but its analgesic and antipyretic potency equals that of aspirin. Oral doses are rapidly and well absorbed. About 80–85% of an acetaminophen dose is metabolized in the liver, and the metabolites and some unchanged analgesic are excreted in the urine. One of the metabolites, para-aminophenol, can cause methemoglobinemia to which children are particularly sensitive.

CONTRAINDICATIONS: May be contraindicated in patients with G6PD deficiency.

PRECAUTIONS: Use cautiously in patients with severe hepatic or renal impairment (drug accumulation). Give doses q8h in patients with severe renal impairment. Children tend to develop methemoglobinemia from the para-aminophenol metabolite more readily than adults do. Use cautiously or avoid in patients with G6PD deficiency (hemolytic anemia may develop).

SIDE EFFECTS/ADVERSE REACTIONS: In normal therapeutic doses acetaminophen is relatively nontoxic. Occasionally, rashes, urticaria, laryngeal edema, and drug fever may occur. Blood dyscrasias (e.g., anemia, thrombocytopenia, neutropenia, leukopenia, pancytopenia) occur rarely, usually with prolonged therapy or large doses. Early signs and symptoms of acute toxic effects (from a single toxic dose or from chronic ingestion) are nausea, vomiting, abdominal pain, diaphoresis, and general malaise; these appear within 2–3 hours of ingestion. Methemoglobinemia may occur. Clinical and laboratory evidence of hepatotoxicity and hepatic necrosis may not be obvious for 48–72 hours after ingestion of toxic doses. The para-aminophenol metabolite may take 2–6 days to produce jaundice, so the patient should be hospitalized for at least several days for observation. Hepatic necrosis is likely if the plasma half-life of acetaminophen exceeds 4 hours on the first day of overdose. Hepatic coma is likely if the first-day half-life exceeds 12 hours (normal is about 3 hours). Azotemia, renal tubular necrosis, hypoglycemia, hypoprothrombinemia, severe rash, and mucosal lesions are also associated with acute toxicity.

DRUG INTERACTIONS: Large doses may potentiate the anticoagulant activity of *coumarin, heparin,* and other *anticoagulants*. Concomitant use with *phenothiazines* may cause profound hypothermia.

ANTIDOTE: Discontinue acetaminophen. If toxic doses were recently ingested, induce emesis with syrup of ipecac or gastric lavage. Activated charcoal may hinder further acetaminophen absorption. Vigorous hydration will enhance excretion. Support ventilation as necessary. Serum levels of acetaminophen greater than 300 µg/ml 4 hours after ingestion are often associated with hepatotoxicity, while levels less than 120 µg/ml are not. Levels greater than 120 µg/ml may require oral acetylcysteine therapy (investigational). This treatment is most beneficial when given within 12 hours following overdose. The oral dosage of acetylcysteine is 140 mg/kg of a 20% solution, followed by 70 mg/kg q4h for 16 doses. (See chapter 33 for more detailed information.) Methemoglobinemia usually disappears within 24–72 hours, but if it is severe, treat with IV infusions of methylene blue (1–2 mg/kg of a 1% solution given over 3–5 minutes).

Aspirin (acetylsalicylic acid [ASA])

ADMINISTRATION

Available Forms: Tablets, 65–650 mg; chewable tablets, 81 mg; sustained-release tablets, 650 mg; enteric-coated tablets, 325, 650 mg; capsules, 325 mg; chewing gum, 230 mg (Aspergum); rectal suppositories, 60, 125, 200, 300, 600 mg, 1.0, 1.3 gm. Also available in combination with acetaminophen, codeine and other narcotic derivatives, phenacetin, antihistamines, and antacids.

Dosage (Oral or Rectal): Varies according to use.
For analgesia or antipyresis: 65 mg/kg/day (1.5 gm/m^2/day) orally or rectally in divided doses (q4–6h). Maximum is 3.6 gm/day. Alternatively, single doses of 60 mg/kg for each year of age up to 5 years can be given 4–5 times/day.
As antirheumatic: 100 mg/kg/day (3 gm/m^2/day) orally in divided doses (q4–6h).

RENAL IMPAIRMENT: Adjustments are necessary.

- Moderate renal impairment: Give doses q6h.
- Severe renal impairment: Avoid use

INDICATIONS: Aspirin is used as an antipyretic, anti-inflammatory, and analgesic agent for relief of mild to moderate pain associated with fever, headache, neuralgia, muscle and joint inflammation, and other integumental, nonvisceral pain. It is not indicated for acute, severe visceral pain.

ACTIONS: Aspirin acts on the hypothalamic temperature-regulating center to produce antipyresis, but toxic doses can cause temperature elevation as a result of increased oxygen consumption and metabolic rate. Its anti-inflammatory and analgesic effect may be due to an inhibition of prostaglandin synthesis or a blockade of pain impulses by depression of peripheral chemoreceptors. Aspirin also inhibits platelet aggregation and may decrease Factor VII levels thereby increasing bleeding and prothrombin times. Aspirin can cause changes in the body's acid-base balance, especially in high or toxic doses. Initially, respiratory alkalosis occurs as a result of hyperventilation caused by central stimulation and an increase in O_2 consumption and CO_2 production. The body compensates by excreting excess base via the kidneys, and metabolic acidosis, especially in young children, is quickly superimposed (see acute toxicity under side effects/adverse reactions).

Aspirin is rapidly absorbed from the GI tract and rapidly hydrolyzed to salicylic acid (salicylate), which is active and is 50–80% protein-bound after therapeutic doses. Salicylate is metabolized, primarily in the liver and possibly in the kidneys, by conjugation with glycine and glucuronic acid to form several metabolites. These metabolites and unchanged salicylate are excreted in the urine. Newborn infants have a low capacity for glucuronide conjugation; this condition may slow salicylate metabolism and lead to toxic serum levels. Alkalinization of the urine accelerates the excretion of unchanged salicylate; this technique is useful in the treatment of salicylate overdose. Cross-sensitization with salicylic acid (sodium salicylate) is uncommon.

CONTRAINDICATIONS: Hypersensitivity to aspirin; active gastric and peptic ulcer disease; asthma; preexisting hypoprothrombinemia, vitamin K deficiency, or bleeding disorders; premature and full-term newborns.

PRECAUTIONS: Use cautiously in patients with asthma, hay fever, nasal polyps, peptic ulcer disease, gastritis, bleeding tendencies, vitamin K deficiencies, or severe renal impairment and in those undergoing concurrent therapy with anticoagulants. Children with preexisting fever and dehydration and infants are particularly susceptible to aspirin toxicity; maintain adequate fluid intake in these patients. Avoid use in children less than 3 years of age. Gastric distress can be diminished by giving oral doses with milk, food, or a full glass of water. Rectal suppositories, although used to avoid gastric irritation, may produce slow, incomplete absorption and rectal irritation. Monitor vital signs, particularly respirations, frequently in infants and young children.

SIDE EFFECTS/ADVERSE REACTIONS: Gastrointestinal symptoms of nausea, vomiting, heartburn, dyspepsia, anorexia, and increased occult blood loss are the most common side effects. Aspirin may exacerbate gastric hemorrhage, gastritis, and peptic ulcer. Hypersensitivity reactions include urticaria, rashes, rhinitis, angioneurotic edema, purpura, bronchospasm, laryngeal edema, and anaphylaxis. (Hypersensitivity reactions are more frequently associated with asthmatics and patients with nasal allergies and polyps.) Bleeding time and prothrombin times are usually prolonged. Mild salicylate toxicity or "salicylism" may occur during prolonged therapy with large doses, as are used in rheumatic disorders. Signs and symptoms, usually associated with plasma levels of 20–40 mg/100 ml or ingestion of 150 mg/kg or more, include tinnitus, headache, dizziness, mental confusion, visual disturbances, fever, sweating, lassitude, nausea, vomiting, diarrhea, hyperventilation, and tachycardia.
Acute aspirin poisoning: Severe and often fatal, acute aspirin poisoning causes disturbances of acid-base balance. Initially, hyperventilation causes respiratory alkalosis, which is quickly replaced by metabolic acidosis in infants and young children. (Older children and adults usually have respiratory alkalosis only.) The early signs of "salicylism" progress to fever, dehydration, hemorrhage, hypoglycemia, hypokalemia, excitement, confusion, delirium, convulsions, oliguria, circulatory collapse, coma, and respiratory and metabolic acidosis.

DRUG INTERACTIONS: Use with *anticoagulants* increases the risk of bleeding. Aspirin may displace *phenytoin, coumarin, oral antidiabetic agents, sulfinpyrazone, probenecid,* and *methotrexate* from their plasma protein-binding sites to increase their serum levels and toxicity. Concomitant use with *alcohol, corticosteroids,* and other *ulcerogenic medications* increases risk of GI ulceration. Aspirin decreases the diuretic effect of *spironolactone* and the uricosuric effect of *probenecid.* Concomitant use with *phenothiazines* may cause profound hypothermia. Large doses (2.4 gm or more daily) interfere with tests for urinary glucose: false-negative reactions with the glucose-oxidase method (Tes-Tape, Keto-diastix) and false-positive reactions with the copper reduction method (Clinitest).

ANTIDOTE: Discontinue aspirin. Immediately draw blood for serum levels of salicylate (a level of 50 mg/100 ml or any toxic signs or symptoms indicate a need for hospitalization). Institute supportive therapy immediately. If less than 4 hours have elapsed since ingestion, induce emesis or perform gastric lavage followed by activated charcoal to remove any remaining aspirin from the stomach. Replace fluid losses with IV fluids and give glucose to correct hypoglycemia and ketosis. Reduce hyperthermia by sponging with tepid water. Monitor and support respiration as necessary. Perform appropriate laboratory studies (blood gases, pH, electrolytes, glucose, ketones, complete blood count, prothrombin time, serum salicylate level, etc.). Administer phytonadione (vitamin K) to reverse hypoprothrombinemia and whole blood replacement for hemorrhage. Alkalinize urine cautiously with IV doses of sodium bicarbonate (2–3 mEq/kg q4–6h) and monitor urine pH (keep it above 7.5). If urine flow and renal function are adequate, give potassium (3–6 mEq/kg/day) in IV solutions to correct hypokalemia and maintain an alkaline urine. Potentially fatal serum levels of salicylate (100–150 mg/100 ml), oliguria, anuria, and cardiac impairment are indications for hemodialysis in older children and for peritoneal dialysis or exchange transfusions in infants. *Do not* give barbiturates for treatment of excitement or convulsions as they may worsen coma.

26
Local Anesthetics

When applied topically or injected into a specific area, local anesthetics produce a loss of sensation and motor activity in that specific area. These agents prevent impulses from reaching the CNS by blocking transmission along peripheral nerves. The blockade is reversible and progressive: First, smaller autonomic fibers are blocked; this is followed by loss of pain and other sensory functions; and, finally, motor activity is lost. Function is regained in the reverse order. The area anesthetized is distal to the point of injection or, in the case of topical anesthetics, is the site of application.

The duration of the anesthetic block depends on several factors, including tissue pH, blood flow in the area, the chemical structure of the anesthetic, the concentration and volume injected, and whether or not a vasoconstrictor (e.g., epinephrine) is added to the solution. In general, larger amounts of more concentrated solutions are required for a successful block of larger, centrally located nerve trunks than are required for block of small peripheral nerves. For most local anesthetics, the concentration required to produce a block is several hundred times the tolerable plasma level, and toxicity can result if the anesthetic is not injected at precisely the appropriate site. Peak plasma levels are reached quickly after injection into highly vascularized areas (e.g., head, neck, intercostal areas) and when solutions without epinephrine are used. The least volume of the most dilute solution that is effective should be given.

Parenteral local anesthetics are classified as either *ester* or *amide* types. The following is a partial listing; trade names are given in parentheses.

- Ester type
    - Benzocaine—topical use only
    - Cocaine—topical use only

- Procaine (Novocain)
- Proparacaine (Ophthaine)—topical use only
- Tetracaine (Pontocaine)

- Amide type
  - Bupivicaine (Marcaine)
  - Dibucaine (Nupercaine)—topical use also
  - Lidocaine (Xylocaine)
  - Mepivicaine (Carbocaine)
  - Prilocaine (Citanest)

The type of linkage (ester or amide) determines primarily the site of metabolism of each agent. Most ester types are partly or completely hydrolyzed by plasma cholinesterases, and the metabolites are excreted in the urine. (Cocaine, however, is metabolized in the liver.) The amide types are degraded in the liver, and urinary excretion of metabolites is insignificant.

There appears to be little or no cross-allergenicity between amide-type and ester-type anesthetics. Thus, a patient hypersensitive to any amide type can usually tolerate an ester type and vice versa.

Many topical and parenteral local anesthetics are available, but only a few are discussed in this chapter:

- **Bupivicaine**
- **Cocaine**
- **Lidocaine**
- **Mepivicaine**

LOCAL ANESTHETICS (GENERAL STATEMENT)

INDICATIONS: Local anesthetics are used for procedures that require local and regional anesthesia: suturing, regional surgery, and insertion of large bore needles and catheters. Some are used topically on intact or broken skin and on mucous membranes of the respiratory and urinary tracts for relief of pain. Others can only be injected SC or into an appropriate tissue space; these are used for infiltration (local); peripheral nerve block; and epidural, spinal, caudal, and regional anesthesia.

ACTIONS: Local anesthetics stabilize neuronal membranes to prevent initiation and transmission of nervous impulses to the central nervous system. Since almost all these agents cause vasodilation (except for cocaine), a vasoconstrictor such as epinephrine is often added to delay absorption, thereby prolonging the anesthesia and possibly reducing systemic toxicity. The vasoconstriction also helps control bleeding and oozing from the trauma site.

CONTRAINDICATIONS: See the individual agents.

PRECAUTIONS: Avoid intravascular injection; always check needle placement by aspiration before injecting the anesthetic; inject solutions slowly. Have resuscitative equipment, oxygen, anticonvulsants, and other resuscitative medications readily available. Avoid use in patients with myasthenia gravis, shock, heart block, or impaired cardiac conduction and in inflamed or infected areas. Use cautiously in patients with a history of allergic reactions or multiple allergies. Patients with impaired renal function or hepatic disease and newborns with undeveloped renal or hepatic function may have low levels of plasma cholinesterase, so they may metabolize ester-type anesthetics more slowly. Severe hepatic impairment can slow metabolism of amide-type anesthetics. Tachyphylaxis or tolerance may develop with repeated injections.
Local anesthetics with epinephrine: Use cautiously in patients with severe cardiovascular disease, peripheral vascular disease, diabetes, hyperthyroidism, or hypertension. Do not use with inhalation anesthetics (epinephrine sensitizes the myocardium to serious arrhythmias). Do not use for nerve blocks in digits, ear, nose, or penis as ischemia and gangrene may result. Epinephrine (in concentrations greater than 1:200,000) can constrict uterine blood vessels, prolong labor, or produce severe hypertension in patients receiving oxytocics. Monitor vital signs frequently during use of local anesthetics.

SIDE EFFECTS/ADVERSE REACTIONS: Side effects and adverse reactions result primarily from high plasma levels caused by inadvertent intravascular injection, rapid absorption rate, slow metabolic degradation, injection into highly vascularized areas, or excessive dosage. Toxic effects on the CNS may begin with an initial but transient excitation phase (restlessness, anxiety, tremors, twitching, blurred vision) that may progress to convulsions. However, these reactions may be minimal or absent in some patients, and the CNS depression phase may be more evident (drowsiness is usually first symptom, progressing to unconsciousness and respiratory arrest). Cardiovascular reactions include peripheral vasodilation, hypotension, myocardial depression, bradycardia, cardiac arrhythmias, cardiovascular collapse, and cardiac arrest. (Note: Reactions may occur within a few minutes if absorption of the anesthetic is rapid or may be delayed 30–40 minutes if absorption is slowed by the addition of epinephrine.) Hypersensitivity reactions include cutaneous lesions, urticaria, edema, and anaphylactoid reactions. A transient burning sensation may be noted at the injection site, and, rarely, prolonged burning, tissue irritation, swelling, neuritis, necrosis, or sloughing may occur. Solutions containing epinephrine may cause anxiety, dizziness, headache, palpitations, tremors, tachycardia, and hypertension.

DRUG INCOMPATIBILITIES: Do not mix with any medications, especially alkaline preparations.

DRUG INTERACTIONS: Ester-type anesthetics may antagonize the action of *sulfonamides*. Local anesthetics with vasoconstrictors may potentiate hypertension if used with *MAO inhibitors* or *tricyclic antidepressants* and may cause serious ventricular arrhythmias if used with *inhalation anesthetics*.

ANTIDOTE: Discontinue the anesthetic. Maintain the patient's airway and support ventilation as necessary. Treat hypotension and myocardial depression with appropriate vasopressors as indicated. Convulsions can be controlled with oxygen and a short-acting barbiturate (e.g., secobarbital, pentobarbital) or diazepam.

Bupivicaine (Marcaine)

ADMINISTRATION

Available Forms: Injectable, 0.25% (2.5 mg/ml), 0.50% (5.0 mg/ml), 0.75% (7.5 mg/ml), with and without epinephrine (1:200,000). Multidose vials contain methylparaben as a preservative.

Dosage: Varies with the area to be anesthetized and with the anesthetic technique employed. Use is not recommended in children less than 12 years old. Do not use 0.75% solutions for infiltration or peripheral nerve blocks.
Usual dose: 2 mg/kg (plain or with epinephrine).
Maximum dose (adult): 175 mg (plain); 225 mg (with epinephrine).
For infiltration block: Use 0.25% solutions.
For peripheral block: Use 0.25–0.50% solutions.

INDICATIONS: Bupivicaine is used for infiltration; peripheral nerve block; and epidural, caudal, or sympathetic block. It is not used for spinal anesthesia.

ACTIONS: See local anesthetics (general statement). With the 0.25% or 0.50% solution, onset of anesthesia is rapid (4–20 minutes), and duration is long (3–7 hours). Single doses usually provide adequate sensory blockade, but repeated doses are usually needed to produce complete muscle relaxation (motor block). Repeat doses should not be given more frequently than every 3–5 hours. Bupivicaine does not appear to cause methemoglobinemia or fetal CNS and cardiovascular depression after use in obstetrical epidural anesthesia.

CONTRAINDICATIONS: Hypersensitivity to bupivicaine and other amide-type anesthetics. (Also check for hypersensitivity to paraben preservatives and epinephrine.)

PRECAUTIONS: See local anesthetics (general statement).

SIDE EFFECTS/ADVERSE REACTIONS: See local anesthetics (general statement).

DRUG INCOMPATIBILITIES: See local anesthetics (general statement).

DRUG INTERACTIONS: See local anesthetics (general statement).

ANTIDOTE: See local anesthetics (general statement).

Cocaine

ADMINISTRATION

Available Forms: Topical solutions, 1, 2, 4, 5, 10%; usually prepared as needed.

Dosage (Topical): Varies with the procedure. Avoid use of concentrations >4% because of a potential increase in the incidence and severity of systemic toxicity. The usual maximum single dose is 1 mg/kg.
For ophthalmic use: 2, 4%.
For ear, nose, throat (ENT) use: 1–4% (5–10% has been used).
For nasal pack in acute rhinosinusitis: 1% in light mineral oil.

INDICATIONS: Cocaine solutions are used for surface anesthesia in the ear, nose, and throat and in bronchoscopy. (Other ophthalmic anesthetics have largely replaced the use of cocaine in the eye.)

ACTIONS: Cocaine is an alkaloid obtained from the leaves of *Erythroxylon coca*. When applied to mucous surfaces, it produces excellent surface anesthesia with intense vasoconstriction. When used in the eye, it also constricts conjunctival vessels, blanches the sclera, and causes mydriasis. Use with epinephrine is unnecessary and may increase the likelihood of cardiac arrhythmias. The onset of action is rapid (about 1 minute after application) and duration is up to 2 hours, depending on the concentration used.

CONTRAINDICATIONS: Hypersensitivity to cocaine.

PRECAUTIONS: Cocaine is readily absorbed through mucous membranes, so use cautiously because of the danger of toxicity. Prior to cocaine anesthesia, a therapeutic dose of a barbiturate can be given to counteract cocaine-induced CNS stimulation. Frequent applications to the nasal mucosa can result in perforation of the septum. Chronic use can lead to psychic dependence and tolerance. Use cautiously in patients with hypertension, severe cardiovascular disease, or thyrotoxicosis. Capillary dilation may result in delayed capillary hemorrhage.

SIDE EFFECTS/ADVERSE REACTIONS: Stimulation of the CNS produces euphoria, excitement, tremors, hypertension, tachycardia, and tachypnea. Acute poisoning causes marked CNS stimulation, nausea, vomiting, abdominal pain, exophthalmos, hyperthermia, and mydriasis; CNS depression follows, and death is from respiratory arrest. Cocaine potentiates endogenous epinephrine and may produce ventricular fibrillation.

DRUG INCOMPATIBILITIES: Cocaine solutions are unstable and decompose upon standing. Do not boil or autoclave solutions.

DRUG INTERACTIONS: Cocaine potentiates the adrenergic effects of *epinephrine, norepinephrine, sympathomimetic amines, guanethidine,* and *MAO inhibitors* (excessive cardiovascular stimulation). Ventricular fibrillation may occur if cocaine is used with *general anesthetics* that sensitize the myocardium to catecholamines.

ANTIDOTE: Discontinue cocaine. Treat adverse reactions symptomatically and supportively.

Lidocaine (Xylocaine)

ADMINISTRATION

Available Forms: Injectable, 0.5, 1.0, 1.5, 2.0%, with or without epinephrine (1:100,000 or 1:200,000); topical, 2% jelly, 2.5 and 5.0% ointment, 2% solution (viscous), 4% solution. Injectable forms are available with or without methylparaben preservative.

Dosage (Parenteral): Use of 0.5 or 1.0% solutions is recommended. Dosage depends on the type of block and on the age and weight of the child. (Consult appropriate anesthesia textbooks for further dosage information.)

For infiltration or peripheral block: Usual dose is 5 mg/kg (plain solution); 7 mg/kg (with epinephrine). Note: Lower doses may be required in children less than 3 years of age since plasma levels of lidocaine are relatively higher in this age group than in older children.

INDICATIONS: Lidocaine is widely used topically for anesthesia and by injection for infiltration and peripheral nerve or sympathetic block. Solutions without preservatives are used for epidural, caudal, spinal, and intravenous regional anesthesia.

ACTIONS: See local anesthetics (general statement). The onset of action is more rapid than that of bupivicaine and duration is shorter (about 60–75 minutes after perineural injection; with epinephrine, up to 2 hours more). In equal concentrations lidocaine is more toxic than procaine but less toxic than bupivicaine. Lidocaine is not irritating and produces relatively little sensitization when used topically.

CONTRAINDICATIONS: Hypersensitivity to lidocaine or other amide-type local anesthetics. (Also check for hypersensitivity to paraben preservatives and epinephrine.)

PRECAUTIONS: See local anesthetics (general statement).

SIDE EFFECTS/ADVERSE REACTIONS: See local anesthetics (general statement).

DRUG INCOMPATIBILITIES: See local anesthetics (general statement).

DRUG INTERACTIONS: See local anesthetics (general statement).

ANTIDOTE: See local anesthetics (general statement).

Mepivicaine (Carbocaine)

ADMINISTRATION

Available Forms: Injectable, 1, 2% (with or without methylparaben preservative), 1.5% (without preservative).

Dosage (Parenteral): Varies according to the patient's weight and age.
Children <14 kg: Total dose should not exceed 5–7 mg/kg (use 0.5–1.5% solutions).
Children <3 years old: Use 0.5–1.5% solutions only.
Usual dose: 5 mg/kg (plain solution); 7 mg/kg (with epinephrine).

INDICATIONS: Mepivicaine is used for infiltration and for peripheral or sympathetic nerve block. Solutions without preservatives are used for epidural or caudal blocks. It is not effective as a topical anesthetic, and it is not used for spinal anesthesia.

ACTIONS: The potency of mepivicaine is similar to that of lidocaine. Concentrations of 0.5–1.0% block sensory and sympathetic conduction without loss of motor function, while 1.5–2.0% solutions provide extensive or complete motor block. The onset of action is more rapid and duration is more prolonged than for lidocaine. Onset of anesthesia is usually 3–5 minutes after injection (up to 20 minutes depending on the type of block, the procedure, etc.), and duration is 2.0–2.5 hours. Mepivicaine produces less vasodilation than other local anesthetics, so use with epinephrine is usually not required. Like lidocaine, mepivicaine produces little irritation or tissue damage.

CONTRAINDICATIONS: Hypersensitivity to mepivicaine or amide-type anesthetics. (Check for hypersensitivity to paraben preservatives.)

PRECAUTIONS: See local anesthetics (general statement).

SIDE EFFECTS/ADVERSE REACTIONS: See local anesthetics (general statement).

DRUG INCOMPATIBILITIES: See local anesthetics (general statement).

DRUG INTERACTIONS: See local anesthetics (general statement).

ANTIDOTE: See local anesthetics (general statement).

VIII
ANTICONVULSANTS AND SKELETAL MUSCLE RELAXANTS

Although convulsive disorders and skeletal muscle spasms can be treated as separate and distinct physiological problems, they require treatment with medications that have similar actions on the nervous system. For this reason, anticonvulsants and skeletal muscle relaxants are included together in a single section.

27
Anticonvulsants

A variety of medications are available for immediate therapy and long-term management of many types of convulsive disorders. These anticonvulsants act centrally to prevent the propagation of a seizure. They stabilize the normal neurons surrounding a seizure focus and thus prevent their detonation by that focus. This effect is often accomplished by increasing the convulsive threshold of the motor cortex to excitatory stimulation and by depressing the transmission of synaptic impulses.

Convulsions can be caused by idiopathic epilepsy or by a variety of pathological conditions such as fever, metabolic imbalances, brain tumors, cerebrovascular accidents, head injuries, drug intoxications, or drug withdrawal. Most idiopathic epilepsy begins during childhood or adolescence. Seizures that occur after birth and during infancy are usually the result of developmental defects in the brain, other congenital birth defects, fever, or metabolic disturbances (e.g., hypokalemia, hypocalcemia, hypoglycemia, edema, metabolic alkalosis, hypoxia, phenylketonuria, and pyridoxine deficiency). Benign febrile convulsions are also commonly seen during this period. Adulthood epilepsy is usually caused by head trauma, brain tumors, or cerebrovascular accidents.

A convulsive disorder can be defined as the expression of a sudden, excessive, unorganized disorderly discharge of neurons in an otherwise structurally normal cortex or in one that is diseased. This event results in an almost instantaneous disturbance of sensation, a loss of consciousness, convulsive movements, or any combination of these. The severity of a seizure can range from an involuntary muscle twitch or a brief lapse in attention to death resulting from blockage of the airway, aspiration, or cardiac arrhythmias. Clinical signs and symptoms of different types of convulsive disorders vary.

For example, a grand mal seizure begins with a sudden loss of consciousness, a cry, and a fall to the ground; tonic (contraction) and then clonic (alternating contraction and relaxation) movements of the muscles of the head and limbs occur; sometimes there is urinary or fecal incontinence. This attack typically lasts two to five minutes. After the motor activity, the patient is in a state of coma for a brief period (up to 30 minutes) and then may waken and complain of mental confusion, drowsiness, or headache.

On the other hand, petit mal (absence) seizures begin with a brief (10 to 30 seconds) loss of consciousness with minimal motor involvement; eye blinks at a rate of 3/sec are typical. This type of convulsive disorder most often occurs from age 4 to adolescence and may be combined with other types of seizures (mixed epilepsy).

During complex partial seizures (including psychomotor epilepsy), the patient is partially conscious, usually for one or two minutes, and the convulsive movements (e.g., facial grimacing, chewing motions, licking or smacking of the lips, tonic spasms of the limbs, or turning of the head and eyes to one side) can last a few seconds to several hours. The patient will have amnesia regarding the period of the seizure. During elementary partial seizures, such as Jacksonian epilepsy, the seizure is said to "march" from one part of the body to others, typically beginning in the fingers or toes on one side, then progressing to the other extremity.

Finally there is status epilepticus in which recurrent generalized convulsions occur so frequently that consciousness is not regained between them. This is a true medical emergency that may lead to serious metabolic and clinical consequences, including circulatory collapse and death. This seizure disorder demands prompt and effective treatment.

A full discussion of the pathology and classification of the many convulsive disorders is beyond the scope of this book. However, a brief classification of seizure types may be helpful. CNS disorders can be divided into four broad categories:

1. Partial seizures (seizures beginning locally)

    - Partial seizures (elementary symptomatology, consciousness usually not impaired)
        - Jacksonian (motor, sensory, or somatosensory symptoms)
        - Autonomic symptoms
        - Compound forms
    - Partial seizures (complex symptoms, usually with impaired consciousness)
        - Temporal lobe seizures (psychomotor epilepsy)
        - Compound forms
    - Partial seizures (secondarily become generalized)

2. Generalized seizures (bilaterally symmetrical and without local onset, usually with loss of consciousness)

- Absence seizures (petit mal, brief loss of consciousness)
- Bilateral massive epileptic myoclonus (usually no loss of consciousness)
- Infantile spasms
- Clonic seizures
- Tonic seizures
- Tonic-clonic seizures (grand mal)
- Atonic seizures
- Akinetic seizures

3. Unilateral seizures (or those predominantly unilateral)
4. Unclassified epileptic seizures (incomplete data to determine type)

While the underlying cause of seizure activity should be determined and treated if possible, the choice of anticonvulsant is based upon the type of seizure pattern rather than the underlying cause. The objective of therapy is to control seizures without causing excessive CNS depression in the patient. Therapy must be individualized, and the anticonvulsant or combination of anticonvulsants used depends upon the type of seizure (as determined through observation, patient history, and EEG patterns) and patient tolerance. The anticonvulsant dosage for children is usually somewhat larger on a weight basis than that for adults. Except for control of acute seizures, patients should be started on small to moderate doses of a suitable anticonvulsant and the dose gradually increased until control of the seizure is achieved or until toxic reactions make further increases inadvisable. Additional anticonvulsants from different chemical classes may have to be added during therapy (determine by titration). Avoid abrupt withdrawal of any anticonvulsant; doing so could precipitate seizures.

The following anticonvulsants are discussed in this chapter:

- **Carbamazepine**
- **Clonazepam**
- **Diazepam (parenteral)**
- **Ethosuximide**
- **Paraldehyde**
- **Phenobarbital**
- **Phenytoin**
- **Pyridoxine**
- **Valproic acid**

Carbamazepine (Tegretol)

ADMINISTRATION

Available Forms: Tablets, 100 mg (chewable) and 200 mg.

Dosage (Oral): Varies according to the patient's age.
Children 6–12 years old: 100 mg bid to start, followed by gradual increases of 100 mg/day (up to 1000 mg/day in 3–4 divided doses if needed). Usual maintenance dose is 400–800 mg/day.
Children 12–15 years: 200 mg bid to start, followed by gradual increases of 200 mg/day (up to 1000 mg/day in 3–4 divided doses).
Alternatively for children 6–15 years old: 225 mg/m^2/day in 2 divided doses to start, then increase gradually to 450–700 mg/m^2/day in divided doses (q6–12h) for maintenance. Maximum is 1 gm/day.

INDICATIONS: Carbamazepine is used in the prophylactic therapy of temporal lobe (psychomotor), major motor (grand mal), and focal seizures and mixed seizure patterns unresponsive to less toxic anticonvulsants; and for symptomatic relief of pain in trigeminal neuralgia.

ACTIONS: Like phenytoin, carbamazepine primarily limits seizure activity by preventing the propagation of a seizure from an irritable focus to the surrounding neurons. It reduces pain in trigeminal neuralgia by reducing synaptic transmission within the trigeminal nerves. It also has sedative, anticholinergic, antidepressant, muscle-relaxant, antiarrhythmic, and antidiuretic effects. Carbamazepine is absorbed slowly from the GI tract, is highly protein-bound, and has a long half-life (14–30 hours); 2–4 days may be needed to reach optimum steady-state levels. Therapeutic plasma levels appear to be 3–14 µg/ml. Carbamazepine crosses the placenta and is excreted in breast milk. It is partially metabolized in the liver to an active metabolite that is further degraded and excreted via the urine. Carbamazepine is structurally related to the tricyclic antidepressants and imipramine.

CONTRAINDICATIONS: Hypersensitivity to carbamazepine or tricyclic antidepressants, previous bone marrow depression, administration of MAO inhibitors within the last 14 days, nursing mothers.

PRECAUTIONS: Abrupt withdrawal may precipitate seizures or status epilepticus. Severe, sometimes fatal, bone marrow depression has occurred; do complete blood counts (CBCs) prior to treatment and repeat them weekly for the first 3 months, then monthly thereafter. Use cautiously in patients with a history of hematological reactions, and discontinue the anticonvulsant if there is evidence of bone marrow depression or infection. Use cautiously in patients with renal, hepatic, or cardiac impairment; increased intraocular pressure; or preexisting visual disturbances. Obtain baseline and periodic hepatic and renal function tests and eye examinations. Discontinue the medication if aggravated liver dysfunction develops. Carbamazepine may cause sedation, mental impairment, and slowed reflexes, so caution the patient accordingly.

SIDE EFFECTS/ADVERSE REACTIONS: Frequent adverse effects include drowsiness, dizziness, ataxia, nausea, and anorexia (can be minimized by increasing the dosage in small increments over 7–10 days). Other neurological effects include headache, confusion, incoordination, speech and oculomotor disturbances, blurred vision, hallucinations, activation of latent psychoses, paresthesias, and muscle and joint pain. Various forms of GI upset, stomatitis, and glossitis may occur. Renal impairment may develop (azotemia, oliguria, renal failure) as well as hepatic abnormalities (abnormal liver function tests, cholestatic jaundice, hepatitis). Various rashes (mild to severe), urticaria, photosensitivity, alopecia, and a systemic lupus-like syndrome have been reported. Hematological toxic reactions may be severe and sometimes fatal. Various blood dyscrasias (leukopenia, agranulocytosis, eosinophilia, leukocytosis, thrombocytopenia), purpura, bone marrow depression, and aplastic anemia may develop (onset may occur 3 weeks to 2 years after the start of therapy). Cardiovascular side effects may be severe and include edema, congestive heart failure, aggravation of hypertension, thrombophlebitis, hypotension, syncope, and collapse. Other effects include fever, chills, pulmonary hypersensitivity reactions (pneumonitis, dyspnea), diaphoresis, lymphadenopathy, and lens opacities.

DRUG INTERACTIONS: Use with *MAO inhibitors* may cause hyperpyrexia, excitability, and seizures. Carbamazepine may stimulate hepatic microsomal enzymes and thus accelerate the metabolism of *phenytoin, phenobarbital,* and *doxycycline.* Concomitant use may decrease the plasma levels of *warfarin* and thus antagonize warfarin's anticoagulant effect.

ANTIDOTE: Discontinue carbamazepine. For acute ingestion, empty the stomach with induced emesis or by gastric lavage. Treat adverse reactions symptomatically and monitor the ECG. Maintain a patent airway, support ventilation, and treat shock and arrhythmias as necessary. Hyperirritability can be treated with parenteral barbiturates unless the patient has taken MAO inhibitors within the last week.

Clonazepam (Clonopin)

ADMINISTRATION

Available Forms: Tablets, 0.5, 1.0, 2.0 mg.

Dosage (Oral): Varies according to the patient's age.
Infants and children (<10 years old and <30 kg): 0.01–0.03 mg/kg/day (up to 0.05 mg/kg/day) in divided doses (q8–12h) to start. Can be increased by 0.25–0.50 mg every 3 days, up to 0.1–0.2 mg/kg/day in divided doses (q8h), unless seizures are controlled at lower doses or side effects preclude further increments.
Older children: Up to 1.5 mg/kg/day in divided doses (q8h) to start. Can be increased by 0.5–1.0 mg increments every 3 days (up to 20 mg/day) until seizures are controlled or the maximum dose is reached.

INDICATIONS: Clonazepam is used either alone or with other anticonvulsants for management of myoclonic spasms, akinetic seizures, infantile spasms, and petit mal variant epilepsy (Lennox-Gastaut syndrome). Its effectiveness in treatment of absence seizures (petit mal) is variable, but it has been used as an alternative anticonvulsant for patients not responding to the succinimides. Investigationally, clonazepam has been used with some success in grand mal and refractory temporal lobe (psychomotor) and focal seizures. The parenteral form (unavailable as yet) has been used with some success in status epilepticus.

ACTIONS: The pharmacological actions of clonazepam are similar to those of diazepam and other benzodiazepine derivatives. It appears to act at the limbic and subcortical levels of the CNS to produce anticonvulsant and sedative effects. Oral doses are well absorbed, and the onset of action is about 6–8 hours in infants and children (up to 12 hours in adults). It has a long and variable half-life of 18–40 hours. Therapeutic plasma levels are 20–80 μg/ml (usually achieved with pediatric doses of 1.5–4.0 mg/day). Clonazepam is almost completely metabolized in the liver and excreted in the urine. It probably crosses the placenta.

CONTRAINDICATIONS: Hypersensitivity to benzodiazepines, significant liver disease, acute narrow-angle glaucoma.

PRECAUTIONS: In combination therapy, use of clonazepam may permit dosage reductions of other anticonvulsants, but paradoxical increases in seizure activity may occur. Clonazepam may precipitate major motor seizures in patients with mixed epilepsy. A decreased anticonvulsant response to the medication may occur after several months of therapy; abrupt withdrawal may precipitate status epilepticus. Use cautiously in patients with renal or hepatic impairment and in patients with chronic respiratory disease (causes respiratory depression and upper respiratory tract hypersecretion). Since clonazepam produces significant CNS depression, caution patients against performing potentially hazardous tasks that require mental alertness. Because it is a benzodiazepine derivative, clonazepam may be habit-forming, especially in addiction-prone patients, and its abrupt discontinuance has precipitated benzodiazepine withdrawal symptoms (e.g., tremors, nausea, vomiting, abdominal and muscle cramps, convulsions). Blood counts and liver function tests should be done periodically during long-term therapy.

SIDE EFFECTS/ADVERSE REACTIONS: CNS depressant effects are the most common adverse reactions (e.g., sedation, drowsiness, ataxia, and behavioral disturbances, particularly in children, that include aggressiveness, agitation, and hyperkinesis). These effects may diminish in time and can be minimized by beginning therapy with low doses and gradually increasing the dosage over 2 weeks. More severe psychiatric disturbances may occur, particularly in patients with a history of psychiatric disorders or preexisting mental retardation or brain damage. Other neurological effects include abnormal eye movements, a "glassy-eyed" appearance, nystagmus, diplopia, respiratory depression, slurred speech, vertigo, tremor, muscle weakness, and pain. Chest congestion, hypersalivation, rhinorrhea, and upper respiratory hypersecretion may be troublesome. Gastrointestinal and genitourinary disturbances include anorexia, vomiting, diarrhea, constipation, gastritis, dry mouth, sore gums, urinary retention, and enuresis. Rashes, anemia and other blood dyscrasias, hepatomegaly, and elevated liver enzymes have been reported. Other minor effects include hirsutism, alopecia, lymphadenopathy, fever, dehydration, palpitations, and general malaise.

DRUG INTERACTIONS: Additive CNS depression may occur if clonazepam is used with other *CNS depressants, alcohol,* or other *antiepilepsy agents.*

27: Anticonvulsants 295

ANTIDOTE: Discontinue clonazepam. Gastric lavage (take care to prevent aspiration) can be used for acute ingestion. Treat respiratory and cardiovascular depression supportively with assisted ventilation, adequate airway maintenance, IV fluids, and vasopressors (e.g., levarterenol) as indicated. *Do not* use respiratory stimulants. Treat withdrawal symptoms symptomatically.

Diazepam (parenteral) (Valium)

ADMINISTRATION

Available Forms: Injectable (IM, IV), 5 mg/ml in 2 ml amps and syringes, 10 ml vials.

Diluent: Give undiluted. Do not mix with any other aqueous injections or IV solutions because precipitation may occur. (Diazepam is in a propylene glycol diluent.)

Dosage (Parenteral): Varies according to use.
For status epilepticus and acute seizure control: Slow IV bolus of 0.1–0.3 mg/kg; can be repeated q3–5min if necessary. Maximum cumulative dose for infants and small children is 5 mg; for older children, 10–15 mg.
Investigational use: Diazepam has been administered rectally in doses of 0.5–0.8 mg/kg to infants and children; this route has proved to be both a safe and effective method of administration. Rapid absorption through the rectal mucosa was noted. Peak plasma levels were usually achieved within 5 minutes, and convulsions were controlled within 5–10 minutes. Rectal doses of diazepam were found to be most effective when given soon after the onset of convulsions (e.g., within 15 minutes). No adverse reactions of respiratory depression or apnea were noted. The undiluted IV solution is drawn up in a plastic syringe to which a blunt-ended plastic tube can be attached for rectal instillation.

Rate: Administer IV boluses over 3 minutes. Do not exceed 5 mg/min.

INDICATIONS: Diazepam (given IV) is generally considered the anticonvulsant of choice in older infants and children for terminating status epilepticus or acute convulsions resulting from drug overdose or poisons. After seizures are terminated, appropriate maintenance anticonvulsant therapy should be started.

ACTIONS: Diazepam appears to act at the limbic, thalamic, or hypothalamic levels of the CNS; it causes antianxiety, sedative, hypnotic, skeletal-muscle-relaxant, and anticonvulsant effects. Diazepam suppresses the spread of seizure activity (possibly by inhibiting the transmission of presynaptic impulses), but it does not abolish the abnormal discharge from a seizure focus. Onset of action after IV use is 1–5 minutes, and the duration of effect is 15–60 minutes. Diazepam is metabolized in the liver to three pharmacologically active metabolites: two hydroxylated derivatives and N-desmethyldiazepam, which has the longest half-life of the three. These are further conjugated, inactivated, and excreted in the urine. In premature infants, neonates, and full-term infants less than 2 or 3 weeks old, hepatic hydroxylation is practically absent and demethylation occurs at a much slower rate than in older infants. After single doses, these infants tend to have higher, more persistent levels of unchanged diazepam and its active metabolite, N-desmethyldiazepam, for up to 48 hours after the dose was given. (Serum half-life of diazepam increases to 20–45 hours in full-term infants and to 40–100 hours in neonates.) The accumulation of these active compounds can subsequently cause both prolonged pharmacological effects and adverse reactions such as respiratory depression and apnea. Consequently, the use of diazepam should be avoided in infants less than 1 month of age. However, if the decision is made to employ diazepam for seizure termination in neonates and full-term infants, reduced doses should be used. Lower doses are also indicated for patients with hepatic impairment. The vehicle for IV diazepam contains sodium benzoate, which can interfere with bilirubin binding in neonates.

CONTRAINDICATIONS: Hypersensitivity to diazepam (or other benzodiazepines), shock, coma, acute alcohol intoxication with depressed vital signs.

PRECAUTIONS: Use of diazepam is not recommended in neonates. Administer the drug directly into a large vein to avoid thrombosis; if this is not feasible, inject it into the tubing of a flowing IV solution as close as possible to the vein insertion (diazepam may precipitate in aqueous solutions). Injections given IM are erratically absorbed. Avoid intra-arterial injection or extravasation as tissue necrosis may occur. To avoid respiratory depression or apnea, give IV doses in children and infants over at least 3 minutes; titrate the dose to the specific desired effect rather than giving it as a rapid bolus. Facilities and equipment for cardiopulmonary assistance should be readily available.

SIDE EFFECTS/ADVERSE REACTIONS: Rapid IV administration may cause hypotension or respiratory depression, apnea, bradycardia, or cardiac arrest. Individual sensitivity to diazepam varies widely; apnea has been reported with doses as low as 2.5 mg.

DRUG INCOMPATIBILITIES: Do not mix with any other medications or IV solutions.

DRUG INTERACTIONS: Concomitant use with *barbiturates* increases the risk of respiratory failure and circulatory collapse. Diazepam may cause additive CNS depression if used with other *CNS depressants* (e.g., narcotics, alcohol, tranquilizers, sedative-hypnotics).

ANTIDOTE: Discontinue the medication. Treat cardiopulmonary depression symptomatically and supportively (e.g., vasopressors and assisted ventilation).

Ethosuximide (Zarontin)

ADMINISTRATION

Available Forms: Capsules, 250 mg; oral syrup, 250 mg/5 ml.

Dosage (Oral): Varies according to the patient's age.
Children 3–6 years old: 250 mg/day to start, followed by increases of 250 mg/day every 4–7 days until optimal clinical response is achieved. Maximum is 1.5 gm/day in divided doses. Normal optimal dose is 20 mg/kg/day.

Children >6 years old: 500 mg/day to start, followed by 250 mg/day increments every 4–7 days until optimal clinical response is achieved. Maximum is 1.5 gm/day in divided doses.

INDICATIONS: Ethosuximide is the anticonvulsant of choice for management of absence (petit mal) seizures. It has been used for myoclonic spasms and akinetic epilepsy with some success, but it is ineffective in temporal lobe (psychomotor) or other major motor seizures (e.g., grand mal) and in patients with severe organic brain damage. If used alone in patients with mixed epilepsy, ethosuximide can increase the frequency of major motor seizures, and so it should be combined with phenobarbital or phenytoin in these cases.

ACTIONS: Ethosuximide elevates the seizure threshold in the cortex and stabilizes normal neurons, preventing their detonation by the seizure focus (i.e., the synaptic response to low-frequency repetitive stimulation is reduced). Oral doses are well absorbed, but it takes 4–7 days of the usual dosage to achieve steady-state plasma levels. Plasma half-life in children is about 30 hours. Therapeutic plasma levels are about 40–80 μg/ml. Most of the medication is metabolized in the liver, and metabolites and unchanged ethosuximide (20%) are excreted in the urine.

CONTRAINDICATIONS: Hypersensitivity to any of the succinimides (e.g., ethosuximide, methsuximide, phensuximide).

PRECAUTIONS: Abrupt withdrawal of ethosuximide may precipitate petit mal seizures and may increase the incidence of grand mal (generalized) seizures in patients with mixed epilepsy. Use cautiously in patients with renal or hepatic impairment; do periodic liver function and urinalysis studies. Periodic blood counts should be done as this medication causes blood dyscrasias (sometimes fatal). Ethosuximide may cause sedation; caution the patient against performing potentially hazardous tasks.

SIDE EFFECTS/ADVERSE REACTIONS: The most common side effects are gastric upset with nausea, vomiting, anorexia, epigastric and abdominal pain, and diarrhea. Effects on the CNS produce drowsiness, dizziness, ataxia, headache, euphoria, and hiccups. Occasionally, hyperactivity, sleep disturbances, and psychological disturbances are seen. Blood dyscrasias include leukopenia, eosinophilia, pancytopenia, agranulocytosis, and aplastic anemia (with fatalities). Hypersensitivity reactions of rashes, urticaria, and pruritus may occur. Other rare reactions include Stevens-Johnson syndrome, SLE, myopia, vaginal bleeding, swelling of the tongue, gum hyperplasia, and hirsutism.

DRUG INTERACTIONS: Use with high doses of *tricyclic antidepressants* or *antipsychotic agents* may precipitate seizures. Ethosuximide may cause a false-positive reaction in the direct Coomb's test.

ANTIDOTE: Discontinue ethosuximide. For acute ingestion, induce emesis or perform gastric lavage to empty the stomach. Treat adverse reactions symptomatically and supportively.

Paraldehyde (USP)

ADMINISTRATION

Available Forms: Injectable (IV, IM), 2, 5, 10 ml amps; solution, 30 ml bottles (nonsterile).

Diluent: For rectal use dilute dose with at least equal parts of mineral, olive, vegetable, or cottonseed oil. For IV use dilute dose in at least 100 ml NS.

Dosage (Oral): Varies according to use.
For sedation: 0.15 ml/kg/dose (6 ml/m^2/dose) diluted in milk or iced fruit juice.
For hypnosis: 0.15 ml/kg/dose (6 ml/m^2/dose) diluted in milk or iced fruit juice; dose can be doubled.

Dosage (Rectal): Varies according to use.
For seizures: 0.15–3.00 ml/kg/dose (6–12 ml/m^2/dose) diluted in equal parts oil (see Diluent) and given by high rectal tube. Flush the tube with 10 ml NS. The patient's buttocks can be taped together.
For sedation: 0.15 ml/kg/dose (6 ml/m^2/dose) diluted in equal parts of specified oil (see Diluent) and given as a retention enema.

Rate: Intravenous administration is usually not recommended for children. If used, give well diluted solutions no faster than 1 ml/min.

INDICATIONS: Paraldehyde is a fast-acting, relatively safe sedative-hypnotic used for the management of acute convulsions, particularly febrile seizures and status epilepticus refractory to other agents. It may also be given for the seizures associated with tetanus and certain poisonings. Paraldehyde can also be used as a sedative.

ACTIONS: Like chloral hydrate and the barbiturates, paraldehyde produces its sedative, hypnotic, and anticonvulsant effects by depressing many levels of the CNS. Therapeutic doses have little effect on blood pressure or respiration, but high doses can cause hypotension or respiratory depression or failure. Like the barbiturates, paraldehyde has no analgesic effects in subanesthetic doses; in fact, it can cause excitement or delirium in patients experiencing uncontrolled pain. Paraldehyde is rapidly absorbed after oral or rectal administration. It takes 30–60 minutes to reach maximal concentrations in the brain, but sleep and anticonvulsant effects occur within 5–15 minutes and last about 8 hours. Paraldehyde readily crosses the placenta. About 80–90% of a dose is metabolized by the liver, primarily to acetaldehyde. A significant amount is excreted unchanged through the lungs, giving the breath a characteristic odor. Only trace amounts are eliminated in the urine. Patients with hepatic disease metabolize paraldehyde more slowly; consequently, the hypnotic effects are prolonged and the risk of toxic reactions is increased.

CONTRAINDICATIONS: Severe liver or bronchopulmonary disease, peptic ulcer (oral doses), hypersensitivity to paraldehyde.

PRECAUTIONS: Use only fresh solutions from tightly stoppered bottles; discard opened bottles after 24 hours. Do not use brownish solutions. Solutions exposed to air or light can decompose to acetic acid, which can cause serious intoxication. Do not use with plastic syringes or containers; use glass cups or syringes only. Oral doses taste unpleasant but can be made more palatable if mixed with iced fruit juice or milk. *Do not give IM or SC.* Avoid IV administration because severe cardiopulmonary problems can occur. Use cautiously, if at all, in patients with asthma or any degree of pulmonary or hepatic impairment. Patients in pain may experience delirium or agitation when given paraldehyde.

SIDE EFFECTS/ADVERSE REACTIONS: Oral doses frequently cause gastric irritation. Decomposed solutions can cause severe corrosion of the stomach or rectal mucosa and metabolic acidoses. Doses given IM or SC often produce pain, sterile abscesses, tissue necrosis, muscle irritation, and possible nerve injury. Intravenous use can result in pulmonary edema and hemorrhage, right ventricular failure, respiratory distress, and circulatory collapse. Paraldehyde often causes an erythematous rash. Overdoses produce rapid, labored respiration; rapid, feeble pulse; coma; pulmonary edema; cardiac failure; metabolic acidosis; liver damage (e.g., toxic hepatitis); and renal impairment (azotemia, albuminuria, and oliguria).

DRUG INCOMPATIBILITIES: Do not mix with any other medications.

DRUG INTERACTIONS: Additive CNS depression may occur if paraldehyde is administered with *barbiturates, alcohol,* or other *CNS depressants.*

ANTIDOTE: For oral overdoses, use gastric lavage (with cuffed endotracheal tube to prevent aspiration); follow with administration (oral or via nasogastric tube) of a demulcent such as mineral oil to relieve gastric irritation. For rectal overdoses, lavage the rectum. Maintain an adequate airway, assist respiration, and administer oxygen as needed. Support circulation. Correct metabolic acidosis with sodium bicarbonate or sodium lactate.

Phenobarbital (Luminal, others)

ADMINISTRATION

Available Forms: Injectable (IM, IV), 65 and 130 mg per milliliter in amps and syringes, 65, 120, 130, 200, 300, 325 mg vials; tablets, 8, 15, 16, 30, 32, 60, 65, 100 mg; capsules, 16 mg; oral elixir, 20 mg/5 ml (4 mg/ml); rectal suppositories, 8, 15, 30, 60, 100, 120 mg (for sedative use only).

Diluent: Reconstitute vials of powder with sterile water for injection and use within 24 hours. Phenobarbital solutions from the manufacturer usually contain alcohol and propylene glycol and can be given undiluted. Further dilution with water, D5W, or NS may cause precipitation of the medication. Use dilutions immediately after mixing.

Dosage (Parenteral): Varies according to use.
For status epilepticus and other active seizures: 5–10 mg/kg IM or slow IV. A second dose can be given in 20–30 minutes if necessary. Maximum cumulative dose is 20 mg/kg.
For maintenance therapy in patients not currently experiencing seizures: Loading dose of 10-15 mg/kg IM or slow IV in divided doses (q12h) for 1 day, then 3–8 mg/kg/day in divided doses (q12h).
For sedation: 6 mg/kg/day IM or slow IV in divided doses (q8h).

Dosage (Oral or Rectal): Varies according to use.
For maintenance anticonvulsant therapy: 3-8 mg/kg/day in divided doses (q8–12h).
For sedation: 6 mg/kg/day in divided doses (q8h).

Rate: For IV infusion do not exceed 60 mg/min.

INDICATIONS: Phenobarbital is one of the most widely used anticonvulsants in pediatric therapy and is usually the initial choice for all forms of epilepsy (except petit mal) because of its broad spectrum and safety. Its principal effectiveness is in generalized tonic-clonic (grand mal) epilepsy, many types of partial (focal) seizures, and febrile convulsions in children. Its effectiveness in myoclonic spasms and in petit mal and akinetic epilepsy is limited. It is often used in combination with phenytoin and other anticonvulsants in the management of epilepsy. Despite its slower onset of action, parenteral phenobarbital is preferred over IV diazepam for termination of seizures in neonates and young infants. It does not interfere with bilirubin binding and has a wider margin of safety in this age group than does diazepam. Phenobarbital's longer duration of action makes it more reliable than diazepam for preventing the recurrence of convulsions.

ACTIONS: In anesthetic doses, all barbiturates are capable of inhibiting convulsions via a generalized CNS depression. Phenobarbital, however, has a selective anticonvulsant effect in nonsedative doses. It appears to raise the seizure threshold of the motor cortex and decrease excitability of the neurons. Phenobarbital, like other barbiturates, can cause all levels of CNS depression, from mild sedation to coma. It also lowers serum levels of bilirubin in neonates and in patients with congenital hyperbilirubinemia by inducing glucuronyl transferase, the enzyme that conjugates bilirubin. Oral doses are slowly absorbed from the GI tract; rectal doses are readily absorbed. Peak levels in the CNS are reached in 10–15 hours after oral administration; IM administration produces peak effects in 20–60 minutes. Phenobarbital has a long half-life (2–3 days in children) and, without loading doses, 3–4 weeks may be required to reach optimum steady-state plasma levels. Therapeutic anticonvulsant blood levels are 15–30 μg/ml; 15 μg/ml are usually necessary to control febrile seizures. Phenobarbital is metabolized in the liver; its metabolite and some unchanged phenobarbital (25%) are excreted in the urine. Severe renal impairment can cause accumulation of the unmetabolized form. Phenobarbital crosses the placenta and is excreted in breast milk.

CONTRAINDICATIONS: Hypersensitivity to barbiturates, history of porphyria, marked hepatic impairment, respiratory disease where dyspnea or obstruction is present, severe renal impairment.

PRECAUTIONS: Drowsiness is common but transient; however, paradoxical hyperactivity may occur in some children (particularly those with evidence of brain damage); excessive hyperexcitability may require discontinuance of phenobarbital. Abrupt termination of therapy may cause barbiturate withdrawal symptoms (e.g., anxiety, delirium, convulsions, cardiovascular collapse). Use cautiously in patients with renal impairment, nephritis, or hepatic impairment (drug accumulation). Phenobarbital may be habit-forming in addiction-prone individuals, but drug dependence is unlikely with the usual anticonvulsant doses. Use cautiously in asthmatics and allergy-prone individuals (higher incidence of hypersensitivity reactions). Monitor vital signs frequently when phenobarbital is given parenterally. Administer IV doses slowly. Blood counts should be done prior to and periodically during long-term therapy.

SIDE EFFECTS/ADVERSE REACTIONS: Drowsiness to which tolerance develops is the most common side effect. Rapid IV rates can cause respiratory depression, hypotension, and circulatory collapse. Paradoxical excitement and hyperkinetic activity may occur in some children, especially infants and toddlers. Oral doses may cause occasional gastric distress with nausea, vomiting, and anorexia. Skin eruptions are uncommon but may be mild or progress to exfoliative dermatitis with hepatitis and jaundice (incidence is higher in patients with asthma, urticaria, or angioneurotic edema). Ataxia occurs occasionally and may require dosage reductions if persistent. Megaloblastic anemia and other blood dyscrasias occur infrequently. Use during pregnancy can cause coagulation defects and hemorrhage in the newborn. Toxic plasma levels (>40 µg/ml) cause CNS depression ranging from sleep to profound coma, hypothermia, shock, respiratory depression, apnea, and death. Plasma levels of 80 µg/ml are potentially lethal.

DRUG INCOMPATIBILITIES: Do not mix with any other medications.

DRUG INTERACTIONS: Phenobarbital may cause additive CNS depression if used with other *sedative–hypnotics, alcohol, tranquilizers, narcotics,* or *antihistamines.* Phenobarbital can stimulate hepatic microsomal enzymes resulting in increased metabolism of other medications and consequently a reduction in their pharmacological effects (e.g., *oral anticoagulants, digitoxin, corticosteroids, doxycycline*). Large doses can competitively inhibit *phenytoin* metabolism and predispose the patient to phenytoin toxicity. Low doses, however, stimulate hepatic enzymes and thus increase phenytoin metabolism (caution is required if phenobarbital is discontinued; observe the patient for signs of phenytoin toxicity in this case).

ANTIDOTE: Discontinue phenobarbital. For acute ingestion—within 30 minutes—give activated charcoal; within 4 hours, use gastric lavage, taking care to prevent pulmonary aspiration. Maintain the patient's airway, assist ventilation, and give oxygen. Monitor vital signs and fluid balance. Administer standard therapy for shock if necessary. If renal function is normal, force alkaline diuresis. If anuric, peritoneal dialysis or hemodialysis may be necessary. *Do not* use analeptic agents to stimulate respiration as they may precipitate seizures.

Phenytoin (Dilantin)

ADMINISTRATION

Available Forms: Injectable (IM, IV), 50 mg/ml in 2 and 5 ml amps and preloaded syringes; capsules, 30, 100 mg; tablets (chewable), 50 mg; oral suspension, 30 and 125 mg per 5 ml; also available as 100 mg capsules combined with 16 and 32 mg of phenobarbital.

Diluent: Give undiluted or dilute dose in NS or LR only. Add 100 mg to 25–50 ml for a concentration of 2–4 mg/ml, which maintains a pH >10 (more dilute solutions have a pH <10 and crystallization results). Use diluted solutions within 1 hour after mixing.

Dosage (Parenteral)
For status epilepticus: Loading dose is 10–15 mg/kg/dose slow IV push. Do not give IM as absorption is erratic and unpredictable.

Dosage (Oral): Initially 5 mg/kg/day (250 mg/m^2/day) divided into 2–3 doses; maximum is 300 mg/day. Usual maintenance dose is 4–8 mg/kg/day divided into 1–2 doses; maximum is 300 mg/day. Alternatively, a loading dose of 500–600 mg followed by 200 mg qd has been used.

Rate: To avoid development of arrhythmias, do not exceed IV infusion rates of 25 mg/min.

INDICATIONS: Phenytoin is used for treatment and prevention of tonic-clonic (grand mal) and psychomotor (temporal lobe) seizures. It is also effective in controlling autonomic seizures and is often combined with phenobarbital or other anticonvulsants such as trimethadione or ethosuximide for management of combined grand-mal-petit-mal epilepsy. It should *not* be given alone for pure petit mal (absence) seizures since it may actually increase the frequency of these convulsions. Phenytoin can also be given parenterally (IV) for prevention and treatment of seizures that occur during neurosurgery and for treatment of status epilepticus; however, parenteral doses of diazepam or phenobarbital are preferred since phenytoin's onset of action is slow. Phenytoin is also used as an antiarrhythmic for treatment of ventricular tachycardia, paroxysmal atrial tachycardia, and arrhythmias due to digitalis toxicity (see chapter 6).

ACTIONS: In the usual doses phenytoin has the advantage of producing antiepileptic activity without causing any significant sedation. It limits the spread of seizure activity from its point of origin (focus) to other surrounding normal neurons. By depressing the synaptic transmission of the nerve impulse, phenytoin prevents the cortical seizure foci from detonating adjacent cortical areas. Phenytoin's antiarrhythmic effects include a suppression of atrial and ventricular automaticity without slowing AV conduction (see chapter 6). Oral doses of phenytoin are well absorbed (except in neonates), but absorption of IM doses is slow and erratic and produces unpredictable blood levels. Since therapeutic plasma levels of 10–20 µg/ml may not be achieved for a week, loading doses are often given. Phenytoin is metabolized in the liver, and its metabolites plus a small amount of unchanged phenytoin (about 1%) are excreted in the urine. Normally, about 95% of phenytoin is protein-bound, but in patients with liver or renal impairment, there is significantly less protein binding, so phenytoin toxicity can occur in these patients at lower plasma levels. Phenytoin interferes with the binding of bilirubin by albumin. Consequently, free bilirubin can further displace phenytoin from the latter's albumin-binding sites, causing increased levels of unbound, active phenytoin. Jaundiced infants have a particularly high risk of developing toxic serum levels of phenytoin from this interaction.

CONTRAINDICATIONS: Hypersensitivity to phenytoin and other hydantoins; for parenteral use: sinus bradycardia, SA or severe AV block, Stokes-Adams syndrome.

PRECAUTIONS: Abrupt withdrawal may precipitate status epilepticus. Use cautiously in patients with hepatic impairment (accumulation of phenytoin may increase the risk of toxicity). Use cautiously in patients with renal impairment or diabetes as large doses have caused hyperglycemia and glycosuria in these patients. Use with caution in jaundiced infants. Congenital enzyme deficiencies in some patients cause a decrease in phenytoin metabolism and an increased risk of toxicity even at low doses. Phenytoin can cause reversible lymph node hyperplasia, a syndrome that resembles malignant lymphoma; if this occurs, discontinue phenytoin and substitute another anticonvulsant if possible. Discontinue the medication if rashes appear. If mild rashes (e.g., measles-like) occur, phenytoin can be restarted after allowing the rash to disappear; if severe rashes occur (e.g., bullous, exfoliative), discontinue phenytoin indefinitely. Scrupulous oral hygiene is necessary, especially in children, because of the high incidence of gingival hyperplasia. Avoid IM use; if this route must be used, a 50% increase in the dose (with respect to the oral dose) should be given to prevent a fall in plasma level. Administer IV doses slowly to avoid cardiovascular collapse and CNS depression. Use only clear solutions; dilute in NS or LR only and mix prior to use. Administer IV doses through an in-line filter as diluted phenytoin may precipitate upon standing. Administer oral doses with full glasses of water or with meals to minimize gastric irritation. Agitate large bottles of oral suspension well prior to giving the dose to ensure a uniform concentration of phenytoin in each dose. Total daily doses can be given in the evening so peak drug levels and any possible side effects will occur when the patient is asleep. Monitor serum levels 6–12 hours after giving a loading dose and then periodically during therapy (keep in mind it may take 5 or more days to reach steady-state levels after each dosage change). Avoid peak levels of 20 μg/ml; observe the patient for nystagmus and ataxia (first signs of overdosage). IV administration of phenytoin is recommended in newborns because their absorption of oral doses is poor.

SIDE EFFECTS/ADVERSE REACTIONS: Gastric upset with nausea, vomiting, and constipation are seen frequently with high doses. Gingival hyperplasia is common and often severe in children; hirsutism is less common but does occur. Signs of CNS toxicity correlate well with plasma levels: more than 20 μg/ml, nystagmus, diplopia; 30 μg/ml, ataxia; 40 μg or more per milliliter, increasing drowsiness, lethargy, slurred speech, irritability; 50 μg or more per milliliter, extreme lethargy progressing to coma. Megaloblastic anemia due to folic acid deficiency occurs occasionally. Mild rashes accompanied by fever may occur, especially in children; rarely, more severe cutaneous forms (e.g., exfoliative, Stevens-Johnson type) have occurred. Other idiosyncratic reactions include pseudolymphomas, hepatitis, bone marrow depression, blood dyscrasias, systemic lupus-like syndrome, hepatitis, liver damage, and jaundice. Large doses may cause hyperglycemia, and osteomalacia has occurred during long-term therapy. Rapid IV administration may cause hypotension, CNS depression, cardiovascular collapse, and asystole. Doses given IM may cause pain, tissue necrosis, and inflammation at the injection site.

DRUG INCOMPATIBILITIES: Phenytoin is highly alkaline (pH is approximately 12). Do not mix with any other parenteral medications.

DRUG INTERACTIONS: Medications or conditions that *stimulate* the hepatic microsomal enzymes responsible for metabolizing phenytoin may cause reduced plasma levels of phenytoin and a decreased anticonvulsant effect; these include chronic *alcohol* abuse, *phenobarbital*, and *carbamazepine*. Many medications *inhibit* metabolism of phenytoin, resulting in higher plasma levels and increased phenytoin toxicity; these include *aminosalicylic acid (PAS)*, *barbiturates* (including large doses of phenobarbital), *chloramphenicol, chlordiazepoxide, diazepam, disulfiram, isoniazid*, and *phenothiazines*. *Salicylates, phenylbutazone, sulfonamides*, and *oral anticoagulants* can displace phenytoin from plasma-binding sites thereby increasing the serum levels and toxicity of phenytoin. Use with *tricyclic antidepressants* can induce seizures. Long-term *folic acid* therapy can antagonize the anticonvulsant effects of phenytoin. Phenytoin stimulates the metabolism of and decreases the pharmacological effects of *corticosteroids, doxycycline, digitoxin*, and *oral anticoagulants*.

ANTIDOTE: Discontinue phenytoin. For ingestion of toxic doses, induce emesis or perform gastric lavage and instill activated charcoal. Hemodialysis and exchange transfusions may be necessary. Monitor cardiovascular and respiratory functions and institute supportive measures as required.

Pyridoxine HCl (Vitamin B$_6$)

ADMINISTRATION

Available Forms: Injectable (IM, IV), 50, 100 mg/ml; tablets, 5, 10, 25, 50, 100, 200, 500 mg. Also available in infant liquid vitamin preparations, infant feeding formulas, and IV caloric and electrolyte solutions.

Diluent: Dilute large doses for IV infusion in D5W or NS. Protect solutions from direct sunlight.

Dosage (Parenteral): Varies according to use.
For acute infantile seizures: 10–100 mg (usual, 50 mg) IM or IV.
For acute toxic reactions to isoniazid: Give a dose of pyridoxine *equal* to the amount of isoniazid ingested. Can be given by IV infusion over several hours, depending on the amount of the dose.

Dosage (Oral)
For prevention of pyridoxine-responsive seizures: 2–100 mg orally qd throughout life.

Rate: Give small doses for seizures over several minutes. Administer large doses via infusion over several hours.

INDICATIONS: Parenteral pyridoxine is used in newborn infants to treat seizures unresponsive to usual therapy. In these infants a hereditary syndrome (possibly because of defective glutamic acid decarboxylase) causes a pyridoxine dependency in which unusually large amounts of this vitamin are needed to prevent seizures. These infants may also have been exposed to large doses of pyridoxine *in utero*. Some clinicians recommend that pyridoxine be given to any newborn infant who has seizures of unknown causes. Intravenous doses have also been given during EEG evaluation for diagnosis of neonatal seizures. Other genetic abnormalities that respond to large doses of pyridoxine include hereditary hypochromic anemia, xanthurenic aciduria, homocystinuria, and cystathioninuria. Parenteral pyridoxine is given along with other anticonvulsants for treatment of convulsions or coma resulting from isoniazid overdoses.

ACTIONS: Pyridoxine is a water-soluble, B-complex vitamin required for metabolism of amino acids, lipids, and carbohydrates. In the body its activated form acts as coenzymes in a variety of metabolic reactions. Pyridoxine appears to be essential in the synthesis of the neurotransmitter gamma-aminobutyric acid (GABA) and of the heme component of hemoglobin. Pyridoxine deficiency in adults primarily affects the skin, mucous membranes, peripheral nerves (neuritis), and blood (hypochromic anemia). In children, however, mainly the CNS is affected, resulting in seizures. Oral doses are readily absorbed. Seizures generally stop in 2–3 minutes if amenable to pyridoxine therapy. Pyridoxine is converted in the liver and red blood cells to its active form, pyridoxal phosphate, and riboflavin is required for this process. Vitamin B_6 is stored primarily in the liver, with lesser amounts in muscle and brain tissue. Total body stores are about 16–27 mg. It crosses the placenta, and fetal plasma concentrations are about five times greater than that of maternal blood. Pyridoxal phosphate is metabolized by the liver, and the resulting inactive compound is excreted in the urine. Pyridoxine deficiency causes an accumulation and urinary excretion of xanthurenic acid and a decreased glutamic-oxaloacetic transaminase activity in red blood cells; measurement of either of these may be used to diagnose pyridoxine deficiency.

CONTRAINDICATIONS: Hypersensitivity to pyridoxine.

PRECAUTIONS: Use of large doses during pregnancy has been implicated in pyridoxine-dependent seizures in neonates.

SIDE EFFECTS/ADVERSE REACTIONS: Pyridoxine is usually nontoxic even in large doses. Doses given IM may produce burning or stinging at the injection site. Very large IV doses have caused convulsions. Nausea, headache, paresthesia, sleepiness, increased SGOT, and decreased levels of folic acid have been reported. Occasional allergic reactions have occurred.

DRUG INCOMPATIBILITIES: Pyridoxine is incompatible with alkaline solutions, iron salts, and oxidizing agents.

DRUG INTERACTIONS: Pyridoxine reverses the therapeutic effects of *levodopa* given for Parkinson's syndrome.

ANTIDOTE: Discontinue pyridoxine. Treat adverse reactions symptomatically.

Valproic acid (Depakene)

ADMINISTRATION

Available Forms: Capsules, 250 mg; oral syrup, 250 mg/5 ml (50 mg/ml).

Dosage (Oral): 15 mg/kg/day to start, followed by weekly increases of 5–10 mg/kg/day until optimal response is achieved. Maximum is 60 mg/kg/day. Doses greater than 250 mg/day should be divided.

INDICATIONS: Valproic acid is used alone or with other agents (e.g., ethosuximide) in the management of simple and complex petit mal (absence) seizures. It is also used in conjunction with other anticonvulsants in the management of mixed epilepsy that includes absence seizures. Investigationally, it shows promise in the treatment of myoclonic epilepsy of children. It has been given rectally (instillation of syrup) or by intragastric drip with some success in the management of status epilepticus refractory to IV doses of diazepam.

ACTIONS: The mechanism of action is not known, but it appears to be related to an increase in brain levels of the inhibitory neurotransmitter gamma-aminobutyric acid (GABA). It may also inhibit neuronal activity by increasing potassium conductance. Valproic acid is rapidly absorbed from the GI tract, and peak plasma levels occur in 1–4 hours. Therapeutic plasma levels are thought to be in the range of 50–100 μg/ml and can be maintained by the usual recommended doses. Valproic acid is excreted in breast milk and may cross the placenta. It is almost completely metabolized in the liver, and metabolites are excreted in the urine.

CONTRAINDICATIONS: Hypersensitivity to valproic acid, hepatic disease or significant hepatic dysfunction, pregnancy (relative contraindication).

PRECAUTIONS: Use cautiously in patients with hepatic impairment; serious or fatal hepatotoxicity has occurred within the first 6 months of therapy; perform liver function tests prior to and periodically during therapy (every 2 months during prolonged therapy). Use cautiously in patients with unusual congenital brain disorders or severe seizure disorders accompanied by mental retardation or organic brain disease. Because valproic acid induces thrombocytopenia and inhibits platelet aggregation, platelet counts, bleeding times, and coagulation studies should be done prior to and periodically during therapy. Withdraw the medication if bruising, coagulation disorders, or hemorrhage develops. Valproic acid may cause sedation and impaired reflexes, so caution patients accordingly. Discontinue the medication if hyperammonemia develops. Local irritation of the mouth and throat may occur if capsules are chewed; do not add the valproate sodium syrup to carbonated beverages as valproic acid will be liberated, which can cause mouth and throat irritation. Gastric upset can be minimized by giving doses with food.

SIDE EFFECTS/ADVERSE REACTIONS: The most frequent side effects are indigestion, nausea, and vomiting. Also reported are hypersalivation, anorexia, cramps, diarrhea, and weight gain or loss. Drowsiness and sedation may occur with combination therapy; however, hyperactivity, aggressiveness, and behavioral changes have been reported in children. Other CNS effects seen rarely are ataxia, dizziness, tremor, headache, dysarthria, nystagmus, diplopia, "spots before the eyes," mental depression, hallucinations, and psychosis. Rarely, paresthesias, muscle weakness, rashes, and transient hair loss or curliness may occur. Hematological reactions include thrombocytopenia, decreased platelet aggregation, leukopenia, lowered fibrinogen levels, bruising, petechiae, epistaxis, and frank hemorrhage. Elevations in liver enzymes, hyperammonemia, hepatotoxicity, and frank hepatic failure have been induced by valproic acid. Hepatotoxicity may be preceded by nonspecific signs and symptoms that include loss of seizure control, malaise, weakness, lethargy, anorexia, and vomiting. Acute toxicity causes somnolence and coma.

DRUG INTERACTIONS: Increased CNS depression occurs with concomitant use of *alcohol,* other *CNS depressants,* and *barbiturates.* Use with *clonazepam* has precipitated petit mal seizures. Valproic acid may increase or decrease plasma levels of *phenytoin,* so adjust phenytoin dosage as the clinical situation dictates. Valproic acid may potentiate the effects of *MAO inhibitors* and other *antidepressants*; it does potentiate the anticoagulant effect of *aspirin, warfarin, dipyridamole,* and *sulfinpyrazone.*

ANTIDOTE: Discontinue valproic acid. Acute toxic effects can cause coma. Treat adverse reactions symptomatically and supportively. Maintain adequate urine output. Naloxone can be given cautiously to reverse CNS depression, but it may also reverse the anticonvulsant effect of valproic acid. Since valproic acid is so rapidly absorbed, gastric lavage is of limited value.

28
Skeletal Muscle Relaxants

The agents used to relieve muscle spasticity do so primarily by reducing muscle tone. While neuromuscular function can be blocked centrally or peripherally, the latter is more effective. The centrally acting agents reduce muscle tone by acting on the central nervous system, but CNS depression is frequently an undesirable side effect. The neuromuscular blockers act peripherally at the myoneural junction. They induce the temporary but profound skeletal muscle paralysis that is necessary for certain surgical and emergency procedures without causing CNS depression; however, assisted ventilation is necessary. Dantrolene is the only agent that acts directly on the muscle cell.

Some skeletal muscle relaxants are used for the short-term treatment of acute local muscle spasm and tetany, while others may be useful in the long-term management of muscle spasms that accompany many neurological disorders (e.g., multiple sclerosis, cerebral palsy).

The following agents are discussed in this chapter:

- **Carisoprodol**
- **Dantrolene**
- **Diazepam**
- **Methocarbamol**
- **Pancuronium bromide**
- **Succinylcholine**

Carisoprodol (Soma)

ADMINISTRATION

Available Forms: Tablets, 350 mg. Also available as 200 mg with caffeine, 32 mg and phenacetin, 160 mg (Soma Compound) and with codeine phosphate, 16 mg (Soma Compound with Codeine).

Dosage (Oral)
Children 5 years or older: 25 mg/kg/day (750 mg/m^2/day) in divided doses qid.

INDICATIONS: Carisoprodol, like other centrally acting muscle relaxants, is used as an adjunct to other measures such as rest, physical therapy, and analgesics for the relief of acute muscle spasms associated with trauma, tension, or inflammation. It is ineffective for muscle spasticity or rigidity caused by drug-induced extrapyramidal reactions or by chronic neurological disorders such as cerebral palsy.

ACTIONS: Carisoprodol is a CNS depressant chemically and pharmacologically related to meprobamate. Its relaxant effects on skeletal muscle are most likely due to its sedative effect. Unlike neuromuscular blockers, it does not depress neuromuscular transmission or muscle excitability, nor does it directly relax skeletal muscle fibers. Carisoprodol is almost totally metabolized in the liver; its metabolites and trace amounts of unchanged drug are excreted in the urine. Drug accumulation may occur in patients with liver or renal disease.

CONTRAINDICATIONS: Acute intermittent porphyria, allergic or idiosyncratic reactions to carisoprodol or meprobamate.

PRECAUTIONS: Carisoprodol may cause drowsiness or impair mental alertness and physical coordination, so caution ambulatory patients accordingly. Use with caution in patients with hepatic or renal disease; dosage adjustments may be necessary.

SIDE EFFECTS/ADVERSE REACTIONS: The most frequent complaints are drowsiness and dizziness. Other CNS effects include ataxia, vertigo, tremor, nervousness, agitation, headache, syncope, insomnia, and mental depression. Gastrointestinal upset with nausea, vomiting, hiccups, and epigastric distress may occur. Cardiovascular effects include tachycardia, postural hypotension, palpitations, and facial flushing. Idiosyncratic reactions have occasionally been reported in patients who have never received carisoprodol before. These reactions usually appear by the fourth dose and last for several hours before subsiding. They are characterized by extreme weakness, ataxia, dizziness, transient quadriplegia, stammering, temporary loss of vision, diplopia, mydriasis, agitation, euphoria, confusion, and disorientation. Allergic reactions range from mild skin eruptions to extensive rashes, fever, angioneurotic edema, asthmatic attacks, smarting eyes, and anaphylactic shock.

DRUG INTERACTIONS: Carisoprodol causes additive CNS depression when used with *tranquilizers, alcohol, sedative-hypnotics, narcotics,* and other *CNS depressants.*

ANTIDOTE: Discontinue carisoprodol. Overdosage produces symptoms similar to meprobamate overdoses: stupor, coma, shock, respiratory depression, and, very rarely, death. Treatment includes induced emesis, gastric lavage, administration of activated charcoal, maintenance of an adequate airway, assisted ventilation, and pressor medications for support of blood pressure as necessary. Treat allergic reactions with epinephrine, antihistamines, and corticosteroids. Phenacetin-containing compounds (Soma Compound) may cause cyanosis and methemoglobinemia; treat these with IV methylene blue.

Dantrolene (Dantrium)

ADMINISTRATION

Available Forms: Injectable (IV), 20 mg (powder); capsules, 25, 50, 100 mg.

Diluent: Reconstitute contents of vial with 60 ml sterile water for injection (*without* preservative); resulting concentration is 333 µg/ml.

Dosage (Parenteral)
For malignant hyperthermia: 1 mg/kg given rapidly IV. Dose can be repeated if needed, up to a total cumulative IV dosage of 10 mg/kg.

Dosage (Oral)
For muscle spasticity:

- Children >5 years old: 0.5 mg/kg bid to start, then tid-qid if tolerated. Increase by 0.5 mg/kg increments at 4–7 day intervals, up to 3 mg/kg bid-qid; maximum is 400 mg/day.

Rate: Use rapid IV push but avoid extravasation.

INDICATIONS: Dantrolene is used to relieve the muscle spasticity and sequelae associated with upper motor neuron disorders such as cerebral palsy, multiple sclerosis, spinal cord injury, and stroke. Although dantrolene frequently causes muscle weakness, it reduces involuntary muscle activity to allow for better motor coordination. It should not be used to relieve acute muscle spasms due to musculoskeletal trauma. It is used IV to treat episodes of malignant hyperthermia.

ACTIONS: Dantrolene substantially reduces muscle tension via a direct effect on the muscle's contractile mechanism. In normal doses it has little effect on cardiac or smooth muscle. It produces generalized muscle weakness, reduces hyperreflexia and stiffness, and causes some CNS depression. It is metabolized in the liver to an active metabolite that is excreted in the urine.

CONTRAINDICATIONS: Active hepatic disease; patients who must utilize spasticity to maintain upright posture, balance, or increased body function.

PRECAUTIONS: Oral doses are not recommended for children less than 5 years of age. Dantrolene is potentially hepatotoxic (sometimes fatal), so monitor liver function tests and enzymes before and frequently during prolonged therapy. Severe muscle weakness or diarrhea may necessitate discontinuance of the medication. Avoid prolonged exposure to sunlight (photosensitivity reactions). Use cautiously in patients with hepatic impairment, obstructive pulmonary disease, epilepsy, or myocardial disease with impaired cardiac function. Warn the patient to use caution when performing potentially hazardous activities that require mental alertness. When using IV doses, discontinue concomitant use of all anesthetics; maintain supportive measures (e.g., cooling procedures, oxygen), treat metabolic acidosis, monitor electrolytes, and maintain urine output. Avoid extravasation. (Continued administration of 4–8 mg/kg/day orally in divided doses for 1–3 days after a hyperthermic episode may be necessary to prevent exacerbation.)

SIDE EFFECTS/ADVERSE REACTIONS: The most common side effects are muscle weakness, diarrhea, drowsiness, dizziness, fatigue, general malaise, nausea, and vomiting. Severe diarrhea or muscle weakness or both (with slurred speech, drooling, and enuresis) may necessitate dosage reductions or discontinuance of dantrolene. Hepatotoxicity, including fatal hepatitis, has occurred (incidence is higher with doses of 300 mg/day for longer than 2 months). Other reported reactions include gastric upset, abdominal pain, severe constipation with abdominal distension and ileus, visual disturbances, hallucinations, increased nervousness, precipitation of seizures, urinary retention, tachycardia, pericarditis, phlebitis, diaphoresis, fever, chills, rashes, urticaria, photosensitivity, and abnormal hair growth.

DRUG INTERACTIONS: Dantrolene produces additive CNS depression when used with other *tranquilizers, sedative-hypnotics, alcohol,* or other *CNS depressants.*

ANTIDOTE: Discontinue the medication. For acute ingestion use gastric lavage. Otherwise, give supportive therapy. Maintain the patient's airway and ventilation, ensure adequate hydration and urine output, and monitor ECG. Resuscitate if indicated.

Diazepam (Valium)

ADMINISTRATION

Available Forms: Injectable (IM, IV), 5 mg/ml in 2 ml amps and syringes and 10 ml vials; tablets, 2, 5, 10 mg.

Diluent: Give undiluted. Do not mix with any other aqueous injections or IV solutions because precipitation may occur. (Diazepam for injection is in a propylene glycol diluent.)

Dosage (Parenteral): Varies according to use.
For tetanus and painful musculoskeletal spasticity:

- Infants (>1 month old) and children: 0.1–0.3 mg/kg slow IV or IM; can be repeated q2–4h if needed; do not exceed 0.6 mg/kg in an 8 hour period.

For status epilepticus: See chapter 27.

Dosage (Oral)
For anxiety, tension, muscle spasm:

- Children >6 months old: 0.12–0.80 mg/kg/day (3.5–24.0 mg/m^2/day) divided into 3–4 doses.

Rate: Administer IV bolus doses over at least 3 minutes.

INDICATIONS: Diazepam is used as adjunctive therapy for relief of acute, painful muscle spasms; tetany; and upper motor neuron disorders. It is also used to treat anxiety, tension, and alcohol withdrawal syndromes and for preoperative sedation. Given IV, it is the medication of choice for termination of status epilepticus and acute seizures (see chapter 27). It is generally ineffective for treatment of depressive reactions or psychoses.

ACTIONS: Diazepam acts at the limbic, thalamic, and hypothalamic levels of the CNS to produce sedative, hypnotic, antianxiety, anticonvulsant, and skeletal-muscle-relaxant effects. It appears to produce skeletal muscle relaxation by blocking excitatory synaptic transmission along spinal afferent nerve pathways. It may also directly depress motor nerve and muscle function without producing extrapyramidal side effects. It can produce CNS depression ranging from sedation to coma and can cause hypotension and bradycardia. Oral doses of diazepam are well absorbed, but absorption of IM doses is slow and erratic. It is metabolized in the liver and excreted in the urine; its half-life is increased in patients with liver disease and in premature and newborn infants. (See diazepam [parenteral] in chapter 27 for further precautions with respect to its metabolism.) Diazepam crosses the placenta and may produce fetal hypotension, hypoactivity, apnea, and kernicterus. It is excreted in breast milk.

CONTRAINDICATIONS: Hypersensitivity to diazepam (or other benzodiazepines), shock, coma, acute alcohol intoxication with depressed vital signs, psychosis, acute narrow-angle glaucoma (relative contraindication).

PRECAUTIONS: When using parenteral doses, monitor vital signs frequently, especially blood pressure, pulse, and respiratory rate. Inject the drug into large veins only; if this is not feasible, inject slowly through IV infusion tubing as close as possible to the site of insertion in the vein. Avoid extravasation or intra-arterial injection as necrosis may occur. Use cautiously in patients with respiratory or cardiovascular impairment, those who are receiving narcotics, and neonates and infants. When oral doses are given over a prolonged period of time, abrupt withdrawal of diazepam may precipitate seizures (in epileptics) or barbiturate-like withdrawal symptoms. Symptoms may not be seen for several days after discontinuing the drug because of the long half-life of its metabolites. Diazepam may be habit-forming. Use cautiously in patients with respiratory, cardiac, hepatic, or renal impairment and in infants.

SIDE EFFECTS/ADVERSE REACTIONS: The most common side effects are drowsiness, dizziness, fatigue, and ataxia. Paradoxical hyperexcitability may occur as well as sleep disturbances, anxiety, hostility, and hallucinations. Visual disturbances (blurred vision, diplopia, nystagmus), rashes, urticaria, urinary retention, gastric upset, constipation, muscle cramps, and jaundice may occur. Diazepam may induce hyperbilirubinemia and kernicterus in newborns. Parenteral use in particular may cause bradycardia, hypotension, syncope, respiratory depression, apnea, laryngospasm, hiccups, muscle weakness, diminished reflexes, and cardiovascular collapse.

DRUG INCOMPATIBILITIES: Do not mix parenteral doses of diazepam with any other aqueous medication or IV solution.

DRUG INTERACTIONS: Diazepam causes additive CNS depression when used with other *CNS depressants*.

ANTIDOTE: Discontinue diazepam. If ingestion was recent, empty the stomach by gastric lavage (avoid aspiration). Treat cardiopulmonary depression symptomatically and supportively. Maintain an adequate airway. Hemodialysis is of limited value.

Methocarbamol (Robaxin)

ADMINISTRATION

Available Forms: Injectable (IM, IV), 100 mg/ml in 10 ml vials (in polyethylene glycol diluent); tablets, 500, 750 mg.

Diluent: For IV infusion dilute with D5W or NS (1 gm/250 ml) if needed.

Dosage (Parenteral)
For tetany: 15 mg/kg (500 mg/m^2) IV q6h with other adjunctive therapy. Do not exceed 1.8 gm/m^2/day for 3 consecutive days.

Dosage (Oral)
Children 12 years or older: 60 mg/kg/day in divided doses (q6h).

Rate: For IV bolus doses do not exceed 3 ml/min (300 mg/min) or 6 mg/kg/min.

INDICATIONS: Oral doses are used as an adjunct with other measures for the relief of acute, painful muscle spasms of local origin, inflammation, or trauma. Parenteral doses are used as adjunctive therapy in tetanus and other acute musculoskeletal spasms. Methocarbamol is not indicated for muscle spasticity due to chronic neurological disorders.

ACTIONS: Methocarbamol acts centrally to produce sedation and muscle relaxation, presumably by blocking spinal polysynaptic reflexes to reduce muscle tone. It does not depress neuronal conduction, transmission, or muscle excitability. Oral doses are rapidly absorbed, and the onset of action is about 30 minutes. The onset of action of parenteral doses is almost immediate. Methocarbamol is probably metabolized in the liver and excreted in the urine.

CONTRAINDICATIONS: Hypersensitivity to methocarbamol, impaired renal function (parenteral form only).

PRECAUTIONS: The polyethylene glycol diluent used in the injectable forms may be nephrotoxic. Use parenteral doses cautiously in patients with renal impairment, metabolic acidosis, or epileptic disorders. Have the patient in a recumbent position during administration. Avoid extravasation as tissue sloughing may occur. Methocarbamol will not mix with blood if the latter is aspirated into the syringe. The sedative effect of oral doses may impair the patient's ability to perform potentially hazardous tasks that require mental alertness. Methocarbamol is not recommended for children less than 12 years old except for parenteral treatment of tetanus.

SIDE EFFECTS/ADVERSE REACTIONS: The most common side effects associated with oral doses are drowsiness, dizziness, vertigo, and light-headedness. Also reported are nausea, anorexia, and allergic reactions (rashes, urticaria, nasal congestion). Parenteral doses may cause sedation, flushing, vertigo, nausea, gastric upset, a metallic taste in the mouth, nystagmus, diplopia, mild ataxia, syncope, hypotension, bradycardia, convulsions, and allergic and anaphylactoid reactions. These can be minimized by keeping the IV infusion rate at or slower than 3 ml/min. Thrombophlebitis and tissue sloughing may occur.

DRUG INCOMPATIBILITIES: Do not mix with any other medications.

DRUG INTERACTIONS: Methocarbamol may cause additive CNS depression if used with other *CNS depressants*.

ANTIDOTE: Discontinue the medication. Treat adverse reactions symptomatically and supportively.

Pancuronium bromide (Pavulon)

ADMINISTRATION

Available Forms: Injectable (IV), 1 mg/ml in 10 ml vials, 2 mg/ml in 2 and 5 ml amps.

Diluent: Give undiluted.

Dosage (Parenteral): Not approved for children less than 10 years of age, but the following doses have been used safely in neonates, infants, and children.
For intubation: Initially, 0.06–0.10 mg/kg IV, then 0.02–0.06 mg/kg if needed. Subsequent doses of 0.01–0.02 mg/kg IV can be given q30–60min as needed to maintain satisfactory muscle relaxation.
Note: Neonates can be given a test dose of 0.02 mg/kg, but usually pancuronium's duration of action is not prolonged in this age group. Children have been given IM doses of 2.5 mg/m^2 with good results.

INDICATIONS: Pancuronium bromide is used to facilitate endotracheal intubation and mechanical respiration and to increase pulmonary compliance during assisted or controlled respiration. It is also used to produce skeletal muscle relaxation after induction of general anesthesia. Succinylcholine is sometimes administered prior to pancuronium during endotracheal intubation to increase the duration and intensity of the neuromuscular blockade.

ACTIONS: This nondepolarizing neuromuscular blocker causes skeletal muscle paralysis by blocking the access of the normal neurotransmitter, acetylcholine, to its receptor sites at the myoneural junction. Thus, neuromuscular transmission and subsequent muscle contractions are inhibited. Pancuronium is approximately five times more potent than tubocurarine. It causes little or no histamine release, ganglionic blockade, hypotension, or bronchospasm. It may increase heart rate, cardiac output, and arterial pressure because of an acetylcholine-blocking (e.g., vagolytic) effect on cardiac receptors. Pancuronium does not impair consciousness or alter the pain threshold. Its action can be altered by dehydration, electrolyte imbalance, renal disease, acid-base imbalance, and concomitant administration of other neuromuscular blockers. The onset of action is 2–3 minutes after administration. Pancuronium's duration of action is dose-related, but single doses usually produce muscle paralysis for 30–45 minutes. Supplemental doses cause a cumulative effect that increases and prolongs the neuromuscular blockade. Large single doses hasten onset and prolong the duration of effect. Pancuronium is eliminated primarily unchanged in the urine.

CONTRAINDICATIONS: Hypersensitivity to pancuronium or to bromides.

PRECAUTIONS: Pancuronium's action may be prolonged by hypokalemia, fever, hypermagnesemia, and myasthenic-like syndromes such as those associated with lung cancer, dehydration, thyroid disorders, collagen diseases, and porphyria. Determine serum levels of electrolytes and arterial pH prior to treatment. Mechanical or manual ventilation should be continued throughout pancuronium's duration of action. Use with caution in neonates and young children and in patients with tachycardia, renal or hepatic impairment, myasthenia gravis, or pulmonary disease.

SIDE EFFECTS/ADVERSE REACTIONS: The most common side effects are skeletal muscle weakness, profound paralysis, respiratory depression, apnea, and increased heart rate. Excessive salivation and sweating may occur in children (especially if no atropine is given prior to pancuronium). Transient rashes, wheezing, and burning sensations along the injected vein have been reported. Malignant hyperthermia is a potential adverse reaction to all neuromuscular blockers.

DRUG INTERACTIONS: The intensity and duration of the neuromuscular blockade are increased when pancuronium is used concomitantly with many *general inhalation anesthetics, succinylcholine, aminoglycosides, clindamycin, polymyxin B, magnesium salts, quinine, quinidine, propranolol,* high-dose *lidocaine,* or *potassium-depleting agents* (e.g., thiazides, potent diuretics, corticosteroids, amphotericin B). *Narcotics* and other *CNS depressants* may potentiate the respiratory depression induced by pancuronium.

ANTIDOTE: Discontinue pancuronium. Maintain a patent airway and provide assisted ventilation. Pyridostigmine bromide preceded by atropine will antagonize pancuronium's effects. Treat adverse reactions symptomatically and supportively.

Succinylcholine (Anectine, Quelicin)

ADMINISTRATION

Available Forms: Injectable (IM, IV), 20, 50, and 100 mg per milliliter; 500 mg, 1 gm (powder for reconstitution).

Diluent: For continuous IV infusion, reconstitute the powder and dilute it to a concentration of 1–2 mg/ml with D5W or NS. The vial solutions can be diluted in the same manner (use this method only for prolonged procedures).

Dosage (Parenteral): If the IV route is not feasible, an IM dose of up to 2.5 mg/kg has been used. Maximum total dose is 150 mg.

Infants and children: Initially, give a test dose of 100 μg/kg. If no apnea occurs or if transient apnea dissipating within 5 minutes occurs, proceed with a normal dose of 1–2 mg/kg IV; this can be repeated as needed, depending on the response to the initial dosage.

INDICATIONS: Succinylcholine is used primarily to produce skeletal muscle relaxation during procedures of short duration (i.e., <3 minutes) such as endotracheal intubation, endoscopic examinations, relief of laryngospasm, and orthopedic manipulations. It has also been used for emergency termination of convulsions.

ACTIONS: Succinylcholine is a depolarizing neuromuscular blocker. After injection, it initially mimics the normal neurotransmitter, acetylcholine, and causes transient muscular fasciculations. This is followed by a prolonged depolarization at the motor end plate of the neuromuscular junction that causes profound flaccid skeletal muscle paralysis. Given IV, succinylcholine has a rapid onset of about 1 minute and a short, effective duration of about 5 minutes. It is rapidly hydrolyzed by plasma cholinesterase, and recovery is usually within 10 minutes. The onset of action of IM doses is slower (about 2–3 minutes) and duration is prolonged (about 10–30 minutes). Succinylcholine does not alter the pain threshold or impair consciousness. It has histamine-releasing properties. It stimulates the vagus nerve and the sympathetic nerve ganglions to produce some complex cardiovascular effects that include bradycardia, hypotension, tachycardia, hypertension, and cardiac arrhythmias. Repeated injections may lead to desensitization and tachyphylaxis. Succinylcholine usually produces transient apnea but does not cause complete or prolonged respiratory paralysis in usual doses. However, assisted mechanical ventilation may be necessary.

CONTRAINDICATIONS: Hypersensitivity to succinylcholine, severe hepatic impairment, severe anemia, patients with genetic plasma cholinesterase deficiency.

PRECAUTIONS: Prolonged apnea and paralysis may occur in patients with low plasma cholinesterase levels (a test dose to determine the patient's ability to metabolize succinylcholine is recommended). Plasma cholinesterase levels may be decreased in patients with genetic predisposition, hepatic disease, severe anemia, dehydration or malnutrition; those who are receiving phenothiazine therapy; and those who have been exposed to organophosphate insecticides. Use cautiously in patients with renal, cardiac, or pulmonary impairment; glaucoma; or myasthenia gravis. Electrolyte disturbances may alter the effect of succinylcholine; high serum levels of magnesium and low serum levels of calcium may potentiate its action. Hyperkalemia may be exacerbated and lead to ventricular arrhythmias (especially in digitalized patients and those with severe burns, massive trauma, brain or spinal cord injuries, or tetanus). Hypothermia can potentiate the action of succinylcholine and fever can lessen it. Use cautiously in patients with fractures or muscle spasms as initial muscular fasciculations can cause pain. Maintain fluid and electrolyte balance; have equipment necessary for artificial respiration readily available.

SIDE EFFECTS/ADVERSE REACTIONS: Dose-related prolonged apnea, residual muscle weakness, pain, and stiffness are the primary side effects. Succinylcholine may cause vagal and ventricular arrhythmias (e.g., nodal arrhythmias, bradycardia and sinus arrest after IV use in children) and hypotension. These effects can be minimized by prior administration of atropine. Hyperkalemia, excessive salivation, bronchospasm, increased intraocular pressure, and histamine release may also occur. A rare complication is malignant hyperthermia (especially during general anesthesia).

DRUG INCOMPATIBILITIES: Do not mix with alkaline solutions or barbiturates. Use only freshly prepared solutions (if using powder for reconstitution).

DRUG INTERACTIONS: The intensity and duration of the neuromuscular blockade caused by succinylcholine are increased with many *general inhalation anesthetics, magnesium salts, aminoglycosides, clindamycin, polymyxin B, quinine, quinidine, propranolol,* and *lidocaine* (high doses). *Narcotics* potentiate the respiratory depression associated with succinylcholine (especially postoperatively).

ANTIDOTE: Discontinue succinylcholine. Prolonged respiratory depression or apnea can be reversed by neostigmine or edrophonium preceded by atropine. Maintain the patient's airway and assist ventilation.

IX
SEDATIVES AND HYPNOTICS

Reassurance, tenderness, and support from parents or loved ones are often all that is needed to calm an anxious and agitated child. However, certain sedative medications are sometimes used to control excessive anxiety and induce cooperation. There are only a few situations in pediatric therapy that warrant the use of sedative-hypnotics, and the reaction of children to these medications, particularly to the barbiturates, is often unpredictable.

Single doses, especially in infants and toddlers, can cause extreme excitement or agitation. Children also have a higher incidence of idiosyncratic reactions to sedatives than do adults. Section IX discusses the few sedative medications used in pediatric emergencies.

29
Sedative-Hypnotics

The barbiturates, certain antihistamines, and chloral hydrate are used for mild sedation in children. For most purposes, a weak sedative such as hydroxyzine (see chapter 15) is a very effective and safe calming agent for simple anxiety and one that is least liable to cause unwanted side effects. Other antihistamines with reliable sedative properties include promethazine and diphenhydramine. Chloral hydrate is also a safe, inexpensive alternative for alleviating excessive agitation and anxiety without causing undue respiratory depression.

Situations in which sedation of the child is indicated include the following:

- Preoperative anesthesia
- Painful diagnostic procedures
- Intubation or tracheostomy for respiratory assistance
- Intractable pain (when used as an adjunct to narcotic analgesics to alleviate anxiety)
- Agitation that can greatly aggravate certain conditions, such as asthma or croup (however, use with extreme caution in these conditions)

Sedation is not the treatment of choice for insomnia or hyperactivity. Some sedatives, notably the barbiturates, can cause paradoxical hyperexcitability in children, especially those 2 years of age or younger, and often under circumstances in which continued stimulation of pain, restraint, or anxiety is present. The barbiturates, however, have two major applications in pediatric emergency medicine: as anticonvulsants and as adjuncts in the management of intracranial hypertension. With regard to the latter, high doses of barbiturates appear to have a protective effect on brain tissue subjected to severe anoxia or injury as may occur after cardiac arrest, severe head injury, near drowning, encephalitis, stroke, and

Reye's syndrome. When treatment is started early, within 2 hours of the anoxic episode, and combined with other techniques, such as controlled hyperventilation, therapeutic hypothermia, and the use of corticosteroids and osmotic diuretics, better recovery rates and preservation of cerebral function ensue. Pentobarbital has been used more frequently than the other barbiturates for this purpose.

The following medications are discussed in this chapter:

- **Chloral hydrate**
- **Pentobarbital**
- **Phenobarbital**
- **Secobarbital**

Chloral hydrate (Noctec, others)

ADMINISTRATION

Available Forms: Capsules, 250, 500 mg; oral syrup, 250 and 500 mg per 5 ml; rectal suppositories, 300, 600, 1000 mg (Aquachloral).

Dosage (Oral): Varies according to use.
For sedation: 25 mg/kg/day (750 mg/m^2/day) in divided doses (q8h).
For hypnosis: 50 mg/kg/day (1.5 gm/m^2/day) as a single dose; maximum is 1 gm.
Prior to EEG examination: 20–25 mg/kg as a single dose.

Dosage (Rectal): Same as oral dosage. Chloral hydrate syrup can be suspended in olive oil or cottonseed oil for use as a retention enema.

INDICATIONS: Chloral hydrate is given to children to produce mild sedation when excessive apprehension and agitation can aggravate respiratory distress (e.g., as in croup or asthma). It may also be combined with mild analgesics or narcotics as an adjunct to control pain after trauma and during postoperative care. Chloral hydrate is also given to induce sedation before EEG examinations.

ACTIONS: Chloral hydrate produces CNS depressant effects similar to those caused by paraldehyde and the barbiturates, but it has no analgesic or anticonvulsant actions in sedative-hypnotic doses. Normal doses appear to cause less respiratory depression and paradoxical excitement in young children than do the barbiturates. In therapeutic doses, chloral hydrate affects respiration and blood pressure little more than does ordinary sleep. Toxic doses, on the other hand, produce anesthesia, severe respiratory impairment, and hypotension by depressing the respiratory and vasomotor centers in the brain. Doses larger than therapeutic ones can decrease myocardial contractility. Chloral hydrate is rapidly absorbed after oral or rectal administration and is rapidly reduced in the liver and blood to the actual active compound, trichloroethanol, which diffuses into the CSF. The drug crosses the placenta readily; however, little of the compound appears in breast milk. Some of the trichloroethanol is further detoxified by the liver to several inactive metabolites, which are excreted slowly, most in the urine and a small amount in the feces. Trichloroethanol is also excreted unchanged in the urine, so both renal and hepatic impairment could cause drug accumulation and an increased risk of toxic effects.

CONTRAINDICATIONS: Hypersensitivity to chloral hydrate, marked renal or hepatic impairment, gastritis, esophagitis, gastric or duodenal ulcers.

PRECAUTIONS: Chloral hydrate is a gastric irritant. Capsules should be swallowed whole with a full glass (6–8 oz) of fluid. Dilute the syrup in one-half glass of water, fruit juice, or ginger ale. Use cautiously in those patients with respiratory impairment (see indications). Avoid large doses in those with severe cardiac disease. The drug may cause excitement and delirium in patients who are experiencing pain. Chloral hydrate may be habit-forming with prolonged use of large doses, and its abrupt discontinuance can precipitate withdrawal symptoms.

SIDE EFFECTS/ADVERSE REACTIONS: The most frequent complaints are gastric irritation with nausea, vomiting, and diarrhea. Sometimes, paradoxical excitement occurs. CNS depressant effects include dizziness, ataxia, drowsiness, vertigo, delirium, and disorientation. Residual sedation ("hangover") rarely occurs. Cutaneous reactions are not common but include various rashes (erythematous, eczematoid, and scarlatiniform), hives, urticaria, purpura, and angioedema. Toxic overdoses cause coma, hypotension, hypothermia, respiratory depression, cardiac arrhythmias, miosis, vomiting, muscle flaccidity, and decreased or absent reflexes. Gastric necrosis, GI hemorrhage, and esophageal stricture may occur. Hepatic and renal function may become impaired, causing jaundice and albuminuria. Death results from hypotension and respiratory failure.

DRUG INTERACTIONS: Additive CNS depression occurs if chloral hydrate is given with other *CNS depressants* (e.g., narcotics, barbiturates, paraldehyde, antihistamines, alcohol). *IV furosemide* (Lasix), given within 24 hours after chloral hydrate, has caused a reaction characterized by sweating, flushing, hot flashes, hypertension, and variable blood pressure changes (primarily in patients with congestive heart failure or myocardial damage). Chloral hydrate may potentiate the hypoprothrombinemic effect of *coumarin anticoagulants,* so reduce anticoagulant doses if the two medications are given together on a long-term basis.

ANTIDOTE: Empty the stomach by gastric lavage; take care to avoid aspiration (use a cuffed endotracheal tube). Maintain an adequate airway, assist respiration, and administer oxygen as needed. Maintain the patient's body temperature and support circulation and blood pressure.

BARBITURATES (GENERAL STATEMENT)

INDICATIONS: The range in the onset and duration of action among the different barbiturates makes this class of medications very versatile. They can be used for almost any condition in which a relatively nonspecific depression of the CNS is desirable. The short-acting or intermediate-acting agents, pentobarbital and secobarbital, are frequently used as preoperative sedatives, usually combined with an anticholinergic (e.g., atropine or scopolamine) to dry secretions and a narcotic analgesic. This preoperative combination is not necessary in neonates but may be beneficial in patients 6 months of age and up. Of the two agents, pentobarbital is the more frequently used and is usually given rectally to children up to 8–10 years old and orally to those 10 years or older. Given rectally or parenterally, pentobarbital and secobarbital are used to provide hypnosis as an adjunct to general, spinal, or regional anesthesia; to induce anesthesia prior to ear, nose, or throat (ENT) procedures; or to facilitate intubation or tracheostomy for respiratory assistance. They are sometimes given IV to sedate an excessively agitated child undergoing controlled, mechanical respiration who is "fighting" the respirator. The ultra-short-acting thiopental is administered IV as the sole anesthetic agent for brief (e.g., 15 minutes) procedures or for induction of anesthesia prior to the administration of inhalation anesthetics. Rapid onset of action is required when the barbiturates are used for emergency treatment of convulsions such as those associated with status epilepticus, tetanus, meningitis, cerebral hemorrhage, and certain poisonings. For this purpose the parenteral route, preferably IM, is used. Although diazepam IV is the treatment of choice for acute convulsive episodes, phenobarbital IM is frequently given as an alternative, especially in neonates. High-dose IV barbiturate therapy has been an effective adjunct in the control of intracranial hypertension refractory to other therapeutic measures. The cerebral protective effect of the barbiturate-induced coma has produced good recovery results in patients with severe head injury, encephalitis, cardiac arrest, Reye's syndrome, and other anoxic injuries. Both pentobarbital and thiopental have been given, but pentobarbital has been used more frequently.

ACTIONS: The barbiturates are capable of producing all levels of CNS depression—from mild sedation to profound coma. However, the degree of depression obtained depends on a variety of factors. These include the dosage, route of administration, and pharmacokinetics of the particular barbiturate being used; the patient's age, physical state, and degree of CNS excitability at the time of administration; and the influence of any other medications being used concurrently. Low doses decrease motor activity, depress the sensory cortex, and produce sedation and drowsiness. However, in some patients euphoria or excitability can occur before drowsiness does. Phenobarbital, in particular, can cause paradoxical hyperactivity and excitement in young children. Larger doses impair mental abilities, further suppress motor activity and respiration, and produce sleep. Still larger doses induce anesthesia and markedly decrease the rate, depth, and volume of respiration (direct action on medullary centers in the brain). Rapidly administered IV doses can cause severe respiratory depression and hypotension. The barbiturates do not produce analgesia except at anesthetic doses. All members of this class exhibit anticonvulsant activity (especially when given parenterally), but only the phenobarbital derivatives are effective prophylactic oral anticonvulsants in doses low enough not to cause sleep. Sedative doses also reduce GI tone and motility through a central depressant action. Barbiturates can lower serum bilirubin levels in neonates, presumably by activitation of glucuronyl transferase, the enzyme responsible for conjugating bilirubin.

Several mechanisms have been given to explain the barbiturates' protective effects against the deleterious conditions produced by cerebral anoxic injury. Proposed mechanisms include (1) reduction in the cerebral metabolic rate (up to 50% when the EEG is flatline); (2) prevention and reduction of cerebral edema; (3) selective vasoconstriction of cerebral blood vessels in undamaged areas of the brain, thereby preferentially shunting and increasing blood flow to the injured, ischemic areas; and (4) controlling the damaging "free radical" reactions that occur in hypoxic-ischemic tissue. In the absence of oxygen, highly reactive "free radical" compounds are produced that appear to damage the mitochondrial membrane lipids in brain cells. The barbiturates seem to act as free radical "scavengers." Additional benefits of high-dose barbiturate therapy are (1) reduction of ICP, which reduces the requirements for osmotic diuretics; (2) lessening the ICP spikes caused by irritating stimuli (e.g., patient position changes, noise, suctioning); (3) anticonvulsant effects; and (4) additional patient immobilization, which, in conjunction with pancuronium and controlled hyperventilation, helps to maintain a reduced ICP.

The absorption of the barbiturates into the bloodstream and, consequently, their onset of action are variable, depending on their route of administration. The rate of absorption and onset is slower when doses are given orally or rectally (15–30 minutes) and slightly faster when administered IM (10–20 minutes). The sodium salts are more rapidly absorbed by all routes than are the acid forms. Taking oral doses on an empty stomach hastens gastric absorption but may cause significant stomach upset. The barbiturates are rapidly distributed to all tissues, but the highest concentrations appear in those that receive the greatest percentage of the blood flow (or the highest perfusion rates), namely the brain and liver.

These medications readily cross the placenta in high concentrations and are excreted in breast milk. The barbiturates also bind to plasma proteins; the more lipid-soluble thiopental, pentobarbital, and secobarbital are more highly protein-bound than the less lipid-soluble phenobarbital. The degree of lipid-solubility is the dominant factor that determines each barbiturate's onset and duration of action, body distribution, and clinical application. For example, thiopental is the most lipid-soluble. It penetrates the blood-brain barrier the fastest to induce anesthesia and exits quickly from brain tissue, so its duration of action is the shortest. Hence, thiopental is used primarily to induce general anesthesia for brief procedures. On the other hand, the less lipid-soluble phenobarbital enters and exits the brain more slowly, so it has a slower onset but longer duration of action. Its principal use in pediatrics is as an anticonvulsant, parenterally for status epilepticus and orally for chronic control of epilepsy.

Three processes are responsible for terminating the CNS depressant actions of the barbiturates: redistribution, metabolism, and excretion. All reduce plasma concentrations and cause the drugs to leave their site of action in the CNS. Termination of the anesthetic effect depends mainly on the redistribution phase; that is, the high CNS levels of barbiturate decline rapidly as the drug shifts or "redistributes" from brain tissue to other tissues, such as muscle, fat, and body water. For example, thiopental has a very brief duration of action, not because it is rapidly metabolized or excreted, but because it is quickly redistributed from the brain cells to primarily muscle tissue in the first 15–20 minutes after IV administration. After that, the declining plasma levels are due to uptake of the drug by body fat and subsequent metabolic destruction. However, repeated doses of thiopental can accumulate in body fat, which then acts as a "reservoir" to slowly release the medication back into the bloodstream. This phenomenon results in a prolonged anesthetic effect as well as the characteristic "hangover" that may last for several hours after emergence from thiopental anesthesia.

The termination of the other actions and side effects of barbiturates depends on the other two processes, metabolism and excretion. All of these medications are eventually degraded chiefly by the liver, and the metabolic products are excreted mainly in the urine and, to a lesser extent, in the feces. Since most of the barbiturates are excreted as inactive metabolites, renal impairment may not cause appreciable accumulation of unchanged drug. (The major exception is phenobarbital; 25% is excreted *unchanged* and dosage reductions are necessary in patients with renal insufficiency.) However, because the barbiturates are extensively detoxified by the liver, hepatic impairment can cause the drugs to accumulate to toxic serum levels, so dosage reductions are necessary here. Also, since these agents are bound to plasma proteins in various degrees (20–80%), patients with uremia, renal disease, or other conditions in which serum proteins are decreased may exhibit an increased sensitivity to the barbiturates. This occurs because the unbound, freely diffusable barbiturate is now circulating at abnormally high levels since there is less plasma protein to complex with it and render it inactive. Consequently, the barbiturates should be used at lower doses and with caution under these conditions.

CONTRAINDICATIONS: Hypersensitivity to any of the barbiturates, a history of porphyria.

PRECAUTIONS: Varies according to the route of administration and type of therapy.
Intravenous use: Solutions of barbiturates are highly alkaline and irritating. Administer IV doses slowly into the infusion line of a well-running IV whenever possible.

Avoid extravasation or accidental intra-arterial injection. Use cautiously in patients with hypertension or hypotension or pulmonary or cardiac disease as IV administration can cause laryngospasm, bronchospasm, severe hypotension, respiratory depression, and cardiac arrhythmias. Monitor blood pressure, respiration, and cardiac function continuously; have equipment for respiration and artificial ventilation on hand (if the patient is not already receiving assisted ventilation).

High-dose IV therapy: (See also pentobarbital.) Patients should have continuous monitoring of their ICP, arterial pressure (with a Swan-Ganz catheter, if possible), ECG, and EEG. Monitor serum barbiturate concentrations periodically (see pentobarbital schedule). Evaluate patients with head trauma periodically; use the Glasgow Coma Scale (GCS). Infuse IV doses slowly with syringe pump or controlled infusion device; use a separate IV line to avoid drug-drug incompatibilities. Barbiturate-induced hypotension may require vasopressors (e.g., dopamine) and colloid infusions to maintain circulating blood volume. Patients may exhibit withdrawal symptoms when emerging from barbiturate-induced coma. Treat them with diazepam, mild sedatives, a quiet environment, and reassurance. To lessen withdrawal symptoms and prevent rebound increases in ICP, taper IV barbiturate doses gradually; prophylactic phenobarbital may be helpful; start it 24 hours before tapering begins.

Intramuscular use: Inject IM doses deeply into a large muscle mass; IM administration can cause tissue necrosis.

In general: Use cautiously in children less than 2 years old. Use cautiously in patients who are uremic, in shock, or who have recently been given other CNS depressants (see drug interactions) as barbiturate action may be intensified. Use cautiously and at reduced doses in patients with impaired liver function. Doses given to patients with severe uncontrolled pain may sometimes produce paradoxical excitement and delirium, which may worsen their condition. Because skin eruptions can precede potentially fatal reactions, discontinue barbiturates if dermatologic eruptions occur. Also discontinue these medications if toxic hematological effects become apparent (as evidenced by blood tests, sore throat, persistent infections, easy bruising, epistaxis, and so forth). When giving oral doses for long-term anticonvulsant therapy, warn ambulatory patients of sedation and possible impaired mental alertness. Laboratory evaluations for renal and hepatic function and blood tests should be done periodically during prolonged barbiturate therapy.

SIDE EFFECTS/ADVERSE REACTIONS: Chief complaints following IV administration are laryngospasm, bronchospasm, coughing, sneezing, and hiccoughing. Intravenous use can also cause thrombophlebitis, pain, injury to nerves adjacent to the injection site, and tissue necrosis. Cardiac arrhythmias and reduced body temperature have also been reported. Too rapid administration of IV doses can produce vasodilation, a profound hypotension, respiratory depression, and apnea. Abrupt discontinuance of high-dose therapy can precipitate withdrawal symptoms (e.g., tremors, agitation, delirium, visual hallucinations, sleep disturbances, difficulty in controlling speech and fine motor movements). All forms of barbiturates can cause various degrees of CNS depression, headache, dizziness, paradoxical hyperactivity, excitement, anxiety, and hallucinations. Cardiovascular effects include bradycardia, hypotension, and syncope. Hypersensitivity reactions include rashes, urticaria, fever, serum sickness, a hepatitis syndrome, angioneurotic edema, and severe forms of dermatitis such as Stevens-Johnson syndrome and others (incidence is higher in asthmatics and other allergy-prone individuals). Barbiturates can cause postpartum hemorrhage and hemorrhagic disease in newborns (treatable with vitamin K). Other reported toxic hematological effects are agranulocytosis, thrombocytopenic purpura, megaloblastic anemia, and precipitation of acute intermittent porphyria attacks in those individuals with a history of this disease. Barbiturates can elevate blood ammonia levels, worsen hepatic coma, and cause hepatic damage.

DRUG INCOMPATIBILITIES: To ensure accurate IV doses, do not mix barbiturate solutions with any other medications. Use separate IV lines.

DRUG INTERACTIONS: Concomitant use with other *CNS depressants* (e.g., sedatives, hypnotics, narcotic analgesics, antihistamines, ketamine, alcohol) produces additive CNS depressant action. Since barbiturates, particularly phenobarbital, induce hepatic microsomal enzymes, accelerated metabolism of certain medications can occur, notably *quinidine, doxycycline, theophylline, digitoxin, corticosteroids, coumarin anticoagulants,* and possibly *phenytoin*. The net effect is that larger doses of these medications may be required to achieve the same effects. Barbiturates can decrease the GI absorption of *griseofulvin* and produce lower serum levels of this antibiotic.

ANTIDOTE: Signs and symptoms of barbiturate overdose include respiratory and CNS depression, possibly progressing to Cheyne-Stokes respiration, absent reflexes, slight miosis (dilation in severe poisonings), oliguria, tachycardia, hypotension, hypothermia, apnea, coma, respiratory arrest, cardiovascular collapse, and death. Maintain an adequate airway, assist ventilation, and administer oxygen as necessary. Treat shock with IV fluids and vasopressors (e.g., dopamine). If renal function is adequate, forced fluid diuresis and alkalinization of the urine may be helpful in *phenobarbital* overdoses only. For oral overdoses (within 4 hours of ingestion), empty the patient's stomach by gastric lavage; take care to avoid pulmonary aspiration. Activated charcoal is beneficial primarily if given within 30 minutes of ingestion. Dialysis may be helpful in those patients who are anuric, in shock, or severely intoxicated. Withdrawal symptoms can be treated with daily oral doses of phenobarbital that are gradually decreased and withdrawn completely over a 2 week period.

Pentobarbital sodium (Nembutal, others)

ADMINISTRATION

Available Forms: Injectable (IM, IV), 50 mg/ml in 1 and 2 ml ampules and prefilled syringes, 20 and 50 ml vials; capsules, 30, 50, 100 mg; oral elixir, 20 mg/5 ml; rectal suppositories, 30, 60, 120, 200 mg.

Diluent: For IV use in high-dose barbiturate therapy, dilute dose in sufficient volume of D5W or NS (e.g., 25–100 ml) to allow administration over 10–60 minutes or by continuous infusion.

Dosage (Parenteral): Varies according to use.
For seizures: 3–5 mg/kg/dose (125 mg/m^2/dose) IM.
For sedation:

- Children > 2 years old: 3 mg/kg/dose IM; can be repeated q8h prn

For intracranial hypertension: Loading dose of 3–5 mg/kg IV (diluted) given over 30–60 minutes. Follow with a maintenance dose of 2 mg/kg/hr by continuous IV infusion (use a syringe pump or controlled infusion device and a separate IV line). For sudden increases in ICP, give an additional dose of 1–2 mg/kg IV (diluted) over 10–30 minutes (or can give mannitol instead, 0.5 gm/kg IV if serum osmolality is less than 320 mOsm). Note: This therapy should be initiated within 12 hours of the cerebral injury and be continued for at least 3 days since cerebral swelling is usually maximal 48–72 hours after injury. Average duration of therapy is about 5 days.

Dosage (Oral): Varies according to use.
For preoperative sedation:

- Children 8 years and older: 3 mg/kg/dose (maximum, 100 mg) given 1.5 hours before surgery. Usually given with IM or SC morphine, 0.75 mg per year of age, up to a maximum of 8 mg.

For general sedation:

- Children > 2 years old: 6 mg/kg/day in divided doses (q8h).

Dosage (Rectal): Varies according to use.
For preoperative sedation:

- Children < 8 years old: 4 mg/kg/dose (maximum, 120 mg) given 1.5 hours before surgery. Usually given with IM or SC morphine, 0.75 mg per year of age, up to a maximum of 6 mg.

For general sedation:

- Children > 2 years old: 6 mg/kg/day in divided doses (q8h).

Rate: For IV infusion administer at 2 mg/kg/hr. For IV push (undiluted) do not exceed 50 mg/min; for diluted IV bolus, 10–30 minutes.

INDICATIONS: Pentobarbital is the most frequently used barbiturate for preoperative sedation in children and for the management of intracranial hypertension. For the latter purpose, it is usually given in conjunction with other therapeutic measures such as controlled hyperventilation, hypothermia, fluid restriction, dexamethasone, furosemide, and mannitol. (See also barbiturates, general statement.)

ACTIONS: See barbiturates (general statement).

CONTRAINDICATIONS: See barbiturates (general statement).

PRECAUTIONS: See barbiturates (general statement). Additional precautions should be taken during high-dose therapy: Continuously monitor the patient's ICP, arterial pressure (use a Swan-Ganz catheter), ECG, and EEG. Perform liver function tests every 2–3 days. Use the Glasgow Coma Scale (GCS) to evaluate head trauma patients. Measure serum concentrations of pentobarbital 12 hours after the start of therapy, 24 hours after each dosage change, and then every 2 days. Maintain a therapeutic level of 2.5–4.0 µg/ml. Adjust dose as necessary to maintain ICP less than 15 torr and mean arterial pressure (MAP) of 60 torr; maintain serum osmolality under 320 mOsm, if possible. Consider stopping therapy if ICP has been less than 20 torr for longer than 24 hours; discontinue barbiturate therapy if it is not effective in 3–7 days. Taper the dosage over 1 to several days to prevent rebound increases in ICP. Prophylactic phenobarbital therapy can be started 24 hours prior to pentobarbital tapering (usual phenobarbital dose is 5 mg/kg/day IM and then orally when feasible). The use of barbiturates for coma therapy has certain disadvantages: It may become impossible to monitor the EEG because the high therapeutic serum levels of barbiturate necessary for coma therapy can depress EEG voltage. Clinical neurological signs cannot be fully assessed during high-dose therapy. Barbiturate-induced hypotension may be significant, especially in unstable patients. Barbiturates cannot reverse the vasospasm and cerebral vasoconstriction that may occur after cerebral anoxic injury; consequently, blood can be shunted away from ischemic areas where it is most needed.

SIDE EFFECTS/ADVERSE REACTIONS: See barbiturates (general statement).

DRUG INCOMPATIBILITIES: See barbiturates (general statement).

DRUG INTERACTIONS: See barbiturates (general statement).

ANTIDOTE : See barbiturates (general statement).

Secobarbital sodium (Seconal, others)

ADMINISTRATION

Available Forms: Injectable (IM, IV), 50 mg/ml in 1 and 2 ml prefilled syringes and 20 ml vials; capsules, 50, 100 mg; oral elixir, 22 mg/5 ml; rectal suppositories, 30, 60, 120, 200 mg.

Diluent: Give undiluted or dilute with sterile water or NS.

Dosage (Parenteral)
For sedation: 3 mg/kg/dose IM.

Dosage (Oral)
For preoperative sedation: Given 1–2 hours before surgery.

- Children 8 years and older: 3–5 mg/kg as a single dose (combined with 0.4 mg atropine IM and 0.75 mg morphine per year of age IM or SC)

Dosage (Rectal)
For preoperative sedation: Given 1–2 hours before surgery.

- Infants at least 6 months old: 30 mg
- Infants and children (>6 months to 3 years old): 60 mg
- Children (>3–8 years old): 60–90 mg

Rate: For IV bolus do not exceed 50 mg/min.

INDICATIONS: Secobarbital is given orally or rectally primarily for preoperative sedation and parenterally to produce rapid sedation for anesthesia to facilitate ENT procedures or intubation.

ACTIONS: See barbiturates (general statement).

CONTRAINDICATIONS: See barbiturates (general statement).

PRECAUTIONS: See barbiturates (general statement).

SIDE EFFECTS/ADVERSE REACTIONS: See barbiturates (general statement).

DRUG INCOMPATIBILITIES: See barbiturates (general statement).

DRUG INTERACTIONS: See barbiturates (general statement).

ANTIDOTE: See barbiturates (general statement).

X
AGENTS FOR HYPERGLYCEMIC AND HYPOGLYCEMIC EMERGENCIES

Regulation of blood glucose and carbohydrate metabolism is under the control of the pancreatic hormones, insulin and glucagon. Insulin lowers blood glucose in response to hyperglycemia, and glucagon raises blood glucose in response to hypoglycemia by mobilizing hepatic glycogen. Malfunctions in the pancreatic secretion of insulin lead to the development of diabetes mellitus, a condition that, if untreated, results in fatal diabetic ketoacidosis (DKA) and coma. Hypoglycemia, especially neonatal hypoglycemia, is a more common syndrome in infants and children. Blood glucose must be restored to normal quickly to prevent the serious complication of mental retardation.

This section discusses the principal agents used for rapid correction of alterations in blood glucose.

30
Glucose-lowering Agents

Management of hyperglycemia in its most severe form (i.e., diabetic ketoacidosis and coma) involves prompt correction of dehydration; prevention and control of complications such as shock, oliguria, cardiac arrhythmias, and electrolyte imbalances; proper handling of precipitating factors (e.g., infection, trauma); and, most importantly, an adequate program of insulin administration. This chapter discusses the use of insulins in the treatment of diabetic ketoacidosis and in the management of diabetes mellitus.

Diabetes mellitus is a chronic systemic disease characterized by disturbances in the metabolism of carbohydrates, fats, and proteins because of partial or complete insulin deficiency. Without insulin the body loses its capacity to use ingested carbohydrates for energy. Instead, fats and proteins are "burned" to secure the necessary energy that can no longer be obtained from carbohydrates. The end result is ketosis, protein wasting, weight loss, hyperglycemia, and glycosuria. The principal early symptoms of diabetes mellitus (e.g., polyuria, polydypsia, and polyphagia) are due to impaired glucose utilization. As the disease progresses, vascular abnormalities develop, producing the characteristic diabetic "triad" of complications: nephropathy, retinopathy, and neuropathy.

For purposes of a simplified discussion, diabetes mellitus can be classified into two major categories: (1) type I, insulin-dependent diabetes mellitus (IDDM), formerly termed juvenile diabetes, and (2) type II, noninsulin-dependent diabetes mellitus (NIDDM), formerly referred to as adult-onset diabetes. A third category includes diabetes mellitus associated with certain conditions such as pancreatic, hormonal, or genetic diseases or with use of certain medications such as thiazide diuretics, adrenal hormones, catecholamines, and so forth.

Classically, type I diabetes, IDDM, is often hereditary and occurs primarily in juveniles; however, the disease can be recognized and become symptomatic at any age. The onset of clinical symptoms is abrupt, and they often appear before the age of 20. The pancreas of the patient with type I diabetes secretes little or no insulin. Treatment with insulin injections and strict dietary adjustments are mandatory for control of the disease. Oral hypoglycemic agents are ineffective in these patients. Ketosis and metabolic acidosis occur frequently unless insulin doses, diet, and exercise are properly coordinated.

On the other hand, patients with type II diabetes, NIDDM, exhibit minimal diabetic symptoms; they may be asymptomatic for years as the disease slowly progresses. Although most patients who develop NIDDM do so after the age of 40, this condition can also occur in young persons; hence the former nomenclature, maturity-onset diabetes in the young. Obesity is a prominent contributing factor in the development of this type of diabetes. These patients are not dependent on insulin injections to prevent ketonuria and are usually not prone to ketosis. However, the patient with type II diabetes may use insulin injections for correction of symptomatic or persistent hyperglycemia and may develop ketosis under special circumstances such as infections or stress. These patients can usually control their disease with diet, weight reduction, and use of oral hypoglycemic medications.

With regard particularly to the type I diabetic, if insulin injections are withheld too long, diabetic ketoacidosis (DKA) and coma may develop. Conversely, if too much insulin is given without proper timing of meals or exercise, hypoglycemic (insulin) coma may occur. Table 30–1 differentiates the two types of coma with respect to their signs, symptoms, and treatment.

The following medications are discussed in this chapter:

- **Insulins (regular)**
- **Insulins (longer-acting preparations)**

TABLE 30–1 Diabetic and Insulin Comas*

	Diabetic (Hyperglycemic) Coma	Insulin (Hypoglycemic) Coma
ONSET	Slow (days)	Sudden (minutes) with regular insulin, gradual (hours) with other insulins
CAUSES	Ignorance, neglect, omission of insulin and food, concurrent disease or infection	Insulin overdose, delayed or omitted meals, excessive exercise before meals
SYMPTOMS	Thirst, headache, nausea, abdominal pain, dimmed vision, constipation, shortness of breath	Nervousness, hyperactivity, weakness, hunger, dizziness, tingling sensations, double or blurred vision, negative behavior (e.g., mental confusion, psychosis)
SIGNS	Florid face, rapid breathing (air hunger) to respiratory paralysis, dehydration (dry skin, rapid pulse, soft eyeballs), reflexes normal or absent, acetone breath, vomiting, coma	Pallor, shallow breathing, sweating (usually), pulse normal to uncharacteristic, eyeballs normal, Babinski's reflex, stupor, convulsions
URINE GLUCOSE	Positive	Usually negative
ACETONE	Positive	Negative
DIACETIC ACID	Positive	Negative
BLOOD GLUCOSE	>250 mg/100 ml (usually)	≤60 mg/100 ml
TREATMENT	Regular insulin (boluses or microdrip infusion), IV fluid replacement (normal saline initially, D5W later), potassium replacement	Dextrose 50% IV, glucagon IV, glucose orally
RESPONSE TO TREATMENT	Usually slow	Usually rapid if due to regular insulin overdose, may be slower if due to other insulins

*Source: *Diabetes Mellitus*, ed 8. Indianapolis, Eli Lilly and Co, 1980; *Managing Your Diabetes*. Indianapolis, Eli Lilly and Co, 1983.

Insulins (regular) (Iletin, others)

ADMINISTRATION

Available Forms: Injectable (IV, IM, SC), various preparations in 10 ml vials (see Table 30–2). Insulin preparations can be stored at room temperature for 1 year without loss of potency.

TABLE 30–2 Regular Insulin Preparations*†

Product (Manufacturer)	Species Source	Strength (units/ml)	Purity (ppm proinsulin)
Actrapid (Novo)	Pork	100	≤1
Human Actrapid (Novo)	Human (semisynthetic)	100	≤1
Humulin R (Lilly)	Human (biosynthetic)	100	—
Insulin, Improved (Squibb)	Pork	40, 100	<25
Insulin, Purified (Squibb)	Pork	100	<10
Regular Iletin I (Lilly)	Beef/pork Beef	40, 100 100	<20
Regular Iletin II (Lilly)	Beef Pork	100 100, 500	<10
Velosulin (Nordisk)	Pork	100	≤1

*Adapted with permission from the *Handbook of Clinical Drug Data*, 5th ed, edited by James E Knoben and Philip O Anderson, published by Drug Intelligence Publications, Inc, 1241 Broadway, Hamilton, IL 62341.
†All can be given IV, IM, or SC

Diluent: Can be diluted in NS for IV infusion ("microdose" method). Compatible with many IV solutions.

Dosage (Parenteral): Varies according to method and use.
High-dose method: 0.5–2.0 units/kg (one-half given IV and one-half given IM or SC); can be repeated as 0.5–2.0 units/kg SC q2h according to the severity of the clinical state and the glucose and acetone content of blood and urine.
Low-dose ("microdose") method: Initial IV loading dose of 0.1–0.5 units/kg (depending on clinical condition), followed by continuous infusion of 0.1 units/kg/hr; maximum is 5 units/hr.
For hyperkalemia: 0.2 units/kg with 200–400 mg/kg glucose (D25W) IV.

INDICATIONS: Regular insulin is used for the rapid reversal of hyperglycemia in DKA. Insulin therapy in patients with severe brittle or complicated diabetes is usually initiated with regular insulin and then gradually replaced by an intermediate-acting insulin for maintenance. The initial total daily insulin dosage is determined by sliding-scale regular insulin coverage in response to urinary glucose determinations done every 6 hours. Regular insulin is sometimes added to IV infusions of dextrose to facilitate the shift of potassium into cells in the treatment of severe hyperkalemia. The highly purified insulin preparations (especially pork and synthetic human insulins) are particularly beneficial for newly diagnosed diabetics, those with type II diabetes, those needing continuous IV or SC insulin, and those with insulin allergy or resistance or excessive lipoatrophy.

ACTIONS: Exogenous insulin elicits the same pharmacological effects as endogenous insulin secreted by the pancreatic beta cells of the islets of Langerhans. Under its influence, blood glucose is transported to adipose tissue and skeletal and cardiac muscle where it is metabolized. (Other tissues require insulin for metabolism but not for transport of glucose.) Insulin stimulates utilization of glucose for energy, promotes conversion of glucose to glycogen, and facilitates glycogen storage in liver and muscle tissue. It also prevents protein breakdown, stimulates protein synthesis, promotes storage of fats as adipose tissue, and prevents the metabolism of fat to ketone bodies, a condition that would result in metabolic acidosis. Insulin also causes an intracellular shift of potassium and magnesium, temporarily decreasing the serum levels of these ions. Its action is antagonized by epinephrine; growth, thyroid, and adrenocortical hormones; and estrogen.

Since the early 1980s more highly purified, less antigenic insulin products have been commercially prepared. Previously all insulin preparations contained large amounts of protein-like impurities such as glucagon, proinsulin, and other polypeptides. Specialized purification procedures now remove most of these potential antigens. The purity of an insulin product is determined by its proinsulin content expressed as parts per million (ppm). Three types of improved preparations have been developed:

1. "Single peak" animal insulins (proinsulin content, 20–25 ppm)
2. Purified animal insulins (proinsulin content, <10 ppm)
3. Biosynthetic and semisynthetic "human" insulins (proinsulin content, ≤1 ppm)

By comparison, older standard insulin products contained 3,000–10,000 ppm of proinsulin; these have been gradually phased out of the market. Beef insulin is the most antigenic of the common insulins; pork insulin, which differs from the human form by only one amino acid, is less antigenic than beef. Biosynthetic and semisynthetic human insulins are the least antigenic because, when properly prepared, they do not differ from the endogenous hormone. ("Human" insulin is produced by recombinant DNA technology utilizing genetically altered *E. coli* [Lilly preparations] or by enzymatic alteration of the pork insulin molecule to make its amino acid sequence identical to that of the human variety [Novo preparations].)

When administered IV, all regular insulin preparations act rapidly (within minutes). After SC or IM injection the onset of action is 30–60 minutes, peak effects occur in 2–4 hours, and the duration of action is approximately 5–8 hours.

CONTRAINDICATIONS: Insulin allergy (rare). Some patients allergic to beef or pork may be able to use insulin derived from the opposite source or the new synthetic human insulins.

PRECAUTIONS: Only regular insulin can be given IV. Use only clear solutions. Laboratory monitoring should include serum levels of glucose, sodium, and potassium; serum and urinary ketones; arterial pH; blood CO_2 content; and BUN. Initial severe acidosis may cause hyperkalemia, which usually reverts to hypokalemia after insulin and fluid therapy; monitor ECG and observe the patient for symptoms of hypokalemia; give potassium supplements if indicated. Avoid correcting acidosis with injections of bicarbonate unless there is no improvement in arterial pH or blood CO_2 content after insulin and fluid therapy. Hyperinsulinism, resulting in exaggerated hypoglycemia, may occur in patients with brittle diabetes or in those receiving an overdose of insulin or IV fluids containing no glucose during the later phases of treatment of DKA. Dextrose infusions may be required after control is achieved to prevent hypoglycemia and to replenish glycogen stores. Beta-blockers (e.g., propranolol) may mask symptoms of hypoglycemia and cause delayed recovery. Double-check all amounts of insulin drawn up for administration; to avoid the danger of overdosage or underdosage, use only syringes calibrated for the particular concentration of insulin being administered (e.g., U-100 syringes for U-100 insulin only). Insulin adsorbs to the surfaces of IV infusion bottles and tubing (up to 80% loss of potency). Monitor blood and urinary levels of glucose frequently and adjust the dosage or flow rate of insulin drips as necessary.

SIDE EFFECTS/ADVERSE REACTIONS: Hypoglycemia is the primary side effect and usually occurs when administered insulin reaches its peak action. Signs and symptoms include hunger, pallor, nausea, fatigue, sweating, headache, shallow respirations, tingling sensations, double or blurred vision, hypothermia, uncontrolled yawning, mental confusion, irritability, tachycardia, stupor, and convulsions. Prolonged hypoglycemia can lead to irreversible brain damage. Transient localized allergic reactions include itching, redness, swelling, and stinging or warmth at the injection site. True insulin allergy is rare; it may be characterized by urticaria, lymphadenopathy, angioneurotic edema, and anaphylaxis. (Allergic reactions can be minimized by using newer, more purified beef or pork preparations or human insulins.)

DRUG INCOMPATIBILITIES: Insulin is incompatible with barbiturates, aminophylline, phenytoin, and sodium bicarbonate.

DRUG INTERACTIONS: The hypoglycemic action of insulin may be potentiated by *alcohol, anabolic steroids, MAO inhibitors, disopyramide, guanethidine, salicylates,* and *oral hypoglycemic agents* and may be antagonized by *thiazide diuretics, furosemide, ethacrynic acid, estrogens, thyroid hormones, corticosteroids,* and *epinephrine.* Concomitant use of *propranolol* interferes with carbohydrate metabolism and poses risks of hypoglycemia and possibly hyperglycemia.

ANTIDOTE: Discontinue insulin. Administer 50% glucose or glucagon IV (see chapter 31).

Insulins (longer-acting preparations)

ADMINISTRATION

Available Forms: Injectable (IM, SC), various preparations in 10 ml vials (see Table 30–3).

TABLE 30-3 Comparison of Insulin Preparations*

Product (Manufacturer)	Species Source	Strength (units/ml)	Purity (ppm proinsulin)	Route
RAPID-ACTING				
INSULIN (REGULAR, SEE TABLE 30-2) (Onset: 0.5–1.0 hr Peak: 2–4 hr Duration: 5–8 hr)				
PROMPT INSULIN ZINC SUSPENSION (SEMI-LENTE) (Onset: 1–3 hr Peak: 2–8 hr Duration: 12–16 hr)				
Semi-Lente Iletin (Lilly)	Beef/pork	40, 100	<20	SC
Semi-Lente Insulin, Improved (Squibb)	Beef	100	<25	SC
Semitard (Nova)	Pork	100	≤1	SC
INTERMEDIATE-ACTING				
ISOPHANE INSULIN SUSPENSION (NPH) (Onset: 1–3 hr Peak: 6–15 hr Duration: 22–28 hr)				
Humulin N (Lilly)	Human (biosynthetic)	100	—	SC
Insulatard NPH (Nordisk)	Pork	100	≤1	SC

*Adapted with permission from the *Handbook of Clinical Drug Data*, 5th ed. edited by James E. Knoben and Philip O. Anderson, published by Drug Intelligence Publications, Inc., 1241 Broadway, Hamilton, IL 62341

TABLE 30-3 continued

Product (Manufacturer)	Species Source	Strength (units/ml)	Purity (ppm proinsulin)	Route
INTERMEDIATE-ACTING continued				
Isophane Insulin, Improved (Squibb)	Beef	40, 100	<25	SC
Isophane Insulin, Purified (Squibb)	Beef	100	<10	SC
NPH Iletin I (Lilly)	Beef/pork Beef	40, 100 100	<20	SC
NPH Iletin II (Lilly)	Beef Pork	100 100	<10	SC
Protaphane (Novo)	Pork	100	≤1	SC
ISOPHANE INSULIN SUSPENSION (70% NPH + 30% REGULAR) (Onset: 0.5 hr Peak: 4–8 hr Duration: 24 hr)				
Mixtard (Novo)	Pork	100	≤1	SC
INSULIN ZINC SUSPENSION (LENTE = 70% ULTRALENTE + 30% REGULAR) (Onset: 1–3 hr Peak: 6–15 hr Duration: 22–28 hr)				
Lentard (Novo)	Beef/pork	100	≤1	SC
Lente Iletin I (Lilly)	Beef/pork Beef	40, 100 100	<20	SC
Lente Iletin II (Lilly)	Beef Pork	100 100	<10	SC

30: Glucose-lowering Agents 343

Lente Insulin, Improved (Squibb)	Beef	40, 100	<25	SC
Lente Insulin, Purified (Squibb)	Beef	100	<10	SC
Monotard (Novo)	Pork	100	≤1	SC
Human Monotard (Novo)	Human (semisynthetic)	100	≤1	SC

LONG-ACTING

PROTAMINE INSULIN ZINC SUSPENSION (PZI)
(Onset: 4–6 hr Peak: 14–24 hr Duration: ≥36 hr)

Protamine, Zinc & Iletin (Lilly)	Beef/pork Beef Pork	40, 100 100 100	<20	SC
Protamine Zinc Insulin, Improved (Squibb)	Beef	100	<25	SC

EXTENDED INSULIN ZINC SUSPENSION (ULTRALENTE)
(Onset: 4–6 hr Peak: 10–30 hr Duration: ≥36 hr)

Ultralente Iletin (Lilly)	Beef/pork	40, 100	<20	SC
Ultralente Insulin, Improved (Squibb)	Beef	100	<25	SC
Ultratard (Novo)	Beef	100	≤1	SC

Dosage (Parenteral)

For diabetic maintenance therapy: Dose must be titrated to clinical response. Give IM or SC (preferred) only.

INDICATIONS: The longer-acting insulins are used as replacement therapy in the management of ketosis-prone, insulin-dependent diabetes mellitus (IDDM). They are also indicated for noninsulin-dependent diabetes mellitus (NIDDM) that is not adequately controlled by dietary regulation, weight reduction, or oral hypoglycemic agents. The highly purified insulins can be particularly beneficial for newly diagnosed diabetics, those patients with local or systemic insulin allergy or resistance, or those with lipoatrophy at insulin injection sites. These insulin suspensions should never be given IV and are not indicated for treatment of acute diabetic ketoacidosis (only regular insulin is indicated in this case).

ACTIONS: See insulins (regular).

CONTRAINDICATIONS: Insulin allergy (rare), hypersensitivity to beef or pork (switch to insulin from the opposite source or to new, highly purified preparations).

PRECAUTIONS: Do not give IV. Monitor serum and urine levels of glucose and ketones at regular intervals throughout the day. Both the patient and the parents must understand the importance of the proper timing of insulin doses, meals, exercise, and blood and urine tests. Double-check all insulin doses; use only syringes calibrated for the particular concentration of insulin being administered. To ensure uniform dosages, shake insulin suspensions well before using them. Insulin requirements may increase because of fever; infection; trauma; surgery; increased food intake; weight gain; reduction in physical exercise; hyperthyroidism; therapy with thyroid hormones, estrogens, or corticosteroids; and various endocrine disorders. Rebound hyperglycemia may develop in patients who are repeatedly receiving overdoses of insulin (initial hypoglycemia stimulates the release of glycogen, catecholamines, adrenal corticosteroids, and growth hormone and thereby antagonizes further insulin activity). Atrophy or hypertrophy of subcutaneous fat tissue may occur at the site of frequent insulin injections. If this happens, rotate injection sites, inject insulin that has been warmed to room temperature, or switch to highly purified pork derivatives or synthetic human insulin. Insulin "resistance" or refractoriness may develop; this is characterized by insulin requirements of >40 units/day in children <6 years old, >60 units/day in children >10 years old, and >150 units/day in adolescents. It may be due to immune or nonimmune mechanisms; treatment with corticosteroids or a switch to another species source of insulin or to the highly purified pork or synthetic human preparations may restore insulin effectiveness. True insulin allergy is rare, but it may require desensitization procedures. Care must be exercised in switching patients from conventional "single peak" insulins to the highly purified preparations (proinsulin content, 1–10 ppm); a 10–20% reduction in the dosage of purified pork insulin or the synthetic human preparations may be required in patients who were previously using other insulins of lesser purity. For those patients with insulin resistance who require large doses, it may be desirable to hospitalize them to make the transition to a highly purified preparation. (Since the older insulins have been largely replaced by the new, improved forms, dramatic changes in insulin requirements are not expected to occur.)

SIDE EFFECTS/ADVERSE REACTIONS: See insulins (regular).

DRUG INCOMPATIBILITIES: See insulins (regular).

DRUG INTERACTIONS: See insulins (regular).

ANTIDOTE: See insulins (regular).

31
Glucose-elevating Agents

Hypoglycemia can be a result of inadequate carbohydrate intake, insulin overdosage, the effects of certain medications on carbohydrate metabolism, pancreatic insulin-secreting tumors, hyperinsulinism due to many causes, malnutrition (especially during fetal development), overwhelming infectious diseases, respiratory distress syndrome, enzyme deficiencies, endocrine disorders, liver disease, and many other factors. In children less than 5 years old, symptomatic hypoglycemia is more common than diabetes mellitus. The incidence of hypoglycemia is highest in low-birth-weight, full-term, immature, or stressed infants. These babies have low carbohydrate reserves that must be restored to provide energy to meet metabolic requirements.

The primary aim of therapy is to determine and treat the underlying cause of hypoglycemia, but, in addition, the acute hypoglycemic episode must be rapidly corrected because prolonged hypoglycemia can lead to irreversible brain damage and mental retardation. Symptoms of neonatal hypoglycemia may include tremors, jitteriness, apnea, cyanosis, tachypnea, lethargy, and convulsions. Treatment with IV doses of dextrose should be instituted when blood levels of glucose fall below the normal range for the age and size of the infant. Normal values for blood glucose are 60–100 mg/100 ml in the newborn and 70–100 mg/100 ml in the child. In a full-sized infant, a level less than 30 mg/ml in the first 48 hours of life and less than 40 mg/ml thereafter is abnormal. In the low-birth-weight neonate, blood glucose levels less than 20 mg/100 ml represent significant hypoglycemia; this condition must be treated immediately.

The following glucose-elevating agents are included in this chapter:

- **Dextrose 50% (IV)**
- **Diazoxide**
- **Glucagon**

Dextrose 50% (IV)

ADMINISTRATION

Available Forms: Injectable (IV), 0.5 gm/ml (50%) in 50 ml syringes (25 gm).

Diluent: Can be diluted to 25% with equal parts of sterile water for injection.

Dosage (Parenteral): Dilute to 25% before use. Initially, 2–4 ml/kg/dose (0.5–1.0 gm/kg/dose) as an IV bolus given slowly over 1–2 minutes; can be followed by constant IV infusion of D10W or D15W 4–8 mg/kg/min (about 3–5 ml/kg/h of D10W).

Rate: Give IV boluses slowly (1 ml/min). Give IV infusions of D10W or D15W at 2–5 ml/kg/h.

INDICATIONS: Dextrose (25–50%) is given for rapid reversal of hypoglycemia due to many causes. Continuous IV infusion of 10% dextrose is used frequently for treatment of neonatal and infantile hypoglycemia.

ACTIONS: Dextrose is utilized quickly by excess insulin, causing reversal of hypoglycemia or insulin-induced coma.

CONTRAINDICATIONS: Intracranial or intraspinal hemorrhage.

PRECAUTIONS: Solutions of 50% dextrose are *extremely hypertonic* (D50W = 2526 mOsm/liter). Avoid use of 50% dextrose as it is highly irritating to veins, causes sclerosing, and may cause thrombosis; dilute it to 25% or less before administration. Give infusions through a large vein. Infusion rates faster than the body's ability to metabolize glucose (e.g., 0.5 gm/kg/hr) may result in osmotic diuresis, dehydration, or significant hyperglycemia. Monitor fluid and electrolyte balance (especially potassium) and blood glucose.

SIDE EFFECTS/ADVERSE REACTIONS: See precautions.

ANTIDOTE: Discontinue the infusion. Give insulin as necessary to treat hyperglycemia. Replace fluids lost through diuresis.

Diazoxide (Proglycem)

ADMINISTRATION

Available Forms: Capsules, 50, 100 mg; oral suspension, 50 mg/ml in 50 ml with calibrated dropper.

Dosage (Oral): 10–15 mg/kg/day, divided into 4 doses.

INDICATIONS: Oral doses of diazoxide are used primarily for management of mild hyperinsulinism (hypoglycemia associated with leucine sensitivity). It is not effective in infants with severe hyperinsulinism associated with pancreatic islet cell hyperplasia, adenomatosis, or adenoma, but it has been used preoperatively in these cases as a temporary hyperglycemic measure and postoperatively if hypoglycemia persists.

ACTIONS: Diazoxide raises blood glucose levels apparently by suppressing the pancreatic secretion of insulin, by stimulating release of catecholamines, by increasing the hepatic release of glucose, or by a combination of these. After oral administration, hyperglycemic effects appear in about 1 hour and last about 8 hours in patients with normal renal function. Diazoxide is highly protein-bound and may displace medications and other substances (e.g., bilirubin) from their protein-binding sites. It is partially metabolized and unchanged diazoxide and its metabolites are excreted in the urine. Diazoxide crosses the placenta, but its excretion in breast milk is undetermined.

CONTRAINDICATIONS: Hypersensitivity to thiazides, management of functional hypoglycemia.

PRECAUTIONS: Monitor levels of blood glucose and urine levels of sugar and acetone carefully until the patient's condition has stabilized. Observe the patient carefully for development of severe hyperglycemia (especially in patients with renal disease, disorders of carbohydrate metabolism, or liver disease). Use cautiously in patients with congestive heart failure or uremia as sodium and water retention occur frequently. Monitor fluid and electrolyte balance; hypokalemia potentiates the hyperglycemic effects of diazoxide. Fetal or neonatal hyperbilirubinemia, thrombocytopenia, and altered carbohydrate metabolism may occur. Periodic hematological monitoring is recommended during long-term therapy.

SIDE EFFECTS/ADVERSE REACTIONS: The primary side effects are sodium and fluid retention, hirsutism, and hyperuricemia. Diazoxide has caused hyperbilirubinemia, kernicterus, thrombocytopenia, severe hyperglycemia, and hyperosmolar coma in infants. Other reported effects include transient hypotension, extrapyramidal symptoms (dose-related), GI upset, accelerated bone maturation, blood dyscrasias, bleeding disorders, azotemia, and decreased renal output and function. Tightness in the chest, dyspnea, muscle and back pain, parotid swelling, salivation, dry mouth, tingling sensations, dizziness, euphoria, anxiety, and visual disturbances have also been reported (probably more prominent after IV use).

DRUG INTERACTIONS: Concomitant administration of *diuretics* may potentiate hyperglycemia, hyperuricemia, and hypotension. Diazoxide may potentiate the hypotensive effects of other *antihypertensives*. It may also displace *warfarin* and other highly protein-bound drugs from their plasma-binding sites, thus increasing their serum levels and possibly their toxicity. It may increase or decrease plasma levels of *phenytoin* (monitor clinical response carefully). Concomitant use with *phenytoin, corticosteroids,* or *estrogens* may potentiate hyperglycemia.

ANTIDOTE: Discontinue diazoxide. Administer insulin as necessary for severe hyperglycemia. Restore fluid and electrolyte balance. Prolonged surveillance is recommended since diazoxide has a long half-life (20–36 hours).

Glucagon

ADMINISTRATION

Available Forms: Injectable (IV, IM, SC), 1 mg (1 unit) and 10 mg (10 units) vials (powder).

Diluent: Use the packaged diluent provided (contains glycerin and phenol).

Dosage (Parenteral): 0.025 mg/kg as a single dose IV, IM, or SC; can be repeated in 20 minutes if necessary (for neonates, 0.3 mg/kg as a single dose).

INDICATIONS: Glucagon is used for emergency treatment of severe hypoglycemic reactions in diabetic patients who are receiving insulin.

ACTIONS: Glucagon is a polypeptide hormone produced by the alpha cells of the pancreatic islets of Langerhans. It elevates blood levels of glucose by converting liver glycogen to glucose; thus, glucagon is effective only when hepatic glycogen is available. Patients whose glycogen stores are decreased (e.g., conditions of starvation, adrenal insufficiency, or chronic hypoglycemia) are unable to respond to glucagon. Glucagon has a positive inotropic and chronotropic action on the heart. Because parenteral administration produces smooth muscle relaxation of the stomach, duodenum, small bowel, and colon, glucagon is useful as a diagnostic aid in the radiological examination of the GI tract. After parenteral administration, maximal hyperglycemic effects occur within 20–30 minutes. Blood levels of glucose return to normal or hypoglycemic levels within 1–2 hours. Glucagon is metabolized by the liver. It is ineffective when given orally.

CONTRAINDICATIONS: Hypersensitivity is a possibility because glucagon is a protein; avoid use in patients with hyperinsulinism.

PRECAUTIONS: Glucagon's hyperglycemic effect is relatively brief. As soon as possible after the patient responds, give supplementary carbohydrates (either orally or IV) to restore hepatic glycogen and to prevent secondary hypoglycemia. (This is especially important in juvenile diabetics as their response to glucagon is less pronounced than that of adults who have stable diabetes.) Failure to respond to glucagon therapy necessitates IV administration of glucose because of the potential deleterious effects of cerebral hypoglycemia. Other causes of coma should be considered if the patient fails to respond to glucagon. The hyperglycemic response may be reduced in emaciated, malnourished patients or in those with uremia or liver disease. Use cautiously in patients with insulin-secreting tumors (may cause rebound hypoglycemia) or pheochromocytoma (may cause hypertension).

SIDE EFFECTS/ADVERSE REACTIONS: Nausea and vomiting may occur, but may be due to hypoglycemia. Hypersensitivity reactions are possible since glucagon is a protein of animal origin.

DRUG INCOMPATIBILITIES: Glucagon is incompatible in any solution with a final pH of 3.0–9.5 (includes almost every commercial IV solution). Do not mix with any other medications.

ANTIDOTE: The hyperglycemic action of glucagon is brief. Treat rebound hypoglycemia with carbohydrate supplements.

XI
ANTIEMETICS, ANTIDIARRHEALS, AND GASTRIC ACID INHIBITORS

Although the GI tract is subject to a number of clinical problems, many of these upsets are uncomfortable but not serious. However, one of the most potentially serious problems in infants and children arises from the severe loss of fluids and electrolytes produced by continuing emesis or diarrhea. Nausea, vomiting, and diarrhea are only indicators of an underlying pathology that must be diagnosed and treated primarily. Antiemetics and antidiarrheals are only adjunctive therapy to aid in reducing fluid and electrolyte losses and to make the child more comfortable. Gastric acid inhibitors are used with antacids and other measures for the management of acute GI bleeding associated with peptic ulcer disease and gastritis.

Antiemetics are discussed in chapter 32 and antidiarrheals in chapter 33. Syrup of ipecac, an over-the-counter agent used to induce emesis, is discussed as an antidote in chapter 35. The gastric acid inhibitor cimetidine is covered in chapter 34.

32
Antiemetics

Nausea and vomiting are common nonspecific indicators associated with a variety of underlying disturbances. Among the many causes for emesis during infancy and childhood are bacterial and viral infections, esophageal dysfunction, intestinal obstructions, peptic ulcer, increased intracranial pressure, intolerance of feeding formulas, food poisoning, metabolic disturbances, uremia, Reye's syndrome, adrenal insufficiency, radiation therapy, painful or noxious stimuli, and emotional distress.

Antiemetic therapy is directed toward diagnosing and treating the cause while replacing the fluids and electrolytes lost through emesis. Use of antiemetics in children is often undesirable since these agents may mask signs of an undiagnosed primary disease with CNS symptoms (e.g., brain tumors, Reye's syndrome, encephalopathies) or other conditions such as intestinal obstruction, appendicitis, or drug overdose. However, antiemetics may be tried when alternative measures have failed to control acute or prolonged vomiting.

Antiemetics prevent or relieve nausea and vomiting by acting centrally on the brain's chemoreceptor trigger zone (CTZ), the vomiting center in the medulla, or by acting on the vestibular apparatus of the ear. Oral forms are more useful for the prevention of emesis; parenteral and rectal forms are preferable for treatment of acute vomiting.

Although the phenothiazines are the most effective antiemetics in adults on a single-dose basis, they can produce severe toxic reactions in infants and children. Prochlorperazine in particular causes a high incidence of severe and disabling extrapyramidal reactions in pediatric patients. For this reason, its use is contraindicated in infants and children so it is not included in this chapter. Antiemetics from the antihistamine class have a lower incidence of toxicity and are preferable for pediatric use.

The following antiemetics are discussed in this chapter:

- **Chlorpromazine**
- **Diphenidol**
- **Hydroxyzine**
- **Promethazine**

Chlorpromazine (Thorazine)

ADMINISTRATION

Available Forms: Injectable (IM, IV), 25 mg/ml in 1 and 2 ml amps and syringes and 10 ml vials; tablets, 10, 25, 50, 100, 200 mg; oral syrup, 10 mg/5 ml; oral concentrate, 30 and 100 mg per milliliter (*not* for pediatric use); suppositories, 25, 100 mg. (Sustained-release capsules are available, but these are used primarily for antipsychotic therapy.)

Diluent: Can be diluted with NS (25 mg/25 ml); IV use is not recommended, however.

Dosage (Parenteral): Varies according to use.
For antiemesis or sedation:

- Infants (>6 months old) and children: 0.55 mg/kg given deep IM q6–8h prn. Half doses can be given slowly IV, but hypotension may be severe.

For control of shivering during induced hypothermia: 0.1–0.2 mg/kg/dose IM or IV.
For drug withdrawal in infants: 1.5–3.0 mg/kg/day IM in divided doses (q6h). Switch to oral doses when feasible.

Dosage (Oral)
For antiemesis or sedation:

- Infants (>6 months old) and children: 2 mg/kg/day (60 mg/m^2/day) in divided doses (q4–6h)

Dosage (Rectal)
For antiemesis or sedation:

- Infants (>6 months old) and children: 1.1 mg/kg q6–8h prn

Rate: Give IV bolus doses over at least 1–2 minutes.

INDICATIONS: Chlorpromazine (CPZ) is a prototype phenothiazine used for control of nausea and vomiting (except that caused by motion sickness), for preoperative sedation, (see DPT cocktail), and for sedation in hyperexcitable or psychotic behavior. It has been given as adjunctive treatment for symptoms of drug withdrawal in infants born to addicted mothers. Small doses help prevent shivering and central pooling when hypothermia must be induced for the management of cerebral edema and CNS resuscitation. Other uses include treatment of intractable hiccups, rheumatic chorea, drug-induced hypertension, and LSD or amphetamine overdoses.

ACTIONS: Chlorpromazine acts centrally to depress both the CTZ and the vomiting center and produces sedation without hypnosis. It relieves anxiety and suppresses combative behavior. It also has antihistamine effects, reduces muscle tone, lowers the convulsive threshold, alters the body's temperature regulation mechanism, and acts on the autonomic nervous system to cause anticholinergic and alpha-adrenergic blocking effects. After parenteral administration onset of action occurs within 30 minutes; duration is usually 3–4 hours, but may be up to 12 hours in children. Oral use produces effects within 30–60 minutes; these last 4–6 hours. Rectal doses have a slower onset of action than oral doses, and duration is shorter, about 3–4 hours. Chlorpromazine is metabolized in the liver and kidney; metabolites and unchanged chlorpromazine are excreted in the urine. It crosses the placenta and is excreted in breast milk.

CONTRAINDICATIONS: Hypersensitivity or toxic reactions to any of the phenothiazines, children less than 6 months of age, comatose states or depressed states due to CNS depressant drugs, bone marrow depression.

PRECAUTIONS: See also promethazine. Chlorpromazine causes extrapyramidal effects, especially in children, but less so than promethazine. Extrapyramidal and antiemetic effects may mask symptoms of CNS disease, brain tumors, Reye's syndrome and other encephalopathies, intestinal obstruction, and overdoses with other medications. Sedation and drowsiness may be troublesome, so caution ambulatory patients accordingly. Reduce doses of narcotics and other CNS depressants by 50–75% when starting chlorpromazine. Use cautiously in patients with seizure disorders, dehydration, fever, chronic respiratory disorders, asthma (especially children), hepatic or cardiac impairment, or conditions aggravated by anticholinergic activity; and in those who are exposed to extreme heat or concomitantly receiving atropine or other anticholinergics. Monitor vital signs frequently (especially blood pressure and pulse). Replace fluid and electrolytes lost by emesis as necessary. Solutions are light-sensitive; do not use if extremely yellowed. Contact dermatitis may occur if solutions come in contact with skin and clothing. Inject IM doses slowly and deeply; avoid SC injections.

SIDE EFFECTS/ADVERSE REACTIONS: As for promethazine. However, sedation is prominent, but extrapyramidal symptoms are less than with promethazine. In addition, use of chlorpromazine is associated with a high incidence of anticholinergic side effects. Cardiovascular effects include hypotension, tachycardia, shock-like syndromes, and cardiac arrest. Mild fever may occur with large IM doses. Chlorpromazine may also induce jaundice.

DRUG INCOMPATIBILITIES: Can be mixed with atropine, scopolamine, morphine, or meperidine in the same syringe if used within 15 minutes. Avoid admixing with any other medications.

DRUG INTERACTIONS: See promethazine. Also, chlorpromazine may reduce the convulsive threshold and precipitate seizures in patients on *anticonvulsants*.

ANTIDOTE: See promethazine.

Diphenidol (Vontrol)

ADMINISTRATION

Available Forms: Injectable (IM), 20 mg/ml in 2 ml amps; tablets, 25 mg; suppositories, 25, 50 mg (contain benzocaine).

Dosage (Parenteral)
Children >6 months old and >12 kg: 0.44 mg/kg deep IM; can be repeated in 1 hour if necessary; give subsequent doses q4h prn. Maximum dose is 3.3 mg/kg/day.

Dosage (Oral, Rectal)
Children >6 months old and >12 kg: 0.88 mg/kg; can be repeated in 1 hour if necessary; give subsequent doses q4h prn. Maximum is 5.5 mg/kg/day (150 mg/m^2/day).

INDICATIONS: Diphenidol is used to control nausea and vomiting associated with surgery, radiation treatment, malignant neoplasms, antineoplastic therapy, infectious diseases, and labyrinthine disturbances. It is also effective in the prevention and treatment of motion sickness and vertigo caused by ear surgery or Meniere's disease.

ACTIONS: Diphenidol is structurally unrelated to antihistamines or phenothiazines. It apparently produces antiemesis by inhibiting conduction through the vestibular-cerebellar apparatus and by depressing the CTZ. It has weak peripheral anticholinergic effects and no appreciable antihistaminic activity. Onset of action after IM administration occurs within 30–40 minutes, and duration of antiemesis is 4–6 hours. Peak blood levels occur 1.5–3.0 hours after oral administration. The metabolic fate of diphenidol is unknown, but most of an oral dose is excreted in the urine as metabolites and a small amount of unchanged antiemetic.

CONTRAINDICATIONS: Hypersensitivity to diphenidol, anuria, hypotension (parenteral use), children less than 6 months old or less than 12 kg in weight.

PRECAUTIONS: Do not administer IV or SC in children. Close medical supervision is necessary during diphenidol administration because it can cause auditory and visual hallucinations, confusion, and disorientation, usually within the first 3 days of use; discontinue the medication if such a reaction occurs. Parenteral administration may cause a decrease in systolic and diastolic blood pressures of up to 20 mm Hg. Use cautiously in patients with conditions aggravated by anticholinergic activity (e.g., glaucoma, pylorospasm or stenosing peptic ulcer, other obstructing GI or genitourinary lesions, organic cardiospasm or tachycardia). The antiemetic effects may mask symptoms of overdoses of other drugs, intestinal obstruction, brain tumors, Reye's syndrome, or other CNS disease. Monitor vital signs (especially blood pressure and pulse). Replace fluid and electrolytes lost through emesis as needed. Diphenidol may cause drowsiness; caution ambulatory patients accordingly.

SIDE EFFECTS/ADVERSE REACTIONS: Occasional side effects are drowsiness, dizziness, and dry mouth. Hypotension may occur after IM use. Discontinue diphenidol if auditory or visual hallucinations or disorientation or confusion occur (usually develops within 3 days and dissipates within 3 days of drug withdrawal). Other reported effects include tachycardia, palpitation, headache, nausea, indigestion, rash, blurred vision, malaise, overstimulation, and sleep disturbances.

DRUG INTERACTIONS: Diphenidol may potentiate the anticholinergic effects of *atropine* and other *anticholinergics*.

ANTIDOTE: Discontinue diphenidol. With early overdose caused by ingestion, gastric lavage may be useful. Treat overdoses with general supportive therapy, including maintenance of blood pressure and respiration.

Hydroxyzine (Atarax, Vistaril)

ADMINISTRATION

Available Forms: Injectable (IM), 25 and 50 mg per milliliter in 1, 2, and 10 ml vials; tablets, 10, 25, 50, 100 mg (Atarax); capsules, 25, 50, 100 mg (Vistaril); oral syrup, 10 mg/5 ml (Atarax); oral suspension, 25 mg/5 ml (Vistaril).

Dosage (Parenteral)
For antiemesis: 1.1 mg/kg (30 mg/m^2) IM as a single dose.

Dosage (Oral)
For antiemesis, antianxiety, or sedation: 2 mg/kg/day (60 mg/m^2/day), divided into 4 doses.

- Children <6 years old: Maximum is 50 mg/day.
- Children >6 years old: Maximum is 100 mg/day.

INDICATIONS: Hydroxyzine is used to control emesis and to reduce preoperative and postoperative narcotic requirements. It is also used as a mild calming agent to reduce anxiety, tension, and agitation associated with emotional or psychoneurotic states. It may be useful in the relief of histamine-induced pruritus and urticaria.

ACTIONS: Hydroxyzine is an antihistaminic compound that exhibits CNS depressant, anticholinergic, antiemetic, antispasmodic, mild gastric antisecretory, and local anesthetic effects. It has some minor skeletal-muscle-relaxant activity and produces only minimal circulatory or respiratory depression. Onset of action of oral doses is within 15–30 minutes, and IM doses probably act more rapidly. The metabolic fate of hydroxyzine is unknown. Hydroxyzine may be teratogenic, and it is not recommended for nursing mothers.

CONTRAINDICATIONS: Hypersensitivity to hydroxyzine, early pregnancy.

PRECAUTIONS: Do not administer IV, SC, or by inadvertent intra-arterial injection. In children inject into the midlateral muscles of the thigh. Hydroxyzine may produce transient drowsiness; caution ambulatory patients accordingly. Reduce dosages of other CNS depressants (e.g., narcotics, sedatives) if used with hydroxyzine. Replace fluid and electrolytes lost through emesis as indicated.

SIDE EFFECTS/ADVERSE REACTIONS: Hydroxyzine has a low incidence of toxicity. Transient drowsiness and dry mouth commonly occur. Doses given IM may produce pain and discomfort at the injection site. Inadvertent intra-arterial injection causes endarteritis, thrombosis, and digital gangrene. Doses given SC cause tissue induration. Rarely (particularly with high doses), involuntary motor activity, tremor, convulsions, dizziness, urticaria, and various rashes have occurred.

DRUG INCOMPATIBILITIES: Do not mix with barbiturates, diazepam, or other benzodiazepines in the same syringe. Hydroxyzine *can* be mixed with atropine, morphine, meperidine, pentazocine, promethazine, or scopolamine in the same syringe, however.

DRUG INTERACTIONS: Hydroxyzine causes additive CNS depression when used with *alcohol, narcotics, sedative-hypnotics, tricyclic antidepressants,* or other *CNS depressants.* (Reduce dosage of these agents accordingly.)

ANTIDOTE: Discontinue the medication. If ingestion was recent, empty the stomach with gastric lavage. Induced emesis may not be effective. Monitor vital signs. Treat adverse reactions symptomatically and supportively. Hypotension can be treated with IV fluids or levarterenol (do not use epinephrine because hydroxyzine antagonizes the vasopressor effect). Support respiration.

Promethazine (Phenergan)

ADMINISTRATION

Available Forms: Injectable (IM, IV), 25 and 50 mg per milliliter in 1 ml amps and syringes; tablets, 12.5, 25.0, 50.0 mg; oral syrup, 6.25, 12.50, and 25.00 mg per milliliter; suppositories, 25, 50 mg.

Diluent: Can be diluted in D5W or NS for IV use. Do not exceed a concentration of 25 mg/ml.

Dosage (Parenteral): 0.5 mg/kg/dose (15 mg/m^2/dose) given q4–6h deep IM.
As antihistamine: Full dose at bedtime and one-fourth dose in the morning or prn.
As antiemetic: 0.25–0.50 mg/kg/dose IM q4–6h prn.
Preoperative dose: 0.5–1.0 mg/kg/dose IM.

Dosage (Oral or Rectal): Same as parenteral dose.
For motion sickness: Full dose repeated q12h prn.

Rate: If given IV administer no faster than 25 mg/min.

INDICATIONS: Promethazine is a phenothiazine derivative with potent antihistaminic properties. It is used primarily as an antiemetic in motion sickness and for nausea and vomiting associated with surgery. Because of its prominent sedative action, it is useful as a preoperative medication and as an adjunct to analgesia with narcotic and non-narcotic analgesics. However, this pronounced sedative effect limits its usefulness as an antihistamine in ambulatory patients.

ACTIONS: Promethazine has antiemetic, antihistaminic, and anticholinergic effects similar to those of other antihistamines. Although it can produce CNS excitation, CNS depression with sedation is more common with therapeutic doses. It has no significant effects on the cardiovascular system in normal doses, but rapid IV administration may cause hypotension. Onset of action is rapid (within 3–5 minutes) after IV administration, and within 20 minutes for all other routes. Promethazine is metabolized by the liver and excreted in the urine and feces.

CONTRAINDICATIONS: Known hypersensitivity to promethazine or other phenothiazines, patients who are comatose or receiving large doses of other CNS depressants.

PRECAUTIONS: Use cautiously in patients with cardiovascular disease, impaired liver function, asthmatic attacks, or conditions aggravated by anticholinergic action. Promethazine may suppress the cough reflex; use it carefully in children with acute or chronic respiratory impairment. Neonates, infants, and children, especially those acutely ill and dehydrated, may be more susceptible than adults to the dystonias and extrapyramidal symptoms. Paradoxical excitability and abnormal movements may follow a single dose. Epileptic patients may experience increased severity of convulsions. Giving excessive amounts for pain without providing adequate analgesic coverage may cause restlessness and motor hyperactivity. Use cautiously in patients with bone marrow suppression since the medication may cause additional leukopenia and agranulocytosis. Inject IM doses slowly and deeply. Chemical irritation and tissue necrosis can occur if doses are given SC or if extravasation occurs during IV administration. Inadvertent intra-arterial injection may cause serious arteriospasm and gangrene. Administer IV doses slowly to avoid hypotension. Solutions are light-sensitive and should not be used if severely yellowed.

SIDE EFFECTS/ADVERSE REACTIONS: The most common adverse reactions are sedation, confusion, and disorientation. Nightmares and CNS excitation may occur in children receiving single high doses of 75–125 mg. Other reported CNS stimulatory effects include tremors, hysteria, convulsive seizures, oculogyric crises, and catatonia-like states. Anticholinergic effects; extrapyramidal symptoms; gastric upset; and cardiovascular effects including tachycardia, bradycardia, hypotension, and hypertension may occur. Hypersensitivity, photosensitivity, and blood dyscrasias occur rarely.

DRUG INTERACTIONS: Use with *barbiturates* and *narcotic analgesics* causes additive sedation and CNS depression. (Reduce doses of each of these by 25–50% when given together with promethazine.) Additive anticholinergic effects occur when promethazine is given with *atropine* and atropine-like compounds. Promethazine reverses the vasopressor effect of *epinephrine*. Additive antihistaminic effects occur when it is used with other *antihistamines*.

ANTIDOTE: Discontinue promethazine. Treat adverse reactions symptomatically and supportively. *Do not use CNS stimulants* or induce emesis. Treat severe hypotension with norepinephrine or phenylephrine (alpha agonists). *Do not use epinephrine* as it may further lower blood pressure. Convulsions can be treated with diazepam or short-acting barbiturates. Anticholinergic antiparkinson medications (e.g., benztropine) or diphenhydramine may control extrapyramidal symptoms. Mechanically assisted ventilation may be necessary.

33
Antidiarrheals

Uncontrolled diarrhea can cause critical dehydration and electrolyte loss in infants and children. It can be chronic or acute and can be caused by a number of factors. These include bacterial, viral, or parasitic infections; intoxication with drugs or other toxic substances; malabsorption syndromes; GI inflammation; metabolic disturbances; cystic fibrosis; allergy; and tumors. The readiness with which diarrhea subsides depends on the underlying cause, which must be primarily diagnosed and treated. Injudicious use of antidiarrheals can mask symptoms of serious GI disease.

Children with acute diarrhea and minimal dehydration are best treated without the use of these medications. Administration of clear fluids, juices, or oral electrolyte-rehydrating solutions (see chapter 10) is usually effective in replacing fluid losses during the first 24 hours. Bland solids can be added after 24–48 hours. Large-volume feedings should be avoided because they stimulate the gastrocolic reflex, which aggravates the problem. Small-volume feedings (30–60 ml) given hourly, as tolerated, are recommended.

Antidiarrheals act either by adsorbing toxins (kaolin-pectin) or by decreasing propulsive contractions of the GI tract to slow gut motility (belladonna compounds, diphenoxylate, paregoric). The value of these medications in infants and young children is questionable, and their use in this age group should be discouraged. If the use of an antispasmodic antidiarrheal, such as diphenoxylate or paregoric, is considered, it should be used sparingly and only in older children or adolescents. In general, antispasmodic agents may give a false sense of security because even when GI spasm is reduced, fluid losses continue to occur into the gut lumen. In addition, use of antidiarrheals that slow GI motility may actually be deleterious in infectious diarrhea because expulsion of the infected GI contents and bacterial toxins may be a protective mechanism and therefore desirable.

Diarrhea caused by infecting pathogens should be treated with the appropriate antibiotics.

There are many antidiarrheal combinations available, but only a representative few are discussed in this chapter:

- **Diphenoxylate with atropine**
- **Paregoric**
- **Paregoric with kaolin-pectin**

Diphenoxylate with atropine (Lomotil)

ADMINISTRATION

Available Forms: Tablets, 2.5 mg diphenoxylate with 0.025 mg atropine; oral liquid, 2.5 mg diphenoxylate and 0.025 mg atropine per 5 ml.

Dosage (Oral): (Dosages are based on diphenoxylate concentration.)
Children 2–5 years old: 6 mg/day (12 ml liquid), in divided doses (q8h).
Children 5–8 years old: 8 mg/day (16 ml liquid), in divided doses (q6h).
Children 8–12 years old: 10 mg/day (20 ml liquid or 4 tablets) divided into 5 doses.
Adults: 15–20 mg/day divided into 4–6 doses.

INDICATIONS: Diphenoxylate with atropine is indicated for adjunctive treatment of nonspecific diarrhea. It should not be used in diarrhea that is secondary to poisonings until the toxic material is eliminated from the GI tract by gastric lavage or cathartics. It should not be used in diarrhea caused by toxigenic bacteria or amoebas.

ACTIONS: Diphenoxylate with atropine acts on the smooth muscle of the intestinal tract to inhibit GI motility and excessive propulsion. Subtherapeutic amounts of atropine are added to discourage abuse of this meperidine cogener, but "atropinism" may occur in young children. Antidiarrheal effects begin about 1 hour after administration and last about 3–4 hours. Diphenoxylate is metabolized in the liver (one metabolite is active) and excreted primarily in the feces and bile (a small amount is excreted in the urine). It crosses the placenta and is excreted in breast milk.

CONTRAINDICATIONS: Hypersensitivity to atropine or diphenoxylate; obstructive jaundice; pseudomembranous colitis; infectious diarrhea caused by *E. coli, Salmonella, Shigella,* or other invasive organisms; children less than 2 years of age.

PRECAUTIONS: Use of this compound is not recommended in infants and young children because they are more susceptible to atropine poisoning. Correct severe dehydration and electrolyte imbalances with appropriate fluid and electrolyte replacements before instituting antidiarrheal therapy since dehydration may predispose the patient to delayed diphenoxylate intoxication. Inhibition of peristalsis may cause fluid retention in the bowel that is great enough to mask and further aggravate dehydration and electrolyte imbalances (especially with acute enteritis in children). Diphenoxylate with atropine may induce toxic megacolon in patients with acute ulcerative colitis. Use in infectious diarrhea may be deleterious because expulsion of intestinal contents is a protective mechanism. Use with extreme caution in patients with advanced liver disease, cirrhosis, or abnormal liver function tests since hepatic coma may be precipitated.

SIDE EFFECTS/ADVERSE REACTIONS: Atropine effects including dry mouth, skin, and mucous membranes; thirst; flushing; urinary retention; tachycardia; hyperthermia; and blurred vision may occur, especially in children. Other adverse reactions include dizziness, drowsiness, sedation, headache, anorexia, nausea, vomiting, paralytic ileus, toxic megacolon, numbness in the extremities, malaise, restlessness, euphoria, mental depression, respiratory depression, and coma. Hypersensitivity reactions include pruritus, swelling of the gums, urticaria, and angioneurotic edema.

DRUG INTERACTIONS: Concomitant use with other *CNS depressants* causes additive CNS depression. Additive anticholinergic effects occur when used with *atropine-like drugs, antihistamines,* or *antispasmolytic agents*. Because it is a meperidine cogener, diphenoxylate with atropine may precipitate hypertensive crisis in patients receiving *MAO inhibitors*.

ANTIDOTE: Discontinue the medication. Maintain an open airway and assist ventilation as necessary. If the patient is conscious, induce emesis or use gastric lavage to empty the stomach and then give activated charcoal. Give naloxone (0.01 mg/kg IV for children) to reverse respiratory depression; dose can be repeated as needed at 2–3 minute intervals. Monitor the patient for at least 48 hours for recurrence of symptoms. Treat "atropinism" with IV doses of physostigmine.

Paregoric (camphorated opium tincture)
Paregoric with kaolin-pectin (Parepectolin)

ADMINISTRATION

Available Forms: Oral liquid, equivalent to 0.4 mg morphine/ml (Paregoric-Schedule III controlled substance). Parepectolin contains 3.7 ml paregoric, 162 mg pectin, and 5.5 gm kaolin per 30 ml.

Dosage (Paregoric): 0.25–0.50 ml/kg/dose, up to 4 times daily.

Dosage (Paregoric with Kaolin-Pectin): 2.5–10.0 ml/dose given after each evacuation; no more than 4 doses in 12 hours.

INDICATIONS: Paregoric with or without kaolin-pectin is used as adjunctive therapy for treatment of nonspecific diarrhea. (Addition of kaolin-pectin is of doubtful efficiency since the antidiarrheal effect is exclusively due to the paregoric constituent.)

ACTIONS: The antidiarrheal effect of paregoric is due to the morphine, which slows GI motility. The action of kaolin-pectin is questionable, but it is claimed to act as an adsorbent and protectant.

CONTRAINDICATIONS: Hypersensitivity to morphine, convulsive states (e.g., status epilepticus, tetanus, or strychnine poisoning), diarrhea caused by poisoning (before the toxic material is eliminated from the GI tract), suspected obstructive bowel lesions (kaolin-pectin).

PRECAUTIONS: *Do not confuse with opium tincture, which is 25 times more potent.* Paregoric may be habit-forming, particularly in addiction-prone individuals; patients on therapy for 1–2 weeks have experienced mild withdrawal symptoms. (Short courses of therapy with the usual oral doses rarely cause problems, however.) All other precautions are the same as those for morphine (see chapter 24).

SIDE EFFECTS/ADVERSE REACTIONS: The usual antidiarrheal doses may cause light-headedness, dizziness, sedation, nausea, or vomiting. Euphoria, dysphoria, analgesia, and respiratory depression may occur with higher doses. Pruritus and constipation may also occur.

DRUG INTERACTIONS: See morphine (chapter 24).

ANTIDOTE: See morphine (chapter 24).

34
Gastric Acid Inhibitors

Peptic ulcer disease with associated gastritis and esophagitis is reported with increasing frequency in childhood. Ulcers in infants and young children often result in bleeding, perforation, or obstruction and can be related to inflammatory disease, sepsis, steroid therapy, burns, CNS disorders, or ingestion of corrosive chemicals. The major therapeutic objective is to control acidity and peptic activity thereby allowing the ulcer to heal. Frequent neutralization with antacids is indicated in acute cases. Control of gastric acid and pepsin secretion is accomplished by the administration of the gastric acid inhibitors, cimetidine (Tagamet) and ranitidine (Zantac). Studies on the use of these agents in pediatric patients are very limited. Since there has been more experience with cimetidine, it is the only gastric acid inhibitor discussed in this chapter.

Cimetidine (Tagamet)

ADMINISTRATION

Available Forms: Injectable (IV), 150 mg/ml in 2 and 8 ml vials; tablets, 200, 300 and 400 mg; oral solution, 60 mg/ml.

Diluent: For intermittent IV infusions doses can be diluted in at least 20 ml of D5W, NS, or other multiple electrolyte solutions. The usual dilution is 300 mg in 50–100 ml.

Dosage (Parenteral): Varies according to the patient's age.
Children <12 years old: 20–40 mg/kg/day IV in divided doses (q6h).
Children >12 years old: 300 mg IV q6h.

Dosage (Oral): Varies according to the patient's age.
Children <12 years old: 20–40 mg/kg/day in divided doses (q6h).
Children >12 years old: 300 mg q6h.

Rate: Give doses for intermittent IV infusions over 15–20 minutes.

INDICATIONS: Cimetidine is used in the management of acute GI bleeding associated with peptic ulcer disease, gastritis, or esophagitis. It is also commonly used for prophylaxis against upper intestinal bleeding. Concomitant administration of antacids to neutralize gastric acid is usually necessary.

ACTIONS: Cimetidine is an H_2-receptor antagonist. By inhibiting the action of histamine on these receptors in gastric parietal cells, cimetidine reduces gastric acid secretion both during fasting and during stimulation by food, insulin, or histamine. It also indirectly diminishes pepsin secretion by decreasing the volume of gastric juice. Peak blood levels are reached immediately after IV administration and within 1 hour after oral doses. Basal gastric acid secretion is diminished 80–100% by peak blood levels greater than 1.0 µg/ml and 50–80% by levels of 0.5 µg/ml. These levels usually persist for 4–5 hours after IV or oral doses. Cimetidine is partially metabolized by the liver, but 50–70% is excreted unchanged by the kidney; severe renal impairment and hepatic impairment can cause drug accumulation.

CONTRAINDICATIONS: None known.

PRECAUTIONS: Give IV doses slowly to avoid possible hypotension and cardiac arrhythmias. If peptic ulcer disease, gastritis, or esophagitis is present, give antacids hourly in a dose of 1 ml/kg (up to 30 ml/dose) to neutralize gastric acid. Magnesium hydroxide antacids (Maalox, Mylanta) can be alternated with aluminum hydroxide mixtures (Amphojel) to prevent diarrhea or constipation. In patients with severe renal impairment, the dosage interval should be reduced to q12h.

SIDE EFFECTS/ADVERSE REACTIONS: Mild and transient diarrhea, dizziness, somnolence, muscle pain, urticaria, transient rashes, and neutropenia have been reported. Rapid administration of IV boluses has been associated with hypotension and rare cardiac arrhythmias.

DRUG INCOMPATIBILITIES: Do not mix with cephalothin, cefamandole, cefazolin, or barbiturates.

DRUG INTERACTIONS: By suppressing the action of hepatic microsomal enzymes, cimetidine can inhibit the metabolism of certain drugs such as *theophylline, phenytoin, diazepam,* and *propranolol.* The result is higher serum levels and possible toxic levels of these medications.

ANTIDOTE: Discontinue cimetidine. Up to 10 gm have been ingested without adverse effects, but potential respiratory failure and tachycardia could occur. Remove unabsorbed drug from the stomach by emesis or gastric lavage followed by activated charcoal. Treat tachycardia with propranolol. Monitor the patient and provide supportive therapy as needed.

XII
TREATMENT OF POISONINGS

Many poisons, including ingested drug overdoses, can be adsorbed and neutralized, or their toxic effects can be antagonized by specific pharmacological antidotes.

Chapter 35 includes drugs used exclusively as antidotes to specific types of chemical and drug poisonings.

Chapter 36 discusses antivenins indicated for treatment of certain poisonous snake and insect bites, and chapter 37 describes antiserums used to provide rapid but brief passive immunity after exposure to certain infectious microorganisms.

A table of routine and specialized immunizing agents has also been provided in the appendix.

35
Antidotes

Poisoning is still one of the most common causes of childhood morbidity and mortality. Children under 5 years of age constitute about 90% of recorded cases of poison ingestion. Fortunately, the frequency of poisonings has decreased because of the more widespread use of safety packaging of toxic and potentially toxic substances and because of better parental education.

Poisonings and drug overdoses can be classified into two categories: (1) those with specific antidotes and treatment, and (2) those for which there is no specific antidote or treatment. Unfortunately, most poisonings fall into this second category. In these cases, one must rely on supportive and symptomatic therapy, including mechanical or chemical removal of the ingested poison; maintenance of fluid and electrolyte balance; stabilization of vital signs; support of respiration, renal, and cardiovascular function; and so forth. The toxicologist's adage, "Treat the patient, not his poison," still underscores the importance of symptomatic and supportive therapy of all poisonings.

Before therapy is begun, the poison must first be identified, and the time of ingestion or exposure must be established through careful questioning and physical examination. A recently ingested toxic substance can usually be removed mechanically by gastric lavage and aspiration or chemically by inducing emesis. These measures should *not* be employed if corrosives (e.g., acids and alkalies) or petroleum distillates have been ingested, if emesis may trigger convulsions (e.g., ingestion of CNS stimulants such as strychnine), or where aspiration of vomitus is possible (e.g., coma, uncooperative or extremely restless states). Many medications and toxins can be adsorbed by activated charcoal and their further systemic absorption thereby prevented. Enemas may sometimes be helpful in removing overdoses of materials given rectally.

If enough time has elapsed between ingestion and initiation of therapy (usually more than 30 to 60 minutes), all or a large part of the chemical may already be absorbed, making gastric removal or the use of activated charcoal ineffective. Enhancing excretion of the toxin by forced fluid or osmotic diuresis, by acidification or alkalinization of the urine, or by use of diuretics may be indicated, but these methods do involve some risk. Severe cases of poisoning may warrant use of exchange transfusions, peritoneal dialysis, or hemodialysis. Exchange transfusions can be particularly effective in small children for poisonings caused by highly protein-bound agents. Peritoneal dialysis is useful for children in instances of electrolyte and acid-base disturbances and for drugs and chemicals that are not so tightly protein-bound or that have a high dialysis clearance across the peritoneum. Hemodialysis and lipid dialysis are less commonly used in pediatric poisonings. (Consult current toxicology texts or regional poison control centers for information regarding dialyzable drugs and poisons.)

This chapter considers some of the more commonly used antidotes, including those that have nonspecific activity against a variety of poisons and those that are direct pharmacological antagonists of a particular drug or group of drugs. The following antidotes are discussed in this chapter:

- **N-Acetylcysteine**
- **Activated charcoal**
- **Cyanide antidote package**
- **Deferoxamine mesylate**
- **Dimercaprol**
- **Edetate calcium disodium**
- **Syrup of ipecac**
- **Methylene blue**
- **Naloxone**
- **Penicillamine**
- **Physostigmine salicylate**
- **Pralidoxime**
- **Sodium polystyrene sulfonate**

Some of the other medications used as antidotes have already been discussed in other chapters: atropine, calcium gluconate, dextrose, diphenhydramine, epinephrine, glucagon, phytonadione, and protamine sulfate.

An extensive discussion of therapy for the many and varied types of poisonings that may be encountered in the pediatric emergency setting is beyond the scope of this book. The reader should refer to the many available toxicology texts for this purpose.

N-Acetylcysteine (Mucomyst)

ADMINISTRATION

Available Form: Topical solution, 10 and 20% in 4, 10, and 30 ml vials.

Diluent: The 20% solution can be diluted with three parts cola, orange or grapefruit juice, or water to achieve a 5% solution, which is approximately isotonic. The mixture should be consumed within 1 hour of preparation.

Dosage (Oral)

For treatment of acute acetaminophen overdosage: Initially, a loading dose of 140 mg/kg, followed by 70 mg/kg in 4 hours and q4h thereafter over a period of 68 hours (i.e., 17 maintenance doses). If the patient vomits any of the doses within 1 hour of administration, repeat the dose. Doses can also be administered by duodenal intubation.

INDICATIONS: N-acetylcysteine has been used investigationally as an effective antidote for acute acetaminophen overdose. Best results are obtained if this preparation is given within 24 hours of the acetaminophen ingestion. Clinical experience indicates that children less than 5 years old appear to be more resistant than adults to the hepatic effects of acetaminophen overdose, and even mild hepatic toxicity is remarkably rare in this age group. However, as in the adult, treatment is recommended. In adults, hepatic necrosis may occur with ingested doses greater than 10 gm or with plasma levels higher than 300 μg/ml at 4 hours (or 50 μg/ml at 12 hours) following acute overdoses. Hepatic damage is likely if the half-life of acetaminophen exceeds 4 hours, and hepatic coma may occur if it exceeds 12 hours (normal half-life is 2.75–3.25 hours in adults and longer in neonates and infants).

ACTIONS: N-acetylcysteine provides cysteine, which is a glutathione precursor. An active intermediate metabolite of acetaminophen is the hepatotoxic entity; it is normally conjugated by glutathione and rendered nontoxic. In acetaminophen overdose, the body's glutathione stores are insufficient to complex and detoxify this metabolite. Oral administration of N-acetylcysteine provides the necessary glutathione for detoxification. The clinical picture of acetaminophen toxicity involves several phases. The first phase begins shortly after ingestion and lasts 12–24 hours. Signs and symptoms include gastric upset, nausea, vomiting, anorexia, pallor, diaphoresis, and methemoglobinemia. If toxicity ensues, a latent period of 24–48 hours (sometimes up to 4 days) may occur in which earlier symptoms abate but hepatic necrosis progresses. Hepatic enzymes, serum levels of bilirubin, and prothrombin time increase, and pain develops in the right upper quadrant as the liver becomes enlarged and tender. If toxicity progresses beyond 3–5 days, further hepatic damage develops and, in severe cases, confusion, stupor, hepatic necrosis with jaundice, coagulation defects, hypoglycemia, encephalopathy, renal failure, and myocardiopathy may occur. Death is usually due to hepatic failure.

CONTRAINDICATIONS: Hypersensitivity to N-acetylcysteine.

PRECAUTIONS: Supportive therapy should include gastric emptying by lavage or by induction of emesis with syrup of ipecac (within 12 hours of acute ingestion). *Do not administer activated charcoal since it will inactivate N-acetylcysteine.* N-acetylcysteine should be given within 24 hours of the toxic ingestion. Draw blood for acetaminophen level *stat* and again in four hours. If the serum level of acetaminophen has decreased to 120 µg/ml or less at the 4 hour determination and there is no clinical or laboratory evidence of toxicity, N-acetylcysteine can be discontinued. Maintain fluid and electrolyte balance. Monitor urine output; liver enzymes (SGOT, SGPT, bilirubin); prothrombin time; and serum glucose, CO_2, and creatinine at 24 hour intervals. Treat hypoglycemia if indicated. Administer phytonadione (vitamin K), and plasma or clotting factor concentrates if the prothrombin time ratio is prolonged (i.e., 1.5–3.0). Avoid use of diuretics, forced diuresis, or dialysis as these measures have been associated with increased morbidity and mortality.

SIDE EFFECTS/ADVERSE REACTIONS: Oral doses of N-acetylcysteine are well tolerated with the exception of possible nausea and vomiting.

Activated charcoal

ADMINISTRATION

Available Forms: Bulk powder.

Diluent: Prepare a slurry in water.

Dosage (Oral): The proper dose is 5–10 times, by weight, the estimated amount of the ingested toxin. Usually 1–2 tablespoons (tbsp) or 0.5–1.0 gm/kg are mixed in 8 oz of water and given orally or instilled into a nasogastric tube (up to 10–12 tbsp or 30–50 grams may be necessary).

INDICATIONS: Activated charcoal is a general-purpose antidote for the immediate treatment of ingested poisons, including many drugs and noncorrosive chemicals. It is *ineffective* against ingested corrosive agents (e.g., alkalies and mineral acids), cyanide, ethanol, methanol, organic solvents, and ferrous sulfate.

ACTIONS: Activated charcoal is a nonspecific adsorbent of a wide variety of drugs and chemicals. It forms a stable complex with the ingested toxic material and prevents further gastrointestinal absorption of the toxic component. Activated charcoal is most effective when given within 30 minutes after ingestion of the chemical or drug, but it has been effective even when administration has been delayed several hours. Repeated doses may be effective for substances that are absorbed slowly or recycled through the enterohepatic system. Large doses are necessary for substances that delay gastric emptying (e.g., anticholinergics) or if there is food in the stomach. Activated charcoal is less effective if the toxic or poisonous materials are rapidly absorbed.

Table 35–1 lists some of the medications and other substances adsorbed by activated charcoal.

TABLE 35–1 Agents Adsorbed by Activated Charcoal

Acetaminophen	Digitalis	Penicillins
Amphetamines	Diphenylhydantoin	Phenol
Antihistamines	Glutethimide	Phenolphthalein
Antipyrine	Iodine	Poisonous mushrooms
Aspirin	Ipecac	Propoxyphene
Atropine	Methylene blue	Primaquine
Barbiturates	Morphine	Quinine
Camphor	Nicotine	Salicylates
Cantharides	Opium	Sulfonamides
Cocaine	Oxalates	Strychnine
Colchicine	Parathion	Tricyclic antidepressants

CONTRAINDICATIONS: All ingested corrosives, alkalies, mineral acids, cyanide, ethanol, methanol, organic solvents, and iron salts; acetaminophen overdose when N-acetylcysteine has been given also.

PRECAUTIONS: The effectiveness of activated charcoal may be enhanced if it is given after emesis has been induced. *Do not give simultaneously with syrup of ipecac* as the charcoal will adsorb the syrup, rendering it ineffective. The slurry is unpleasant to drink and compliance may be difficult to achieve; a small amount of concentrated fruit juice or chocolate syrup can be added to improve palatability. *Do not* use ice cream or sherbert for this purpose as they decrease the adsorptive capacity of the charcoal. Activated charcoal makes endoscopy difficult.

Note: Burnt toast, charcoal tablets, granules, capsules, or the "universal antidote" containing charcoal, magnesium oxide, and tannic acid are all *ineffective* substitutes for activated charcoal.

SIDE EFFECTS/ADVERSE REACTIONS: None.

Cyanide antidote package (Lilly brand)

ADMINISTRATION

Available Forms: Injectable (IV), package includes sodium nitrite, 300 mg/10 ml (2 vials) and sodium thiosulfate, 12.5 gm/50 ml (2 vials); inhalation, amyl nitrite perles, 0.3 ml each.

Diluent: Give injections undiluted.

Dosage (Amyl Nitrite Perles): Initially, break the perles one at a time in a gauze sponge and hold the sponge under the patient's nose or over an Ambu-bag intake valve for 15–30 seconds out of each minute. The interrupted schedule is important because continuous use of amyl nitrite can prevent adequate oxygenation. Discontinue amyl nitrite when IV doses of sodium nitrite are ready to be given.

Dosage (Sodium Nitrite): Give 6–8 mg/m^2 (0.2 ml/kg) slowly IV at 2.5–5.0 ml/min; monitor blood pressure carefully. Maximum dose is 10 ml. Leave the needle in place for injection of the sodium thiosulfate.

Dosage (Sodium Thiosulfate): Inject 30–40 ml/m^2 (1 ml/kg) slowly through the same IV needle used for the administration of the sodium nitrite.

INDICATIONS: The cyanide antidote package is used exclusively for treatment of cyanide poisoning. Inhaled cyanide is lethal within minutes, but when absorbed through skin or ingested, the onset of symptoms may be delayed for several minutes, with death ensuing in untreated cases within 3–4 hours. Cyanide poisoning can stem from many sources. Certain fumigants used to control rodents and insects contain hydrocyanic acid (prussic acid). Cyanide salts are present in photographic chemicals and metal cleaners. Organic cyanide compounds can be found in certain fertilizers. Children may develop cyanide toxicity after ingesting certain plants or parts of plants (e.g., apricot, pear, bitter almond, and peach pits; apple seeds; choke cherry pits; elderberry leaves or shoots; hydrangea leaves or buds; sorghum species; and cassava beans or roots). (Refer to standard toxicology texts for other sources.)

ACTIONS: Cyanide is a protoplasmic poison that induces cellular hypoxia. Cyanide complexes with and thereby inhibits the enzyme cytochrome oxidase, which promotes the cellular utilization of oxygen. Amyl nitrite and sodium nitrite combine with hemoglobin to form methemoglobin, which combines readily with complexed cyanide. This reaction leads to the production of a cyanomethemoglobin complex and the liberation of cytochrome oxidase. Sodium thiosulfate then combines with the cyanomethemoglobin complex to produce methemoglobin and thiocyanate. The thiocyanate is excreted in the urine, and the methemoglobin is rapidly converted to functional hemoglobin via normal erythrocyte metabolism. Because of the rapid action of cyanide, the cyanide antidote kit should be used prior to attempts to induce emesis or gastric lavage, even if the toxic substance was ingested. Signs and symptoms of cyanide toxicity include local irritation, which results in a burning sensation in the mouth; nausea; and increased salivation. Neurological signs and symptoms include headache, faintness, diaphoresis, vertigo, excitement, and anxiety. These are followed by drowsiness, prostration, paralysis, convulsions, stupor, coma, and death. Patients may initially exhibit tachypnea and dyspnea, which are followed by respiratory depression and cyanosis. Cardiovascular effects include initial hypertension; reflex bradycardia; and sinus, AV nodal, or idioventricular arrhythmias. Later, tachycardia, hypotension, and QRS changes with T wave elevations are noted. The early clinical picture may be confused with carbon monoxide poisoning.

CONTRAINDICATIONS: None, because of the emergency nature of cyanide poisoning.

PRECAUTIONS: Maintain continuous ventilation with 100% oxygen. After using the cyanide antidote kit, consider emesis followed by gastric lavage with 5% sodium thiosulfate, 1% potassium permanganate, or diluted 3% hydrogen peroxide (1:5). *Do not use activated charcoal* as cyanide inhibits its action. Draw blood for cyanide levels. Keep the patient under close observation for 24–48 hours. Severe poisonings may require repeat doses of each antidote at 50% of the initial dosage.

SIDE EFFECTS/ADVERSE REACTIONS: Vomiting, syncope, headache, and stupor may occur early on during the administration of sodium nitrite. Severe hypotension may occur during either sodium nitrite or thiosulfate administration; this can be minimized by giving the infusions slowly and using the Trendelenburg position.

Deferoxamine mesylate (Desferal)

ADMINISTRATION

Available Forms: Injectable (IM, IV), 500 mg (powder).

Diluent: For IM use reconstitute with 2 ml sterile water for injection. For IV infusion further dilute in D5W, NS, or LR.

Dosage (Parenteral): Initially, 20 mg/kg (600 mg/m^2) IM (preferred) or *slow* IV; can be followed with 10 mg/kg (300 mg/m^2) q4h for 2 doses. Subsequent doses of 10 mg/kg (300 mg/m^2) can be given q4–12h, depending on the clinical response. Maximum is 6 gm/day or 3.5 gm/m^2/day.

Rate: For IV infusion do not exceed 15 mg/kg/hr (450 mg/m^2/hr).

INDICATIONS: Deferoxamine is used as an adjunct in the treatment of acute iron intoxication. It is most effective when given early after the acute ingestion.

ACTIONS: Deferoxamine is a potent, highly specific iron-chelating agent. It readily complexes with ferric ions (and ferrous ions, to a lesser extent) to form ferrioxamine, a stable, water-soluble chelate, which is then excreted in the urine. This complex turns the urine a characteristic reddish-brown, which indicates elevated serum levels of iron and the need for further therapy. Maximal iron excretion usually occurs at the beginning of treatment. Deferoxamine can also remove loosely bound stored iron from ferritin, hemosiderin, and transferrin but not from bone marrow or hemoglobin. This effect has been applied experimentally in the treatment of secondary hemochromatosis that occurs after the multiple transfusions used in treatment of various sickle cell anemias, etc.

CONTRAINDICATIONS: Severe renal impairment or anuria.

PRECAUTIONS: Do not use deferoxamine as a sole substitute for other measures such as induced emesis, gastric lavage (with 5% sodium bicarbonate solution), suction, airway maintenance, peritoneal dialysis, and control of shock and acidosis. Because serum levels of iron are not always an accurate indication of the severity of intoxication, and because potentially fatal necrosis of the GI tract can occur despite low serum levels, treatment with deferoxamine should be started even before elevated serum levels of iron are confirmed. The IM route of administration is preferred in children. Avoid rapid IV rates as hypotension and shock may occur.

SIDE EFFECTS/ADVERSE REACTIONS: Deferoxamine is relatively nontoxic in recommended doses. Rapid IV infusion can cause generalized erythema, urticaria, hypotension, tachycardia, and shock (due to histamine release). Doses given IM cause pain and induration at the injection site. Long-term use for chronic iron storage disease may cause allergic reactions (e.g., wheals, pruritus, rash, anaphylaxis), blurred vision, abdominal discomfort, diarrhea, leg cramps, fever, and cataracts.

Dimercaprol (British anti-lewisite [BAL], Dimercaptopropanol)

ADMINISTRATION

Available Form: Injectable (IM), 100 mg/ml in 3 ml amps (10% in peanut oil).

Dosage (Parenteral): Do not exceed 5 mg/kg/dose for any of the following conditions.
For arsenic, mercury, or gold poisoning (mild): All doses given deep IM. First day, 2.5 mg/kg q4h for 6 doses; second day, 2.5 mg/kg q6h for 4 doses; third day, 2.5 mg/kg q12h for 2 doses; then 2.5 mg/kg qd for 10 more days. For severe poisoning increase the dosage by 25%.
For severe symptomatic lead poisoning: 4 mg/kg IM q4h for 5–7 days with 250 mg/m^2 calcium disodium EDTA given IM in a different site.
For acrodynia in infants and children: 3 mg/kg IM q4h for 2 days, then q6h for 1 day, then q12h for 7–8 days.

INDICATIONS: Dimercaprol is the antidote of choice for acute arsenic (except arsine gas, A_5H_3), mercury, or gold poisoning caused either by ingestion of the metal salts or by overdosage with metallic therapeutic agents. It is usually ineffective for treatment of chronic poisoning due to these heavy metals. Dimercaprol is particularly useful for acute hemorrhagic arsenic encephalitis and gold-induced dermatitis, or thrombocytopenia (e.g., dermatitis or thrombocytopenia induced by gold). In acute mercury poisoning, it is most effective when given within 1–2 hours after ingestion, but it cannot reverse mercury-induced renal damage. Infants and children with acrodynia ("pink disease"), caused by mercury hypersensitivity, respond to dimercaprol. It is also beneficial when given together with calcium disodium EDTA for treatment of acute, severe lead encephalopathy or when serum levels of lead exceed 100 µg/100 ml. Dimercaprol has been used successfully in the management of some cases of antimony, bismuth, chromium, copper, nickel, tungsten, or zinc poisoning. It should *not* be used for iron, cadmium, selenium, or uranium poisoning because the complexes formed between dimercaprol and these metal ions are more toxic than the metal ions alone.

ACTIONS: Dimercaprol forms complexes with certain heavy metal ions, and these complexes prevent or reverse the binding of metallic cations to some of the body's essential enzymes. The complexes are then excreted in the urine. Since the dimercaprol-metal complex can dissociate in an acid medium (thus releasing the metal to exert its toxic effects), it is advisable to keep the urine alkaline. The dosage of dimercaprol must be sufficient to produce a surplus of this agent to ensure that all the excess metal will be complexed. Dimercaprol usually does not cause a depletion of the body's trace elements. After IM injection, peak plasma levels are reached in 30–60 minutes. The antidote is well distributed in all body tissues. Excess dimercaprol (uncomplexed) is rapidly metabolized and is excreted in the urine.

CONTRAINDICATIONS: Severe renal or hepatic impairment, anuria.

PRECAUTIONS: Supportive therapy should include gastric lavage with 2–5% sodium bicarbonate or 5% sodium formaldehyde sulfoxylate. Keep the urine alkaline throughout therapy. Monitor vital signs, especially blood pressure, frequently as dimercaprol may cause hypertension. Dimercaprol is potentially nephrotoxic, so dosage reductions are indicated for patients with renal impairment. Doses greater than 5 mg/kg are associated with vomiting, stupor, convulsions, and coma. Fever occurs frequently in children, especially after the second or third dose. Hemolysis may be induced in G6PD-deficient patients. Prophylactic administration of an antihistamine may relieve mild side effects. Give *deep* IM injections.

SIDE EFFECTS/ADVERSE REACTIONS: (Closely dose-related, especially when dosage exceeds 5 mg/kg.) Signs and symptoms of an adverse reaction may appear within 15–30 minutes after injection; these include nausea, vomiting, hypertension, headache, sweating, fever, anxiety, nervousness, throat constriction, muscular weakness, aches and pains, and tingling of the extremities. Blepharal spasm, lacrimation, salivation, rhinorrhea, and conjunctivitis may occur (treat with antihistamines). Dimercaprol may impart a strong mercaptan-like odor to the breath and may cause a burning sensation in the lips, mouth, throat, eyes, and penis. Complaints of tooth pain have been reported. Dimercaprol may cause metabolic lactic acidosis. Drug fever and a reduction in polymorphonuclear leukocytes occur frequently in children. Local pain and sterile abscesses at the injection site may occur, especially if the antidote is not given by *deep* IM injection. Nephrotoxicity (especially with prolonged and high doses) includes proteinuria, capillary damage, excessive fluid loss, and vascular collapse. Coma and convulsions have occurred.

DRUG INCOMPATIBILITIES: Dimercaprol is unstable in aqueous solution.

DRUG INTERACTIONS: Dimercaprol forms extremely toxic complexes with iron. Do not give the medication during *iron therapy* or for *iron poisoning*. Uptake of iodine[131] may be decreased.

ANTIDOTE: Discontinue dimercaprol. Maintain hydration and keep the urine alkaline. Treat adverse reactions symptomatically and supportively. Correct acidosis and hypertension.

Edetate calcium disodium (calcium EDTA) (Calcium Disodium Versenate)

ADMINISTRATION

Available Forms: Injectable (IM, IV), 200 mg/ml in 5 ml amps; tablets, 500 mg.

Diluent: For IV use dilute dose with D5W or NS to a concentration of 2–4 mg/ml.

Dosage (Parenteral): (Total dose depends on the severity of lead poisoning and on the patient's response and tolerance to the antidote.)
For acute lead poisoning: (Serum levels of lead 50–100 μg or more per 100 ml.) 30–50 mg/kg/day (1.0–1.5 gm/m^2/day) IM (preferred) in divided doses (q12h) for up to 3–5 days. Follow with a rest period of 2 days; then repeat the course of therapy if indicated. (Children may often require two treatment courses.) Maximum dose is 70 mg/kg/day (1.7 gm/m^2/day).

Dosage (Oral): Not recommended as it may enhance gastric absorption of lead.

Rate: If IV infusion is used, the dose can be administered over 2 hours in a symptomatic patient, but 6–8 hour infusions are preferred.

INDICATIONS: Edetate calcium disodium, or calcium EDTA, is the chelating agent of choice for acute and chronic lead poisoning. Acute lead encephalopathy in children and patients with serum levels of lead greater than 100 μg/100 ml are preferably treated with a combination of calcium EDTA and dimercaprol. Calcium EDTA is less effective in poisonings caused by copper, cadmium, chromium, manganese, zinc, nickel, and some radioactive and nuclear fission products. It is *not* indicated for gold, mercury, or arsenic poisoning.

ACTIONS: Calcium EDTA chelates the heavy metal ions to form stable, water-soluble complexes, which can then be excreted in the urine. It does not produce a negative calcium balance as does disodium EDTA because it is already fully saturated with calcium. It is most effective when given early in the course of acute poisoning. After parenteral administration, urinary excretion of chelated lead usually begins in 1 hour, and peak excretion occurs within 24–48 hours. Calcium EDTA is excreted unchanged by glomerular filtration. Oral use should be avoided; when given by this route, calcium EDTA is poorly absorbed, its action is delayed, and it may enhance the absorption of any lead present in the GI tract.

CONTRAINDICATIONS: Anuria, increased intracranial pressure (IV doses).

PRECAUTIONS: Therapy should be started in asymptomatic patients who have serum levels of lead greater than 50–80 μg/100 ml and in all patients with symptoms of lead toxicity (e.g., lead encephalopathy, moderate to severe lead colic, early nephropathy). Do not use any chelating agent prophylactically. Calcium EDTA can cause fatal toxic renal tubular necrosis; use cautiously in patients with renal impairment and reduce the dosage.

Establish a good urine flow with IV fluids before giving the first dose (avoid fluid excess in lead encephalopathy, however). Monitor renal function (e.g., serum creatinine, BUN) before and during therapy. Monitor blood and 24 hour urine lead levels. Daily urinalysis is recommended; discontinue calcium EDTA if proteinuria, hematuria, or renal epithelial cell counts increase. Monitor ECG and serum levels of calcium and phosphorus during therapy. Do not exceed the recommended daily dosage. Avoid extravasation with IV use. Concentrated IV solutions (5 mg or more per milliliter) are associated with thrombophlebitis.

SIDE EFFECTS/ADVERSE REACTIONS: Calcium EDTA may cause pain at the injection site (area can be infiltrated with lidocaine before IM administration). Rapid IV injection may cause lethal increases in intracranial pressure. Occasionally, fever, chills, malaise, thrombophlebitis, thirst, and histamine-like reactions (e.g., nasal stuffiness, sneezing, lacrimation) may occur 4–8 hours after IV infusion. Parenteral administration may also cause anorexia, nausea, vomiting, headache, numbness, tingling, myalgia, hypercalcemia, hypotension, and ECG changes (inverted T waves). Prolonged therapy with large doses produces transient bone marrow depression and skin and mucous membrane lesions. High doses can cause toxic and fatal renal tubular necrosis.

DRUG INCOMPATIBILITIES: Do not mix in D10W, 10% invert sugar, Ringer's solution, LR, or protein hydrolysates.

DRUG INTERACTIONS: Calcium EDTA chelates zinc and may interfere with the duration of action of *zinc insulin* preparations.

ANTIDOTE: Discontinue calcium EDTA. Treat adverse reactions symptomatically and supportively (see precautions).

Syrup of ipecac (USP)

ADMINISTRATION

Available Form: Syrup, 30 ml.

Dosage (Oral)
Infants <1 year old: 5–10 ml.
Children >1 year old: 15 ml, followed by water or milk; can be repeated after 15–30 minutes if emesis has not occurred; if patient still does not vomit after the second dose, remove the dose by gastric lavage.

INDICATIONS: Syrup of ipecac is used to induce vomiting in the early management of acute poisonings caused by ingestion of toxic substances. Since emesis may not remove all the ingested toxin, the patient should be observed for signs of increasing intoxication. Activated charcoal can be given after emesis has occurred to prevent further absorption of the ingested toxic material. (If given before emesis, the charcoal will adsorb the ipecac, thus rendering it ineffective.) Syrup of ipecac should be used only when the ingested substances are noncorrosive and noncaustic.

ACTIONS: Syrup of ipecac acts locally and centrally; it produces emesis by irritation of the gastric mucosa and by stimulation of the CTZ in the medulla (only when medullary centers are responsive). Onset of emesis usually occurs within 20 minutes of administration.

CONTRAINDICATIONS: Ingestion of corrosive poisons, strong acids or alkalies. petroleum distillates of low volatility, volatile oils, strychnine or other CNS stimulants; ingestion of antiemetics more than 1 hour before; simultaneous use of activated charcoal; patients who are unconscious, semicomatose, severely inebriated, convulsing, or in shock or who have lost the gag reflex.

PRECAUTIONS: Do not confuse syrup of ipecac with ipecac *fluidextract* (which is 14 times more concentrated and toxic). Use cautiously in digitalis overdoses because vomiting potentiates vagal activity and AV block. Emesis may precipitate seizures in patients who have ingested convulsive agents. Ipecac may be cardiotoxic if it is systemically absorbed instead of vomited; if it does not induce emesis, it should be removed from the stomach by aspiration and gastric lavage or by administration of activated charcoal.

SIDE EFFECTS/ADVERSE REACTIONS: There are usually no adverse reactions with doses of 30 ml or less. Higher doses, if absorbed, may cause cardiotoxicity (e.g., myocarditis, tachycardia, T wave depression, atrial fibrillation, depressed myocardial contractility). Other signs and symptoms of toxic overdose include nausea, bloody stools and vomitus, abdominal cramping or pain, hypotension, dyspnea, shock, convulsions, coma, and heart failure. (Acute toxicity has, so far, been reported only for accidental use of *fluidextract* instead of *syrup* of ipecac.)

DRUG INTERACTIONS: Ingestion of *antiemetics* (late) counteracts ipecac's emetic effect. *Activated charcoal* adsorbs ipecac.

ANTIDOTE: Treat the patient symptomatically. Gastric aspiration and lavage and activated charcoal can be given to remove the ipecac.

Methylene blue (injectable, USP)

ADMINISTRATION

Available Forms: Injectable (IV), 10 mg/ml (1%) in 10 ml amps.

Diluent: Give undiluted or dilute in a sufficient volume of NS to ensure slow IV administration.

Dosage (Parenteral): 1–2 mg/kg/dose (0.1–0.2 ml/kg/dose) given slowly IV. Can be repeated as necessary within 1–2 hours to reduce serum levels of methemoglobin to less than 40%. (Oxygen administration is also indicated.)

Rate: Administer IV doses over 5 minutes.

INDICATIONS: Methylene blue is given IV to reverse acute methemoglobinemia induced by nitrates and nitrites, both organic and inorganic. Exposure can occur from a variety of sources. Nitrates and nitrites are available as prescription and nonprescription medications (e.g., nitroglycerin, amyl nitrite, isosorbide dinitrate, sulfonamides, quinones, bismuth subnitrate, silver nitrate solutions). They are present in certain room deodorizers as butyl and isobutyl nitrite, in well water contaminated with fertilizer or decaying animal and vegetable matter, and in many dyes and solvents (nitrobenzene). Nitrites are used as curing agents and preservatives in certain foods, particularly smoked and cured meats (sausage, bacon, ham, lunch meat, smoked fish) and cheese. Inorganic nitrates occur naturally in certain vegetables, including carrots, spinach, cabbage, and beets. The toxicity of dietary nitrates results from their conversion in the GI tract to nitrites. Methemoglobinemia from these dietary sources of nitrates is most common in infants less than 4 months of age because they do not yet secrete gastric acid at normal levels. This consequently permits an overgrowth of certain bacteria (notably *E. coli*) capable of reducing these nitrates to the nitrite forms that cause methemoglobinemia if high levels accumulate. Methylene blue is not recommended for methemoglobinemia induced by cyanide poisoning or carbon monoxide.

ACTIONS: Nitrates and nitrites are oxidizing substances that can oxidize hemoglobin to methemoglobin, which is incapable of transporting oxygen in the blood. The patient becomes cyanotic. Typically, the mucous membranes take on a brownish hue; arterial blood appears chocolate brown and does not revert to bright red when shaken (in a test tube) after oxygen has been bubbled through it. Tissue hypoxia from methemoglobinemia and cardiovascular collapse from the extensive vasodilation caused by nitrates and nitrites are the major toxic effects. Cyanosis usually first appears when blood levels of methemoglobin are greater than 10–15%. At 20–40% headache, dizziness, weakness, flushing, tachycardia, hypotension, and rapid respiration occur. At levels of 40–50% or more there is significant tissue hypoxia, metabolic acidosis, sinus tachycardia, lethargy, stupor, and possibly coma or convulsions. At levels of 60–70% severe metabolic acidosis, respiratory depression, convulsions, cardiovascular collapse, and death from asphyxia can occur. Other complications of prolonged severe hypoxia, such as pulmonary edema and postanoxic encephalopathy, should be anticipated.

Methylene blue produces two opposite effects on hemoglobin. At low doses, it converts methemoglobin back to hemoglobin. This is accomplished within intact red blood cells through a process involving certain enzymes (methemoglobin reductases). In high doses, however, methylene blue acts as an oxidizing agent, which can convert the ferrous iron of hemoglobin to ferric iron; this results in the formation of more methemoglobin.

CONTRAINDICATIONS: Intraspinal injection of methylene blue.

PRECAUTIONS: Avoid exceeding recommended dosage. Inject IV doses slowly over several minutes to prevent local high concentrations of the compound from producing additional methemoglobin (see actions). Measure arterial blood gases (ABGs) and methemoglobin levels in arterial blood as soon as possible; levels of 40% or more require immediate treatment with methylene blue and oxygen. If ABGs and methemoglobin levels cannot be rapidly determined and the patient is obviously cyanotic, the aforementioned treatment should be started anyway. (A quick bedside test is to place a drop of the patient's blood and a control drop of normal blood on a piece of filter paper; when dry, a chocolate brown color indicates greater than 15% methemoglobin.) Monitor vital signs frequently.

Additional therapeutic measures include emesis, lavage, and activated charcoal for oral poisoning; bathing the skin in soapy water or irrigating it with saline for cutaneous exposure; and putting the patient in a horizontal or head-down position, giving IV fluids, and (rarely) administering dopamine or norepinephrine for hypotension. Patients with G6PD deficiency usually do not respond to methylene blue because they also have a deficiency in the necessary methemoglobin reductase enzymes. Consider using exchange transfusions and hyperbaric oxygen for these cases.

SIDE EFFECTS/ADVERSE REACTIONS: Large or rapidly infused IV doses cause nausea, vomiting, dizziness, mental confusion, abdominal and chest pain, sweating, hypertension, grayish-blue cyanosis, and further formation of methemoglobin. Young infants are particularly susceptible to severe hemolytic reactions.

DRUG INCOMPATIBILITIES: Do not mix methylene blue with any other medications.

DRUG INTERACTIONS: None.

ANTIDOTE: Discontinue methylene blue infusion. Most side effects are self-limiting and benign. Severe methemoglobinemia, complicated by excess methylene blue, may require exchange transfusions or hyperbaric oxygen.

Naloxone (Narcan)

ADMINISTRATION

Available Forms: Injectable (IM, IV, SC), 0.4 mg/ml in 1 ml amps, 0.01 mg/ml in 2 ml amps (Neonatal Narcan).

Diluent: Give undiluted or further dilute with sterile water or NS for injection.

Dosage (Parenteral): Varies according to use.
For neonatal respiratory depression: 0.01 mg/kg injected into the umbilical vein; can be repeated at 2–3 minute intervals (can also be given IM or SC).
For narcotic-induced respiratory depression in infants and children: 0.01 mg/kg IV, IM, or SC. Dose can be repeated at 2–3 minute intervals.

INDICATIONS: Naloxone is used to reverse the respiratory depression induced by natural and synthetic narcotics (opiate derivatives only), pentazocine (Talwin), propoxyphene (Darvon), diazepam (Valium), butorphanol (Stadol), and nalbuphine (Nubain). It is ineffective for cocaine overdose and for respiratory depression caused by barbiturates, other sedative-hypnotics, anesthetics, or other non-narcotic CNS depressants. Naloxone is also indicated for diagnosis of suspected acute narcotic overdosage. It is usually injected into the umbilical vein to reverse neonatal respiratory depression caused by the administration of narcotics during labor and delivery.

ACTIONS: Naloxone is essentially a pure narcotic antagonist: it competitively inhibits the action of narcotics at their CNS receptor sites (other mechanisms may also be involved). It has no pharmacological effects of its own and does not produce physical dependence or tolerance. Even in large doses naxolone reverses all degrees of narcotic-induced respiratory depression, mild to severe, without increasing the degree of existing depression. Naloxone's onset of action is rapid (within 2 minutes after IV injection and 2-5 minutes after IM or SC administration). Its duration of action (about 45 minutes) is shorter than that of most narcotics, so repeated doses are often necessary to treat respiratory depression effectively. It readily crosses the placenta and is metabolized in the liver.

CONTRAINDICATIONS: Known hypersensitivity to naloxone.

PRECAUTIONS: Naloxone may precipitate severe withdrawal symptoms in patients addicted to opiates, propoxyphene, or pentazocine. Maintain supportive treatment with oxygen, assisted ventilation, vasopressors, and so on as necessary. If no response is noted after 3 doses, suspect another cause of coma or respiratory depression. Following the use of narcotics during surgery, excessive doses of naloxone may significantly reverse analgesia, increase blood pressure, and induce nausea and vomiting. Keep the patient under continued surveillance for at least 24 hours.

SIDE EFFECTS/ADVERSE REACTIONS: There are virtually no side effects or adverse reactions. IV doses have caused hypertension, tachycardia, and ventricular irritability in patients with coronary disease (causal relationship not established).

Penicillamine (Cuprimine, Depen Titratabs)

ADMINISTRATION

Available Forms: Tablets, 250 mg (Depen); capsules, 125, 250 mg (Cuprimine).

Dosage (Oral): For those who cannot swallow tablets or capsules, capsule contents can be administered in 15-30 ml of chilled pureed fruit or fruit juice. Duration of treatment varies; 1-6 months may be required, depending on serum levels of lead and symptoms.
Infants >6 months old and children: 250 mg qd in fruit juice (or 20-40 mg/kg/day).
Older children: 1 gm/day (or 20-40 mg/kg/day).

INDICATIONS: Penicillamine is an oral metal-chelating agent used in the treatment of lead poisoning. It is less potent or efficient than EDTA and dimercaprol, which are used in severe, acute cases. However, its relatively low toxicity and ease of administration make it valuable for moderate, asymptomatic lead poisoning; for chronic cases requiring long periods of de-leading; and for diseases associated with excess storage of metals (e.g., Wilson's disease, copper). Penicillamine may be particularly useful as follow-up therapy after lead poisoning has been treated initially with EDTA or dimercaprol. It may also be useful in poisonings with alkyl lead compounds (e.g., tetraethyl lead).

ACTIONS: Penicillamine acts in much the same manner as does dimercaprol. It chelates copper, iron, lead, mercury, and probably other heavy metals to form stable soluble complexes that are readily excreted by the kidneys. It does not remove lead from erythrocytes. Penicillamine is readily absorbed from the GI tract, and peak levels are attained in about 1 hour. It is believed to be metabolized in the liver and excreted in urine and feces, but very little of the drug exists as uncomplexed penicillamine.

CONTRAINDICATIONS: Previous penicillamine-related aplastic anemia or agranulocytosis, severe renal impairment, possible cross-allergenicity with penicillin (rare).

PRECAUTIONS: During prolonged therapy, take the patient's temperature nightly for the first few months and observe the skin and mucous membranes frequently for allergic reactions. If fever or rashes occur, discontinue the drug until allergic reactions subside (these can be treated with antihistamines). Then, reinstitute therapy with smaller doses, gradually increasing to full dosage. If allergic reactions occur a second or third time, systemic corticosteroids may be necessary. Discontinue penicillamine if bleeding into the skin, hemoptysis, or pulmonary infiltrates occur. Urinalysis, differential blood counts, WBC and platelet counts, and hemoglobin determinations should be done every 3–7 days for the first month, every 2 weeks for the next 3 months, and then monthly. Observe the patient for signs of toxic hematological reactions (fever, sore throat, chills, bruising, or bleeding). Watch for the development of proteinuria and hematuria, which may be a sign of nephrotic syndrome. Monitor renal and liver function tests. Use cautiously in patients with renal disease. Because iron will bind chelating agents, discontinue iron therapy before starting chelation therapy. If iron deficiency anemia develops, iron supplements can be given for short periods, if necessary, but administer the doses of iron and penicillamine at least 2 hours apart. Mineral supplements should be avoided as penicillamine increases excretion of zinc and other metals.

SIDE EFFECTS/ADVERSE REACTIONS: Incidence of allergic reactions is high (approximately 30%), and they may reoccur after therapy is restarted. The most common allergic reaction is an early rash (generalized, pruritic, erythematous, maculopapular, or morbilliform), which usually disappears a few days after penicillamine is discontinued. A late rash (intensely pruritic, scaly, macular lesions or pemphigoid-type) may occur after 6 months or more of therapy. It may persist for weeks after discontinuance of penicillamine and may require systemic corticosteroids. Fever, joint pain, and lymphadenopathy may accompany the rash. Drug fever is common and usually appears within 2–3 weeks after the start of therapy. Gastrointestinal side effects include nausea, vomiting, anorexia, epigastric pain, dyspepsia, and diarrhea. A metallic taste in the mouth and oral ulcerations have also been reported. Hematological effects include leukopenia, eosinophilia, thrombocytopenia, hemolytic and iron-deficiency anemias, granulocytopenia, and aplastic anemia. A systemic lupus-like syndrome may occur. The skin may become excessively wrinkled and easily bruised or broken. Toxic renal effects may appear as hematuria, proteinuria, rare glomerulonephritis, development of nephrotic syndrome, or renal vasculitis. Pulmonary infiltrates, hemoptysis, allergic alveolitis, and intra-alveolar hemorrhage have occurred, but rarely. Hepatic dysfunction, cholestatic jaundice, and pancreatitis have been reported also.

DRUG INTERACTIONS: *Oral iron* or *mineral supplements* can bind penicillamine and decrease its effectiveness.

ANTIDOTE: Discontinue penicillamine. Treat severe allergic reactions with systemic corticosteroids. Treat other adverse reactions symptomatically.

Physostigmine salicylate (Antilirium)

ADMINISTRATION

Available Form: Injectable (IM, IV), 1 mg/ml in 2 ml amps (salicylate salt).

Diluent: Give undiluted or dilute with D5W, sterile water, or NS for injection.

Dosage (Parenteral)
To reverse anticholinergic effects of atropine or scopolamine preanesthetic medications: 0.03–0.05 µg/kg IM as a single dose; can be repeated in 15–20 minutes if necessary.
For anticholinergic poisoning: Initially, 0.5 mg slow IV. Dose can be repeated every 5 minutes until the desired response occurs, cholinergic signs appear, or 2 mg has been given.

Rate: Inject IV bolus doses slowly over at least 2 minutes.

INDICATIONS: Because of its cholinergic effects, physostigmine is used to reverse the toxic effects of atropine, scopolamine, and other belladonna alkaloids. It is also used to treat the toxic cardiac and CNS anticholinergic effects induced by tricyclic antidepressants (e.g., amitryptyline, doxepin, imipramine, nortriptyline) and, sometimes, phenothiazines and antihistamines.

ACTIONS: Physostigmine is an anticholinesterase inhibitor. It prevents destruction of acetylcholine by this enzyme, thereby prolonging and intensifying acetylcholine's effects. The resulting cholinergic responses include miosis, increased tone of GI smooth muscle, bronchoconstriction, sweating, and salivation. Unlike pyridostigmine or neostigmine, physostigmine crosses the blood-brain barrier to counteract the CNS toxicity (e.g., delirium, agitation, hallucinations, coma) of the belladonna alkaloids. High doses of physostigmine can cause CNS depression and a direct blocking action at autonomic ganglia, ultimately producing tremor, convulsions, coma, a depolarizing skeletal muscle block, and death from respiratory paralysis. Physostigmine is readily absorbed after parenteral administration by all routes. Onset of action appears in 3–8 minutes, and effects last 0.5–5.0 hours. Its metabolic fate is not completely understood. Since it crosses the blood-brain barrier, it is expected to cross the placenta also.

CONTRAINDICATIONS: Asthma, chronic airway obstruction, gangrene, diabetes, cardiovascular disease, mechanical obstruction of the intestinal or genitourinary tracts, concomitant use with depolarizing neuromuscular blockers (e.g., succinylcholine).

PRECAUTIONS: Atropine should always be available to reverse excess cholinergic effects. Use cautiously in patients with epilepsy, parkinsonism, or bradycardia. Reduce the dose if excessive nausea, vomiting, or sweating occurs. Facilities for mechanical ventilation and bronchial aspiration should be available.

SIDE EFFECTS/ADVERSE REACTIONS: The cholinergic (parasympathetic) effects include nausea, vomiting, epigastric pain, miosis, sweating, lacrimation, dyspnea, and bronchospasm. Overdoses can precipitate a "cholinergic crisis" characterized by excessive salivation, sweating, miosis, nausea, vomiting, diarrhea, bradycardia, tachycardia, hypotension or hypertension, confusion, convulsions, coma, severe muscle weakness, respiratory paralysis, and pulmonary edema.

DRUG INTERACTIONS: Physostigmine causes increased muscle paralysis if given with depolarizing *neuromuscular blockers* (succinylcholine). Additive cholinergic effects occur when it is given with other *choline esters* (e.g., bethanechol).

ANTIDOTE: Discontinue physostigmine. Reverse cholinergic toxicity with IV doses of atropine (equivalent to one-half of the injected physostigmine dose). Provide supportive therapy, including mechanical ventilation and frequent bronchial aspirations. Pralidoxime chloride may be effective in reversing skeletal neuromuscular blockage and respiratory paralysis.

Pralidoxime (2-PAM) (Protopam)

ADMINISTRATION

Available Forms: Injectable (IV, IM), 1 gm (powder); tablets, 500 mg.

Diluent: Reconstitute contents of the vial with 20 ml sterile water for injection (concentration is 50 mg/ml). For IV infusion further dilute calculated dose in 100 ml NS. Dilute IV bolus doses to a concentration of 5%.

Dosage (Parenteral): 25–50 mg/kg given slowly IV; can be repeated every 10–12 hours if needed. In the presence of severe muscarinic symptoms, 1 mg of atropine should be given simultaneously IV or IM and repeated q5–30min as necessary until muscarinic symptoms disappear or until mild symptoms of "atropinism" appear.

Rate: Administer IV infusions over 15–30 minutes. If a more rapid effect is desired, a 50 mg/ml solution can be given by slow IV injection over 5–10 minutes.

INDICATIONS: Pralidoxime is used as an adjunct to atropine and supportive assisted ventilation to reverse the respiratory muscle paralysis in poisonings caused by organophosphate anticholinesterase pesticides, chemicals, and drugs. Simultaneous administration of atropine is necessary to treat symptoms of poisoning at the respiratory center in the CNS where pralidoxime is ineffective. Pralidoxime is most effective if given within 24–36 hours after exposure to the toxic substance. However, if the poison has been ingested, toxicity may be prolonged because of slow GI absorption. In these cases, pralidoxime treatment may need to be continued for several days. Pralidoxime is not equally effective against all cholinesterase inhibitors (e.g., neostigmine, pyridostigmine, and ambenonium). Check the manufacturer's literature for a list of substances treatable with this agent.

ACTIONS: Pralidoxime is a cholinesterase reactivator. In organophosphate poisoning, it reacts with the *recently* inactivated phosphorylated form of this enzyme to form a complex, which then breaks down to liberate active cholinesterase. If the inhibited enzyme is allowed to "age" (e.g., after 36 hours), it usually cannot be reactivated. Enzyme reactivation occurs primarily at the skeletal neuromuscular junction and autonomic ganglia; it reverses respiratory and skeletal muscle paralysis and other nicotinic effects (muscle twitching, tachycardia, elevated blood pressure). Since pralidoxime produces little CNS activity, atropine is given to improve central respiratory function and to alleviate the muscarinic effects of anticholinesterase poisoning (bronchoconstriction, dyspnea, increased secretions, salivation, nausea, vomiting, abdominal cramps, miosis, hypotension). Parenteral use is recommended since absorption of oral doses is variable and incomplete. Peak levels occur within 5–15 minutes after IV administration and within 10–20 minutes after IM use. Pralidoxime is partially metabolized in the liver, and both unchanged and metabolized pralidoxime are excreted in the urine.

CONTRAINDICATIONS: Carbaryl (Sevin) poisoning; use with theophylline, succinylcholine, or respiratory depressants.

PRECAUTIONS: Pralidoxime must be given early, within 24–36 hours after exposure to the toxic agent. Maintain a patent airway, assist ventilation, and administer oxygen as necessary. Use gastric lavage if the poison was ingested. Determinations of erythrocyte and plasma cholinesterase may be helpful in assessing the degree of intoxication. If the poison was absorbed through the skin, remove the patient's clothing and wash the skin with sodium bicarbonate or alcohol. Be aware of signs of "atropinism," which may occur earlier when atropine is used with pralidoxime. Avoid rapid IV rates as tachycardia and laryngospasm may occur. Reduce the dosage in patients with renal impairment. Pralidoxime may precipitate myasthenic crisis if the patient has myasthenia gravis. Exposure to anticholinesterase inhibitors should be avoided for several weeks after pralidoxime therapy.

SIDE EFFECTS/ADVERSE REACTIONS: Pralidoxime may cause dizziness, diplopia, blurred vision, impaired accommodation, headache, drowsiness, nausea, tachycardia, hyperventilation, hypertension, maculopapular rash, and muscular weakness. (Note: It may be difficult to differentiate the toxic effects produced by atropine or the organophosphates from those produced by pralidoxime.) Rapid IV injection may cause tachycardia, hypertension, laryngospasm, muscle rigidity, and transient neuromuscular blockade. Administration of IM doses may produce mild pain at the injection site.

DRUG INCOMPATIBILITIES: Do not mix with any other medications.

DRUG INTERACTIONS: Avoid concomitant use of *succinylcholine, theophyllines, barbiturates,* and other *respiratory depressants* as they potentiate anticholinesterase toxicity.

ANTIDOTE: Treat pralidoxime-induced hypertension by slowing the IV infusion rate, discontinuing the medication, or giving IV doses of phentolamine.

Sodium polystyrene sulfonate (Kayexalate)

ADMINISTRATION

Available Forms: Powder for oral or rectal use, 450 gm.

Diluent: Mix 50 gm with 40 ml of 70% sorbitol and 80 ml of water to yield a 150 ml suspension; the concentration is 1 gm/3 ml. Shake well before using.

Dosage (Oral): 1 gm/kg/dose (as a suspension) given in 4 divided doses.

Dosage (Rectal): 1 gm/kg/dose (as a suspension) given in 4 divided doses. Have the patient retain the dose for 30–45 min; tape the buttocks together.

INDICATIONS: Sodium polystyrene sulfonate is an ion exchange resin. It is used in the treatment of hyperkalemia associated with severe renal impairment, sudden oliguria, overdoses of potassium-containing medications or potassium-sparing diuretics (spironolactone, triamterene), and the like. It should be used as an adjunct to other therapeutic measures such as restricted intake of potassium and control of metabolic acidosis. Since its action is slow, the resin should not be used alone to treat severe hyperkalemia (serum levels of 7–8 mEq of potassium per liter and associated ECG changes). Such cases require rapid-acting emergency therapy such as IV sodium bicarbonate, glucose and insulin infusions, and IV calcium gluconate. The resin can be used to supplement these measures.

ACTIONS: Oral doses of the resin are converted to the hydrogen form in the stomach. As it passes through the intestines and, particularly, the colon, each gram of resin exchanges 1 mEq of its sodium ions for 1 mEq of potassium ions. (It also binds some calcium, magnesium, and ammonium ions.) The resin, with its bound potassium ions, is then excreted in the feces. The action is slow; usually 12–24 hours are required for full control of hyperkalemia.

PRECAUTIONS: Shake suspensions well before administering them. To increase the exchange surface area, the resin mixture should be a fluid suspension, *not* a paste. Sorbitol must be added to prevent intestinal impaction. For rectal use, give an initial cleansing enema. Place the resin suspension high in the sigmoid colon, have the patient retain it 30–45 minutes (up to 4 hours), then remove it with a saline enema. Monitor serum potassium levels daily or q12h; discontinue the exchange resin when serum levels have decreased to 4–5 mEq/liter. If therapy continues for more than 3 days, monitor serum calcium also. Since the resin releases sodium into the body, observe the patient for the possible development of edema.

SIDE EFFECTS/ADVERSE REACTIONS: Side effects include constipation, intestinal impaction, nausea, vomiting, anorexia, hypokalemia, hypomagnesemia, hypocalcemia, increased sodium load, and edema.

DRUG INTERACTIONS: Oral doses can bind the magnesium and calcium of *oral antacids*. This process interferes with the normal action of these ions in the intestine (i.e., to neutralize bicarbonate ions, which normally balances the neutralization of gastric acid by the antacid). The resulting excess bicarbonate can cause systemic alkalosis. (The use of rectal doses may avoid this interaction.)

ANTIDOTE: Discontinue the resin. Remove it from the colon with cleansing enemas. Treat other side effects symptomatically.

36
Antivenins

An antivenin is an antitoxin, a serum prepared by immunizing animals (usually horses) with the venom of certain poisonous insects, snakes, or other creatures. When administered parenterally to patients who have been bitten and envenomated by a poisonous reptile or insect, the antivenin neutralizes the absorbed venom and prevents or minimizes its toxic effects. Venoms contain multiple proteolytic enzymes that are capable of causing massive tissue destruction, hemolysis, coagulation abnormalities, hemorrhage, renal damage, and cardiac and neurological toxicities that may lead to shock, respiratory paralysis, and death.

Poisoning by snake venom is a medical emergency. It is imperative that treatment be initiated within the first few critical hours since most symptoms of systemic toxicity appear within a few minutes to a few hours after envenomation. Before treatment with antivenin is begun, it must be established that the snake involved was poisonous and that the patient was envenomated when bitten, not simply bitten. Failure to make these determinations can result in the use of therapeutic measures that may cause needless discomfort or even harm to a patient who was not envenomated.

Treatment of snake venom poisoning should include appropriate amounts of antivenin, fluid and blood replacements if indicated, antibiotics and tetanus antitoxin if the bite is contaminated, and supportive measures for hypovolemia, shock, and renal or respiratory failure.

The amount of antivenin used depends on several factors:

- Severity of the bite
- Age, size, and general health of the victim
- Species and size of the snake
- Nature, location, depth, and number of bites

- Amount of injected venom
- Patient's sensitivity to the venom
- Degree and kind of first aid treatment received when the bite occurred
- Onset and severity of the symptoms

In general, a small child who is bitten by a large snake on the face, neck, or trunk will require more antivenin than an adult who is bitten by the same size snake on the extremities.

An estimation of the severity of envenomation must be made as soon as possible since the initial dose of antivenin is based on this information. The severity of a bite can be graded as follows:

- No envenomation: No local or systemic manifestations
- Minimal envenomation: Local swelling, skin discoloration, and other local changes; no systemic manifestations; normal laboratory findings
- Moderate envenomation: Swelling and edema progressing beyond the site of the bite, one or more systemic manifestations (e.g., nausea, vomiting, chills, numbness), abnormal laboratory findings (e.g., decreased hematocrit, decreased platelets)
- Severe envenomation: Marked local responses (e.g., severe swelling, petechiae, ecchymoses), severe systemic manifestations, significantly abnormal laboratory findings

Children generally require more antivenin than adults because they are less resistant and have smaller amounts of body fluids with which to dilute the poison. The IV route of administration is preferred because adequate blood levels of antivenin are achieved rapidly and the infusion can be stopped immediately if systemic hypersensitivity reactions develop. Since antivenins are prepared from horse serum, skin tests for hypersensitivity must be done according to the instructions in the package insert before full doses of antivenin are given. (Vials of horse serum are provided for this purpose.) Conjunctival sensitivity testing is not recommended. A positive test (i.e., appearance of an urticarial wheal with surrounding erythema in 10–15 minutes) may indicate a need for desensitization procedures (also outlined in the package insert). In life-threatening poisonings where the patient has a positive skin test reaction but must receive the antivenin or die, some clinicians have pretreated these patients with antihistamines and corticosteroids and then, with facilities for treatment of anaphylaxis readily available, given the antivenin very slowly IV over several hours.

The following antivenins (of equine origin) are discussed in this chapter:

- *Crotalidae* **polyvalent antivenin**
- *Latrodectus mactans* **antivenin**
- *Micrurus fulvius* **antivenin**

Crotalidae polyvalent antivenin (equine)

ADMINISTRATION

Available Form: Injectable (IV, IM). Not less than 6000 antivenin units/vial with 1 ml vial of horse serum for hypersensitivity testing and desensitization.

Diluent: Reconstitute with the enclosed vial of bacteriostatic water for injection. For IV use further dilute 1:1 or 1:10 with NS or D5W (can use 500–1000 ml volumes).

Dosage (Parenteral): The IV route is preferred.
For no envenomation: No antivenin.
For minimal envenomation: 2–4 vials.
For moderate envenomation: 5–9 vials.
For severe envenomation: 10–15 or more vials.

Rate: Allow the initial 5–10 ml of the diluted solution to infuse slowly over 3–5 minutes; observe the patient carefully for untoward reactions. If none appear, the infusion rate can be increased according to the patient's status. If systemic hypersensitivity reactions occur, temporarily discontinue the infusion and administer epinephrine or antihistamines or both as needed. The infusion can sometimes be continued at a slower rate.

INDICATIONS: This antivenin is indicated exclusively for treatment of envenomation by crotalids (pit vipers) native to North, Central, and South America; Asia; and the tropics. Among those crotalids included are rattlesnakes, cottonmouths or water moccasins, copperheads, bushmasters, bothrops, and cantil species. *Crotalidae* antivenin is ineffective against true vipers (e.g., cobras, puff adders) and noncrotalid snakes (e.g., coral snakes). The antivenin should be used in all patients who, within 30–60 minutes following the snake bite, show progressive swelling of the bitten area; numbness or tingling of the scalp, mouth, fingers, or toes; or any other systemic symptoms of poisoning.

ACTIONS: Polyvalent crotalid antivenin neutralizes the absorbed venom of the specified snakes, thus preventing or minimizing the venom's toxic effects. Because of the short latent period (5–15 minutes) between the bite and the appearance of clinical symptoms, antivenin therapy should be started as soon as possible, preferably within 4 hours after the bite. The effectiveness of the antivenin decreases dramatically if given 8 hours after the bite, and its value is questionable if given after 12 hours. The IV route of administration is preferred as therapeutic serum levels are achieved more rapidly than with the IM route.

Local signs and symptoms of poisoning develop rapidly, usually within 24 hours. These include fang marks and pain and swelling of the bite area (within 5–15 minutes) and then progressive spreading of edema to the extremities (1–24 hours). Skin discoloration and ecchymoses occur in a few hours; these are followed by vesicles, petechiae, necrosis, and hemorrhagic bullae, usually within 8–36 hours after the bite. Systemic signs and symptoms include weakness; sweating; chills; faintness; nausea; numbness or tingling around the mouth, scalp, fingers, toes, and the bite; muscle fasciculations; hypotension; prolongation of bleeding and clotting times; frank bleeding; hematuria; proteinuria; renal toxicity; and neurological toxicities leading to shock and respiratory failure.

CONTRAINDICATIONS: Hypersensitivity to horse serum (requires desensitization procedures).

PRECAUTIONS: Hospitalization is required for treatment and observation. Ingestion of alcoholic beverages should be avoided (resulting vasodilation can enhance the spread of venom). Immobilize the affected body part to minimize lymphatic movement. Use of tourniquet, incision, suction, and cryotherapy is *no longer* recommended. Administer a skin test dose of horse serum before full doses of antivenin are given (conjunctival testing is no longer preferred). Give the antivenin as soon as possible. Do not inject it into fingers or toes. Maintain plasma volume with IV fluids (two IV lines are suggested—one for antivenin infusion and one for supportive therapy). If transfusions are necessary, type and crossmatch blood early before venom alters the blood proteins. Extensive hemolysis may require infusions of whole blood or platelets. Monitor vital signs frequently (especially blood pressure and respirations). Measure the circumference of swollen extremities q15–30min to monitor progression of edema. Laboratory monitoring should include CBCs, coagulation studies, renal function tests, and urinalysis. Tests to determine hematocrit and hemoglobin and platelet counts should be done several times a day during the critical period. Other supportive therapy includes assisted ventilation, oxygen, epinephrine, corticosteroids, antibiotics, and tetanus immune globulin. Use sedatives and narcotics cautiously, particularly if respiration is already depressed. Narcotics may aggravate nausea and vomiting.

SIDE EFFECTS/ADVERSE REACTIONS: Immediate reactions (usually occurring within 30 minutes) include shock and anaphylaxis, preceded by anxiety, flushing, itching, urticaria, cough, dyspnea, cyanosis, vomiting, angioneurotic edema, and collapse. A delayed serum-sickness-like reaction (incidence 30–75%, depending on the dose) usually occurs 5–24 days after antivenin administration; signs and symptoms include malaise, fever, urticaria, nausea, vomiting, joint pain, lymphadenopathy, muscle weakness, and peripheral neuritis.

ANTIDOTE: Discontinue the antivenin infusion. Treat systemic hypersensitivity reactions with epinephrine, antihistamines, corticosteroids, and supportive care. Sometimes the infusion can be restarted at a slower rate.

Latrodectus mactans antivenin (equine)

ADMINISTRATION

Available Form: Injectable (IM, IV), not less than 6000 units/2.5 ml vial (powder for reconstitution) with 1 ml vial of horse serum for hypersensitivity testing and desensitization.

Diluent: Reconstitute contents of the vial with the enclosed sterile water for injection. For IV use dilute further with 10–15 ml NS.

Dosage (Parenteral): Give a test dose first (intradermal or conjunctival). If there is no hypersensitivity reaction, give the entire contents of the prepared vial IM (preferably in the anterolateral thigh); can be repeated in 1–3 hours if necessary.
For children <12 years old, severe cases, or shock: Give contents of the vial slowly IV.

Rate: Infuse diluted dose over 15 minutes.

INDICATIONS: *Latrodectus mactans* antivenin is used to treat black widow spider bites. For greatest effectiveness it should be used as soon as possible after envenomation.

ACTIONS: The contents of 1 vial should counteract the venom and provide symptomatic relief. The sequential development of signs and symptoms usually depends on the location of the bite. The venom acts on the myoneural junctions or individual nerve endings or both to cause motor paralysis and destruction of nerve endings. Local muscle cramps usually begin within 15 minutes to several hours after the bite; the sequence is usually cramps in the shoulder, back, and thigh followed by abdominal rigidity. Signs and symptoms may mimic those of an acute abdominal syndrome. As pain increases, the patient may become restless, anxious, and delirious and develop a feeble pulse, cold, clammy skin, and labored breathing and speech. Convulsions may occur, especially in small children. Nausea, vomiting, urinary retention, cold sweats, cyanosis, and shock may occur. Except in fatal cases, toxicity usually peaks in a few hours to a day and then subsides over 2–3 days even without treatment. Residual muscle spasm and tingling may persist for several weeks or months.

CONTRAINDICATIONS: Hypersensitivity to horse serum (desensitization procedures can be undertaken in life-threatening cases).

PRECAUTIONS: Immobilize the affected extremity and apply cold packs to the bite. Hospitalize the patient for continued treatment and observation. Administer antivenin as soon as possible. Supportive therapy includes warm baths, IV doses of 10% calcium gluconate or muscle relaxants for muscle cramping, and morphine for relief of pain. Barbiturates given for restlessness may potentiate respiratory paralysis, so use them cautiously. Have epinephrine readily available to treat hypersensitivity reactions; corticosteroids may or may not be effective. Local treatment of the site of the bite (e.g., incision, suction, tourniquet) is of no value. Observe the patient for 8–12 days for the development of serum sickness.

SIDE EFFECTS/ADVERSE REACTIONS: Hypersensitivity reactions (to the horse serum) and anaphylaxis may occur immediately. A delayed serum-sickness-like reaction can occur 8–12 days after the administration of the antivenin, so observe the patient closely during this time period.

ANTIDOTE: Give epinephrine for hypersensitivity reactions. If the antivenin is given IM in the recommended anterolateral area of the thigh, apply a tourniquet to this site to slow systemic absorption of the antivenin.

Micrurus fulvius antivenin (equine)

ADMINISTRATION

Available Form: Injectable (IV), unit vial (powder for reconstitution). Available from Wyeth Laboratories, PO Box 8299, Philadelphia, PA 19101 or from Immunobiologics Activity, Bureau of Laboratories, Centers for Disease Control, Atlanta, GA 30333; telephone (404) 633-3311 or (404) 633-2176 (off-duty hours).

Diluent: Reconstitute the contents of the vial with the enclosed 10 ml vial of bacteriostatic water for injection. Can be further diluted in NS for IV infusion.

Dosage (Parenteral): If the patient has definitely been bitten and there is immediate pain, or if any other signs or symptoms of envenomation develop, administer 3–5 vials of antivenin slowly IV. Up to 7 vials may be required for severe poisoning.

Rate: Administer the IV infusion slowly; give the first 1–2 ml over 3–5 minutes and observe the patient for any hypersensitivity reactions. Then administer at a rate determined by the patient's fluid status.

INDICATIONS: *Micrurus fulvius* antivenin is indicated only for treatment of envenomation caused by eastern coral snakes (*M. fulvius fulvius*) and Texas coral snakes (*M. fulvius tenere*). It will not neutralize the venom of the Arizona or Sonoran coral snake.

ACTIONS: This antivenin is a concentrated and lyophilized preparation of serum globulins from horses immunized with eastern coral snake venom, and it will neutralize the absorbed venom of the two species of coral snakes mentioned (see indications). Severe or fatal envenomation may occur without the local tissue necrosis seen in crotalid poisoning. Coral snakes may produce one or several tooth marks that may be difficult to find. Scratch marks usually mean the strike was superficial, and in this case envenomation rarely occurs. In true bites some pain may occur; it may be confined to the bite area, or it may radiate to the extremities and across the chest area. The severity of the pain is related to the amount of venin injected. There is usually little swelling, but within 2 hours numbness or weakness in the affected area may develop. There is often a delay of several hours (sometimes up to 8 or more) before systemic signs and symptoms of envenomation appear. Such a delay makes it difficult to determine the severity of poisoning and the amount of antivenin to use. Signs and symptoms of coral snake bites include a feeling of drowsiness or oncoming unconsciousness, apprehension, weakness, fasciculation and tremor of the tongue, difficulties in swallowing, excessive salivation, nausea, vomiting, paresis of extraocular muscles, pinpoint pupils, and dyspnea. Paresis and paralysis spreading to the limbs may occur within 2 hours, as well as hypotension and convulsions. Death is usually associated with respiratory and cardiac failure. Once signs and symptoms appear, it may not be possible to prevent or reverse the toxic effects of coral snake venom. It is wisest to begin antivenin treatment as soon as possible.

CONTRAINDICATIONS: Hypersensitivity to horse serum (desensitize if necessary).

PRECAUTIONS: All patients with either fang marks or scratches should be hospitalized. Immobilize and disinfect the affected area. Observe the patient and monitor vital signs for several hours. Begin antivenin at the first appearance of systemic signs of envenomation. Maintain fluid and electrolyte balance. Administer an appropriate antitetanus agent. Support respiration with intubation, assisted ventilation, and oxygen if respiratory difficulties develop. Suction off excessive salivary secretions as necessary. Avoid the use of sedatives and narcotics as they may further depress respiration. Maintain supportive symptomatic treatment throughout therapy.

SIDE EFFECTS/ADVERSE REACTIONS: Immediate and delayed hypersensitivity reactions to the horse serum may occur (see *Crotalidae* polyvalent antivenin).

ANTIDOTE: Discontinue or slow the infusion. Administer epinephrine for anaphylactic reactions. Treat adverse reactions symptomatically and supportively.

37
Antiserums

The antiserums or hyperimmune globulins discussed in this chapter are derived from humans immunized with certain bacteria, bacterial toxins, or viruses. These serums therefore contain antibodies specific for these agents. Some preparations are composed of whole serum, while others contain the gamma globulin (antibody) fraction. Unlike vaccines that induce active, life-long immunity, these antiserums impart immediate but short-lived passive immunity. They can be given prophylactically following exposure to an infectious agent (e.g., rabies, hepatitis virus) or therapeutically as adjunctive therapy for tetanus, diphtheria, or botulism.

The following antiserums are discussed in this chapter:

- **Hepatitis B immune globulin**
- **Immune human serum globulin (for IM use only)**
- **Immune human serum globulin (for IV use only)**
- **Rabies immune globulin**
- **Tetanus immune human globulin**
- **Varicella-zoster immune globulin**

Hepatitis B immune globulin (H-BIG, Hyperhep, Hep-B-Gammagee)

ADMINISTRATION

Available Form: Injectable (IM), sterile solution of 10–18% human immunoglobulin that has a high titer of antibody to hepatitis B surface antigen (HBsAg), in 1 and 5 ml vials.

Dosage (Parenteral): Varies according to use.
For exposure to HBsAg-positive materials: 0.06 ml/kg IM given as soon as possible after exposure (preferably within 7 days); repeat the dose 28–30 days after exposure.
For newborn infants whose mothers have acute hepatitis B or have HBsAg in their serum: 0.13 ml IM as a single dose; repeat in 7 days.

INDICATIONS: Hepatitis B immune globulin is used to provide passive immunity to hepatitis B to persons (usually laboratory personnel) exposed to HBsAg-positive materials such as blood, plasma, or serum. This is the only use approved by the FDA. The exposure may be parenteral (e.g., "accidental needle-stick"), direct mucous membrane contact (e.g., accidental splash), or oral ingestion (e.g., pipetting accident). Investigationally, it has been given to infants whose mothers had acute hepatitis in the third trimester of pregnancy or HBsAg in their serum at the time of delivery. Hepatitis B immune globulin is not indicated for treatment of acute hepatitis B, and it is ineffective in the treatment of chronic active or fulminant forms of hepatitis B (stage II–IV hepatic encephalopathy). Hepatitis B immune globulin has been shown to be more effective than immune human serum globulin without anti-HBsAg for prophylaxis of individuals exposed to patients with acute hepatitis B infections (not approved by FDA).

CONTRAINDICATIONS: Patients with HBsAg in their serum; concomitant administration of live virus vaccines (e.g., measles) as the antibodies in hepatitis B immune globulin may interfere with the induction of active immunity by the vaccine.

PRECAUTIONS: *Do not administer IV.* Use cautiously in patients who have had hypersensitivity reactions to preparations containing immune human serum globulin. Give IM doses into the gluteal or deltoid muscle.

SIDE EFFECTS/ADVERSE REACTIONS: Transient local pain, tenderness, swelling, or rash may occur at the injection site. Also reported are urticaria, erythematous rash, nausea, dizziness, fever, faintness, syncope, weakness, muscle and joint pain, and angioedema.

ANTIDOTE: Treat hypersensitivity reactions with epinephrine if necessary.

Immune human serum globulin (IM use only) (Gamastan, Gammagee)

ADMINISTRATION

Available Form: Injectable (IM), 2 and 10 ml vials (15–18% immunoglobulin G[IgG]).

Dosage (Parenteral): Varies according to use.
For measles (rubeola) prevention: (Primarily in infants) 0.2 ml/kg IM within 4–6 days after exposure. Dose should be increased after 10 days postexposure.
For measles (rubeola) modification: (Primarily in children) 0.04 ml/kg IM within 6 days after exposure.
For use with measles vaccine (live, attenuated): 0.02 ml/kg IM in the opposite arm; increase to 0.04 ml in the stressed patient (TB, cystic fibrosis, febrile convulsions).
For poliomyelitis prevention: 0.3–0.4 ml/kg IM given during the first 5–7 days of the incubation period or prior to exposure. Dose can be repeated in 5–6 weeks if necessary.
For infectious hepatitis prevention and modification: 0.02–0.04 ml/kg IM within 7 days of exposure. If prolonged, intensive exposure, increase dose to 0.06–0.10 ml/kg IM. Doses can be repeated in 3–6 months if necessary. (Immune serum globulin is not indicated in infectious hepatitis [HAV] if 5–6 weeks have elapsed since the exposure.)

INDICATIONS: Immune human serum globulin (ISG) passively supplies antibodies for prevention or attenuation of the following infectious diseases:

- Measles (rubeola) in exposed, nonimmune infants less than 2 years old and all nonimmune children, especially those who are stressed because of severe illness (e.g., burns, rheumatic fever, cystic fibrosis, pertussis)
- Poliomyelitis if given promptly after exposure (within the first 5–7 days of the incubation period)
- HAV (hepatitis A) in nonimmune, exposed patients if given early during the viral incubation period

ISG is usually administered with the live, attenuated measles vaccine to minimize the associated reactions of fever and rash. It has been given as replacement therapy and as prophylaxis against infections in patients with acquired and congenital gamma globulin deficiencies, but the preparation for IV use is preferred. Immune human serum globulin is considered less effective than hepatitis B immune globulin for postexposure prophylaxis of hepatitis B (serum hepatitis). It should not be used in children to prevent rubella (German measles) or chickenpox.

ACTIONS: Immune human serum globulin is a fraction of pooled plasma from normal donors and has 15–25 times more gamma globulin than normal plasma. It contains many antibodies normally present in human blood (e.g., neutralizing antibodies effective against diphtheria, poliomyelitis, infectious hepatitis, and measles). Doses of ISG are well distributed after IM administration, and antibodies are available for utilization within 48 hours. Immunity to measles lasts about 3–4 weeks, but immunity to HAV may be prolonged up to 3–6 months. Immunity to poliomyelitis may last up to 5–6 weeks.

CONTRAINDICATIONS: Known hypersensitivity to human gamma globulin preparations or to thimerosal (used as a preservative).

PRECAUTIONS: *Do not administer IV* (may cause severe hypotension and anaphylactic reactions). Do not use turbid solutions. Do not skin test with ISG since intradermal use will cause a local inflammatory reaction that can be misinterpreted as a false-positive allergic reaction. Doses greater than 5 ml should be divided among different injection sites (midthigh muscles preferred). Do not mix with any vaccines in the same syringe because the vaccine may be neutralized. Sensitization may occur with repeated injections or because of prior blood transfusions.

SIDE EFFECTS/ADVERSE REACTIONS: Infrequent, mild reactions include local tenderness, pain, muscle stiffness, and erythema at the injection site; low-grade fever; urticaria; headache; and malaise. Systemic reactions of angioneurotic edema, nephrotic syndrome, hypotension, and anaphylaxis have been reported (especially after accidental IV use).

ANTIDOTE: Treat hypersensitivity reactions with epinephrine as necessary.

Immune human serum globulin (IV use only) (Gamimune 5% IV)

ADMINISTRATION

Available Form: Injectable (IV), 5% solution of human gamma globulin in 50 and 100 ml vials (in 10% maltose).

Diluent: Can be further diluted in D5W.

Dosage (Parenteral): 100 mg/kg (2 ml/kg) given every month by IV infusion. Can be increased to 200 mg/kg (4 ml/kg) if necessary.

Rate: Begin infusion at 0.6–1.2 ml/kg/hr. If no untoward reactions are observed during the first 30 minutes, can increase to 1.2–2.4 ml/kg/hr.

INDICATIONS: Immune human serum globulin for IV administration is used for maintenance therapy of immune deficiency syndromes characterized by the absence or low levels of gamma globulin (e.g., congenital agammaglobulinemia, common variable hypogammaglobulinemia, immune deficiency of immunoglobulin M [IgM], or a combination of these). It is used primarily in patients who have small muscle masses or bleeding tendencies where IM use would be contraindicated or who require a rapid increase in their level of IgG.

ACTIONS: Immune human serum globulin for IV administration provides antibody for immediate use. In contrast, with the preparation for IM use there is a 2–7 day delay before peak antibody titers are achieved. Serum half-life of these antibodies is about 3 weeks.

CONTRAINDICATIONS: Hypersensitivity to any human gamma globulin preparations.

PRECAUTIONS: Do not use if the solution is turbid or if it has been frozen and thawed. Hypotension may occur.

SIDE EFFECTS/ADVERSE REACTIONS: See immune human serum globulin (IM use only).

ANTIDOTE: Treat hypersensitivity reactions with epinephrine.

Rabies immune globulin (Hyper-Rab)

ADMINISTRATION

Available Form: Injectable (IM), 150 international units (IU)/ml in 2 and 10 ml vials. (Derived from pooled plasma from donors who have been hyperimmunized with rabies vaccine.)

Dosage (Parenteral): 20 IU/kg; one-half given IM, one-half infiltrated into wound area. Dose is given at the same time as the first dose of rabies vaccine.

INDICATIONS: Rabies immune globulin provides passive immunity to rabies in the initial prophylactic treatment of individuals exposed to the rabies virus. Because of its low antigenicity, this preparation is preferred over the equine antirabies serum. Rabies immune globulin should be used in conjunction with the rabies vaccine series for all patients who have been severely bitten by any of the following:

- Known rabid animals or certain wild animals (e.g., bats, skunks, foxes, coyotes, raccoons, wild dogs or cats)
- Unknown dogs or cats (especially those showing signs suggestive of rabies)
- Otherwise healthy dogs or cats that develop rabid symptoms during the 10 day observation period

Severe bites from healthy dogs or cats that show no rabid symptoms after 10 days require only local treatment. The immune globulin should be given as soon as possible (preferably within 24 hours) to every patient when indicated. (For more detailed information, see the appendix.)

ACTIONS: Specific antibodies present in this immune globulin neutralize the rabies virus so that the virus's infective and pathogenic properties are destroyed. The antibodies are ineffective against virus that is already fixed to nerve tissue, so it is imperative that rabies immune globulin be administered as soon after the bite as possible. The immune globulin may also increase the incubation period of the disease, thus allowing more time for the concurrently administered rabies vaccine to produce active immunity. Rabies immune globulin may partially suppress the antibody response to the rabies vaccine, but this interference can apparently be overcome by giving the serum in a single early dose, followed by the assigned schedule of rabies vaccine doses and boosters. After IM administration, measurable levels of antibodies to rabies appear in the blood within 24 hours and peak in 3–9 days. Passive immunity lasts about 3 weeks.

CONTRAINDICATIONS: Repeated doses given after treatment with rabies vaccine have been started (the immune globulin may interfere with production of active immunity by the vaccine), concurrent corticosteroid therapy.

PRECAUTIONS: *Do not administer IV.* Do not give more than 5 ml into any one IM site; divide doses larger than 5 ml. Do not physically mix rabies immune globulin and rabies vaccine in the same syringe; neutralization of the vaccine may result. Withhold corticosteroids or ACTH during prophylactic rabies therapy because they may interfere with the antibody response to the vaccine. Observe the patient for possible hypersensitivity reactions (rare). Immediately flush and thoroughly cleanse all bite wounds and scratches; use soap and water, followed by iodine, alcohol, or other disinfectants. Immediate suturing of wounds is not advised.

SIDE EFFECTS/ADVERSE REACTIONS: Soreness, redness, and induration at the injection site and slight fever (sometimes lasting up to 3 days) have been reported. A few cases of angioneurotic edema, nephrotic syndrome, and anaphylactic shock have been reported.

ANTIDOTE: Treat hypersensitivity reactions with epinephrine if necessary.

Tetanus immune human globulin (Hyper-Tet, Gamatet)

ADMINISTRATION

Available Form: Injectable (IM), 250 units in vials and preloaded syringes. (Contains 15–18% gamma globulin prepared from the venous blood of humans hyperimmunized with tetanus toxoid.)

Dosage (Parenteral): Varies according to use.

For tetanus prophylaxis in children: 4 units/kg IM given with tetanus toxoid (use opposite extremity; give series). It is recommended that the whole 250 unit dose be given to children regardless of their size since the same amount of toxin will be produced by the tetanus organism in a child as in an adult.

For active tetanus therapy:

- Neonates: 500 units IM
- Infants and children: 200 units/kg IM (up to a total of 2000–6000 units)

INDICATIONS: Tetanus immune human globulin (TIG) is used to provide immediate passive immunity to patients whose wounds are potentially contaminated with *Clostridium tetani*. Because of its low antigenicity, it is preferred over tetanus antitoxin (equine origin).

TIG is especially indicated for those patients with little or no immunity to tetanus toxin or those with an uncertain history of immunization (e.g., no tetanus toxoid given within the last 5 years). It is also used as an adjunct to appropriate antibiotics in the treatment of active tetanus infections.

ACTIONS: TIG contains antibodies that specifically neutralize the free form of the exotoxin produced by *C. tetani*. The antibodies are ineffective against exotoxin already bound to nervous tissue. Passive immunity reportedly lasts for 24–32 days following IM administration.

CONTRAINDICATIONS: Known hypersensitivity to human gamma globulin or thimerosal (used as a preservative).

PRECAUTIONS: *Do not administer IV* (severe hypotension and anaphylaxis may occur). Skin tests with TIG should not be done because it causes a localized inflammation that can be mistaken for a positive allergic reaction. Tetanus immune human globulin is *not* a substitute for active immunization. A tetanus toxoid series or booster should be initiated (inject into a different site and use a different syringe). Do not mix TIG and tetanus toxoid in the same syringe. Maintain proper wound care and cleansing. Administer appropriate antibiotic therapy when indicated.

SIDE EFFECTS/ADVERSE REACTIONS: Infrequently, local tenderness, soreness, or stiffness at the injection site; erythema; or low-grade fever may occur. Reported systemic allergic reactions include angioneurotic edema, nephrotic syndrome, and anaphylaxis.

ANTIDOTE: Treat systemic hypersensitivity reactions with epinephrine.

Varicella-zoster immune globulin (VZIG)

ADMINISTRATION

Available Forms: Injectable (IM), 50 units/ml in 2.5 ml vials. Available from regional distribution centers (see list at end of chapter).

Diluent: Give undiluted.

Dosage (Parenteral)
For prevention or modification of varicella infections: Give a single IM dose within 72–96 hours after exposure.

- Children up to 10 kg: 125 units (2.5 ml)
- Children up to 20 kg: 250 units (5.0 ml)
- Children up to 30 kg: 375 units (7.5 ml)
- Children up to 40 kg: 500 units (10.0 ml)
- Children > 40 kg: 625 units (15.0 ml)

A second dose can be given in 4 weeks. Maximum is 625 units/dose.

INDICATIONS: Varicella-zoster immune globulin (VZIG) is reserved for the prevention or amelioration of varicella in susceptible immunocompromised children exposed to chickenpox or herpes zoster. It is also recommended for prophylaxis in newborn infants of women who develop a chickenpox rash from 5 days before to 2 days after delivery. Children whose immunity has been suppressed by disease (e.g., leukemia, immune deficiency syndromes) or medications (e.g., high-dose corticosteroids) appear to have the highest risk of developing serious, life-threatening, disseminated varicella infections. Newborns may suffer multiple birth defects after first, second, or third trimester infections. Chickenpox in otherwise healthy children with normal immune systems is usually benign and confers life-long immunity. It is therefore recommended that VZIG be reserved primarily for those high-risk patients who have no known history of chickenpox or no antibodies to varicella-zoster in their serum. While VZIG may be beneficial in preventing or modifying varicella infections, there is little evidence to support its effectiveness as a curative in the therapy of established, disseminated infections.

ACTIONS: VZIG is human gamma globulin prepared from pooled plasma that has high titers of varicella-zoster antibodies. The plasma, which is screened for these high titers, is obtained from volunteer donors. When administered within 72 hours after household or hospital exposure to varicella-zoster, VZIG provides antibodies that can prevent both clinical and serological evidence of disease. In those immunosuppressed children who develop chickenpox after receiving VZIG, the illness is often milder than is usually experienced by these patients. The duration of protection after one dose of VZIG is not well established. Patients who have continued or repeated exposure to the virus (and no clinical infection or serological evidence of immunity due to a subclinical infection) should probably be given a second dose about 4 weeks after the first one.

CONTRAINDICATIONS: Hypersensitivity to human gamma globulin.

PRECAUTIONS: Give IM injections deep into the gluteal muscle; doses greater than 5 ml should be divided into two injections. VZIG should be given as soon after exposure as possible (within 72 hours); after 96 hours, its value is uncertain. Its effectiveness in newborn infants, pregnant women, or other adults has not been established.

SIDE EFFECTS/ADVERSE REACTIONS: Adverse reactions are similar to those caused by gamma globulin. Pain, redness, and swelling can occur at the injection site. Allergic reactions have been reported rarely.

DRUG INTERACTIONS: Unknown.

ANTIDOTE: Treat allergic reactions symptomatically.

VZIG REGIONAL DISTRIBUTION CENTERS

- Massachusetts: Massachusetts Public Health Biologic Laboratories, 375 South St, Jamaica Plain, MA 02130, (617) 522-3700
- Maine: American Red Cross Blood Services, Northeast Region, 812 Huntington Ave, Boston, MA 02115, (617) 731-2130, ext 146

- Connecticut: American Red Cross Blood Services, Connecticut Region, 209 Farmington Ave, Farmington, CT 06032, (203) 677-4531, (203) 677-4538 (night)
- Vermont, New Hampshire: American Red Cross Blood Services, Vermont-New Hampshire Region, 32 North Prospect St, Burlington, VT 05402, (802) 658-6400
- Rhode Island: Rhode Island Blood Center, 551 North Main St, Providence, RI 02917, (401) 863-8366
- New Jersey, New York: The Greater New York Blood Program, 150 Amsterdam Ave, New York, NY 10023, (212) 570-3067, (212) 570-3068 (night)
- Delaware, Pennsylvania: American Red Cross, Penn-Jersey Region, 23rd & Chestnut St, Philadelphia, PA 19103, (215) 299-4114
- Maryland, Virginia, West Virginia, Washington, DC: American Red Cross Blood Services, Washington Region, 2025 E St NW, Washington, DC 20006, (202) 857-2021
- Alabama, Georgia, Mississippi, North Carolina, South Carolina, Puerto Rico: American Red Cross Blood Services, Atlanta Region, 1925 Monroe Dr NE, Atlanta, GA 30324, (404) 881-9800, ext 244, (404) 881-6752 (night)
- Florida: South Florida Blood Service, PO Box 420100, Miami, FL 33142, (305) 326-8888
- Indiana, Michigan, Ohio: American Red Cross Blood Services, Southeastern Michigan Region, 100 Mack Ave, PO Box 351, Detroit, MI 48232, (313) 949-2715
- Iowa, Minnesota, North Dakota, South Dakota, Wisconsin, Northern Illinois (Chicago): The Blood Center of SE Wisconsin, 1701 Wisconsin Ave, Milwaukee, WI 53233, (414) 955-5003
- Arkansas, Kansas, Kentucky, Missouri, Southern Illinois, Tennessee, Nebraska: American Red Cross, Missouri/Illinois Regional Blood Services, 4050 Lindell Blvd, St Louis, MO 63108, (314) 658-2000
- Louisiana, Oklahoma, Texas: Gulf Coast Region Blood Center, 1400 La Concha, Houston, TX 77054, (713) 791-6250
- Arizona, Colorado, New Mexico: United Blood Services, PO Box 25445, Albuquerque, NM 87125, (505) 247-9831
- Hawaii, Southern California: American Red Cross Blood Services, LA-Orange Counties Region, 1130 South Vermont Ave, Los Angeles, CA 90006, (213) 739-5620
- Nevada, Utah, Wyoming, Northern California: American Red Cross Blood Services, Central California Region, 333 McKendrie St, San Jose, CA 95110, (408) 292-6242, (408) 292-1626 (night)
- Alaska, Idaho, Montana, Oregon, Washington: Puget Sound Blood Center, Terry at Madison, Seattle, WA 98104, (206) 292-6525
- Canada: Canadian Red Cross Blood Transfusion Service, National Office, 95 Wellesley St East, Toronto, Ontario, (416) 923-6692
- All other countries: American Red Cross Blood Services, Northeast Region, 60 Kendrick St, Needham, MA 02194, (617) 449-0773

Appendix

The appendix has been designed to provide the health practitioner with concise and readily available information regarding vaccines, immunization schedules, pediatric dosage calculations, and other pertinent data that may be useful for the safe and effective administration of pediatric emergency medications. Dosage calculations and IV administration rates must be determined with accuracy and precision. The information provided includes a table listing the average body weights of infants and children, a pound-to-kilogram conversion chart, and a mathematical review to assist the practitioner in dosage calculations and IV drop rates for use with certain infusion pumps. A brief summary of commonly used emergency medications (listing doses, infusion rates, and significant precautions) is included as an aid for cardiopulmonary resuscitation. A chart of common drug incompatibilities is also provided.

VACCINES FOR ROUTINE CHILDHOOD IMMUNIZATIONS

Table A-1 presents the vaccines used for routine immunization against diphtheria-pertussis-tetanus, mumps, measles, rubella, and poliovirus.

VACCINES FOR SPECIFIC NEEDS

Table A-2 describes the vaccines used for patients who are at high risk or who have been exposed to the following microorganisms:

- Hepatitis B virus
- Influenza virus
- Pneumococci
- Rabies virus

TABLE A–1 Vaccines for Routine Childhood Immunizations*

Vaccine	Content	Indicated for	Dosage	Contraindications†	Adverse Effects/Comments
Diphtheria-Pertussis-Tetanus (DPT)	Aluminum-adsorbed diphtheria and tetanus toxoids, killed *B. pertussis* (thimerosal preservative)	Infants >6 wk Unimmunized children <7 yr	0.5 ml IM at 2, 4, and 6 mo *Booster* at 18 mo and at 4–6 yr (deep IM injection)	Hypersensitivity to pertussis or thimerosal, severe febrile illness, evolving neurological disorders; children 7 yr or older	Local pain, swelling, and erythema; low-grade fever; malaise; systemic allergic reactions; severe reaction to pertussis component‡
Tetanus-Diphtheria (adult) (Td)	Aluminum-adsorbed diphtheria and tetanus toxoids (thimerosal preservative)	Unimmunized children 7 yr and older	0.5 ml IM for 2 doses 2 mo apart, then 1 dose 6–12 mo later *Booster* every 10 yr (deep IM injection)	Children <7 yr, hypersensitivity to any component, severe respiratory illness (except when emergency booster is necessary)	Local pain, swelling, and erythema; low-grade fever; malaise (can be severe if Td given too often); postvaccinal neurological disorder (rare)
Tetanus-Diphtheria (pediatric) (TD)	Aluminum-adsorbed diphtheria and tetanus toxoids (thimerosal preservative)	Infants >2 mo and children 6 yr and under when pertussis is inadvisable or contraindicated	0.5 ml IM for 2 doses 2 mo apart, then 1 dose 6–12 mo later *Booster* of TD at 18 mo, then subsequent boosters of Td q10yr (deep IM injection)	Children 7 yr and older, other contraindications as for Td	As for Td TD (pediatric) has 5–10 times the diphtheria toxoid concentration of Td (adult)
Mumps§	Live, attenuated virus grown in chick embryo cell cultures	Children 12 mo and older‖	0.5 ml SC for 1 dose	Hypersensitivity to neomycin, altered immune status, immunodeficiency	Low-grade fever, transient rash, soreness, local swelling, erythema;

Measles§	Live, attenuated virus grown in chick embryo cell cultures (contains neomycin)	Children 15 mo and older#	0.5 ml SC for 1 dose	As for mumps; also: recent immune globulin injection, pregnant women	As for mumps
Rubella§ (Human diploid cell)	Live, attenuated virus grown in human diploid cells (RA 27/3 strain) (contains neomycin)	Children 12 mo and older‖	0.5 ml SC for 1 dose	As for mumps and measles vaccines	Low-grade fever, rash, sore throat, lymphadenopathy; rubella-like symptoms in 2–3 wk; arthralgia and arthritis increasing with age; encephalopathy (rare); suppressed response to TB skin test

*Adapted with permission from Abramowicz M (ed): *Handbook of Antimicrobial Therapy*, rev ed. New Rochelle, NY. The Medical Letter, Inc, 1980, pp 52–54.
†General contraindication is concurrent immunosuppressive therapy with anti-inflammatory steroids, antineoplastic agents, radiation therapy, etc.
‡Severe, sometimes fatal reactions to the pertussis component have occurred. Signs and symptoms include high fever, screaming fits, infantile spasms, shock, collapse, pseudotumor cerebri, neurological derangements, CNS damage (occasionally permanent), hemolytic anemia, and thrombocytopenic purpura.
§Can be given as combined measles-rubella or measles-mumps-rubella vaccine; if the combined product containing measles antigen is used, the first dose should be deferred until the child is 15 months old.
#Measles vaccine is not routinely given before 15 months of age because persisting maternal antibodies may prevent a satisfactory immunological response. Although there is a slightly lower seroconversion rate in children vaccinated at 12 months, the ACIP currently states that children vaccinated with the live, attenuated preparation at 12–15 months do not need to be revaccinated. Children, adolescents, and young adults who have not had measles and were not vaccinated with the *live* vaccine (i.e., prior to 1968) should be revaccinated.
‖Do not administer to infants <12 months of age because persisting maternal antibodies may interfere with a satisfactory immune response.

TABLE A–1 continued

Vaccine	Content	Indicated for	Dosage	Contraindications†	Adverse Effects/Comments
Poliovirus, Live, Oral (TOPV) "Sabin"	Trivalent, live, attenuated virus grown in monkey kidney cell cultures	Children 2 mo to 18 yr	1 dose given orally at 2 and 4 mo Booster at 18 mo and at 4–6 yr	Immunodeficiency, altered immune status, acute or debilitating illness, persistent vomiting or diarrhea, recent immune globulin injection (within 3 mo)	Rare vaccine-associated paralytic disease Unimmunized young adults and adults coming into contact with live, attenuated virus (TOPV) should receive primary immunization with *inactived* polio virus (IPV)

TABLE A-2 Vaccines for Specific Needs*

Vaccine	Content	Indicated for	Dosage	Contraindications†	Adverse Effects/Comments
Hepatitis B (Heptavax-B)	Aluminum-adsorbed inactivated hepatitis B surface antigen (HBsAg) (thimerosal preservative)	Patients 3 mo and older exposed to or at increased risk of infection	Children (3–10 mo): 0.5 ml IM initially; repeat in 1 and 6 mo Older children: 1.0 ml IM initially; repeat in 1 and 6 mo	Hypersensitivity to any component or thimerosal; pregnancy (Ineffective in preventing hepatitis A, non-A or non-B hepatitis)	Local soreness, swelling, and erythema; low-grade fever; systemic reactions (rare) of rash, malaise, arthralgia, myalgia. Can be given with hepatitis B immune globulin in the opposite arm Do *not* freeze or use thawed solutions
Influenza, trivalent	Inactivated whole or virus subunits ("split-virus"), types A, A', and B, grown in chick embryo cells	High risk patients Children 13 yr and older may receive whole virus preparation Children <13 yr should receive only the "split-virus" preparation	Children 13 yr and older: 0.5 ml SC or IM; can repeat in 1 mo Children <13 yr: 0.5 ml SC or IM; can repeat in 1 mo ("split-virus" preparation only)	Allergy to eggs or egg products; acute respiratory or other active, febrile infections	Local swelling, soreness, and erythema; low-grade fever; chills; malaise; backache

*Adapted with permission from Abramowicz M (ed): *Handbook of Antimicrobial Therapy*, rev ed. New Rochelle, NY, The Medical Letter Inc, 1980, pp 52–54.
†General contraindication is concurrent immunosuppressive therapy with anti-inflammatory steroids, antineoplastic agents, radiation therapy, etc.

TABLE A-2 continued

Vaccine	Content	Indicated for	Dosage	Contraindications†	Adverse Effects/Comments
Pneumococcus, polyvalent (Pnu-imune 23)	Antigenic polysaccharides from 23 pneumococcal types	High risk patients 2 yr and older who have not been previously immunized with any polyvalent pneumococcal vaccine	0.5 ml SC or IM as a single dose. Do not give booster injections	Children <2 yr, known hypersensitivity to this vaccine, pregnancy, acute febrile or respiratory infections (unless benefit outweighs risk)	Local swelling, soreness, and erythema; mild fever (more severe if revaccinated within 3 yr)
Rabies (Human Diploid Cell Strain) (Wyvac, Imovax)	Killed virus (HDCS WI-38 strain), grown in human diploid cell cultures (neomycin, gentamicin, or amphotericin B added)	Preexposure for high risk patients (e.g., veterinarians and other animal handlers) Postexposure for bite victims	Preexposure: 1.0 ml IM on day 0, 7, 21 and 28; booster q2yr; test antibody titers q2yr Postexposure bite victims: 1.0 ml IM on day 0, 3, 7, 14, and 28 plus 1 dose of rabies immune globulin on day 0 (opposite arm)	Preexposure: febrile illness, pregnancy Postexposure: none	Mild local pain, rash, swelling, and erythema; fever; headaches; muscle aches; malaise; rarely, neuroparalytic reactions, anaphylaxis, lymphadenopathy Consider concomitant tetanus prophylaxis in postexposure treatment

IMMUNIZATION SCHEDULES

Table A-3 lists the recommended schedules for immunization against diphtheria-pertussis-tetanus, poliovirus, measles, rubella, and mumps and gives the age for tuberculin skin tests. These schedules include recommendations for children not immunized in early infancy.

TREATMENT OF RABIES

Table A-4 is a guide for treatment of persons who have been bitten by or exposed to possibly rabid animals. It is only a guide and should be applied in conjunction with knowledge of the animal species involved, circumstances of the bite or other exposure, vaccination status of the animal, and presence of rabies in the area. Consult local and state public health officials if necessary.

TETANUS PROPHYLAXIS IN WOUND MANAGEMENT

Table A-5 gives the indications and types of preparations for tetanus prophylaxis according to the type of wound and the immunization status of the patient.

PEDIATRIC DOSAGES OF COMMONLY USED EMERGENCY DRUGS

Table A-6 lists drugs and dosages used to treat conditions commonly encountered in the emergency department.

AVERAGE PEDIATRIC WATER REQUIREMENT

Table A-7 gives the range of average water requirements for children of different ages under ordinary conditions.

COMPOSITION OF COMMONLY USED IV SOLUTIONS

Table A-8 lists the composition of commonly used IV solutions and provides a formula for calculating the amount of sodium necessary to replace sodium deficits.

TABLE A-3   Immunization Schedules*

Normal Infants and Children

AGE	PREPARATION†
2 mo	DPT #1, TOPV #1
4 mo	DPT #2, TOPV #2
6 mo	DPT #3
1 yr	PPD
15 mo	MMR‡
18 mo	DPT #4, TOPV #3
4–6 yr	DPT #5, TOPV #4
14–16 yr	Td (and every 10 yr thereafter)

Children Not Immunized in Early Infancy

TIMING	PREFERRED SCHEDULE†	ALTERNATIVE SCHEDULES†§ A	B	C
First visit	DPT #1, TOPV #1, PPD	MMR PPD	DPT #1, TOPV #1, PPD	DPT #1, TOPV #1, MMR, PPD
1 mo after first visit	MMR	DPT #1, TOPV #1	MMR, DPT #2	DPT #2
2 mo after first visit	DPT #2, TOPV #2	—	DPT #3, TOPV #2	DPT #3, TOPV #2
3 mo after first visit	(DPT #3 if TOPV #3 is not to be given until 10–16 mo)	DPT #2, TOPV #2	—	—
4 mo after first visit	DPT #3, (TOPV #3)#	—	(TOPV #3)#	(TOPV #3)#
5 mo after first visit	—	DPT #3, (TOPV #3)#	—	—
10–16 mo after last dose	DPT #4, TOPV #3 or #4	DPT #4, TOPV #3 or #4	DPT #4, TOPV #3 or #4	DPT #4, TOPV #3 or #4
Preschool‖	DPT #5, TOPV #4 or #5	DPT #5, TOPV #4 or #5	DPT #5. TOPV #4 or #5	DPT #5 TOPV #4 or #5
14–16 yr old	Td (and every 10 yr thereafter)	Td (and q10yr)	Td (and q10yr)	Td (and q10yr)

*Adapted with permission from *Report of the Committee on Infectious Diseases*, ed 19. Copyright American Academy of Pediatrics, 1982.

†DPT = diphtheria-pertussis-tetanus toxoid; do not give to children age 7 or older. TOPV = trivalent oral polio vaccine, types 1, 2, and 3. PPD = purified protein derivative for tuberculin skin tests (intradermal Mantoux preferred); frequency of tests depends on local epidemiology; annual or biennial testing is recommended unless local circumstances dictate less frequent or no testing. MMR = measles-mumps-rubella combined vaccine. Td = combined tetanus and diphtheria toxoids, adult strength; do not give to children age 7 and under.

‡Measles vaccine is not routinely given before 15 months of age, but the combined series can be given at 1 year as MMR vaccine (see Table A–1 also).

§Alternative schedule A can be used in those patients more than 15 months old if measles is occurring in the community. Alternative schedule B allows for more rapid DPT immunization. Alternative schedule C should be reserved for those whose access to medical care is compromised by poor compliance.

#TOPV #3 is optional for areas of likely importation of polio (e.g., some southwestern states).

‖The preschool dose is not necessary if DPT #4 or #5 is given after the child's fourth birthday.

TABLE A-4 Treatment of Rabies*

Animal Species	Condition of Animal at Time of Attack	Treatment of Exposed Person†
Domestic: Dog and cat	Healthy and available for 10 days of observation	None, unless animal develops rabies‡
	Rabid or suspected rabid	Rabies immune globulin§ and rabies vaccine‖
	Unknown (escaped)	Consultation with public health officials. If treatment is indicated, give rabies immune globulin§ and rabies vaccine‖
Wild: Skunk, bat, fox, coyote, raccoon, bobcat, and other carnivores	Regard as rabid unless proved negative by laboratory test#	Rabies immune globulin§ and rabies vaccine‖
Other: Livestock, rodents, rabbits, and hares	Consider individually. Provoked bites of squirrels, hamsters, guinea pigs, gerbils, chipmunks, rats, mice, and other rodents or rabbits and hares almost never call for antirabies prophylaxis. Local or state public health officials should be consulted about questions that arise about the need for rabies prophylaxis.	

* Adapted from Wyeth Rabies Vaccine (WYVAC®) package insert with permission of Wyeth Laboratories, date of issuance Aug. 9, 1982.
† All bites and wounds should be thoroughly cleansed with soap and water immediately. If antirabies treatment is indicated, both rabies immune globulin and rabies vaccine should be given as soon as possible, *regardless* of the interval from exposure.
‡ Begin treatment with rabies immune globulin and rabies vaccine at the first sign of rabies in biting domestic animals during the usual holding period of 10 days. The symptomatic animal should be killed immediately and tested.
§ If rabies immune globulin is not available, use antirabies serum of equine origin. Do not use more than the recommended dosage.
‖ Discontinue the vaccine if fluorescent antibody tests of animal are negative.
The animal should be killed and tested as soon as possible. Holding for observation is not recommended.

TABLE A-5 Tetanus Prophylaxis in Wound Management*

History of Tetanus Immunization (Number of Doses)	Clean, Minor Wounds		All Other Wounds	
	Td†	TIG‡	Td†	TIG‡
Uncertain	Yes	No	Yes	Yes
0–1	Yes	No	Yes	Yes
2	Yes	No	Yes	No§
3 or more	Yes‖	No	No#	No

* Adapted with permission from package insert for Tetanus Immune Globulin (Human), Cutter Biological, Emeryville, Calif.
† Td = tetanus-diphtheria toxoids, adult strength.
‡ TIG = tetanus immune globulin.
§ Unless wound more than 24 hr old.
‖ Unless more than 10 yr since last dose.
Unless more than 5 yr since last dose.

TABLE A–6 Pediatric Dosages of Commonly Used Emergency Drugs*†

Drug (How Supplied‡)	Dosage	Comments
Atropine (1 mg/10 ml, PLS)‡	0.01–0.03 mg/kg IV or via endotracheal tube (minimum dose = 0.1 mg)	For bradycardia. Can repeat dose in 5 min. Maximum = 1.0 mg. Do not mix with sodium bicarbonate.
Bretylium (50 mg/ml)	5–10 mg/kg/dose slow IV push; can repeat in 15–30 min (maximum cumulative dose = 30 mg/kg)	For refractory ventricular tachycardia and fibrillation, especially when lidocaine fails. Follow dose with electrical defibrillation attempt. Rapid IV rates produce hypotension.
Calcium gluconate (10%, 4.8 mEq/10 ml)	1–2 ml/kg slow IV push	For myocardial stimulation and low cardiac output. Do not mix with sodium bicarbonate.
Calcium chloride (10%, 13.6 mEq/10 ml, PLS)	0.2–0.5 ml/kg slow IV push	As for calcium gluconate.
Dextrose (50%, 500 mg/ml, PLS)	2–4 ml/kg slow IV push (25% solution)	For hypoglycemia. Dilute 50% solution 1:1 with water to get 25% concentration. Give slow IV bolus over 1–2 min. Hypertonic, sclerosing.
Digoxin (0.25 mg/ml, adult) (0.1 mg/ml, pediatric)	0.03–0.05 mg/kg IV or IM (deep) = total digitalizing dose (TDD)	As cardiotonic for pulmonary edema and congestive heart failure or as antiarrhythmic for supraventricular tachycardia. Use lower TDD if patient is arrhythmia-prone. Avoid use with calcium salts.
Dopamine (40 mg/ml in amps) (80 mg/ml in vials)	2–30 μg/kg/min by IV infusion (titrate to desired effect)	For shock. Dilute 200 mg in 500 ml D5W to give 400 μg/ml. Maximum rate is 50 μg/kg/min.
Epinephrine (1 mg/10 ml of 1:10,000 solution, PLS)	0.1 ml/kg IV push or via endotracheal tube	Myocardial stimulant. Use with defibrillation. Can repeat dose q5–10min. Do not mix with sodium bicarbonate.
Furosemide (10 mg/ml)	1–2 mg/kg slow IV push	Diuretic for edema, congestive heart failure, pulmonary edema. Ototoxic if IV rate rapid.

*Source: *Textbook of Advanced Cardiac Life Support.* Dallas, American Heart Assoc, 1983.
†See text for additional comments and precautions.
‡PLS = preloaded syringe.

TABLE A-6 continued

Drug (How Supplied‡)	Dosage	Comments
Hydralazine (20 mg/ml)	0.15 mg/kg IV or IM q6h; can increase by 0.1 mg/kg q6h prn until desired response	For hypertensive crisis.
Isoproterenol (1:5000 = 0.2 mg/ml or 200 µg/ml)	Usual IV infusion range, 0.1–0.5 µg/kg/min. Titrate to effect with heart rate, blood pressure. IV bolus dose = 0.010–0.025 mg (10–25 µg)	Myocardial stimulant, bronchodilator. For complete heart block, cardiogenic shock, severe bronchospasm. Dilute 1 mg (1 amp) in 250 ml D5W to give 4 µg/ml for IV infusion.
Lidocaine (100 mg/5 ml = 20 mg/ml, PLS)	Initial IV bolus of 1 mg/kg followed by IV infusion of 10–50 µg/kg/min. Titrate to response. Do not exceed infusion rate of 5 mg/min. Bolus dose can be given via endotracheal tube	Myocardial depressant for ventricular arrhythmias. Dilute for IV infusion, 1 gm/500 ml D5W = 2 mg/ml. IV bolus dose can be repeated in 5–10 min prn (maximum is 5 mg/kg/dose or 100 mg/hr). Do not mix with sodium bicarbonate. Toxic levels may cause seizures.
Morphine (2–15 mg/ml)	0.1–0.2 mg/dose IV, IM, or SC	Narcotic analgesic for pain, pulmonary edema, restlessness. Dilute doses with saline for slow IV push.
Naloxone (0.4 mg/ml, adult) (0.02 mg/ml, pediatric)	0.01 mg/kg/dose IV push	For narcotic-induced respiratory depression. Can repeat dose q2–3min as needed.
Phenytoin (50 mg/ml)	1–5 mg/kg/dose slow IV push (rate not to exceed 25 mg/min)	Antiarrhythmic for ventricular tachycardia due to digitalis toxicity. Dilute dose in saline just prior to use or give undiluted.
Potassium chloride (KCl) (2 mEq/ml)	0.3 mEq/kg/dose slow IV infusion over at least 1 hr	For digitalis toxicity, severe hypokalemia. *Must be diluted before use.* Do not exceed 40 mEq/500 ml. Monitor with ECG.

‡PLS = preloaded syringe.

TABLE A–6 continued

Drug (How Supplied‡)	Dosage	Comments
Procainamide (100 mg/ml)	2 mg/kg (diluted) slow IV push (rate not to exceed 25 mg/min)	Antiarrhythmic for ventricular tachycardia and other ventricular arrhythmias. Dilute IV bolus dose in D5W or saline for slow administration. Maximum is 100 mg/dose. Can repeat bolus q10–15min prn up to 1 gm total cumulative dose.
Propranolol (1 mg/ml)	0.05–0.15 mg/kg slow IV as a single dose given over 10 min; can be repeated once in 10 min	Cardiac depressant for supraventricular tachycardia, ventricular arrhythmias, digitalis toxicity. *For IV use only.* Dilute for slow administration. Maximum dose is 10 mg.
Sodium bicarbonate (1 mEq/ml)	1–2 mEq/kg/dose slow IV over several minutes (dilute 1:1 for infants)	Correction of acidosis during CPR. For neonates and infants, dilute 1:1 with water, etc. to give 0.5 mEq/ml. Give slowly to avoid hypernatremia. Do not mix with calcium salts.
Verapamil (2.5 mg/ml)	Infants (up to 1 yr), 0.1–0.2 mg/kg, IV push over 2 min (maximum is 0.75–2.00 mg) Children (1–15 yr), 0.1–0.3 mg/kg IV push over 2 min (maximum is 2.5 mg)	For supraventricular tachyarrhythmias. Can repeat bolus dose in 30 min for 1 dose.

‡PLS = preloaded syringe.

TABLE A–7 Average Pediatric Water Requirement*

Age	Average Body Weight (kg)	Total Water in 24 hr (ml)	Water/kg/24 hr (ml)
3 days	3.0	250–300	80–100
10 days	3.2	400–500	125–150
3 mo	5.4	750–850	140–160
6 mo	7.3	950–1100	130–155
9 mo	8.6	1100–1250	125–145
1 yr	9.5	1150–1300	120–135
2 yr	11.8	1350–1500	115–125
4 yr	16.2	1600–1800	100–110
6 yr	20.0	1800–2000	90–100
10 yr	28.7	2000–2500	70–85
14 yr	45.0	2200–2700	50–60
18 yr	54.0	2200–2700	40–50

*Adapted with permission from Vaughan VC III, McKay RJ Jr, Behrman RE (eds): *Nelson's Textbook of Pediatrics*, ed 11. Philadelphia, WB Saunders Co, 1979.

TABLE A–8 Composition of Commonly Used IV Solutions

Description	Dextrose (gm/100 ml)	Calories/liter	Na$^+$	K$^+$	Ca^{++}	Mg^{++}	Cl$^-$	HPO$_4^{--}$	Acetate	Lactate	Comments
D5W	5	170	0	0	0	0	0	0	0	0	Provides water for maintenance of plasma volume, supplies calories. Do not mix with blood; use separate IV line or Y-site tubing. Infusion rate should not exceed 0.5 gm dextrose/kg/hr (10 ml D5W/kg/hr). Solutions with NaCl also replace mild sodium deficits.
D10W	10	340	0	0	0	0	0	0	0	0	
D5/0.2NS	5	170	34	0	0	0	34	0	0	0	
D5/0.45NS	5	170	77	0	0	0	77	0	0	0	
D5/NS	5	170	154	0	0	0	154	0	0	0	
0.45NS	0	0	77	0	0	0	77	0	0	0	For maintenance of plasma volume, administration of blood, replacement of mild sodium deficits, use in diabetics.
NS	0	0	154	0	0	0	154	0	0	0	
3% NaCl	0	0	513	0	0	0	513	0	0	0	Correction of severe hyponatremia. Infusion rate should not exceed 10 ml/kg/hr. Use cautiously in those with edema or cardiac disease.
5% NaCl	0	0	855	0	0	0	855	0	0	0	

To calculate amount of sodium necessary to replace deficits, use the following formula: mEq Na$^+$ needed = (desired serum level [mEq/liter]) – (patient's serum level [mEq/liter]) × body weight (kg) × 0.6.

TABLE A-8 continued

Description	Dextrose (gm/100 ml)	Calories/liter	Na+	K+	Ca++	Mg++	Cl-	HPO4--	Acetate	Lactate	Comments
D5LR	5	170	130	4	3	0	109	0	0	28	Lactated solutions correct mild acidosis and replace fluids and electrolytes, especially following burns. Also supplies calories.
LR (Hartmann's)	0	0	130	4	3	0	109	0	0	28	
D5R	5	170	147	4	4	0	155	0	0	0	Balanced solutions for fluid and electrolyte replacement; contains an excess of chloride, so observe for hyperchloremic acidosis.
Ringer's	0	0	147	4	4	0	155	0	0	0	
Isolyte P with D5W	5	170	25	20	0	3	22	3	23	0	Provides water for hydration, carbohydrates to minimize ketosis, and balanced amount of electrolytes for replacement and maintenance therapy in neonates and infants.
D5W with Electrolyte No. 48	5	170	25	20	0	3	22	3	0	23	
Isolyte M with D5W	5	170	40	35	0	0	40	15	20	0	Like Isolyte P but for children and adults. Same as Ionosol T with D5W solution.
D5W with Electrolyte No. 75	5	170	40	35	0	0	40	15	0	20	

KILOGRAM CONVERSION CHART

Table A–9 gives information for converting weight in pounds (lb) to weight in kilograms (kg) and vice-versa.

TABLE A–9 Kilogram Conversion Chart

lb	kg	kg	lb
1	0.5	1	2.2
2	0.9	2	4.4
4	1.8	3	6.6
6	2.7	4	8.8
8	3.6	5	11.0
10	4.5	6	13.2
20	9.1	8	17.6
30	13.6	10	22.0
40	18.2	20	44.0
50	22.7	30	66.0
60	27.3	40	88.0
70	31.8	50	110.0
80	36.4	60	132.0
90	40.9	70	154.0
100	45.4	80	176.0
150	68.2	90	198.0
200	90.8	100	220.0

1 lb = 0.454 kg   1 kg = 2.204 lb

AVERAGE BODY WEIGHTS

Table A–10 gives the average weight in kilograms and pounds for children from birth to 12 years.

TABLE A–10 Average Body Weights*

Age†	Girls kg	Girls lb	Boys kg	Boys lb
Birth	3.36	7.4	3.40	7.5
3 mo	5.62	12.4	5.72	12.6
6 mo	7.26	16.0	7.58	16.7
9 mo	8.71	19.2	9.07	20.0
1 yr	9.75	21.5	10.07	22.2
18 mo	11.11	24.5	11.43	25.2
2 yr	12.29	27.1	12.56	27.7
2½	13.43	29.6	13.61	30.0
3	14.42	31.8	14.61	32.2
3½	15.38	33.9	15.56	34.3
4	16.42	36.2	16.51	36.4
4½	17.46	38.5	17.42	38.4
5	18.78	41.4	19.41	42.8
6	21.09	46.5	21.91	48.3
7	23.68	52.2	24.54	54.1
8	26.35	58.1	27.26	60.1
9	28.94	63.8	29.94	66.0
10	31.89	70.3	32.61	71.9
11	35.74	78.8	35.20	77.6
12	39.74	87.6	38.28	84.4

*Source: Adapted from Vaughan VC III, McKay RJ Jr, Behrman RE (eds): *Nelson's Textbook of Pediatrics*, ed 11. Philadelphia, WB Saunders Co, 1979; Wong D, Wholey L: *Clinical Handbook of Pediatric Nursing*. Springfield, Ill, The CV Mosby Co, 1981, p 65. The portion adapted from Vaughn et al was modified from studies by Howard V Meredith, Iowa Child Welfare Research Station, The State University of Iowa.

†Age in years unless otherwise specified.

COMPATIBILITY OF DRUGS COMBINED IN A SYRINGE

Table A–11 gives the chemical compatibility of various medications when they are combined in the same container.

CALCULATION OF DOSAGES

This section is intended as a quick review of mathematical formulas used to convert available medications to usable dosages. By using the following equation, you can obtain the proper calculated amount:

desired dosage/unknown amount (X) to be given = dosage available/units in dosage available

Example 1: An injectable preparation with a concentration of 1 mg/ml.
   desired dosage = 0.5 mg
   dosage available = 1 mg

Appendix 431

TABLE A–11 Compatibility of Drugs Combined in a Syringe*

	Atropine	Butorphanol (Stadol)	Chlorpromazine (Thorazine)	Codeine	Diazepam† (Valium)	Diphenhydramine (Benadryl)	Hydroxyzine (Vistaril)	Innovar	Meperidine (Demerol)	Morphine
Atropine		C	C	P	X	C	C	C	C	C
Butorphanol (Stadol)	C		P		X		C	C		
Chlorpromazine (Thorazine)	C	P		C	X	C	P	C	C	C
Codeine	P		C		X		C		P	
Diazepam† (Valium)	X	X	X	X		X	X	X	X	X
Diphenhydramine (Benadryl)	C		C		X		C	C	C	C
Hydroxyzine (Vistaril)	C	C	P	C	X	C		C	C	C
Innovar	C	C			X	C	C		C	P
Meperidine (Demerol)	C		C	P	X	C	C	C		X
Morphine	C		C		X	C	C	C	X	
Pentazocine (Talwin)	C		C	P	X	C	C	A	A	A
Pentobarbital† (Nembutal)	P				X	X	X	X	X	X
Phenobarbital† (Na Luminal)					X	X	X	X	X	X
Prochlorperazine (Compazine)	C			C	X	C	C	C	C	C
Promethazine (Phenergan)	C			C	X	X	C	C	P	C
Scopolamine	C		C	C	X	C	C	C	C	C
Secobarbital (Seconal)		X			X		X		X	

*C = compatible. X = incompatible. P = provisional compatibility; use within 15 min. A = pentazocine may antagonize narcotic analgesia.
†It is recommended that diazepam or barbiturates not be mixed with any other medications in the same syringe.

TABLE A-11 continued

	Atropine	Butorphanol (Stadol)	Chlorpromazine (Thorazine)	Codeine	Diazepam† (Valium)	Diphenhydramine (Benadryl)	Hydroxyzine (Vistaril)	Innovar	Meperidine (Demerol)	Morphine	Pentazocine (Talwin)	Pentobarbital† (Nembutal)	Phenobarbital† (Na Luminal)	Prochlorperazine (Compazine)	Promethazine (Phenergan)	Scopolamine	Secobarbital (Seconal)
Pentazocine (Talwin)	C		C	A	X	C	C	A	A	A		X			C	C	
Pentobarbital† (Nembutal)	P		X	X	X	X	X		X	X	X		X	X	X	C	X
Phenobarbital† (Na Luminal)			X	X	X	X	X		X	X		X			X	C	X
Prochlorperazine (Compazine)	C		C	C	X	C	C	P	C	C	C	X			C	C	
Promethazine (Phenergan)	C		C	X	X	C	C	C	C	C	C	X	X	C		C	
Scopolamine	C	C	C	P	X	C	C	C	C	C		C	X	C	C		
Secobarbital (Seconal)		X	X	X	X	X			X					X	X		

†It is recommended that diazepam or barbiturates not be mixed with any other medications in the same syringe.

units in dosage available = 1 ml
unknown amount to be given = X
set up equation: $\dfrac{0.5 \text{ mg}}{X} = \dfrac{1 \text{ mg}}{1 \text{ ml}}$
cross multiply: (1 mg) (X) = (0.5 mg) (1 ml)
reduce equation: 1X   = 0.5 ml
amount to be given   = 0.5 ml

Example 2: An oral solution with a concentration of 250 mg/5 ml.
desired dosage = 375 mg
dosage available = 250 mg
units in dosage available = 5 ml
unknown amount to be given = X
set up equation: $\dfrac{375 \text{ mg}}{X} = \dfrac{250 \text{ mg}}{5 \text{ ml}}$
cross multiply: (250 mg) (X) = (5 ml) (375 mg)
reduce equation: 250X = 1875 ml
                                   X = 1875/250 ml
amount to be given   = 7.5 ml (or 1½ tsp)

Example 3: An injectable preparation with a concentration of 8 mg/ml.
desired dosage = 2 mg
dosage available = 8 mg
units in dosage available = 1 ml
unknown amount to be given = X
set up equation: $\dfrac{2 \text{ mg}}{X} = \dfrac{8 \text{ mg}}{1 \text{ ml}}$
cross multiply: (8 mg)(X) = (2 mg) (1 ml)
reduce equation: 8X = 2 ml
                                  X = 2/8
amount to be given   = 0.25 ml

Example 4: A digoxin injection of 0.5 mg/2 ml.
desired dosage = 0.1 mg
dosage available = 0.5 mg
units in dosage available = 2 ml
unknown amount to be given = X
set up equation: $\dfrac{0.1 \text{ mg}}{X} = \dfrac{0.5 \text{ mg}}{2 \text{ ml}}$
cross multiply: (0.5 mg) (X) = (0.1 mg) (2 ml)
reduce equation: 0.5X = 0.2 ml
                                X = 0.2/0.5
amount to be given   = 0.4 ml

CALCULATION OF IV DROP RATES

The following formula can be used to calculate the drop rate (number of drops per minute) needed to infuse a given volume of solution over a specified period of time.
flow rate in drops/min =
(drops in 1 ml) × (total ml)/(desired total time in min for infusion)

Example 1
  drops in 1 ml = 60 (microdrip IV set)
  total ml = 100
  desired infusion time = 3 hr (180 min)
  flow rate in drops/min = X
  X = (60 × 100)/180 = 33 drops/min

Example 2
  drops in 1 ml = 20 (macrodrip IV set)
  total ml = 100
  desired infusion time = ½ hr (30 min)
  flow rate in drops/min = X
  X = (20 × 100)/30 = 67 drops/min

Example 3
  drops in 1 ml = 15
  total ml = 50
  desired infusion time = 25 min
  flow rate in drops/min = X
  X = (15 × 50)/25 = 30 drops/min

Example 4
  drops in 1 ml = 10
  total ml = 100
  desired infusion time = 1 hr (60 min)
  flow rate in drops/min = X
  X = (10 × 100)/60 = 17 drops/min

CALCULATION OF INFUSION RATES FOR DRUGS GIVEN IN µg/kg/min*

Doses of medications such as dopamine, dobutamine, isoproterenol, lidocaine, levarterenol, and sodium nitroprusside are given in µg/kg/min. Determining the infusion rates and concentrations of these diluted solutions can be confusing, particularly when the standard concentrations used in adults are too concentrated for pediatric use. The following formulas should be helpful in computing desired infusion rates, solution concentrations, and dosages.

Equation 1: $C = \dfrac{60\,DW}{R}$

Equation 2: $D = \dfrac{CR}{60\,W}$

Equation 3: $R = \dfrac{60\,DW}{C}$

where   C = concentration of the final solution in µg/ml
    60 = proportionality constant for 60 min/hr
    D = dose in µg/kg/min

*Source: Zenk KE: Dosage calculations for drugs administered by infusion. *Am J Hosp Pharm* 1980;37:1304.

W = body weight in kilograms
R = rate of infusion in ml/hr

Example 1. A 9 lb infant requires a dopamine infusion to be started at 10 μg/kg/min. A solution of 200 mg of dopamine in 500 ml D5W is prepared. What should be the infusion rate in ml/hr?

W = 9 lb (about 4 kg; see Table A–9)
D = 10 μg/kg/min
C = 200 mg/500 ml = 0.4 mg/ml or 400 μg/ml

Using equation 3: Solve for R (rate of infusion in ml/hr).

$$R = \frac{60\ DW}{C}$$

$$= \frac{(60)(10)(4)}{400}$$

$$= 2400/400$$

$$= 6\ ml/hr\ (or\ 6\ drops/min\ if\ a\ microdrip\ IV\ tubing\ is\ used)$$

Example 2. An IV solution of 400 mg dopamine in 500 ml D5W is begun on a 45 lb child at an arbitrary infusion rate of 30 ml/hr (e.g., 30 drops/min using a microdrip IV set). The physician wants to know what μg/kg/min dose this patient is receiving at the current rate of infusion.

W = 45 lb (about 20 kg; see Table A–9)
R = 30 ml/hr
C = 400 mg/500 ml = 0.8 mg/ml or 800 μg/ml

Using equation 2: Solve for D (dose in μg/kg/min).

$$D = \frac{CR}{60W}$$

$$= \frac{(800)(30)}{(60)(20)}$$

$$= \frac{24000}{1200}$$

$$= 20\ μg/kg/min$$

Bibliography

1. Abramowicz M (ed): *Medical Letter on Drugs and Therapeutics: Handbook of Antimicrobial Therapy*, rev ed. New Rochelle, NY, The Medical Letter Inc, 1980.

2. Abramowicz M (ed): *Medical Letter on Drugs and Therapeutics: Handbook of Antimicrobial Therapy*, rev ed. New Rochelle, NY, The Medical Letter Inc, 1982.

3. *AMA Drug Evaluations*, ed 3. Littleton, Mass, PSG Publishing Co Inc, 1977.

4. Aranda JV, Grondin D, Sasyniuk BI: Pharmacologic considerations in the therapy of neonatal apnea. *Pediatr Clin North Am* 1981;28:113–133.

5. Aranda JV, Sitar DS, Parsons WD, et al: Pharmacokinetic aspects of theophylline in premature newborns. *N Engl J Med* 1976;295:413–416.

6. Avery ME, Taeusch HW: *Diseases of the Newborn*, ed 5. Philadelphia, WB Saunders Co, 1984.

7. Benowitz NL: Nitrite and nitrate poisoning. *CHSP Voice* 1983;10:90–92.

8. Bunney WE Jr (moderator): Basic and clinical studies of endorphins—an NIH conference. *Ann Intern Med* 1979; 91(2):239–250.

9. Caplik JF, Walter JK: *Guidelines for the Preparation of Intravenous Admixture Solutions*. Berkeley, Calif, Cutter Medical Laboratories, 1980.

10. Classification and diagnosis of diabetes mellitus and other categories of glucose intolerance—National Diabetes Data Group. *Diabetes* 1979;28:1039–1057.

11. Cunha BA, Ristuccia AM: Clinical usefulness of vancomycin. *Clin Pharm* 1983;2:417–424.

12. Davies JG, Taylor CM, White HR, et al: Clinical limitations of the estimation of glomerular filtration rate from height/plasma creatinine ratio: A comparison with simultaneous ^{51}Cr edetic acid slope clearance. *Arch Dis Child* 1982;57:607–610.

13. Del Vecchio PJ: Apnea after IV diazepam administration. *JAMA* 1978;239:614.

14. Driscoll DJ, Gillette PC, McNamara DG: The use of dopamine in children. *J Pediatr* 1978;92:309–314.

15. Eichenwald HF: Prescribing cephalosporins in children—Drug therapy. *J Clin Ther* 1983;13:221–231.

16. Elliot GT, Quinn SL: Intravenous nitroglycerin. *Drug Intell Clin Pharm* 1982;16:211–217.

17. *Fluid and Electrolytes: Some Practical Guides to Clinical Use.* Chicago, Abbott Laboratories, 1970.

18. Fuquay D, Koup J, Smith AL: Management of neonatal gentamicin overdosage. *J Pediatr* 1981;99:473–476.

19. Gahart BL: *Intravenous Medications: A Handbook for Nurses and Other Allied Health Personnel.* St Louis, The CV Mosby Co, 1977.

20. Geffner ES (ed): *The Hospital Pharmacy Compendium of Drug Therapy.* New York, Biomedical Information Corp, 1982.

21. Gelband H, Rosen M: Pharmacological basis for the treatment of cardiac arrhythmias. *Pediatrics* 1975;55:59–67.

22. Goetzman BW, Sunshine P, Johnson JD, et al: Neonatal hypoxia and pulmonary vasospasm: Response to tolazoline. *J Pediatr* 1976;89:617–621.

23. Goldfrank L, Kirstein R: Toxicologic emergencies: The Tea Party. *Hosp Physician* 1977;13:4.

24. Goodman LS, Gilman A: *The Pharmacological Basis of Therapeutics,* ed 6. New York, Macmillan Publishing Co Inc, 1980.

25. Graef JW, Cone TE (eds): *Manual of Medical Therapeutics.* Boston, Little Brown & Co, 1975.

26. Hansten PD: *Drug Interactions,* ed 3. Philadelphia, Lea & Febiger, 1976.

27. Heinemann CJ: *Emergency Drug Reference.* Kettering, Ohio, Kettering Medical Center, 1981.

28. Hoecker J, Pickering LK, Swaney J, et al: Clinical pharmacology of tobramycin in children. *J Infect Dis* 1978;137:592–596.

29. Holden KR, Freeman JN: Neonatal seizures and their treatment. *Clin Perinatol* 1975;2:3–13.

30. Hopefl AW: Clinical use of IV acyclovir. *Drug Intell Clin Pharm* 1983;17:623–628.

31. Hume AL, Kerkering TM: Ketoconazole. *Drug Intell Clin Pharm* 1983;17:169–174.

32. Kagan BM: *Antimicrobial Therapy,* ed 2. Philadelphia, WB Saunders Co, 1974.

33. Knudsen FU: Rectal administration of diazepam in solution in the acute treatment of convulsions in infants and children. *Arch Dis Child* 1979;54:855–857.

34. Lesar TS, Rotschafer JC, Strand LM, et al: Gentamicin dosing errors with four commonly used nomograms. *JAMA* 1982;248:1190–1193.

35. Management of Acetaminophen Overdose with N-acetylcysteine, monograph. Fort Washington, Pa, McNeil Consumer Products Co, 1979.

36. Manufacturers' product package inserts for medications.

37. Masaki BW: Physiologic basis for pediatric drug therapy. *US Pharmacist,* Nov/Dec 1978, pp 36–49.

38. Mattila MAK, Ruoppi MK, Ahlström-Bengs E, et al: Diazepam in rectal solution in premedication in children, with special reference to serum concentrations. *Br J Anaesth* 1981;53:1269–1272.

39. Maxwell MH, Kleeman DR: *Clinical Disorders of Fluid and Electrolyte Metabolism.* New York, McGraw-Hill Book Co Inc, 1962.

40. McCracken GH, Nelson JD: *Antimicrobial Therapy for Newborns*. New York, Grune & Stratton, 1977.

41. McIntyre KM, Lewis JA (eds): *Textbook of Advanced Cardiac Life Support*. Dallas, American Heart Assoc, 1981.

42. Meyers BR: *Antimicrobial Prescribing*. Princeton, NJ, Antimicrobial Prescribing Inc, 1983.

43. Milligan N: Rectal diazepam in the treatment of absence status: A pharmacodynamic study. *J Neurol Neurosurg Psychiatry* 1981;44:914–917.

44. Mitenko PA, Ogilvie RI: Rational intravenous doses of theophylline. *N Engl J Med* 1973;289:600–603.

45. Oski FA: *Hematologic Problems in the Newborn*, ed 3. Philadelphia, WB Saunders Co, 1982.

46. *Parenteral Solutions Handbook: A Guide to Optimal Utilization*. Berkeley, Calif, Cutter Laboratories, 1965.

47. Pascoe DJ, Grossman M: *Quick Reference to Pediatric Emergencies*. Philadelphia, JB Lippincott Co, 1973.

48. Pasternak GW: Endogenous opiod systems in brain. *Am J Med* 1980;68:157–159.

49. Pfeifle CE, Adler DS, Gannaway WL: Phenytoin solubility in three intravenous solutions. *Am J Hosp Pharm* 1981;38:358–362.

50. Pieper JA, Slaughter RL, Anderson GD, et al: Lidocaine pharmacokinetics. *Drug Intell Clin Pharm* 1982;16:291–294.

51. Prober CG, Yeager AS, Arvin AM: Effect of chronologic age on the serum concentrations of amikacin in the sick term and premature infants. *J Pediatr* 1981;98:636–640.

52. Rapp RP, Young B, Perrier D, et al: Phenytoin dosing in infants. *Drug Intell Clin Pharm* 1977;11:462–464.

53. Raymond G, Day P, Rabb M: Sodium content of commonly administered intravenous drugs. *Hosp Pharm* 1982;17:560–561.

54. Reilly MJ (ed): *The American Hospital Formulary Service*. Washington, DC, American Society of Hospital Pharmacists Inc, 1982.

55. Russell FE: *Snake Venom Poisoning*. Philadelphia, JB Lippincott Co, 1980.

56. Russell WL, McKenzie MW: Drug usage in newborn intensive care units. *Hosp Form* 1983;18:625–638.

57. Safe blood for transfusion. *Med Lett* 1983;25:93–95.

58. Salam-Adams M, Adams RD: The convulsive state and idiopathic epilepsy, in Isselbacher KJ, Adams RD, Braunwald E, et al (eds): *Harrison's Principles of Internal Medicine*, ed 9. New York, McGraw-Hill Book Co, 1980, pp 131–139.

59. Sardemann H, Colding H, Hendel J, et al: Kinetics and dose calculations of amikacin in the newborn. *Clin Pharmacol Ther* 1976;20:59–66.

60. Schulte-Steinberg O: Neural blockade for pediatric surgery, in Cousins MJ, Bridenbaugh PO (eds): *Neural Blockade in Clinical Anesthesia and Management of Pain*. Philadelphia, JB Lippincott Co, 1980, pp 504–505.

61. Schwartz GJ, Haycock MB, Edelman CM, et al: A simple estimate of glomerular filtration rate in children derived from body length and plasma creatinine. *Pediatrics* 1976;58:259–263.

62. Shirkey HC (ed): *Pediatric Therapy*, ed 5. St Louis, The CV Mosby Co, 1975.

63. Simmons MA, Adcock DW, Bard H, et al: Hypernatremia and intracranial hemorrhage in neonates. *N Engl J Med* 1974;291:6–10.

64. Soyka LF: The rational use of digoxin in infants and children. *Hosp Form* 1979;14:546–555.

65. Sutherland VC: *A Synopsis of Pharmacology,* ed 2. Philadelphia, WB Saunders Co, 1970.

66. Trissel LA: *Handbook on Injectable Drugs*. Washington, DC, American Society of Hospital Pharmacists Inc, 1977.

67. Weinberger M. Hendeles L: Poisoning patients with intravenous theophylline, editorial. *Am J Hosp Pharm* 1980; 37:49–50.

68. Yeager AS: Use of acyclovir in premature and term neonates. *Am J Med* 1982;73(suppl):205–209.

69. Zenk KE: Drug dosing in children, in Pagliaro LA, Levin RH (eds): *Problems in Pediatric Drug Therapy*. Hamilton, Ill, Drug Intelligence Publications Inc, 1979, pp 209–286.

70. Zenk KE: Guidelines for the safe use of digoxin in infants and children. *Infusion* 1982;6:76–84.

71. Zenk KE, Amlie RN: Neonatal emergency transport box. *Drug Intell Clin Pharm* 1982;16:122–125.

Index

A

Absorption, drug, 11
Acetaminophen, poisoning from, N-acetylcysteine for, 371–378
N-Acetylcysteine
   as antidote, 377–378
   as bronchodilator, 137
Achromycin, 220–221
Acid-base balance, 79–80
   disorders of, agents for, 79–90. *See also* Electrolyte replacements
Activated charcoal as antidote, 378–379
Acyclovir as antiviral agent, 230–232
Adrenalin in cardiopulmonary resuscitation, 27–28
Adrenergic blockers in cardiopulmonary resuscitation, 35–38
   phentolamine as, 36
   tolazoline as, 37–38
Adrenergic receptors, 23*t*
Adrenergics in cardiopulmonary resuscitation
   dobutamine as, 25–26
   dopamine as, 26–27
   epinephrine as, 27–28
   isoproterenol as, 29–30
   norepinephrine as, 30–31
   phenylephrine as, 31–32

   type of, and primary receptor type stimulated by, 24*t*
Age-appropriate time frames, 4*t*
Albumin (human) as plasma volume expander, 94–95
Albumisol as plasma volume expander, 94–95
Albutein as plasma volume expander, 94–95
Albuterol as bronchodilator, 138–139
Allergy, antihistamines for, 127–133. *See also* Antihistamines
Alupent as bronchodilator, 145–146
Amicar as coagulant, 103–104
Amikacin as aminoglycoside, 154–155
Amikin as aminoglycoside, 154–155
Aminoglycosides, 151–162
   actions of, 153
   amikacin as, 154–155
   antimicrobial spectrum of, 153
   contraindications for, 153
   drug interactions with, 154
   gentamicin as, 156–157
   indications for, 153
   kanamycin as, 158–159
   neomycin as, 159–160
   precautions with, 153–154
   renal impairment and, 152–153
   side effects of, 154
   streptomycin as, 160–161

Page numbers followed by *t* indicate tables.

442 INDEX

tobramycin as, 161–162
Aminophyllin as
  bronchodilator, 139–140
Aminophylline as bronchodilator
  oral, 140–143
  parenteral, 139–140
Amoxicillin, 198–199
Amoxil, 198–199
Amphotericin B as antifungal
  agent, 232–234
Ampicillin, 199–201
Ancef as first-generation
  cephalosporin, 169–170
Anectine as skeletal muscle
  relaxant, 316–317
Anesthetics, local, 279–285. *See also*
  Local anesthetics
Anspor as first-generation
  cephalosporin, 173–174
Antiarrhythmics in cardiopulmonary
  resuscitation, 39–47
  bretylium tosylate as, 40–41
  lidocaine as, 41–42
  phenytoin as, 42–43
  procainamide as, 43–45
  propranolol as, 45–46
  verapamil as, 46–47
Antiasthmatics, 135–146
Antibiotics, 147–259
  aminoglycosides, as, 151–162. *See
    also* Aminoglycosides
  cephalosporins as, 165–183. *See
    also* Cephalosporins
  penicillins as, 185–206. *See also*
    Penicillins
  sulfonamides as, 207–213. *See also*
    Sulfonamides
  tetracyclines as, 215–221. *See also*
    Tetracyclines
  for urinary tract infections, 223–228.
    See also Urinary tract anti-
    infectives and antiseptics
Anticoagulants, 98, 110–112
Anticonvulsants, 289–307
  carbamazepine as, 292–293
  clonazepam as, 293–295
  diazepam as, 295–296
  ethosuximide as, 296–297
  paraldehyde as, 298–299
  phenobarbital as, 299–301
  phenytoin as, 302–304

pyridoxine hydrochloride
  as, 304–305
valproic acid as, 306–307
Antidiarrheals, 365–369
  diphenoxylate with atropine
    as, 367–368
  paregoric as, 368–369
  paregoric with kaolin-pectin
    as, 368–369
Antidotes, 375–395
  N-acetylcysteine as, 377–378
  activated charcoal as, 378–379
  cyanide antidote package
    as, 379–381
  deferoxamine mesylate as, 381–382
  dimercaprol as, 382–383
  edetate calcium disodium
    as, 384–385
  methylene blue as, 386–388
  naloxone as, 388–389
  penicillamine as, 389–390
  physostigmine salicylate
    as, 391–392
  pralidoxine as, 392–393
  sodium polystyrene sulfonate
    as, 394–395
  syrup of ipecac as, 385–386
Antiemetics, 355–363
  chlorpromazine as, 357–358
  diphenidol as, 359–360
  hydroxyzine as, 360–361
  promethazine as, 361–363
Antifungal agents
  amphotericin B as, 232–234
  griseofulvin as, 244–246
  ketoconazole as, 249–250
  miconazole as, 252–253
  nystatin as, 254
Antihemophilic factor
  as coagulant, 100–101
  cryoprecipitated, as
    coagulant, 101–107
Antihistamines for allergy, 127–133
  chlorpheniramine as, 128
  dimenhydrinate as, 128–129
  diphenhydramine as, 130
  hydroxyzine as, 131–132
  premethazine as, 132–133
Antihypertensives in cardiopulmonary
  resuscitation, 55–63
  diazoxide as, 56–57
  hydralazine, 57–58

Antilirium as antidote, 391–392, 393
Antiserums, 405–412
  hepatitis B immune globulin as, 406
  immune human serum globulins as, 407–409
  rabies immune globulin as, 409–410
  tetanus immune human globulin as, 410–411
  varcella-zoster immune globulin as, 411–412
Antivenins, 397–403
  Crotalidae polyvalent, 399–400
  Latrodectus mactans, 400–401
  Micrurus fulvius, 402–403
Antiviral agent, acyclovir as, 230–232
Apresoline in cardiopulmonary resuscitation, 57–58
AquaMEPHYTON as coagulant, 107–109
Arsenic, poisoning from, dimercaprol for, 382–383
Asthma, agents for, 135–146. *See also* Bronchodilators
Atarax
  as antiemetic, 360–361
  as antihistamine, 131–132
Atropine
  in cardiopulmonary resuscitation, 33–34
  diphenoxylate with, as antidiarrheal, 367–368
  pediatric dosages of, 424*t*
Autonomic nervous system, 16–17
  effects of, 18*t*

B

Bactrim, 211–212
Barbiturates
  in intracranial hypertension management, 321–322
  as sedative-hypnotics, 324–331
    actions of, 325–326
    antidotes for, 328
    contraindications for, 326
    drug incompatibilities with, 328
    drug interactions with, 328
    indications for, 324–325
    pentobarbital as, 328–330
    precautions with, 326–327
    secobarbital as, 330–331
    side effects of, 327–328

Benadryl as antihistamine, 130
Black widow spider bite, *Latrodectur mactans* antivenin for, 400–401
Blockers
  adrenergic, in cardiopulmonary resuscitation, 35–38. *See also* Adrenergic blockers
  cholinergic, in cardiopulmonary resuscitation, 33–34
Blood volume, agents affecting, 91, 93–96
Body weight(s)
  average, 430*t*
  loss in, and dehydration, relationship between, 75*t*
Brethine as bronchodilator, 146
Bretylium, pediatric dosages of, 424*t*
Bretylium tosylate in cardiopulmonary resuscitation, 40–41
Bretylol in cardiopulmonary resuscitation, 40–41
Bricanyl as bronchodilator, 146
Bronchodilators, 135–146
  N-acetylcysteine as, 137
  albuterol as, 138–139
  aminophylline as
    oral, 140–143
    parenteral, 139–140
  isoetharine as, 143–144
  metaproterenol as, 145–146
  terbutaline as, 146
Bronkosol as bronchodilator, 143–144
Buminate as plasma volume expander, 94–95
Bupivicaine for local pain relief, 282–283

C

Calan in cardiopulmonary resuscitation, 46–47
Calcium chloride
  for acid-base disturbances, 81–83
  pediatric dosages of, 425*t*
Calcium gluconate
  for acid-base disturbances, 81–83
  pediatric dosages of, 425*t*
Camphorated opium tincture as antidiarrheal, 368–369
Carbamazepine as anticonvulsant, 292–293
Carbenicillin, 201–203

Carbocaine for local pain relief, 285
Cardiopulmonary resuscitation (CPR)
 adrenergic blockers in, 35–38
 adrenergics in, 23–32. See also
  Adrenergic(s) in cardiopulmonary
  resuscitation
 agents for, 15–63
 antiarrhythmics in, 39–47. See also
  Antiarrhythmics in cardiopulmonary
  resuscitation
 antihypertensives in, 55–63
 cardiotonics in, 49–53
 cholinergic blockers in, 33–34
 nervous system and, 15–21
 vasodilators in, 55–63
Cardiotonics in cardiopulmonary
 resuscitation, 49–53
Carisoprodol as skeletal muscle
 relaxant, 310–311
Ceclor as second-generation
 cephalosporin, 175–176
Cefaclor as second-generation
 cephalosporin, 175–176
Cefadroxil as first-generation
 cephalosporin, 168–169
Cefadyl as first-generation
 cephalosporin, 172–173
Cefamandole as second-generation
 cephalosporin, 176–177
Cefazolin as first-generation
 cephalosporin, 169–170
Cefotaxime as third-generation
 cephalosporin, 181–182
Cefoxitin as second-generation
 cephalosporin, 177–178
Cephalexin as first-generation
 cephalosporin, 170–171
Cephalosporins, 165–183
 actions of, 166
 antimicrobial spectrum of, 165–166
 contraindications for, 166
 first-generation, 167–174
 indications for, 166
 precautions with, 166
 renal impairment and, 165
 second-generation, 174–178
 side effects of, 167
 third-generation, 179–183
Cephalothin as first-generation
 cephalosporin, 171–172
Cephapirin as first-generation
 cephalosporin, 172–173

Cephradine as first-generation
 cephalosporin, 173–174
Charcoal, activated, as
 antidote, 378–379
Child, crying, dealing with, 5
Chloral hydrate as sedative-
 hypnotic, 323–324
Chloramphenicol as
 antimicrobial, 234–236
Chloromycetin as
 antimicrobial, 234–236
Chlorothiazide as diuretic, 68–69
Chlorpheniramine as antihistamine, 128
Chlorpromazine as antiemetic, 357–358
Chlor-Trimeton as antihistamine, 128
Cholinergic blockers, in cardiopulmonary
 resuscitation, 33–34
Cimetidine as gastric acid
 inhibitor, 371–372
Claforan as third-generation
 cephalosporin, 181–182
Cleocin as antimicrobial, 236–239
Clindamycin as antimicrobial, 236–239
Clonazepam as anticonvulsant, 293–295
Clonopin as anticonvulsant, 293–295
Cloxacillin, 192–193
Coagulant, 97–110
 antihemophilic factor (factor VIII)
  as, 100–101
 cryoprecipitated antihemophilic
  factors as, 101–103
 epsilon-aminocaproic acid
  as, 103–104
 factor IX as, 104–106
 fresh frozen plasma as, 106–107
 phytonadione (vitamin K)
  as, 107–109
 protamine sulfate as, 104–110
 vitamin K as, 107–109
Coagulation, mechanisms of, 98
Cocaine for local pain relief, 283–284
Colloid plasma volume expanders
 albumin (human) as, 94–95
 plasma protein fraction as, 95–96
Comas, diabetic and insulin, 337t
Complex partial seizures, 290
Convulsions, control of, 289–307. See
 also Anticonvulsants
Coral snake, poisoning by *Micrurus
 fulvius* antivenin for, 402–403
Corticosteroids, 115–126
 actions of, 118–119

antidote for, 127
contraindications for, 119
desoxycorticosterone as, 121–122
dexamethasone as, 122–123
drug incompatibilities of, 120
drug interactions with, 120
hydrocortisone as, 123–124
indications for, 118
methylprednisolone as, 124–125
precautions with, 119–120
prednisone as, 125–126
relative potency of, 116t
side effects of, 120
"Craniosacral" system, 17
Crotalidae polyvalent
   antivenin, 399–400
Crotalids, poisoning by, *Crotalidae*
   polyvalent antivenin for, 399–400
Crying child, dealing with, 15
Cryoprecipitated antihemophilic factor as
   coagulant, 101–103
Cuprimine as antidote, 389–390
Cyanide antidote package, 379–381

D

Dantrium as skeletal muscle
   relaxant, 311–312
Dantrolene as skeletal muscle
   relaxant, 311–312
Decadron for inflammation, 122–123
Deferoxamine mesylate as
   antidote, 381–382
Dehydration
   and loss in body weight, relationship
      between, 75t
   oral rehydrating solutions for, 75–78
Deltasone for inflammation, 125–126
Depakene as anticonvulsant, 306–307
Depen titratabs as antidote, 389–390
Desferal as antidote, 381–382
Desoxycorticosterone acetate (DOCA) for
   inflammation, 121–122
Dexamethasone for inflammation,
   122–123
Dextrose 50% (IV) for hypoglycemic
   emergencies, 348
Dextrose, pediatric dosages of, 425t
Diabetes mellitus, 335–336
   insulins for, 338–345
      intermediate-acting, 341–343t
      long-acting, 340, 343t, 344–345

   regular, 338–340, 341t
Diabetic comas, 337t
Dialysis, peritoneal, for poisoning, 376
Diarrhea, agents for, 365–369. *See also*
   Antidiarrheals
Diazepam
   parenteral, as anticonvulsant,
      295–296
   as skeletal muscle relaxant, 312–314
Diazoxide
   in cardiopulmonary resuscitation,
      56–57
   for hypoglycemic emergencies,
      348–349
Dicloxacillin, 193–194
Digoxin
   in cardiopulmonary resuscitation,
      49–53
   pediatric dosages of, 425t
Diiodohydroxyquin as antimicrobials,
   239
Dilantin
   as anticonvulsant, 302–304
   in cardiopulmonary resuscitation,
      42–43
Dimenhydrinate as antihistamine,
   128–129
Dimercaprol as antidote, 382–383
Diphenhydramine as antihistamine, 130
Diphenidol as antiemetic, 359–360
Diphenoxylate with atropine as
   antidiarrheal, 367–368
Diphtheria-Pertussis-Tetanus
   Vaccine, 416t
Diuretics, 67–74
   chlorothiazide as, 68–69
   ethacrynic acid as, 69–70
   furosemide as, 70–72
   glycerol as, 72
   mannitol as, 73–74
Diuril as diuretic, 68–69
Dobutamine in cardiopulmonary
   resuscitation, 25–26
Dobutrex in cardiopulmonary
   resuscitation, 25–26
Dopamine
   in cardiopulmonary resuscitation,
      26–27
   pediatric dosages of, 425t
Dosage, calculation of, 9, *10*, 430, 433
Doses, oral and parenteral, measuring
   solutions of, 6

Doxycycline, 218–219
Dramamine as antihistamine, 128–129
Drug(s). *See also* Medications, administration of
 absorption of, 11
 compatibility of, combined in syringe, 431*t*
 emergency, pediatric dosages of, 424–426*t*
 infusion rates for, calculation of, 434–435
 intravenous drop rates for, calculation of, 433–434
 volume-of distribution of, 11–12
Drug-metabolizing enzymes, 12
Duricef as first-generation cephalosporin, 168–169
Dynapen, 193–194

E

Edecrin as diuretic, 69–70
Edetate calcium disodium as antidote, 384–385
E.E.S. as antimicrobial, 240
Electrolyte replacements, 79–90
 acid-base balance and, 79–80
 calcium chloride as, 81–83
 calcium gluconate as, 81–83
 magnesium sulfate as, 83–85
 potassium acetate as, 85–87
 potassium chloride as, 85–87
 potassium phosphate as, 85–87
 sodium bicarbonate as, 87–88
 tromethamine as, 89–90
Emesis, agents for, 355–363. *See also* Antiemetics
Endocrine system, 15
Enzymes, drug-metabolizing, 12
Epilepsy, agents for, 289–307. *See also* Anticonvulsants
Epinephrine
 in cardiopulmonary resuscitation, 27–28
 pediatric dosages of, 425*t*
Epsilon-aminocaproic acid (EACA) as coagulant, 103–104
Erythrocin as antimicrobial, 240
Erythrobycin as antimicrobial, 240
Ethacrynic acid as diuretic, 69–70
Ethambutol for tuberculosis, 242–243
Ethosuximide as anticonvulsant, 296–297

Exchange transfusions for poisoning, 376

F

Factor VIII as coagulant, 100–101
Factor IX complex as coagulant, 104
Fluid and electrolyte imbalances, 65–90
 diuretics for, 67–74. *See also* Diuretics
 electrolyte replacements for, 79–90. *See also* Electrolyte replacements
 oral rehydrating solutions for, 75–78
 therapy for, goals of, 65
Fresh frozen plasma (FFP) as coagulant, 106–107
Fulvicin as antifungal agent, 244–246
Fungizone as antifungal agent, 232–234
Furadantin for urinary tract infections, 226–228
Furosemide
 as diuretic, 70–72
 pediatric dosages of, 425*t*

G

Gamastan, 407–408
Gamatet, 410–411
Gamimune 5% IV, 408–409
Gamma benzene hexachloride as scabicide/pediculicide, 243–244
Gammagee, 407–408
Gantanol, 210–211
Gantrisin, 212–214
Garamycin as aminoglycoside, 156–157
Gastric acid inhibitors, 371–372
Gentamicin as aminoglycoside, 156–157
Geocillin, 201–203
Geopen, 201–203
Globulins, hyperimmune, 405–412. *See also* Antiserums
Glucagon for hypoglycemic emergencies, 350–351
Glucose-elevating agents, 347–351
 dextrose 50% as, 348
 diazoxide as, 348–349
 glucagon as, 350–351
Glucose-lowering agents, 335–345
 insulins as, 338–345
  intermediate-acting, 341–343*t*
  long-acting, 340, 343*t*, 344–345
  regular, 338–340, 341*t*
Glycerin as diuretic, 72

Glycerol as diuretic, 72
Gold, poisoning from, dimercaprol for, 382–383
Gonococcal infections, spectinomycin for, 256–257
Grand mal seizures, 289–290
Grifulvin V as antifungal agent, 244–246
Gris PEG as antifungal agent, 244–246
Grisactin as antifungal agent, 244–246
Griseofulvin as antifungal agent, 244–246

H

Helminthic infections, mebendazole for, 250–251
Hemodialysis for poisoning, 376
Hemorrhage
  causes of, 97
  control of, coagulants in, 98–110. See also Coagulants
Hemostasis, agents affecting, 91, 97–112
Henderson-Hasselbalch equation, 80
Heparin as anticoagulant, 110–112
Hepatitis A, prevention of, immune human serum globulin for, 407–408
Hepatitis B immune globulin, 406
Hepatitis B Vaccine, 419t
Hydralazine
  in cardiopulmonary resuscitation, 57–58
  pediatric dosages of, 425t
Hydrocortisone for inflammation, 123–124
Hydroxyzine
  as antiemetic, 360–361
  as antihistamine, 131–132
Hyperbilirubinemia, reduced protein-binding capacity and, 11
Hyperglycemic emergencies
  glucose-lowering agents for, 335–345
  insulins for, 338–345
    intermediate-acting, 341–343t
    long-acting, 340, 343t, 344–345
    regular, 338–340, 341t
Hyperimmune globulins, 405–412. See also Antiserums
Hyperkalemia, sodium polystyrene sulfonate for, 394–395
Hyper-Rab, 409–410

Hyperstat (IV) in cardiopulmonary resuscitation, 56–57
Hyper-tet, 410–411
Hypertension, intracranial, barbiturates in management of, 321–322
Hypoglycemic emergencies
  dextrose 50% for, 348
  diazoxide for, 348–349
  glucagon for, 350–351
  glucose-elevating agents for, 347–351
Hypnotics, 321–331. See also Sedative-hypnotics

I

Iletin, 338–340, 341t
Ilosone as antimicrobial, 240–242
Ilotycin as antimicrobial, 240–242
Immune deficiency syndromes, immune human serum globulin for, 408–409
Immune human serum globulin
  IM use, 407–408
  IV use, 408–409
Immunizations, childhood
  routine, vaccines for, 416–418t
  schedules for, 422t
Inderal in cardiopulmonary resuscitation, 45–46
Inflammation, agents affecting, 113, 115–126. See also Corticosteroids
Influenza vaccine, 419t
Infusion rates, calculation of, 434–435
INH for tuberculosis, 246–249
Injections
  intramuscular, location of, 6–7
  intravenous, location of, 7
Insulin comas, 337t
Insulins
  intermediate-acting, 341–343t
  long-acting, 340, 343t, 344–345
  regular, 338–340, 341t
Intracranial hypertension, barbiturates in management of, 321–322
Intramuscular injections, location of, 6–7
Intravenous injections, location of, 7
Intravenous solutions, composition of, 427–428t
Intropin in cardiopulmonary resuscitation, 26–27
Iodoquinol as antimicrobial, 239

Iron, poisoning from, deferoxamine
    mesylate for, 381–382
Isoetharine as bronchodilator, 143–144
Isoniazid for tuberculosis, 246–249
Isoproterenol
    in cardiopulmonary
        resuscitation, 29–30
    pediatric dosages of, 425t
Isoptin in cardiopulmonary
    resuscitation, 46–47
Isuprel, in cardiopulmonary
    resuscitation, 29–30
Ivadantin for urinary tract
    infections, 226–228

K

Kanamycin as aminoglycoside, 158
Kantrex as aminoglycoside, 158–159
Kaolin-pectin, paregoric with, as
    antidiarrheal, 368–369
Kayexalate as antidote, 394–395
Keflex as first-generation
    cephalosporin, 170–171
Keflin as first-generation
    cephalosporin, 171–172
Kefzol as first-generation
    cephalosporin, 169–170
Ketoconazole as antifungal
    agent, 249–250
Kidney(s)
    function of, pharmacology
        and, 12–13
    impaired. See Renal impairment
Kilogram conversion chart, 429t
Klebcil as aminoglycoside, 158–159
Konȳne as coagulant, 104–106
Kwell as scabicide/
    pediculicide, 243–244

L

Lanoxin in cardiopulmonary
    resuscitation, 49–53
Larotid, 198–199
Lasix as diuretic, 70–72
Latrodectus mactans antivenin, 400–401
Lead poisoning
    edetate calcium disodium
        for, 384–385
    penicillamine for, 389–390
Levarterenol in cardiopulmonary
    resuscitation, 30–31

Levophed, in cardiopulmonary
    resuscitation, 30–31
Lidocaine
    in cardiopulmonary
        resuscitation, 41–42
    for local pain relief, 284–285
    pediatric dosages of, 425t
Local anesthetics, 279–285
    actions of, 281
    antidotes for, 282
    bupivicaine as, 282–283
    cocaine as, 283–284
    drug interactions with, 282
    drug incompatibilities with, 282
    indications for, 281
    lidocaine as, 284–285
    mepivicaine as, 285
    precautions for, 281
    side effects of, 281–282
Lomitil as antidiarrheal, 367–368
Luminal as anticonvulsant, 299–301

M

Macrodantin for urinary tract
    infections, 226–228
Magnesium sulfate for acid-base
    disturbances, 83–85
Mandelamine for urinary tract
    infections, 224–225
Mandol as second-generation
    cephalosporin, 176–177
Mannitol as diuretic, 73–74
Marcaine for local pain relief, 282–283
Measles, prevention of, immune human
    serum globulin for, 407–408
Measles vaccine, 417t
Mebendazole for helminthic
    infections, 250–251
Medications, administration of, 3–7. See
    also Drug(s)
    dealing with crying child in, 5
    by intramuscular injections, location
        for, 6–7
    by intravenous injections, location
        for, 7
    measuring solutions of oral and
        parenteral doses for, 6
    oral, 5–6
Medrol for inflammation, 124–125
Mefoxin as second-generation
    cephalosporin, 177–178
Mephyton as coagulant, 107–109

Mepivicaine for local pain relief, 285
Mercury, poisoning from, dimercaprol for, 382–383
Metaprel as bronchodilator, 145–146
Metaproterenol as bronchodilator, 145–146
Methcillin, 194–195
Methemoglobinemia from nitrates and nitrites, methylene blue for, 386–388
Methenamine mandelate for urinary tract infections, 224–225
Methocarbamol as skeletal muscle relaxant, 314–315
Methylene blue as antidote, 386–388
Meticorten for inflammation, 125–126
Mezlin, 203–204
Mezlocillin, 203–204
Micrurus fulvius antivenin, 402–403
Minocin, 219–220
Minocycline, 219–220
Morphine, pediatric dosages of, 425t
Moxalactam as third-generation cephalosporin, 182–183
Moxam as third-generation cephalosporin, 182–183
Mucomyst
  as antidote, 377–378
  as bronchodilator, 137
Mumps vaccine, 416t
Muscles, skeletal relaxants of, 309–317.
  See also Skeletal muscle relaxants
Myambutol for tuberculosis, 242–243
Mycifradin as aminoglycoside, 159–160

N

Nafcillin, 195–196
Nalidixic acid for urinary tract infections, 225–226
Naloxone
  as antidote, 388–389
  pediatric dosages of, 425t
Narcan as antidote, 388–389
Narcotic analgesics
  actions of, 264–265
  antidote for, 266
  contraindications for, 265
  drug incompatibilities with, 266
  drug interactions with, 266
  indications for, 264
  precautions for, 265–266
  side effects of, 266
Narcotics, poisoning from, naloxone for, 388–389
Nebcin as aminoglycoside, 161–162
NegGram for urinary tract infections, 225–226
Nembutal as sedative-hypnotic, 328–330
Neomycin as aminoglycoside, 159–160
Nervous system
  autonomic, 16–17
  functional divisions of, 16
  parasympathetic, 16–17
  peripheral, 16
  sympathetic, 16–17
Neonate(s)
  drug absorption in, 11
  drug-metabolizing enzyme activity in, 12
  pharmacology for, 9–13
  plasma protein-binding capacity in, 11
  renal function in, 12–13
  volume of distribution of drugs in, 11–12
Neo-Synephrine in cardiopulmonary resuscitation, 31–32
Neurotransmitters, definition of, 16
Nipride in cardiopulmonary resuscitation, 60–61
Nitrates, poisoning from, methylene blue for, 386–388
Nitrites, poisoning from, methylene blue for, 386–388
Nitrofurantoin for urinary tract infections, 226–228
Nitroglycerin (IV) in cardiopulmonary resuscitation, 59–60
Nitroprusside in cardiopulmonary resuscitation, 60–61
Nizoral as antifungal agent, 249–250
Noctec as sedative-hypnotic, 323–324
Norepinephrine in cardiopulmonary resuscitation, 30–31
Nydrazid for tuberculosis, 246–249

O

Omnipen, 199–201
Oral doses, measuring solutions of, 6
Oral medications, giving, 5–6
Oral rehydrating solutions, 75–78
Organophosphates, poisoning from, pralidoxime for, 392–393
Osmitrol as diuretic, 73–74
Oxacillin, 196–198

P

Pancuronium bromide as skeletal muscle relaxant, 315–316
Paraldehyde as anticonvulsant, 298–299
Parasympathetic nervous system (PANS), 16–17
  fibers of, 17, *19–20*
Paregoric as antidiarrheal, 368–369
Parenteral doses, measuring solution of, 6
Parepectolin as antidiarrheal, 368–369
Pavulon as skeletal muscle relaxant, 315–316
Pediatric patients
  administration of medications to, 3–7
  dosages of commonly used emergency drugs for, 424–426*t*
  pharmacology for, 9–13
  special considerations for, 1–13
Pediculosis, gamma benzene hexachloride for, 243–244
Penicillamine as antidote, 389–390
Penicillin(s), 185–206
  actions of, 186
  antimicrobial spectrum of, 185
  contraindications for, 186
  extended-spectrum, 197
  indications for, 185–186
  penicillinase-resistant, 191–192
  precautions with, 186
  renal impairment and, 185
  side effects of, 186
Penicillin G, 186–188
  oral, 190–191
  parenteral, 188–190
Penicillin V, 186–188, 190–191
Penicillinase-resistant penicillins, 191–192
Pentid, 190–191
Pentobarbital sodium as sedative-hypnotic, 328–330
Pen-Vee, 190–191
Pen-Vee K, 190–191
Peptic ulcers, gastric acid inhibitors, for, 371–372
Peripheral nervous system, 16
Peritoneal dialysis for poisoning, 376
Petit mal seizure, 290
Pharmacology, 9–13
  clinical studies of, 13

  drug absorption in, 11
  drug-metabolizing enzyme activity in, 12
  plasma protein-binding capacity in, 11
  renal function and, 12–13
  volume of drug distribution in, 11–12
Phenazopyridine for urinary tract infections, 228
Phenergan
  as antiemetic, 361–363
  as antihistamine, 132–133
Phenobarbital as anticonvulsant, 299–301
Phentolamine in cardiopulmonary resuscitation, 36
Phenylephrine in cardiopulmonary resuscitation, 31–32
Phenytoin
  as anticonvulsant, 302–304
  parenteral, in cardiopulmonary resuscitation, 42–43
  pediatric dosages of, 425*t*
Physostigmine salicylate as antidote, 391–392
Phytonadione as coagulant, 107–109
Piperacillin, 204–205
Pipracil, 204–205
Plasma, fresh frozen, as coagulant, 106–107
Plasma protein-binding capacity, 11
Plasma protein fraction as plasma volume expander, 95–96
Plasmanate as plasma volume expander, 95–96
Plasmatein as plasma volume expander, 95–96
Pneumococcus vaccines, 420*t*
Poisonings, treatment of, 373–412
  antidotes in, 375–395. *See also* Antidotes
  antiserums in, 405–412. *See also* Antiserums
  antivenins in, 397–403. *See also* Antivenins
Poliomyelitis, prevention of, immune human globulin for, 407–408
Poliovirus vaccines, 418*t*
Polycillin, 199–201
Polymox, 198–199
Potassium acetate for acid-base disturbances, 85–87

Potassium chloride
  for acid-base disturbances, 85–87
  pediatric dosages of, 425*t*
Potassium phosphate for acid-base disturbances, 85–87
Pralidoxime as antidote, 392–393
Prednisone for inflammation, 125–126
Priscoline in cardiopulmonary resuscitation, 37–38
Procainamide
  in cardiopulmonary resuscitation, 43–45
  pediatric dosages of, 426*t*
Proglycem for hypoglycemic emergencies, 348–349
Promethazine
  as antiemetic, 361–363
  as antihistamine, 132–133
Pronestyl in cardiopulmonary resuscitation, 43–45
Proplex as coagulant, 104–106
Propranolol
  in cardiopulmonary resuscitation, 45–46
  pediatric dosages of, 426*t*
Prostaphlin, 196–198
Protamine sulfate as coagulant, 109–110
Protein-binding capacity of plasma, 11
Protopam as antidote, 392–397
Proventil as bronchodilator, 138–139
Pyridium for urinary tract infections, 228
Pyridoxine hydrochloride as anticonvulsant, 304–305

Q

Quelicin as skeletal muscle relaxant, 316–317

R

Rabies, treatment of, 423*t*
Rabies immune globulin, 409–410
Rabies vaccine, 420*t*
Receptors, adrenergic, 23*t*
Regitine in cardiopulmonary resuscitation, 36
Rehydrating solutions, oral, 75–78
Relaxants, skeletal muscle, 309–317.
  See also Skeletal muscle relaxants
Renal function, pharmacology and, 12–13

Renal impairment
  acyclovir and, 230
  aminoglycosides and, 152–153
  amphotericin B and, 232
  ampicillin and, 200
  carbenicillin and, 202
  cefaclor and, 176
  cefadroxil and, 169
  cefamandole and, 177
  cefazolin and, 170
  cefotaxime and, 181
  cefoxitin and, 178
  cephalexin and, 171
  cephalosporins and, 165
  cephalothin and, 172
  cephapirin and, 173
  cephradine and, 174
  chloramphenicol and, 234
  ethambutol and, 242
  isoniazid and, 247
  ketoconazole and, 249
  methicillin and, 194
  mezlocillin and, 203
  minocycline and, 220
  moxalactam and, 182
  penicillin G and, 189
  penicillins and, 185
  piperacillin and, 204
  sulfamethoxazole and, 211
  sulfamethoxazole with trimethoprim and, 212
  sulfisoxazole and, 213
  tetracycline and, 221
  ticarcillin and, 206
Reserpine in cardiopulmonary resuscitation, 61–63
Resuscitation, cardiopulmonary, agents for, 15–63. *See also* Cardiopulmonary resuscitation (CPR)
Robaxin as skeletal muscle relaxant, 314–315
Rubella vaccine, 417*t*
Rubeola, prevention of, immune human serum globulin for, 407–408

S

Scabies, gamma benzene hexachloride for, 243–244
Secobarbital sodium as sedative-hypnotic, 330–331
Seconal as sedative-hypnotic, 330–331
Sedative-hypnotics, 321–331

barbiturates as, 324–331
chloral hydrate as, 323–324
indications for, 321
pentobarbital as, 328–330
secobarbital as, 330–331
Seizures
classification of, 290–291
control of, 289–307. *See also*
Anticonvulsants
description of, 289–290
Septra, 211–212
Serpasil in cardiopulmonary
resuscitation, 61–63
Shock, colloid plasma volume expanders
for, 93–96
Silvadene, 209–210
Silver sulfadiazine, 209–210
Skeletal muscle relaxants, 309–317
carisoprodol as, 310–311
dantrolene as, 311–312
diazepam as, 312–314
methocarbamol as, 314–315
pancuronium bromide as, 315–316
succinylcholine as, 316–317
Snake venom, poisoning by, antivenins
for, 397–400, 402–403
Sodium bicarbonate
for acid-base disturbances, 87–88
pediatric dosages of, 426t
Sodium polystyrene sulfonate as
antidote, 394–395
Solu-Cortef for inflammation, 124–125
Soma as skeletal muscle
relaxant, 310–311
Somatic nervous system, 16, 19–21
Spider, black widow, *Latrodectus
mactans* antivenin for, 400–401
Staphcillin, 194–195
Staphylococcal infections, vancomycin
for, 257–259
Status epilepticus, 290
Streptomycin as
aminoglycosides, 160–161
Succinylcholine as skeletal muscle
relaxant, 316–317
Sulfamethoxazole, 210–211
with trimethoprim, 211–212
Sulfisoxazole, 212–214
Sulfonamides, 207–213
actions of, 208
antimicrobial spectrum of, 208
contraindications for, 208
drug interactions with, 209

indications for, 208
precautions of, 208–209
side effects of, 209
silver sulfadiazine as, 209–210
sulfamethoxazole as, 210–211
sulfamethoxazole with trimethoprim
as, 211–212
sulfisoxazole as, 212–214
Sumycin, 220–221
Sympathetic nervous system
(SANS), 16–17
Syringe, drugs combined in, compatibility
of, 431t
Syrup of ipecac as antidote, 385–386

T

Tagamet as gastric acid
inhibitor, 371–372
Tegretol as anticonvulsant, 292–293
Terbutaline as bronchodilator, 146
Tetanus-Diphtheria vaccines, 416t
Tetanus immune human
globulin, 410–411
Tetanus prophylaxis in wound
management, 423t
Tetracyclines, 215–221
actions of, 216–217
antimicrobial spectrum of, 216
contraindications for, 217
doxycycline as, 218–219
drug incompatibilities with, 218
drug interactions with, 218
indications for, 216
minocycline as, 219–220
precautions with, 217
side effects of, 217–218
THAM for acid-base
disturbances, 89–90
Theophylline, oral, as
bronchodilator, 140–143
Theophylline ethylenediamine as
bronchodilator, 139–140
Thoracolumbar system, 17
Thorazine as antiemetic, 357–358
Ticar, 205–206
Ticarcillin, 205–206
Time frames, age-appropriate, 4t
Tobramycin as
aminoglycoside, 161–162
Tolazoline in cardiopulmonary
resuscitation, 37–38

Transfusions, exchange, for
    poisoning, 376
Tridil in cardiopulmonary
    resuscitation, 59–60
Trimethoprim, sulfamethoxazole
    with, 211–212
Tris buffer for acid-base
    disturbances, 89–90
Tromethamine for acid-base
    disturbances, 89–90
Tuberculosis
    ethambutol for, 242–243
    isoniazid for, 246–249
    rifampin for, 254–256

U

Ulcers, peptic, gastric acid inhibitors
    for, 371–372
Ultracef as first-generation
    cephalosporin, 168–169
Unipen, 195–196
Urinary tract anti-infectives and
    antiseptics, 223–228
    methenamine mandelate as, 224–225
    nalidixic acid as, 225–226
    nitrofurantoin as, 226–228
    phenazopyridine as, 228

V

Vaccines
    for routine childhood
        immunizations, 416–418t
    for specific needs, 419–420t
Valium
    as anticonvulsant, 295–296
    as skeletal muscle relaxant, 312–314
Valproic acid as
    anticonvulsant, 306–307
Varicella-zoster immune
    globulin, 411–412
    distribution centers for, 412–413
Vasodilators in cardiopulmonary
    resuscitation, 55–63
    nitroglycerin as, 59–60
    nitroprusside as, 60–61
    reserpine as, 61–63
V-cillin, 190–191

V-cillin K, 190–191
Velosef as first-generation
    cephalosporin, 173–174
Venom, snake, poisoning by, antivenins
    for, 397–400, 402–403
Ventolin as bronchodilator, 138–139
Veracillin, 193–194
Verapamil
    in cardiopulmonary resuscitation,
        46–47
    pediatric dosages of, 426t
Vermox for helminthic infections,
    250–251
Vibramycin, 218–219
Vistaril
    as antiemetic, 360–361
    as antihistamine, 131–132
Vitamin B_6 as anticonvulsant, 304–305
Vitamin K_1 as coagulant, 107–109
Vomiting, agents for, 355–363. See also
    Antiemetics
Vontrol as antiemetic, 359–360

W

Water, pediatric requirements for, 426t
Weight(s), body
    average, 430t
    loss in, and dehydration, relationship
        between, 75t
Wound management, tetanus prophylaxis
    in, 423t

X

Xylocaine
    in cardiopulmonary resuscitation,
        41–42
    for local pain relief, 284–285

Y

Yodoxin as antimicrobial, 239

Z

Zarontin as anticonvulsant, 296–297
Zovirax as antiviral agent, 230–232